COURTROOM PSYCHOLOGY
—— and ——
TRIAL ADVOCACY

Richard C. Waites, J.D., Ph.D.

2003

ALM Publishing

New York, New York

Cover Design: *Michael Ng*

Interior Page Design & Production: *Amparo Gra*f

Library of Congress Cataloging-in-Publication Data

Waites, Richard, 1951-
    Courtroom psychology and trial advocacy / by Richard Waites.
        p. cm.
    Includes bibliographical references.
    ISBN 0-9705970-9-6
    1. Trial practice—United States. 2. Psychology, Forensic. I. Title.

KF8915 .W355 2002
347.73'75—dc21   2002034474

Contents

Introduction

Every day in courtrooms all across America, men and women of all ages and backgrounds are called upon to make decisions in cases. Some of them have never been inside a courthouse before. Others make a career out of judging and arbitrating cases. Nonetheless, they are all just people trying to do their best. They come to the courtroom with all their joys and sorrows as well as their successes and failures. They are filled with knowledge about life's circumstances. They feel deeply. They think about things that are important to them and their families. They have hundreds of opinions and attitudes that help direct them in their daily lives. Most important, they bring all these attitudes, life experiences, thoughts, and feelings with them to the courtroom.

This book is about using information we have about the psychology of judges, jurors, and arbitrators to increase attorneys' persuasive power in the courtroom. The strength of our justice system rests in the ability of opposing advocates to make their best case to the people who will decide the outcome. In order to make that case, it is vital to know how the decision makers regard circumstances like those in the litigation if we hope to convince them that we are right.

The poet Robert Frost once wrote, "The jury consists of twelve persons chosen to decide the better lawyer." His sentiment is shared by many people. However, one might ask, what makes a better lawyer? Is a better lawyer one who has superior knowledge of the rules or is a better lawyer simply better at engaging in treachery, as many critics believe? Perhaps the latter is true. However, in order to inspire and motivate judges, jurors, and arbitrators, the better lawyer may need other capabilities such as understanding (1) what the decision makers need to know, (2) how to help them learn what they need to know, (3) the self-interest of the decision makers, and (4) how they look at the world.

Until now, trial advocacy reference books have focused on teaching lawyers how to improve their presentation skills and thereby increase the effectiveness of their courtroom advocacy. The ideas presented in these works relied primarily upon traditional principles of advocacy and conventional wisdom in making suggestions to trial lawyers and those who work with them. These suggestions focus on the skills of trial lawyers, but they say little about understanding the perceptions and mental processes of judges, jurors, and arbitrators whom the trial lawyers must persuade.

Rather than dealing solely with the trial lawyer's skills, the material in this book focuses on the audiences the trial lawyer wants to persuade, and makes recommendations for developing and presenting more powerful, persuasive presentations. I believe that in order for a trial lawyer to successfully persuade decision makers by using good trial advocacy skills, the substance of his or her argument must be relevant and compelling to the particular audience that the lawyer wishes to persuade.

Even after twenty-three years in the courtroom as a lawyer and trial psychologist, I learn something new almost every day. The most important thing I have learned is that change is inevitable, but growth is optional.

I have also learned that the more experienced one becomes in presenting cases, the more one begins to question the process by which we present cases. And as we question our assumptions, we learn more about ourselves and about the people we are trying to persuade. This book is intended to address the complex, insightful questions that experienced trial attorneys and their clients often raise, questions for which—until now—there have been few answers.

At the core of everyday jury research work are people—many hundreds of jurors or mock jurors and the many judges or arbitrators who have allowed us to study their decision-making processes. We are deeply grateful for their allowing us a limited intrusion into their thinking processes. They tell us that they often feel a mixture of delight and curiosity about why we want to listen to what they have to say.

My premise is that when trial attorneys for both plaintiffs and defendants stop to research and listen to judges, jurors, and arbitrators before trial, and then thoughtfully analyze and use the new information they have gained, the persuasive power of their advocacy is greatly increased and a higher measure of justice is achieved. In this sense, indeed, information is power.

I had three goals in writing this book. The first is to share with you some of the information that I have come across in the course of my work that I hope will help you in the course of your work. The second is to create one more building block toward a meaningful application of scientific psychology for lawyers who are working hard every day to develop their most powerful cases for their clients. The third is to provide a solid foundation for the belief that our system of justice is stronger when we make the jury system work better through more skillful, knowledgeable trial advocacy.

Richard C. Waites, J.D., Ph.D.

Acknowledgments

No book of this nature can be written without the collaborative effort of many people. As you will see, the most important contributions have come from thousands of men and women (trial judges, jurors, and arbitrators) who have allowed scientific researchers to watch and listen as they made important decisions in legal cases. In conducting the research for the book, I had the opportunity to review and analyze hundreds of published articles that discussed the methods and results of scientific studies of how trial judges, jurors, and arbitrators make important decisions. I have found that the people who conduct this type of research are exceptionally bright and talented. I have also found that each of them is willing to sit down and talk about their research whenever possible. The names and qualifications of all these remarkable people are too many to list. Fortunately, their work is available to anyone who wishes to read it. Most notable among them are Shari Diamond, Sol Fulero, Valerie Hans, Gary Moran, Steven Penrod, Neil Vidmar, and Richard Weiner.

I have also had the good fortune to read most of the trial advocacy reference books that have been published over the past twenty years. The quality of the authors' ideas and their dedication is an inspiration to all of us who want to excel in the courtroom. Although many fine authors have written on the subject, the following are worthy of special mention: Sonya Hamlin, Steven Lubet, Thomas Mauet, James McElhaney, and Michael Tigar, whose works have helped many trial advocates. Of special note is the great work of the psychological educators at the National Institute for Trial Advocacy, who over the past thirty years have developed ways to help lawyers enhance their trial advocacy skills.

I cherish the helpful observations shared with me by many good friends who are successful judges and trial attorneys throughout the country. By choice, I spend most of my days around trial lawyers or corporate counsel who are working hard to represent their clients in the courtroom. For every new creative idea I share with them, they teach me something in return.

Some of these great people have agreed to share some of their ideas with you in this book. The depth of their experience and the quality of their ideas exemplifies how they became so successful in their trade.

The most remarkable trial advocacy teacher I have ever met was K. Byron McCoy of the University of Houston Law Center. He was an inspiration to hundreds of aspiring young law students and lawyers during his short lifetime. Those of us who knew him were indelibly changed by him.

I am also greatly indebted to Robert Gordon, one of the great trial consultants of our time. During the years that I worked alongside him, he provided me with many insights about how trial lawyers can benefit from the use of scientific information in practical ways.

In the course of my work I have also been privileged to work with other successful trial consultants who have forged new ways of thinking about the role of science in understanding courtroom decision making. Their unique insights and commitment to helping trial attorneys enhance their power in the courtroom have led to many new friendships for me. Because of her limitless energy and creativity, my friend Amy Singer deserves special mention.

Every day I recall something important that I learned in my doctoral work in psychology. At that time, I was already a board-certified civil trial attorney. My course in life was already charted to continue my work in the courtroom. But I felt it was important to undergo the same training as all other psychologists. I am deeply grateful for the acceptance I received among my graduate school professors and for the new way of thinking about people in the courtroom that I learned under their guidance. In this respect, I am especially grateful to Will Wilson, John Flynn, and Ray Klein, all distinguished professors of psychology.

Should you find yourself in the position of writing a book one day, I hope you will be as lucky as I have been in working with the people at American Lawyer Media and its Law Journal Press subsidiary. Neil Hirsch, Dory Green, Elizabeth Delfs, Caroline Sorokoff, and Patricia Rainsford, all of whom have worked with me closely on this project, have been supportive in so many ways.

Finally, I will never be able to repay the debt of love and understanding that I owe my family, friends, and co-workers at The Advocates,[1] our trial consulting firm. They have been consistently supportive and persevered with me over the three years that it has taken to research and produce this work. In this respect, I am especially grateful to Tony Greisinger, Connie Zeller, Curt Wills, Nancy Wenning, Cynthia Zarling, Alice Singer, Geoff Tudor, and Helen Edmondson. Each of them provided inspiration and insight at times when it was needed the most.

---

[1] www.theadvocates.com

I hope you will find that something in the book touches your life and makes a difference for you.

The editors and I are deeply indebted to the following outstanding trial lawyers for their contributions to this work: Kim J. Askew, Partner, Hughes & Luce LLP; Kenneth R. Chiate, Partner, Pillsbury Winthrop LLP; Nancy J. Geenen, Partner, Foley & Lardner; Frank G. Jones, Partner, Fulbright & Jaworski L.L.P.; Scott D. Lassetter, Partner, Weil, Gotshal & Manges LLP; R. Laurence Macon, Partner, Akin Gump Strauss Hauer & Feld LLP; Randy J. McClanahan, Partner, McClanahan & Clearman, L.L.P.; Kerry E. Notestine, Partner, Littler Mendelson, P.C.; Barbara Radnofsky, Partner, Vinson & Elkins L.L.P.; Stephen Rasch, Partner, Thompson & Knight LLP; John S. Serpe, Partner, Sheehy, Serpe & Ware, P.C.; Job Taylor, III, Partner, Latham & Watkins; Robert S. Walker, Partner, Jones, Day, Reavis & Pogue; and Edward M. Waller, Jr., Partner, Fowler White Boggs Banker. These remarkable men and women have dedicated themselves to the pursuit of excellence in their profession and, consequently, their clients benefit greatly from their superior advocacy skills every day.

We are especially indebted to Hon. Charles A. Legge (Ret.) who served with distinction for seventeen years as a trial judge in the United States District Court for the Northern District of California. Judge Legge has presided over more than 5,000 cases in his judicial experience and he honors us all with his observations and insights in this book. Judge Legge is currently associated with the San Francisco office of JAMS, a premier provider of alternative dispute resolution services in the United States.

CHAPTER 1

The Decision-Maker Oriented Approach
to Trial Advocacy

CHAPTER CONTENTS

1

> *"He makes people pleased with him by making them first pleased with themselves."*
>
> — Lord Chesterfield (1694-1773)

§ 1.01 | WHAT IS DECISION-MAKER ORIENTED TRIAL ADVOCACY?

When we ask a judge, jury, or arbitration panel to accept our arguments and to decide a case in our favor, we are asking them to allow us into their world. It is like asking someone to let us come into his or her home for a visit. The occupant must be the one who unlocks and opens the door from the inside.

What is at the heart of persuasion? Winston Churchill once said, "My most brilliant achievement was my ability to be able to persuade my wife to marry me." Without knowing Clementine Churchill, you might suspect that in accepting his proposal of marriage, she was simply acting in her own self-interest. After all, what eligible woman would not want to marry a handsome, wealthy, and adventurous man like Winston Churchill?

It so happens, however, that Clementine Churchill was a striking and well-educated woman who was not easily persuaded. Nonetheless, Winston worked hard to attract her and, luckily for him he struck a chord with her. His letters to her were passionate and interesting. After first meeting her at a ball in London in 1904, he wrote a private note to her that read, "What a comfort and pleasure it was to me to meet a girl with so much intellectual quality and such strong reserves of noble sentiment." He treated her as if she were the only woman in the world who interested him. During their four-year courtship, upon leaving for an overseas business trip, he once wrote, "Goodbye my darling. I feel there is no room for anyone but you in my heart—you fill every corner." Thus began a fifty-seven-year marriage that remains a monument to passion and romance.

Skeptics might argue that successful persuasion in a personal relationship between two people is a matter of fate and chemistry rather than the matching of two people who work to attract each other and have the same self-interest. However, that argument is too simplistic. People are complex. They use their logic and emotions in varying degrees to make decisions that will help them to experience pleasure and avoid pain. One way in which people experience pleasure is to make decisions that make them feel good about themselves. This principle holds true in persuading judges, juries, and arbitrators.

To motivate people in the courtroom to listen to you and to take action in your favor, you must understand their needs and what inspires them. Using the most correct, appropriate trial advocacy technique is not enough.

Persuading people in the courtroom involves meaningful two-way communication between the trial lawyer and the people whom he or she wishes to convince. No lawyer ever won a case by telling a judge, jury, or arbitration panel what to do. A case is won because the fact finder(s) can identify with the lawyer's moral interpretation of the case.

Note that during interaction between trial attorneys and courtroom decision makers, lawyers cannot dominate fact finders. Lawyers can only inspire and motivate them. Fact finders make their own decisions about how to respond.

It is a fallacy to believe that decision makers in the courtroom are passive participants in the trial. Even though they may be separated by tables, walls, or benches from the lawyers and witnesses, they are visualizing and imagining the circumstances of the case and interpreting them in accordance with their attitudes and life experiences. They are working vigorously trying to understand the meaning of the case for themselves.

No matter who the decision makers are in your case, their images and interpretations of the circumstances of the case are uniquely their own. For decades post-trial interviews of jurors have revealed that each of them develops his or her own version of a case story by the end of trial. Most have begun to form the story before the end of opening statement.

It is immensely helpful to know before trial how the decision makers in a particular case are likely to view the circumstances of the case. For example, in product liability cases evidence often shows that some manufacturers have undertaken cost-benefit analyses to determine the cost-effectiveness of designing their products in certain ways. Armed with this information, a plaintiff attorney might argue that the manufacturer had reduced the value of life to dollars and cents and that a jury should impose punitive damages to punish the company for being so callous. A defense attorney might respond that conducting such analyses is beneficial since the cost to the public of implementing a new design would be prohibitive, considering that perhaps only one of a great number of products might result in someone's death.

Before developing arguments on the issues for trial, one might therefore want to know more about how a jury will view those issues. Once this information is available, a lawyer might craft an argument that coincides with the fact finders' likely views. One way to obtain this information would be through the use of scientific focus groups or mock trials to better understand how jurors are likely to perceive issues. If there are budgetary or time constraints, there are now hundreds of peer-reviewed journal articles that publish the results of scientific research about how people in the jury population think about certain issues that arise often in the courtroom.[1]

After three decades of experimenting with the use of scientific decision-maker research, we have learned that the most powerful, creative way to present an argument is to gather information about the decision makers by using an objective process, and then to brainstorm ways to incorporate this information into the development of the argument.

To some extent we have become conditioned to believe that our performance in the courtroom is about us and how well we present a case. Although three decades of intensive trial advocacy training have helped us to enhance our communication skills, this is only the first step. The next step is to use our skills to engage fact finders in powerful ways. After all, their decision is about themselves, not us.

The most effective trial lawyers realize that working with judges, juries, and arbitrators is a cathartic experience. They realize that in order to be effective they must let down their personal barriers and engage decision makers in intimate, meaningful ways. They must be in touch with that part of their own spirit that unleashes real personal power. They realize that their role is to stimulate and motivate decision-makers, not to control them.

---

[1] Some of the scientific journals that often publish studies related to judge, jury, and arbitrator decision making include:
- Law and Human Behavior (the official journal of the American Psychology Law Society: Division 41 of the American Psychological Association),
- Journal of Applied Psychology (published bimonthly by the American Psychological Association),
- Psychology, Public Policy & Law (published quarterly by the American Psychological Association),
- Journal of Personality & Social Psychology (published monthly by the American Psychological Association),
- Journal of Experimental Psychology (published quarterly by the American Psychological Association), and
- Group Dynamics: Theory, Research and Practice (published quarterly by the American Psychological Association).

These journals are available by subscription from the publisher or for review at most university libraries that have substantial social science collections.

It is not *our* power that results in a favorable verdict. It is the power within the decision maker that creates the magical experience that results in a decision.

As trial lawyers, we give homage to this power of the decision maker. We honor and respect that power and should not try to upstage it. To the contrary, one of our goals is to empower fact finders by acknowledging their supreme authority.

§ 1.02 | THE NEW AGE OF TRIAL ADVOCACY AND COURTROOM PSYCHOLOGY

The world around us is changing. The practice of trial advocacy is changing. Historically, we have depended solely upon self-reliance and intuition in developing and presenting cases in the courtroom, as we were taught to do. We have relied solely upon trial advocacy skills that we learned from law professors, seminar speakers, and our mentors. We have developed our themes and case theories from ideas that sounded persuasive to us, that we generated ourselves, or that we borrowed from other sources.

However, despite our emphasis upon self-reliance, a revolution has occurred in how we develop and present cases to judges, juries, and arbitrators. This revolution began about thirty years ago with the founding of the National Institute for Trial Advocacy (NITA) and other teaching organizations that are dedicated to assisting lawyers in enhancing their trial advocacy skills. NITA and the other groups believe that the ideals of our system of justice are furthered when attorneys work to develop their skills as advocates.

The effect that NITA and other similar groups have had is profound. Thousands of attorneys have participated as teachers or students in the advocacy programs. Improvements in the quality of legal representation in the courtroom that have resulted are noticeable. Many of these improvements involve the incorporation of persuasive techniques that have been developed through practice and scientific research. The fact that these fundamental improvements have occurred in such a short time is remarkable considering the conservative nature of our judicial system and general legal practice.

Why have these changes taken hold so rapidly? There are three reasons. First, the improvements in our trial advocacy system evolved out of the ideals of traditional law practice in the United States. Second, they conform with our beliefs that the public has a right to be represented by lawyers who have access to the most reliable, useful information available. Finally, the use of improved persuasive techniques and scientifically based information in the courtroom reflects advancements taking place in the rest of our modern world.

One of the effects of the drive to be more successful as a trial advocate has been the need for more reliable, useful information about how our case presentations will be perceived by judges, jurors, and arbitrators. Scientific decision-maker research is just one source of this information. There are many others.

As we learn more about how judges, jurors, and arbitrators make decisions, we discover new ways to apply this information to make the work of trial advocates more effective. By focusing case presentations on the needs of the decision makers to better understand cases and their meaning, we can help those decision makers do a better job of making appropriate decisions. This all improves the trial advocacy system.

In this book we spend a great deal of time looking at the results of scientific research and how to apply what we have learned. In the process, however, we may sometimes fail to acknowledge that advocacy is an art. It is one of the highest forms of art. It involves the use of oratory and expression that focus on the meaning of life's circumstances.

We have spent years making sacrifices to learn this art. But now the basic learning is over. It is time to use our skills and all of the resources available to us to create a masterpiece—a trial—that is meaningful in the lives of our clients and the decision makers as well.

§ 1.03 | HOW TO INSPIRE JUDGES, JURORS, AND ARBITRATORS TO DECIDE IN YOUR FAVOR

Being the most competent trial lawyer in the courtroom is not enough. It takes more than oratorical skills and courtroom savvy to convince decision makers to decide in favor of your client. To win a case, the substance of your presentation must be compelling, meaningful, and inspiring.

Some of the most brilliant trial lawyers in the United States tell us that they view themselves as messengers. They tell us that fact finders are most persuaded by the message and content of their arguments. They tell many war stories about trials in which a less skilled trial advocate defeated them because the substance of the winning argument was more compelling.

The role that we play in the courtroom is historic. In their morality plays and in their oratory, the ancient Greeks sought to persuade their audiences to accept certain moral principles as the motivating force for behavior. They talked about the dilemmas in which people found themselves and they suggested resolutions that incorporated ethical and moral considerations. Two thousand years later, our audiences in the courtroom continue to be inspired by ethical and moral reasoning that motivates them to resolve dilemmas consistent with their beliefs and life experiences.

Developing an effective trial strategy that will make a judge, jury, or arbitration panel enthusiastic about deciding in your favor is dependent largely upon framing an argument in a way that is meaningful and motivational to them. The themes and case theory you rely upon must be in accordance with the fact finders' attitudes about specific issues in the case, relevant life experiences, and other personal characteristics that will influence the verdict.

People do not make decisions in a vacuum. No judges, jurors, or arbitrators have ever made a decision without first considering their perceptions of the world around them and their previous life experiences.

§ 1.04 | THE SECRET TO MOTIVATING JUDGES, JURORS, AND ARBITRATORS

The world of trial advocacy is unique in many respects, but the fundamental dynamics of persuasion are the same everywhere. Because trial advocacy takes place within a legalistic environment laden with complicated rules and procedures, we sometimes forget that the people we try to persuade in the courtroom are the same people who spend most of their time outside the courtroom. Jurors in particular may enter a courtroom only once or twice in their lifetimes.

Whether we want to admit it or not, trial advocacy is selling. It is the highest form of selling in the sense that we are selling ideas that will affect people's lives.

Why do people buy products or ideas? The answer is simple. They buy out of self-interest. Benjamin Franklin once said, "If you would persuade, you must appeal to interest rather than intellect."

The practice of persuading people in the courtroom seems complex because of the hundreds of details that make up every case and because different decision makers will view the case differently. Nevertheless, the objective is to frame the issues and presentation of a case to address the needs of the decision makers. They want to learn as much information as they can, and they need to make a decision that makes them feel good about themselves.

In essence, therefore, decision makers make important decisions the same way you do. Think about how you go about making decisions about family matters, law practice matters, and personal matters. Do you make important decisions completely rationally and considering only the information that someone tells you is admissible? That is highly unlikely.

How would you feel if over dinner your spouse told you that she had been offered a promotion with her company, but the job was located in a different city? Think of all of the issues that would come up in such circumstances. What would you need to do before you could express your opinion or make a decision about the ramifications of the proffered promotion? Because the decision is important to you, you would want to learn everything you could and you would want to be free to respond any way you see fit—logically or emotionally.

The same is true for the people you will be persuading in the courtroom. They take their jobs seriously. Jurors have been overheard to say things such as, "This is the most important thing I will ever do."

For those of us who practice in the courtroom, we encounter what sometimes seems to be an endless stream of disputes. After all, our job is centered around helping people to resolve their differences. However, sometimes we become so caught up in the legal details that we forget that decision makers have no personal stake in the disputes, but are viewing the case as a moral dilemma that they must resolve.

The more you are sensitive to the needs of decision makers to form a story about what happened and why, the better equipped you will be to develop themes and messages in the case that are meaningful and powerful to them. Decision makers need to learn the important aspects of the case as clearly and simply as possible. Overwhelming them with details makes their work more difficult. Because they know nothing about the case, they have no idea who to believe and what to believe. They do not know what is really important and what is simply unnecessary detail.

But there is another important aspect of presenting a case that all successful trial lawyers must understand. Judges, jurors, and arbitrators will make their decision in your case based on their own attitudes about specific issues in the case, their own life experiences, and their own set of life's influences. Throughout this book we will discuss what we know about the psychology of judges, jurors, and arbitrators and how they make decisions in cases like yours. We will also discuss how you can put this information to work for you today.

CHAPTER 2

The Psychology of Communication and Persuasion

CHAPTER CONTENTS

"The difference between the right word and the almost right word is the difference between lightning and a lightning bug."

— Mark Twain (1835-1910)

§ 2.01 | OVERVIEW OF THE COMMUNICATION/ PERSUASION PROCESS

We tend to use terms such as *communication* and *persuasion* loosely in describing the process through which we present our case to jurors. Most trial lawyers are talkative and assertive. But how do we know if we are communicating? Is communication all about words and body language? Or maybe it goes deeper than that. And what is persuasion, really?

Each of us has thousands of opinions that came from somewhere. Persuasion is inevitable. Persuasion is everywhere. It is at the heart of sales, politics, courtship, negotiating, parenting, religious evangelism, and, of course, courtroom decision making.

Why do some persuasion efforts fail whereas others are wildly successful? Whether you are a minister, a sales manager, or a trial lawyer, what can you do to make yourself, and your message, more persuasive? In order to answer such questions, we study the effects of various factors on the listener's perceptions and behavior, which we will discuss in more depth in the chapters on jury psychology and jury research.

The persuasive process begins with basic communication. Let's begin our discussion with an analysis of the communication process as it relates to persuasion.

COMMUNICATION

Intentional and purposeful interaction between at least two people, primarily through the use of verbal and nonverbal symbols.

PERSUASION

Motivating someone to action.

---

§ 2.02 | THE PROCESS OF COMMUNICATING

[1]—Basic Characteristics of Communication

Because communication is inherently interactive, the communicator and the observer are interdependent. In the courtroom we communicate with jurors, judges, co-counsel, opposing attorneys, support staff, court staff, and others. In each of our communications we are dependent upon the other participant for a response. Otherwise, the interaction rapidly dissipates.

Some conversation is *interactive* but not necessarily communicative. For example, people often say things in the courtroom that are meaningless and intended only to fill silence. At times these meaningless interactions detract from the message to be communicated. It is not surprising that judges and jurors are easily irritated by arguments or evidence that does not directly relate to the central issues.

The best communicators, however, remain true to their message. They remain focused on the idea to be communicated. They work hard to make sure that all of their words, actions, and tools communicate *pure* messages without any distractions.

Regardless of the culture or setting, we think and communicate in symbols. A *symbol* is a sound, behavior, letter, or visual image that stands for something else. The most highly organized symbols we usually call *language*. A typical trial is filled with symbols, each of which will mean something to one or more jurors. Therefore, we have to pay attention to the symbols we use and project so that the correct message is presented to and, it is hoped, received by the jurors and judges.

[2]—Inner Selves and Communication

Our internal states both begin and end communication. The perceptions and mental state of the communicator are the source of the information to be communicated. Conversely, the perceptions and mental state of the listener shape the end product of the communication.

One might argue that the things in our environment about which we are communicating are definite and that perceptions of the same object must be the same for everyone. After all, the sky is usually blue and trees are usually green. However, our memories and perceptual systems are highly selective about what they acknowledge, and even more selective about the information that is retained in temporary or long-term memory. Each person perceives the sky or a tree in a unique way. In this sense, our perceptions are not directly tied to specific events or objects, but are created by our individual perceptual systems.

[3]—Tools for Creating and Changing Perceptions

There are many interesting tools that humans have created or used over the millennia to create, maintain, and change perceptions. These tools are derived from our understanding about our cognitive (thinking) processes and our affective (feeling) processes. We will look at three of these tools that are most useful in the courtroom. They are language, schemas, and affect.

[a]—Language

Language is a powerful communication tool in many respects. In a very basic way, it helps us organize our thoughts and information in systematic ways. Language can be used as words, concepts, or style of expression. Words convey meaning and concepts, and the same words can be spoken or displayed in many ways. Language is flexible and, in this sense, is a tool, not a constraint.

As children, we acquire language at an early age as symbols and concepts. It is not until we are somewhat older that we learn the spelling of the words and the formal rules of grammar. For this reason, when we present a case in trial, it is more important to be concerned about the concepts and the connotations of our presentation than the actual words we use. Once the concepts are right, the words will follow.

However, often as lawyers we perceive language to be a technical construct rather than a free-flowing mode of communicating. We tend to be hypertechnical about our use of particular words that fit legal patterns rather than focus on central concepts and messages that jurors must hear and see if we are to be persuasive.

Perhaps we should approach the use of words as an opportunity to create mental pictures. For example, fiction writers are taught to use words to convey interesting aspects of a character's behavior, thus revealing the character's inner thought processes.

[b]—Schemas

As human beings, we tend to form preconceptions and expectations as a result of our previous life experiences. Technically, psychologists refer to these preconceptions and expectations as *schemas*.

A schema is a group of concepts and perceptions and the systems we use to organize them. They are a type of mental shorthand. Schemas help us to quickly make sense of the things that are happening around us. For example, when we are driving behind a car down the interstate highway and that car begins to swerve from a blown tire, we consult our schemas to try to understand what is happening and what, if anything, we need to do about it.

Depending upon one's proximity to the event, immediate evasive action might be prudent if one senses danger based upon past direct or indirect experience. At some later point, one might consider the reasons that the tire blew out. Was it an old tire that should have been changed? Was the tire underinflated? Was the tire manufactured improperly?

Interestingly, all of these thoughts might be prompted from one's perceptions of a single event. Our brains tend to store information in an order that seeks to make sense or order out of life's events and to avoid disorder or inconsistencies.

When jurors are listening and watching your trial presentation, they are constantly testing and comparing the thoughts and messages in your presentation with their own life experiences in order to make sense out of the presentation. If there is an identical match between jurors' schemas and the messages in the presentation, the jurors will readily accept the new information. If the jurors' schemas are different from the messages or ideas in the presentation, they will generally feel uncomfortable with them, and may even reject them. If the jurors have no schema with which to compare the ideas in the presentation, they will consider the attendant circumstances and how much they trust the presenter in order to form a new schema. Or they might reject the ideas in the presentation altogether.

Consider this example: If a trial lawyer tries to describe his corporate client as a company that makes decisions based upon its business interest in keeping customers happy, jurors will likely accept the message. This message will make sense to them, based upon their own life experiences. However, if the trial lawyer tries to portray his corporate client as a company that makes decisions solely on the basis of humanitarian considerations, jurors will likely reject the message. Their experience tells them that this message is generally not true.

When there is a match between the jurors' schemas and the messages, the relationship between the jurors and the trial lawyer is enhanced. When jurors reject a message, however, the relationship between the jurors and the trial lawyer suffers.

One of the primary reasons for conducting pretrial jury research is to identify the schemas that jurors will use to process a specific case and reach a decision. We have learned through experience that when we try to guess which schemas jurors will use, we are often wrong. Scientific jury research also helps us to identify which of the schemas that jurors use which will be dominant vis-à-vis reaching a verdict.

Jurors, like the rest of us, often form schemas around subjects. Consider the example of banks. Jurors expect to walk into a bank and see a bank president, loan officers, tellers, vaults, cash drawers, expensive rugs, and elegant wood paneling. We expect banks to make loans to people with good credit and to deny loans to people who have bad credit. We often expect bankers to be more interested in making money than in benefiting society. In addition to these perceptions, each of us has many other perceptions about banks and the people who work in them. If a trial involves a bank or banking issue, these schemas will come into play. It is therefore important during pretrial development of the case to discover in advance how these schemas and representations will figure into jurors' thinking.

Schemas are formed primarily by perceptions and ideas that have been related to us by others. Socialization is perhaps the most powerful influence on how schemas (and stereotypes) are formed, maintained, and changed. The significant people in our lives have a profound influence on how we view the world.

Jurors' perceptions are highly individualized. Even when the facts of a case are not disputed, each juror will likely have a different version of the same schema to understand what happened, why things happened as they did, and what the verdict should be. Since jurors' schemas are pre-existing, therefore, the trial lawyer must set the stage with powerful messages that will cause a juror to put these schemas into motion.

Interestingly, the key to changing attitudes or perceptions often lies within the framework of our schematic structure. Our value structure forms the backbone of our belief system and can be of great use to a trial lawyer who wishes to change the perceptions that jurors might have at the outset of a trial.

Consider the example of a medical malpractice case brought against a hospital and an ob/gyn relating to brain deficiencies suffered by a newborn baby girl. In the facts of our case, we discover that the mother, a lawyer, had had a fairly normal pregnancy until the morning of the delivery. At 6:00 A.M. she called her doctor's office to report bleeding. A nurse returned the call, and after some discussion determined that the bleeding was slight and not abnormal. Several hours later the mother went into labor and was taken to the hospital for delivery. Within fewer than twelve hours after delivery, the nursing staff noticed that the baby's blood chemistry showed signs of brain damage due to oxygen depletion and they began treating the baby immediately.

Clearly this is a case where causation would be in issue. But jurors may have little experience with professionals who deal with pregnancy and hospitals, depending upon their life experiences. Research and experience tell us that most jurors will come to one of three conclusions. They will either believe that the hospital is omnipotent and could have prevented brain damage altogether, that the cause of the brain damage was apparent before the mother arrived at the hospital and that the hospital could not be liable, or that brain damage is simply an act of God. In order to decide causation, therefore, jurors will compare the information learned about the case to their schemas, which are limited by their knowledge about the subject.

Research and experience also tell us that juries decide in favor of medical malpractice plaintiffs in fewer than one case in three, and their decisions on liability are not related to the severity of the injury suffered by the plaintiff. Further, studies have shown that jury verdicts in medical malpractice cases coincide with the findings of medical investigations of the same events. This tells us that, for most jurors, the schemas they have of health care providers are historically positive (although there are more recent findings that indicate that this positive bias may be changing).

This medical malpractice case example demonstrates how schemas are deeply integrated into jurors' attempts to make sense out of the information that jurors receive at trial. Later in this chapter we will discuss how changing or switching schemas can have a powerful persuasive effect.

[c]–Affect

The last tool that we will discuss is *affect*. In contrast to our thinking processes, we share experiences with jurors through our feelings. To demonstrate the differences, let's assume that you missed an important filing deadline in a trial court. On one hand, you know what happened factually from your cognitive processes. On the other hand, you are probably quite upset and perhaps even frightened about the possible consequences. These emotional reactions or emotional states we call affect.

In our example, the cognitive processes brought about the emotional state because we have learned through our experience to associate the two. In other words, we have learned to link certain cognitive thoughts and perceptions to certain sets of emotions. The emotions arise as a result of our perception that a certain state of events or facts exists.

Now if we change the perception, what will happen? Suppose the trial judge issues an order extending the filing deadline? The facts have now changed. Our perception of the state of the world has changed. And of course, our mental state changes from anxiety to calm.

Let's see what happens when we apply these principles to a particular case. This time let's examine a contract and fraud dispute between two businesses. One company is a Fortune 500 company that manufactures computer hardware and software. The company uses small companies to manufacture certain parts of its computer equipment. One such small company complains that the big company promised to order 1 million parts a year for ten years, and that in reliance on this promise, it borrowed and spent money to expand its plant size and machinery capacity. The small company also complains that the big company is now ordering only 200,000 parts per year. The big company responds by saying that the 1 million parts number was only a projection, not a promise. Further, the big company makes a new promise that it will order more parts when the economy in the industry improves and its customer demand increases.

What will jurors think? How will they feel about the big company? Will they mistrust the officers of the big company under the assumption that officers of big companies will lie to protect their jobs? Will they feel sorry for the small company because it had less power and control? Will they believe that the drop in the number of parts ordered was due solely to the unexpected changes in the industry, and therefore, was not a breach of contract or result of fraud?

To be sure, each new set of facts and circumstances in the case will prompt different cognitive and emotional responses from jurors based upon their attitudes, life experiences, personality traits, values, and demographic influences. The keys to success at trial, therefore, lie in understanding the jury's attitudes, life experiences, and beliefs. By understanding which attitudes, life experiences, and beliefs will dominate the jury's thinking, we have a better chance of developing a targeted presentation that will be persuasive. In addition, by understanding the breadth and depth of thinking or feeling about the issues that a jury will experience, we can shape the arguments and communication opportunities so that they coincide with jurors' schemas as well as with jurors' cognitive and affective processes. This important information about jurors is also one of the objectives of pretrial jury research.

The construction of a powerful argument is the product of systematic analysis and methodical development of messages and information that can be communicated effectively. An unforgettable example is the powerful words, "If it doesn't fit, you must acquit."

[4]—Measuring Effectiveness of Communication in the Courtroom

There are generally two ways to measure the effectiveness of communication in the courtroom. The first is to judge the quality of the communication by comparing the actual communication to its purpose. The second is to observe whether the recipient of the communication is motivated to behave in accordance with the purpose of the communication. The first measure is a more subjective measurement, whereas the second is more objective.

Regardless of how you judge effectiveness, the central determination is: *Does the communication have its desired effect?*

This topic is important for trial lawyers because the effectiveness of trial advocacy is so often measured subjectively (i.e., whether the lawyer believes he or she did a good job in presenting the case), rather than by the more objective standard. As a result, the trial lawyer's communication efforts are often ineffective even though the trial lawyer has communicated with great social skill.

For example, during voir dire we all want jurors to like us. In order to get them to like us, each of us has learned to communicate in a style that has resulted in getting people to like us in the past. Some trial lawyers have used voir dire as an opportunity to simply fraternize with jurors in order to curry favor. Assuming they are successful, jurors may feel that these trial lawyers are likable, and perhaps even credible. But what have the lawyers learned about the jurors in order to determine whether these jurors can be fair and impartial? What have they communicated to the jurors which would persuade them to consider the lawyers' clients' position on the issues in a favorable way?

In this example, each patronizing lawyer reached one stated goal—the jury liked him or her. But were all the goals realized? If there were three goals in the exercise—to uncover biases of jurors, to educate and persuade them, and to establish rapport with them—then perhaps the third goal was reached although the other two goals were ignored. The point of this part of our discussion is, therefore, to clearly identify the purpose(s) of a courtroom presentation and to focus effort on those purpose(s).

§ 2.03 | THE IMPORTANCE OF LISTENING AND MAKING JURORS WANT TO LISTEN

Some people say that listening is an art. Perhaps that's true. Certainly one of the best ways to understand another person is to listen to him or her. But the ability to listen is also a skill that can be enhanced with understanding and practice. Listening is an active behavior, not a passive one. Our success in listening to judges, jurors, and arbitrators while convincing them to listen to us can be markedly improved once we consider how the listening process works.

[1]–How Listening Works

Listening in the courtroom is critical to the process of communication and persuasion. Jurors must listen to understand the case. Lawyers must listen to jurors in voir dire (and sometimes in trial) in order to understand jurors' perceptions and to measure how well the case is being presented and accepted. Lawyers must listen to judges in order to pick up legal and procedural cues, as well as any bias of the judge in favor of or in opposition to their cases.

However, as human beings, we do not listen to everything we hear, and, conversely, not everything we hear is important enough to pay much attention to. Many things affect our listening ability. For example, we are sometimes accused by others of selective listening. Sometimes the selection process is deliberate and other times it is unconscious.

As trial attorneys we have an obligation to train ourselves to listen carefully to jurors, judges, arbitrators, witnesses, and other lawyers, and to minimize the selectivity that we might be tempted to use outside the courtroom. Courtroom decision makers, however, do not have the same motivations. They feel quite free to listen when they want, or alternatively, not to listen, either consciously or unconsciously.

The most effective communicators are usually good at short-term listening. For example, during voir dire and examination of witnesses, listening to someone's responses is important in creating a productive flow of conversation and learning the basic story of a case.

Judges, jurors, and arbitrators will generally listen to the testimony and arguments that coincide with their self-interest in knowing about the case and making a decision which makes them feel good about themselves. They will generally listen to a lawyer unless the lawyer has made them angry or created some other obstacle to acceptability.

Like most people, courtroom decision makers also listen selectively due to unconscious attitudes about the subject, the speaker, or some other element of the case. In addition, there are always competing stimuli in a courtroom.

By and large, however, the biggest physical obstacle to communication in a trial is the striking difference between the presentation rate of information and the assimilation rate with which jurors absorb that information. Most people speak at a rate of between eighty and 120 words per minute. However, ordinarily judges and jurors, like most people, can absorb words and pieces of information at a much greater speed.

The difference in the presentation rate with which most trial teams present their cases and the assimilation rate at which jurors absorb them generally leads to some difficulties. Daydreaming, sleeping, and sometimes even frustration and anger are often the result of lethargic trial presentations, which are often unnecessarily detailed and could be presented in more interesting, efficient ways.

[2]—Memory and Retention of Information in the Courtroom

Retaining information long enough to make a decision is an essential part of judge and jury decision making. Retention involves memory. To better understand how memory works, try this exercise. Answer the following questions using your memory:

(1) What is the name of street where you live?
(2) What was your mother's maiden name?
(3) What are the names of Santa's reindeer?
(4) What was the name of your first-grade school bus driver?

To be able to answer these questions, the answers must have been encoded, stored, and retrieved. Memory refers to our ability to acquire, retain, and use information or knowledge.

Jurors retain information in several ways. Memories are stored in either short-term memory or long-term memory. Short-term memory is that part of our memory which is currently active and can change quickly when our focus of attention is shifted. We usually keep short-term information active in our minds for less than ninety seconds. For example, you might be trying to remember a telephone number when suddenly a friend asks you a question such as, "What time does the train arrive?" You may instantly forget the telephone number you were trying so hard to remember.

Long-term memory, however, is the repository of everything that we know. Generally, any piece of information that we retain in our brains for more than an hour is considered to be long-term. Long-term memory is virtually limitless. However, memory can fool us. Sometimes we remember things differently than the way they actually happened. Moreover, sometimes we fail to remember things that we thought we knew very well.

In these ways, human memory is different from computer memory. Computers store information digitally in exactly the same form in which it was input. Computers do not create nuance or context without being instructed. Computers do not make judgments. Computers do not color memory with emotional responses. However, human memory is more complex, and can store information in forms that include events or facts as well as associated context, perceptions, judgments, and visual images.

Computers can generally recall every bit of data that was input even once. Human beings only store information in long-term memory that appears to be important or useful for future reference.

What is the benefit of short-term memory in the courtroom? It aids the learning process.

In courtroom persuasion we attempt to activate a decision maker's long-term memory in a number of ways, typically by association and repetition. If we can associate new information with information that is already stored in a juror's long-term memory, storage of the new data will be facilitated. In addition, if new data are repeated enough times (by reference, not by rote repetition), they will usually be transferred to long-term storage.

There has been much recent innovative research that relates to *working memory* (a rapidly fading set of "engrams" that stores only recent events in our brains) and to *reference memory* (all of the stable images and facts that we have learned and committed to long-term memory). This research has focused primarily on how memory is transferred from working memory to reference memory. Since many of the memory functions of judges and jurors involve the success or failure of this transfer process, we will continue to explore how to enhance long-term reference memory with working memory.

However, the psychological messages that are the most persuasive and powerfully compelling in the courtroom are those which are already reflected in a juror's long-term reference memory. In other words, themes used in trial that conform to a juror's pre-existing belief structure or life experience have a better chance of becoming part of a juror's long-term memory about the case than themes that are new or conflict with a juror's pre-existing experience. For this reason, some trial attorneys and trial scientists believe that a case is decided before jurors ever enter the courthouse.

§ 2.04 | HOW PERSUASION WORKS IN THE COURTROOM

Persuasion is communication that is intended to reinforce, shape, or change responses of the audience. A trial lawyer in the courtroom who uses persuasion is trying to influence, reinforce, shape, or change attitudes and behavioral intentions (decision-making) of the judge or jury. Clearly, persuasion is more than merely communicating objective facts and information. If persuasion in the courtroom simply consists of relating the facts of a case, we would not need lawyers and jurors. We would simply type in the facts on a computer and the computer would decide who wins the case.

Human beings are obviously more complex. An example is the national campaign to persuade people to wear their seat belts. In the 1970s, it was uncommon for people to wear seat belts and, indeed, many cars did not even have seat belts. Thereafter, for almost a decade, the United States government and many public interest groups ran graphic (even gruesome) television, magazine, and newspaper ads to motivate people to visualize the consequences of not wearing seat belts. Laws were passed providing for criminal penalties for the failure to wear seat belts. Driver safety courses taught the use of seat belts as required behavior. As a result of this massive attempt to persuade the public, today most people wear seat belts, according to statistics provided by the National Safety Council.

For the most part, persuasion (to motivate someone to do something he would not ordinarily do) occurs when a credible source of information presents an idea or attitude that differs from ideas or attitudes that are already held by our "audience." In the courtroom, our audience (i.e., the judge, jury, or arbitration panel) may have no preconceived ideas about the topic at hand or may have different ideas or attitudes about the same topic. As a result of the presentation of a new or different idea, the audience will feel momentary tension that produces a kind of dissonance or incongruity. Because of the discomfort that the audience feels, they are motivated to try to remove the dissonance by (1) accepting the new idea readily, (2) rejecting it, or (3) reconciling it with previously held ideas and attitudes.

These days it seems that most people have an opinion about most topics. Nonetheless, most people, including judges and jurors, are open to new ideas and attitudes. So long as these new ideas or attitudes conveniently fit in with previously held ideas and attitudes, the job of persuasion is relatively simple. However, sometimes these new ideas or attitudes are in complete opposition to a person's previously held beliefs. In that case, the job of persuasion is more challenging. In other cases, the difficulty of persuasion falls somewhere in between, such as when new ideas or attitudes do not actually conflict with pre-existing beliefs, but some adjustment is required.

Attitudes are visceral and implicit for most people. We are often known for our opinions about specific topics. We have attitudes about Republicans and Democrats, the safety of air travel, the importance of "family values," and countless other topics. Most of the time we are not even aware that we have these attitudes. At other times, we are quite surprised to find that other people do not share our views. The same is true for jurors. But once an attitude is in place, it is difficult to change.

Clearly, the best option for counsel when faced with a pre-existing attitude is to find a way to reconcile that attitude with the new idea that counsel wants the audience (the decision maker) to accept. For example, if we want jurors to believe that our corporate client has a justifiable defense to punitive damages, we would have a difficult task if the corporation has acted badly. However, if we state that we agree that punitive damages are justified in cases where corporations have acted badly, but that this particular corporation has acted in such a way and demonstrated its contrition so that punishment is not necessary, the persuasion process becomes easier.

Much of our work in courtroom decision-maker research is designed to identify these pre-existing attitudes and discover ways to create themes and a case story that foster acceptance by a likely jury rather than rejection. Basically, we are working to understand the audience and learn how best to make a case that coincides with a likely jury's attitudes and life experiences.

§ 2.05 | THE ELEMENTS OF PERSUASION

In order for attorneys to be persuasive in the courtroom, we must understand the elements that make up a persuasive communication. There are essentially four such elements: the communicator, the message, how the message is communicated, and the audience.

[1]—The Communicator and Credibility

Who the communicator is and how the communicator conducts himself or herself is important to credibility, and credibility is critical to persuasion. Let's say, for example, that you are watching television news this evening. There is a story about a political demonstration in front of the United States Supreme Court building in Washington. In the news tape there is a slovenly dressed middle-aged man with long hair screaming into the camera, "Whenever government becomes oppressive, it is the right of the people to alter or to abolish it!" What would be your reaction? Do thoughts about radical left-wing terrorists come to mind? Most likely, if you were sitting on the steps of Independence Hall in Philadelphia in 1776 and you witnessed Thomas Jefferson reading aloud the Declaration of Independence—which uses essentially the same words—you might feel quite differently.

Now let's complicate the situation a little. Let's say that, instead of the political statement, the demonstrator simply says, "Parents should be better examples to their children." In this instance the message is not controversial and the credibility of the speaker is not really an issue.

Credibility is a complex issue. Most highly educated people would ordinarily accept a conclusion stated in an official publication of the National Academy of Sciences before they would accept one from a tabloid newspaper. So what does this tell us? It tells us that expertise and trustworthiness are critical factors in determining credibility. An organization or person with a reputation for expertise and trustworthiness will generally be perceived as credible.

It is also important to understand that source credibility (credibility attributed to the source as opposed to the content) often diminishes over time, and the message may fade as the source of the message is forgotten or even dissociated from the message. Conversely, the effect of a message sometimes increases over time even though the messenger may not have been perceived as credible (with no perceived expertise or trustworthiness). For example, one of the trial lawyers may be obviously young or inexperienced but have a powerful message, whereas the opposing attorney is more experienced and steady in the courtroom. In these circumstances, jurors will often tend to remember the message better than the messenger. We sometimes refer to this as the *sleeper effect*.

This writer has always found this principle to be a powerful argument for making sure that the messages presented in trial are the most well-researched and effective we can create. There will often be one or more jurors who like or trust one attorney more than another, but who will give a favorable verdict to the client of the attorney whom they believe is less likeable or credible, but whose message is more profound and therefore more persuasive. Credibility can also emanate from a speaker's bearing.

For the most part, people perceive expertise when the speaker appears to be knowledgeable and speaks directly and confidently. Lawyers are generally knowledgeable about the case in trial, and if they are not, jurors will soon discover this intuitively. Sometimes, however, when a trial lawyer who really does know the case equivocates, even slightly, his or her credibility is lost.

In any discussion of expertise and persuasiveness, it is important to note the difference between *similarity* and *credibility*. For example, many people who buy items in a hardware store to remedy a problem tend to rely upon the advice of other people who have experienced the same problem rather than the word of an expert. However, when people discuss a more technical topic such as the composition of ozone, they tend to rely solely upon experts and will scoff at the opinion of a mere neighbor down the street.

After much research we now understand that in some cases similarity is more important than credibility. If the topic relates to a subjective preference (i.e., personal choice), people tend to prefer the opinion of someone who shares their personal values, tastes, or way of life. But when they make judgments about facts or objective reality—such as whether Madrid receives more rainfall than Rome—people prefer the opinion of someone with objective credibility.

In essence this means that in some instances it may be more powerful for trial lawyers to use familiar analogies and references rather than expert testimony. Post-trial interviews often reveal that jurors trusted familiar analogies to everyday circumstances more than the opinions of a learned expert. Moreover, an expert who uses similarity in creating everyday analogies in support of an opinion can be extremely effective. For example, jurors understand what it's like to shop at the hardware store and make decisions about which paint to buy. Some of the most persuasive analogies used by experts in trials have come from such routine experiences.

Trustworthiness is a more difficult issue for lawyers in the courtroom. For the most part, jurors tend to try to speculate about the lawyer's or witness's bias or motives in making important statements. As a result, the audience trusts the communicator more when he or she is not trying to persuade them or has no self-interest. They also trust a speaker more when the speaker admits a failing or accepts blame that appears to be against his or her self-interest.

Research in social psychology has supported the principle that only a credible and trustworthy speaker (someone difficult to discount) can cause marked change when advocating an idea that is greatly discrepant (different) from the pre-existing attitude held by the listener. One's own family experience will probably mirror this research finding. For example, a father's favorite or most trusted child has a better chance of persuading father to radically change a position or attitude than a child who is not as favored.

For this reason, one of the most important goals for a trial attorney at the outset of trial is to gain credibility as soon as possible. It is like building up the balance in a bank account before spending the money. Experience tells us that no matter how strong your case appears to be, there will come a time during the trial when you will need extra credibility to surmount a difficult moment in the trial.

[2]–The Content of the Message

When we talk about the content of a message, we are referring to the substantive information and themes that are being transmitted as well as the style with which it is being conveyed. There are many lively debates in trial advocacy about a number of issues that relate to the content of our messages. Consider the following questions:

(1) Which is more persuasive—a carefully reasoned message or one that arouses emotion?

(2) Is it better to advocate an idea that is slightly different from a juror's or to advocate an extreme point of view?

(3) Should a message express only one side of the argument, or should it try to present the opposing view?

(4) Does the order of speaking (first, second, or last, as the case may be) give the speaker any advantage?

The answers to these questions are found in the published and private scientific research that is available to us as trial advocates.

The first question, the "reason versus emotion" debate, must be answered from an understanding of the particular audience. If an audience is made up of well-educated or analytical people, the rational appeal will usually obtain a better response than if it is presented to less-educated or less analytical people. Thoughtful, involved audiences are generally more responsive to reasoned arguments. Audiences which are less accustomed to analytic thinking or are not interested in the subject tend to make their decisions based upon their perceptions of the communicator and the message, rather than the logic of the argument.

The content of messages also become more persuasive as they become associated with good feelings inside the decision maker. Similarly, happy (contented) people tend to make quick decisions and unhappy people tend to make slow decisions. Therefore, if you cannot make a strong case on the facts, it would be wise to help the jury feel more positive about your case story. This does not always work, but if both cases have equally powerful messages, the odds are better that you will win.

Conversely, some messages are very effective because they invoke negative emotions. For example, fear and anger are strong motivators.

How do you handle a situation when you know in advance that some jurors will find one of your arguments hard to accept? Do you try to "soft-peddle" the new idea or do you present it directly in its most blunt form? We know that some new ideas or attitudes will produce discomfort, and sometimes discomfort causes people to change their opinions in response to a new idea. So we might argue that a more direct and bold approach is preferable. However, sometimes a message that is uncomfortable causes a trial lawyer to lose credibility with a juror.

For example, there have been many instances where politicians and news reporters have taken positions different from a listener, and the listener then interpreted the speaker as biased, inaccurate, and untrustworthy. For the most part, therefore, people are most open to conclusions within their own range of acceptability. Greater disagreement between the new idea and the listener's pre-existing attitude will produce less change in the juror's attitude.

Research has indicated that jurors and arbitrators who are already personally and deeply involved in the subject matter of the trial will be able to accept only a narrow range of new perceptions and attitudes. To these people, even a moderately different message may seem radical. Therefore, if—and only if—counsel has gained credible authority and jurors are only moderately involved in the issue, an attorney should feel freer to advocate a more radical position.

One final thought about advocating a different view from that of jurors or arbitrators and arbitration panels: Most juries consist of people with widely ranging views on most topics. The smart advocate will construct an argument that will appeal to people with all these different perceptions. To be in a position to do that, it is most important to identify these widely ranging viewpoints using scientific decision-maker research or other research techniques, and to experiment with the combinations of messages that will form a stronger composite argument.

As for addressing the opponent's arguments, there is no common sense answer that works 100% of the time. There are situations when we run the risk of weakening our own argument and confusing the audience. However, our message might seem more fair and perhaps even disarming if it recognizes and refutes the opposition's arguments.

For the most part, trial scientists believe that acknowledgment and perhaps refutation of the opposing argument, and addressing evidence damaging to one's own case, strengthens credibility and provides friendly jurors with counterarguments.

One of the more common psychological principles recognized in trial advocacy is the "primacy and recency effect." Most of the long-standing research indicates that the person or argument making the first impression has the most influence on the decision outcome. For example, read both of the following statements slowly and carefully:

(1) Carol is intelligent, industrious, impulsive, critical, stubborn, and envious.
(2) Carol is envious, stubborn, critical, impulsive, industrious, and intelligent.

Now, what is your impression of Carol, positive or negative? Statements like these have been used in research studies which have concluded that the initial impression would be positive.

That is, the *primacy effect* after reading the first statement generally leaves a positive impression. The *recency effect* from the second statement for most people would not be powerful enough to overcome the positive effect from the first statement. A statement such as the second one merely causes most readers to believe that even though Carol's description is mostly positive, Carol has some negative characteristics that make her more human. Previous research has indicated that initial impressions color one's perception of information obtained later in the course of events.

A similar principle applies to the timing of arguments in trial. The primacy effect would tell us that in the short term, the first argument is the most influential, all things being equal. However, we have also learned that a responsive argument is best presented directly after the first argument, and *before* the plaintiff's or prosecution's case.

This is true for two reasons. The first is that judges, jurors, and arbitrators, like everyone else, think in terms of duality. That is to say, they view every argument on a continuum with the truth lying somewhere between the two extremes. We have been conditioned to believe that there are two sides to every story or argument. Second, the recency effect is also powerful, even though, because it comes on the heels of the first argument, it is generally incrementally less powerful than the primacy effect, all things being equal.

But what about the overall recency effect? Research has indicated that, after some passage of time, the primacy effect fades from cognitive and affective memory (i.e., our active thoughts and feelings). Therefore, forgetting has the effect of creating a more powerful recency effect when sufficient time separates the two messages and the jury must come to a decision soon after the second argument.

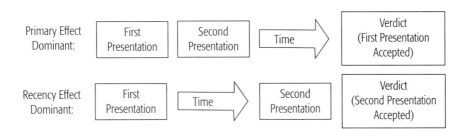

[3]—How the Message Is Conveyed

When we talk about how a communication is delivered, we are primarily talking about the channel of communication—whether the message is delivered face-to-face, in writing, on film, or through some other means. Regardless of the medium, however, there are a number of factors that must be considered. Will the audience pay attention to the message? Will they comprehend it? Will they believe it? Will they remember it? Will they behave accordingly?

Perhaps one of the most frustrating aspects of communication and persuasion is that rarely does one medium of communication seem to be the most powerful. For example, let's consider the spoken word. Over the years we have heard, and perhaps delivered, stirring and powerful speeches and lectures. But try as we might, words are fleeting and memories fade. In addition, only approximately one-third of people rely primarily on their sense of hearing to learn new information. For most people, it is the message in the speech that is more powerful and lasting than the speech itself.

What about written words? We know from experience and research that jurors rely heavily on the words contained in written agreements and communications. However, in the scheme of things, jurors make their decisions based upon the overall messages that stimulate their belief systems. In addition, written words that convey messages are more powerful than written words that have no message, despite their being technically accurate. Therefore, a trial lawyer would be well-advised to use words judiciously and to use words in visual aids that convey messages and mental pictures.

What about videotaped depositions or presentations? Research has indicated that messages that are simple to understand are most persuasive when they are supported or supplemented by a videotaped presentation. Complex or difficult messages are more persuasive when they are written or illustrated (they force the listener to think through the idea). Therefore, the level of difficulty of the message interacts with the medium to determine the persuasiveness of the message.

It would generally be wise to use more than one medium to convey the most powerful messages in a case. Simple techniques such as using text captions to track conversation in videotapes can be very effective. There is an authoritative anchoring effect that builds confidence in a message when courtroom decision makers see and hear that message repeated in different forms in different media.

[4]—The Audience: The Judge, Jury, or Arbitration Panel

Regardless of the specific courtroom audience, it is important to have an understanding of their characteristics before developing or presenting a persuasive argument. These characteristics generally fall into five categories:

    (1) attitudes about specific issues in the case,

    (2) life experiences relevant to specific issues in the case,

    (3) personality traits,

    (4) general values/beliefs, and

    (5) influential demographics.

Attitudes and life experiences relevant to specific issues in a case are often significantly or moderately related to verdict decisions. Research by social psychologists has found that these relationships are perhaps the most important characteristic to know about the judge, jury, or arbitration panel before attempting to persuade them. One of the many advantages to performing scientific decision-maker research in advance of trial is to identify the case-specific attitudes and life experiences that will shape the listening and mental processing of the likely courtroom decision makers in the case.

What about personality traits? For the most part, general personality traits of a judge or jury will not predict their responses to an argument. A particular trait may enhance the effectiveness of one argument or another for a particular judge or jury or, alternatively, may work against it. We know from research that jurors who suffer from low self-esteem are slower to comprehend an argument. However, jurors who have high self-esteem comprehend an argument much faster, but are often prone to change their opinions because their opinions are held more confidently.

The characteristics most often used (although they are the least reliable in predicting behavior) are demographics. As a general matter, demographics of jurors are not helpful in predicting how they will process the case or how they will vote. But a demographic characteristic can often raise a question or create a hypothesis in a particular case that can be helpful in forming a composite understanding of a juror.

Consider this example of a juror's demographics: In a case that involves technical issues, such as patent, trade secrets, or toxic waste, a juror who has a background in science may find it easier to comprehend the details and arguments, but may also have pre-existing ideas that favor one side or the other of the argument.

That is, personal traits, general values, and demographics of the judge or jury can clearly influence their perceptions and their decision. However, in order to be able to predict an outcome one must have a complete picture of the audience's attitudes about specific issues, life experiences relating to specific issues, certain personality traits, general values and beliefs, and demographic influences.

In developing a complete, thorough picture of a judge, juror, or arbitrator, the only reliable information comes from responses to specific questions. The more specific the question, the more reliable the response. The best way to gain a reliable understanding of particular jurors is with questions that are case-specific asked in oral voir dire or a pre-trial juror questionnaire. Many successful trial presentations have incorporated specific references from sitting jurors' responses in oral voir dire or in pre-trial questionnaires. References to statements or ideas in juror responses (without referring to the source) can be a powerful persuasive tool.

§ 2.06 | PATHS TO PERSUASION

There are two psychological routes to persuading someone in the courtroom. The first is the central route that takes place when the communicator and the listener are both focused on the same arguments, and the listener responds favorably or unfavorably. The second route is the peripheral route that takes place when people are influenced by incidental cues, such as the communicator's likeability or credibility, rather than the argument itself.

For the most part, jurors who are motivated to think through an issue will be more persuaded by a direct (central) route that brings out systematic arguments that will in turn stimulate favorable responses. There are many examples around us of persuasion using the central route. For instance, businesses that advertise discount prices and Internet ads that advertise new products to help make work less stressful both appeal to the intellect.

In the courtroom, almost all cases involve issues that require the use of intellect to be able to understand what happened and how a particular party views the remedy(ies) that have been suggested. Jurors who are more intellectually inclined or detail-oriented will be more easily persuaded to connect mentally with central arguments than other jurors.

However, using the central route to persuasion does not necessarily mean that only cognitive faculties are involved. Using the direct approach to making a persuasive argument can also motivate jurors emotionally in a very powerful way.

Research and experience indicate that the central route to persuasion is more thoughtful and less superficial than the peripheral route. As a result, the central route to persuasion is more long-lasting and more likely to influence the behavioral change intended by the argument.

However, the peripheral route generally causes less conscious opposition because it is a subtle approach to an argument. It is more inferential. The peripheral route is persuasive because listeners are often persuaded to accept someone or something associated with the idea, rather than the idea itself.

The most obvious persuasive examples around us are ads that promote soft drinks and clothing. Billboards and magazine ads imply that if we buy a particular soft drink or brand of clothing, we will be more attractive or happy. If we buy this brand of tennis racket or golf clubs, then our scores will increase.

One use of peripheral persuasive techniques occurred in a case that involved a breach of a partnership agreement. The case was essentially a shouting match between a general partner and two limited partners whom he sued for not performing under an agreement to invest several million dollars in capital for the development of a large retirement community. Because the defendants did not proffer their capital, the community was never built and the business failed.

The general partner put into evidence the agreement itself and its breach. The limited partners claimed and put into evidence information suggesting that they were excused from performance due to alleged misrepresentations made by the general partner. Jury research before trial indicated that all the parties had some credibility obstacles to overcome. To tilt the balance toward the plaintiff, the general partner called another limited partner, who had invested the money he had promised, to testify.

This third limited partner just happened to be a former U.S. Postmaster General who by his elegant and thoughtful bearing made a very credible witness. Since he was no longer an investor in the general partner's business, he had no obvious bias. His demeanor and warmth at trial were exemplary. His appearance was more in keeping with an appearance before Congress than a state circuit court jury. As a result, his testimony that he had kept his promise and that he was disappointed that the defendants had not was persuasive for the plaintiff. In addition, the Postmaster General's corroboration testimony that the plaintiff was a man of integrity and honesty also helped the plaintiff win his case.

There are many other examples of how the peripheral route can be used to bolster a central argument in the courtroom. A well-crafted argument will include all appropriate routes and methods to communicate to and persuade the jury.

§ 2.07 | REFERENCES

Aristotle (translated by Barnes), *The Complete Works of Aristotle,* Vol. 2 (Princeton: Princeton University Press, 1984).

Aristotle (translated and organized by Ross, Ross, Ackrill & Urmson), *The Nicomachean Ethics (Oxford World's Classics)* (Oxford: Oxford University Press, 1998).

Aubuchon, *The Anatomy of Persuasion* (New York: American Management Association, 1997).

Bell, *Developing Arguments: Strategies for Reaching Audiences,* (Belmont, CA: Wadsworth Publishing Co., 1990).

Bostrom, *Communicating in Public* (Minneapolis: Burgess Publishing, 1988).

Cialdini, *Influence: Science and Practice* (Needham Heights, MA: Allyn & Bacon, 2000).

Perloff, *The Dynamics of Persuasion* (Mahwah, NJ: Lawrence Erlbaum Associates, 1993).

Thompson, *Persuading Aristotle: The Timeless Art of Persuasion in Business, Negotiation, and the Media* (St. Leonards, Australia: Allen & Unwin, 1999).

CHAPTER 3

Jury Psychology and Decision Making

CHAPTER CONTENTS

> *"[T]o the natural law belongs everything to which a man is inclined according to his nature. Now different men are naturally inclined to different things; some to the desire of pleasures, others to the desire of honours, and other men to other things. There is not one natural law for all."*
>
> — St. Thomas Aquinas (1226-1274)

§ 3.01 | PSYCHOLOGY AND THE JURY DECISION-MAKING PROCESS

Every day thousands of men and women sit on juries across America. Each juror has a private story to tell about his or her successes and failures in life. All of them have a family history that has helped make them who they are. Each of them has a unique life outside the courtroom that influences the way he or she will view the issues during trial.

Regardless of their achievements or lack of achievements, every one of these people deserves our respect and admiration. They usually know little if anything about the dispute at hand, and yet we have interrupted their normal lives and forced them to learn about a dispute and decide how that dispute should be resolved. Most of them believe firmly that their jury service is important. As one San Francisco juror (the general manager of a well-known restaurant) put it, "This is the most important thing I will ever do."

We do not give jurors very much instruction about how to resolve a case. We give them a few legal instructions and tell them, basically, "you're on your own." And if our philosophy about jury trials is correct, then we are also correct in expecting jurors to use their *common sense* in deciding the case. It is appropriate, therefore, for a trial lawyer and client to try to understand what the *common sense* of the jury will be when considering and deciding how the case should be resolved.

In recent years there has been a concerted effort by some judges, legislators, and corporate leaders to undermine the decisions of jurors. The trend toward taking courtroom decision making away from juries is disturbing because of the assumption that juries are not competent to make important decisions. However, trial attorneys and litigants who make the effort to understand and engage juries are finding that the chances of their success in the courtroom are greatly increased and the results more satisfying than they might have anticipated.

This chapter will explore some of the things we know about the mental processing of jurors in the courtroom, and how that affects their behavior when deciding how a case should be resolved. We will discuss what *common sense* for jurors really is and how we can understand how it will be applied by a likely jury in a given case. We might even discover something about ourselves in the process.

§ 3.02 | OVERVIEW OF THE JURY DECISION-MAKING PROCESS

For many centuries, collective (small group) decision-making in both private and public affairs has been a hallmark of Western societies. The conventional wisdom is that small groups of individuals who share a common purpose make better-quality decisions than individuals acting alone. To better understand group decision-making in a courtroom setting, one must analyze the social structure and process within a jury as they affect each individual juror and the jury as a whole.

The influences that will shape the way a juror feels and thinks about a case begin long before trial. As a result, the decision-making process for a juror in any particular case begins as soon as he or she enters the courtroom and starts making assessments of the people and information that are presented.

Researchers who have studied the decision-making behavior of jurors have identified three levels of analysis. The first level refers to the decision-making behavior of individual jurors. The second level of analysis concerns social events that occur before and during the deliberation of the case. The third level of analysis is a review of the cognitive and affective experiences of individual jurors in the context of social interaction before and during deliberation (i.e., how the jury as a whole reaches a decision).

Understanding how a jury reaches its decision requires a review of each of these levels, so we shall consider each level separately. It is important to emphasize that the most effective trial presentations should incorporate powerful themes that appeal to both individual jurors and the jury as a whole.

[1]—Jury Decision-Making Model for Individual Jurors and the Group as a Whole

Scientific research into juror decision making has concluded that there is a three-stage model which best describes the process a typical juror will undergo on his or her journey to making a decision. First, the juror evaluates the facts, arguments, and technical evidence and constructs a mental summary in the form of a narrative story. Second, the juror comprehends the judge's instructions concerning the legal verdict alternatives that are available as decision categories. Third, the juror attempts to find a match between his or her story of the case and a verdict category in order to classify the story into the category it best fits. After individual jurors complete this mental procedure, the members of the jury then interact with each other to negotiate a solution that helps each juror reach the maximum goal of making a decision that gives meaning to the jurors' experiences and helps them to feel good about themselves.

This general three-stage model for decision making is referred to by social scientists as an *explanation-based model*. Within this mental structure, the juror attempts to summarize the case by forming an explanation and creating a story of the case which is used in reasoning toward a verdict. This process begins as soon as the juror begins learning about the case from direct and indirect cues in the courtroom.

[a]—Construction of a Mental Summary

There are both *cognitive* (thoughtful and intellectual) and *affective* (emotional) processes which occur during this first stage of individual decision making. This formation of a summary of the evidence is the same process that occurs when each of us tries to make sense of other events which we encounter in everyday living. Beginning with the initial stages of the courtroom presentation, jurors assign meaning to the case by incorporating into or overlaying on the actual case one or more reasonable explanations or narrative stories that explain the events about which the lawyers and the witnesses have talked. This search for meaning is perhaps the most profound explanation for why jurors behave the way they do.

Perhaps the most eloquent explanation of the role of narrative meaning (i.e., meaning in the context of a story) is reflected in the writings of Jerome Bruner, a famous educational and developmental psychologist, in his work *Acts of Meaning*.[1] In this work, Bruner explains that the central concept of human psychology is *meaning*, along with the processes and transactions involved in the construction of meaning. Bruner states that culture shapes human life and the human mind, and gives meaning to the events and behaviors by creating an

---

[1] See references in § 3.04 *infra.*

interpretive system. He says that our interpretations and perceptions are highly individualized in many ways, but are also greatly influenced by forces around us. He refers to this interpretive system as *folk psychology* or *common sense*. Bruner writes that this *folk psychology* is a system by which people organize their experience in, knowledge about, and transactions with the social world.

The vehicle with which people learn, organize, and relay meaning and understanding is the *narrative* or *story*. Bruner states that the function of *story* is to create an explanation, to provide understanding, and to rationalize events, behaviors, and mental states of other people with whom an individual interacts. In this way, an individual and group can compare acceptable and normal cultural patterns with actions which deviate in matters of legitimacy, moral commitment, and values.

Another interesting and provocative writer on this subject is Joseph Campbell, the great social philosopher and cultural anthropologist. In his work *The Power of Myth*,[2] Campbell explains his belief that the basic driving force for mankind is the search for *meaningful experience*. Throughout his lifetime Campbell immersed himself in the cultural philosophies of human societies around the world and reached back into prehistoric times. Just before his death in 1987, Campbell stated in his last interviews and writings that he had reached the conclusion that it was not enough for man to discover the meaning of something intellectually in an objective way. He determined that it was more important for us to actually *experience* the meaning—to internalize it and feel its effects—in order to undergo a more subjective reaction.

The use of stories, myths, parables, and fables to encourage acceptable behaviors and motivations and to discourage unacceptable ones is well-documented in nearly all primitive and modern cultures. Anthropologists who have studied dispute resolution in Western and non-Western societies have found clear and convincing evidence that unwritten laws or codes for conduct exist and are passed on from generation to generation in the form of stories.

The conclusions of these authors are important to us in the courtroom in one significant respect—we must develop and present the facts of a case with real substantive meaning and experience for every juror. Otherwise, we are simply going through the motions and will have made a case presentation that offers neither meaning nor experience with which a juror can identify and to which that juror can commit.

---

[2] *Id.*

A typical juror concludes the initial stage of the decision-making process with a single dominant story in mind. In fact, researchers have determined that a sizable percentage of jurors have established a clear preference in the case by the end of the opening statement (prior to any exposure to witnesses or evidence). This would mean that, for most jurors, the actual trial presentation is a process of filtering through the evidence to test their individual hypotheses about the case—to either confirm or to alter their original notion of what the case story really is.

Jurors make decisions by:

(1) Forming a new story of what happened
(2) Filtering through the evidence to find support
(3) Comparing their stories to the allegations
(4) Trying to make the stories and the allegations fit together
(5) Negotiating with other jurors

Jurors tend to reason *deductively* (determining the important principles of the case and fitting the facts into them), whereas most of us who are trial attorneys tend to reason *inductively* (determining the facts and details of the case and following them to their logical conclusion). Jurors are not really different from the rest of us, most of whom go through our lives making most important decisions deductively. Our choice of spouse, our selection of career, our purchase of the car we drive—all are usually made using deductive reasoning despite our pride in using the best *logic* we can muster.

In the course of determining the narrative story of the case, jurors will refer back to their life experiences, stereotypes, schemas, attitudes, and any other references in their minds that will help them to understand and find meaning within the particular facts and issues in the case. As we have discussed in Chapter 2, jurors' cognitive structures (everything jurors know and how they reason) are fairly inflexible, and they will make every effort to fit their perceptions of the facts and circumstances of a case into the story they have formed.

[b]—Learning Legal Decision Alternatives

The second stage of the decision-making process usually begins as soon as the jury learns the legal allegations. Most of the time jurors get this information from piecing together random comments from the judge, the trial attorneys, and the witnesses before the charge is read to them prior to deliberations. Rarely do jurors first discover the legal allegations when the charge is actually read.

Regardless of when or how jurors find out what the legal issues are, each juror attempts to comprehend and learn the decision alternatives available in the law as represented by the court. This stage is known as the *verdict representation*. In this stage of the process, each juror attempts to form a concept of the legal framework within which the juror fits the narrative structure or story that the juror has formed about the case. That is, the jurors attempt to fit their own stories of the case into their perceptions of the overall legal framework about which the trial lawyers seem to be talking.

Although brief, this stage is critical to the persuasion process, because it is at this point that jurors begin to formalize their thinking about whether the actions of any party are right or wrong for purposes of their tasks in the courtroom. Most of the time jurors are alternating between the first two stages of the decision-making process. However, in stage two, jurors begin to conclude whether the actions of a party amount to a legal or illegal act *from a layman's point of view*, apart from any legal distinctions and definitions.

Let's consider the example of a medical malpractice case in which a patient died during surgery. In addition to medical negligence, suppose the plaintiff's lawyer claims that the actions of the hospital staff and doctors constituted murder. The jury charge will probably define murder as an intentional act. However, before a juror hears or sees the jury charge, the lawyers will have discussed the concept all the way through the trial. It is here, in stage two, that jurors will decide for themselves whether the actions of the hospital staff and doctors indeed constituted an intentional act resulting in murder.

Once the jurors have reached their own conclusions, the individual characteristics of each juror will determine the strength of his or her convictions about these conclusions. These pre-charge conclusions are difficult to change. It is more likely that jurors will try to interpret the ultimate jury charge so as to conform to their pre-charge conclusions than to alter their conclusions to meet any strict definitions in the charge.

[c]–Classification

This brings us to the third and final stage in the decision process, known as "classification." This final stage, which usually takes place during deliberations, provides the juror with an opportunity to make a match between classification of the episode or story structure and one of the verdict categories prescribed by the court. In this stage, the juror scrutinizes features in the verdict category as they apply to events or relationships that the juror believes are true and are imbedded in his or her internalized version of the story of the case.

During this stage of decision making, jurors freely interact with each other to test their story of the case with the other jurors. This stage of decision making is part of the general socialization process through which jurors reach an ultimate decision.

[2]—Direct Influence of Attitudes in Jury Decision Making

As we discussed in Chapter 2, every juror evaluates what transpires in the courtroom on the basis of his or her life experiences, attitudes, and predispositions. Jurors obviously do not come to the courtroom with blank minds. Their beliefs, values, attitudes, and morals are well-entrenched, and everything that is heard and experienced will be filtered and colored by them.

Changing strongly held attitudes often involves a journey through the process of exposure to the case and its participants, acceptance or rejection of all or parts of the presentation, filtering, discomfort, anxiety, distortion, minimization, rejection, and cognitive dissonance. Most theorists believe that throughout this journey, attitudes not only summarize past experience with the object or subject of those attitudes, but they also play a role in determining future behavior. Research in the field of cognitive psychology has indicated that attitudes direct or guide human behavior in one direction or another, whereas our individual needs for self-actualization motivate us. Therefore, attitudes may be considered to enter the picture predominantly at crucial decision junctures. There are thousands of published scientific studies designed to understand the formation, maintenance, and change of attitudes that are available to us as reference tools.

In the context of decision making in the courtroom, salient beliefs and attitudes will guide individual jurors and the entire jury to reach a decision which conforms to their beliefs and attitudes about the specific issues present in the case.

[3]—How Juror Attitudes and Belief Systems Are Formed and Changed

Understanding the role of attitudes in jury decision making requires an acknowledgment that individual jurors bring their life experiences (including things they have learned as well as their learned thinking processes) with them to the courtroom. It is beyond the scope of our discussion to explore the myriad of earlier life experiences which jurors bring with them into the decision-making process. However, it is important to explore the role these experiences play in the decision-making process as well as the role that socially shared experience plays in that process.

As we have seen, the results of recent social science studies have clearly demonstrated that a juror's cognitive life experiences have shaped the juror's emotional processing, personality, persuadability, perceptions of causal attribution, perceptions of damages, and reactions to attorneys and witnesses. It is equally clear that individual jurors and the jury as a whole are influenced by emotional or affective processing.

A juror's appraisals of *attitude objects* (e.g., people, events, institutions, etc.) are likely to influence that juror's subsequent emotional reactions to them. Conversely, a juror's emotional reactions to an attitude object can yield information for us by inducing thoughts within the juror's mind about it. In practical terms it does not matter if emotion influences thoughts or, in the alternative, if thoughts influence emotion. The result is the same: An attitude which influences the outcome of a decision is, as a rule, based on a juror's emotional *and* thought experiences.

Jurors' attitudes and beliefs are formed in response to information learned through personal experience, through information relayed by other people, and through present moment observation. The formation of attitudes and beliefs is a juror's way of understanding and experiencing the rest of the world around that juror. As a result, in order for us to understand how jurors perceive the issues, parties, and facts of our case, we must make the effort to identify the attitudes and beliefs of likely jurors and understand how they were formed, why they have been maintained, and how they might be changed if necessary.

Attitudes are comprised of *affect* (emotions and instincts), *cognition* (perceptions, thoughts, and interpretations), and *behavior* (intention to act in accordance with the attitude). For example, consider a juror's reaction in a trade secret case. A juror may feel strongly that anyone who steals a secret and sells it to someone else is a bad person (feeling), that anything which a company keeps private is a secret (perception), and that, if given a chance to punish someone for stealing a secret, he or she would do so (behavioral intention). This same pattern can be adapted to any attitude about any subject.

In scientific jury research we closely study these types of patterns in order to identify areas of weakness and strength of a particular issue in a case. We closely study jurors' attitudes, the life experiences that are associated with them, and the role they will play in juror decision making about the case. By studying attitudes we learn a great deal about how to capitalize on the attitudes that likely jurors will have that will be beneficial to us. Conversely, we will also learn about the attitudes that may not be beneficial to us, and how to disarm or change them.

However, it is important to be aware that, like most people, jurors apply different standards to others than they apply to themselves (for reasons associated with self-esteem). For example, in conducting research in tobacco cases, we learned that when asked whether they, themselves, are influenced by advertising and marketing, potential jurors denied this. However, when asked whether *other people* are influenced by advertising and marketing, they usually said "of course!"

This brings us to an interesting observation about attitudes: Jurors will only apply those attitudes that are *salient*. Salient attitudes are those that are actually prompted to appear in jurors' minds by the case presentation, in contrast to attitudes that we predict should apply to the case, but which jurors do not find applicable. Every juror, like every other person, has thousands of attitudes about something. The question is always, "Which ones will you encounter in your case?"

The only way to know which attitudes, beliefs, values, life experiences, and mental processes likely jurors will utilize to decide a particular case is to refer to case-specific experience or to undertake some kind of pretrial research (whether scientifically conducted or not) to identify them, understand them, and learn how to work with them to develop a powerful and persuasive case. There are many different methods to conduct such research that are discussed in a separate chapter on scientific jury research.[3]

Jurors have many belief systems about almost every object, person, institution, life challenge, etc., that they have encountered in their lifetimes. And, for the most part, jurors form attitudes that are consistent with their views of the world around them and consistent with their other attitudes and beliefs.

For counsel to avoid being frustrated by attitudes that at first appear to be insurmountable, one must understand a number of important characteristics of attitudes. Although it is true that jurors are committed to their own perceptions, it is also true that there are a number of weaknesses in the attitude

---

[3] See Chapter 6 *infra.*

formation process that make many of them more susceptible to adaptability and change.

The first weakness in attitude formation is that there is a value hierarchy which most people have in their overall belief system that often allows one attitude to be superseded by another, more important, attitude. For example, imagine a case against a major financial news publisher alleging that the newspaper wrongfully published a critical exposé of an investment brokerage company. The brokerage company alleges that the article was based upon false or misleading information and, as a result, that the company had to terminate its business due to the adverse effects of the article on its reputation. At trial, the plaintiff argues that the author of the article and the publisher had unsavory motives that interfered with their objectivity. It argues that the publisher knew the kind of effect that critical articles could have on such a company. It argues that because of the loss of the company, 100 innocent employees lost their jobs with a company where they loved to work.

In defense, the publisher states that it had no ill intent and that if the published information was false, the responsibility for any errors lay with the sources of information, not the publishing company. The publisher also implied that the company failed due to poor management.

Can you predict the following?

(1) Which of the themes for each party would prevail?
(2) What juror attitudes would arise and which would predominate?
(3) How would jurors feel about the parties and the issues? Surely some jurors would see the struggle as a David vs. Goliath matter, but how sympathetic would they be toward wealthy investment brokers or a newspaper publisher?
(4) Would jurors be preoccupied by their perceptions of how a newspaper reporter researches and corroborates information for such an article?
(5) Which themes and attitudes would affect jurors more deeply and motivate them toward a verdict—issues about corporations and publishing or issues about everyday people losing their jobs so a publisher could sell more newspapers by publishing a sensational article?

Most likely, if the plaintiff in the case relied solely upon juror attitudes about businesses suing other businesses or about proper publishing procedures, it would be litigating on the defendant's turf and presenting its arguments from a position of weakness. The publisher in this case has a good reputation among most businesspeople and certainly is the expert when it comes to publishing procedures. Most important, however, attitudes of most jurors about business and publishing topics are equivocal and not based upon much experience. They would have a difficult time being motivated by them alone.

Nevertheless, most jurors have a lot of experience with losing jobs and how painful that can be. Surveys and private jury research also show that jurors believe that most large companies are not loyal to their employees, and that companies will sacrifice employees for profit.

Even the most experienced trial lawyers and trial consultants cannot always accurately predict which of the attitudes and belief systems of a likely jury will be activated in a particular case without conducting empirical jury research before trial. However, once the attitudes and perceptions of a jury are activated, they will most surely influence the jury's decision in the case.

Experience in the courtroom tells us that waiting until oral voir dire to find out which attitudes a jury will have is a classic case of *too little, too late*. Even with recent voir dire reforms, some trial courts will still not allow attorneys to ask many questions about juror attitudes and beliefs. In addition, even when a trial court allows the trial attorneys to ask questions about jurors' attitudes about specific issues in the case, jurors often do not tell the whole truth about their opinions. Most oral voir dire questions are fairly transparent to jurors and they will often give answers which are politically correct or which simply tell the trial lawyer what the lawyer wants to hear. In addition, it should not escape our notice that if the only objective data we have obtained about likely juror attitudes are obtained during oral voir dire, it is rather late to be of any use in the development of themes and a case story. Even information obtained in a written pre-trial juror questionnaire gives the trial team a little more time to make the information useful prior to opening statement.

Therefore, investigating likely juror attitudes and experiences before trial is a good idea.

[4]—How Jurors Process Arguments and Evidence

Through this book we will discuss why case themes and stories must be presented in simple yet varied forms in order to touch the hearts and minds of different jurors whom we are likely to encounter in the courtroom. In this section we will discuss individual differences in juror characteristics and what they mean in terms of presenting information (argument and evidence) at trial.

[a]—Individual Characteristics of Jurors

The characteristics of jurors that are the most observable are also the least reliable when one is trying to predict their attitudes and verdict choice. Anyone who has watched actual or mock jurors before and during deliberations has been surprised many times when certain physical cues a juror gave out (such as nodding, writing, or smiling) turned out not to be predictive of his or her verdict preference. Why? Jurors—like the rest of us—are complex creatures in every respect. We often give off cues that point in one direction to someone who does not know us, but at the same time think something quite different from the perceptions that the other person has formed. We might remember an old cliché—*charm* is saying one thing, but thinking something else.

As we will see later in this chapter, there are many factors that influence each juror's decision in a particular case, most of which are not detectable without precise, focused inquiry and observation. For purposes of this section, we will examine how differences in attitudes, life experiences, personality traits, values/beliefs, and demographic influences cause jurors to process information differently.

So, how do we know if our themes and case story are being accepted by a jury? How do we know if the jurors are receiving our signals accurately? There are actually four sources of information we can draw from to answer these questions.

First, if our jury research is conducted scientifically, it is likely that the actual jury is responding similarly to our research jury panels, and perhaps better if we have learned how to enhance the case. Previous comparisons between mock trial results and actual trial results tell us that.

Second, the information we acquire about each juror during jury selection will tell us a lot about how individual jurors will approach the case differently. This means that voir dire should be as thorough as possible in terms of learning about jurors' feeling and thinking styles, including their attitudes. Written questionnaires are useful both in selecting a fair and impartial jury and in understanding how the jurors who are actually empanelled will process the case.

Third, we need to regularly study the latest objective information about juror psychology and juror decision making. The more we, as trial lawyers, understand jurors from an objective point of view, the more we can supplement and add power to our natural intuition.

Finally, the more we realize that our natural instincts are biased, the more we will want to seek out observations from other professionals (usually other skilled attorneys or experienced trial consultants) to give us a broader perspective. Like everyone else, we are limited by our personal biases about the circumstances of a case. In order to be sharp and effective, we must develop methods for obtaining and confirming information about what an actual or mock juror is actually thinking at any given time. However, there are some important things to know that will give us an advantage in such an effort.

At the outset we should understand that, despite frequent attempts to analogize the human brain to a computer, the comparison is imprecise in many important ways. First, people have feelings and intuition, and computers do not. Moreover, computers can recall information in exactly the same format that it was encoded no matter how long the information was stored, and human beings cannot.

[b]—Juror Decision-Making Styles

Jurors tend to fall into two categories regarding styles of decision making. They are either affective thinkers or cognitive thinkers.

Affective thinkers tend to rely on their emotions when making important decisions. They are highly selective and judgmental about the information they receive, and often make impulsive decisions. They tend to be more affected by symbols and meaning and are less logical in their decision making. Affective jurors tend to be conceptual and are more affected by the use of who and what the parties represent to them in the internal stories they develop about a case. They may be liberal or conservative. Most affective jurors have often studied or are employed in social science fields such as social work. Of course, these characteristics are general and do not in themselves predict verdict preference.

Cognitive jurors tend to be more logical in their approach to making decisions. All their lives they have been conditioned to think about important things in some detail, and in making well-considered, thorough decisions. They will generally tend to wait until they have heard both sides of a story before making any decisions.

Affective jurors are sometimes a frustration to trial attorneys. They tend to make decisions intuitively and may easily disregard factual evidence that is inconsistent with their perceptions of the case. In truth, most problems persuading affective jurors lie more with presentations of a case which ignore the individual needs and characteristics of jurors than with the jurors themselves. It is a pretty good rule of thumb that we should present a case with a special focus on the characteristics and needs of affective jurors, and depend on cognitive jurors to note the details of the case in the course of the trial. It is also important to remember that both cognitive and affective jurors are searching for the meaning of the case, and hence both kinds of jurors will be affected by the themes and the story that we tell.

[c]—How Jurors Make Sense Out of Evidence

Often in this book we discuss the influences of attitudes and life experiences on juror decision making. However, for purposes of this section we should talk about some of the technical aspects of juror psychology and the ways jurors make sense out of a large quantity of data. As a result, we can understand how to use this information in developing our most powerful and persuasive case.

When jurors try to understand the evidence, arguments, and the meaning of both, they tend to think either *systematically* (following the arguments and the progression of the evidence) or *heuristically* (looking for cues outside the evidence to help them take a mental shortcut). Most jurors will make a significant effort to follow each lawyer's presentation of evidence and the arguments, and to form a story of what happened and what that story means.

Because listening to a lengthy case presentation can be very tedious, jurors will listen only when they are motivated to do so. They are usually highly motivated at the outset of trial and less motivated once they begin to believe they have things figured out. Jurors are also motivated by subject matter and how interesting the case themes, personalities, and story seem to be. Hence, at the outset of the trial and if and when the subject matter and evidence are interesting, jurors will tend to think more systematically.

When jurors are not as motivated by the subject or case story to follow the details, they tend to resort to mental shortcuts such as heuristics. There are many types of heuristics that jurors use to make sense out of a case. Each of us uses heuristics every day in making large and small decisions. For example, when our favorite golf pro begins a game with a few poor shots, we tend to believe that he or she is having a bad day and that the rest of the game will suffer as well. Why? There are usually no specific facts to bring us to that conclusion. One might then say that "life experience" leads us to such a conclusion. Experience at what? How surprised we then are when the golf pro succeeds in making up the early losses and winning the tournament. And of course we will rationalize the change in outcome by thinking that *somebody must have given him a pep talk* or *she must have changed caddies.*

What about statements about the economy? Let's say that your next-door neighbor tells you that interest rates are coming down next month and that stock prices will go up. Would you believe him? Why or why not? Would you believe it if you heard it in a speech that the Federal Reserve Chairman made on CNN? How about the Chairman of the SEC?

Jurors use the same types of rules of thinking that the rest of us do. In a case that is mundane and uninteresting, jurors tend to rely on heuristics to process the case. Also, the more complex the subject matter of a case, the more jurors rely on heuristics to try to understand the story of the case and what it means. They will usually try very hard to understand the technicalities, even though they may have avoided studying complex or scientific methods throughout their educational experiences. But in the end they will rely on simple principles that have guided them for most of their lives. This means that regardless of how intelligent or educated a jury panel seems to be, a trial lawyer's time simplifying the case and developing a powerful story is time well-spent.

In cases where the parties or attorneys are well-known, pre-trial publicity has been extensive, or the issues are particularly timely, jurors will tend to think about cases more systematically at first to determine if the elements of the case conform to their stereotypes or schemas. However, ultimately jurors are more likely to resort to heuristics in reaching their conclusions. And, as we have indicated before, cognitive jurors tend to think more systematically for longer periods of time than affective jurors.

We should not equate systematic thinking with accurate thinking. Systematic thinking is not any more accurate than heuristic thinking. Both styles of mental processing can be equally accurate or inaccurate.

Since jurors regularly engage in heuristic thinking, let's take a closer look at some additional characteristics of heuristic thinking. When jurors think in terms of heuristics, they are simply trying to make sense out of events that they did not personally experience by comparing what they are hearing in the courtroom to things that they already know. They may be right (accurate) or they may be wrong.

For example, one of the most common questions encountered at trial regards causation. If a company makes a product that, according to its own studies, has a one in 1 million chance of failing and hurting someone based on a sample of 10,000 people, what will jurors focus on in determining fault and causation as a general proposition? Will they focus on the 999,999 times that the product performed safely or the one time that it did not? What if the plaintiff offers another study that the chances are one in ten based upon a sample of 100 people? Jurors typically do not understand scientific methodologies and will believe whatever conforms to their story of the case based upon cues they have received in the case.

Research and experience tell us that if jurors have reason to suspect that a company has bad motives, they may very well disregard the study with the larger sample in favor of the smaller one offered by the plaintiff because the latter study conforms to their perceptions of the company. In addition, they may well focus on the one time the product failed, and determine that the company had prior notice of a defective product. This type of conflicting and detailed evidence is precisely the type of evidence that affective jurors enjoy disregarding.

Jurors also tend to believe that the more wealthy and powerful a company, the more likely the chance that the company knew everything there was to know about the effect of its products and services, even if direct evidence is lacking. Of course, if we are defending a large corporation and we know something about heuristics, we can literally change the focus or reframe the issues in order to force other heuristics to arise that will make jurors less angry and/or more understanding of the company's position.

Perhaps the most common type of heuristic has to do with a juror's determination of whether the people or the evidence is representative of the stereotypes or beliefs they have previously formed. The more representative a party or its behavior is perceived to be, the more a juror will act in accordance with the heuristic. However, the more genuinely different the person or facts seem to be from the jurors' preconceived ideas, the more jurors will scrutinize the evidence to be certain of that difference. If jurors are convinced that the object of their scrutiny is genuinely different from the heuristic, they will usually resolve or rationalize the difference in a way that avoids the effect of the heuristic.

For example, consider the heuristic or belief among some jurors that large companies will fire people who have less power in a company in order to improve the company's profit margin. But suppose the undisputed evidence indicates that the company conducted a company-wide survey to determine which people were producing better-quality work, and then laid off those employees who were not productive in response to a drop-off in sales. Let's also present evidence that the company spent a great deal of effort and money helping the people who were laid off to find new jobs.

Most probably, jurors will scrutinize the company's efforts closely to make sure that they are genuine. Along the way, an enterprising opposing lawyer might posit the argument that the company's efforts were a ruse to cover up its true intentions. Since the idea of a ruse and cover-up is in accordance with some jurors' mistrust of corporations, this argument has some natural strength. It will be up to the company, its managers, and its attorneys to make persuasive arguments to the contrary.

Sometimes a heuristic is so powerful that to overcome it would take much work and some lucky breaks. For example, let's consider a medical malpractice case where a patient suffered an unusually severe loss of blood during surgery at the hands of a surgeon who had had a previous problem with misuse of barbiturates. Suppose also that there was no evidence of drug use by the doctor during the surgery and no testimony from anyone present at the hospital that he appeared to be under the influence. However, the plaintiff also presents evidence in the form of tearful testimony from a former wife about the times the doctor deceived her about his misuse of drugs and her suspicions that he performed surgery while secretly under the influence.

What will a jury think? Will they refer back to life experiences where they know of people (perhaps themselves) who secretly abused drugs or alcohol and who were never caught despite the damage that was done? How will they feel about a doctor caught up in such circumstances? Research indicates that jurors are greatly angered when someone whose heuristic tells them should be above reproach has instead acted in a way that runs counter to the heuristic and has therefore hurt someone severely.

Another phenomenon that is characteristic of juror thinking is finding order or a direct link between events where the evidence is tenuous or at best suggestive. Perhaps the most difficult task for a juror is piecing everything together in a way that is coherent and makes sense in the juror's own frame of reference. During trial, lawyers often leave out details or offer only sketchy information about facts, events, or issues that jurors believe are important. They want to know more, but in most jurisdictions they are not allowed to ask questions, even through the presiding judge. Therefore, lawyers must anticipate the jurors' questions and address them or suffer the consequences when jurors imagine what the answers must be and fill in the blanks for themselves out of whole cloth.

One of the mental techniques that jurors use to answer questions about people or events is *representativeness*. Jurors will often determine whether someone is good or bad by a perception of the person as a member of a certain class in the juror's mind (e.g., self-serving corporate executives). They will often determine causation by looking at the consistencies they see in someone's past behavior or in a juror's own life experiences to determine the probability that one action caused a certain consequence.

[d]—Juror Decisions About Causation

In summary, the following factors are essential to juror causation decisions:

♦ What is the consistency in the actor's previous behavior?
♦ Is the actor's behavior consistent with how other people would behave under the same circumstances?
♦ Is the actor's behavior distinctively appropriate or inappropriate?

§3.03 | INDIVIDUAL AND GROUP DECISION MAKING IN JURIES

In essence, decisions made by individuals who constitute a group determine verdicts (and other intermediate decisions) reached by a jury. In this context, it is important to understand the cognitive and affective factors which affect the decisions of each individual, as well as those which impact the entire jury group.

[1]—Factors Which Influence Jury Decision Making

Before we can understand how jurors make decisions and prepare effective trial presentation strategies to impact those decisions in favor of our clients, we must understand the wide variety of factors that influence jurors' decision-making processes in a case and how those factors influence juror thinking. Such understanding clearly enhances development of an effective trial and jury selection strategy.

Once we are aware of the many factors which influence learning, comprehension, evaluation, and decision making, the legal standard imposed on jurors to be impartial and to "decide the case strictly on the facts of the case" seems absurd. In American jurisprudence, jurors are instructed to reach verdicts by utilizing facts and evidence while at the same time ignoring their pre-existing biases, feelings, and the like.

However, substantial research indicates that there are a multitude of factors which are not part of the formal evidence but which influence jury decisions.

The diagram which follows demonstrates the primary factors that are found to affect jury behavior and decision making.

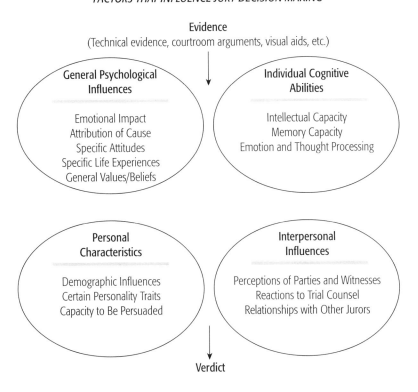

FACTORS THAT INFLUENCE JURY DECISION MAKING

Evidence
(Technical evidence, courtroom arguments, visual aids, etc.)

General Psychological Influences

Emotional Impact
Attribution of Cause
Specific Attitudes
Specific Life Experiences
General Values/Beliefs

Individual Cognitive Abilities

Intellectual Capacity
Memory Capacity
Emotion and Thought Processing

Personal Characteristics

Demographic Influences
Certain Personality Traits
Capacity to Be Persuaded

Interpersonal Influences

Perceptions of Parties and Witnesses
Reactions to Trial Counsel
Relationships with Other Jurors

Verdict

[2]—The Role of Individuals in Jury (Group) Decision Making

It is difficult (if not impossible) for a single juror to comprehend all of the facts, events, and nuances contained in a courtroom case presentation. No matter how intelligent or experienced a juror may be in making important decisions, every juror (like every person) has limitations. For example, individual jurors engage in a variety of coping mechanisms which "filter" information and shape perceptions so as to create understanding and comfortable feelings, and to minimize dissonance. Individual jurors are also limited in their decision-making abilities by varying emotional reactions, differing assessments of attribution, varying intellectual capacities, varying abilities to recall, differences in cultural views and sensitivities, widely varying life experiences, and many other factors.

As a result, individual jurors construct different stories or assessments of the same court case even though every juror is exposed to the same facts, evidence, and arguments in the case. They construct their own versions of the facts and motivations of each of the trial participants. This process of applying a juror's understanding of life and the creation of a narrative or story for the case being presented to the juror in court is the driving force behind an individual juror's decision about the case. Once a narrative has become firmly visualized, jurors will rarely change their opinions about what happened, although they will occasionally change their minds about how the events in the case should be legally classified.

Ironically, the same limitations and characteristics of jurors which give meaning to individuality are also strengths to aid the jury group as a whole to arrive at a fair and equitable decision. Differing insights and differing views of events and motivations provide the group with a more complete perspective from which better-quality decisions can be made.

[3]—Group Influences on Individual Juror Decision Making

There are a number of ways in which various processes within a jury influence each juror's individual decision making. For example, in the context of group decision making, information is exchanged as a by-product of the social interaction which occurs within the group. Group interaction can cause knowledge to be acquired that might not otherwise have become apparent to individual, inexperienced, unworldly individuals without that interaction. It is at this critical point in the jury deliberation process, for example, that jurors with any relevant life experience will generally speak up, and sometimes become *instant experts.*

It is human nature for jurors to talk to each other about the case during the trial despite court admonitions, and they are of course directed to talk to each other during deliberations. But regardless of when substantive interaction begins, each member of the group typically begins with a set of ideas about his or her own goals and alternative choices. As discussion emerges, individuals share their ideas with others, and in a larger jury of eight to twelve people they are especially likely to share their ideas with other members of a subgroup with whom they share characteristics. Gradually, the sharing of ideas through juror social interaction influences the development of each individual's cognitive representations of the case and the decision to be reached, as well as those of the entire jury or any subgroup.

The information exchanged by members of the group includes both cognitive and affective information (i.e., how each of the jurors thinks and feels about the issues in the case). The differences in the effects of each are interesting and profound. As a practical matter, it is difficult if not impossible to separate one's thinking about a set of circumstances from one's emotional reaction to them. However, in the process of sharing cognitive and affective information, the recipient of a shared idea will likely react differently than the originator, although the recipient may be motivated to act in concert with the originator. As a result, jurors will often (if not usually) arrive at the same conclusion, although their thoughts and feelings (rationale) about it may differ.

Similarly, in the quest to comprehend and solve any dilemmas presented in a case, jurors almost always learn and understand the case more completely only after discussion within the group. There are many reasons which form the basis for this principle. For example, the group as a whole usually has a more complete data base for problem-solving than any of its individual members. It is not likely that any individual member of the jury has acquired or has access to all of the pieces of information needed to undertake the group's obligations.

Significantly, as a general proposition the knowledge presented in a case in court is not developed or presented in an explicitly stated, usable form that individuals may easily adapt in making a complete decision. For this reason, one of the most important challenges for any trial attorney is to arrange the case into a simple, easily digestible story form that conforms with the way jurors resolve a case.

Because of the severe limitations that an individual juror experiences in internal formation of a trial story which explains the case—due to restrictions on evidence available to him—a narrative that at first appears to be complete to the trial team is often determined to be inadequate or inappropriate once it is expressed before the rest of the jury group. The checks and balances offered by a multiple-person jury help to ensure what is often referred to as *justice*. Whether there is more justice dispensed by a six-person jury or a twelve-person jury we will leave to the philosophers.

Finally, the interaction of a group can provide motivation to arrive at a more complete and morally supportable decision than a decision made by one individual juror acting alone. Interpersonal energy among jurors, either positive or negative, tends to enliven and stimulate more complete, acceptable discussion and results.

[4]—The Active Role of Individual and Shared Attitudes in Jury Deliberations

Trial lawyers and social scientists generally regard the jury deliberation process as a highly complex, easily misunderstood system of social interchange. Yet it has remained a mystery to many people. Our focus here will be to take a closer look at the social events which occur in the jury deliberation process in order to better understand juries' verdict decisions.

In general, the jury deliberation process is less systematic than individual decision making. However, recent research has concluded that there are generally three models that describe the social process for sharing information, and for learning and comprehending during many jury deliberations: (1) *evidence-driven* deliberation style, (2) *verdict-driven* deliberation style, and (3) a combination of the two.

In the evidence-driven deliberation sequence, individual jurors simply recount their understanding of the events and evidence previously described to them in the courtroom. During deliberation, the jury will begin by attempting to reach a consensus about "what happened" in the circumstances described in the courtroom. It is common for individual jurors to have reached differing accounts or conclusions about the underlying sequence of events in the story that was revealed to them. The fact that other jurors have visualized a different narrative is usually surprising to jurors. During consensus building, jurors will pool information about their alternative versions of the story and attempt to influence other jurors' opinions. In the last stages of the deliberation, jurors tend to reach agreement about the definitions and instructions given to them by the judge and to match the circumstances or conclusions they have reached to the appropriate verdict category that was presented to them by the court.

By contrast, in verdict-driven deliberations jurors tend to discuss piecemeal parts of the complete narrative of events and organize them around the elements of the verdict or instructions from the court as a form or outline for their discussion. Verdict-driven deliberations are usually chosen by juries whose prime opinion-makers are more focused on the task at hand than on an overall understanding of the case story.

One dramatic contrast between verdict-driven and evidence-driven styles of deliberation is the degree of consensus reached by jurors. Evidence-driven juries tend to reach a greater level of consensus than verdict-driven juries. This is presumably true because individual jurors share their understanding and comprehension of the complete narrative or story throughout jury deliberations and, therefore, the entire jury discusses its ultimate decision in terms of understanding and comprehending the complete story. Conversely, verdict-driven juries tend to segment their discussion around particular verdict issues and, therefore, it becomes difficult at times to reconcile the pieces into an overall, comprehensible, coherent story.

There are a number of discussion tools that have been reported consistently in actual and mock jury deliberations as social influence tactics to reach group consensus. The first mechanism is that jurors pool information relevant to the truth about events or law under discussion. Second, jurors make appeals to values, beliefs, morals, right or acceptable conduct, and other attitude- or value-motivated subjects in order to persuade other jurors. Finally, there has been substantial evidence of other social behaviors which we might label as *reward and punishment.*

The pooling of information is how jurors collectively share their acquired knowledge from their life experiences and from the courtroom presentation. Social interaction within the jury plays an important role in this pooling and acquisition of knowledge. Efforts to comprehend the case become both an individual enterprise and a social activity.

When jurors share information and put together a group sense of the case, they use many social tools they have learned over time to facilitate this process. For example, at least some members of the group will be interested in how and why events occurred. They will ask questions and invite others to comment about their ideas about the case. Because there is a finite set of information available from all the jurors on any topic raised in the deliberations, jurors move from one subject to another in a natural sequence of events to satisfy their own needs for resolution.

In their efforts to comprehend the activities and ramifications presented in a case, jurors try to achieve insight or to find satisfactory explanations for the occurrences or series of events. This requires that jurors coordinate pieces of old and new information in order to build a full, sensible representation of what factors define or delineate the case.

As a practical matter, the social structure of the jury may facilitate or restrict interaction among its members depending upon the personality and leadership styles of the jury opinion-makers. Similarly, subgroups may develop within the jury which form cohesive bonds between themselves and no-one else. These subgroups often share a perspective and knowledge base which are dramatically different from those of the remainder of the jury, thereby making consensus difficult to achieve.

Utilizing these social tools, jurors tend to forge a spontaneous structure in which to reach a decision. This multilevel (individual, subgroup, and group) perspective of the case reached through information sharing encourages us to maintain a broader view of how jurors make decisions than that offered by traditional trial advocacy texts and simplified reviews of jury verdicts.

[5]—What Goes On in the Jury Room?

One of the first comprehensive studies of the dynamics of jury discussion during deliberation was conducted by Bridgeman and Marlowe in 1979.[4] In this study, the researchers contacted 120 jurors following the completion of ten felony trials, and sixty-five of the jurors agreed to be interviewed.

When they were asked about the effect of the deliberation itself on their individual decisions, only fifteen of the jurors mentioned deliberation as being one of the main reasons they eventually voted the way they did. Eleven of the jurors said that the opinions of other jurors most influenced them, and no-one felt that his or her vote was determined by the foreperson. (All of the jurors stated that the foreperson was nominated spontaneously by another juror and was selected quickly as someone who could help the group stay focused on the task at hand.)

When the jurors were asked at what point in the trial they first became convinced of the defendant's guilt or innocence, twenty-three jurors (35%) said they made their minds up near the beginning or the middle of trial, thirty-one (48%) said they reached a conclusion near the end of the trial, but before deliberations, and only eleven (17%) said they were undecided until deliberations. (Jurors were admonished from the beginning of trial to keep an open mind and listen to all the evidence before deciding the case.)

A word of caution: All of the data received in this study are the results of juror self-reports. Whether the responses the jurors gave were politically correct responses rather than completely truthful responses we do not know. However, later published and private studies have indicated that between 70% and 85% of jurors establish a clear leaning in a case by the end of opening statement. These later data were obtained most often in a controlled environment by asking mock research jurors to state their preferences about

---

[4] See references in § 3.04 infra.

who should win and who should lose the case at the end of opening statement, and then taking the same measurement again at the end of trial.

We also know that during deliberations jurors tend to organize the evidence in the same way as the attorneys in the case, provided that the information was presented and organized in a way that makes decision making simple. For example, if one or both of the trial attorneys use time lines to organize their presentation of the case and to make their arguments, jurors will try to follow the same time lines to such a great extent that they will create their own time line if the court has not allowed the demonstrative time lines to be entered into evidence.[5]

We have already discussed the tendency of jurors to share information about the case from their memories to allow the jury to collectively recall details. Based upon studies which have looked at the accuracy of juror recall, we estimate that jurors who have not shared their recollections of the case with each other recalled only about 60% of the information directly stated in testimony and less than 30% of the information contained in material evidence. In contrast, a jury group that has shared recollections of proceedings tends to recall more than 90% of the information directly stated in testimony and more than 80% of the information contained in material evidence.

However, these statistics do not mean that jurors will change their opinions about the case just because more accurate information has been recalled during deliberations. As we have discussed earlier, jurors are very resistant to changing their constructions of the evidence and their stories of what they believe happened once they have been formed and stabilized. The only jurors who can generally be persuaded to change their perceptions of the case during deliberations are those jurors who are genuinely undecided, and they are usually a very small minority.

For reasons related to self-esteem, jurors may vigorously avoid admitting that they misunderstood the evidence, that they misjudged the credibility of a witness, or that their stories of the case are not plausible. It is much easier to persuade such jurors that they misunderstood the legal instructions and definitions. A juror who can claim that he or she misunderstood the legal issues possesses a gracious, less embarrassing stratagem to resolve any dilemmas he or she has with the other members of the jury.

---

[5] In several cases juries actually taped key pieces of evidence including documents to a wall in chronological order to re-create the demonstrative time line that had been presented by the attorneys for one or both of the parties during trial but which had been denied admissibility by the trial court.

A FINAL WORD: HOW JURORS THINK

To win a jury trial, you need to understand how jurors think, and create a compelling story and themes that lead jurors to the result you want.

Jurors think about justice as "good" or "bad," and decide cases based on their perceptions of "good" or "bad" conduct, or "good" or "bad" people. Jurors cannot be expected to decide "objective truth." Instead, jurors vote for the party they think is "good" and vote against the party they think is "bad." It is an imperfect system of "gut justice." Reliable research confirms that more than 75% of all jurors believe that, "Whatever the judge says the law is, jurors should do what they believe is the right thing."

To win, a trial lawyer must weave the evidence into a vivid tapestry of themes and stories that will help jurors *feel* they are "doing the right thing." When faced with complex facts, jurors filter and selectively listen to and store evidence by adopting a story with moral themes to help them decide who is "good" and who is "bad"—e.g., "profits over people," "personal responsibility," "fairness," and who should win. If the lawyer does not offer a fitting theme and story at the outset of the trial, the jurors will create one on their own.

To *feel* they are "doing the right thing," jurors typically decide: (1) What did each of the parties *know* before the event at issue? (2) What could the parties have done (*power* and *ability*)? (3) Why did each of the parties choose his or her particular course of action (*motive*)? Evidence of document destruction, evasive answers, incessant objections, and other "hiding" reflects negatively on a party's *knowledge, power/ability,* and *motives* because "good people have nothing to hide." By contrast, evidence of a party's outward concern for customers, employees, and others can reflect the selfless compassion we associate with heroes.

Winning trial lawyers use stories and themes to organize and present facts that answer the jurors' key questions, and make jurors *feel* their vote in a client's favor is the "right thing" to do. A lawyer without a good story is like a warrior without a weapon.

– Kenneth R. Chiate, Partner
Pillsbury Winthrop LLP

§ 3.04 | REFERENCES

Abelson, Kinder, Peters & Fiske, "Affective and Semantic Components in Political Person Perception," 42 J. Personality & Social Psychology 619-630 (Apr. 1982).

Ajzen, "The Directive Influence of Attitudes on Behavior," in Gollwitzer & Bargh, eds., *The Psychology of Action: Linking Cognition and Motivation to Behavior* (New York: The Guilford Press, 1996).

Benson, "Attributional Measurement Techniques: Classification and Comparison of Approaches for Measuring Causal Dimensions," 129(3) J. Social Psychology 307-323 (June 1989).

Boyll, "Psychological, Cognitive, Personality and Interpersonal Factors in Jury Verdicts," 15 Law & Psychology Rev. 163-184 (Spring 1991).

Brekke, Enko, Clavet & Seelau, "Of Juries and Court-Appointed Experts," 15(5) Law and Human Behavior 451-475 (Oct. 1991).

Bridgeman & Marlowe, "Jury Decision Making: An Empirical Study Based on Actual Felony Trials," 64 J. Applied Psychology 91 (Apr. 1979).

Davis, Kameda, Parks, Stasson & Zimmerman, "Some Social Mechanics of Group Decision Making: The Distribution of Opinion, Polling Sequence, and Implications for Consensus," 57 J. Personality & Social Psychology 1000-1012 (Sept. 1989).

Eagly, Mladinic & Otto, "Cognitive and Affective Bases of Attitudes Toward Social Groups and Social Policies," 30 J. Experimental Social Psychology 113-137 (Mar. 1994).

Forster, Lee, Horowitz & Bourgeois, "Effects of Notetaking on Verdicts and Evidence Processing in a Civil Trial," 18(5) Law & Human Behavior 567-578 (Oct. 1994).

Haney, Hurtado & Vega, "'Modern' Death Qualification: New Data on Its Biasing Effects," 18(6) Law & Human Behavior 619-633 (Dec. 1994).

Hastie & Pennington, "Cognitive and Social Processes in Decision Making," in Resnick, Levine & Teasley, eds., *Perspectives on Socially Shared Cognition* 308-327 (Chicago: American Psychological Ass'n., 1996).

Hatano & Inagaki, "Sharing Cognition Through Collective Comprehension Activity," in Resnick, Levine & Teasley, eds., *Perspectives on Socially Shared Cognition* 308-327 (Chicago: American Psychological Ass'n., 1996).

Houston, Joiner, Uddo, Harper & Stroll, "Computer Animation in Mock Juries' Decision Making," 76 Psychological Reports 987-993 (June 1995).

Malouff & Schutte, "Shaping Juror Attitudes: Effects of Requesting Different Damage Amounts in Personal Injury Trials," 129(4) J. Social Psychology 491-497 (Aug. 1989).

Mayer, *Thinking, Problem Solving, Cognition* (New York: W. H. Freeman & Co., 1997).

Moran, Cutler & De Lisa, "Attitudes Toward Tort Reform, Scientific Jury Selection and Juror Bias Verdict Inclination in Criminal and Civil Trials," 18 Law & Psychology Rev. 309-328 (Spring 1994).

Neck & Moorhead, "Jury Deliberations in the Trial of U.S. vs. John Delorean: A Case Analysis of Groupthink Avoidance and an Enhanced Framework," 45 Human Relations 1077-1091 (Oct. 1992).

Ogloff & Vidmar, "The Impact of Pretrial Publicity on Jurors," 18(5) Law & Human Behavior 507-525 (Oct. 1994).

Resnick, "Shared Cognition: Thinking as Social Practice," in Resnick, Levine & Teasley, eds., *Perspectives on Socially Shared Cognition* 1-20 (Chicago: American Psychological Ass'n., 1996).

Schwarz & Bohner, "Feelings and Their Motivational Implications: Moods and the Action Sequence," in Gollwitzer & Bargh, eds., *The Psychology of Action: Linking Cognition and Motivation to Behavior* (New York: Guilford Press, 1996).

Scudder, Herschel & Crossland, "Test of a Model Linking Cognitive Motivation, Assessment of Alternatives, Decision Quality, and Group Process Satisfaction," 25(1) Small Group Research 57-82 (Feb. 1994).

Tindale, Davis, Vollrath, Nagao & Hinsz, "Asymmetrical Social Influence in Freely Interacting Groups: A Test of Three Models," 58 J. Personality & Social Psychology 438-449 (Mar. 1990).

Ward & Reingen, "Sociocognitive Analysis of Group Decision Making Among Consumers," 17 J. Consumer Research 245-262 (Dec. 1990).

Wicklund & Steins, "Person Perception Under Pressure: When Motivation Brings About Egocentrism," in Gollwitzer & Bargh, eds., *The Psychology of Action: Linking Cognition and Motivation to Behavior* (New York: Guilford Press, 1996).

Wiggins & Breckler, "Special Verdicts as Guides to Jury Decision Making," 14 Law & Psychology Rev. 1-41 (Spring 1990).

CHAPTER 4

Juror Perceptions about Common Issues in Personal Injury and Business Lawsuits

CHAPTER CONTENTS

"The truth is more important than the facts."

– Frank Lloyd Wright (1867-1959)

§ 4.01 | INTRODUCTION

Those of us in the trial professions are often apprehensive that the judge, jury, or arbitration panel might not share our view of a case. We have learned from experience that our theoretical perspective of the evidence may be based upon our best thinking, but it may not be the most effective approach for persuading particular fact finders. For many reasons, we develop biases in the development of cases for trial or mediation that blind us to the view that the prospective fact finders will have. We might not be aware that there are different ways to view the evidence. Even the most experienced, successful trial attorneys suffer from the effects of their own limited perspective.

For example, attorneys who are dedicated to the protection of plaintiffs' rights sometimes tend to view the behavior of all large corporations as predatory and believe that jurors will naturally feel the same way. By adopting this view, a plaintiff's attorney might take a superficial approach to a case that simply indicts every corporation for the same bad behavior without looking deeper in a case for a more powerful, substantive approach to winning.

Conversely, attorneys who are dedicated to the protection of the rights of corporate defendants sometimes view plaintiffs as opportunistic and jurors as too sympathetic. Defense attorneys too often buy into the public relations of "civil justice reform" advocates who claim that their efforts have persuaded all right-thinking judges and jurors that most lawsuits are frivolous. An attorney in this situation might be tempted to believe that he or she can persuade any jury with a standard, but superficial, appeal to second-guess the plaintiff's case on tort reform grounds.

Using any superficial or standard approach to try a case is necessarily chancy because it does not take into account the underlying meaning of the case to different juries or the subtle, but powerful, circumstantial differences between cases. Taking the time to study the likely perceptions of jurors may seem eccentric, but making the effort to develop a case for trial without understanding the likely jurors' perceptions is extremely risky.

There are many questions about likely juror perceptions that plague us as we try to develop a case that will please our clients and win fact finder approval.

Is it true, as some people say, that jurors are most sympathetic to plaintiffs? Will jurors ignore key facts in order to award a verdict against a company with a "deep pocket"? Are jurors prejudiced against large corporations? Are jurors more influenced by an attorney's behavior than the themes or facts of a case? Is the jury system an obstacle for corporations or businesses?

Certainly, people around us such as clients and other attorneys can have strong opinions about answers to these and other questions. However, do the other people with whom we associate really know the answers? When do we question the assumptions that we (and other people) have made about juror perceptions?

Each of us has a method for keeping a well-balanced perspective on a case so that we can recognize danger signs and make decisions that consider the actual fact finders' perspective. Most of us recognize that we must consult with other people who may have an unbiased view of the issues in a case. Consulting with others about our cases is a tradition in law practice.

However, we are fortunate these days to have many reliable sources of information about how a likely jury is going to view a case. Published studies of juror thinking, published verdict reports, and private jury research can all be helpful.

In this chapter we will focus on information we have gained from scientific study of juror decision making, including how jurors perceive common issues contained in lawsuits between individuals, professional people, and companies. We will discuss how jurors sort out the issues and assign responsibility. We will analyze how jurors view claims for actual and punitive damages, and how they determine the amount, if any, that should be awarded. The information contained in this chapter draws from studies of actual jury verdicts, post-trial interviews, general juror interviews, and public opinion polling.

§ 4.02 | HOW WE KNOW WHAT JURORS ARE THINKING

We know what jurors are thinking by asking them and by listening and observing them as they process information about a case. Over the past thirty years, we have accumulated a great storehouse of responses from jury-eligible people who have actually served on juries or who have participated in scientific research studies. Using post-trial interviews, community attitude surveys, focus groups, and simulated trials, we have gathered substantial information to help us understand how jurors think about certain issues.

Although the process of asking questions and getting responses from jurors may seem simple, obtaining reliable, useful information is actually quite complicated. For example, if a jury in a particular venue ruled against a plaintiff in a patent prosecution case, will the next jury in a similar patent prosecution case view the same issues in the same way? Even though 81% of the average jury population nationwide may not trust corporate executives to tell the truth, will they trust corporate officers who testify in a particular case?

Obtaining information about juror perceptions that is reliable and useful in preparing your next case for trial is a matter of gathering information about juror perceptions methodically and interpreting the information accurately. We all have a natural tendency to overgeneralize. It is human nature for us to take skimpy amounts of information and extrapolate from them to create expectations about how future events will occur or how people will behave in the future.

We are fortunate that social science research techniques have been developed to help us answer difficult questions about how people, especially jurors, think. The scientific literature comprises thousands of scientifically conducted studies about the formation, maintenance, and change of attitudes that affect how people make important decisions. Hundreds of scientific studies of jury decision making and jury behavior have been published and are still in print or otherwise available.

Some research techniques are more scientific than others. For example, opinion polls taken on news Web sites do not incorporate true scientific methods, but they do produce interesting, provocative responses. Since more than 50% of the American population has access to a computer for browsing the Internet, some of the opinion polls accumulate thousands of responses. One could argue that although these data-gathering methods are not particularly scientific, the huge number of responses makes the data somewhat useful and reliable regarding the issues that are presented. Moreover, the reliability of computer-based research in conducting focus groups and gathering opinion data is increasing rapidly.

We should also discuss sources of information where reliability is questionable. For example, "conventional wisdom" about jurors is the most common source of information that is often unreliable. For decades, trial advocacy books and articles have often repeated information about jurors that has little or no scientific or statistical support. Consequently, well-intentioned trial attorneys have developed and presented cases in court based upon ideas about jurors that were not true.

Unfortunately, those of us who have practiced law for many years have become comfortable with conventional wisdom about jurors. It is sometimes difficult for us to accept new ideas about how jurors will perceive our case.

But there are a number of very important reasons to seek out new information about how jurors perceive issues. First, and most important, information is power. Second, creative uses of information can enhance power. Finally, the world is constantly changing and we must change with it.

Let us now move on to discuss what we know about juror attitudes and perceptions on specific issues that you might face in your next trial.

§ 4.03 | ATTITUDES AND JURY DECISION MAKING

Juror attitudes and perceptions have three basic characteristics that are important to understand. First, they are identifiable and can be measured. Second, they are fluid and therefore subject to change. Third, changes in juror attitudes are usually the result of changes in context, rather than changes in substance. In other words, juror attitudes are founded upon bedrock beliefs that may be applied differently depending upon the nature of a particular situation.

Why are attitudes so important to us? We know that an attitude is essentially a favorable or unfavorable evaluation about something or someone that is expressed through one's beliefs, feelings, or intended behavior. That is, we size up the rest of the world using attitudes and personal perceptions.

In order for us to be able to understand jurors (as well as judges and arbitrators), we must be able to understand the attitudes and perceptions that motivate them to arrive at their decisions.

[1]—The Importance of Attitudes and Life Experiences in Jury Decision Making

In previous chapters we discussed the importance of attitudes in juror decision making. One concept we discussed involved the principle that the more specific and relevant a juror's attitude is, the more that attitude will likely factor into a juror's ultimate decision about the case. We also discussed the concept that all of us tend to take shortcuts in trying to understand the world around us. We often stereotype people and institutions in our culture, and we presume that people and companies behaved in the past as we would have expected them to.

Jurors are subject to the same laws of psychology as the rest of us. They have expectations of people and institutions in our culture, and they expect people and institutions to behave in accordance with those expectations. Indeed, fact finders, like the rest of us, resist notions that a person or group could have acted in a way that runs counter to our perceptions, even if there is solid evidence that would support a departure from our natural inclinations. Thankfully, as we learned in Chapters 2 and 3, many techniques will assist us in persuading fact finders either to avoid perceptions that are contrary to our position in a case or to overcome initial perceptions that may be contrary to that position.

Rarely are people's perceptions identical. Each of us has had life experiences that "individualize" our views of the world. However, most perceptions do fall within patterns and categories that have been created for us by our social environment.

For this reason, it is important for us to know about certain key attitudes and perceptions that jurors have about personal injury, product liability, medical malpractice, business litigation, and intellectual property disputes. Once we are aware of general juror perceptions, we can identify important questions about specific juror perceptions of fact patterns and themes that should be studied in particular cases. Awareness of these perceptions can also serve as a roadmap as we develop our case story for presentation to the actual fact finders.

[2]—Forming Perceptions: Jurors' Psychological Stages

Juror perceptions about a case develop in phases or stages much like we download graphic images from a Web site or travel down a foggy roadway. The first perceptions of jurors are fuzzy and unclear. As jurors gather more information about the case, their perceptions become more focused. There are critical junctions along the way where key themes and evidence will cause them to begin to frame the evidence and meaning of the case. In the final phases, their attitudes and perceptions are clear enough to help them to make key decisions about the case.

The stages that jurors go through in developing their perceptions of a case tend to be universal, although their individual attitudes and the speed or rate with which they progress will vary. These stages include:

+ Angst and confusion
+ Information gathering
+ Matching information with life attitudes and experience
+ Verification
+ Motivation to act
+ Challenge and confrontation with other jurors
+ Closure

[a]–Angst and Confusion

Even the most self-confident jurors are anxious about their role as a juror. The more complex the case, the more jurors are concerned about their ability to measure up to the task. In addition to their normal concerns about being able to function as a productive member of a group, they also have concerns about how to maintain their self-esteem in the company of strangers and in a courtroom environment. They instinctively know that they will be called upon to decide the case outcome, and they want to make a decision about which they will feel proud. (Research indicates that judges and arbitrators experience some of these same feelings.)

Much of the anxiety that jurors feel results from pressures that include normal stresses of home and work life, as well as the experience of being forced into an unfamiliar, highly structured environment like a courtroom.

In addition to anxiety, jurors are confused. Although we believe strongly in the value of the advocacy system, it fosters a great deal of confusion at the outset of most cases. Jurors have often commented after trial that they felt convinced after the initial plaintiff's presentation during voir dire or opening statement, only to be confused when they were also persuaded or convinced by the defendant's opening presentation. Their state of confusion is usually only momentary as they adjust their thoughts and feelings to the conflicting accounts of the case.

From a psychological standpoint, jurors are confused because they have a natural tendency to rapidly form a coherent story about what happened in the case and what it means to them. We have discussed this principle in some depth in Chapter 3. At the outset of trial, the motivation to rapidly form perceptions and draw upon life attitudes and experiences to understand the meaning in the case is strong. In addition, confusion and uncertainty about their perceptions also produces considerable angst. As a result, there is a powerful drive to understand the information in the case and to make decisions about it rapidly.

However, the advocacy process forces jurors to observe and consider the opposing information early in the case, at the same time as they are forming their perceptions. Most trial courts even instruct jurors to keep an open mind until after final argument. Therefore, although most jurors (like most other people) can prolong decisions for a limited time, they try to comply with courts' requests, thus prolonging the confusion phase.

The real problem is that the longer jurors are anxious or confused, the more frustrated they become and the less attention they pay to the details of a case. We spend a great deal of time in jury research studying ways to present cases so that they start out with simple, yet powerful information and progress in complexity as the jurors become ready to accept more complex aspects of the case. If jurors are too anxious to give us their full attention, this careful preparation is wasted.

It is a good idea for a trial lawyer who is preparing for trial to make mental lists of jurors' likely worries as well as aspects of the case that may cause confusion. Such lists will help provide counsel with a real appreciation for how jurors are thinking and feeling during trial.

This awareness will likely result in an added measure of sensitivity that will benefit you in many obvious and some not-so-obvious ways. For example, once you are acutely aware of the pressures that jurors are feeling, you will be motivated to find ways to "get to the point" faster and to present information to jurors in more powerful, clear ways.

[b]—Information Gathering

Jurors begin gathering information about the case immediately upon hearing or seeing anything relevant in the courtroom. They have an almost insatiable desire to learn everything they can about the people and the circumstances to begin the process of forming a meaningful story.

This information-gathering stage may continue throughout the testimony, and in a few instances, into closing argument. The duration of this phase will depend upon the complexity of the facts and the clarity with which they are presented, as well as the mental acumen of individual jurors.

However, in most instances, jurors will have received enough information to begin forming opinions about the case by the end of opening statement. Once these opinions begin to form, jurors, like most decision makers, will filter through the remaining information about the case looking for evidence that will corroborate their beliefs about the case. Evidence that contradicts their initial beliefs about the case is usually held in abeyance until jurors are more comfortable about their conclusions.

[c]—Matching Information with Life Attitudes and Experience

From the outset, jurors will be constantly comparing the information they are receiving in trial to their long-held attitudes and previous life experiences. In this process, facts and themes in the case that are already familiar to them gain a higher degree of understanding and acceptance early in the process.

One of the important benefits of knowing juror attitudes and beliefs prior to trial is the ability to present a case that matches the jurors' expectations. If jurors determine that the circumstances in the case are recognizable and they agree with your themes at the outset, you have a head start.

There will be trial situations where the themes and circumstances you espouse will not be familiar to jurors or where those of your opponent have more early popularity with the jurors. Advance jury research should be helpful in finding ways to meet and overcome these situations with themes and strategies that will neutralize the early popularity of the opposing case. It is in precisely these types of situations that scientific jury research and experienced trial consultants can be of greatest value.

As we have discussed in other chapters, each juror is searching for the most important personal meaning in the case. Jurors usually discover this meaning at the point where they begin to feel that the themes or circumstances in the case resonate with their long-held beliefs or life experiences.

[d]—Verification

Even as they are matching circumstances in the case with their attitudes and experiences, jurors are at the same time seeking verification that their impression or preliminary story about the case is true. Once jurors have begun forming identifiable perceptions about the case, it only takes a minimal amount of supportive information to verify their impression or preliminary case story.

For example, if a juror intuitively feels that a company has acted badly or has bad motives, any supportive information, no matter how slight, may be enough for a juror to verify his or her beliefs. Like most decision makers, jurors will look for verifying evidence to the exclusion, perhaps, of more voluminous information that would contradict their beliefs. Conversely, if jurors feel intuitively that a company is a good company and had good motives, they will look for verification of this belief and discount information to the contrary. This is all part of the natural filtering process.

There are a few jurors who will need little verification for their perceptions. They will view the raw information in the case and make rapid conclusions without waiting for verification. These are jurors who perhaps should have been eliminated during voir dire. However, since we realize that voir dire does not usually exclude all biased jurors, it is best to know the prevailing attitudes and perceptions before trial to be able to develop strategies to persuade jurors who might draw quick conclusions against your case.

Regardless of the amount of verification needed by a particular juror, there are some interesting behaviors attached to verification. Often when jurors perceive that a lawyer or witness is corroborating their perceptions, they will nod or smile in recognition. When jurors perceive that a lawyer or witness is contradicting their perceptions, they will look confused, furrow their eyebrows, or even disengage altogether while staring blankly into space.

[e]–Motivation to Act

Once jurors have formed conclusions and verified them, they usually begin to feel more comfortable about the case and confident enough to visualize a potential decision in the case. They begin to feel more powerful and self-reliant. At the point when a juror feels empowered, it becomes exponentially difficult to convince the juror to change his or her mind.

For some jurors in some cases, the point at which they feel empowered can occur very early in the case. Afterwards, they will continue to filter evidence and look for continual verification, but they become easily bored. It will take a dramatic (and usually cathartic) event to cause them to reconsider their opinions about the case.

For most jurors, however, the point of empowerment occurs at some unexpected point in the trial proceedings when they have gauged the verifying evidence and found that the evidence that would contradict their perceptions about the case can be comfortably discounted, or even dismissed. They have reached a level of assurance wherein their dominant attitudes and relevant life experiences are reflected in the circumstances of the case.

Some jurors in some cases do not feel empowered at any time during the trial. The circumstances of the case have not resonated with them, and they will be easily persuaded by other jurors to accept the other jurors' perceptions about the case and to rely on the most scant information to make a decision. Final argument is important to these jurors. They are struggling to reach conclusions about which they can feel confident.

However, at the point when average jurors feel a level of significant power and confidence about the case, they are so motivated to act (make a decision) that they begin to visualize the upcoming deliberations. They begin thinking about ways to cement alliances with like-minded jurors and to convince other jurors. Your ability to persuade them to accept ideas that conflict with their new convictions is then minimal.

If jurors are feeling empowered and their perceptions of the case are favorable to you, it will be beneficial to present information that is consistent with their beliefs. You will also want to make every effort to insure that the jurors who are favorable to you and are empowered are leaders among the jury. However, even if jurors are beginning to be empowered and their perceptions are not favorable to you, all is not lost.

There are many ways to persuade jurors who are already feeling empowered, but whose perceptions may be somewhat unfavorable to you. One way is to more directly address the pivotal issue that would change their opinions and offer information that would neutralize the adverse position. There are a number of powerful visual strategies that will get attention and successfully contrast the two sides of an issue.

Regardless of the strategy used to persuade jurors, it is important to help jurors feel confident enough to make a statement about your case at or before the time they are feeling empowered. Your efforts will support their need to enhance their self-esteem. Keep in mind that your efforts should be directed at those jurors who are likely to be opinion-makers or leaders in the group.

[f]—Challenge and Confrontation with Other Jurors

It surprises most jurors that the other jurors in their group have different perceptions and opinions about the case. Their surprise is quickly overcome, however, with an instinctive need to evaluate how other jurors feel and determine how to challenge and confront them so that they can all move forward together to accomplish the task of making a uniform decision.

This stage of decision making is usually reached during deliberations, but not always. Jurors often discuss evidence and issues with each other in an effort to better assimilate what they have seen and heard. In the process, they sometimes reach consensus without being aware of it. Jurors have a natural tendency to look for agreement from other jurors and to convince those who may think differently about the case.

During this phase, jurors will try to convince the other jurors with observations and evidence that they have acquired during the trial. The opinion-makers on the jury will usually frame the discussion. Those jurors who do not have any strong opinions to share will generally let the opinion-makers lead the way.

At the end of most trials, the jurors are generally split in their thinking about liability or damages issues. You might view the situation as having friends and enemies on the jury. One of your tasks, therefore, in final argument, is to equip your friends with themes and information to help them prevail in their challenge from and confrontation with the other jurors. You might even want to restate the pivotal questions that jurors will face in deliberation and demonstrate how the evidence and themes in the trial support the outcome you advocate.

[g]–Closure

Jurors want to reach a point in their experience in the case where they feel satisfaction and closure. In other words, they want to feel a deep, abiding sense that they have "done the right thing."

It will be beneficial in final argument to help jurors visualize how they will reach this closure by deciding the case in your favor. One helpful technique, often used in cases where a party's position becomes more acceptable after additional careful consideration of the evidence, is to ask the jury not to make a decision until they feel that they have considered everything and are ready to reach a decision that is consistent with their attitudes and life experiences. By reminding jurors of the long-term considerations of the case and the importance of the case to the outside world, you help jurors visualize the deeper sense of closure they will receive by this broader, more careful consideration.

[3]–The Complicated Link between Juror Attitudes and Jury Decision Making

For thousands of years scientists, philosophers, theologians, and educators have studied connections between thoughts and behavior, character and conduct, and private thoughts and public actions. Because of this effort, we generally believe that our private beliefs (attitudes) and feelings determine our behavior in public. Therefore, we assume that if we want to influence how people act, we must influence their thoughts and feelings. If we want to change how people act, we must cause changes in their hearts and minds.

However, we learned in the first twenty years of social psychological research (ca. 1945-1965) that changing one's attitudes does not always change behavior. This means that simply causing favorable changes in jurors' attitudes will not always result in a favorable verdict.

Similarly, the attitudes that people express will not always predict their behavior. In the courtroom context, just because jurors express certain attitudes (either in voir dire or in jury research) does not mean necessarily that you can predict their decisions at the end of trial.

Consider, for example, the famous Andrea Yates murder case (the mother who drowned her five children). In that case, the jurors indicated that they felt sympathy for a mother who had severe postpartum depression and possibly bipolar disease. Without asking further questions, one might believe that these jurors would be pro-defendant and acquit her. However, the jurors were also angry that a mother would drown her children. They felt strongly that they had a responsibility to state as a group that the murder of children by their parents (especially mothers) should not be tolerated under any circumstances. However, they also felt strongly that the death penalty should be reserved for people who have committed heinous crimes and who are a danger to society. They did not believe that Mrs. Yates should be executed under all the circumstances in her case.

From an objective point of view, these attitudes may or may not predict the behavior of a jury. Even though juror attitudes may seem straightforward and simple, the truth is never clear until it is published in a verdict.

The attitudes that we express and our behavior are subject to many external influences. People—including jurors—do not always act in accordance with their stated beliefs because there are other influences present in their decision-making process. Some of these influences may include:

 ◆ Other strongly held attitudes that neutralize the first attitude;
 ◆ Social influences from other jurors;
 ◆ Likes or dislikes of different key people in the case (e.g., attorneys or witnesses); and
 ◆ Life experiences that neutralize the effects of the attitude.

Juries in tobacco cases often reflect the dynamic nature of attitudinal influences in jury decision making. Most jurors do not trust corporate executives in large corporations. Jurors believe that they often lie. Similarly, jurors believe that nicotine is addictive and unhealthy. However, jurors generally believe that individuals have a responsibility to themselves to avoid the use of products that they know in advance are unhealthy.

Even though there are jurors in virtually every tobacco trial who hold these competing attitudes, the verdicts in these cases have been quite varied from venue to venue and jury to jury. Why? Attitudes *do* often predict behavior when:

♦ The decision maker perceives that the attitude is directly connected to the situation or circumstances,
♦ Other influences are minimized, or
♦ The attitude is powerful in the decision maker's thinking process.

§ 4.04 | LOOKING AT EVIDENCE

Attorneys and jurors live in different universes that sometimes overlap. To an attorney, evidence is whatever the court and rules of evidence allow into the court record. To jurors, however, everything is evidence.

It is interesting sometimes to watch jurors during trial when a comment or item of information has made its way into the court record only to draw an objection that is sustained. Sometimes a judge will even turn to the jury and instruct them to ignore the information that they have just seen and heard. Whether or not jurors can successfully ignore the information is a purely academic matter. Research (and common sense) has indicated that jurors cannot erase information that has been encoded in their brains, especially if the court highlights it with a "pay-no-attention" instruction. Published scientific studies have conclusively proven that court instructions to ignore evidence are not usually effective.

Jurors believe instinctively that in order for them to understand a case and make a decision, they must know everything there is to know, without exception. They are especially interested in knowing about the character and motivations of the parties and key witnesses in the case. They want to know about the character and sincerity of the trial attorneys in order to decide how much to trust the attorneys and believe what they say.

With these points in mind, we will now discuss some common attitudes and perceptions that jurors have of evidence in different types of cases.

§ 4.05 | ATTITUDES ABOUT LAWSUITS AND
        TORT REFORM

A number of reliable studies have indicated that between 65% and 85% of jury-eligible people in the United States believe that there are too many frivolous lawsuits filed. Between 35% and 50% believe that jury awards are too high.

The prevalence of these beliefs may be due, in part, to the activities of people and groups who support civil justice reform. According to the Web site of the American Tort Reform Association,[1] a bipartisan coalition of more than 300 businesses, tort reform proponents have been able to accomplish a number of changes in state laws:

  ◆ Forty-five states and the District of Columbia have enacted tort reform changes in their laws;
  ◆ Thirty states have modified the law of punitive damages;
  ◆ Thirty-three states have modified the law of joint and several liability;
  ◆ Twenty-one states have modified the collateral source rule;
  ◆ Twenty-nine states have penalized parties who bring frivolous lawsuits;
  ◆ Seven states have enacted comprehensive product liability reforms; and
  ◆ Medical liability reforms have also been enacted in most states.

But, what effects, if any, has the promotion of tort reform or civil justice reform had on the attitudes of everyday jurors in the average court trial?

[1]—The McDonald's Coffee Case

Discussions about the McDonald's coffee case seem to work their way into most voir dire proceedings. According to a nationwide poll of jury-eligible adults commissioned by *The National Law Journal,* 44.6% of respondents believed that the jury's decision in that case was a bad decision. Only 6.7% of respondents agreed with the jury's decision.

But what about the attitudes of the jurors who actually sat on the McDonald's case? Were these jurors mindless, pro-plaintiff, Robin Hood jurors who were willing to award millions of dollars in damages at the drop of a hat?

---

[1] www.atra.org.

Part of the answer is revealed in an article written by Andrea Gerlin, a writer with *The Wall Street Journal*.[2] Ms. Gerlin reported interviews with the actual jurors in the case.

In these interviews, the jurors stated that at the beginning of trial they did not understand why they should have to sit on a case that involved a mere coffee spill. However, during the trial the evidence indicated that the plaintiff, seventy-nine-year-old Stella Liebeck, had suffered severe burns and that McDonald's had received over 700 complaints of coffee burns in the previous ten years, many of which had been settled.

The jurors also mentioned their concerns that the McDonald's company executives admitted that they were aware of the possibility of severe burns, but they had not consulted any experts about how to deal with the issue, had no plans to warn customers, and also had no plans to change the temperature or methods by which the coffee was made.

At trial, the McDonald's trial team argued that the severity of the burns was the fault of the plaintiff. They argued that she should have immediately removed her coffee-soaked clothing in order to take the heat away from her skin. They argued that because she was an older person, her skin was thinner than that of a younger person, and thus more vulnerable to injury.

As you might suspect, the jurors did not agree with the McDonald's trial defense. They believed that the company showed a "callous disregard" for the welfare and safety of its customers. They felt that in light of the company's defense, the best way to send a message to the company that its behavior would not be tolerated should involve awarding $2.7 million in punitive damages.

---

[2] Gerlin, "How a Jury Decided That a Coffee Spill Is Worth $2.9 Million," The Wall Street Journal, p. A1 (Sept. 1, 1994). Note that the media reported a number of incorrect facts: (1) that the plaintiff was driving, when in fact she was a passenger in a vehicle driven by her grandson; (2) that the vehicle was moving when the spill occurred, when in fact the vehicle had stopped so that the plaintiff could add milk and sugar to the coffee; (3) that the coffee was really not that hot, when in fact the coffee was kept at a temperature well above that deemed safe by the industry—between 180 and 190 degrees Fahrenheit; (4) that the plaintiff's injuries were minimal, when in fact the plaintiff suffered burns that were severe, painful, and long-lasting; (5) that the plaintiff could have minimized the burns by disrobing, when in fact the spilled coffee permeated the plaintiff's sweat pants for a sustained period of time, holding the scalding liquid in proximity to Mrs. Liebeck's body; (6) that the jury exonerated Mrs. Liebeck of all fault, when in fact it found her to be 20% contributorily negligent, which reduced the award for compensatory damages; (7) that the plaintiff always sought the largest damage award she could, when in fact she had been rebuffed in her pre-lawsuit effort to settle with McDonald's for $20,000 to pay her medical bills; (8) that the $2.7 million punitive damages verdict stood, when in fact the trial judge in New Mexico reduced it to $480,000, or three times the final compensatory damage award of $160,000; and (9) that the plaintiff actually collected the full amount of the award, when in fact she later entered into a secret agreement with McDonald's, the terms of which have not been released to the public, and was required to make some payment toward her medical bills.

Knowing more about the details of the trial in the McDonald's case helps us to better understand why the jurors in the case made the decision that they made. However, few people are aware of the details of the case; most have heard only of the sensational jury verdict.

Fortunately, a number of researchers followed the course of media coverage of the case. One study, conducted by researchers at the University of Washington and the University of Puget Sound discovered that once the verdict was announced, most other media accounts and commentary disregarded the details of the case and simply continued to discuss the sensational verdict.[3] The result of this limited and misleading discussion has been that many people have disagreed with the jury's decision in the case.

[2]—Media Coverage and Tort Litigation

In 1996, researchers conducted a content analysis of 249 articles published in Time, Newsweek, Fortune, Forbes, and Business Week between 1980 and 1990 to examine the media coverage of tort litigation.[4] In their analysis, the researchers compared the frequency of various types of tort lawsuits reported in court system statistics with those reported in the media. They learned that the magazine articles consistently overstated the relative frequency of some forms of litigation, such as product liability and medical malpractice, overstated the proportion of disputes resolved by trial (as opposed to settlement), and overstated plaintiffs' victory rates and average jury awards.

In addition to general media coverage, there are documented accounts of tort reform advocates sponsoring specific advertising campaigns designed to affect public opinion. One such situation occurred in 1997, when the Dow Chemical Company sponsored an advertising campaign in Louisiana to promote its corporate image just when several breast implant cases were ready for trial in New Orleans. A second advertising campaign sponsored by the American Tort Reform Association happened to be under way at the same time, promoting the positive medical uses of silicone. This second campaign was highlighted by photographs of a young woman with a silicone shunt in her

---

[3] Aks, Halton & McCann, "Media Coverage of Personal-Injury Lawsuits and the Production of Legal Knowledge," Paper presented at the annual meeting of the Law and Society Association, St. Louis (May 31, 1997). And see Haltom, *Reporting on the Courts: How the Mass Media Cover Judicial Actions,* pp. 223-229 (Chicago: Nelson-Hall Publishers, 1998).

[4] Bailis & MacCoun, "Estimating Liability Risks With the Media as Your Guide: A Content Analysis of Media Coverage of Tort Litigation," 20 Law & Human Behavior 419-429 (1996).

brain. In the ads for this campaign, the young woman's mother stated, "Silicone is not the problem. The personal-injury lawyers and their greed is the problem."[5]

Have juror decisions been affected by the public discussions—and public relations—regarding tort reform and civil justice reform? We might recall our previous discussions about how attitudes affect decisions. We discussed how powerful attitudes that seem to be directly related to specific circumstances will usually prevail over less powerful attitudes that are too general in nature or that are not perceived to be related to those circumstances. We also discussed how attitudes or perceptions that have been recently uppermost in the mind of the decision maker may be more influential than, perhaps, other not-so-recently considered attitudes, and that if a situation is sufficiently vague or ambiguous, the decision maker might apply his or her most recently considered attitude.

[3]–Relationship Between Attitudes toward Tort Reform and Verdicts

Researchers have discovered that although attitudes toward tort reform can sometimes predict individual juror verdicts, jurors will more often continue to try to formulate decisions that they believe are appropriate, regardless of tort reform laws. In one important study, researchers studied the attitudes about tort reform of 785 potential jurors and compared these attitudes to their verdicts in four different types of cases.[6] The researchers found that there was a significant relationship between attitudes toward tort reform and verdicts. Jurors who opposed tort reform were more likely to support plaintiffs and render verdicts in their favor, whereas jurors who believed in tort reform were more likely to favor the cases of corporate defendants. As a result, it appears that these attitudes may be useful in jury selection.

One eminent jury research team conducted an exhaustive study of the relationship between attitudes about tort reform and verdicts under a grant from the National Science Foundation.[7] In this study, the researchers conducted interviews with hundreds of jurors who were divided into thirty-four groups, ten of which considered versions of a case in which liability evidence was strong and twenty-four groups that reviewed cases with ambiguous liability

5 Schmitt, "Can Advertising Sway Juries?" Wall Street Journal, pp. B1, B3 (March 3, 1997).

6 Moran, Cutler & De Lisa, "Attitudes Toward Tort Reform, Scientific Jury Selection, and Juror Bias: Verdict Inclination in Criminal and Civil Trials," 18 Law & Psychology Rev. 309-328 (1994).

7 Hans, *Business on Trial: The Civil Jury and Corporate Responsibility* (New Haven: Yale University Press, 2000).

evidence. Prior to being exposed to the evidence, each of the participants was asked questions about his or her perceptions of the state of litigation in the nation. The researchers created a score for each juror from that juror's responses on a rating scale known as the "Litigation Crisis Scale," as well as an average score for each jury group. After responding to these questions, the jurors were then exposed to the evidence in their cases. At close of evidence, the jurors reached a verdict. The researchers then compared the scores in the "Litigation Crisis Scale" to the verdicts.

The researchers found that there was a statistically significant relationship between the jurors' litigation crisis scale scores and their verdicts. This relationship suggests that attitudes about civil litigation influence how a juror interprets evidence and decides a lawsuit. These studies also show, however, that attitudes about civil litigation would be *less* influential in cases where the evidence and arguments presented at trial created an ambiguous situation in the jury's perception (i.e., where the plaintiff and defendant present equally strong cases). In such situations, a pro-tort reform juror might decide in favor of a plaintiff and an anti-tort reform juror might decide in favor of a defendant.

Other researchers have looked at the behavior of jurors when they have been given court instructions that reflect the effects of tort reform laws. Two independent studies analyzed potential jury behavior when the jurors were faced with either a law capping punitive damages or one that prohibited awarding punitive damages at all.[8] In essence, the researchers were trying to determine the extent to which jurors could successfully compartmentalize compensatory and punitive damages.

Both studies were conducted at a time when tort reform advocates had made great strides in amending laws relating to damage awards. In both studies, however, jurors were more likely to inflate compensatory damages when the defendant's conduct was egregious, especially when they were not given an option of awarding punitive damages. Conversely, jurors moderated their punitive damages awards when they were instructed that the law capped such damages.

The jurors' comments in each of the studies revealed their thinking. Even though the jurors may have had some disagreements about particular amounts

---

[8] Anderson & MacCoun, "Goal Conflict in Juror Assessments of Compensatory and Punitive Damages," 23 Law & Human Behavior 313-330 (1999); Greene, Coon & Bornstein, "The Effects of Limiting Punitive Damage Awards," 25 Law & Human Behavior 217-234 (2001).

of damages, they all tended to agree that the extent of their compensatory award was intended to (1) make up for the losses incurred by the plaintiff, (2) punish the defendant when appropriate, and (3) deter the defendants and other similarly situated people from future similar conduct when necessary in the jurors' view.

The bottom-line results of these and other scientific research studies suggest that regardless of jurors' exposure to tort reform information, jurors tend to award similar total amounts of money whether the awards include both compensatory and punitive damages or compensatory damages alone. These findings also seem to be supported by statistical reports of verdicts that indicate that the number of plaintiff verdicts appears to be diminishing somewhat (arguably the result of judicial intervention), whereas the average jury award has not changed, and might even be growing larger.

All of the studies indicate that there is a pervasive belief among many jurors that there is a litigation crisis. For those of us who are involved in jury selection and preparing cases for trial, it would be helpful to know which people believe that there is a litigation crisis and what it means to us in terms of their decision-making processes in the courtroom. This issue is important regardless of whether you represent a plaintiff or a defendant because we need to know when the litigation crisis attitude will be relevant to a case and how to address it most effectively in jury selection.

To suggest that those jurors who believe that there is a litigation crisis acquired their attitudes because of media influence is not helpful, and ignores a fundamental insight into human nature. Those jurors who adhere to tort reform beliefs and will apply them to achieve a more conservative verdict are also more likely to believe that individuals have a great deal of responsibility for their own conduct and outcomes. Those jurors are also less likely to hold a corporation or anyone else responsible for someone's injuries absent clear evidence and strong arguments. However, these same jurors *will* hold someone responsible for causing injuries to someone else when the evidence and arguments are powerful enough to motivate them to decide for a plaintiff.

In essence, much of the public discussion and legislation concerning tort reform has occurred in the absence of empirical research. That is, laws appear to be created, eliminated, or changed without lawmakers truly knowing the effects they will have on jury verdicts. The research that has been conducted suggests that efforts to influence jury verdicts by applying changes in the law may have unintended consequences.

Until more research has been conducted to study the effects of tort reform on jury verdicts, the author suggests that trial lawyers and clients focus their attention on developing the most powerful and persuasive case to present to a judge or jury. In those rare instances where tort reform is directly relevant to the specific issues in a case, the presentation at trial can be fashioned to incorporate an appropriate argument. Otherwise, the only time the subject of tort reform is likely to be relevant is during jury selection, when we are trying to determine whether certain jurors will be supportive of or unsympathetic toward one party after they have heard and seen all the evidence.

§ 4.06 | PERCEPTIONS IN PERSONAL INJURY AND PRODUCTS LIABILITY CASES

We tend to think that juror attitudes about issues are concrete and can easily be discerned with a few superficial questions in jury selection, mock trials, or post-trial interviews. However, people who study trends in jury decisions have discovered that juror attitudes and perceptions are quite fluid, run very deep, and can be applied differently to different situations. These factors are especially true in personal injury and products liability cases.

[1]—Antecedents in American History

Just as current legal theories have their roots in *stare decisis*, juror (and public) perceptions and attitudes have their roots in historical experience. In the nineteenth century, American citizens were accustomed to day-to-day hardship. When something went wrong, they generally attributed it to bad luck, the natural consequences of everyday life, or the failure of someone to carry out his or her personal responsibilities.[9] They did not generally look to others as being responsible for their injuries.

For most of the nineteenth century, workers were deemed to assume the risks of their workplaces. Workers who held dangerous jobs were generally paid more than workers who held less dangerous jobs and were, thus, compensated for the increased risk.

---

[9] Friedman, *A History of American Law,* 2d ed. (New York: Simon and Schuster, 1985); Schwartz, "Tort Law and the Economy in Nineteenth-Century America: A Reinterpretation," 90 Yale L. Rev. 1717-1775 (1997).

Workers were often precluded from recovery in situations where they were injured by a fellow worker (under the fellow-servant rule). In those cases where juries were allowed to hear cases of employer liability, their judgments were often conservative due to the prevailing belief that people are responsible for themselves.

In addition, for most of the nineteenth century, the jury held an unchallenged, prominent role in deciding the outcome of civil cases. However, as the U.S. judiciary became more professionalized and trained, some of the jury's powers shifted to trial judges.[10] Even though the Seventh Amendment to the United States Constitution recognized the right to a trial by jury in civil cases, there was a concerted effort to whittle away much of the jury's authority. This tendency continues to the present time.

The impetus for this trend of "chipping away" at a jury's authority is unclear. Moreover, it was presumed by many pro-business constituencies that juries have always tended to be pro-plaintiff even though, by today's standards, early jury verdicts were quite conservative.

By the end of the nineteenth century, some differences between the views of the judicial system and those of jurors began to surface. At that time, contributory negligence was often an absolute bar to recovery. However, in most jurisdictions where questions of contributory negligence went to a jury, both liability and some award of compensation were often elements of the jury's verdict.

A number of important factors have contributed to a shift in juror perceptions that causes jurors to question the behavior of big companies. One such factor has been the significant rise in the number of industrial accidents. Even though the industrial revolution contributed to a better standard of living for most people, it also contributed to record numbers of injuries.[11]

In the case of railroads, Lawrence Friedman said it best:

> "Almost every leading case in tort law was connected, mediately or immediately, with this new and dreadful presence. The railroad was the prince of machines, both as symbol and as fact. It was the key to economic development. It cleared an iron path through the wilderness. It bound cities together, and tied the farms to the cities and the

---

[10] Horwitz, *The Transformation of American Law, 1780-1860* (Cambridge: Harvard University Press, 1977).

[11] Hans, *Business on Trial: The Civil Jury and Corporate Responsibility* (New Haven: Yale University Press, 2000).

seaports. Yet, trains were also wild beasts; they roared through the countryside, killing livestock, setting fires to houses and crops, smashing wagons at grade crossings, mangling passengers and freight. Boilers exploded; trains hurtled off tracks; bridges collapsed; locomotives collided in a grinding scream of steel."[12]

The notoriety and frequency of industrial accidents reached alarming levels. At the start of the twentieth century, there were about 2 million injuries and 35,000 deaths related *each year* to industrial accidents. When compared with the population of the country at that time (approximately 76 million), these figures mean that 2.6% of the people in the nation were experiencing industrial injuries each year.

Despite these statistics, judges and juries were slow to change their views that favored business. Most of the people injured were never compensated because of legal impediments to recovery or because of juror beliefs that most of the injuries were due to plaintiff error, not business error.

One high-profile case illustrates this point.[13] In 1911 the Triangle Shirtwaist Factory, which was located on the east side of Washington Square Park in New York City, caught fire. One hundred forty-six (146) workers, mostly poor Jewish immigrant women as young as thirteen, were killed. Although the company was found to have committed many violations of safety regulations (such as locking fire exit doors to keep workers at their sewing machines and failing to properly maintain fire escapes that then collapsed during the fire under the weight of the frantic workers), a jury acquitted the owners of the company of manslaughter charges. The fire occurred in the top three of ten floors, which contributed to the high death toll because most of the stranded workers could not safely escape from such a great height.[14]

Only one employee was able to maintain a civil case all the way to trial. This case was dismissed after a jury became deadlocked. Twenty-three (23) other cases were settled for $75 each.

---

[12] Friedman, N. 9 *supra* at 468.

[13] McEvoy, "The Triangle Shirtwaist Factory Fire of 1911: Social Change, Industrial Accidents, and the Evolution of Common-Sense Causality," 20 Law & Social Inquiry 621-651 (1995).

[14] There were numerous reports of workers jumping or falling to their deaths onto the sidewalks below in front of the gathering crowd, and the newspaper accounts of the tragedy painted a gruesome scene.

After the conclusion of the case that went to trial, attempts were made to interview the jurors. One of the jurors summed up the attitudes of many jurors throughout the nation in tort cases. He said,

> "I can't see that anyone was responsible. . . . [I]t must have been an act of God. I think the factory was well managed and was as good or better than many others. I think that the girls, who undoubtedly have not as much intelligence as others might have in other walks of life, were inclined to fly into a panic."[15]

These prevailing attitudes had a number of interesting effects. First, the inquiry and the evidence were focused on the responsibilities of the injured person, not the company. Second, there was an unstated assumption that the corporate defendants were innocent or the victims of circumstances, and that the plaintiffs must have wittingly or unwittingly put themselves in harm's way.

By the second half of the twentieth century, notable shifts occurred in political, judicial, and juror perceptions. The sheer number of situations that could not be attributed to plaintiff negligence or an act of God often made it difficult for absolute legal bars to stand. Jurors themselves began to perceive that many of the injuries suffered by workers resulted from decisions made by businesses and not from workers' lack of responsibility. Because most jurors had some experience in the workplace, they were aware that sometimes businesses had power, control, and knowledge that caused or contributed directly to injuries. It made sense to them that businesses should have to pay for the damages they caused.

The political and social shifts that occurred during this time were profound. The Great Depression laid the foundation for the institution of the New Deal and the creation of Social Security. A fundamental increase in social sensitivity and interest in the welfare of common citizens arose. Businesspeople and union leaders negotiated worker compensation and health care plans that provided income and health care for injured and ill employees, while at the same time decreasing corporate liability. State courts, legislatures, and federal agencies expanded the exposure of businesses through loosened contributory negligence provisions, enactment of comparative negligence doctrines, and the establishment of strict liability laws.

---

[15] McEvoy, N. 13 *supra* at 637.

These changes in culture have contributed to shifts in the current attitudes of jurors. In the nineteenth century, judge and jury decisions heavily favored businesses and corporations. In the mid-twentieth century the behavior of businesses was more often placed in the spotlight, and the pendulum swung against businesses. Finally, by the late twentieth century, tort reform efforts had succeeded in making jurors aware of the possibility of excesses in the judicial system.

As a result, jurors' perceptions at the beginning of the twenty-first century seem more balanced, with fewer swings in favor of either plaintiffs or defendants in civil cases. In general all parties to litigation are placed under great scrutiny by juries.

[2]–Perceptions of Plaintiffs

[a]–Are Jurors Guided by Sympathy?

For more than 150 years, there has been a common belief that jurors are naturally sympathetic to plaintiffs. In 1852, Justice Barculo of New York wrote,

> "We can not shut our eyes to the fact that in certain controversies between the weak and the strong—between a humble individual and a gigantic corporation, the sympathies of the human mind naturally, honestly, and generously, run to the assistance and support of the feeble, and apparently oppressed; and that compassion will sometimes exercise over the deliberations of a jury, an influence, which, however honorable to them as philanthropists, is wholly inconsistent with the principles of law and the ends of justice."[16]

More than a century later Peter Huber, a popular author, concurred:

> "Juries face accidents up close, viewing them in the lurid setting of an individual tragedy already completed. . . . The only human reaction to the individual tragedy viewed close up, is unbounded generosity, which any large corporation or insurer can surely afford to underwrite."[17]

---

[16] Haring v. New York & Erie Railroad, 13 Barb. 2, 15 (N.Y. 1853), quoted in Landsman, "The History and Objectives of the Civil Jury System," in Litan, ed., *Verdict: Assessing the Civil Jury System,* p. 45 (Washington, D.C.: Brookings Institution, 1993).
[17] Huber, *Liability: The Legal Revolution and Its Consequences,* p. 185 (New York: Basic Books, 1988).

These views are shared by many people both in the general public and in the legal professions. The majority of respondents in one national poll agreed that plaintiffs had a better chance of winning their cases with juries than with judges.[18] In another poll taken of law professors, dispute experts, and law students, the overwhelming majority stated that plaintiffs in product liability and medical malpractice cases would win more often in jury trials than in bench trials.[19] The respondents as a group believed that plaintiffs would win 63% of the time before a jury, but only 44% of the time before a judge.

Professor Valerie Hans, one of the preeminent jury researchers of our time, argues that this apparent consensus is wrong.[20] She states,

> "The belief that jurors are universally compassionate to injured plaintiffs is simplistic. It does not capture the complexity of the approach that jurors take in assessing the claims of the injured party in a lawsuit against a corporation. Jurors often show doubts about, and sometimes even hostility toward, injured plaintiffs."[21]

Research that has been conducted in scientific jury research studies using both actual cases (pre-trial and post-trial) and hypothetical cases (laboratory mock trial studies), support Professor Hans's point. Like jurors of the nineteenth century, today's jurors scrutinize a plaintiff's claims carefully. They want to know if the plaintiff behaved in accordance with the norms that they expect from someone in the same or similar circumstances.

Typical cases are those where children were injured while under the supervision of their parents. In most such cases, jurors will scrutinize the parents' behavior very closely to determine if they were negligent in watching over the child. Jurors will usually measure the parents' behavior by their own standards. They will make such statements as, "If I were those parents, I would have . . . ."

[b]—Are Jurors Guided by a Standard of Social Duty?

Realistically, a minute number of jurors in the eligible juror populations in most venues will want to find liability and award some damages regardless of real fault. They feel that organizations with more resources than the plaintiff

---

[18] Saks, "Public Opinion About the Civil Jury: Can Reality Be Found in the Illusions?" 48 DePaul L. Rev. 221, 243 (1998).

[19] Clermont & Eisenberg, "Trial by Jury or Judge: Transcending Empiricism," 77 Cornell L. Rev. 1124-1177 (1992).

[20] Hans, N. 11 *supra* at 23.

[21] *Id.*

have a social duty to help the plaintiff. However, the overwhelming majority of jurors have a natural aversion to rewarding bad behavior of a plaintiff and punishing defendants that have done nothing wrong, in their view.

There are also many instances where the defendant may have been negligent or reckless, but jurors believe that the plaintiff made bad choices that caused his or her own injuries. A high-profile example is the subject of tobacco personal injury litigation. Regardless of the venue, many jurors believe that a plaintiff smoker made a choice to smoke tobacco. The question of liability often turns on whether the plaintiff's choice was a "free choice" or the result of an addiction.

If jurors believe that the plaintiff is culpable, they will generally not hesitate to say so. They hold plaintiffs to an elevated standard of conduct, although they may hold corporations to an even higher standard of conduct. If they feel that the plaintiff is trying to manipulate the system or is being deceitful in any way, they will usually place blame on the alleged victim and send the plaintiff on his or her way.

[c]—Perceptions of Plaintiff Competence

Jurors tend to view plaintiffs as less competent than they are themselves. A number of interesting scientific studies conducted in connection with product liability lawsuits indicated that most jurors (like most other people) believe that they themselves are not influenced by advertising, but that other people are. They believe that they, themselves, are careful in their use of products, but that others are not as careful.

The lack of competence that jurors expect of others coupled with the elevated standard to which they hold plaintiffs can cause precisely the uphill battle that most plaintiffs have in the courtroom. As we will discuss later, jurors will also scrutinize the defendant(s) closely. However, the plaintiff must first jump the hurdle to show that his or her hands are clean. A plaintiff must clearly demonstrate that victimization occurred.

Unless these beliefs are refuted, jurors believe that plaintiffs would not do something to injure themselves, and therefore, that they must have fallen victim to someone else's injurious behavior or to their own lack of competence. In every instance, jurors will compare the trial facts to their own life experiences.

[d]—Impact of Jurors' Life Experiences

Jurors' considerations of their own life experiences may lead to interesting results. As many plaintiff attorneys will attest, jurors who have received injuries are not always sympathetic to a plaintiff. For example, a juror who has a family member who was severely handicapped in an automobile accident and lived through the horrors of ripped and broken body parts, is not likely to be very sympathetic to a plaintiff in a crash case who suffered only temporary soreness and occasional headaches.

Jurors' scrutiny of plaintiffs is especially apparent with regard to loss of consortium claims. Many jurors feel that such claims are contrived. Others feel that it is a duty of a spouse to care for the other spouse and that no award is appropriate. It is with this type of claim that juror attitudes and life experiences concerning a specific issue can be determinative of the outcome. Jurors who place a high value on consortium or who have particularly close relationships with their spouses will be more supportive of the plaintiff's claims.

It is also important to note that jurors will watch plaintiffs very closely in the courtroom to determine if their character and behavior are consistent with their claims. For example, jurors will notice whether a husband and wife sit closely together and appear supportive during trial to determine whether one should be entitled to recovery for loss of consortium.

In summary, Professor Hans is right. Jurors' perceptions are complex. Their view of a plaintiff is dictated by their expectations of someone in the plaintiff's position. These expectations will be influenced by each individual juror's life experiences as well as the circumstances of the case.

[3]—Views of Corporations and Businesses

Jurors' perceptions of corporations reflect the ambiguity with which the rest of society views corporations. In the law, corporations have many of the same rights and responsibilities as human beings. Trial judges even instruct jurors that they are to treat corporations as individuals.

[a]—How Corporations and Businesses Differ from Individuals

Corporations are organizations or legal entities, not people. They do not have "people" names and they do not live where people live. They do not have families in the traditional sense. Corporations do not have physical bodies that do things or brains that think and motivate them. Companies are only known by their reputations, corporate images, or the behavior of the people within the organizations.

As a result, jurors are somewhat confused by legal instructions that deal with corporations. They are not capable of judging corporations the same way they assess individuals.

Individual parties to lawsuits have advantages and disadvantages with jurors that corporations lack. Individuals have faces and bodies on which jurors focus attention in order to judge their behavior. Jurors may feel sympathy with or disdain for individuals more readily than with regard to corporations.

However, businesses also have an advantage over individuals such as individual plaintiffs or other defendants. They can create and change character more easily than an individual. That is, most jurors believe that a person's character is stable and continuing, whereas the personality of companies can change. Psychological research has indicated that most of us do not form impressions about groups as readily as we form impressions about individuals.

[b]—How Smaller Businesses Fare vs. Large Corporations

These principles have been supported by research that compared the liability of big corporations with that of small business owners in identical fact patterns. Research indicates that jurors are slightly more inclined to find liability against corporations than small business owners. But even more important, jurors tend to attribute less comparative responsibility to small business owners than to big, anonymous corporations. This difference can be attributed to jurors' identification with small business owners and to their belief that corporations have more power, control, and knowledge than small business owners.

[c]—Corporate Identity and Company Officials in Trial

Corporate identity often stays in the background in personal injury litigation. For example, in most automobile accident cases, the evidence in the case usually does not include much information about company officials or company business. This is probably true because jurors do not believe that the company itself was involved in a typical automobile accident.

However, in some situations where the company business itself and the way it is conducted affect the public welfare, company officials, company policies, and company information become highly relevant to jurors. Examples include chemical plant explosions, toxic waste incidents, and product liability cases.

In cases where company business is relevant to jurors, the presence of company officials to express their care and concern about the case and the people who have suffered injuries in the case can be very important. Jurors believe that decision makers in a company whose business affects the public should be present at trial, particularly at the beginning and the end of the trial. They also believe that the company should have an authoritative presence during the entire trial through company representatives.

The absence of company officials often allows the opposing party to shape a company's personality in unflattering ways. Post-trial interviews have revealed that jurors feel strongly that if a company really cares about a verdict, it will have a high-profile courtroom presence.

The majority of jurors in most jurisdictions believe that the behavior of a company can be understood by analyzing the behavior of the individuals who act on behalf of the company. For example, in many product liability cases jurors often decide whether a product was defective by analyzing the attitude of the people inside the company, both in the design and manufacturing departments.

Another advantage that corporations have in litigation against individuals is that the financial interest of a corporation in the outcome of the litigation is more diffuse than that of an individual plaintiff. That is, jurors understand that a corporation in a personal injury or product liability suit wants to avoid having to pay money. But jurors more readily focus on the financial interest of the plaintiff in the outcome of the litigation rather than that of the defendant.

To overcome this advantage, many good plaintiff's lawyers will focus on the power, control, knowledge, and wealth of the defendant corporation. This shift in focus (by highlighting the corporation's characteristics and de-emphasizing the plaintiff's characteristics) is often successful in framing the issues in the case in a pro-plaintiff perspective.

[d]—Standards by Which Jurors Scrutinize Corporate Behavior

It may seem paradoxical that even though jurors do not equate corporations with individuals, they often measure or judge the behavior of corporations by standards applicable to individuals. For example, jurors will not likely view a large corporation like the now-infamous energy giant Enron Corporation the same as they would view an individual actor. However, they expect Enron to behave by the same standards that we expect of individuals. That is, they expect Enron to live by the Golden Rule and to treat employees the way the company wants to be treated by others. For this reason, Enron has entered into an era of ever-expanding civil and criminal litigation fueled by furious employees, retirees, and other shareholders who allege substantial losses caused by nefarious misrepresentations and fraud of Enron management who, at the same time, reaped huge salary and stock windfalls.

Jurors often try to understand a corporation's behavior by referring to analogies or life experiences. In cases involving worker injuries, for example, jurors view the employer as a parent. Jurors expect employers to care about workers' welfare and to make efforts to protect them. Jurors often become angry when they believe that a company has neglected workers in a way that is analogous to the individual crime of child neglect.

Why do jurors apply different standards to corporations than to individuals? Are jurors prejudiced against corporations? Do jurors believe that the "for profit" aspect of business life requires companies to take on more responsibility than individuals?

Research indicates that there is a statistically important relationship between a defendant's identity and the outcome of the case. The more "corporate" the defendant appears to be, the greater the likelihood it will be found responsible. This "corporate" characteristic implies "for profit" factors, higher levels of organization, extensive resources, distant, unapproachable management, and sophistication.

Despite the instructions and evidentiary decisions of a trial judge, jurors will often admit that they attribute higher standards to corporations than to individuals. More than 50% of most jury-eligible populations believe that these higher standards are justified. Opinion polls indicate that more than 60% of the general population agree with their assessment. Research also indicates that the more education a person has, the less likely he or she is to agree that corporations should be held to higher standards.

Published scientific studies have also indicated that there are a number of demographic factors that appear to affect how a juror might make judgments about corporate standards. These factors include age, political leaning, union membership, and a juror's job responsibilities. Younger jurors believe that corporate status is more important than do older jurors. Jurors who hold non-managerial jobs will be more likely to believe that corporate status is an issue. Jurors who have never belonged to a union and politically conservative jurors more often believe that corporate status is not an issue.

These demographic factors do not necessarily weigh against corporations for jurors who fall into each of these categories. However, these jurors are more likely to pay attention to a particular corporation's characteristics.

Some people have hypothesized that jurors who have positive attitudes about business in general will not be as likely to believe that corporations should be held to higher standards. However, research indicates otherwise. In fact, there is significant evidence to show that a juror's general support for business, confidence or lack of confidence in business, or beliefs that companies have too much or too little power are not related to whether a corporation should be held to a higher standard or whether a standard was violated in a particular situation.

There is some statistical support for the notion that jurors who are less advantaged in life will favor holding corporations to higher standards of responsibility. And, in fact, research has indicated that jurors who feel that they have less influence and power believe that corporations should be held to higher standards.

In general, jurors who believe that corporations have higher standards also tend to believe that corporations have a "privileged" status in our culture, that they have more resources and special knowledge than individuals, and that they profit from activities that sometimes cause injuries to others. Most research has indicated, however, that the degree of commercial activity involved in a company's behavior is a less important factor in jurors' assessments than the company's care and concern about individual workers and consumers.

[e]–Relationship Between Bad Corporate Behavior and Corporate Responsibility

There is also a direct relationship in juror thinking between the possible *impact* of a corporation's bad behavior and the percentage of responsibility attributed to the corporation. The greater the possibility of serious injury due to a particular behavior, the more likely a jury will attribute responsibility to the corporation. Classic examples are severe losses as a result of plant explosions, training collisions, and other catastrophic events. In most disastrous loss cases, there is a high likelihood of finding liability because of the infrequency of such events, and the existence of corporate control over the circumstances. In such cases, the battle in the courtroom usually centers around the question of damages, rather than liability. In instances where such defendants have escaped liability, those defendants were generally able to redirect the blame to another person or entity that had more power, knowledge, and control.

One of the important advantages of pretrial jury research is the opportunity to understand the life experiences and attitudes that jurors will apply to a given fact situation. Knowing in advance how the likely jurors in the case will view a corporation and its behavior is helpful in developing a strategy that coincides with jurors' beliefs, and enhances the persuasive power of the case presentation.

[4]—Views of Subsequent Remedial Measures

One of the most wrenching debates among trial lawyers and trial consultants has been whether or not to present evidence of subsequent remedial measures. Historically, most of the consternation occurs on the defense side of the case. Defense lawyers often believe that evidence of subsequent remedial measures will cause a jury to believe that the defendant company has tacitly admitted fault by employing measures to remedy future recurrences of an injurious situation. Plaintiff attorneys are usually delighted to offer evidence of subsequent remedial measures.

However, scientific jury research has revealed that there are other issues that come into play that may adversely affect both parties in such circumstances. In some cases, jurors believe that subsequent remedial measures are evidence that a defendant corporation has taken steps to make sure that other people are not injured in the future, and, therefore, that a message to be sent by punitive damages is not necessary. These same jurors may believe that subsequent remedial measures constitute evidence of fault, but not fault which needs to be punished.

In a case where a defendant is likely to be saddled with some or all of the responsibility for injury, evidence of subsequent remedial measures may be an effective method for containing the risk of exposure to damages. Conversely, a plaintiff might successfully argue that the defendant corporation only employed subsequent remedial measures because of the threat of future litigation or the litigation at hand.

The effect of subsequent remedial measures on likely juror perceptions is often studied in pretrial jury research. One of the most effective ways to study this issue is to divide the research into two phases, one of which studies juror reactions without evidence of subsequent remedial measures and a second one which studies juror reactions with such evidence.

§ 4.07 | PERCEPTIONS IN MEDICAL
         MALPRACTICE CASES

Jurors are often maligned because of their decisions in medical malpractice cases. Some people believe that of all of the problems in the American civil justice system, the extent of adverse jury verdicts in this area is the most pervasive.

A task force for the American Medical Association declared in 1988 that:

> "In the medical liability context, a source of at least some of the problem for physicians and other health care providers . . . appears to many to be the jury. . . . [Problems with the jury] include decisions that are not based on a thorough understanding of the medical facts and awards that increase at an alarming rate and in a fashion that seems uniquely to disadvantage physicians as compared with other individuals who have acted negligently."[22]

Newspaper columns, journal articles, and books allege that medical malpractice jury verdicts are generally unjustifiable and need regulation. As one author stated,

> ". . . judges and juries were, for the most part, committed to running a generous sort of charity. If the new tort system cannot find a careless defendant after an accident, it will often settle for a merely wealthy one."[23]

Even legal authors have taken up the mantra that juries are playing Santa Claus in medical malpractice cases and wreaking havoc in the civil justice system. One author wrote:

> ". . . [J]uries have become accustomed to huge award requests and they are more willing to reach into the deep pocket of malpractice insurers to compensate the victims generously—more willing than when they encounter the victims of automobile accidents, for in these cases the

---

[22] American Medical Association Specialty Society Medical Liability Project, *A Proposed Alternative to the Civil Justice System for Resolving Medical Liability Disputes: A Fault-Based Administrative System*, 7-8 (1988).

[23] Huber, *Liability: The Legal Revolution and Its Consequences*, at p. 12 (New York: Basic Books, 1988).

insurance premiums at risk are paid directly by the jurors themselves."[24]

The insurance brokerage firm Johnson and Higgins even took out an advertisement in *The Wall Street Journal* declaring that a litigation crisis existed because juries "tripled their awards in just one decade." The ad further stated that the average medical malpractice award in 1984 was $950,000.[25] The factual or statistical basis for these statements remains unclear.

The accusations leveled against juries in medical malpractice cases might be summarized as follows:[26]

- Over time, juries have increasingly favored plaintiffs over physicians and hospital defendants.
- Jury damage awards are increasing at an alarming rate.
- The amounts of unjustifiable awards are also increasing at an alarming rate.
- Juries are biased against doctors, hospitals, and other health care providers.
- Juries often award damages out of sympathy despite lack of evidence.
- Juries award larger amounts of damages against doctors and health care providers than against other defendants because the former have deeper pockets.
- Punitive damages are awarded too frequently without proper foundation.
- Juries are not competent to decide technical issues in medical malpractice cases.
- Juries are easily confused by experts and evaluate evidence in irrational ways.
- Juries are not reliable, and are arbitrary in their decisions about both liability and damages.
- Doctors, judges, and arbitrators make better decisions in medical malpractice cases than juries.

---

[24] Weiler, *Medical Malpractice on Trial,* at p. 48 (Cambridge: Harvard University Press, 1991).

[25] See Daniels, "The Question of Jury Competence and the Politics of Civil Justice Reform: Symbols, Rhetoric, and Agenda-Building," 52 Law & Contemp. Probs. 269-310 (1986).

[26] Vidmar, *Medical Malpractice and the American Jury,* at p. 7 (Ann Arbor: University of Michigan Press, 1997).

In 1997 Professor Neil Vidmar of Duke University published a book that contained a comprehensive review of these charges against juries.[27] In his book Professor Vidmar takes a careful look at the allegations about juries and compares them to the findings of extensive scientific research. The results of his work reveal astonishing differences between the published opinions against juries and the actual statistics—which the authors of those research findings did not discuss.

For example, Professor Vidmar lists the results of twenty-two different published studies of jury verdicts in jurisdictions all over America which revealed the plaintiff "win" rates over various two- to four-year periods. When averaged together, the actual "win" rate for plaintiffs was 29.86%. Whether such a "win" rate amounts to a crisis in civil justice is questionable.

That is, a closer look at medical malpractice cases which go to a jury trial (and verdict) reveals that they are composed primarily of cases in which evidence of defendant liability is weak.[28] Cases where defendant liability appears to be strong (based on the facts) settle prior to trial. Most defendants and insurance companies tend to fight cases in which they have a better chance of winning, and then settle the rest. The fact that less than 30% of medical malpractice cases that proceed to trial and verdict are won by plaintiffs is an indication that juries tend to view the circumstances of a case in a manner similar to attorneys and other professionals who evaluate such cases prior to trial.

The allegation that jurors do not always "get it right" assumes that there is a "right" answer. We must remember that in most medical malpractice trials, there is a divergence of medical opinions about the treatment that was given to the plaintiff. In other words, even the medical professionals cannot agree on the "right" answer.

Perhaps the closest we can come to arriving at a consensus about a medical malpractice question is to look at those instances where medical panels and doctors are in agreement and compare their decisions with those of juries. A review of medical panel decisions and jury verdicts in New Jersey and Florida has indicated that there is a "high concordance between doctors' assessments of negligence and jury verdicts."[29]

---

[27] *Id.* Neil Vidmar is Professor of Social Science and Law, Duke University School of Law, and Professor of Psychology, Duke University.

[28] *Id.* at 83.

[29] *Id.* at 176.

Jurors tend to believe that doctors, hospitals, and other health care providers should be held to a high standard for a number of reasons. First, in a typical health care scenario, the health care provider has more power, control, and knowledge than the patient. Second, the patient in most instances is vulnerable and, in some instances, the patient's life is in the health care provider's hands. Third, the nature of health care service has a significant effect on an individual patient's life. Fourth, health care providers have special education, skills, and resources that patients and other individuals do not have.

However, jurors are generally hesitant to find liability against health care providers. Jurors want to believe that doctors, hospitals, and other health care providers will provide them with safe medical care and comfort in their time of need. They do not want to believe that doctors and hospitals make mistakes that injure or kill patients.

For these reasons, we often hear jurors say positive things about health care providers in jury selection. In those instances where jurors do not like a particular health care provider such as a large hospital chain, their views are often colored by a mixture of negative media images and personal experiences. When jurors express their views about a particular health care provider in jury selection, their feelings often run deep. They sometimes feel that the health care provider has betrayed patients' trust.

Jurors scrutinize medical malpractice plaintiffs closely. Even jurors who might lean toward the plaintiff will wonder if the plaintiff is a malingerer. They will also want to know if the plaintiff followed the health care providers' instructions. Although jurors will not tolerate an unwarranted attack against a medical malpractice plaintiff, they will be willing to listen to evidence that the plaintiff shares some of the blame or that the plaintiff's claim is wrong.

As in most types of lawsuits, jurors are more persuaded by what happens in the courtroom than what happened outside the courtroom. For example, jurors will watch the plaintiff to see how injured he or she appears to be. Plaintiffs who appear to be normal but who are suffering from mental or nonapparent physical injuries as a result of medical malpractice are sometimes at a disadvantage. In such cases the trial team would be well-advised to carefully plan how to convey such injuries persuasively.

Defendants and their representatives in the courtroom are also scrutinized carefully. Jurors will want to know how caring and comforting the health care provider would be if the jurors themselves were under the provider's care.

Substantial jury research which has been conducted in medical malpractice cases indicates that the likelihood of natural jury bias against doctors and health care providers is extremely remote. There is more likely a tendency to believe that doctors and health care providers should not be liable without clear proof.

One of the most celebrated legal doctrines in medical malpractice is the "captain of the ship" doctrine. According to this principle, a doctor is deemed to supervise and be responsible for a team of health care people who perform surgery or provide other treatment to a patient. Conversely, a hospital is not supervised by a physician and is not responsible for the behavior of people who are under the doctor's supervision. A hospital would only be liable for its own behavior or that of its employees while they are under its supervision.

Jurors do not understand the complex arrangements and legal boundaries that govern interactions between health care providers. Most jurors believe that everyone who provides them with health care is jointly responsible for carrying out necessary treatment. In other words, all health care providers are "lumped" together. Therefore, efforts to distance health care providers from each other in trial are often unsuccessful.

In exceptional cases, a medical malpractice defendant may have behaved in a way which was contrary to the behavior of the other defendant health care providers, either positively or negatively. In those cases, it may be possible for one health care provider to be singled out as having behaved especially well or badly.

The technical aspects of medical malpractice cases often present challenges to trial teams for plaintiffs and defendants. Even though jurors will most likely decide the outcome of the case based upon the totality of the situation, rather than the technical explanations, the use of expert witnesses and persuasive demonstrative exhibits is important to help the jury comprehend the facts.

Jurors understand the trial advocacy system well enough to have ideas about whom they can trust and whom they cannot trust. They realize that each of the opposing parties has retained the best and most persuasive expert possible. They often judge experts by their apparent motivation and their behavior. However, jurors will listen closely to expert witnesses to glean information that will be helpful to them in understanding the circumstances of the case.

Perhaps the most underutilized persuasive tools in medical malpractice cases are effective demonstrative aids. Even though a trial lawyer and an expert witness may be skilled at explaining medical procedures and their effect on the mind and body, there are often visual aids that can transform vague, complex ideas into clear, simple images. For example, the effect of an oral explanation that the plaintiff lost five liters of blood pales in comparison to showing the jury five liter-sized bottles containing a red liquid. Another example might be an animation demonstrating the progressive steps of an operation that is alleged to have been conducted negligently by a defendant doctor.

Since most of the trial attorneys and expert witnesses in medical malpractice cases tend to specialize in this field, their tactics and persuasive tools also tend to be specialized and somewhat sophisticated. However, the technical sophistication of health care continues to increase rapidly, and the necessity for new and inventive ways to study jury perceptions in these cases and for more creative ways to persuade juries therefore also increases.

§ 4.08 | PERCEPTIONS IN LABOR AND EMPLOYMENT LITIGATION

One of the fastest growing areas of litigation is the field of labor and employment law. Some people are alarmed at the recent number of lawsuits filed and the magnitude of the jury verdicts that have been rendered throughout the United States.

A significant amount of jury research indicates that business finds itself in a cultural vice. Until recently, generations of Americans have relied upon big companies to provide stable, secure places to work and generate income for their families. It is not uncommon for us to have parents and grandparents who worked at the same company for thirty years or more. Despite the complaints that people have had about the excesses of corporate culture, they relied upon seniority and longevity to provide them with job security.

Things have changed dramatically in recent years. Jurors and others close to them have experienced painful dislocations when they were laid off from jobs where they had faithfully carried out their responsibilities for many years. Many of them have witnessed behavior by employers that they believe was an abuse of power.

Most jurors, like most adults, have deeply felt anxieties which result primarily from fear of an uncertain future. Many them are angry at employers whom they believe have betrayed their loyalty. They are also angry because they believe that principles upon which they have relied have turned out to be inaccurate or inappropriate in today's economy.

However, despite the changing economic environment, people still tend to develop their self-concept around their jobs. To many employees, the people they work with are as close to them as their regular family members. They often spend more time with people at work than with people at home.

Jurors often relate to work groups as an extended family. The president or boss in the company plays a role that is like a father or mother. The head of a company or senior manager of a large work group assumes the same kind of power, control, and responsibilities that the heads of families assume. In the same way, employees may view themselves as children and expect to be treated as parents would treat their children.

Jurors expect companies to protect vulnerable employees. Some of the largest jury verdicts against companies have come after an employee successfully proved extensive failure by a company's management to respond to claims of sexual harassment and other employee abuse.

Jurors expect employers to provide safe working conditions and to provide guidance for the welfare of the employee as well as the company as a whole. Jurors expect employers to provide counseling, coaching, training, and feedback to workers. They expect employers to provide substantial, clear warnings to employees about the consequences of poor performance in advance of punishment or severance. They expect employers to have and to follow clear written policies about key issues that affect employee welfare. For these reasons employee handbooks are often used by companies to provide important information to employees. (It is also this same written material that can provide the starting point for wrongful conduct by employers.)

Jurors expect employers to be honest with employees. When employees are not performing well, jurors expect employers to be truthful with them about their nonperformance and to document each incident. Jurors expect performance reviews to be conducted fairly.

Our jobs are important to us. When we experience joy in our work, it is deeply felt. Similarly, when we experience pain in our work, it, too, is deeply felt. Sometimes the pain that we experience from a bad situation on the job is more long-lasting than any other type of pain. If one of our friends or someone in our family does something that is painful to us, we can usually go to them and work it out. But in the workplace, painful situations may not be resolved so easily. For example, we may be fired without receiving any notice and under circumstances that may be humiliating.

Consequently, when jurors are faced with making judgments in disputes between employers and employees, they draw upon their life experiences as employees and tend to become instant experts in the subject. We have said that in pretrial and post-trial jury research, we often find that jurors relate their previous life experiences to the circumstances of a particular lawsuit. When jurors are asked about their reactions to a particular fact or circumstance of alleged employee abuse, they often state that the case reminds them of "a company I used to work for."

Jurors' beliefs and attitudes about job-related incidents are often as important as the facts of a particular case. To the casual observer, it may appear that jurors disregard evidence in making their decisions in labor and employment cases. It may even appear that jurors disregard a judge's instructions.

Even though a juror may not be able to relate to legal boundaries in considering evidence, jurors seem to know instinctively that inside every labor and employment dispute there is usually a deeper meaning that should be discovered. For example, it is common in lawsuits between executives and their former employers for lawyers in the case to view the dispute as simply a business dispute with employment trappings (i.e., a rich person suing a wealthy employer). However, even though jurors may initially adopt the lawyers' approach to the case, they will almost always gravitate to an understanding of the case based upon their own life experiences as an employee or employer.

Jurors will usually resolve such a case with reference to attitudes about employees and employers that they have developed over their lifetimes. They will scrutinize each employee and employer very closely to determine whether their behaviors were appropriate or not. They will look for the consistencies in their behavior. They will try to understand the motivations of each employee and employer.

Whistleblower cases offer special challenges to both plaintiffs and defendants. On one hand, jurors are very sympathetic toward an employee who tries to warn employers and others of serious problems at work. Jurors can become angered that warnings go unheeded, and even more angered if there is clear evidence of retaliation. On the other hand, jurors are also on the look-out for employees whom they believe are "whining" or exaggerating.

In judging the behavior of an employer, jurors will look at the fairness with which the employer made decisions, and they will look at the fairness of the decision itself. Jurors will decide for themselves, based on their own perceptions of fairness, whether the behavior of the employer was appropriate or not.

Jury selection is an important part of an employment case whether you are representing a plaintiff or a defendant. A juror's attitudes about specific issues in the case and relevant life experiences will often predict how a juror will approach the evidence.

It is generally not a good idea to rely upon demographic characteristics to make decisions about potential jurors in a labor and employment case. For example, a long-term, seemingly loyal employee in the human resources department of a local company may not turn out to be a very good juror for a defendant. In fact, such a juror could devastate a defendant's case and wind up being a good juror for the plaintiff.

Jurors base their decisions in these cases largely on their own life experiences and attitudes. Perhaps more than in most cases, the evidence often is tailored to fit their views of the world.

§ 4.09 | PERCEPTIONS IN BUSINESS LITIGATION

The dynamics of jury decision making in business litigation is dramatically different than in most personal injury litigation. In the usual automobile negligence or product liability case there is often a clear dichotomy in power and control between the plaintiff and defendant(s). However, in business litigation, two large, sophisticated organizations often are suing each other.

For this reason, it may appear that jurors will have difficulty in determining where their sympathies lie. If both parties are wealthy and self-sufficient, a jury may have difficulty deciding which of the parties is worthy of a judgment, and if it rules for the plaintiff, how large a judgment would make the plaintiff whole.

In the context of business litigation, there may be many claims, counterclaims, affirmative defenses, matters in avoidance, and other legal issues that require a fact finder's decision. Some of these matters will be familiar to jurors whereas others will not. Most jurors have not had any legal experience or education. They can only relate to their own life experiences and attitudes.

For the most part, it is usually futile to try to explain some legal concepts, such as breach of a fiduciary duty, in the same terms that we learned in law school. Explaining breach of fiduciary duty as "a violation of the duty of loyalty and care" will make little impression on the jury. However, explaining the concept as a "betrayal by someone who agreed to look out for you" as revealed by a "smell test" (or, "You know it when you see it") may get you a lot farther.

Similarly, questions about waiver, statutes of limitations, and other legal concepts should be tested with a focus group or mock jury on a case-by-case basis. Experience tells us that the more "legal" our case appears to be, the less persuasive it will be to a jury.

If the case focuses only on the terms of a contract, the dynamics of the trial and, indeed the dynamics of the jury's decision-making process, will be fairly monotone in nature and not likely to cause powerful emotional reactions which might elevate the damages award. Conversely, if the case includes evidence of more interesting behavior that might give rise to such claims as betrayal, fraud, dishonesty, deceit, or greed, the case may take a decidedly different turn.

In one such case, a manufacturer sued a supplier of chemicals for alleged overcharging for its products over a period of several years. A written contract in the case had been interpreted by a trial judge as stating that, under ordinary circumstances, the manufacturer should have been given a discount. In response, the supplier argued that the manufacturer had waived its claim to the discount by paying regular monthly invoices at the higher amount.

However, there were some other interesting facts that were revealed in discovery that caused the case to take a different turn. During the contractual period in question, the manufacturer held three of the five seats on the board of directors of the supplier's corporation. (In other words, the manufacturer had a great deal of power and influence over the supplier's operations.) At the end of this period of time, the manufacturer sold its interest in the supplier's company to the remaining owners. In addition, the president of the supplier (Mr. X) resigned and became the president of the manufacturer.

A review of internal e-mails of both companies revealed that even as Mr. X was negotiating a job with the manufacturer, he was also discussing ways for the manufacturer to withhold its claim for a refund until after the supplier's company stock changed hands and he became president of the manufacturer. The implication of the behavior of Mr. X and the owners of the manufacturer was that they wanted to keep the value of their shares in the supplier artificially high until after they were sold. At that point, they would file suit against the supplier and demand a refund, in effect making a windfall profit.

After conducting a series of focus groups, the supplier learned that it could also argue that the manufacturer (the plaintiff) had breached its fiduciary duty to the supplier (vis-à-vis the manufacturer's dominant position on the board of directors of the supplier company) and, in the process, had committed fraud and other deceitful acts.

The information obtained during the initial phase of jury research led the supplier's trial team and its trial consultant to believe that it might be possible to reinvent the case. Even though a likely jury might split a decision between the two parties, there was a substantial chance of achieving a complete victory if the supplier could successfully persuade the jury that the manufacturer had committed particularly bad acts.

After refocusing the case on the plaintiff's conduct and testing the case again in a mock trial research study, it became apparent that the chances of a complete victory had increased. Consequently, the trial team developed a strategy for maintaining the focus of the trial on the manufacturer's conduct, and the case went to trial before a federal court jury.

The jury heard testimony from Mr. X and all the other key executives from both companies, as the plaintiff's trial team attempted to keep the focus of the case on the written contract. The plaintiff's attorneys knew that jurors tend to rely heavily on written documents and they hoped that the inquiry would end with the contract.

However, more than 80% of the trial focused on the behavior of the manufacturer, its members on the supplier corporation's board of directors, and, of course, Mr. X. The focus included simple, clear presentations of damages by the defendant's trial team.

In the end, the jury decided to give the supplier a complete victory. They awarded the manufacturer nothing, but awarded the defendant more than $16 million (exactly what the defendant had requested) for the betrayal it had suffered, along with an additional $2 million in attorneys' fees.

This case scenario reflects the perceptions of jurors in most business litigation. In essence, jurors want to make equitable decisions. They want to reward good behavior and punish bad behavior.

For this reason, we often find trial teams fighting for the moral high ground in business litigation. Jurors want to know who the good guy is so that they can support him (or her) and be on the winning team. Conversely, jurors also want to know who the bad guy is so that they can punish him.

§ 4.10 | PERCEPTIONS IN INTELLECTUAL PROPERTY CASES

Intellectual property cases offer many challenges to trial attorneys. The stakes are usually high for their clients and there is a great deal of pressure to win the case. Businesspeople are at the heart of the internal decision-making process and they tend to be risk-averse. Faced with high stakes, risk-averse clients, and decisions that may ultimately be made by a disinterested judge or jury, intellectual property attorneys are constantly looking for ways to outperform the opposition and gain the advantage in the courtroom.

[1]—Intellectual Property Trials Generally

Experienced intellectual property trial lawyers have learned that the trial team must work its way through a mountain of complexities in a case in order to simplify the case and then persuade a judge and jury. An example is the relatively simple case of a copyright infringement claim brought against the Baltimore Ravens football team by a fan named Bouchat who was a security guard. The plaintiff, Bouchat, had designed a suggested logo with a raven holding a shield and faxed it to the team's home office. Shortly thereafter, the team revealed its new logo, which looked "strikingly similar" to the one that Bouchat had faxed to the office. However, the Ravens disputed that they had used his design idea.

The case proceeded to a jury trial after the trial judge ruled that there was sufficient evidence to raise a fact issue. Many months of intense legal research and technical study ensued in which the opposing trial teams fought over every legal and technical detail they discovered. In the end, however, a jury decided that the case was simple. After looking at the timing of events and the similarity of the design, the jury decided that someone with the Ravens' organization had, indeed, copied Bouchat's design. There had been a copyright infringement.

Whether a case involves unauthorized disclosure of trade secrets, antitrust violations, copyright or patent infringement, unlawful use of trademarks, or any other type of intellectual property claim, most jurors work hard to try to understand the details. However, jurors' greatest interest lies in the simple human story that is at the center of every controversy. They want to know and understand the meaning that is at the core of the case. As has often been stated, "Inside every complex case is a simple story struggling to get out."

[2]—Patent Infringements

Patent cases offer particular challenges. The details of patent cases are often so complex and technical that we even require most patent lawyers to have academic degrees in a field of science or technology to supplement their legal training.

However, jurors generally decide that there is a simple dispute at the heart of most patent cases. They believe that the plaintiff must prove that the defendant is using his or her idea (invention), and the defendant must prove that the ideas (mechanisms) being used are not the same as those owned by the plaintiff.

In making their decisions, jurors have been proven to be equally capable as most trial judges of understanding the important details of a case and rendering a well-reasoned decision. Like trial judges, jurors have little self-interest in most patent disputes and, therefore, they scrutinize each party and its expert witnesses closely.

Jurors tend to respect decisions of the United States Patent Office and will disregard a governmental decision only when there is clear evidence that the patent examiner "got it wrong." One such case occurred in 1999 when a federal court jury decided that the "hash-and-sign" digital time-stamping used in encryption technology by Entrust Technologies predated Surety.com's patent establishment. The trial lasted for six days of grueling testimony with mind-boggling details that would challenge the most sophisticated audience. In the end, the jury decided that the invention was not new, based upon the chronology of events.[30]

Most jurors are concerned about protecting inventors' rights, but not in a way that stifles other inventors or causes obstacles in the evolution of new products to enhance our standard of living. Jurors are interested in fairness and want to make decisions that they think are just.

[3]—Trade Secret and Copyright Infringements

Trade secret and copyright infringement cases offer significant opportunities for trial teams to tell an interesting story. Although many of the issues in these cases will be decided by a trial judge, there are often attention-grabbing fact circumstances that may be presented to a jury.

---

[30] Surety Technologies, Inc. v. Entrust Technologies, Inc., 71 F. Supp.2d 520 (E.D. Va. 1999).

By the time most trade secret and copyright infringement cases go to trial, liability is unclear and damages are hotly contested. If a case involves situations where a defendant was "caught red-handed" while stealing or copying ideas or materials, the case would not likely go to trial, and if it did, the jury would not take long to decide the case.

Trade secret cases often involve a specific set of circumstances within larger scenarios. For example, it is common for companies to sue former employees if they believe that they have taken trade secrets with them to their new places of employment. Such circumstances offer many opportunities for opposing trial teams to argue from different perspectives.

The plaintiff employer might argue that the employee signed an employment agreement promising not to take trade secrets if the employee should ever resign. The employer might also argue that even though the employee did not take any documents or things belonging to the company when the employee left, the trade secrets of the employer remained in the employee's head. The employer might also argue that the employee will inevitably be required to utilize trade secrets of the employer when working at his or her new place of employment.

In his defense, the employee will remind the jury that he or she did not take any documents or things upon resigning from the company. The employee will also state that he or she will continue to honor his or her promise not to use trade secrets of the former employer at any time.

The central argument in this scenario is generally over the meaning of the term "trade secret." The employer (or any owner of a trade secret) will want to argue that the term "trade secret" should have a broad meaning and encompass all private information of the company, virtually anything that the employee learned while employed by the company. The employee, however, will argue that the term should have a more narrow meaning and should encompass only information that was developed by the employer (or under the employer's supervision) and is essential to the employer's operations.

In cases like these where legal definitions are central to a case, some education of a jury is required. They need to know the scope of their inquiry. However, jurors are sophisticated enough in the world of business and employment to know that they must figure out whether all of the information that the employer believes constitutes trade secrets are in fact trade secrets. Both parties will put on fact and expert witnesses to discuss how much of the information is already in the public domain. If, after hearing the evidence, jurors still have questions about the essential facts, they will, like any other fact finder, simply judge the credibility of the witnesses who have testified.

After determining which information, if any, constitutes a trade secret, jurors can then determine whether the employee is unjustifiably using a previous employer's trade secrets at the employee's new place of employment. In making this determination, jurors scrutinize the employee closely. They also make judgments about the credibility and likeability of each of the witnesses and parties in order to determine who to believe.

One of the most interesting issues in these circumstances is the overlap between juror perceptions in employment cases and juror perceptions in intellectual property cases. We have learned that jurors are sophisticated enough to know whether a former employer is wrongfully trying to inhibit an employee from working for a competitor by accusing the employee of stealing trade secrets. In this instance, jurors are often persuaded that a plaintiff employer is essentially trying to interfere with the freedom of an employee to work wherever he or she wants to work. They believe that an employee must be free to make employment decisions that benefit the employee's family without interference from a former employer.

Winning a trade secret or copyright infringement case is often a matter of successfully framing the argument so that it is favorable to your client. By keeping the "bad guy" on stage and causing the jury to scrutinize his/its behavior closely, you generally place yourself and your client in a stronger posture.

[4]—Trademark Infringements

In trademark infringement cases, the issues for a jury are fairly straightforward. Jurors are uniquely qualified to say whether two trademarks are similar and whether the allegedly infringing trademark causes confusion for people about the plaintiff's trademark. After all, in most cases, they are the ultimate consumers.

However, as was discussed previously, everything is evidence. Jurors make decisions about who they believe and who they like, and those decisions affect how they filter the evidence. If, for example, they believe that the plaintiff trademark holder is trying to gain a competitive advantage over a small start-up company without justification, they will make decisions that they feel are fair and equitable. Nevertheless, they are sophisticated enough to know when a defendant has embarked on a parasitical creation of income for itself based upon the plaintiff's good reputation in the marketplace. They intuitively know when a defendant is trying to cause product confusion in order to siphon off some of the plaintiff's business.

During the trial, jurors work hard to identify good and bad character as well as good and bad behavior. Therefore, framing the issues is critical at trial.

§ 4.11 | PERCEPTIONS OF TRIAL LAWYERS

Even though jurors base their decisions primarily on the meaning of the case and the messages contained in the case, their perceptions of the messenger are important. Jurors make judgments about a trial lawyer's credibility, honesty, and character that affect the way they view the evidence.

[1]—Attitudes and Opinions about Lawyers

It will come as no surprise that, in general, jurors appear to have negative views of attorneys. In opinion polls, when people are asked to associate the concept of lawyers with something else in their lives, their responses are often not publishable. When asked why their opinions are so negative, people often cite excesses they have witnessed in lawyer behavior, the high cost of attorneys' fees, and the claims made by people who support civil justice reform. Many jurors believe that lawyers are motivated by greed and that they are loyal to no-one except themselves.

However, these generally negative views are often outweighed by other, more favorable beliefs about lawyers or by a particular lawyer's good behavior that they have personally witnessed. A slight majority of jurors believe that much of the criticism of lawyers is not deserved. A larger majority of jurors believe that lawyers are valuable and important in modern culture. They believe that everybody is entitled to be represented by a good lawyer.

In fact, most people believe that the difference between winning or losing a case depends upon having a good lawyer. They even believe that is more important for a party to have a good lawyer than to have favorable facts.

These opinions about lawyers may seem contradictory, as do many other aspects of jury decision making. However, a closer look at the perceptions of jurors reveals consistency in their thinking.

Jurors' assessments of lawyers can be divided into two areas: (1) their views about a lawyer's motivations and personal characteristics and (2) their views about a lawyer's utility, competency, and effectiveness. Jurors may assess a lawyer as competent and effective while at the same time being greedy and dishonest. Defense lawyers seem to be the most vulnerable to jurors' beliefs that their positions in cases are superficial and dishonest. Plaintiff lawyers seem to fare better because even though jurors believe that they are also motivated by fees, they are also usually representing someone who cannot otherwise afford legal representation.

In post-trial interviews, jurors often express warm feelings about particular trial lawyers who presented a case to them in the courtroom. They judge a lawyer by a standard which is very personal to them. They make conscious and unconscious decisions about whether they would want a particular lawyer to represent them in the future based upon that lawyer's behavior during the court case in which they sat as jurors.

Jurors' perceptions of a particular lawyer are individualized at the outset of trial and often adjust to those of other jurors during the trial process. For the most part, jurors are more persuaded by lawyers who are prepared, honest, committed, and cognizant of the jury's needs. The credibility of a lawyer is often affected by the messages that the lawyer espouses. The more acceptable the messages and behavior of the lawyer, the more accepted the messenger and the message will be by jurors. Conversely, the more inappropriate the messages and behavior of the lawyer, the more rejected the messenger and the message will be.

[2]—Media Images and Juror Attitudes

Almost 90% of Americans have witnessed lawyer advertising and lawyer images in the media. Television channels frequently broadcast glitzy lawyer advertisements and yellow page directories devote many pages to lawyer advertising. Moreover, most general cable television channels, including the major networks, carry at least one regular dramatic series that features lawyers who represent clients in litigation. Each year new feature films are released that focus on lawyers and litigants.

With regard to media advertising, nevertheless, opinion polls have indicated that approximately 80% of people do not believe that the best lawyers and law firms advertise their services. Most people believe that it is permissible for lawyers to advertise, with certain restrictions. However, many jurors believe that lawyer advertising can be blamed for advancing greed and increasing the number of lawsuits.

There is little evidence that lawyer advertising has affected the views of most jurors in particular cases. As we have discussed, jurors' general perceptions about non-case related issues are not very useful in determining how they will decide specific issues in specific cases.

Most of the media images of lawyers, however, simply reinforce jurors' previously held views. It is up to a particular lawyer in a particular case to determine whether his or her behavior is going to enhance the case or detract from it.

§ 4.12 | PERCEPTIONS ABOUT DAMAGES

Juror perceptions about damages depend upon the evidence and the context of the case. In order to better understand jurors' perceptions, we will divide our discussion into topics relating to various types of cases.

[1]—Personal Injury and Product Liability Cases

The damages that are sought in personal injury and product liability cases generally fall into three areas: economic damages, noneconomic damages, and punitive damages. We will discuss economic and noneconomic damages in this subsection, and turn to punitive damages later in this section.

The dispute over economic damages generally revolves around past and future medical care and past and future loss of income. Jurors' perceptions of awards for economic damages are usually the result of their reasoned understanding of the actual evidence, their feelings of wanting to help the plaintiff resume a normal lifestyle (under the circumstances), and their level of emotional response to the case. They believe that plaintiff attorneys usually ask for more than is needed, and that the defense attorneys want to keep the award as low as possible.

The dispute over noneconomic damages often concerns whether there has been sufficient "mental anguish" or "pain and suffering" to warrant the imposition of such damages. Jurors' approaches to awarding noneconomic damages are highly individualized. Jurors who are more concrete, logical, rigid, and cognitive (reasoned) in their thinking tend to award less money. Jurors who are more abstract, emotional, and flexible in their thinking tend to award more money.

As with questions of liability, jurors' attitudes and life experiences are more predictive of jurors' approaches to damages awards than demographic or personality characteristics. Jurors who object to awarding noneconomic damages come from all walks of life and from most demographic backgrounds. Conversely, jurors who favor awarding noneconomic damages in particular fact situations also have varied personal characteristics. The most effective way to know in advance how an individual juror might approach the question of damages in a case is to ask probative questions during jury selection.

Statistically, the amount of money awarded in product liability cases exceeds that of other types of personal injury cases (with the exception of medical malpractice cases). Although the circumstances of each case will differ, jurors tend to believe that the consequences of the production of a defective product by a manufacturer or distributor affect more people than an average roadway accident case. Perhaps the larger jury verdicts therefore reflect a desire by the jury to "send a message" to the defendant to stop putting the public at risk.

Jurors are generally not surprised at the large sums of money discussed in trial. They have heard of huge awards in so many different contexts through the news media that a $10 million to $100 million judgment does not necessarily seem like a large amount of money. Research indicates that, as a general rule, the more money a plaintiff requests, the more money a jury will award (up to the point where the plaintiff is clearly being greedy).

In response to most damages questions, there are often a few jurors who will want to award everything the plaintiff requests and a few jurors who want to award the plaintiff very little money. Most jurors fall somewhere in between. The question of damages is often a matter of consensus building within the jury group.

Scientific research has indicated that the severity of a plaintiff's injury is not usually related to a jury's finding of liability. This would seem to indicate that juries take their obligation to pay strict attention to the evidence seriously. However, the severity of an injury is often related to the amount of a jury's award once liability has been determined.

Dr. Michael Saks, a highly respected jury researcher for more than thirty years, has concluded that, "in the aggregate, jury awards are remarkably predictable. Over half the variation can be accounted for merely by knowing the severity of the plaintiff's injuries."[31]

Although some commentators have expressed their beliefs that juror decision making in the area of damages is irrational, the evidence points to the contrary. In fact, jurors consider not only the factors that the litigants espouse in their arguments, but also other factors that they, themselves, believe are relevant to their decision. They use a reasoning process that is broader than the sometimes simplistic factors that are listed in a jury charge.

Jurors intuitively want to reach an award that is meaningful to them. Although they may "split the difference" at the end of a long day, the process that they used to arrive at that point is much more sophisticated. Jurors factor in their beliefs about the evidence, the parties, and the meaning that they wish to attach to their awards. In other words, they try to reach an amount that they intuitively believe is fair.

For jurors, the question of damages is often more difficult than the question of liability. After all, in response to a liability question, they generally have two choices: "Yes" or "No." Regardless of the opinions stated by published authors, jurors usually consider every aspect of an award prior to making their decision. They will discuss the evidence, the appropriateness of various awards, the effect on future insurance premiums, and many other factors. In the end, however, they will award an amount that they feel is fair and justifiable according to their own perceptions.

Research has indicated that jurors often feel that they are not equipped to make judgments about damages.[32] Jurors rarely walk into the jury deliberation room with a particular damages award in mind. They need help with direction and focus. If the damages theory that a party supports is too complicated or inappropriate in the jurors' minds, jurors will most likely just " tune out."

If they are inclined to award liability, jurors will often use the plaintiff's damages request as a benchmark for the beginning of their discussions. However, there are documented cases where the amount offered or suggested

---

[31] Saks, "Do We Really Know Anything about the Behavior of the Tort Litigation System—and Why Not?" 140 U. Pa. L. Rev. 1147 (1992).

[32] Mott, Hans & Lindsay, "What's Half a Lung Worth? Civil Jurors' Accounts of Their Award Decision Making," 24 Law & Human Behavior 401-419 (2000).

by a defendant became the benchmark. Jurors will then engage in a discussion about whether the amount suggested by the defendant was too high or too low.

For this reason, trial lawyers are well-advised to be as clear and precise with their explanations of the amounts of money they believe are justified in the case and the commonsense justification for those amounts. To enhance the clarity and precision of their presentations, lawyers are also well-advised to use visual aids that present the amounts and the justification and/or formulas to be used in calculating those amounts.

[2]–Medical Malpractice Cases

According to the National Law Journal, three of the top ten verdicts in the United States during the first quarter of 2002 were entered in medical malpractice cases. They ranged in amount from $64 million to $95 million. These verdicts raise questions about whether they are typical of medical malpractice verdicts and whether juries are awarding damages in an appropriate way.

Superficially it appears that the average medical malpractice jury award is incrementally larger than the average award for most other types of personal injuries. However, as Professor Vidmar found in his research that compared awards in medical malpractice and automobile negligence cases, "jurors did not give statistically different awards as a function of whether the injury was caused by medical or automobile negligence."[33]

However, it is more common in medical malpractice cases than in other types of personal injury cases for a jury to find that the plaintiff was contributorily negligent. Jurors often believe that a medical malpractice plaintiff assumed the risk by consenting to elective surgery or contributed to the problem in some other way.

As with damages questions in other types of personal injury cases, jurors will discuss every factor of which they are aware. They consider the evidence, the consequences of awarding damages against the doctor and a hospital, the effect on health care and insurance premiums, the likelihood that the defendant is covered by insurance or has the ability to pay a judgment, and their personal concerns for the doctor and those close to him or her.

---

[33] Vidmar, *Medical Malpractice and the American Jury,* at p. 217 (Ann Arbor: University of Michigan Press, 1997).

Juries tend to worry less about financial consequences for defendants when they deliberate about injuries to children and elderly people than when they consider other types of personal injury or medical malpractice cases. In cases involving very young or elderly plaintiffs, jurors tend to be so emotionally responsive (perhaps like most other people) to the helpless nature or frailty of the plaintiff that they sometimes overlook or forget about other considerations. As a result, jury awards in these types of cases are often fairly large when liability is determined against a health care provider. In these situations, the defense is often relegated to trial strategies that focus on damage control.

Because of the large amounts of money at stake in medical malpractice cases, it is advisable that counsel study likely juror reactions in advance of trial.

[3]—Labor and Employment Litigation

The explosion in the number of labor and employment cases is a fairly new development. There is not yet a great deal of published scientific jury research that has focused on whether jurors make damages decisions in labor and employment litigation differently from their decisions in other types of litigation.

One survey performed by Jury Verdicts Northwest[34] compared the average damages awards in all jury verdicts reported in the State of Washington in employment cases between 1995 and 1997. Following are the results:

Year	Average Jury Verdict
1995	$317,890
1996	$690,273
1997	$1,012,142

The sizable increases in awards over just three years in these types of cases may indicate the existence of a number of phenomena. First, the number of cases being filed in state and federal courts may be growing rapidly and judgments may simply reflect this trend. Second, employees may be filing suits that they would not have filed previously. That is, there may be a cultural trend that encourages plaintiffs to come forward. Third, the number of cases

---

[34] Jury Verdicts Northwest, 1998 study published on the Web site of the National Association of State Verdict Publishers: www.juryverdicts.com/articles/jvnwz.html.

going to a jury trial may not have changed, but it may be that more and larger verdicts are being reported to verdict reporting services. Finally, it is also possible that changes in the law may be contributing to more lawsuits and larger awards.

Regardless of the reason for the sharp rise in the average reported verdict, more attention is being given to ways that plaintiffs and defendants can influence damages decisions of judges and juries. Trial teams for employees and employers are increasing their use of tactics to better understand how juries might react to particular case circumstances.

Based upon significant private jury research and post-trial interviews, we believe that there is little difference between how jurors determine damages in labor and employment litigation and how they assess damages in personal injury and product liability cases. Jurors will try to base their awards on what they perceive to be the needs of the plaintiff in a way that they believe is fair under the circumstances.

Jurors scrutinize employees' claims closely and are not usually inclined to make employees rich. Even though jurors may identify with an employee's situation, they are inclined to award only amounts that can be justified in considering both economic and noneconomic issues.

They are not likely to consider the financial resources of the employer in determining liability or damages, although there are two exceptions to this principle. First, jurors may adjust an award downward if they believe that the employer has meager financial resources and that there may be unintended consequences such as bankrupting the company and causing innocent workers to lose their jobs. Second, approximately one-third of the jurors will consider the financial resources of the employer in determining the extent of punitive damages.

[4]—Business Litigation

Perhaps more than in any other type of litigation, the amounts of jury awards can vary wildly and unexpectedly for most business people in business litigation. Because there are relatively few caps on damages in business litigation, the risk for plaintiffs and defendants can be more problematic than in personal injury cases. In business litigation, jurors' attitudes and life experiences with business people and in connection with business situations can dramatically affect the amount of jury verdicts.

Because the potential awards in business cases can be quite high, they are often the subject of extensive pretrial scientific jury research. It is common for opposing parties to test alternative theories of their case well in advance of trial.

In our previous discussion about liability in business litigation[35] we focused on a jury's need to determine the equities in a case and, thus, internalize the meaning of the case. Jurors use the same process in determining damages. A jury's attempt to determine an equitable decision with respect to damages will encompass every aspect of the case and all of the jurors' attitudes and life experiences.

Juries rely heavily on written contracts and other written materials, including electronic mail. They want to anchor their decision to some clear, concise pieces of evidence.

However, jurors are also mindful of their need to reach a decision which they believe is fair and just under the circumstances. They want to make a decision of which they can be proud.

[5]—Punitive Damages and Bifurcation of Trials

From a legal standpoint, the purpose of punitive damages is to deter others from wrongful behavior or to punish the defendant for past wrongful conduct. As in most other subject areas in jury decision making, there is a difference in the way the law defines and applies the concept of punitive damages and the way a jury approaches the subject.

Research has indicated that there are two prongs to consideration by jurors of punitive damages: (1) their beliefs about the defendant's misuse of power, control, and knowledge, and (2) their level of outrage. Noticeably absent from these factors are considerations of liability or, as some people say, the facts of the case.

By the time punitive damages become the focus of the trial, jurors have often already made important decisions about their perceptions of the parties and the circumstances of the case. They may or may not be feeling anger.

With most punitive damages awards, jurors have satisfied themselves that the defendant has misused its power, control, and knowledge, and have

---

[35] See § 4.09 *supra.*

implied that they are outraged by the defendant's conduct in the past and in the courtroom as well. They feel motivated by their anger to "send a message" to the defendant and others in the defendant's position that the wrongful behavior will not be tolerated.

The extent of punitive damages may also be enhanced by the extent of financial resources or net worth of the defendant. Jurors tend to believe that the wealthier the defendant, the more money it takes in punitive damages to get its attention. They believe that their judgment is meaningless and that their time has been wasted if a wealthy defendant has committed particularly bad acts and yet only a small punitive damages award is entered. They believe that such a defendant would slough off such a small award. This is precisely the reason that small compensatory damages awards are sometimes accompanied by huge punitive damages awards.

The question of whether to bifurcate a trial for the consideration of gross misconduct or punitive damages has been the subject of recent scientific study. The results of this study conflict with conventional wisdom. Until now, many of us have believed that the plaintiff receives an advantage when the financial resources or net worth of a wealthy defendant are discussed before the jury has decided questions of liability. Underlying this belief is the notion that juries will more likely find liability and higher damages against a wealthier defendant.

However, as we have discussed earlier in this chapter, we now know that juries do not often consider the financial resources of a defendant in determining either liability or compensatory damages. We know that juries make their decisions about punitive damages to punish a defendant for misusing power, control, and knowledge and to express outrage. We also know that the question of financial resources and net worth of a defendant are normally considered by jurors only when they are trying to determine the amount of punitive damages to award, if any.

As a result of this knowledge, it appears that when a trial is bifurcated the jurors gain a second opportunity to express anger against the defendant, rather than being limited to one such opportunity had the trial not been bifurcated. In other words, in most trials jurors are not told that the trial will be bifurcated and they believe that they will only have one opportunity to award damages. Therefore, if jurors are not aware that they will be given an opportunity to express their outrage through punitive damages or they know that there is a cap or limitation on punitive damages, they will often assess compensatory damages at a significantly higher level than jurors who are aware that they will have an opportunity to award punitive damages separately.[36]

Researchers have also found that a plaintiff's requested amounts of punitive damages can have a dramatic effect on actual awards.[37] The higher a plaintiff's request, the higher the award is likely to be.

A secondary issue studied in this research was the effect of a party's geographic identity. The jury researchers found that local plaintiffs were often awarded greater compensatory damages than plaintiffs from other communities.[38] Conversely, they found that the geographic identity of a defendant, whether or not local, did not appear to have any effect on the amount of damages awarded, if any. To apply these research findings to specific cases, it appears that when a jury is likely to be outraged by a defendant's conduct, bifurcation seems to benefit the plaintiff, not the defendant. To determine whether these general rules apply to a particular case, you might consider reviewing the published research in more detail or even conducting your own scientific jury research in the case prior to trial.

[6]–"Deep Pockets"

The question of whether a jury really considers a defendant's wealth or ability to pay damages in determining liability or damages awards has been the subject of considerable scientific study over the past few years.

Some research has indicated the possibility that although jurors do not often consider a defendant's wealth in determining liability, they will sometimes award amounts of money at a higher level of the range of damages that they believe are appropriate against those who have deeper pockets. Conversely, if they determine that a defendant's wealth is minimal, they will award an amount at the lower end of the range.

The greater weight of findings based upon scientifically conducted research indicates, however, that jurors do not differentiate between wealthy and poor

---

[36] Anderson, Chernikoff & MacCoun, "Goal Conflict in Juror Assessments of Compensatory and Punitive Damages," 23 Law & Human Behavior 313-330 (1999); Greene, Coon & Bornstein, "The Effects of Limiting Punitive Damages Awards," 25 Law & Human Behavior 217-234 (2001).

[37] Hastie, Schkade & Payne, "Juror Judgments in Civil Cases: Effects of Plaintiff's Requests and Plaintiff's Identity on Punitive Damage Awards," 23 Law & Human Behavior 445-470 (1999).

[38] Id.

defendants in either liability decisions or monetary awards.[39] Although it is difficult to be certain which factors appear to be the most influential in jury awards, the fact that a number of different reputable research teams have arrived at this same conclusion is persuasive. Therefore, we believe that financial resources of the defendant do not have a measurable impact on either liability or the size of jury awards. Similar research has also concluded that bifurcation often has the effect of augmenting both compensatory and punitive damages awards.[40]

There is substantial other reliable research that indicates, however, that jurors may adjust an award downward if they believe that the defendant has no insurance or that the defendant does not have the ability to pay a judgment. Most juries do not want to put a defendant company out of business and cause its innocent employees and their families to suffer.

A defendant's ability to pay a judgment comes up for discussion by the jury more often in punitive damages cases than in cases that do not involve punitive damages. One hypothesis for this distinction is that the question of a company's net worth or financial resources is not usually entered into evidence for consideration by the jury unless punitive damages are requested. Another hypothesis is that a court's instructions may imply that the net worth or financial resources of the corporation should be considered when the jury assesses punitive damages.

To summarize these research findings, we might simply conclude that jurors usually form perceptions of a defendant's ability to pay a judgment as they try to understand the parties and the case. However, the financial resources of a defendant usually only come into focus for jurors when they are trying to determine if the defendant has the ability to pay a judgment and how much in punitive damages would inflict appropriate punishment on a defendant for wrongful conduct.

[7]—Making Alternative Damages Arguments

There are a number of important questions about how to approach damages issues with a jury that lawyers often debate. Attorneys who represent plaintiffs

[39] Hans, "Attitudes toward Corporate Responsibility," Nebraska L. Rev. 69, 186 (1990); Vidmar, *Medical Malpractice and the American Jury: Confronting Myths about Jury Incompetence, Deep Pockets, and Outrageous Damage Awards,* at pp. 203-222 (Ann Arbor: University of Michigan Press, 1995).

[40] Greene, Woody, Douglas & Winter, "Compensating Plaintiffs and Punishing Defendants: Is Bifurcation Necessary?" 24 Law & Human Behavior 187-205 (2000).

in personal injury, business, and intellectual property cases are often concerned about how much to ask for in damages and how to present their arguments. Attorneys who represent defendants are concerned about whether to argue against damages at all or to present alternative arguments asking the jury to find no damages or at least an amount substantially less than the plaintiff's request.

A precise answer to these questions is available by studying general jury research and by conducting private jury research in a particular case. However, we have learned much in recent years about how juries respond to various approaches.

We have learned, as a general rule, that the more money a plaintiff requests, the more money the plaintiff will receive if the jury finds liability. This rule appears to be applicable up to the point that a plaintiff begins to appear to be avaricious. Determining the point of apparent greed can be accomplished in two ways. The first is to look at previous jury awards in similar cases. The second is to include a study of the maximum amount of money a jury is likely to award with other pretrial jury research that is being conducted in the case.

Whether to present alternative damages arguments from a defensive standpoint is more a question of *how* to do it as opposed to *whether* to do it. Substantial research conducted in post-trial interviews and mock trial jury studies indicates that jurors want to hear as many appropriate alternatives as possible. It is common for jurors at the conclusion of trial to express frustration that a defense team did not address the possibility of alternative damages awards. If you fail to provide enough alternatives, you may force a jury to make a decision that is unpalatable to your client.

From a psychological standpoint, jurors are capable of comprehending alternative arguments if they are placed in context. For example, a defense attorney might argue,

> "We believe that the evidence in this case does not support an award of *any* damages to this plaintiff. Even if you believe the other party's case, then the amount of money that is justified by the evidence is no more than _____ dollars."

At this point in our discussion we should realize that jurors are much more sophisticated in their thinking than we often believe. They are quite capable of and ready to make reasoned decisions based upon alternative arguments from both plaintiff and defendant. In the experience of many veteran trial professionals, actual jury awards are often significantly different from amounts requested by either the plaintiff or defendant.

There are a few cases, however, where the question of liability is so close that it might be best for a defendant not to make alternative arguments. In those cases, making an argument that would imply that the plaintiff might be entitled to any damages at all could be counterproductive. Jury research in those specific cases will provide insight on how to handle the situation.

§ 4.13 | REFERENCES

Aronson, Rovella & Van Voris, "Jurors: A Biased, Independent Lot," The National Law Journal, pp. A1, A24-A25 (Nov. 2, 1998.)

Feigenson, Park & Salovey, "Effect of Blameworthiness and Outcome Severity on Attributions of Responsibility and Damage Awards in Comparative Negligence Cases," 21 Law & Human Behavior 597-617 (1997).

Hans, "Attitudes toward Corporate Responsibility," Nebraska L. Rev. 69, 158-189 (1990).

Hans, *Business on Trial: The Civil Jury and Corporate Responsibility* (New Haven: Yale University Press, 2000).

Hans & Appel, *Handbook of Jury Research* (Philadelphia: American Law Institute, 1999).

Vidmar, *Medical Malpractice and the American Jury* (Ann Arbor: University of Michigan Press, 1997).

CHAPTER 5

Developing Powerful Stories
and Themes

CHAPTER CONTENTS

"Of course it is all storytelling—nothing more. It is the experience of the tribe around the fire, the primordial genes excited, listening, the shivers racing up your back to the place where the scalp is made, and then, breathless climax, and the sadness and tears with the dying of the embers, and the silence. . . . The problem is that we, as lawyers, have forgotten how to speak to ordinary folk. . . . Lawyers long ago abandoned ordinary English. Worse, their minds have been smashed and serialized, and their brain cells restacked so they no longer can explode in every direction—with joy, love, and rage. They cannot see in the many colors of feeling. The passion is gone, replaced with the deadly droning of the intellect. And the sounds we make are all alike, like machines mumbling and grinding away, because what was once free—the stuff of storytelling—has become rigid."

— Gerry Spence
American Bar Association, 1986

§ 5.01 | WHAT IS STORYTELLING?

Storytelling is nothing more than sharing a narrative tale of experiences, either real or imaginary, with someone else. It is essentially a cultural art form for preserving and transmitting thoughts, perceptions, images, motives, and emotions with others.

We have done it all our lives and do it every day. In the evening when your spouse and the kids come home, everybody talks about their experiences during the day. We are inundated with stories—stories in newspapers, stories in television news, stories from our friends at lunch, stories from strangers in the check-out line.

Some stories are more interesting than others, depending upon the content, the storyteller, and the listener. Consider this passage from a wonderful book written by a Spanish countess who had been a spy for the United States in Spain during World War II:

"When we arrived at the highway, the driver turned left, taking a different road to the city, I supposed. Then his strange detour brought me back to the present with a jerk.

"'Why are we taking this road,' I asked.

"'Shorter,' he replied.

"I looked out at the open country of the unpopulated northwestern border of the city. Some instinct warned me even before he pulled the car to the side of the road.

"As he came to a stop, I jumped out and started to run and in a second was in thick underbrush. I heard him following, and although it was pitch black, I feared he would hear my steps racing through the crackling underbrush. As I ran, I grabbed my Beretta .25, letting my bag fall. His pursuit, crashing through the bushes, became louder each second. My long dress was catching on thorny branches, my heels were sinking into the sandy earth, making it difficult to run. I knew I had to do it.

"I turned and without hesitation crouched and shot at the shadowy form rushing at me, fifteen feet away. I must have missed, because he lunged for me and grabbed my throat. He was strangling me! Using my last bit of strength, I shoved the gun at him, not knowing or caring where I was aiming this time. I was sinking into unconsciousness when I heard the sound of a shot. My own! But now it seemed to echo from afar; then there was silence."[1]

This passage is contained within a larger story that is full of intrigue, excitement, terror, and ordinary people doing extraordinary things in order to undermine the German Third Reich. It is full of heroes and villains.

There are many reasons that we tell stories to each other. Sometimes we experience something that affects us strongly and we feel a need to share the experience with those around us. When we tell stories we feel more connected and alive. When we tell stories we learn something about ourselves and about other people to help us utilize our perceptions, thoughts, feelings, and values. Storytelling is a kind of catharsis or process through which we reconcile conflicts and bring about a better understanding between ourselves, whoever is listening, and the events about which we speak.

One of the most disconcerting aspects of storytelling for those who are trying to improve their skills is that storytelling is personal and may change depending upon the audience. It is not a rigid exercise. It is a process in which

---

[1] Aline, Countess of Romanones, *The Spy Wore Red* (New York: Random House, 1987).

the storyteller reaches out and says, "You and I have the same needs and I want to be closer to you." Storytelling is more intimate than most forms of entertainment.

Storytelling has become the primary method by which we learn as children.

§ 5.02 | WHY STORYTELLING IS SO PSYCHOLOGICALLY POWERFUL

Storytelling is one of the most powerful ways of communicating with other people. Why? Because since the time we were babies, storytelling has been the fundamental way for us to learn about life.

Anthropologists tell us that our primitive ancestors began the process of telling stories in order to share their experiences with each other. The tradition of storytelling began in prehistoric times so that one member of a tribe could explain the hazards he or she had encountered during the day to help others avoid impending threats to their survival. In fact, language and alphabets were developed in part to help with this process.

The most recent research in developmental and cognitive psychology tells us that people begin learning about the world around them immediately after birth through observation and experimentation. One published psychological study found that children between the ages of two and three years of age observe an average of eight and one-half new vignettes of life each day through the stories and revelations of their parents. In this process of learning, children begin to record these vignettes or "storiettes" as if they were actual life experiences, and even adopt the judgments and conclusions relayed to them by their parents.

Looking at this process more closely, we know that each of these storiettes contains all the elements of any other story. They have a beginning, a middle, and an end. They occur in chronological sequence. They contain characterizations of other people, the storyteller, and the circumstances. They contain facts. They contain emotional appeal. They contain the moral values and messages that give the story meaning.

Moving one step further, then, we can understand how people would feel comfortable with the process of storytelling as the most acceptable way to learn new information about other people's perceptions and experiences. It is part of our conditioning.

§ 5.03 | STORYTELLING AS AN ART FORM

It is often hard to imagine a time when there were no books, televisions, computers, telephones, automobiles, or even cities and governments. Nonetheless, since the beginning of known history, ancient people gathered to share their experiences and thoughts through music and prose. For people of many cultures, storytelling was a way of preserving knowledge as well as a way of romanticizing their past and their heroes.

In many Eastern and Western cultures, troubadours and minstrels earned a living traveling from town to town, entertaining people with the stories they had developed. In this sense, storytelling evolved from a cultural necessity to a form of entertainment. Even today, ballads and fiction novels have evolved as a contemporary form of storytelling.

Ancient storytellers used mythology and drama to relate their experiences and perceptions. We can envision players re-enacting comedies and tragedies on the stages of ancient Greece. People came from faraway places just to share the experience. The same is true of the people who lived in medieval Europe.

Even in those days, great orators were also called upon to speak for citizens involved in legal disputes. Some of the disputes dealt with life and death issues, whereas others dealt with personal liberties and disputes over property and contract rights.

Those of us in the field of trial advocacy romanticize a time in American history when public debate and storytelling brought about turning points in cultural evolution. Examples include the 1776 debates over the wording of the United States Declaration of Independence and the 1926 Scopes "monkey" trial on the teaching of scientific evolution in public schools.

Good storytellers realize that a modern audience expects to hear interesting, entertaining stories in public debates, including courtroom trials. Jurors search for meaning in a trial that both touches and entertains them.

§ 5.04 | Selecting the Story to Tell

There are several important considerations to bear in mind when one tells a story in the courtroom. Obviously, one is limited to the evidence and the inferences that can reasonably be drawn from that evidence. However, within the confines of these broad limitations, there are many wonderful opportunities to develop a story that is both entertaining and persuasive. If one were to argue that the evidence is so limited that a strong and compelling story cannot be told, one might also argue that the storyteller has not worked hard enough or been creative enough to find the most powerful story to tell in the case.

When you select which story to tell, it is important to tell a story that you like and that makes you feel confident and committed in telling it. One should enjoy telling the story of a case because a good story only gets better with time.

Conversely, a story that is difficult to tell either because it does not feel comfortable or truthful to the storyteller, becomes more troublesome with time. The process is like trying to fit a square peg in a round hole. Both judge and jury will feel uncomfortable.

The story and style of telling should both complement the style and character of the lawyer who tells the story. For example, a lawyer who is extroverted will feel comfortable using exaggerated body language and style, whereas a more introverted lawyer may tell the same story more quietly, relying upon themes and message content to carry the day.

It is most important, however, that the lawyer agree with the content of the story and messages. Some people have insisted that a good storyteller can make an argument with which he or she does not agree. Experience indicates, however, that disbelief on the part of a storyteller is usually apparent in subtle ways. Storytellers who try to "fake it" are not usually successful no matter how skillfully they tell stories.

Conversely, some limited research indicates that audiences will assume that a storyteller believes the story even when they are told otherwise. However, those same audiences experience trepidation about the story and the storyteller when they perceive that the storyteller is not being genuine. In the final analysis, stories are more powerful when the storyteller believes the story and its messages.

A good story contains a small universe in itself. The characters and their activities must be believable in the confines of the story. That is, a good story places everything in context and all the story parts fit together within that context. Otherwise, the story would seem odd to the audience, even though they might be unable to articulate why it seems odd.

A story should be simple enough for an audience to follow without difficulty. It need not have a plot, although most stories do. Nonetheless, a good story has a simple point or moral that demonstrates purpose and meaning to the audience.

Most persuasive stories have an opening that adequately sets the scene, introduces the major characters, and relates the chronology of the story. The opening also briefly explains the background necessary to understand the story.

Most good stories also have action and suspense to keep the audience interested. They contain sensory imagery in order to enrich the experience of the audience. For example, powerful and colorful adjectives that describe people can often provide characterizations that quickly lead the audience to conclusions about the actors.

The most effective stories are brief and do not contain much dialogue. The most effective writers and speakers use sparing, but powerful words in describing people, behavior, and events. Brevity should be a standard.

Finally and most important, the development of a powerful story is not an event; it is a process. Developing a story is like painting on canvas. It starts with a vision of the outcome and is slowly and carefully developed through trial and error, letting creative intuition take you to the finished end product.

§ 5.05 | DEVELOPING COMPELLING STORY THEMES

Every work of art has a concept or "theme" that comprises the message the artist wishes to convey. Theme, then, is the message that gives meaning.

There are three principles that significantly affect the development of central themes for the case story.

First, there are two types of themes: *descriptive themes*, which characterize particular pieces of evidence, and *evaluative themes*, which characterize the overall principles for which the case stands. Descriptive themes are rarely determinative of case outcome because they are often localized to a particular event or transaction. However, evaluative themes are so important to a case that if the lawyers fail to provide them, jurors will provide them instead. For example, a descriptive theme that seeks to show that a particular signature was forged is not nearly as powerful as an evaluative theme to the effect that the forger was "greedy," "dishonest," and "didn't care who he hurt."

The second principle to remember when formulating themes is that compelling themes help jurors organize case information along the lines that the presenter wishes, and help them to overcome disputes or conflicts with specific evidence. For example, with regard to a medical malpractice case, a theme which asserts that "the doctor didn't care enough to help a mother in distress" assists jurors to focus on trial information that substantiates that the doctor did not care (did not return telephone calls, did not go to the hospital for ten hours after getting an emergency call, etc.). This theme would also help jurors to overcome some inconsistent but isolated evidence to the contrary.

Finally, compelling themes must fit well with jurors' preconceived attitudes and life experiences, and must outrank or "trump" the opposing party's themes in fundamental importance. Themes and messages are at least as important as the key facts of the case.

Determining the best themes and psychological messages prior to trial should involve intense research. Places to search for effective themes are ubiquitous. Themes are all around us every day. Newspapers, television shows, movies, fiction books, children's story books, collections of fables and fairy tales, and mythology books are a few excellent sources of basic themes that might apply to a particular case. Other ideas can come from a review of previous jury verdicts, news stories about other cases, and post-trial interviews in other similar cases; these sources can help to focus on the issues and rationale of a likely jury. The most effective, reliable method of identifying the most powerful themes and case story for a particular case is to conduct scientific jury research that focuses on the specific circumstances of the case.

THE MOST PERSUASIVE THEMES

❍ *Transcend the facts of the case*

❍ *Are emotionally powerful (generally take the moral high ground)*

❍ *Address the larger significance of the case*

❍ *Evoke powerful images*

❍ *Can be expressed visually, in words, and through tangible means*

❍ *Match juror needs to "do the right thing"*

❍ *Provide consistency throughout the case presentation*

❍ *Also provide consistency with other themes*

❍ *Also provide consistency with the evidence and testimony*

As in any presentation, the audience will pay more attention and become more involved when the messages in the case have a level of importance that transcends the case itself. Therefore, the themes that are presented in court must rise to a level of significance so that they touch the hearts and minds of the judge and jury. It should also be noted that expanding one's consciousness beyond the case facts exponentially increases the possibilities for powerful themes.

In other words, an effective theme is easy to remember, appeals to common sense, is in accord with jurors' concepts of fairness and justice, and is consistent with the evidence. What's more, an effective theme resonates throughout the case. It is repeated one way or another in every phase of the trial, unlike specific items of evidence that rarely reappear. Effective themes are revealed over and over again in attorney argument, visual aids, and witness direct and cross-examinations.

§ 5.06 | IDENTIFYING THE RIGHT THEMES FOR THE CASE

One question should enable a lawyer to identify the right themes for a case, i.e., "What is the most powerful story we can tell about the case based upon the experiences and attitudes of the likely jurors?"

In other words, the themes we select must be those that touch the hearts of likely jurors and motivate them to decide in our favor. Even though we and other members of the trial team may think that a particular theme is right, it must be subjected to scrutiny to determine what likely jurors will think. Most jurors generally view the world quite differently than lawyers.

For the most part, trial lawyers have historically developed their themes and case stories through a rather haphazard process. We generally operated under the principle that, "if it feels good, it must be okay." However, a more methodical approach is recommended.

The first step, therefore, is to make a list of all the potential themes that should be considered. The possibilities can come from many sources.

SOURCES FOR POSSIBLE THEMES

- ○ *Fables/Fairy Tales*
- ○ *Greek Mythology*
- ○ *Accounts of Historical Events*
- ○ *Native American Mythology*
- ○ *Fiction and Non-Fiction Stories*
- ○ *Mock Trial Jury Research*
- ○ *Newspaper Stories*
- ○ *Magazine Articles*
- ○ *Television News and Commentary*
- ○ *Personal Experience*

Once a complete list of the possible alternative themes is compiled, we can begin ranking them in order of their appeal to a likely jury (or judge). This ranking process requires both good intuition and objective testing in the context of the evidence and the story to be told.

One of the great benefits of the most recent developments in scientific research methodology is that we can test our best ideas about possible themes and case story presentation (using focus groups or mock trial research methods) and receive reliable data upon which to develop a stronger presentation. Almost every case can benefit from an objective testing phase. These days, scientifically based information is quite varied, and the cost of obtaining scientifically based recommendations for enhancing themes can be tailored to a case. Information based upon reliable jury research methods is available in every case regardless of budget.

No matter what testing mechanism is used (whether scientific or not), it is wise to scrutinize every possible theme closely so that one's own biases do not cause more powerful ideas to be overlooked. Essentially, therefore, developing powerful themes requires creative thinking and rigorous testing.

§ 5.07 | STORY STRUCTURE AND ORGANIZATION

A story may be formed in many ways, but most stories have a plot. Within the plot, two opposing forces meet. One is the protagonist who wants something. The other is the antagonist who tries to prevent the protagonist from getting whatever the latter seeks. The protagonist is generally an individual. The antagonist is generally a force or condition (and sometimes an individual) that is demonstrated largely in the central character's relationships with others.

For example, the famous actor John Wayne often played the role of an individual struggling to bring justice and fairness to the aid of those who were being tormented by greedy, evil forces. Many powerful, persuasive themes were embedded in the scripts for his characters. Sometimes it even seemed that the dialogue for Wayne's character contained nothing more than a continuing stream of themes and psychological messages which revealed the true nature of all the characters and behaviors in the story, from the narrator's perspective.

More modern applications of themes can be seen in stories such as the 2000 movie *Saving Private Ryan*, in which an American Army captain in the World War II Normandy invasion was ordered to locate one lone private whose three brothers had been killed in various battles around the globe. The United States military had made the decision to locate this private and send him home in order to prevent the death of the family's only remaining son. The story contained many plots and subplots, most of which pitted an individual soldier against the pressing demands of the world around him to do things that were extraordinarily good or reprehensible, depending upon the context of the action and the viewpoint of the observer.

Every story has an "inciting incident," which is a pivotal point at which the balance between the protagonist and the antagonist is disturbed. At this point, the action begins to build and the protagonist's problem becomes more intense.

Rhetorical questions begin to form. Does the protagonist know what is happening? Does the protagonist realize he is endangered? Will the protagonist be able to hold back the evil forces?

The suspense builds to a climax. The struggle continues to escalate until something definitive and irreversible happens. The story has reached a turning point. At this point the protagonist generally realizes that he or she will either prevail or lose the struggle. Suddenly, the end of the story arrives and the protagonist has either won or lost.

But the story does not stop here. There is the aftermath. There are the consequences.

§ 5.08 | DEVELOPING THE STORY CHARACTERS

Jurors are vitally interested in the character of the parties and witnesses in a trial. Research and experience indicate that character is often the most important element of a story, if not *the* most important element. Character is certainly equally important as any other element. In many stories, character *is* the story. It is therefore important to analyze key individuals in a trial and identify important characteristics that will help you to present them more effectively. Such characterizations of people should ordinarily be simple, direct, and powerful. The more important characters will require more detailed analysis and character development.

CHARACTER DEVELOPMENT CONSIDERATIONS

1. Where is the person from and how old is he or she?

2. What kind of family relationships does the person have and how does that affect the person's integrity?

3. How likeable is this person? Why?

4. What kind of relationship does the person have with others in the story? Why?

5. What kind of business background does the person have and how does that affect his or her attitudes and behavior?

6. What are the views of the person about his or her relationships to other people in reference to specific subjects? Why?

7. What are the person's motives and beliefs about the important issues? Why?

8. What have been the major influences on this person's life that relate to specific issues in the case?

9. What emotions does the person feel about the people and events in the case?

10. What personality traits does the person have which may have affected his or her behavior and perceptions?

It is often helpful to try to view the characters more objectively and from a perspective that jurors would anticipate in the setting of the case. For example, counsel for a plaintiff worker who was injured in a plant explosion would probably portray that plaintiff as competent, loyal, and hardworking, whereas the plant manager would be characterized as spending most of the day counting the plant's weekly profits and devising ways to improve worker productivity so that the plant can make even more money. Conversely, the defense would portray the worker as competent, honest, and hard-working, but careless about the mechanism that caused the explosion. The plant manager would be portrayed by the defense as always out among the work force, helping to make the work more safe and productive from the worker's perspective.

These examples demonstrate how the themes of the case can be effectively interwoven with the personal characterizations that make the story believable, from a juror's viewpoint. Since we know that jurors look for consistencies in a case, they will probably agree with the position of the trial team that best portrays consistency among character, behavior, and events.

Let's try another example. Let's say the plaintiff is a Fortune 500 corporation which developed a special software application that speeds up the processing of mutual fund investment transactions and allows customers to confirm changes in their account balances instantly. The corporation's team of inventors worked hard on the product and it now enjoys a market share approaching 80%. The defendants are two of the inventors who broke away from the corporation to form their own small company that developed a version of the same software that they had helped to invent while they were employed at the big corporation. The allegations in the suit state that the defendants took trade secrets and are using them in their new software. There is a counterclaim that the big corporation is in violation of antitrust laws by trying to prevent a small start-up company from competing.

When you think the way jurors think, first you must know what kinds of people are involved, in terms of their character traits and motivations. Once you have that information, the themes that help tell the story generally make perfect sense.

If we are representing the plaintiff big corporation we would probably want to characterize it as a company that listens to its employees (here, inventors) and that listens to the public to determine what software applications are needed to make our lives better. We would want to highlight the individual inventors who are still employed at the company to show that they are loyal, trustworthy, and honest (compared to the defendants, who are not).

To summarize, the character traits of actors must be consistent with the themes and the perspective of the story in order for jurors to accept and believe that story. Conversely, if there is any inconsistency, jurors will feel uncomfortable with the characters or the story and will find it less acceptable and credible.

To follow up our last example, if defense counsel can establish that the big corporation is heartless and uncaring toward either workers or the public, the plaintiff's story will be less successful even though it may be completely supported by the facts. For this reason, it is important that the characterizations chosen and the story be consistent with undisputed facts—unassailable wherever possible. It is important for the trial attorney to be fundamentally committed to both the characterizations and the story. To have a "clean" characterization (undisputed) is sometimes hard work in the heat of battle where the opposing party is trying to paint a party as the antithesis.

One of the most interesting techniques for developing character is telling vignettes that reveal character traits. Our life experiences are full of spontaneous activities that reveal the true character of people as well or more specifically than more grand behaviors or behaviors which occurred while a person was under scrutiny.

Finally, it is most helpful for a key witness who is also a central actor to look at jurors directly and tell them in clear terms how he or she feels about a certain issue or is so certain about what happened in the case. In other words, it is very persuasive for a witness to reveal the truth about himself or herself under direct or cross-examination in addition to the narrated descriptions of the trial lawyers.

§ 5.09 | ADDING CREATIVITY TO STORYTELLING

> *"The magic, the joy of preparation: Ah, preparation! There is where the magic begins! Yet young lawyers seem disappointed when I tell them so. They yearn for an easy formula that will permit them to bypass the stodgy stuff called work. I wish I could explain to them that true preparation is not work. It is the joy of creating. Preparation is wading into life, languishing in it, rolling in it, embracing it, smearing it over yourself, living it. . . . I doubt you could have gotten Mozart to admit he ever worked. But his life, his breath, was his music. His argument, rendered with immortal notes, was the product of intense preparation— preparation that consumed him every day of his life."*
>
> – Gerry Spence[2]

One of the remarkable things about storytelling is that every time a story is told, it changes just a little. Why? Whether we are telling a story from personal experience or relating a story that someone has told us, we tend to recall the essence of the story from the pictures and feelings we have stored in our brain

---

[2] Gerry Spence, *How to Argue and Win Every Time* (New York: St. Martin's Press, 1995).

rather than the lexicon with which the story was told to us. The same is true of jurors in their attempts to recall the story.

Listeners therefore tend to give a storyteller license to be creative, and in fact prefer that a storyteller interject personal style and emphasize changes so that they can capture the essence of a story for themselves. For this reason, learning to tell a particular story is easier than learning to recite or to repeat very specific lines as an actor in a play.

The key to presenting a story is to commit the essence of the story and key phrases to memory, and link them together in a spontaneous way. For most people, this may mean constructing a written form of the story using facts and themes which have been researched, and then reading the story over and over, silently and aloud, until the key phrases and expressions are committed to memory. You might also try substituting other phrases and expressions which more graphically and/or accurately tell the same story.

As you continue to read and "practice" telling the story, you might concentrate on the images that arise in your mind. You might think about the meaning and essence of how the images affect you. Certainly the way you perceive those images will be different from the way the people in your audience will perceive them. Rarely do two people see the same images in their minds even when they hear identical words. Nevertheless, the essential meaning and essence of the dialogue will be communicated and received. It is important to note, however, that powerful images are created with a blend of facts and descriptions that convey powerful meaning. Consider the following examples:

> ALTERNATIVE 1: "The man was walking across the sandy beach after a long swim."

> ALTERNATIVE 2: "Soaked and breathless, the man trudged up onto the beach as if he had been chased in the ocean for miles by something dangerous lurking below the surface."

There are few undertakings in life more pleasurable than reading, listening, and creating powerful, interesting stories.

Finally, it may be helpful to memorize the opening sentence to the story and the sequence of events. Some storytellers prefer to write out the opening line and create a time line as a visual aid in telling the story.

Utilizing the method described above allows the storyteller a great deal of license and spontaneity in telling a story. As a result, the story is more effective in obtaining the audience's attention and creating the impression that the storyteller is truly committed to the story. In addition, it eliminates any barriers (e.g., reliance on notes and books) between the storyteller and audience.

§ 5.10 | RELAXING AND GETTING IN THE MOOD

Over the years we have all been given advice about relaxing and getting into the mood for making a presentation or telling a story to an audience. Most of this advice relates to behavioral things we can do such as dressing comfortably, arranging the setting in advance, stretching or shaking our arms and hands until they feel loose, breathing deeply, and meditating to clear our minds. These behaviors can probably help to a limited degree.

However, relaxing and getting in the mood are more a matter of mental attitude than physical state. Few people tell a story to an audience that they do not want to tell. We choose to tell the story. It is our gift to the audience.

It is actually helpful to be a little bit nervous. It keeps us alert and "on our toes." Nervousness is also a reminder that we want the audience to like us and to believe the story. A little anxiety is a good thing.

Sometimes we are so caught up in our self-consciousness we forget that the only reason we are telling this story in the courtroom is to help the fact finder understand what happened and to convince him or her (a judge) or them (a jury) that our client's version of a story is correct. In other words, storytelling in the courtroom is not about the individual as storyteller, but it is about the story and, more important, the audience. Therefore, changing the focus from our own self-consciousness to helping the audience by telling a good story should be a good antidote for stage fright.

§ 5.11 | CONCLUSION

Since judges and jurors are most affected by the essence and meaning of the story, it seems logical that a great deal of effort should be spent on creating a powerful and moving story. No matter what kind of case is being presented to the court, there is a compelling and persuasive story lying just underneath the factual surface waiting to be discovered.

A FINAL WORD: TELLING THE STORY AROUND ONE CENTRAL THEME

The mark of a good trial lawyer is the consistent advocacy of one central theme during all aspects of the trial. In one sentence you must be able to tell the jury what the fight is about and why your client should win it. Lawyers sometimes abandon the approach of one central theme because they are afraid of relinquishing a possible winning argument. However, tossing out multiple potential themes lessens, rather than increases, the chances of winning.

In developing your one central theme of the case, you must answer one critical question: after hearing all of the testimony, what facts will every juror believe to be true? You must clearly think through your case in advance so that you may determine what, in all probability, the jury will believe the truth to be after all the evidence is presented. You must come up with a simple understandable case theory which accounts for all the central facts and persuasively explains why it is fair for your client to win the case. I have twelve-year-old twin daughters. If I cannot explain the case to them with one sentence that persuades them to agree that my clients should win, I know that my theory of the case needs work.

Once you have developed your one central theme, the remainder of the trial involves building a story that gives meaning to your theme. The story must appeal to the heart and soul—not just the mind—of each juror. Keeping in mind that a trial is essentially a credibility contest, the story you are telling the jury must always ring true. Transforming one's case into a story appeals to jurors because people are accustomed to storytelling in ordinary conversation, and because arguments are ordinarily more sensible through storytelling. Storytelling is the most effective technique to communicate information in a persuasive manner because it allows the advocate to evoke a strong emotional response from jurors. Honest emotion is a powerful force in the courtroom. Because of its explanatory power, storytelling allows jurors to place themselves in the case scenario from your client's perspective. An attorney who employs the technique of storytelling to develop one central trial theme adds moral force to the client's position and maximizes the chance of achieving the desired outcome.

— Stephen Rasch, Partner
Thompson & Knight LLP

§ 5.12 | REFERENCES

Aristotle (translated and organized by Ross, Ross, Ackrill & Urmson), *The Nicomachean Ethics (Oxford World's Classics)* (Oxford: Oxford University Press, 1998).

Bruner, *Acts of Meaning* (Cambridge: Harvard University Press, 1990).

Campbell, *Hero With a Thousand Faces* (Princeton: Princeton University Press, 1972).

Campbell & Moyers, *The Power of Myth* (New York: Anchor Books, 1991).

Danilewitz, "Once Upon a Time . . . The Meaning and Importance of Fairy Tales," 75 Early Child Development & Care 87-98 (Oct. 1991).

Erdoes & Ortiz, *American Indian Myths and Legends* (New York: Pantheon Books, 1984).

Lucas & McCoy, *The Winning Edge* (New York: Wiley Law Publications, 1993).

Parry, "Why We Tell Stories: The Narrative Construction of Reality," 27 Transactional Analysis J. 118-127 (1997).

Reilly, "How to Tell a Good Story: The Intersection of Language and Affect in Children's Narratives," 2 J. Narrative & Life History 355-377 (1992).

Spence, *How to Argue and Win Every Time* (New York: St. Martin's Press, 1995).

Walton & Toomay, *The Writer's Path: A Guidebook for Your Creative Journey* (Berkeley: Ten Speed Press, 2000).

CHAPTER 6

Scientific Jury and
Decision-Maker Research

CHAPTER CONTENTS

> *"Thus, it is Foreknowledge that enables a Brilliant Leader to Triumph over others wherever they move, while producing useful achievements for the numerous."*
>
> — Sun Tzu (ca. 480-221 B.C.)
> *The Art of Strategy*

§ 6.01 | INTRODUCTION

Science is about answering hard questions. It is a method of inquiry. Some of the questions scientists have answered are historic, i.e., "Is the earth round or flat?" "What causes electricity?" Many questions are less historic, but important nonetheless.

When we think of science, we have a tendency to focus on mechanical sciences or what some people called "hard sciences." We think of men and women wearing long white coats in laboratories working with tangible, physical materials. However, the knowledge we have about our mental processes and behavior has also come to us through scientific study. For example, why would one child in a family become a hardened criminal while the other becomes a dedicated public servant? Why do men and women sometimes evaluate circumstances differently? Why would a person evaluate one set of circumstances with cold indifference and another set of circumstances with passionate anger?

Consider this quotation from William James, once a psychology professor at Harvard University, who is considered to be the father of modern psychology in America:

> "If we knew thoroughly the nervous system of Shakespeare, and as thoroughly all his environing conditions, we should be able to show why at a certain period of his life his hand came to trace on certain sheets of paper those crabbed little black marks for which we for shortness' sake called the manuscript of 'Hamlet.'"[1]

True psychology is the scientific study of behavior and mental processes. This definition includes the study of feelings, desires, cognition, reasoning,

---

[1] William James, *The Principles of Psychology* (New York: Henry Holt & Co., 1890).

decision making, and anything affecting the mental and emotional aspects of our lives. Every meaningful human action involves mental processing and behavior. We study psychology to understand the connections between mental processes and actual behavior.

Even though you may not have an academic degree in a field of science, you have been conducting scientific research throughout your life. You answer hard questions every day. You may not have used the most objective and rigorous methods of conducting research to answer these questions, but you managed to answer the questions even though you may have gotten mixed results. By increasing your knowledge and awareness of scientific methods, you can sharpen your skills in conducting research and probably get better results. The purpose of this chapter is to help you in this process.

Decision making which takes place in the courtroom affects all of us. Every courtroom decision greatly affects the judge, jurors, trial attorneys, parties, and even non-party witnesses in the case. Some decisions affect thousands if not millions of other people as well, directly and indirectly. To be successful as trial advocates, we must know why people make the decisions they do in the courtroom. We have a vested interest in having enough information before trial to be able to make our best case.

Our trial court system is based upon centuries of tradition in which trial advocates wished to understand their audience in advance in order to craft their most compelling arguments. Nothing is new about this. What is new, however, is the availability of reliable, scientifically based information to use in understanding the judge, jurors, or arbitrators in advance of trial.

We tend to take psychology for granted. Perhaps this is because psychology is like air and water: It is everywhere. We sometimes feel that because we are experienced in the world and in the courtroom, there is little chance that a scientist can tell us something that we do not already know. However, the world is constantly changing and there are many new tools that science is making available to us as trial advocates that help us make more informed strategic decisions and be more effective in persuading the decision makers in our cases.

Some of the questions that every trial lawyer asks in preparation for trial are quite difficult and very important to the parties in the case:

- Should we try this case before a judge, an arbitrator, or a jury?
- What is our best venue for the case?
- What are the real issues that a jury will think are important in the case?

- Who or what will a jury think caused the plaintiff's damages?
- What will the jury think about our argument on damages?
- Will the jury think our client is worthy of a large judgment?
- Will the jury want to punish our client for some reason?
- Which argument or theme is our most persuasive argument?
- Who is our ideal juror?
- Whom should we avoid?
- How can I help a key witness give more effective testimony?

In this chapter we will discuss the contribution that science has made to our understanding of courtroom decision making. We will demonstrate how rigorous and accurate scientific research methods can help every trial attorney and party discover new insights in making decisions about the trial or settlement of a case. The methods we will discuss are general and are currently in use by trial attorneys, corporations, and trial consultants all over the United States. More experienced researchers have developed their own variations or individualized additions to the ideas in this chapter that seem to work well for them.

We will discuss the application of scientific knowledge and research methods for developing a reliable understanding about how a judge, juror, or arbitrator will likely process evidence presented in a specific case. The information and insights from such research will help us use all the other topics we discuss in this advocacy treatise. Ultimately, our primary focus is the development of the most persuasive and compelling presentation of the case, either in trial, arbitration, or mediation.

§ 6.02 | APPLYING SCIENCE TO DEVELOPMENT OF THE CASE FOR TRIAL OR SETTLEMENT

In general, there are three ways in which science can contribute to the development of the case. The first is the application of knowledge that we have about the decision-making processes of people in general, as well as judges, jurors, arbitrators, and opposing parties in particular. The second is the application of specific research tools to the study of each case to help us understand how the decision maker will process and decide the outcome for the case. The third is the application of objective and scientific therapeutic and interpretation techniques that help us to understand and apply the information that we collect in research.

In this chapter we will focus on the application of studied scientific research techniques in order to describe for the reader the requirements necessary to conduct reliable, useful research in specific cases. We will also discuss some of the pitfalls for those readers without scientific research training. Generally, the magnitude of benefit of conducting any kind of research is in proportion to the effort and resources invested. As in any endeavor, the more trained and experienced one is in the conduct and application of scientific research, the more powerful and useful the information gained in the research.

Let us begin with an example of a typical business dispute. The plaintiff is a large, Denver-based corporation that conducts research and development for sophisticated data communications systems. We will call the plaintiff "TFC," which stands for "The First Company." Five principals founded TFC fifteen years ago, one of whom was a famous research scientist we will call "Ms. Garth." TFC has now grown to a $75 billion corporation with several thousand employees. The company enjoys an 82% market share in its niche market. Over the past few years, however, Ms. Garth has gradually stopped enjoying management of such a large organization.

As a result, two years ago Ms. Garth sold her interest in TFC for $133 million and moved to Phoenix. She is an avid golfer and enjoys the year-round availability of challenging golf courses in nearby Scottsdale. When she sold her interest and left TFC, she refused to sign any agreements other than the simple contract for transfer and sale of her stock. She did not take any TFC company documents with her.

Upon arriving in Arizona, Ms. Garth immediately began setting up her own company to develop and manufacture software and hardware for the same market as TFC. The name of her new company is TSC ("The Second Company"). Ms. Garth believes that she has the capability of producing quality products and services for the market at a competitive price. She established a research and development office in Phoenix, and marketing and sales offices in Chicago, New York, Miami, Houston, Denver, Seattle, and Los Angeles.

In the course of setting up her new company, Ms. Garth contacted several of the key engineers at TFC and asked if they would like to apply for important jobs in her new company. She offered them 10% pay raises and a significant number of shares in her new corporation. She was successful in hiring seven of the top engineers from TFC.

The hiring of these seven engineers was a severe blow to TFC's upper management. Much of the company's talent was included in this group. The remaining founders were angry that someone they had worked with closely for so long was now a competitor. They felt Ms. Garth had betrayed them. They also believed that she was trying to steal their trade secrets by hiring away key employees. A preliminary investigation has discovered that one of the key employees downloaded several important engineering documents to disks at his home several days before leaving TFC's employment. TFC has therefore turned to both its general counsel and to outside trial counsel to determine possible avenues of legal recourse.

There are many legal issues involved: What causes of action should they bring? How should venue be determined? Should the case be brought in state court or federal court? In what court would the company most likely obtain the best remedy? What are the relevant laws of the various states involved, which are procedural, which are substantive, and which are likely to be applicable?

However, there are also many important nonlegal questions: In which of the two possible trial locations will local attitudes and opinions among judges and the jury population likely favor TFC if the case were to proceed to trial? What are the issues which will most likely be important to a judge and jury at trial? How will the likely judge and jury view such a big company suing a new start-up company? Where will their sympathies lie? How can we focus our available resources and legal talent on the issues that a jury will find to be important? We know from experience that there will be many more such questions in the course of developing a case for trial or settlement.

As noted above, scientists search for reliable answers to difficult questions. In this case, science offers us a number of tools with which to answer each of the questions we have listed above and any other similar or more specific questions that may arise in the course of case development. Appendix "B"[2] indicates some of the scientific tools that can be used to assist the trial team at different stages of case development.

We can first address choice of venue in the TFC vs. TSC example. Pretrial research can benefit TFC vis-à-vis selection of venue for filing of the action, and can benefit TSC relative to any claims of a more appropriate alternative venue.[3]

---

[2] See Appendix B, "Trial Science in the Life of a Lawsuit," *infra.*

[3] Even though TSC may allege it was sued without warning and hence could not conduct pretrial venue research, in all likelihood pre-filing communications would have put TSC on notice that an action was imminent (and indeed, in some states for some causes of action, such written warning is a prerequisite to filing suit as well as a statutory attempt to encourage mediation and settlement without suit). Cautious, competent counsel for TSC should therefore have conducted at least minimal pretrial venue research in the circumstances outlined above.

Research and experience have taught us that interview surveys of local citizens in the jury population, analysis of local news and opinion publications, post-trial interviews of jurors in similar cases in the different venues, analysis of previous jury verdicts and judge decisions in similar cases within the various venues, and focus groups in each of the venues are all valuable research tools that should be explored. Each of these research tools has its advantages and disadvantages to be discussed in more detail later in this chapter.

Assuming that a particular venue has been selected, we must next address the question of making important strategic decisions about the development of our most compelling case. Whether you are the plaintiff or defendant, your case will be inherently stronger the earlier you begin to focus on the perceptions of the likely judge and jury.

Once TFC has selected the venue and filed suit, questions immediately arise for both TFC and TSC about the issues that will be important to a likely judge, jury, or arbitrator. Other questions relate to the strengths and weaknesses for both parties regarding stated or prospective causes of action. In the course of pretrial discovery, TFC and TSC can benefit greatly from information obtained through the use of live and Internet-based focus groups, community attitude surveys, analysis of previous verdicts in the venue, examination of published scientific research articles about courtroom decision making, and small, less expensive mock trials. In preparation for pretrial hearings, it can be helpful to conduct mock bench hearings with the services of experienced attorneys or retired judges.

Although it is important to recognize good, solid legal research and aggressive discovery, the ultimate fact finder, if the case goes to trial, will be a jury of people who have no knowledge or awareness of the legal research and most of the discovery that was conducted. Even if the ultimate fact finder is a judge or arbitrator, research indicates that he or she will be more persuaded by the themes and story of the case than the fine legal research and voluminous discovery that were prepared in advance of trial. Published scientific research indicates no significant differences in the judgments awarded by judges, arbitrators, or jurors in trial on fact issues.

Scientific research is especially useful if its findings are incorporated in preparation for trial or arbitration hearings. If we have not done adequate research relating to the decision-making processes of our fact finders, we could likely find ourselves appearing in trial filing legal briefs that might please our law professors but offer courtroom arguments that fall flat, or worse, anger the fact finders. Unfortunately, this occurs every day in courtrooms all over the United States.

In TFC's case as plaintiff, a number of very important questions and strategic decisions must be addressed throughout the case. For example:

- What is the most powerful story that can be told to depict Ms. Garth's actions as bad and unethical?
- Should the key employees Ms. Garth hired away from TFC be sued and described as bad characters, or alternatively, should they be treated as innocent pawns?
- Will a judge and jury sympathize with TFC because its employees were lured away, or with TSC as a competitive new start-up company?
- Will the trial judge eliminate a cause of action for theft of trade secrets because no documents were actually taken from TFC by Ms. Garth?
- Will the trial judge grant a preliminary or permanent injunction against Ms. Garth and her new company?

These are only a few of the questions that will inevitably arise.

In TSC's case as defendant, other important questions should be answered:

- What is the most compelling story that can be told in defense of Ms. Garth and her new company?
- How can Ms. Garth's hiring away key employees be presented in its most favorable light?
- How will a judge or jury respond to the evidence that one of TSC's new key employees downloaded critical files from TFC just prior to departure?
- Since Ms. Garth is wealthy, will a jury automatically award damages against her under a deep pockets theory?

There are many other such questions that will be posed on TSC's behalf.

Answering these questions requires using a combination of trial advocacy skills and experience, along with the most powerful sources of available information. Scientifically based information and research are the best available to us as trial advocates. We therefore have an obligation to our clients to utilize this information to benefit them and take much of the guesswork out of trial preparation.

There are many scientific tools that are available to a trial team as trial preparation begins. Using our case example, TFC and TSC could choose from among the following tools:

- Case consultation/strategic planning with trial scientists;
- Analysis of published scientific studies that are related to courtroom decision making;
- Psychological analysis of previous judgments and verdicts in the same venue;
- Focus groups to study the best presentation for specific issues, demonstrative aids, or the most effective pretrial juror questionnaire;
- Mock trial study (with one to three panels of research jurors);
- Mock bench trial study;
- Mock arbitration study;
- Trial advocacy coaching; and
- Media coaching.

In the course of resolving a dispute, settlement discussions arise informally or during formal mediation. There are certain tools that have been developed through the use of scientific methods that can assist in mediation advocacy (persuading the opposing party to settle the case on mutually favorable terms). In this regard, see our discussion about mediation advocacy later in this treatise.[4]

Let's examine some of these research techniques more closely.

§ 6.03 | GENERAL PRINCIPLES APPLICABLE TO ALL COURTROOM RESEARCH PROJECTS

The purpose in using the research tools is to discover, in a reliable, objective manner, important aspects of the likely decision-making process of fact finders in our cases. No matter how intelligent or experienced we are, we can benefit from information that is not tainted by our personal biases, and which can generate new ideas that we had not previously considered.

[1]—Reasoning Errors That Science Can Remedy

Even though we are experienced and skilled as trial advocates, we are still human. We are prone to making the same kinds of errors in our inquiries as other human beings. Unfortunately, we are all generally pretty careless as observers of life's events. Many times we fail to observe things that occur right

---

[4] See Chapter 16 *infra.*

in front of us, and we sometimes "see" things that never happened. Most of our observations are made unconsciously. Scientific observation, however, is made deliberately and consciously in a way that reduces or eliminates the influence of our personal biases.

Another error that we make in normal observation is that of over-generalization. We observe what we at first deem to be a relationship between two things, and then, without a good explanation, generalize it to be true in all circumstances. This phenomenon is rampant in the legal community. How many times have you heard people mention a significant jury verdict and then say that all jury verdicts have gotten too high? How many times have you heard a lawyer tell about one juror—perhaps an engineer who voted against the lawyer's client—who then declares that he will never allow another such juror (engineer) on the jury? All of us, no matter how experienced as lawyers or scientists, have this natural tendency.

Overgeneralization can lead to selective observation. Once we have concluded that a particular relationship or pattern exists in situations around us, we then pay attention only to circumstances which corroborate our conclusion, and we ignore circumstances which do not. For example, once you have concluded that scientific methods or trial consultants do not offer any advantage, you may select or interpret only information you encounter that supports your conclusion and ignore other information that may support a different conclusion.

The same principle affects personal observations made during focus groups and other kinds of research. It may be tempting to begin research with certain conclusions and then use the research feedback to support our conclusions even if there is significant other information that would counter these conclusions. Although our intuition about issues in a case often prove to be supported by the research, it is critically important to our success to go into research questioning our assumptions. If our intuition is confirmed by our research, we can use the research to enhance and improve our position. If our intuition is not confirmed, we must then alter our position in order to strengthen the case presentation to a likely judge or jury. To do otherwise would be counterproductive to our client's position.

Sometimes we attribute other people's reasoning incorrectly. For example, suppose we use a focus group in the TFC vs. TSC case. As plaintiff, we may wish to attack Ms. Garth as being greedy and disloyal to her previous business partners. However, during the focus group most of the male and female research jurors reacted angrily to such attack on the grounds that it was too vicious. As observers, we may react in a number of ways. We might believe that the focus group reacted inappropriately and that a likely jury will agree with the attack. We might choose to believe that the people in the focus group are not representative of the likely jury. Alternatively, we might not attack her so viciously. Any of these results would be supported by the feedback if we stopped our inquiry at that point.

If, however, we continued with the inquiry to probe the research jurors' reasoning to determine why they reacted as they did and what would change their minds, we might come to a different conclusion. We may discover, as often happens, that jurors will indeed dislike Ms. Garth if more evidence of subversive acts is introduced.

Scientific research methods are designed to avoid the fallacies of illogical reasoning. They are designed to help us to avoid the problems that our egos cause. They help us question our assumptions and continue an inquiry until all of the available information has been obtained and analyzed. Scientific inquiry is designed to be more careful than casual inquiry.

[2]—Principles for Constructing the Research Project

Scientists often talk about research design. In doing so, they are really talking about developing a framework and process by which important and reliable information can be obtained and analyzed as we answer a research question. For example, if we represented either TFC or TSC, we would want to identify as early as possible the issues which will be important to a likely jury. We can then undertake discovery in terms of these issues, and begin developing themes and a case story which coincide with the tenor of the evidence that is being developed through that discovery.

So to begin our research, we would pose a very simple question: "What issues that arise out of the evidence are most important to a likely jury?" Our research project would then be designed to answer this question in a reliable way.

[a]—What Is the Purpose of the Research Project?

Approaching the construction of the research project with precision is essential to its success. No matter what you are trying to learn, science offers you many ways to find the answer. However, there are two simple steps that must be taken to get started. The first is that you must specify precisely what you want to learn. The second is that you must develop the best way to discover that information.

Ultimately, scientific inquiry is a process of making observations and interpreting what you have observed. If you have asked the wrong question or developed an unreliable method of making observations and interpreting information, the research is not likely to be productive. A poorly designed research project can be a disaster and the effects on the case can be catastrophic.

Most of the relevant research studies have several purposes. The first is to explore your research topic to become more familiar with the issues and direction on which your case presentation may be based. Focus groups and community attitude surveys can both be helpful in obtaining a general understanding of how a likely jury will process the facts and issues. Usually, exploratory studies are designed to form a general understanding of the direction that a case may take, and form the basis for more extensive later mock trial studies.

The second purpose of a research study is to define and describe the nature of the information to be obtained in the study that helps answer the ultimate question(s). The third purpose of such a study is to explain the information obtained in the study in a manner that is helpful in answering the research question.

If we re-examine our example of a focus group in the TFC vs. TSC case, in the course of the study we would present basic information about the case to the research jurors, and then gather and analyze their responses. In this focus group we will pose questions to explore the mental processing of the participants, and then we will gauge the most important information and ideas based upon the nature of their responses. At some point we will ask the participants for explanations about their perceptions, and we will make observations of our own based upon the research participants' behavior that they are unable to articulate.

[b]—Focal Points During the Research Study

In all of the studies that we will be performing we will be focusing on three things:

(1) the characteristics of the people in our study,

(2) their orientations (their attitudes, beliefs, personality traits, values, prejudices, predispositions, stereotypes, etc.), and

(3) their actions (their decisions).

By studying these three focal points, we can better understand the process that a likely judge, jury, or arbitrator will use in making a decision in the case.

[c]—The Core of Every Research Study: Stimulus and Response

At the center of every study in social science is the principle of stimulus and response. For example, if you want to know how likely jurors will react to your argument on damages, you have to expose them to it and then review their responses.

The stimulus in a study is the information that you present to the research participants to which you want them to react. The stimulus might include just bare facts or any other aspect of the case that is suggested by the research question(s) to be answered. The stimulus must be clearly defined.

The method used to obtain responses is as important as the stimulus. In fact, the method of questioning and obtaining responses is perhaps the single most important element in designing a reliable study. The method of measuring the responses must be exacting, designed not to interfere with the essence of the responses. The questions must be neutral, yet provocative.

[d]—Generalizability, Validity, and Reliability

Perhaps the most important reason why we conduct research studies of the perceptions of the ultimate decision maker(s) is that we are uncertain about how all of the factors and elements in the case will be perceived. This is true of both lucrative and less profitable cases, although every case is important to the litigants.

As lawyers, we are accustomed to taking risks. Most of our lives we have heard people state conclusions about judges, jurors, and other decision makers. But how accurate are these conclusions? When our colleagues advise us about judges, jurors, witnesses, and other aspects of trial presentation, how do we know how valid these suggestions are? With all of the useful research tools currently available to us, it is relatively simple to test the hypotheses that various people propose.

The ability to verify and trust the methods and conclusions of a scientific study is paramount to trial attorneys, clients, and research scientists. In the world of science, the concepts of generalizability, validity, and reliability are part of the scientific "Holy Trinity."

Generalizability refers to the degree to which a finding or conclusion we make in our research can be expected to recur in a different setting, such as a live courtroom during trial. That is, to what extent can we expect the data and findings from our research to actually be present in the actual trial or hearing? A well-designed study can ensure generalizability.

To answer all our important questions about case strategy, we require useful, reliable data to form helpful recommendations for developing the best strategy for the case. In research studies that focus on the decision making of judges, jurors, and arbitrators, it is vital that the information we are obtaining is valid.

The term *validity* has a specific meaning in science. It refers to the truth or correctness of data, findings, or statements. In layman's terms, a valid argument is one that is solid, well-grounded, justifiable, convincing, and powerful. This definition also applies to scientific research studies. Two of the core questions relating to validity are: "Are we measuring what we think we are measuring?" and "Are our observations of the research decision maker(s) accurately reflecting the issues or variables that we are interested in studying?" The essence of validity is accuracy and usefulness.

The concept of *reliability* refers to a different aspect of scientific research. That is, if we conduct another study using a format that is identical to that of the first study, the findings should be the same. In order to predict any aspects of a courtroom decision maker's behavior, we must have undertaken or possess a relevant research study that has been conducted rigorously enough to support reliability. Otherwise, even a hundred poorly designed jury studies would all be unreliable.

[e]—Gathering Information in the Research Project

There are two types of methods for gathering data. The first is the *quantitative method* (using numbers) and the second is the *qualitative method*. A quantitative method poses a specific theory or hypothesis of cause and effect and then seeks to determine whether it is true or not. During a quantitative study, we can develop generalizations that help us to understand the theory that we proposed and to better predict, explain, and understand some of the phenomena involved in the fact finder's decision.

For example, in a mock trial study a trial attorney will pose a theme and argument for obtaining a favorable answer in the jury verdict. His or her success in obtaining the verdict will be measured by the questionnaires that research jurors answer. The success or failure of the proposed theme or argument will, therefore, be measured by the votes either in favor of the theme or argument or against one or both of them. Other typical quantitative studies are opinion polls and, most notably, elections.

Quantitative methods of gathering information are helpful in determining the existence and strength of relationships. They can also be helpful in explaining and predicting future actions by people who resemble the research participants. Their usefulness, however, does not generally extend beyond the nature of the specific questions asked.

Gathering responses using a quantitative measure and a written questionnaire requires understanding of the precise hypothesis you are testing. For example, if you want to determine what characteristics a pro-plaintiff juror will have in a particular case, you would ask questions to identify a research participant's characteristics and whether such a participant would render a verdict for the plaintiff or defendant. You might also want to know what themes and versions of the case story seem to be the most powerful for plaintiff or defendant jurors. Oral questioning and written questionnaires are both possible tools for gathering responses to these types of questions.

As we have indicated, the second method of collecting information involves *qualitative methods*. Most free-flowing discussions in focus group and mock trial studies result from qualitative practice methods. By posing thoughtful, neutral questions to research participants, we can collect valuable data in the context of the case coupled with the individual jurors' patterns of thinking; we can then interpret the jurors' logic.

Hence, qualitative research techniques are often helpful for exploring the thinking processes of a likely judge, jury, or arbitration panel. By engaging research participants in guided interviews, you can learn a great deal about the patterns of thinking that fact finders will have in response to a particular case. The questioning style of an experienced qualitative interviewer may at first seem directionless and unstructured. However, many research scientists believe that the most relevant data derives from qualitative research methods. As famous research scientist James P. Spradley commented:

> "I want to understand the world from your point of view. I want to know what you know in the way you know it. I want to understand the meaning of your experience, to walk in your shoes, to feel things as you feel them, to explain things as you explain them. Will you become my teacher and help me understand?"[5]

---

[5] Spradley, *The Ethnographic Interview,* p. 34 (New York: Holt, Rinehart & Winston, 1979).

A qualitative interview process is intended to exhaust the knowledge of the research participant about a particular topic. A qualitative interview uses ordinary language and does not necessarily try to quantify the information obtained. A good qualitative interview allows the research participant to control the content of the data expressed while at the same time directing the interviewee (research participant) toward answering the ultimate questions. A qualitative interview is designed to expose the research participant's perceptions and the meaning that is attached to them.

A successful qualitative interviewer, whether an attorney or scientist, approaches the research participants with openness and naiveté rather than with predisposed ways of thinking that may result in limiting or skewing the data. In addition, a skilled interviewer will instinctively know when to provoke further thinking by exposing contradictions in a research participant's responses or testing the boundaries and limits of a research participant's perceptions. Sometimes this may mean provoking the research participant to determine what would change his or her mind about a topic.

[f]—Identifying and Obtaining the Best Sample of People for the Study

Another important factor is identification of the best research participants for the project. Typically, you will want to "mirror" the actual or likely decision maker(s) in your case. That is, each of the decision makers will be a member of a larger population of people who have many similar characteristics. We have learned that we can understand the mental processes and behavior of people by studying the mental processes and behavior of other people who are like them. Therefore, the research participants we choose for our project will be our "sample" from that larger, similar population.

The more representative the sample from the jury population and the more accurately they match the "average" jury in the venue, the more reliable and useful the information from the study will be. A wide cross-section of people who have served as jurors in the venue will probably provide more reliable and useful information than a random sample of people in a shopping mall. We have learned over the past thirty years that randomly selecting citizens from the general population for most pretrial research is extremely expensive and rarely reliable. However, choosing test subjects based upon community attitude surveys can be helpful due to the large sample for such surveys. Conversely, the more representative the sample is of the actual or likely fact finder, the less expensive the research and the more reliable the results will be. At times you will know in advance who the actual fact finder(s) will be (i.e., a particular judge or arbitrator). In that instance, you can match the characteristics of the research participants with those of the actual fact finder(s). We even refer to this sampling technique as "matched sampling."

[g]–Why Specific Questions and Answers Are More Reliable and Useful

Finally, we should note that answers to *specific* questions posed to representative samples of people from the population to be studied are more reliable and useful than answers to *general* questions and/or responses from general samples of people from the overall population.

[3]–Designing the Research Project

After considering the concepts discussed above, the next step in planning a research project is designing the actual project. Although we should already understand what questions we would like to have answered, we must begin organizing and formalizing the process so that the energy and resources we invest in research will be well spent and the results will be reliable and helpful.

Following is an outline of the steps to take in designing any courtroom research project.

(1) *Identify the specific purpose for the study.* Identify what you are interested in knowing, what ideas you want to explore, and the theories you wish to test.

(2) *Choose the research format that will best address the purpose.* The usual alternatives are community attitude surveys, focus groups, mock trials, mock bench hearings, mock arbitrations, and mock mediations.

(3) *Determine who makes up the population you are studying and who makes up the sample.* The more refined and representative the sample, the more reliable the data collected. The larger the sample, the more powerful and reliable the results will be.

(4) *Design a study format for collecting the data.* Set up a research event that will bring the sample subjects together, expose them to the stimulus material, and gather data from them that can be analyzed to help answer research questions.

(5) *Carry out the study and collect the data.* Be careful to strictly control the environment so that the data are collected in an uninterrupted fashion without interference that may destroy the usefulness of the data.

(6) *Collate or assemble the data into a useful form.* A typical study will amass a great deal of data in different formats. If the data are collected so that they can be easily analyzed later, this enhances the usefulness of the study.

(7) *Analyze the data.* If you have meticulously followed Steps 1 to 6 above, the data you collected should provide clearly useful information for answering the research question(s). By carefully analyzing the data, you will likely identify trends and relationships that are useful in understanding the data.

(8) *Apply the knowledge gained.* The final, most useful step in the conduct of research is the application of the knowledge gained by the study. Every trial team must know what the data mean and how to implement strategies that make the case stronger. In addition, any new or old issues that need further study can be identified.

[4]—Cost of Scientific Research

Until recently, the cost of conducting private scientific research in a case was inflexible and expensive. The scientists who were developing services for trial attorneys and their clients had little experience with the economics of law suits and were focused only on developing new research methods. There have been two consequences to this lack of attention to cost. The first has been that scientists were rightly concerned with excellence and were therefore able to set high standards of quality for truly scientific research methods. As a result, we now have some powerful research tools available to lawyers and trial consultants. The second consequence has been an entrenched conventional wisdom among some trial attorneys and clients that scientific research is an extravagance that is not warranted in most cases.

Within the past five years, however, trial scientists have responded to the demands of the legal community for more budget-conscious services that could be available to every lawyer in every case. There are now a wide variety of services available to trial attorneys and clients at every stage of a case and in all price ranges.

Therefore, let us next apply this outline to specific research formats that are useful in both developing and presenting powerful, persuasive cases to judges, jurors, and arbitrators.

§ 6.04 | COMMUNITY ATTITUDE
SURVEYS

Philosophically and realistically, a jury represents the consciousness of a community. This consciousness may reflect long-held attitudes and beliefs or may reflect perceptions of current events. Since, as we have established, surveys are a useful tool in determining the best venue for the case, part of that determination is affected by community perceptions of our client and the issues in our cases. Surveys are also useful for beginning the process of narrowing the issues that are likely to be important to the jury.

The first high-profile use of a community attitude survey was in preparation for the 1972 conspiracy trial of the so-called "Harrisburg Seven."[6] The alleged conspirators included seven anti-Vietnam War protestors who were accused by the United States government of conspiring to raid draft boards, destroy government records, kidnap presidential advisor Henry Kissinger, and blow up heating ducts in federal buildings in Washington, D.C. In that case, the FBI and the U.S. Justice Department carefully reviewed all three federal venues within Pennsylvania for the trial to determine which venue contained more Americans with conservative philosophies who were more likely to convict the defendants than in other parts of Pennsylvania.

In so doing, Harrisburg, Pennsylvania, was chosen as the venue for the case. In response, the attorneys for the accused employed a group of social scientists to assist in developing a persuasive defense argument and in helping to seat a jury that would be less likely to convict than the prosecution had anticipated. After conducting a lengthy series of telephone surveys (840 respondents) and in-depth interviews (252 respondents) about media contact, knowledge of the case, attitudes and beliefs about government, religious beliefs, public responsibilities, and acceptable anti-war activities, an ideal juror profile and a jury selection strategy were developed, as well as a set of themes and case stories that favored the defense psychologically. After sixty days of trial, the jury began deliberating the case. On the third day of deliberations, the jury announced that they had found defendants Father Philip Berrigan and Sister Elizabeth McAlister guilty of smuggling letters contrary to federal prison policy, but that they were hopelessly deadlocked (ten for acquittal, two for guilty) on the principal charges of conspiracy.

---

[6] United States v. Berrigan, 347 F. Supp. 912 (M.D. Pa. 1972), *aff'd in part, rev'd in part* 482 F.2d 171 (3d Cir. 1973). See also Schulman, Shaver, Colman, Emrich & Christie, "Recipe for a Jury," Psychology Today 37-44, 77-84 (May 1973).

Because of the sensational nature of the trial, there was great interest in the mental impressions of the jurors and the use of social science to assist in the case. Several of the jurors were interviewed about the jury's decision-making process and their perceptions of the case. As a result, interest was quickly expressed by legal and psychological professionals in the use of scientific means to understand juror characteristics and their influence on decision outcomes.

[1]—What a Community Attitude Survey Does

Community attitude surveys are designed to survey jury-eligible members of the community to identify pretrial characteristics of their respondents that are associated with various attitudes and life experiences which are relevant to issues in the case and, ultimately, to a verdict. Surveys can help to identify the attitudes, biases, sentiments, and feelings existing in the community where the case will be tried. In cases with high-profile parties or high-profile issues, community attitude surveys are obviously valuable. However, surveys are also helpful in communities where attitudes and sentiments are not known.

The information and analysis provided by community attitude surveys can affect decisions about venue, selecting a fair and impartial jury, and developing a more focused, persuasive style of argument to members of a local community. Surveys can also be helpful in developing a database from which a sample of research jurors may be selected for further research in the case.

Surveys give us advance information about a community's perceptions that are relevant to many questions we may have early in a case. For example:

- What is the local sentiment about companies that produce certain types of products or services?
- What kind of public relations campaigns are effective in the community?
- How are plaintiffs' requests for intangible damages such as pain and suffering perceived?
- What are local perceptions about awards for punitive damages?
- How will people in the community react to one of our specific arguments?
- What attitudes, life experiences, personality traits, beliefs, and demographics will the ideal juror have during jury selection?
- What areas of inquiry are most important for oral voir dire?

Community attitude surveys are useful in developing a formula and/or classification procedure for predicting a prospective juror's opinion (in the event there is enough information available about a prospective juror to compare his or her profile with the survey information). Surveys are also useful in providing information with which to answer any of the types of questions listed above.

[2]—Developing a Sample of People to Be Interviewed

A community attitude survey is designed to interview randomly selected members of the jury-eligible population in the local venue. In order to determine who is eligible, local statutes and court rules must be consulted. In addition, allowance must be made for people who would be automatically ineligible, including witnesses in the case.

A practical means of identifying respondents is by choosing names and residential telephone numbers from the local telephone directory. Although this method of obtaining respondents is convenient, it also omits people whose telephone numbers are not listed. In some instances people with unlisted numbers are a small percentage of the population, but in other communities the percentage may be large, thus skewing the study.

Lists of people who previously served as jurors are theoretically the best source of interviews. However, many jurors become hostile when they are called at home, and complaints to local authorities have, in effect, impounded some of these lists.

As an alternative, some governmental authorities will make general or even randomly selected lists of drivers available for research. As a practical matter, however, a telephone survey can identify those people with drivers' licenses for inclusion in the survey without the trouble and expense of obtaining the list from local authorities. Moreover, in many communities, especially rural and suburban ones, most of the people who would be contacted in a telephone survey tend to have drivers' licenses.

There are no firm standards for sample size. In trying to persuade a judge to change venue, a sample of sixty to 100 eligible jurors (whose opinions reflect the concerns of the moving party) is usually sufficient. Such an argument would deal only with local sentiment about a high-profile case; a modest sample is generally sufficient to provide that information. The size of a sample that a judge will deem adequate is determined by the court's discretion.

However, for purposes of conducting pretrial research that will benefit a trial team in making informed strategic decisions, the most reliable samples are much larger. In such cases, the number of questions to be asked is much greater and the relationships between the characteristics of the respondents and their attitudes and decisions is so complicated that a rather large number of people must participate in order to determine whether any such relationships exist and how strong they are.

[3]—Developing the Survey Questionnaire

The average questionnaire takes a trained scientist a week or so to design. Therefore, someone who is not trained in developing survey questionnaires will need more time. The developer of the questionnaire must understand the central story and theories in the case as well as the key words and phrases that are likely to stimulate a larger quantity and quality of information from the respondents. The survey questions must be neutral, yet designed to obtain the maximum amount of focused information known by the respondent. The survey must be developed so that it can be completed within a ten-to-fifteen-minute interview. The longer the questionnaire, the more probable it is that a larger number of people will refuse to participate (and the greater the wasted interviewer time).

The questions should not be designed to influence or educate respondents. The only successful challenges to the use of community attitude surveys have persuaded some trial judges that the design of the questionnaire used by an opposing party was intended to influence the jury-eligible population with reference to the particular case. A well-designed questionnaire would not have this effect. Questionnaires which seek to influence respondents produce unreliable, skewed results.

The order of the questions posed is not generally important. However, in the course of producing a smooth and efficient interview, it is best to begin with general questions and proceed to more specific ones.

Once a draft of the questionnaire is completed, it should be tested with a small sample of people to make sure that the flow and organization of the questionnaire will work well. It is unlikely that the questionnaire will work flawlessly without testing and insertion of last-minute changes.

The questionnaire itself should include a set of instructions for each interviewer, a standardized introduction to be read to each respondent, and questions about specific facts, selected issues, and the respondent's demographics. The introduction usually states that the survey is a public opinion survey concerning the justice system and the legal case in the local county. The respondent will be advised that there are no right or wrong answers and that the responses will remain confidential. The interviewer will ask for permission to ask the questions and, if permission is given, will proceed quickly into the interview. It is generally prudent to end a questionnaire with open-ended questions asking for final comments from the respondent.

[4]—The Interviews

In order for the interviews to be standardized, it is important that the interviewers be well-trained and that they be oriented to the questionnaire and procedure to be used. Most interviews take place between 6:00 P.M. and 10:00 P.M. or during weekends. This schedule helps to ensure that the widest range of respondents is contacted. Otherwise, people who work during the day, and who constitute a large part of the jury population, might be excluded, thus raising questions about reliability and usefulness.

It is important that the interviewers be trained and skilled at telephone interviewing. The interviewers must remain neutral and professional at all times. They should be adept at probing for clear answers from the respondents. They should record exactly what the respondents say, word for word. They should generally be trained as a group in the use of the specific questionnaire.

[5]—Types of Questions to Be Included

The purpose of the survey will dictate the nature of the questions to be included. Most questionnaires will include some of the following types of questions.

- Jury qualification questions (e.g., age, citizenry, voter registration, driver's license);
- Knowledge and opinions about the particular case, including inadmissible information;
- Familiarity with and opinions about the parties or people like them;
- Knowledge and opinions about key issues in the case;
- Questions about the respondent's sources of information;
- Questions about the respondent's demographics; and
- A final question asking for other comments.

[6]—Coding, Tabulating, and Analyzing the Data

One important aspect of developing a questionnaire is to make it easy to score and tabulate the data. Most of the questions will provide for quick responses such as "yes" or "no," or scales which give the respondent the choice of answers on a continuum. A few questions may be more open-ended.

By keeping the responses standardized, the data can then be easily input into a data management software program such as SPSS.[7] Such a program can contrast and compare all the data and identify the strength and weakness of possible relationships within seconds.

Most of the analysis conducted with community attitudes surveys is performed using statistical and inferential analysis. The statistical phase of the analysis is based solely upon the calculations used in interpreting the data. The inferential phase is based upon interpretations and inferences that can be drawn from the results of the statistical analysis, and then applied to answer the original questions which prompted the research.

If a community attitude survey is conducted with scientific precision, it can be especially useful in understanding the characteristics (attitudes, sentiments, feelings, perceptions) of the general juror population in a local venue. To those who are not familiar with statistical analysis, it may seem illogical to use a modest group of people to represent the characteristics of the entire population. However, once you have used a community attitude survey that was properly conducted, you will understand how remarkably useful and revealing a survey can be.

§ 6.05 | LIVE FOCUS GROUP RESEARCH

Live focus groups have been a staple of market research for decades. Most large corporations will not introduce a new product line without having conducted extensive focus group research. In the past fifteen years, trial attorneys and corporate clients have also undertaken regular use of focus groups to help them develop their most powerful, compelling arguments in trial.

A focus group is a research tool that is used to explore topics and issues of all kinds. It is essentially a guided small-group discussion set in a laboratory-

---

[7] Statistical Package for the Social Sciences.

like environment. A focus group is designed to promote the free flow of ideas and, therefore, is less structured than a mock trial. Because of the group dynamics involved, a focus group often brings out aspects of an issue that would not have been anticipated by either the researcher or the trial team. In addition, group dynamics tend to produce more and better quality information than individual interviews with any of the research participants.

[1]—When to Use a Focus Group

A focus group is a reliable way of obtaining information about the perceptions of likely fact finders toward any aspect of a case presentation. Although you may have some preconceived ideas about how a likely jury or panel of judges will react to the entire case or special issues within the case, a focus group is useful for exploring fact finders' perceptions and expanding your awareness of how the case or the issues will be perceived. If we refer back to our case example, TFC vs. TSC,[8] there are a number of specific questions that can be answered with the use of focus groups:

(1) Which of the issues will be most important to a likely jury or panel of arbitrators?
(2) How should we handle certain case weaknesses?
(3) How should we present our strongest points?
(4) What is our most powerful story?
(5) How will the likely jurors or arbitrators react to our key facts and expert witnesses?
(6) Which causes of action should we pursue and which ones should we dismiss?
(7) What important issues have we overlooked?
(8) How will jurors or arbitrators respond to particular witnesses?
(9) How will they respond to our demonstrative exhibits?
(10) Which members of the trial team should handle which parts of the case presentation?
(11) What is the best way to present complicated aspects of the case?
(12) What is the likely range of damages a jury would award in response to particular causes of action?
(13) How do we handle the issue of punitive damages?
(14) What is our best voir dire strategy?

---

8 See § 6.02 *supra*.

These and many other questions can be answered using focus groups. Although many of the same questions can be addressed in a simulated mock trial, there are several important differences regarding the usefulness of the two research tools. First, focus groups are generally used many months before trial to help specify and direct the development of the case for trial or for settlement. Second, the focus group format does not limit the feedback from the research jurors to a specific trial presentation, like that used in the conduct of a simulated mock trial. In this sense, the focus group format is more free-flowing and promotes creativity in the case development process. Third, focus groups are more flexible than simulated mock trials and, if conducted properly, follow the instincts of the research participants. Finally, focus groups are less expensive because there is less production cost and staffing involved.

Besides these research advantages, there are a number of other advantages to a trial team in the use of focus groups. They offer an excellent opportunity for the trial team to rehearse certain parts of the trial presentation as development of the case proceeds. The preparation for a focus group presentation itself is an important mental tool for organizing an attorney's thoughts about the case. Clients can attend the focus group sessions and see first-hand how a likely jury will react to certain aspects of the case.

[2]–Organizing a Focus Group

There are hundreds of different kinds of focus group formats that can strengthen and help evaluate an entire case or specific issues of a case. As with all other research tools, before you try to organize a focus group, it is important to identify the purpose of such a group and the questions to be answered by it.

[a]–Identifying the Best Research Jurors for the Focus Group

Focus groups to aid in preparation of a jury trial case typically engage twelve to sixteen research participants who "mirror" the widest range of characteristics (demographics, attitudes, beliefs, life experiences, and thinking patterns) that define an average jury in the local venue. Focus groups in preparation for an arbitration hearing typically hire six to eight research participants who incorporate the characteristics of the likely arbitration panel. For purposes of this discussion we will concentrate on preparation for trial even though some of the same steps can be taken in organizing focus groups for other purposes, such as giving feedback about specific witnesses, visual aids, or issues.

Identification of the sample of research jurors to be used in a focus group can be accomplished in many ways. First you create a database of people who have volunteered to serve as research jurors, and then you select from that database a cross-section of people who will "mirror" the widest range of characteristics in an average jury in the venue. Some people prefer to run anonymous ads in local newspapers and create a database from the people who respond. Others prefer to use respondents to a telephone community attitudes survey as the database from which to select research jurors. Still others prefer to contact people who have served as jurors in the local venue, if they can be readily identified. Occasionally, when too few people respond to an advertisement, it will be necessary to hand pick people through recruiting services to help complete the sample.

There is no magic way to obtain appropriate research jurors for focus group or mock trial research. It is considered good practice to use a combination of random telephone solicitation, anonymous advertisements, and recruiters to achieve a stratified random sample. However, the end objective should be the same—the seating of a group of people who exhibit the widest range of characteristics that you will usually find in an average jury in the local venue.

We use an average jury as our research target partially because it simply makes common sense and partially due to statistical probabilities. It is more likely that you will encounter an average jury when you go to trial than one that is skewed in some way. We have certainly all witnessed juries that exhibited characteristics that were not typical of juries in a given venue. For example, it is unlikely that you will encounter a jury pool with thirty-eight men out of forty-five potential jurors, but it has happened. Nonetheless, even when an actual jury is somewhat unusual, if the focus group research was carefully conducted to include the widest range of likely characteristics, the results of the research will still be useful.

[b]—The Best Setting for the Study

There are a number of considerations in selecting the location and set-up for the study. It is best to use a facility that is easily accessible to a cross-section of research jurors and promotes free, spontaneous thought processes. There should be one very large conference room for the presentations which seats all the research jurors. If more than one panel of focus group jurors is seated, all the research jurors should observe the same live presentation, after which each panel should proceed to its own discussion room. Each of the jury panels will engage in a guided discussion with a trained facilitator who can obtain the necessary data to answer the ultimate question.

There should be one observation room for each focus group panel with closed-circuit television or two-way mirrors to allow researchers to observe each of the panels. Private viewing rooms permit one to listen to a panel in progress without distracting its members while at the same time providing a private place for the focus group panel to discuss the case.

It is generally not a good idea for a focus group to meet in a lawyer's office because the identity of the sponsor would then be revealed, placing the focus group's impartiality in question and jeopardizing the validity of the results. In addition, most office space is not well-designed for the use of the necessary audio and video equipment to observe the research jurors and document the questions and answers (the data) during the study. Finally, most office space is not designed to accommodate twelve to sixteen jurors, three to six attorneys and study support staff, two or three clients, and one or two audio-visual technicians.

[c]—Agenda for the Study

Each focus group will have a somewhat different agenda because both the questions and the circumstances for each group will differ. Each presenter has his or her own unique presentation style and content. Despite the differences, however, there is a general structure for focus groups that has been developed and used by most research scientists and that will be useful as a starting point.

The style of interaction between the presenters, research participants, and the research interviewer(s) is inherently informal in order to promote free thinking and creativity. However, some simple formalities should be observed. Once the research participants are brought into the presentation room and seated around the table (assuming they constitute only one panel of research jurors), the research interviewer (attorney or trial consultant) will introduce the study, explain the format to be used, and briefly orient the research jurors to the essence of the case. Different members of the trial team will then present the information which will form the stimulus for the study, generally in a nonargumentative style. Often the stimulus phase of the study presents opposing viewpoints on the issues to be studied. However, there are a myriad of ways to present information during this phase of the study. The end of the stimulus phase often consists of an opportunity for the research jurors to ask questions of the presenters about the events and facts of the case.

Once the stimulus has been delivered (i.e., the presentations are completed), the research interviewer will begin asking questions of the research jurors either orally or in writing, using qualitative or quantitative methods of obtaining information. When the thought processes of the research jurors have been explored and the knowledge of the group exhausted, the study ends and the focus group participants are dismissed.

[d]–Maintaining Confidentiality Among the Research Jurors

Foresight and control are required to maintain confidentiality following a live focus research group study. The setting should be neutral so that the research jurors will not know which litigant is sponsoring the study. For ethical reasons, scientists are obligated to advise research jurors of the identity of the company that is conducting the study and the general purposes for which the information gathered may be used. However, there is no obligation to disclose information that would skew the results of the study. In addition, research jurors generally sign a confidentiality agreement and release of the information to be used for purposes designated in the agreement.

It is generally good practice to address the issue of confidentiality directly with the research jurors. They should be reminded that they have signed a confidentiality pledge, and they should agree to continue to keep the information they learn in the study confidential. Although there have been rare reports of research jurors who have tried to disclose to newspapers and others what they learned in a study, their efforts were thwarted for a number of practical reasons. First, newspapers will generally not report information which appears to be confidential unless it is confirmed by another source—in this case the trial team or trial consultant. At the first point of contact with an editor, one of the trial lawyers or trial consultants will advise the editor that any such study is confidential by agreement with the research juror and that any publication of confidential information will subject the publication to liability.

Second, there is a code of honor among most experienced trial teams and trial consultants who regularly engage in jury research. Any attempt to sell or give confidential jury research information belonging to an opposing party usually results in the information being returned to the party who conducted the research.

Third, unethical research jurors usually misunderstand and misstate what actually occurred in the jury research study. They are not scientists and do not understand the process in which they participated. Similarly, they do not understand the importance or lack of importance of the information they are trying to relay to the outside party.

Finally, if both the opposing parties are conducting well-designed scientific jury research, they should both uncover the same data. There is hence no need to steal the data from the opposing party. In addition, the data from the opposing party may be flawed because of poor research design or for some other reason. Professional trial consultants know instinctively that data are always mistrusted unless the complete process in which they were obtained is reliable. There is no way of knowing if the information is reliable without access to the complete plan and mental processes of the research designers of the opposing party.

There have been reports of attempts by a party to send "contaminated" research jurors to take part in the opposing party's study. Having conducted jury research in hundreds of cases, many of which were high-profile, the author doubts the truth of these reports. Indeed it would be almost impossible for an opposing party to "slip in" a contaminated research juror given the system used to locate and recruit research participants. However, in cases where the possibility of research sabotage is suspected, a number of security precautions can be taken.

In the scheme of things, it makes no sense to steal information from the opposing party. With all of the risk inherent in a case, it is much better to conduct one's own research and be able to trust the results.

Having addressed these sensitive issues, a trial team and client should always move aggressively to conduct the research they need to develop their most powerful, persuasive case. Any necessary precautions will be apparent as the team proceeds.

[e]–Analyzing and Applying Information Gained in the Study

As we have stated, the purpose of a primarily qualitative study such as a focus group is to describe and interpret the thought processes of research jurors regarding their own experiences. Note that analysis occurs both throughout the course of a focus group study and afterwards. The research participants discover new relationships and thoughts as they analyze their own and others' statements and perceptions. They discover new connections in their own experiences, apart from any interpretation by the research interviewers. This reaction is similar to juror self-discoveries during actual trial deliberations.

In addition, during the course of the interview the interviewer constantly condenses and interprets what each research participant expresses and relays that meaning back to the research participant. The discussions between the interviewer and research participant continue until the essence of the participant's perception is clear and is placed in context.

The final step in the analysis phase of a study occurs after the end of the focus group interaction. Most of the time the focus group interaction is videotaped or transcribed, and a review of the videotapes and transcription can be useful in obtaining an objective view of the data that were collected. In this part of the analysis, it is helpful to structure the large, complex body of material either manually or with the use of new software programs that provide computer analysis of qualitative material. Once the data are structured, it is helpful to clarify and distill the data to their essential meanings, revealing the most important information learned as well as any relevant trends.

Finally, after the data has been "boiled down" to their most important elements, the trial team must understand the meaning of the resulting data in the context of the case. This process of further condensation, categorization, structuring of the narrative portions of the data, making inferences and interpreting the data, and applying knowledge gained from experience and other research will help in applying the findings of the study and answering the original research questions that constituted the purpose of the study.

§ 6.06 | INTERNET-BASED FOCUS GROUP RESEARCH

Online focus group services are one of the most recent developments in the field of focus group research. Although online focus groups are new to trial and settlement science research, they have been used in marketing research for several years. Online focus groups incorporate the same central elements of a live focus group but function through a private, password-protected chat room on the Internet.

An online focus group study site will include a main presentation "room" and an "observation room" for observers. The research jurors will not have access to the "observation room." Only the research scientist or moderator has access to all the rooms. In addition, each of the observers can communicate in private with the research scientist or moderator through individual chat capabilities.

For those trial attorneys and clients who are comfortable with the Internet, online focus groups are fun and challenging.

[1]—Advantages and Disadvantages of Online Focus Groups

There are a number of ingenious advantages to conducting online focus groups. The content and value of the data collected during an online focus group are comparable to that of a live focus group. Comparison of the findings between an online focus group and a live focus group indicate that similar results are obtained.

In addition, the sincerity and thoughtfulness of the comments made by research jurors in online focus groups are more apparent than some of the spontaneous comments made by research jurors in live focus groups. The physical act of typing out one's thoughts appears to incorporate a measure of authenticity that adds to the value of the comments.

Online focus groups also take less time to organize so that an experienced researcher can set up an online focus group within hours. Because the interactions among the researcher, the research jurors, and any observers are made in written text, the transcription occurs simultaneously with those interactions, and the data analysis therefore occurs much faster. A written report with analysis and recommendations to the trial team can be completed within seventy-two hours after the focus group is requested.

Online focus groups are also more convenient. Live focus groups require that everyone gather at a particular place in order to participate in or observe the focus group study. Because online focus groups take place on the Internet, anyone with access to a computer can participate or observe the focus group study from wherever he or she happens to be. The research jurors, trial team, client, and research scientist can be anywhere in the world as long as they have access to the Internet, a computer-based browser, and the password. The flexibility in location is attractive to trial teams and clients who reside in different cities. It is also attractive to research jurors because they never have to leave their homes or offices.

Online focus groups also decrease the cost of doing focus group research. There are no travel costs. There is no cost associated with a facility rental or audiovisual equipment and operators. The total cost of conducting an online focus group is roughly one-third to one-half the cost of live focus group research.

Internet-based focus groups also support the kind of security needs that most trial teams require. A password is required to enter the Internet site where the focus group study will take place. Anyone who signs on also has a visual (typographical) presence that can be monitored by the research scientist who oversees the study.

There are also some disadvantages to conducting online focus group research. Because the focus group study is not conducted face to face, it is best to limit the study to no more than three issues. In a live focus group, you could be more flexible. Moreover, even though a member of the group may be signed on, he or she may also be inattentive and/or uninvolved, which cannot be monitored by computer.

As this book goes to press, the streaming technology necessary to bring videotaped deposition excerpts or videotaped attorney presentations to an online focus group study has not been perfected. In addition, the slow speed of many home computers will not allow replaying of such complicated software presentations.

[2]—Who Operates Online Focus Groups

The development of an Internet site on which to produce and operate online focus groups requires a significant investment of time, money, and expertise. Marketing research companies such as Protocon have offered online focus group capabilities for rent and moderators to operate them since 1998 (see Protocon's Virtual Research Room[9]). The first trial consulting firms to offer online focus group services to trial attorneys and corporations were The Wilmington Institute[10] and Trial Consultants, Inc.[11]

Over the next few years, more full-service trial consulting firms will begin to offer online focus group services because of the advantages they afford. However, because of the complexities associated with producing and operating an online focus group it is generally recommended that you hire an experienced online research scientist to handle the setup, jury recruitment, moderating of the study, and analysis of the results.

---

[9] See www.vrroom.com.

[10] See www.virtualjury.com.

[11] See www.trialconsultants.com.

[3]—Setting Up the Study and Recruiting Research Jurors

The setup of an online focus group is similar to that of a live focus group. First, the research question(s) to be investigated and issues to be studied are identified. Then the research jurors are recruited in the same ways that any other research jurors are recruited except that the online research jurors must have access to a computer which has the ability to connect to the research site on the Internet. Most research jurors have computers at home or at work, whereas others may have to go to a public facility or obtain access from the computer of a family member or friend.

However the participants obtain Internet access, their characteristics in an online study will be similar to those of research jurors in a live focus group study. Because of the widespread computer access to the Internet among the general juror population, no differences in the quality or quantity of data collected appear to have resulted. An initial concern that people who have access to the Internet are somewhat different in their views than people who serve as actual courtroom jurors has not been supported by any evidence.

An online focus group session will last approximately one to two hours. Such sessions are conducted using the same agenda as for live focus groups. The only obvious difference is that the communication between the research scientist and the research jurors is completely text-based (written). Nonetheless, the expressions and feelings associated with research juror comments and online focus groups are remarkably revealing. Trained online moderators can sense the need for appropriate follow-up on comments from individual research jurors in order to provide the same quality and richness of data that we expect from live focus group studies.

In advance of the study, the research scientist or moderator will contact each of the participants and observers in the study to give them directions to the Internet site and the appropriate password. A contact telephone number should also be given out to allow people having trouble gaining access to the study site to contact someone for help.

[4]—Collecting and Analyzing the Data

The data collection and analysis in an online focus group is virtually the same as for a live focus group. The moderator will be collecting information in the course of the discussion and reacting appropriately to each of the research jurors. The rest of the analysis process is also the same as for a live focus group.

Ultimately, the information obtained in the study must be used to answer the original questions which the study was designed to answer.

§ 6.07 │ MOCK TRIAL RESEARCH

It is now commonplace for courtroom combatants to prepare for trial or settlement negotiations with important information gained from a mock trial study. One such case was a little-publicized but important medical malpractice trial in central Florida. The plaintiffs were a family consisting of a married couple with three children, of whom the husband had suffered brain damage due to a severe loss of blood during back surgery. There were allegations that the surgeon was addicted to painkillers, which might have interfered with his paying careful attention to the extensive blood loss during surgery. There were also allegations that the anesthesiologist had left an inexperienced nurse in charge of monitoring blood loss and obtaining adequate replacement units of blood. The surgeon, the anesthesiologist, and the hospital were all defendants.

In the course of trial preparation, the trial attorneys for the plaintiffs and the defendants each engaged trial consultants and conducted scientifically based mock trial studies. The plaintiffs' attorneys concentrated on how to prove that the surgeon must have been taking painkillers at the time of the surgery, although there was no direct evidence of this. They wanted to know how best to demonstrate the connection between brain damage and blood loss. They wanted to know how to tell their most compelling story using themes that would be persuasive to the jury. They wanted to know what the likely range of damages would be.

Similarly, the defendants' attorneys were concerned about how the jury would perceive each of the defendants and their behaviors. They wanted to know whether the good reputation of the health care providers would be useful in defending them. They wanted to know what the likely range of damages would be. They wanted to know how to minimize the possibility that the jury would be angry at the health care providers and award significant punitive damages. They wanted to know what story would best provide themes with which to help minimize the risk to the health care providers. Finally, they wanted to know the best way to persuade the plaintiffs and their attorneys that they were winning the case in trial, even if they were not. There was a possibility that the plaintiffs would enter into a high-low settlement agreement, so that all of this information would be helpful.

In their separate jury research studies, both sides learned their most powerful themes and case story. They both learned the likely range of damages, which were remarkably similar even though separate research studies had taken place. They both discovered that a sympathetic jury would likely award a huge amount of money in actual and punitive damages. They also learned about their respective weaknesses. They learned that if the defendants took a position of being contrite and caring, the jury would be less angry and the amount it would likely award would decrease.

Of course, at trial the defendants did express contrition and caring and the parties were able to enter into an agreement for a high-low settlement that would assure the plaintiffs a significant amount of money, although less than they were requesting.

The jury research that both sides had conducted accurately predicted the issues that were important to the actual jury, and provided accurate information about how best to present each party's most compelling case. The research also predicted the actual jury award within 2%.

Simulated or mock trial research like that conducted by these parties is the most widely used, comprehensive research tool available. Attorneys and research scientists who use these types of studies frequently place great value on them because they reveal otherwise unknown information about likely jury deliberations.

Most of the published scientific studies of juror decision making also utilize various mock trial study techniques. These studies have been instrumental in developing mock trial study methods that are adaptable to every case.

[1]–The Purpose of a Mock Trial Study

There are a number of important questions that can be answered with the use of a mock trial study to collect the data. They include the following:

- How are the themes and case story going to be perceived by the actual jury, and how can we make them more persuasive?
- What themes and messages should we emphasize that will make our entire case presentation more compelling?
- Are there are any parts of our case that we should eliminate because they weaken other parts of our case?

- How do we handle our weaknesses so as to make the rest of our case more powerful?
- How will a likely jury perceive our key fact witnesses, and what must we do to help them be more credible and helpful to the jury?
- How will the jury perceive our expert witnesses and what can we do to help them be more effective and persuasive?
- How will a likely jury perceive our demonstrative exhibits and how can we improve their persuasiveness?
- What is our standard for the ideal juror against which we will compare all of the prospective jurors during jury selection?
- What specific questions should we ask to identify those jurors who might be biased against us?
- What important aspects of our case have not been apparent to us before?

The comprehensiveness and flexibility of a mock trial study make it an ideal method for testing the effectiveness of an entire case prior to trial. In addition, a well-planned mock trial study can provide an excellent opportunity for the trial team to think through their case presentation and rehearse it well in advance of trial. Developing a case presentation for trial is a process, not a single event. The case presentation and rehearsal are especially useful if computer-assisted demonstrative aids will be used at trial.

Mock trial studies provide an opportunity for the client and trial team to evaluate the risk in the case. Many trial lawyers and corporations regularly use mock trial studies to establish a likely range of verdicts for use in making strategic and settlement decisions.

[2]—When to Use a Mock Trial Study or a Focus Group

A mock trial study is most useful when you want to test the effectiveness of an entire case, not just certain issues. Because a mock trial study is a scientific experiment, you are attempting to test the most important elements of the trial presentation as if the case were actually going to trial on the day of the study. You are in effect recreating reality in a laboratory environment and testing the persuasiveness of the presentation with a representative sample of people from the jury population in the case venue.

Focus group studies are primarily used in the early stages of case development to help give direction to the case and establish how the issues are likely to be processed in the jurors' minds. They can also be used just prior to trial to help work out important last-minute decisions on certain issues or specific elements of a trial presentation.

Mock trial studies, however, are usually conducted two to six months prior to trial once the elements of the case are finally pieced together. The information obtained through the studies helps in making important strategic decisions about trial and settlement of the case.

[3]—Locating and Recruiting Research Jurors

The same methods that are used to recruit research jurors for focus groups can be used in locating and recruiting research jurors for mock trial studies. The target audience is the same—the average jury which is likely to be seated in the case. Research jurors for mock trials come from the same population of people as the actual jury. In effect you are trying to match the broad characteristics of the average jury which is seated in the local venue.

On rare occasions you may be conducting focus group or mock trial studies after the jury in your case has been sworn in. In those instances, you will recruit jurors who exhibit as closely as possible the profiles of the jurors in the case. You will look for people with characteristics similar to those exhibited in the actual jurors. This process is called "*matched sampling.*"

Occasionally, your case may be set for trial in a lightly populated area and you may be concerned that rumors about the study or information produced during the study will be passed along to the opposing trial team. As discussed earlier, it would not be advisable for an opposing trial team to rely on any information they receive from a research juror in the other party's study. However, sometimes there is simply the discomfort or uneasiness of knowing that the opposing trial team is aware you have conducted jury research, although it can conduct its own research at any time. To allay any concerns you might have about mischief of your opposing counsel, social science has a remedy. That is, consider conducting the research study in a nearby county or venue with jury population characteristics similar to those of the case venue.

[4]—Designing the Study and Developing the Agenda

In scientific terms, a mock trial study is an experimental study. The term "experimental" does not mean that the mock trial study method is untested. The scientific method is quite sound and traditional. The term "experimental" refers to the scientific procedure you will be using to experiment with the case as it is currently structured to test its persuasiveness.

There are a number of considerations that affect a determination of how many panels of research jurors to use and how many jurors should compose each panel. One panel of jurors is helpful in understanding the basic dynamics of the case. A second panel is helpful in verifying the decision trend in the first panel and in widening the breadth and depth of jury experience which is brought to the study. Two panels is adequate for most cases. However, a third panel adds more statistical power and may also add to the validity and reliability of the study findings.

The number of jurors for each panel is partly a preference question and partly a statistical question. Most trial attorneys prefer twelve research jurors for each panel when there will be twelve jurors in the trial jury box, and six research jurors for each panel when there will be six jurors in the trial jury box. Experience tells us that nine or ten research jurors per panel is about the perfect number. With twelve or more jurors, just like in a real trial, a few of the jurors will loaf and not participate without special attention. In addition, if the recruiting and sampling of jurors successfully provides a broad cross-section of jurors, nine or ten should be sufficient. Using twelve jurors adds statistical power, however, and may add some incrementally helpful information. Using only six jurors, however, diminishes the volume of information, and the jurors generally will come to a consensus very quickly. Small panels will often deprive you of valuable information that never surfaces because the jurors reach their decision more quickly than you can study their decision.

We generally do not waste much time in the research study with free-flowing deliberations. Attorneys and trial consultants who are trained in observing discussion among jurors in the research study can spot the important issues, themes, and dynamics which will probably affect the likely jury without requiring the mock jury to actually undertake such deliberations. Structured discussions using the real jury charge are much more helpful and are also a more efficient use of money and resources. Free-flowing deliberations can be helpful, however, if you have extra time at the end of a mock trial study and you want to observe how opposing factions in a jury will argue the issues.

In addition, we already know from experience that the actual jury will likely have "opinion-makers" who will lead the discussion in deliberations. We also know that the opinion-makers in our research studies will not be the same opinion-makers as those in the actual trial. We will have to identify the case opinion-makers during jury selection and trial if we can.

The agenda for every mock trial study is going to be somewhat different because the research questions and the case circumstances will differ. Each presenter has a unique style and presents his or her own information content to the research participants. Despite the presenters' stylistic differences, however, there is a general structure for mock trial studies that has been developed and used by most research scientists and that is useful as a starting place.

Because a mock trial study seeks to study the essence of a complete case presentation as if it were going to trial on the day of study, the style of interaction among the presenters, research participants, and the research interviewer(s) is inherently more formal. The laboratory environment of the study dictates that a courtroom-like environment be re-created, complete with the visual trappings of a courtroom. This does not mean, however, that all the rules of evidence need be followed or that there should be live witnesses complete with direct and cross-examination. Such a study would take days if not weeks to perform without any advantage from a scientific point of view. In fact, such a barrage of detail could obscure the essential elements of the case and juror reactions to them.

The purpose of creating a courtroom-like environment is to study the decision-making process of the research jurors in the context of a court case. Since the only aspects of the case that you will be studying are the essential themes, case story, attorney presentation style, witness effectiveness, reactions to demonstrative aids, and other case essentials, you need only present sufficient stimuli to cover those aspects of the case. The case essentials will form the basis upon which jurors will create their own impressions and decisions about the case.

An average mock trial study with two panels of jurors should not take longer than ten hours from start to finish. In more complex cases, there may be too much material to cover in one day and an additional day may be necessary.

Once the research participants are brought into the presentation room and the jury box, the research interviewer (attorney or trial consultant) will introduce the study, explain the format to be used, and briefly orient the research jurors to the essence of the case. Then different members of the trial team will present the information which will form the "stimulus" for the study, generally in a nonargumentative style. Often the stimulus phase of the study presents opposing viewpoints on the issues. However, there are a myriad of ways to present information during this phase of the study. The end of the stimulus phase often consists of an opportunity for the research jurors to ask questions of the presenters about the events and facts of the case.

Once the stimulus has been delivered (i.e., the presentations are completed), the research jurors might have fact questions for the trial attorneys. These questions are important because they will give you advance warning of the types of questions that jurors in the actual trial will have. Following the questions, the jurors will be divided into their panels, and they will begin discussing the case using whatever guidelines you provide. Generally, these guidelines involve the use of a simplified version of the jury charge, and an opportunity for each research juror to speak out. Once the research jurors have finished discussing the case, the research interviewer(s) (one for each panel) will begin asking questions of the research jurors either orally or in writing, using qualitative or quantitative methods of obtaining information from the research jurors. When it appears that all of the thought processes of the research jurors have been explored and the knowledge of the group exhausted, the study ends and the mock trial study participants are dismissed.

[5]—Maintaining Confidentiality Among the Research Jurors

The considerations for maintaining confidentiality of research jurors in a mock trial study are identical to those used in a focus group study.[12] The importance of confidentiality cannot be overemphasized.

[6]—Analyzing and Applying the Information Gained in the Study

A mock trial study is both a quantitative and qualitative study. It is quantitative in that you are trying to study the relationships between the different variables (e.g., your themes and the verdict, or your case story and the verdict). It is qualitative because you are trying to track and understand the mental processes that jurors will experience when deciding the case as you have presented it. Most of the information you will obtain during a mock trial study will come from the qualitative interviewing you will be doing.

The analysis part of the research will describe and interpret the thought processes of research jurors as they refer to their own experiences. Just as in a

---

[12] See § 6.05[2][d] *supra.*

focus group study, you will be analyzing the jurors' mental processes throughout the course of the study itself as well as afterwards. In addition, as in focus group studies, the research participants themselves discover new relationships and thoughts as they analyze their own and others' statements and perceptions.

During the debriefing of jurors after their group discussions, the interviewer constantly condenses and interprets the meaning of the research participants' comments, confirming those meanings with the research participants. The discussions between the interviewer and each research participant continue until the essence of each participant's perception is clear and has been placed in context.

Just as with focus group studies, the final step in the analysis phase of a study comes after the end of the mock trial event. Most of the time, the research jurors' interactions are videotaped or transcribed, and a review of the videotapes and transcription can be useful in obtaining an objective view of the data that were collected. Once the data are structured, it is helpful to clarify and distill them down to their essential meanings, thus revealing the most important and/or instructive information that has been gleaned from the study.

Finally, after the data have been "boiled down" to their most important elements, one must interpret the meaning of the resulting data in the context of the case. This process of further condensation, categorization, structuring of the narrative portions of the data, making inferences and interpreting the data, and applying knowledge gained from experience and other research will help in applying the findings of the study to answering the original research questions that formed the purpose of the study.

§ 6.08 | MOCK ARBITRATION PANEL STUDIES

One of the newest applications of scientific research in the field of trial advocacy is the study of arbitration panel decision making to help in the preparation of an important arbitration hearing. We have learned that arbitration hearings are very expensive to prepare for and that the risk of losing is just as great as if the case were going to a jury trial. We know from our research that arbitrators make decisions the same way jurors do. They try to form a story of what happened in a case, they filter through the evidence and their life experiences to find corroboration for the story, and they make a decision that they think is just and fair. In short, they want to do the right thing.

Because the stakes are just as high as in any other trial, we have to use all our skills and resources during an arbitration to persuade the fact finders. We will have to use our best themes and case story. We are obliged to develop our most powerful, compelling case. The only real difference between an arbitration hearing and a jury trial is the number of fact finders. The casual feel of an arbitration hearing should never deceive you into thinking that you do not have to work as hard to put on your case. In many ways you have to work harder on your themes and case story because arbitrators are generally more aggressive at expediting a hearing than a judge might be in trial.

The most useful scientific tool we have in preparing for an arbitration hearing is a mock arbitration panel study. Such a study is conducted in an arbitration hearing style setting using mock arbitrators who have characteristics that match those of the actual arbitrators in a case. In the same way that "trials" are presented to mock juries to recreate trial conditions, arbitration hearings in a laboratory type setting proceed as if the case were going to hearing the day of the study.

Recruiting mock arbitrators requires attention to detail. You will want to match as many characteristics of the actual arbitrators as you can ascertain, including type of practice, academic background, demographics, and general attitudes about the issues in the case. In most instances, without the use of scientific methods, you will have taken many of these steps already. The use of scientific research methods helps you to increase the usefulness of the information you will have obtained about the actual arbitrators and put it to work for you in a different, more powerful way.

If you refer to the discussions presented previously in this chapter, you will already be familiar with considerations for setting the agenda (which will mirror the anticipated proceedings) and the analysis (which is similar to that of a focus group or mock trial, depending upon the research questions you are asking). There are very few differences between the information-gathering phase of a mock arbitration study and that of a mock trial study. The arbitrators will discuss the case using a format that you select, perhaps with some kind of charge. The trial team and client can observe the discussions either by audio link or audiovisual link. After the arbitrators' decision is made, the research scientist or study moderator will engage the research arbitrators in a qualitative interview similar to that of a mock trial study.

Because there will ordinarily be only three research arbitrators, it will be hard to generalize their decision to the actual case unless you have conducted extremely conscientious sampling in choosing the research arbitrators. If the research arbitrators are an almost identical match to the real arbitrators, the perceptions they form and the decision they reach in the mock arbitration study will be more likely to forecast the perceptions and decision of the actual arbitration panel.

The degree to which there are differences in characteristics may or may not indicate that there will be differences in the perceptions of the actual panel. Nonetheless, experience tells us that there is much inherent value in conducting the mock arbitration panel study because many, if not most, of the perceptions of the mock arbitrators will be close enough to those of the actual arbitration panel that the data will be valuable in developing recommendations for themes, case story, and other aspects of the actual presentation.

§ 6.09 | MOCK BENCH HEARINGS AND TRIAL STUDIES

As a result of recent legislation and appellate court rulings, many important, dispositive decisions that were formerly made by juries are being made by judges. Trial judges are now making important decisions about patent interpretations, expert witness qualifications, class certifications (and many other matters) in addition to continuing their traditional role as fact finders in bench trials. The types of decisions and the risk associated with trial judges make preparation for bench hearings and trials as important as that for any jury trial or arbitration.

We know that trial judges are just as concerned about making the right decision as are jurors and arbitrators. Judges form a story in their minds regarding events in a case about which they are asked to make a decision that is governed to a great extent by judges' attitudes about specific issues in the case, their previous life experiences, and other factors. Judges will filter information and assess credibility just like jurors and arbitrators. Judges want to make decisions that they can be proud of and that are meaningful.

It is therefore important that we learn the kinds of perceptions and attitudes the judge will bring to a case. The best research tool we have available to us to study how the actual judge will approach the case is by conducting private research that involves people who have been judges and have characteristics similar to that of the judge who will be making the decision in the case.

The population of retired or former judges is smaller than that of the population of arbitrators or jurors, so the need for carefully matched samplings is even more important. However, there is an interesting phenomenon which we have discovered among judges who have sat on the bench for more than a year or two. Trial judges, like most other small, exclusive groups of people in our society, tend to take on characteristics of the group even if they are not naturally similar people. Many factors, including pressure for uniformity from appellate courts, judicial schools, and other sources, cause trial judges to approach certain types of issues (e.g., procedural or legally defined matters) in similar patterns. However, decisions about general life issues, such as those that would be encountered in a bench trial, are more often dictated by a judge's general approach to life than by his or her approach to procedural matters.

Regardless of the kind of decision you will be asking a judge to make, you will benefit from a mock bench study. By learning the perceptions and approaches that a judge who is similar to the trial judge will utilize in making decisions in your case, you have a better chance of developing the themes and story that will make a favorable ruling more likely. There is also some inherent value in the rehearsal process.

§ 6.10 | MOCK APPELLATE HEARINGS

The appellate courts have long played an important role in the resolution of cases. Many times we presume that appellate judges are robotic and will simply apply our interpretation of law or that of our opposing party based only upon some thread of legal consciousness implied in the laws and Constitution. Sometimes we are led to believe by news accounts and conventional wisdom that appellate judges may be influenced by some ideological or political bent.

However, research and experience tell us that the decision-making process used by appellate judges in their opinions is much more complicated. If the thinking processes of appellate judges were so simple and predictable, how would we explain a reportedly conservative judge upholding an enormous jury trial damages verdict or making a decision which favors liberal causes? How could we explain a reportedly liberal judge making decisions which favor conservative causes?

Although appellate judges are indeed primarily concerned with the correct application of law, they are also heavily influenced by their views of the world and their desire to do the right thing in a specific situation. They form a story in their minds of what happened in the underlying case and in the trial court proceedings. They filter all of the information they are receiving about the case through their individual life experiences, attitudes, and other life influences.

Appellate judges make interesting research subjects because they are generally so highly skilled at reconciling all of the conflicting elements of an underlying dispute with the rules and mores of our society as a whole. However, there is no way for them to escape their own personal biases.

One of the most important tools that we have available to us to study how individual judges on an appellate panel will perceive the issues in a case is a mock appellate panel research study. There is no magic to understanding how an appellate judge will rule in a case. Appellate judges, like trial judges, are conditioned to their roles and share many views and attributes of other appellate judges. Even judges who have different ideological characteristics share some similar traits because of their conditioning as appellate judges.

By now you should be familiar with the process of matching research participants to the characteristics of the person or people who will be acting as the decision maker(s) in your case. In conducting a mock appellate panel study, you will want to locate former appellate judges to participate as private research participants to review the briefs, listen to the anticipated oral arguments, and then give meaningful feedback. Such an appellate panel study should include briefs and oral hearing identical or similar to those that would be utilized if the appellate hearing were to take place on the day of study. You will want to use the best arguments and the best demonstrative aids that each side would use. You will want to use the surest, best themes and the most appropriate, persuasive style of argument that you can develop for each side of the case.

After the presentations are complete, the research judges will retire to consider the case and may allow you to listen to their deliberations through a closed audio circuit. For documentation purposes, it would also be a good idea to audiotape the deliberations for later reference. You should be aware that retired judges and appellate judges will many times qualify their opinions to you by stating that they are not giving you official rulings. You should appreciate their position and agree with it. You are not asking for any official rulings.

Retired judges and sitting appellate judges who agree to participate in this kind of decision-making study provide a very important service. They help us to better understand how judges make decisions. People who engage in such private judicial research gain much more respect and admiration for how judges go about deciding difficult disputes.

Finally, we should discuss the analysis process in this type of study. Since the sample of people used in the study is so small, trying to make quantitative findings such as who would win in the actual oral argument would be futile. However, the information about the judges' thinking processes is of great value. If the sample of people you have chosen as research judges reflects the fundamental characteristics of the appellate judges in the actual case, then their attitudes, life experiences, and beliefs about the law and life can help your conclusions rise to predictive levels.

One word of caution: Appellate judges, like most other successful, intelligent people, often are not able to articulate the real reason they are making decisions. They will often be able to be express their legal reasoning, but are not able to express their underlying thought processes because they may appear to be inappropriate for a judge. It seems only fair that appellate judges should be free to express their true feelings about a situation. However, we have conditioned them to be hesitant to reveal those feelings. The judges do not want to appear to be applying nonlegal principles or beliefs to a legal question.

In a bench or appellate panel study, you or the research scientist should help the judges to feel at ease in expressing their true feelings about the case. In real life, judges are influenced by their feelings and it is impossible to obviate that influence. Do not be afraid to probe into the underlying factors and feelings that may affect a judge in a research study. We respect the feelings of judges and admire them for their candor and participation in furthering our knowledge of judicial decision making.

§ 6.11 | PSYCHOLOGICAL REVIEW OF PLEADINGS AND BRIEFS

Most experienced trial lawyers and corporate counsel are aware of the power that their pleadings and briefs will have in influencing a judge—especially an appellate judge—prior to a hearing or trial. It is common for a judge to ascend to the bench and immediately announce that he or she has read the pleadings and briefs and has already made a decision. Even in those cases where the judge has read the pleadings and is still willing to listen to oral arguments, the psychological impact of the pleadings and briefs is often apparent.

In our training as lawyers, we focus much of our attention on legal research and writing. We have a case and we have a sense of our optimal legal position. We try to develop a legal argument that will support that position. Our opposing counsel is probably approaching his or her legal research the same way. We focus all of our effort on making an argument that sounds more legally correct than that of our opponent.

At this point in our discussion, you are probably aware that there is more to a judge's decision making than simply rubber-stamping whichever argument is more legally correct. But until now, there has been very little information available to us about the psychological impact of a pleading or brief. In addition, there is the dilemma of how to incorporate important psychological considerations with statements about the law.

Knowing that judges and appellate judges are influenced by many factors, every litigant would be wise to give more attention to the psychological impact of pleadings and briefs. For example, sometimes words or phrases in a pleading or brief which appear to be saying something supportive for your case may in fact be interpreted differently by the trial judge. No two people always see or interpret the same things the same way.

One of the more recently developed tools in research is a psychological review of themes and briefs using the services of retired trial and appellate judges. A study of such matters would be conducted in similar fashion to mock bench studies and mock appellate panel studies. The only difference is that there would be no need to present a practice oral argument unless the trial team and client wish to do so. The pleadings and briefs would be provided to the retired judges along with a questionnaire about their mental processes in response to their reading of these documents. The analysis phase of such a study would focus on patterns of thinking and motivations for thinking and behavior that are apparent from the answers to the questionnaire.

Just as with any other type of study, it is often a good idea to use the research scientist or intermediary to conduct a study of this nature. The results will often be more reliable and neutral, and the recommendations will often be more objective and creative.

§ 6.12 | SHADOW JURIES

[1]—Lawyer Experiences with Shadow Jurors

A shadow jury, or mirror jury, consisting of people who are similar to sitting jurors, is often used by trial lawyers and trial consultants to observe actual trial proceedings and, following the conclusion of portions of the trial and/or the complete trial, to give feedback that can be used to measure the performance of the trial team and the perceptions of jurors in the trial. In effect, a shadow jury is a specialized form of focus group with some unique characteristics regarding how it is formed and utilized. Such a jury is not told which of the litigants has recruited its members and is seeking its advice.

There is much debate about the proper use and effectiveness of shadow juries. Most of the debate is initiated by trial attorneys. Some trial attorneys have used shadow juries in their trials for decades to give them meaningful contemporaneous feedback about the sitting jury's likely perceptions of the case presentations. Other trial attorneys have concerns about the effectiveness of a shadow jury or about the confidentiality of the shadow jury.

In 1995, a Chicago securities law firm was defending in a securities fraud case in which the defendant company was charged with insider trading. There was no dispute that insiders sold stock just prior to the release of a disappointing earnings report. The sequence of events could easily have led the jury to believe that there had been insider trading. Nevertheless, the defendant chose not to hire a trial consultant to assist with the preparation for trial.

Before the trial began, the firm's client offered to settle the case for several million dollars. In light of the factual evidence, such an offer seemed prudent. The offer stayed on the table until the end of opening statements.

Between the end of jury selection and the beginning of opening statements, the law firm employed a trial consulting firm to organize a shadow jury for the case. The firm had used shadow juries for more than fifteen years and thought that a shadow jury would enhance the trial team's efforts. The shadow jurors were recruited based upon a profile of the sitting jury in the case. Many of the demographic and background characteristics of the shadow jurors matched those of the actual jurors.

At the end of the first day of trial, the shadow jurors were interviewed by the trial consultant to gain an understanding of how the actual jury might respond to the case presentations. During the interviews the consultant learned that the shadow jurors had listened intently to the plaintiff's case presentation, but did not understand the essence of the plaintiff's case. Because the defendant now believed that the plaintiff's case might not be persuasive, the defendant retracted the settlement offer and the case proceeded.

Every afternoon at the end of the court proceedings, the trial consultant interviewed the shadow jurors. The shadow jurors discussed their perceptions and how they were learning about the case. The comments of the shadow jurors were candid and unbiased. They forthrightly talked about their reactions to the attorneys and witnesses. They even commented about individual jurors. After the interviews each day, the trial consultant developed a report which translated the perceptions of the shadow jurors and made recommendations to the trial team. The report was transmitted to the trial team by e-mail and followed by a telephone conference each evening.

At the end of the long trial, the defense prevailed despite the bad facts. The trial team and the client believed that the shadow jury and the recommendations of the trial consultant were helpful in making strategic decisions that were beneficial to the persuasive power of their case.

Some trial attorneys are suspicious about the use of a shadow jury. They are concerned that a shadow jury will inevitably find out which party is sponsoring them and that their feedback will therefore be biased. Other trial attorneys believe that day-to-day observations are not helpful and say candidly that the only important part of trial is deliberations. They believe that the quality of the feedback from shadow jurors is doubtful, arguing that the only perceptions that count are those of the actual jurors. They believe that shadow jurors see and hear evidence that is not presented to the actual jury and, therefore, that the perceptions of the shadow jurors may be misleading.

[2]—Organizing an Effective Shadow Jury

There are perhaps two reasons why some lawyers have had questionable experiences with shadow juries. The first is that most shadow juries are loosely organized to simply observe, rather than to serve as scientific research participants. In order to be effective, the shadow jury must be organized such that the jurors are as closely matched psychologically to the actual jurors as possible. The shadow jurors must be trained and oriented so that their role as scientific research participants is clear, and all biases and influences which might skew the results of the experiment are eliminated or controlled.

The second reason that some attorneys do not benefit from shadow jurors is that the interviewing process at the end of the day must also be conducted objectively. The more superficial the questions and answers, the less helpful the shadow jury is to the trial team. For example, it may be interesting to know which of the shadow jurors liked the clothing or the demeanor of each of the lawyers, but neither shadow jurors nor actual jurors make most of their important decisions in cases based upon the clothing of the trial participants.

Obviously, the more provocative and insightful the questions and answers, the more helpful the experience will be for the trial team and the trial consultant. Asking questions of the shadow jurors relating to the quality of the information and visual aids used to explain a party's position can provide considerable information about the effectiveness of each of the parties in teaching the actual jury about the case. Focusing questions on the hierarchy of facts and themes recalled by the shadow jurors can help the trial team in understanding which of the facts and themes the actual jury will likely recall during deliberations.

If the matching process at the beginning of the trial is effective, information from the shadow jurors about their intellectual and emotional reactions to the evidence highlight the effectiveness of the themes and case story that a trial team has presented. Often, the themes and case story which have been developed for trial must be revised or adjusted to meet the psychological profiles of the actual jurors in the case.

An insightful, well-trained interviewer, whether a trial lawyer or trial consultant, can often detect perceptions and mental processes of shadow jurors that are likely to be mirrored in the actual jury, but which the shadow jurors cannot articulate. They can also detect whether a shadow juror has become biased and ascertain how this bias has occurred. If bias results directly from the trial presentations, it is possible that the bias is shared by the actual jury as well. If bias exists because of some glitch in the shadow jury recruitment or interviewing process, the problem can be remedied by either replacing the shadow juror or simply discounting some of the observations that he or she makes.

In addition, a skilled interviewer can spontaneously detect unexpected issues that must be addressed immediately by the trial team. Often the trial team can then test new ideas in front of the shadow jury to determine how they should be addressed before the actual jury.

In essence, the effective use of a shadow jury is commensurate with the quality with which it is organized and utilized. A shadow jury is a valuable tool that is relatively inexpensive and offers a powerful method for keeping the trial team focused on its most persuasive and compelling case presentation.

[3]—Some Additional Tips

Most trial attorneys and trial consultants who use shadow juries for conducting research during a trial have discovered a number of potential problems that can be avoided with planning and proper supervision. If a trial team will approach the use of a shadow jury with the precision required for a scientific study, the experience with the shadow jury will likely be a good one. Following are some specific recommendations:

(1) The decision to use the shadow jury should be made long before trial. The responsible people on the trial team should be ready to recruit the shadow jurors immediately upon the seating of the actual jury. Sources for recruitment should be on alert and ready to proceed once the profiles of the actual jurors are known.

(2) If jury selection is completed early in the day and opening statements are made on the same day, it may be necessary to recruit the initial shadow jurors before trial and later adjust the group with people who more accurately match the characteristics of the actual jury.

(3) It is important to spend some time training the shadow jurors about the shadow jury process before seating them in the courtroom. They need to understand their role and the tasks they are to perform along the way. They must be specifically trained about how to organize their notes, how to conduct themselves during the day, and where to go immediately after trial for interviews.

(4) A supervisory person must accompany the shadow jury at all times in and around the courthouse. This person must be specifically trained to be an advocate for the shadow jury in the event issues arise, such as problems raised by the opposing party. There is no legal reason for excluding a shadow jury, but a trial team must be confident enough to withstand challenges.

(5) In order for the feedback from the shadow jurors to be reliable and useful, the shadow jurors must see and hear *only* the evidence and arguments that the actual jury sees and hears. The shadow jurors should be in the courtroom only when the actual jury is in the jury box.

(6) To prevent bias in the shadow jury process, the shadow jurors should not have any direct meaningful contact with a member of the trial team for either side. They should be recruited and supervised only by a third party who has no obvious contact with anyone in the case. Some trial teams and trial consultants prefer that the shadow jurors be interviewed by teleconference, whereas others prefer live interviews. Either method can be effective. Nonetheless, the shadow jurors must be trained so that their curiosity about their sponsor is diminished.

A FINAL WORD:
WHY SHOULD YOU CONDUCT DECISION-MAKER RESEARCH?

Our clients expect us to win. We apply science to everything in life. Why not use it to enhance the persuasiveness of your case? Full and creative use of scientific research to better understand a judge, a jury or an arbitration panel assigned to a case and how to persuade them is a weapon without which we should not go into battle. The information and insights you can discover from conducting some type of focus group or mock trial research can help you to gain a powerful advantage or at least level the playing field in almost any case.

In our practice, we might use trial science to test a venue before filing a lawsuit (community attitude survey), develop issues on which to request discovery (think-tank type group of judicial and psychological experts), evaluate the believability of fact and expert witnesses, prepare witnesses for deposition or trial testimony, prioritize and clarify issues for trial (focus group or mock trial), develop themes and strategies for trial or arbitration, refine themes until I find what wins, evaluate a case for settlement, prepare for argument of an important motion or appeal (mock panel of former judges), determine how the actual jury is likely receiving the evidence (shadow jury), adjust themes or cross-examination "in the heat of battle" (courtroom trial consultant), prepare for closing argument, and conduct post-verdict interviews of jurors.

CONTINUED

Like picking stocks to buy, some trial lawyers attempt to conduct scientific research themselves. I do not. While I am confident that with time and dedication I could acquire the necessary skills, I have other interests. Trial science is too important to be left to amateurs, especially lawyer-amateurs.

I spent the first seventeen years of my practice with a large national firm, where I had hundreds of partners and the best support staff a client's money could buy. I now have the honor of helping to lead a specialized boutique litigation firm. We represent plaintiffs in complicated business and intellectual property litigation, frequently suing Fortune 500 companies, sometimes on a contingent fee. I have learned that trial science can be the key to David slaying Goliath. I have used it in every aspect of a case, from before the complaint is filed to preparing for oral argument on appeal. Sometimes I use trial science to decide whether to take a case. Rejecting a case that I can't win is the most important decision I can make.

Trial lawyers don't have to understand the research or methodology of trial science, or how to assess its reliability. They are artists and craftsmen, not scientists. For that reason, I want a trial science consultant with battle-hardened experience. I am not afraid to ask "silly" questions or to listen to good advice. I measure the value of the feedback I receive, and I decide what to use and what not to attempt. Sometimes my consultant stretches my creativity and encourages me to courageously try something new.

— Randy J. McClanahan, Partner
McClanahan & Clearman, L.L.P.

§ 6.13 | REFERENCES

Abbott & Batt, eds., *A Handbook of Jury Research* (Philadelphia: American Law Institute/American Bar Association, 1999).

Babbie, *The Practice of Social Research*, 7th ed. (Belmont, CA: Wadsworth Publishing Co., 1995).

Beed & Stimson, *Survey Interviewing: Theory and Techniques* (Sydney: Allen & Unwin, 1985).

Cohen, *Statistical Power Analysis for the Behavioral Sciences*, 2d ed. (Hillsdale, NJ: Lawrence Erlbaum Associates, Inc., 1988).

Creswell, *Research Design* (Thousand Oaks, CA: Sage Publications, 1994).

Davis, Hulbert, Au, Chen & Zarnoth, "Effects of Group Size and Procedural Influence on Consensual Judgments of Quantity: The Examples of Damage Awards and Mock Civil Juries," 73 J. Personality & Soc. Psych. 703-718 (1997).

Fowler, *Survey Research Methods*, 2d ed. (Newbury Park, CA: Sage Publications, 1993).

Heiman, *Basic Statistics for the Behavioral Sciences* (Boston: Houghton Mifflin Co., 1996).

Jorgensen, *Participant Observation: A Methodology for Human Studies* (Newbury Park, CA: Sage Publications, 1989).

Kvale, *Interviews: An Introduction to Qualitative Research Interviewing* (Thousand Oaks, CA: Sage Publications, 1996).

Levin, Fox & Fox, *Elementary Statistics in Social Research* (Needham Heights, MA: Allyn & Bacon, 1999).

McDonough, "Me and My Shadows: 'Shadow Juries' Are Helping Litigators Shape Their Cases—During Trial," The National Law Journal, pp. A1, A16 (May 21, 2001).

Mishler, *Research Interviewing: Context and Narrative* (Cambridge, MA: Harvard University Press, 1986).

Morgan, *Focus Groups as Qualitative Research*, 2d ed. (Thousand Oaks, CA: Sage Publications, 1997).

Morgan, *Successful Focus Groups: Advancing the State of the Art* (Newbury Park, CA: Sage Publications, 1993).

Nunnally & Bernstein, *Psychometric Theory*, 3d ed. (New York: McGraw-Hill, 1994).

Seal, Bogart & Ehrhardt, "Small Group Dynamics: The Utility of Focus Group Discussion as a Research Method," 2 Group Dynamics: Theory, Research & Practice 253-266 (1998).

Stewart & Shamdasani, *Focus Groups: Theory and Practice* (Newbury Park, CA: Sage Publications, 1990).

Wolcott, *Transforming Qualitative Data: Description, Analysis, and Interpretation* (Thousand Oaks, CA: Sage Publications, 1994).

Bench Trials

CHAPTER CONTENTS

"A judge is not supposed to know anything about the facts of life until they have been presented in evidence and explained to him at least three times."

— Lord Chief Justice Parker (1900-1972)

§ 7.01 | Introduction

Judges are people too. Before they were judges, they were lawyers, and before they were lawyers, they were just ordinary people like the rest of us. The probability is that the judge in your next case thinks of himself or herself as a person who is eminently fair, has the highest ethics, works hard to serve the public, and is completely devoted to family and friends. In all likelihood, this is true.

Judges have responsibilities that weigh heavily on them. They feel the importance of making decisions that are fair and that will set an important precedent. They feel powerful and are sometimes afraid of their power. They are aware of their humanity and concerned about the possibility that they might make a wrong decision.

In this chapter we will discuss how judges make decisions, and we will then generate some ideas about developing and presenting a powerful, compelling case in your next bench trial.

§ 7.02 | Why Judges Present Special Challenges to Attorneys

Trial judges present special challenges to attorneys. Most of the difficulties we have persuading trial judges are self-imposed. We often make decisions about how to persuade judges based upon insufficient information and inaccurate assumptions.

It is possible that you have believed trial judges to be powerful, inaccessible, and enigmatic. Because trial judges sometimes feel compelled to demonstrate fairness and objectivity, they occasionally engage in a number of behaviors intended to remind us to keep our distance. Unfortunately, we may interpret their actions as unfriendly or as evidence that judges are different from other people.

Nevertheless, we know instinctively that we must understand how a particular judge is likely to process the issues in our case in order to be able to persuade him or her. How do we go about understanding how a trial judge will approach the case? How do we distinguish between the methods we might use to persuade one judge from the methods that we need to persuade a different judge? Would you present the case differently to a trial judge than to a jury or to an arbitration panel?

The challenges that the persuasion of judges present to us are best resolved with an astute understanding of trial judges' perceptions and how judges make decisions.

§ 7.03 | Bench Trial Considerations

You might try a case to a trial judge rather than to a jury for many reasons. Regardless of the particular reason, it would be wise to develop and present the case as if it were the most important case you have ever tried anywhere, any time.

We often have preconceived notions about particular judges that may or may not be accurate or helpful. Some of our ideas about them are based upon extensive experience with particular judges, but it is difficult to generalize sketchy information about a few judges to all judges. We may like judges in our cases because we know that they are working hard to make fair decisions. However, sometimes we are unsure or perhaps even anxious about them because we see them as powerful and judgmental. When trial judges chastise you in open court, you are instantly reminded of their authority and control.

Perhaps our discomfort with trying to persuade someone who has dominance over us is at the core of our unease. If we could step back and be less subjective, however, we would see that each trial judge is a unique person who has a job to do. That job is not to make our lives easier, but rather to ensure that the principles of the institution that judges represent are upheld and that a fair and just decision is made in each of our cases.

[1]—What Judges Think about You and Your Case

Trial judges realize that they hold a dominant, powerful position. They want to use their power to resolve cases fairly and to make them feel good about themselves.

Trial judges instinctively want you to be the most persuasive, compelling trial lawyer they have ever heard in their courtroom. They want you to convince them that your client should win the case.

If you take the time to review the background of most trial judges, you will better understand their perceptions of you and your case. Because they were trial lawyers and probably associate almost exclusively with trial lawyers, they have a number of traits with which you might be able to identify. These include:

- A high level of self-confidence,
- An extraordinary drive to achieve and perform,
- Love of competition and a need to win,
- A need for the excitement of persuading and motivating other people,
- Love of adventure and brinkmanship,
- An inner satisfaction from analyzing difficult problems and creating solutions, and
- The joy of watching another trial lawyer perform in an outstanding way.

Imagine if you had all these energizing motivations, but were confined to a passive role as an observer only—day after day. Eventually you might begin to be critical of trial lawyers who appear before you. You might often feel frustration as you watch a trial lawyer perform in an ineffective way. You might want to come down from your bench and offer to demonstrate ways to accomplish whatever the lawyer is trying to achieve.

Conversely, you might feel somewhat intimidated by a high-powered trial lawyer who does an outstanding job. You might feel some animosity for having to share the spotlight.

Like everyone else, trial judges cannot dissociate themselves from their previous life experiences. Most of them studied law, courtroom procedure, and trial advocacy methods for many years. They know the ideals that everyone aspires to reach as a trial lawyer. They are sometimes judgmental toward trial lawyers for not working harder to reach those ideals.

Trial judges know instinctively whether a trial lawyer is prepared and whether the trial lawyer is sincerely working hard to perform at a high level. Conversely, they also know when a trial lawyer is not prepared and is trying to pull the wool over the judge's eyes.

Many persuasive techniques we have discussed in other chapters will help you in these situations. For example, being organized and working hard to get to the core of your case (from a psychological standpoint) will leave you free to focus on observing the trial judge and addressing his concerns and questions about the case. A direct approach also displays confidence that, in itself, is often persuasive.

Even though trial judges have a wealth of life experiences and attitudes about specific issues that may arise in your case, they work hard to set aside the influence of those experiences and attitudes. However, because trial judges are only human, they are often unaware of the influence of those life experiences and attitudes.

Depending upon your viewpoint, our judicial system has strengths or weaknesses (or both). One of the strengths is that judges, jurors, and arbitrators are complex human beings who think and feel things that should affect conflict dispute resolution. Some people argue that the human factor in our judicial system is also one of its weaknesses.

The trial advocacy element in the system seems to work well most of the time. Theoretically, all parties to a case have equal access to information about the decision makers. In the case of bench trials, each of the opposing parties has an opportunity to develop and present the most powerful, compelling case presentation for that party. Each side has opportunities to study the way a trial judge is likely to process the issues and circumstances in the case before trial. As we discussed in Chapter 6, there are scientific methods that can be used to study the likely perceptions of the judge in a particular case.

Any belief that trial judges are free of human influences is a myth. Judges are not computers. Each trial judge you appear before is going to have preconceptions about lawyers and about the issues and circumstances in your case. It will be enormously helpful for you to understand those preconceptions before trial. Knowing in advance the issues and values that are important to a trial judge can be extremely useful in developing and presenting a persuasive case.

[2]—What Judges Need from Counsel

Most judges feel a sense of excitement when they first sit on the bench. They feel an overwhelming sensation of power and a desire to use it in a way that will make the world a better place.

It does not take long for them to realize that there are many limitations on their power. All of a sudden, the special authority they are given becomes burdened with a number of challenges. In order for them to be able to do their job, they need help from you and the other attorneys in the case.

[a]—Freedom from Separation and Isolation

Those of you who are solo practitioners can perhaps understand how separated and isolated trial judges feel sometimes. They spend most of their day working alone, having little interaction with colleagues and usually having no-one with whom to brainstorm ideas about a case. Their interactions with court staff are generally administrative in nature. Thanks to computers and electronic mail, they can converse with other judges and colleagues in a limited way, but these methods cannot replace human contact. Those few judges who have law clerks rely upon them heavily to brainstorm legal reasoning, while at the same time recognizing the limitations of their youth. The only friendly contact judges have each day occurs during a few rushed moments with their families, court staff, and occasionally, another judge.

In some ways, trial judges adjust to these circumstances, but they often feel some inner loss. Before they came to the bench, they had jobs just like yours and mine. They generally had the freedom to come and go from the office whenever they wished. They could stop and chat with a colleague in the office to discuss business matters or just to talk about personal things. How would you feel if all of the human interaction that you experience freely each day suddenly disappeared? Would you feel lost? Would you be angry? Different trial judges deal with these issues in different ways.

Part of the isolation that judges feel is acceptable to them. They realize that their role as independent decision makers requires some solitude. Nevertheless, many trial judges feel a deep desire for meaningful human interaction. You can help them by providing a case presentation that focuses on the key issues in a thoughtful, interesting way. If you can adequately convey the powerful meaning of your case to a trial judge, it helps him or her feel that his or her sacrifices have been worthwhile.

[b]—Help in Dealing with Time Pressures and Obstacles to Concentration on Your Case

During a jury trial, twelve men and women will work as a team to gather the information in the case and make a decision. In a bench trial, however, there is only one juror.

Think about all of the work that the trial judge must do during a bench trial. He enforces the rules of court. He rules on objections. He listens to every detail from each of the attorneys and each of the witnesses. He studies each of the documents and other pieces of material evidence. He tries to make sense out of the case and form a story about what happened. Ultimately, he makes a difficult decision. During all of these activities, the judge is called upon to resolve continual quarrels over a few important things and countless less important matters.

While trying diligently to perform in his role as the sole fact finder, the judge is interrupted by spontaneous objections and motions and is expected to make instantaneous rulings that could have the effect of undermining the case for one of the parties. Each of the objections made during trial resembles a flashcard in a children's learning game, requiring an almost reflexive response.

Here is the scene: During a witness examination, one of the lawyers asks a question. With great fanfare the opposing attorney jumps to his feet and in a self-righteous and thoroughly disgusted manner shouts, "Objection, hearsay!" Suddenly the flashcards appear in the judge's mind. The first card reads, "Is it hearsay?" The other side of the card says, "Yes." Then the second card appears. It reads, "Is it an exception to hearsay?" The other side of that card reads, "Yes." The judge then authoritatively states "Overruled" without hesitation. (Judges feel that they must rule decisively out of concern that someone may mistake hesitation for indecisiveness.)

This mental game continues for hours and days and, sometimes, weeks, during which time the judge is quite busy trying to understand the case and make important decisions. Is it any wonder that judges occasionally become a little testy? Do you blame them?

There are many ways that you can help a trial judge. The most important is to use courtroom time in an efficient, focused way. Making points clearly and succinctly is not only appreciated by the court, but is also more persuasive.

Much of the communication we have with trial judges in the courtroom is the result of efforts to pander to the judge. The main problem with pandering is that it is so obvious that judges feel insulted and demeaned by it. Pandering also wastes precious time.

Most trial judges have hundreds of cases on their dockets. Even though only a hundred or so are active at any particular time, there are demands being placed on the court in each of those cases at the same time the judge is sitting and listening to you and your case. Prior to court, during a recess, or after hours your trial judge may have to decide matters related to a dozen other pending cases, which further distracts him or her from concentrating on your trial.

Therefore, if you demonstrate your sensitivity to the time pressures on the judge and if you use the precious time you have in an effective way, your efforts will be noticed. As we have already discussed, fact finders such as judges are more disposed to listen to you and help you if you demonstrate that you are sensitive to their needs.

[c]–Relief from the Stress of Ruling

Even though judges often show a public side of themselves that is businesslike, confident, and compassionate, they worry about whether the decisions they make are the right decisions. They try to balance all of the information they have about a case (the characteristics of the parties, the attorneys, the evidence, the circumstances, and the competing moral issues) in order to make a decision of which they can be proud.

Often they find themselves faced with dilemmas. Perhaps an attorney has been obnoxious during trial and has angered the judge, and the judge is therefore worried that her reaction to the attorney may disadvantage the attorney's client.

Being the sole judge (or juror) in a case is stressful. Trial judges feel compelled to consider every aspect of a case. Most of them have achieved a good deal in their lives due to their diligence and attention to detail.

Trial judges are also trained to see opposing arguments just like you. Once they begin making decisions in their minds, they begin doubting themselves. They begin asking themselves questions such as, "I really believe that _____ is going on here, but what about _____?"

To help meet the judge's needs, think through your case theory and themes until they are solid and convincing. The more considered your presentation is, the more committed you will be to it and the more solid it will feel to the judge. The judge needs reassurance that your case has been carefully developed and that the meaning of your case is important.

[d]–Dealing with Community and Appellate Pressures

In addition to pressures that arise from within the job description, a trial judge often feels pressure to consider the wishes of the court's constituencies in the community, as well as appellate courts that will review the court's decisions. Judges are aware that people who do not attend trial and listen to the evidence are, nevertheless, sometimes critical of the decisions made in courtrooms. Some of these people might be influential political leaders or members of the media.

In addition, trial court judges are keenly aware that an appellate panel will review many of their decisions. They want to feel comfortable about their rulings should an appellate panel accept an appeal from their courts. They feel pressure to ensure that their decisions are defensible from the point of view of appellate judges who were not present in the courtroom at the time of trial.

Trial judges feel more comfortable making decisive rulings when they have based them upon clear, justifiable evidence and arguments that they believe are morally and legally correct. This is where you come in. Your job is to provide the judge with such a strong, persuasive case (clearly supportive evidence, appropriate case theory, and morally persuasive themes) that he or she feels comfortable ruling in your favor. In those rare instances where you ask the court to defy current precedent, you must have the moral high ground on your side.

[e]–Help in Combining Courtroom Ritual and Humanistic Concerns

One of the challenges for trial judges is how to adhere to the court's ritual and the need to impose justice while at the same time recognizing the humanity in the law and the circumstances of the case. Different judges view the need for ritual differently. Some judges require more formality than others. As always, you will simply abide by the rules of a particular court. However, even in situations where adherence to ritual is the most formal and strict, trial judges still want to know the human side of a case. One might even argue that those judges who are the strictest about procedure are also the most sensitive to the human side of a case.

It is helpful to view ritual as simply constituting the trappings of the courtroom, in the same way that different religions require different rituals for weddings and funerals. Just because courtroom rituals require strict adherence to procedure does not lessen the depth and impact of the feelings and circumstances that form the substance of your case.

[f]–Respect

Because of the pressures and demands on a trial judge, a strong ego is an important necessity for survival. Sometimes people resent a judge's actions that might suggest the presence of such an ego. However, the author would respectfully suggest that a better way to approach interaction with a trial judge is to treat him or her with extraordinary respect and a measure of sympathy for having to make decisions in cases where the opposing parties and their attorneys themselves cannot agree. Having sympathy for someone like a trial judge may seem inappropriate at first. However, it is a powerful way to make tension disappear.

Even though we may strongly disagree with a decision of a judge, we would feel less stress if we would separate the judge from the judge's decision. We know that the personal characteristics of a judge inevitably influence a decision. It is counterproductive to expect a trial judge to behave in a way that is contrary to the judge's characteristics. Therefore, experience tells us that we will be much more successful if we study the characteristics of a trial judge and work hard to prepare a powerful case based upon this information. The psychological aspects of your case are much more persuasive than its legal aspects.

[3]—Judges and Jurors: Similarities and Differences

There are more similarities than differences between trial judges and jurors. Judges have families, friends, pets, homes, automobiles, and most of the other aspects of daily living just like jurors. They have dreams and aspirations, likes and dislikes, like all of us.

Neither judges nor jurors are exempt from life's influences. They developed their basic perceptions of the world and their value systems while they were children, like everyone else. They are influenced by the behavior and attitudes of other people. Moreover, most trial judges had no experience on the bench before the age of thirty-five or forty. It was during the first three or four decades of life that they developed their attitudes about many specific issues.

Most of the important decisions that trial judges and jurors make are influenced by those early life experiences and attitudes and, to a limited extent, their individual personality traits. These influences are part of the mental fabric of judges and jurors that cannot be erased.

Of course, trial judges are expected to mentally dissociate themselves from these natural influences. Trial judges wrestle with these expectations during their tenure on the bench. They are told that the public expects them to make decisions that are not influenced by their personal attitudes. They try to comply, but with varying results.

Different judges address their inner conflicts in different ways. Some judges refuse to recognize that they are influenced by their life experiences and attitudes. Others agree that they hold certain attitudes and have had certain life experiences, but they claim to endeavor not to allow those attitudes and experiences to inappropriately influence their decisions. Still others do not hesitate to agree that their life experiences and attitudes influence their decisions.

In all these ways, judges and jurors are alike. However, they also differ in some ways. Judges are more conditioned to be aware of inappropriate influences from their life experience and attitudes than are jurors. Sometimes they are successful in avoiding these influences; at other times they are not so successful.

In addition, judges must consider the legal aspects of their decisions and try to resolve any conflicts between their perceptions of legal requirements and their perceptions of the moral (justice) requirements in particular circumstances. They need to feel that the positions that trial attorneys advocate are in accordance with legal principles. For this reason, the most powerful arguments to trial judges rely heavily on blending the psychological and legal aspects of the case. Case presentations that do not include both aspects or fail to attempt to resolve any conflicts between legal and moral issues are often doomed to failure.

In other words, trial judges work hard to understand the circumstances of the case and to find the meaning in the case for themselves (just like jurors). One of the focuses of pretrial decision-maker research, therefore, is the successful development of a blended argument or case theory.

One factor regarding trial judges differs from those of jurors, i.e., trial judges are more experienced and sophisticated regarding trial advocacy technique. Your trial presentation at a bench trial must consider this sophistication. On one hand, trial judges are aware of the trial advocacy and persuasion techniques you may be using in your presentation. They are knowledgeable about the basis for your behavior and the reasons why you espouse certain positions on the issues. They have seen this many times before.

On the other hand, however, trial judges have a deep appreciation of professionalism, good trial advocacy technique, and powerful, well-developed case theories. More important, they appreciate your use of well-crafted, descriptive demonstrative aids to help them learn about the facts of the case and your use of powerful psychological messages to help them learn about the compelling human side of your case.

[4]—Trial Advocacy Techniques for Bench Trials and Jury Trials: Similarities and Differences

Despite the subtle differences between trial judges and jurors, there should be no significant differences in the trial advocacy techniques that you would use in persuading a trial judge as compared to a jury. Just like jurors, trial judges must learn the circumstances of the case and make an important decision at the end of trial that should resolve the dispute.

Good trial advocacy technique is part educational and part persuasive. The educational techniques you use to help the trial judge to learn about the case are no different from those that you use with a jury. Indeed, since a trial judge is in effect a jury of one person, he or she needs more help in learning about the case than do twelve people who have more natural resources, i.e., jurors can exchange observations, compare arguments during deliberations, and collectively retain more information about the case.

As we have discussed, there are some differences in the persuasive part of the technique that you would use for a bench trial. First, your position should blend the story of the case with good legal principles. Second, you might consider ways to obtain feedback from the judge that indicates whether he or she is following your case presentation. Generally a judge is ahead of your presentation and might even be bored. However, obtaining regular feedback from the judge and asking for any questions will be helpful to you and to the judge. Third, because trial judges need your respect and deference, you should demonstrate respect subtly and spontaneously.

[5]—Persuasive Techniques for Bench Trials

Since trial judges will view a case from a perspective that draws upon their life experiences both as people and as judges, you would use persuasive techniques in a bench trial that are essentially the same as those you would use in a jury trial. We will divide our discussion into two parts to address the special pet peeves of trial judges and to consider general persuasive techniques.

[a]—Judges' Criticisms of Trial Lawyers

Most trial judges are comfortable sharing their views of how trial lawyers should perform in their courtrooms. They realize that their jobs are made simpler when trial lawyers know the rules of engagement in advance. Following are some of the recommendations that have been made by many judges. Most of these recommendations are applicable to bench trials as well as jury trials:

(1) The biggest complaint of trial judges is that many lawyers do not use court time efficiently. Judges (like a lot of other people) have seen trial lawyers who try to monopolize time in the courtroom and who seem to be unaware of the large amount of time they take to present simple information.

(2) The second biggest complaint is that some lawyers seem to have no clear theory of the case or objectives to be reached.

(3) The third biggest complaint is that some lawyers tend to be unprepared, disorganized, and too verbose. Most judges feel that if a trial lawyer is prepared, he can present the heart of a case efficiently and clearly. They believe that the essence of a case can be stated succinctly in one short, powerful paragraph.

(4) Judges are also concerned that some trial lawyers tend to rely too heavily on technical legalities and deprive the court of any significant emphasis on the human story involved in the case. Although trial judges have an appreciation of good legal arguments, in the course of a bench trial and many important motion hearings, they are often more concerned about the human issues in the case. Sometimes they go out of their way to make you think otherwise.

(5) Trial judges often complain that some trial lawyers are so rigid in their presentations that they do not respond well (or at all) when the judge requests the attorney to emphasize different issues or to behave differently.

(6) Judges complain about redundancy and repetition of facts. Although, like jurors, judges want to be reminded of the themes and the meaning in a case, they do not want to hear the same facts repeated over and over.

(7) Trial judges are becoming increasingly concerned about the lack of civility between trial attorneys in the courtroom. They believe that the lack of courtesy and professionalism is distracting and disrespectful.

(8) Judges are also often concerned that trial lawyers do not consider the court's timetable and the needs of the opposing party when scheduling witnesses. Judges believe that a trial lawyer who wants to change the witness schedule should be more considerate of the court and the opposing party before making last-minute alterations without notice to the court or the opposing party(ies).

(9) Despite decades of complaints by trial judges about the number and subject matter of evidentiary objections, they continue to be frustrated by trial lawyers who either do not state their objections accurately and efficiently or who make needless objections.

(10) Trial judges often feel that trial lawyers are trying to make them experts in the details of complex or technical fact circumstances. They believe some trial lawyers have an obsession with overwhelming detail and with dumping all of that detail on the judge. However, judges want to know just enough about the highlights of the case to know the direction of a case and no more. To force a judge to endure a hailstorm of detailed information can be counterproductive.

[b]—Persuasive Techniques

Persuasive techniques for use in a bench trial are generally the same as those you should consider for use in a jury trial. We discussed many of those techniques in Chapter 2.

However, your most important consideration should be the needs of the particular judge in your case. You should therefore focus the development and presentation of the case on that judge, not simply demonstrate general technique. This will increase your chances of success significantly.

Let us discuss ways to apply this principle.

(1) You might consider taking some time before trial to find out as much as possible about the trial judge and to learn about his or her life experiences, attitudes about specific issues in the case, and the judge's needs in the case. By developing themes and a case presentation that appropriately address these characteristics of a particular judge, you have a better chance of gaining the psychological rapport you need to persuade that judge.

(2) If you present your case in a professional and efficient way, without trying to curry favor or pander to the court, this will be noticed and appreciated by a judge.

(3) You should consider starting out with a powerful, but brief, opening statement that tells a compelling story. Experience and research tell us that speaking for thirty minutes or less is most effective.

(4) It will also help if you develop an awareness of your appearance for being organized and professional. Not only do you want to be prepared in your mind, you want to demonstrate your organization

and clarity by your behavior. Inevitably, something will happen during trial that is unexpected and important. You want to be in a mental position to be able to deal with a crisis and instantly resume your position on a previous point.

(5) Because time management is such an important subject to most trial judges, you should demonstrate sensitivity to this issue by being agreeable (whenever possible) with the court and the opposing attorney regarding exhibits and time constraints. This should prevent a trial judge from unconsciously holding you in disfavor.

(6) Closely akin to general trial time management is witness testimony management. In a bench trial, judges usually feel free to ask any questions they like of a lawyer or witness. If you want to make sure that the judge has no questions or that the judge is not uncertain about something, you might consider advising the judge that the witness will be glad to answer any questions that the judge may have. In addition to such a comment being a respectful gesture, this procedure might stimulate the judge to articulate something about which he or she is unclear. Regardless of the method you use, it is important that the judge's concerns be addressed. One way to do this is to avoid cluttering or diluting a witness examination with unnecessary detail.

(7) Although opening statement and closing argument have different purposes, they must both be persuasive. Trial judges rarely like to be drenched in emotional arguments. However, they do want to understand the human story contained in the circumstances of the case both in opening statement and in closing argument. Just as in the opening statement in a jury trial, you must briefly and clearly explain to the court what the evidence will show, including the human side of the case. In closing argument, you must explain the importance of the evidence that has been demonstrated and put it in the context of the human story. It is usually a mistake to forego telling a powerful story just because the judge appears to be resistant to a presentation that is void of any emotional content.

(8) The use of extensive visual and demonstrative aids is always recommended. Trial judges need as much help as you can give them in understanding the concepts and issues in a case. Because of the intensity of the judge's role in a bench trial, the judge is always interested in some variety in the visual ways cases are presented. It

helps them to maintain interest and avoid some of the mind-numbing experiences that they often undergo in a bench trial.

(9)   As with juries, it is helpful to begin the case presentation before a judge in a bench trial with powerful but general information that summarizes the issues that will be presented next in the case. By moving from general information to specific information, you help the judge to understand the hierarchy of issues with less effort. The easier you make the judge's job, the more appreciated your case presentation will be.

(10) Most trial judges do not like to be thought of as biased or as easy targets for members of one side of the bar. If you feel that you have an advantage with a judge for any reason, it is best to consider your position as disadvantaged and expect that you will have to work even harder to earn a favorable ruling.

A FINAL WORD: WHAT JUDGES AND ARBITRATORS THINK

You may initially view your trial judge or arbitrator as an object of fear, with a personality that is both cold and egotistical. But we view ourselves as a bunch of warm and fuzzy guys and girls, who are genuinely interested in *helping* you get your case resolved fairly.

You will probably do some research on the prior decisions of your trial judge or arbitrator. But don't try to use that information to hit our psychological hot buttons. And don't pander by quoting or fawning over our prior decisions, unless they are really on point. Play it straight, not slanted to a personality.

We look for the same things that all judges do. We want a presentation that is organized, with your objectives clearly recognized and stated, and with arguments and evidence that are direct, simple and clear.

Cut the dramatics. Your judge or arbitrator has undoubtedly had sufficient experience not to be impressed by the emotional or accusatory dramatics which you do so well in a *jury* trial. Indeed, they may backfire because we might conclude that the muddy waters are hiding a shallow bottom.

CONTINUED

Grasp your nettles firmly. Every case has some problems. If everything were one-sided, the case wouldn't even be in litigation. Recognize your problems, admit that they may raise some questions for the judge, and address them in an upfront manner.

Object to procedure and evidence only where absolutely vital. As do juries, we want to see the whole case—warts and all—and feel uncertain if too many objections are made.

Don't forget about damages. Damages are not an add-on for the end of your liability case. They are a vital part of your case. That evidence should be as understandable and as recallable later, as your most important liability bell-ringer. At least at the beginning and the end of your case, tell us precisely what you want a result to be. Don't just say "victory," or even "justice." Spell out the exact judgment you want us to enter.

Prepare for trial or arbitration backwards. It is a great organizer and simplifier. That is, first draft the judgment you want us to enter. Then, prepare an outline of your final argument that will get you that judgment. Then, outline the legal elements of your case you are going to integrate into that argument. Then, and only then, organize the evidence that will support your argument. In that way you will sort out a lot of the evidence as being useless to the end result, and it you will just focus on that which will get you your judgment.

Welcome, don't resist, questions from the bench. Answer them immediately and directly. Even if you have a full response prepared for later, give us the short-hand answer that foreshadows it.

If you have time problems, either in the presentation of your evidence or the date by which a decision must be made, let us know early. We will do our best to accommodate.

What do you want the *form* of our decision to be? Is a verbal (albeit on the record) thumbs-up or thumbs-down enough? Is a memorandum opinion needed by you and your client? Or do you

---

CONTINUED

require formal and detailed findings of fact and conclusions of law? If you need the findings and conclusions, help us out by submitting your own draft. Whether we ultimately agree with them or not, you will have our undying gratitude for having simplified that job.

Finally, by way of client relations, let your client come to see us. Have the client present for at least part of the trial or arbitration. This is not to impress us by your client's presence, but to assist you in dealing with your client, who will then have seen the decision maker in action.

— Hon. Charles A. Legge, Judge (Ret.)
United States District Court, Northern District of California
Judicial Arbitration and Mediation Service (JAMS),
San Francisco

---

§ 7.04 | REFERENCES

Gafni, "Gafni on Advocacy in Non-Jury Trials" (Harrisburg, PA: Pennsylvania Bar Institute, 1992).

Hochstein, *If It Pleases Their Honors* (New York: New Books, 1988).

Lempert, "Civil Juries and Complex Cases: Let's Not Rush to Judgment," 80 Michigan L. Rev. 68 (1981). Reprinted in part in Monahan & Walker, *Social Science in Law: Cases and Materials* (New York: Foundation Press, 1985). Also reprinted in part in Levine, Doernberg & Nelken, *Civil Procedure Anthology* (Cincinnati: Anderson Publishing Co., 1998).

Lind, *Logic and Legal Reasoning* (Reno, NV: National Judicial College Press, 2001).

National Center for State Courts, http://www.ncsconline.org/index.html.

National Conference of State Trial Judges, *The Judge's Book*, 2d ed. (Reno, NV: National Judicial College Press, 1994).

Smithburn, *Judicial Discretion* (Reno, NV: National Judicial College Press, 1991).

CHAPTER 8

Making the Choice: Arbitration, Bench Trial, or Jury Trial

CHAPTER CONTENTS

"I was married by a judge. I should have asked for a jury."

– Groucho Marx (1895-1977)

§ 8.01 | INTRODUCTION

Making a choice among a jury trial, a bench trial, and an arbitration hearing has been a time-honored crapshoot for most trial lawyers. One day we may hear or read something that causes us to lean in one direction, only to learn other information the next day that causes us to think differently. Each of us has dealt with this choice in the past by using the best information and intuition we can muster although we may continue to wonder if we made the correct choice.

Perhaps one of the best lessons we can learn from listening to others and reading other people's opinions about choosing a forum is not to believe everything you hear or read. An independent investigation and some creative thinking are likely to improve the quality of your decision considerably.

In this chapter we will discuss how to supplement your intuition with some reliable research information and a method for making a more objective decision. This chapter will not teach you which choice you might make in a particular case. Every case is different and every decision maker is different.

Because some readers feel more comfortable making important decisions on the run whereas others prefer taking more time to organize their thoughts, this chapter is designed to meet the needs of both groups. The next two sections in this chapter contain information that will likely be of interest to everyone. The fourth section provides some ideas about organizing information that is necessary to make your choice.

§ 8.02 | DECISION-MAKING CHARACTERISTICS OF VARIOUS FACT FINDERS

These days we have a great deal of information about decision makers based upon experience and recent research. Let's examine some of that information as we take a closer look at the characteristics of jurors, judges, and arbitrators.

[1]—Jurors

The characteristics of all decision makers, including jurors, may be divided into five categories:

+ Attitudes about specific issues in the case,
+ Relevant life experiences,
+ Relevant personality traits,
+ General values and beliefs, and
+ Demographics.

These particular categories seem to contain information about the characteristics of the decision makers that would most likely influence their decisions.

Because a jury consists of six to twelve people, there will be a wide array of individual characteristics that must be considered. For purposes of making important decisions about whether to take a case to a jury trial, you would probably want to consider the characteristics of the "average" jury in the venue of the case. (When conducting jury research, we generally base our selection of research participants in mock jury panels on this "average "jury concept. We then add research jurors who possess extreme attitudes and other unusual characteristics that often surface within juries in that same venue.)

From the study of social psychology and other fields of behavioral science, we have learned that it is possible to identify and study the perceptions of any group of human beings by studying the mental processes of a representative group of people from the larger group.

In the case of jurors, we have studied the perceptions of jury populations all over the United States by studying the perceptions of a representative sample of people from those populations. As a result, we have learned a great deal about how jurors make decisions in many different circumstances.

Although there are individual juror characteristics to consider in designing the case theory and themes for a case, the jury group also has its own characteristics that are more relevant for the choice between the jury trial, a bench trial, or an arbitration hearing. By definition, for example, juries are a group of people who are appointed to gather information as a group and make a group decision. Their job, in other words, is to work together to learn about a case and make a consensual decision.

As we discussed in Chapter 3, jurors begin the decision-making process by applying their individual efforts and perceptions at the beginning of trial.

Throughout the trial, the jurors try to understand the human story involved in the case and make a decision that they believe is morally and socially appropriate.

As they become more socialized to each other and to the case, they begin to share ideas and opinions that ultimately are incorporated in a decision or verdict during deliberations. The individual perceptions, particularly those of the opinion-makers on the panel, will greatly influence the outcome.

The consensus building part of jury trials is relevant to this chapter. We have been able to conclude that juries are *somewhat predictable* and that *their decisions tend to be moderated* by the opposing views of other jurors who hold conflicting views.

The danger with juries seems to arise most often when we are not aware that individual jurors possess certain attitudes or perceptions about the case. It is possible that if we knew about the key attitudes and perceptions of jurors in a particular case in advance of trial, there would be less danger of an adverse verdict.

There is often a fear of uncertainty about juries that causes attorneys and their clients to be more concerned about juries than about judges or arbitrators. In other chapters we have discussed the results of substantial scientific studies that indicate that most of the fears that people have about juries are based upon poor sources of information.

As a result, the decision whether or not to take a case to a jury trial should be based upon objective information rather than upon unsubstantiated speculation.

[2]—Judges

A bench trial has one juror, the trial judge. In Chapter 7 we discussed how important it is to understand that the judge in a bench trial must understand the human side of the story and how your perception of the case comports with the law of the jurisdiction.

Trial judges are subject to the same influences as jurors, although they try to moderate their attitudes and recollections of life experiences in order to make a more "objective" decision. Different trial judges experience varying degrees of success in tempering their natural influences.

We know from experience and research that trial judges work exceptionally hard to understand a case and make a decision that they believe is fair and just.

Because a judge is a jury of one person, he or she needs as much help as possible in understanding the circumstances of a case.

By definition, the decision of a trial judge is moderated only by his or her own perceptions of the case, the law, and the appropriate outcome. For this reason, researchers have found that the decisions of trial judges are *less predictable* than those of juries and *not subject to the moderating influences* that occur within a group of jurors.

There are two ways to study the decision-making possibilities of a particular judge. One is to study the decision-making patterns of the sitting judge with regard to similar issues that he or she has encountered in past cases. Another is to study the perceptions and mental processes of other judges who have characteristics that are similar to those of the sitting judge in a particular case. We discussed this kind of research in Chapter 6.

[3]—Arbitrators

Arbitration panels are essentially juries of three or more selected professional people who may or may not have some expertise in the subject matter of the case. Most panels consist of two arbitrators who were chosen by the opposing parties separately and a third arbitrator who was chosen by the two other arbitrators, or because he or she is a disinterested person, or by some other previously agreed upon procedure.

Most arbitration panels include accountants, attorneys, doctors, stockbrokers, or others who may specialize in the subject matter of the case. Because they are professional people, information about their personal characteristics (attitudes about specific issues in the case, relevant life experiences, personality traits, general values and beliefs, and demographics) are likely to be more available for study than when the fact finders are either judges or jurors.

Arbitrators tend to view themselves as having the same kind of power that a trial judge might have. They generally work hard to understand a case and reach a decision that they believe is fair and just. In this respect, they want to make a decision that makes them feel good about themselves, as do judges and juries.

Because arbitrators make up a decision-making group, they often take on some of the same characteristics as a jury. You might even refer to an arbitration panel as a "professional jury." As a result, arbitrators usually tend to make decisions based upon their individual perceptions that later become socialized as they share ideas and insights with each other. Arbitrators, like jurors, make consensual decisions that are the result of the moderated input of all members of the arbitration panel. Their decisions tend to be *less predictable* than those of juries and *less moderated* than those of juries.

Although some attorneys or clients may believe that a panel of professional arbitrators will be favorable to one position, this assumption should be made with caution and should be tested before it is relied upon. Arbitrators who are familiar with the subject matter of a case will consider themselves to be instant experts in the case. They will apply their own experience and frame of reference in the case, which may differ from those of your client.

Because we have access to information about the individual characteristics of arbitrators, we have good opportunities to study the likely perceptions of a particular arbitration panel. We can study previous decisions by the arbitrators in similar cases, and we can study the perceptions of other people who have personal characteristics that are identical or similar to those of the sitting arbitrators.

§ 8.03 | COMPARISONS OF DECISION-MAKING PATTERNS

When we draw upon the resources available to us through experience and research, we can compare the decision-making patterns of juries, judges, and arbitrators by the use of the same criteria. Because cases and individual decision makers vary so much, it is difficult to measure or predict the likely decisions that juries, judges, and arbitrators will make in particular cases. However, the information that we have at our disposal is quite interesting.

[1]—Judge vs. Jury Decisions

Of the three kinds of decision makers, jurors are generally more predictable than either judges or arbitrators. Even though there is variability between juries even in cases with similar circumstances, there appears to be even more variability between judges' decisions. Studies of judge decisions in trial and on appeal indicate that there is substantial disagreement among judges on both matters of fact and matters of law.[1] One such study of United States Supreme

---

[1] Diamond, "Order in the Court: Consistency in Criminal Court Decisions," in Scheirer & Hammonds, eds., *Psychology and the Law,* Vol. 2 of *The Master Lecture Series,* pp. 123-146 (Washington, D.C.: American Psychological Association, 1993)

Court opinions indicated that 60% of the Court's opinions from 1953 through 1990 were not unanimous.[2]

Today's popular wisdom seems to support the notion that juries are generally more pro-plaintiff than pro-defendant. However, in fact there is no scientific research support for the proposition that juries are more favorable toward plaintiffs than judges.[3]

There are a number of interesting, reliable studies indicating that there is little variation between the decisions that judges and jurors would make in the same civil case. In one of the earliest studies comparing the decisions of judges and juries, researchers who studied cases dating from the 1950s to the early 1960s found that judges and juries found for plaintiffs and defendants in the same ratios.[4]

Another study, conducted in Arizona in 1998, focused on how often judges and juries agreed in cases where corporations and businesses were defendants.[5] The results of the study indicated that juries were no more likely to find for a plaintiff under such circumstances than were trial judges.

Other research has compared damage awards of judges and juries. We know from this research that juries struggle with questions of whether to award non-economic damages and how to determine the size of any award. Jurors are given little if any guidance about how to measure damages. Of course, judges and legal professionals are more familiar than juries with amounts awarded in previous verdicts and the "going rate" for different types of damages. Because of jurors' lack of such knowledge, there is great variability in the amounts that individual jurors would award in specific cases.

Based upon our understanding that judges have more information about previous verdicts, we might conclude that judges generally award less money than juries do. In particular, we might conclude that judges' awards for non-economic damages would be lower than those of juries.

However, published studies which have compared the awards of arbitrators, trial judges, and juries have concluded that, of the three, juries typically award less money than either arbitrators or judges, even though the

---

[2] Hensley & Scott, "Unanimity on the Rehnquist Court," 31 Akron L. Rev. 387-408 (1998).

[3] Hans, *Business on Trial: The Civil Jury and Corporate Responsibility* (New Haven: Yale University Press, 2000).

[4] Kalven & Zeisel, *The American Jury* (Boston: Little, Brown, 1966).

[5] Hans, "Illusions and Realities in Jurors' Treatment of Corporate Defendants," 48 DePaul L. Rev. 327-353 (1998).

differences are not statistically significant. One such study compared the decisions of arbitrators, trial judges, and jurors in medical malpractice cases.[6]

Aside from scientific studies as an aid to understanding jury verdicts, it is common for trial judges to invite juries to visit with them to discuss the case at the conclusion of trial. Comments made by many of these trial judges on and off the record often indicate their understanding and agreement with a jury's thinking.

Of course, these statistical studies do not take into account specific trial judges and specific circumstances. There may well be times when the decision of a particular judge regarding a particular kind of case can be predicted. However, those situations appear to be the exception.

Trial judges often indicate that they will make special efforts not to favor people with whom they have had previous associations. The circumstances of each relationship with a trial judge are relevant and should be taken into consideration. However, nothing should ever be taken for granted when you try a case to either a judge or a jury.

If it is true, then, that in most circumstances the decision of a judge and a jury would be similar, why would a party elect a bench trial rather than a jury trial? In most cases such a decision depends upon how much reliance a party wishes to make on the law of the case as opposed to the factual evidence. Trial judges are trained to understand the letter of the law and to uphold legal principles. Juries want to abide by the law in most circumstances, but they often do not have a clear understanding of what the law is or how to uphold it. Therefore, if you believe that someone with a better understanding of the law would be more likely to find in your favor, you might consider a bench trial over a jury trial.

Aside from statistical and experiential information, most practitioners seem to believe that bench trials take less time than jury trials. Therefore, the former may be more economical.

[2]—Arbitration Panels and Professional Panels vs. Jury Decisions

Conventional wisdom seems to hold that the decisions of arbitrators or professional panels are more predictable and conservative than the decisions of

---

[6] Vidmar, *Medical Malpractice and the American Jury: Confronting Myths about Jury Incompetence, Deep Pockets, and Outrageous Damage Awards,* at 224-225 (Ann Arbor: University of Michigan Press, 1997).

juries. However, if you have ever tried a case before an arbitration panel or panel of professionals and received a decision, you might disagree with conventional wisdom.

Recall our discussion about the similarities and differences in the perceptions of jurors and arbitrators. Those similarities and differences generally boil down to comparisons between characteristics of the two types of decision makers (i.e., their attitudes about specific issues in a case, relevant life experiences, general values and beliefs, and demographics). Our working hypothesis is, therefore, that people with similar characteristics will be operating under similar influences and, as a result, will make similar decisions.

The effect is that when arbitrators and jurors have similar characteristics, they will make similar decisions. If arbitrators have fundamental differences from jurors in their perceptions of the circumstances of a case, they will likely come to a different conclusion from jurors. We should therefore ask whether arbitrators have fundamental differences from jurors in the way they view the stories and circumstances of human beings who engage in disputes that come before them.

Fortunately, we have several helpful scientific studies that have compared the decisions of arbitrators, professional panels, and juries. Neil Vidmar, professor of psychology at Duke University, and a team of research scientists conducted a review of some of these studies.[7] Vidmar's research was conducted in the context of medical malpractice. His research team compared the decisions of medical panels (comprised of doctors), legal panels (comprised of lawyers), and juries in similar cases.

As part of his research, he reviewed the data collected in a study of New Jersey malpractice cases conducted by Mark Taragin and another team of research scientists.[8] This data included 8,231 malpractice claims that were made between 1977 and 1992. With respect to each of the case files, an insurance company (New Jersey Medical Insurance Exchange) reviewed the claim and made an internal assessment to determine whether the doctor's behavior was in accordance with the necessary standards of medical care. The assessment was based exclusively on medical criteria, not on litigation or legal concerns.

---

[7] Vidmar, *id.*

[8] Taragin, Willet, Wilczek, Trout & Carson, "The Influence of Standard of Care and Severity of Injury on the Resolution of Medical Malpractice Claims," 117 Annals of Internal Medicine 780-784 (1992).

Taragin's team of researchers used the same assessment classifications that the insurance company used for each of the 8,231 cases. They were classified as indefensible, defensible, or unclear. Whenever an insured physician agreed that physician error had occurred, the claim was classified as indefensible. If the physician claimed that no error had occurred, the insurance company sent the file to an independent physician or panel of physicians for review and classification as indefensible, defensible, or unclear. After completing the analysis, it was determined that 62% of the cases were classified as defensible, 25% were classified as indefensible, and 13% were classified as unclear. The research team then further divided the cases into categories according to the severity of the injuries that the plaintiff or claimant alleged.

Twelve percent of the total number of claims had also been decided by a jury. Of the claims that proceeded to a jury trial, 15% were classified as defensible, 5% were classified as indefensible, and 10% were classified as unclear. In the cases that proceeded to a jury trial, the awards ranged from $3,281 to $2,576,377. The median award was $114,170.

In Taragin's study, the researchers found a positive and significant correlation between the jury verdicts and the assessments of the neutral physicians who had reviewed the claims.[9] In other words, the neutral physicians and the jurors *agreed* most of the time. However, no correlation was found between the severity of a plaintiff's injury and the probability that a plaintiff would win the case with a jury. This would indicate that jurors did not determine liability just because a plaintiff's injury was severe.

In other studies, Vidmar compared the decisions of legal professionals with those of juries.[10] Overall, there was *no statistical difference* in how legal professionals and jurors perceived particular case circumstances. This was true for both liability and damages issues.

Another study was conducted by Donald Wittman of the Economics Department at the University of California at Santa Cruz. Note that California courts must provide official court-sponsored arbitration in certain kinds of cases. Hence, in essence, before such a case can be tried to a jury it must be tried to an arbitration panel. The arbitration decision is not binding.

Wittman's study reviewed a number of questions, including, "How do the decisions made by arbitrators compare to the decisions made by juries?" To

---

[9] *Id.*

[10] Vidmar, N. 6 *supra* at 221-235.

answer this question, the researchers reviewed the decisions made by professional arbitrators and juries in 380 automobile accident cases that were tried in California over a nine-year period. The results of the trials had been published in a California periodical *Jury Verdicts Weekly*. The researchers studied the average awards, the percentage of plaintiff verdicts, and possible explanations for any variances.

The results of this study are consistent with the studies of other researchers who have compared the decisions of arbitration panels and juries. Wittman found that arbitrators ruled in favor of the plaintiff 98% of the time, whereas juries ruled in favor of the plaintiff 73% of the time.[11] In addition, the average arbitration verdict was $22,521, whereas the average jury verdict was $19,227. In other words, arbitration verdicts were on average 17% higher than jury verdicts.[12]

In statistical terms, the correlation between jury awards and arbitration awards in Professor Wittman's study was 74%. This means that a jury award and an arbitration award would be the same 74% of the time. The data from the study also indicate that 26% of the time, the arbitration award would be *higher or much higher* than a jury verdict.

The differences in the decisions between arbitrators and juries may be understood in a number of ways. For better or worse, we have kept some cases away from juries. From an advocate's point of view, it might appear that the client would fare better with arbitrators in some instances since they are a panel of professional people who are familiar with the subject matter of the case. Before relying on this hypothesis, however, we must undertake a more detailed review of the actual arbitrators' characteristics; moreover, a consideration of the arbitrators' perceptions in a case would also be advisable.

[3]—Arbitration Panels vs. Judge Decisions

One of the apparent advantages of an arbitration panel over a bench trial may relate to the issue of foreseeability of outcome. You can select arbitrators, but not judges. However, you can generally only select one of three arbitrators. The

---

[11] Wittman, "Lay Juries, Professional Arbitrators and the Arbitrator Selection Hypothesis," Amer. L. & Economics Rev. (forthcoming 2003). Also available at www.econ.ucsc.edu/faculty/wittman/arbitrsjury.pdf.

[12] *Id.*

opposing party can select one. A more objective process generally selects the remaining arbitrator.

Nevertheless, research indicates that the decisions of arbitrators are *just as variable* as those of trial judges and *less predictable* than the decisions of juries. Even though arbitrators may have some professional experience or expertise in a matter similar to your case, there is no assurance that their perceptions of the human story in your case will coincide with yours.

One of the advantages of arbitration panels may be the arbitrators' expertise in the subject matter of the case. However, this "advantage" only means that the arbitrators will be more likely to understand the subject matter. It does not mean that you will have to work less hard to present your case and tell the human story. Arbitrators, like other fact finders, want to make decisions in a case which they believe fits with their view of the world and makes them feel good about themselves.

There are other advantages to arbitrations that will be important to some litigants. One of these is the certainty of an outcome and resolution of the matter. This advantage is not available when cases are taken before a judge or jury. Arbitrations can be scheduled at any time the parties can agree rather than waiting for a court date to become available. Also, arbitration procedure is usually more relaxed than trial procedure. Certainly, arbitration offers many other advantages that should be considered before making a decision.

One of the disadvantages of arbitration is that there is still a significant risk of losing despite the more relaxed environment. Moreover, if you lose, your clients will have no appellate remedy, unlike a courtroom resolution where trial judges have someone looking over their shoulder.

§ 8.04 | Deciding among an Arbitration Panel, a Trial Judge, and a Jury

One of the important contributions that science has made to trial advocacy is the ability to better organize our information-gathering systems and structure our decision-making process so that we maximize our results. At the same time, however, being better organized does not always mean that our decisions are any different or any better than if we relied upon old-fashioned intuition. Nevertheless, sometimes we make better decisions when we spend more time gathering relevant information and organizing our thinking.

As lawyers and scholars, we take pride in the quality of our decisions. Sometimes we take exception to anyone who suggests that our decision-making processes are not very rational. At other times we take pride in our decisions even though we realize they may not be rational.

Curiously, although a number of the most important decisions we make in life are notoriously irrational, most of us manage somehow to live full, successful lives. Some of our most celebrated, irrational decisions include whom to marry, what career to follow, what house to live in, and whether to have children.

One could argue, of course, that we expect those important choices to be based mostly on intuition. And yet, clients expect us to make thorough, completely rational choices before making important decisions or recommendations in their cases. The more sophisticated our clients, the more they expect us to use objective methods as part of our decision-making process.

There are many seminars and treatises on the subject of making good decisions in business situations. In this chapter we will not discuss all of the methods that different authors or scholars promote even though we would all likely benefit from more research on this topic.

Nevertheless, we shall discuss one general method that has been helpful in making many different kinds of decisions in trial advocacy. Psychologists refer to this method as the "rational decision-making method."

In this section, we will apply some of the principles that we have learned using this method to choose a decision maker.

[1]—The Process of Making Decisions

Following is the basic decision-making model. It may look complicated, but it is not. It is actually quite simple. The model structures the decision-making process in an order that you have probably been using for years.

Try using it just once. Letting yourself experience the process will help you to see what you might have been missing. Moreover, after you try this process you may decide to adapt it to your own operations method.

MAKING THE CHOICE OF DECISION MAKER

STEP 1.   List the alternatives.

STEP 2.   Identify the criteria you will use.

STEP 3.   Assign a weight to each criterion.

STEP 4.   Develop information for each alternative (as objectively as possible).

STEP 5.   Evaluate the information for each criterion and each alternative (e.g., determine if each piece of information is "favorable" or "unfavorable" on a 1-to-10 scale).

STEP 6.   Select the best course of action.

---

[2]—Assumptions for Making Rational Decisions

There are a number of assumptions to consider before we start the process of making an important decision. At the risk of repeating what you probably learned in basic science, we will list general assumptions that may be important to you. They include:

(1) The overall goals and objectives have been clearly defined.

(2) The question, problem, or choice must be clear and unambiguous.

(3) The options (arbitration, bench trial, or jury trial) must be known. You can identify all the relevant criteria and list all the viable alternatives. You must be aware of all the possible consequences of each alternative.

(4) The criteria and alternatives can be ranked and weighted to reflect their importance.

(5) The preferences must be constant. The decision criteria are constant, and the values assigned to them are stable over time.

(6) Eligible decision criteria must theoretically include all known criteria. The decision maker should therefore include all criteria known to him or her for consideration. Criteria should not be avoided arbitrarily. Criteria should be stated as specifically as possible and should be clear to observers.

(7) There must be no time or cost constraints on the decision-making process itself.
(8) Maximum results must be preferred. You must choose the alternative that promises to yield the highest perceived value.

(*Caveat:* Information gained later in the process or trial may cause the criteria, weight, or evaluation of each alternative to change.)

[3]—Developing the Criteria

Developing the criteria to use in your comparison between the different decision makers is easy. However, the criteria that you use must be the same for each of the alternatives that you are considering. Here are a few of them:

- *The facts of the case;*
- *Characteristics of the fact witnesses;*
- *Characteristics of the experts;*
- *Admissible vs. inadmissible evidence;*
- *Characteristics of the decision makers;*
- *Outcome of decision-maker research;*
- *Appeal of the case theory and themes to decision makers;*
- *Amount of attorneys' fees;*
- *Other litigation costs;*
- *Range of a likely verdict;*
- *Likelihood of favorable results (liability and damages);*
- *Time availability; and*
- *Chance of success on appeal.*

[4]—Gathering Information About Fact Finders

Gathering the information to determine how each of the alternative decision makers will rate within each of the criteria requires some work and some intuition. Once you clearly define the answer for each criterion and each of the decision makers, you still might want to use your best guess about how particular decision makers will view the case within each criterion.

For example, you might be trying to choose between a bench trial and a jury trial. To make a more objective decision, you would gather information about the trial judge and about a likely jury regarding each of the criteria that you think is important. If the first criterion is how the decision makers will perceive the facts of the case, you would want to find out how the trial judge and a likely jury would look at those facts. If the second criterion is how the decision makers will view the characteristics of the fact witnesses, you want to find out that information.

Your assessment of how the alternative decision makers will perceive each criterion may be based upon your best guess or it may be based upon research that you have conducted. The time and resources available to you will often dictate the amount and reliability of the information that you receive.

Given a choice, however, you will likely prefer to have information that is more objective than your intuition. One of the advantages to scientific judge or jury research is that you collect objective, reliable data upon which to make such important decisions.

[5]—Comparing the Data

After you have collected the information that is relevant to each of the criteria, it is helpful to have a concise, well-organized format for summarizing the information and comparing the two alternative sets of decision makers according to the same criteria.

While we are experimenting with new ways to organize information, perhaps we can come up with a format—a table actually—to use for summarizing what we learn. If you prepare a table like the one that follows for each of the types of decision makers you are considering, you can compare each of them to the other more directly.

Decision Criteria	Weight (Percentage)[13]	Evaluation for Each Alternative (1-to-10 Scale)[14]	Score
1. The facts of the case.			
2. Admissible vs. inadmissible evidence.			
3. Characteristics/effectiveness of fact witnesses.			
4. Characteristics/effectiveness of expert witnesses.			
5. Remedy being sought (damages or other remedy).			
6. Likely range of verdict.			
7. Chance of receiving a judgment in your favor.			
8. Chance of success on appeal.			
9. Chance of collecting a judgment.			
10. Chances of prevailing on the legal issues.			
11. Characteristics of the likely decision maker(s).			
12. Themes and story that will most likely persuade the decision maker (judge, jury, arbitrator, etc.).			
13. Results of decision-maker research.			
14. Cost or expenses involved.			
15. Others.			
	(Total) 100%	/////////////	Total:[15]

[13] Indicates the percentage of influence the criterion has on the decision to be made.

[14] Indicates the attorney's and client's perceptions of how much the information obtained relating to these criteria favors the client's position. "1" = "Unfavorable" and "10" = "Favorable."

[15] Favorability rating for this alternative (1-to-10 scale).

A FINAL WORD: ADVOCACY IN ARBITRATION

Arbitration agreements appear frequently in all types of contracts and are a fact of life in most litigation disputes. Lawyers should keep a few tips in mind as they handle arbitration disputes.

1. Know thy arbitrators and your tribunal. Know what type of expertise you need in an arbitrator and the procedure for selecting him. Does each side select an arbitrator favorable to it and then a neutral? Is the arbitrator an industry or subject matter expert?

2. Develop a theme. Arbitrators are no different than judges or juries and relate to a compelling story.

3. Keep it simple. Develop those complex agreements and issues so that they are more easily understood.

4. Use opening and closing arguments as a way to explain the case and summarize evidence.

5. Develop a strategy for resolving legal issues such as statutes of limitations and the application of damage or warranty limitation provisions. If there are issues subject to summary judgment or limine, alert the arbitrators that they must be resolved prior to other issues. Be prepared to explain how the resolution of legal issues impacts the case.

6. On multi-arbitrator panels, use the expertise of the arbitrators to help you carry the issues on your case. Lawyers can assist with procedural and evidentiary issues. Industry experts can assist the other arbitrators in understanding the industry or subject matter issues as they relate to your client. Present that case so that both the lawyer and non-lawyer arbitrators understand the issues.

7. Understand the "people" aspects in any arbitration. Arbitrators are people and may feel quite differently about a business dispute between commercial giants than an employment dispute that impacts a single employee.

CONTINUED

8. Demonstrative aids can greatly assist arbitrators in reviewing voluminous or complex information. Use them, but don't overdo it, especially in certain employment and consumer cases

9. Don't be surprised when arbitrators ask direct questions to you or the witness. Answer them directly and persuasively. Questions often provide an opportunity for the lawyers to evaluate how an arbitrator may be viewing a particular issue. Decide whether the arbitrator raised an issue that you should later address through witnesses or argument.

10. Lawyers and the witnesses should be "teachers" in many complex arbitrations. Teaching can help you to win.

— Kim J. Askew, Partner
Hughes & Luce LLP

---

§ 8.05 | REFERENCES

Aronson, Rovella & Van Voris, "Jurors: A Biased, Independent Lot," The National Law Journal, pp. A1, A24-A25 (Nov. 2, 1998).

Feigenson, Park & Salovey, "Effect of Blameworthiness and Outcome Severity on Attributions of Responsibility and Damage Awards in Comparative Negligence Cases," 21 Law & Human Behavior 597-617 (1997).

Hans, "Attitudes Toward Corporate Responsibility," Nebraska L. Rev. 69, 158-189 (1990).

Hans, *Business on Trial: The Civil Jury and Corporate Responsibility* (New Haven: Yale University Press, 2000).

Vidmar, *Medical Malpractice and the American Jury: Confronting Myths about Jury Incompetence, Deep Pockets, and Outrageous Damage Awards* (Ann Arbor: University of Michigan Press, 1997).

CHAPTER 9

Pretrial Publicity

CHAPTER CONTENTS

"I don't care what is written about me so long as it isn't true."

– Katharine Hepburn

§ 9.01 | INTRODUCTION

Twenty years ago the only pretrial publicity that most trial attorneys experienced was an occasional mention of a case buried deep in the local newspaper. But times have changed. With the advent of faster communications and Web-based news sites, news organizations find out about court trials more rapidly and can arrive at the scene or in your office within minutes. It is common for trial attorneys everywhere to find themselves being interviewed by a news reporter in person or even in front of a television camera.

What does pretrial publicity have to do with trial advocacy and psychology? In a word, everything. Jurors are often greatly affected by the information concerning cases that they receive from news and media sources. Although people in the media do not generally cause attitudes to be formed, they often frame the discussion and select the issues to be discussed. For these reasons, a trial attorney would be wise to understand the effects of pretrial publicity on judges and jurors and develop communication skills to influence the media in his client's favor.

Often the publicity surrounding a trial is chaotic. News organizations pay thousands of dollars for private interviews with witnesses and litigants. Sometimes people who have an interest in the litigation make overt efforts to control the outcome of the case in the public domain. Some people will even "try" their cases in the news media. In many of these situations there are no controls over either content of or participation in media coverage other than professional obligations of attorneys and occasional court orders.

To the media and the public, the trial and attendant circumstances are news. However, to a trial team and client, the coverage is publicity, whether positive or negative. This chapter will examine both how pretrial publicity can affect a juror's perspective and how to influence that publicity. After all, as trial advocates we know that there are many ways to tell a story.

§ 9.02 | THE EFFECTS OF PRETRIAL
         PUBLICITY IN TRIAL

The criminal trial of John Wayne Bobbitt in 1993 in Manassas, Virginia, offers us a good place to begin our discussion. Prior to the trial, a criminal charge of malicious wounding had been made by John Bobbitt against his estranged wife Lorena for cutting off his penis following what Lorena claimed was a series of assaults and rapes by her husband. (The penis was immediately surgically reattached.) Mr. Bobbitt and his attorney felt compelled to respond to the accusations of domestic violence made against him in the press by his wife, who had been found not guilty in the same court of the charge against her by reason of temporary insanity (due to an "irresistible impulse"). The media accounts of Mrs. Bobbitt's statements were carried nationwide. The subject of the rape trial became front-page news (as had Mrs. Bobbitt's trial) in almost every newspaper, television station, and news Web site in the United States. The accusations against Mr. Bobbitt became the subject of scorn by support groups for victims of domestic violence, and the rights of the accused and accuser were discussed, often with contempt and/or amusement, in editorials and columns in national and legal publications.

Mr. Bobbitt's trial team had no money for a media consultant. They had to rely on their traditional skills as attorneys to try to contain any damage in an effort to protect their client's rights to a fair trial. Regardless, the media was having a field day framing the issues in the case.

During jury selection, Mr. Bobbitt's lead trial attorney carefully asked each of the jurors if they had experienced any domestic violence problems. Jurors who expressed problems were dismissed and the trial proceeded. After the trial was over, two of the trial jurors revealed that they had been domestic violence victims. When asked why they had lied, they said that they just wanted to be on the jury.

Although this episode will not surprise most experienced trial attorneys, we are left wondering how the extensive pretrial publicity affected the jurors who actually sat on the case, but did not or could not admit that they had been affected by the publicity. Let's begin our discussion with a review of available research and reliable information about the effect of pretrial publicity.

[1]—How We Study the Effects of Pretrial Publicity

Over the past forty years, social scientists have studied the effects of pretrial publicity, and have found justification for concern by courts and litigants.

Information contained in pretrial publicity has been found to influence the following factors for jurors: (1) their evaluations of a litigant's likeability, (2) their sympathy for a litigant, (3) their perceptions of a litigant's culpability, and, of course, (4) the final jury decisions. Field surveys and experimental studies (under controlled conditions) have been used to study these effects.

In field surveys, actual and potential jurors have been used to examine the effects of pretrial publicity on a juror's judgments about actual cases. Typically, participants in the surveys are asked how many news sources they had been exposed to and how often they were exposed. They are asked to recall or recognize information about specific cases and to evaluate the persuasiveness of the arguments made by both parties and the likelihood of a defendant or respondent's culpability.[1] In these types of studies, researchers tried to identify any correlations between the extent of pretrial publicity to which an individual juror was exposed and the extent and nature of that juror's prejudgment about the case.

Field studies are sometimes used to support a motion for change of venue. Because of the speed with which information is available and the saturation of our culture with news outlets, frequently large numbers of people in a potential jury pool are familiar with many of the facts or allegations in particular court cases. As a result, some people may have formed preliminary opinions about the case, depending upon a number of factors.

One interesting study was conducted by Gary Moran and Brian Cutler, two of the most experienced jury research scientists in the United States.[2] In this study, the researchers surveyed 704 potential jurors regarding their knowledge of information that involved the investigation, arrest, and indictment of defendants in two unrelated cases. The first case involved the distribution of large quantities of marijuana, and the second involved the murder of a police officer in a drug sting operation. The study was conducted following a year of regular newspaper coverage about each case. The researchers asked the jurors about their knowledge of each case, their general attitudes about crime, and their attitudes about each particular case.

---

[1] In order to assure that respondents are being truthful or accurate, researchers will sometimes include bogus questions or items of information that were not part of the actual case.

[2] Moran & Cutler, "The Prejudicial Impact of Pretrial Publicity," 21 J. Applied Social Psychology 345-367 (1991).

The studies revealed that pretrial knowledge of either case was related to prejudgment about that case. In addition, researchers found that the proportion of the research jurors who said there was "a lot of evidence" against a defendant increased as the amount of information about the case that a juror could recall increased. Furthermore, there was a significant correlation between a juror's knowledge of the case specifics and that juror's perceived culpability of one or more of the defendants. However, jurors were not willing to admit partiality or bias.

As a result, the researchers ultimately concluded that even modest amounts of pretrial publicity might prejudice potential jurors, and that self-reports of a juror's impartiality were not reliable.

Experimental studies typically use a controlled environment to expose a research juror to a specific quantity and type of real or simulated pretrial "publicity," followed by a trial presentation which may or may not discuss the same issues as those stated in the "publicity." Analysis of the results focuses on the effects of the type and amount of pretrial publicity on jurors' perceptions of the litigants, evaluations of the evidence, and verdict decisions.

The perfect experiment would be to present actual jurors in trial with a pretrial questionnaire about their knowledge of the case, their attitudes about information they learned from pretrial publicity, and their pretrial assessments of litigants and issues in the case. During the trial and after the trial is over, jurors would be asked about their assessments of the litigants, their counsel, the witnesses, and the evidence. The jury would then deliberate and reach individual and group decisions about the case. Afterwards, researchers would look for any correlations between pretrial characteristics of the jurors' perceptions, their processing of the evidence, and their verdicts. Of course, interruption of an actual case to gather these impressions could skew the outcome and, in any event, would not be tolerated by the court or the parties.

These types of experimental studies are currently being used by litigants prior to jury trials and arbitrations. By choosing a representative sample from the likely jury population or mock arbitrators to correspond to the actual arbitrators, litigants are able to understand the effects of pretrial publicity prior to trial and to develop strategies to deal with their situations.

One major advantage to using experimental studies to understand the effect of pretrial publicity is that they can be adapted to any real-life situation. Regardless of subject matter and regardless of venue, an experimental study can identify and measure the likely influence of pretrial publicity in a particular case and yield information to develop a strategy for dealing with that influence.

[2]—How Pretrial Publicity Can Affect Jurors

Using research techniques similar to the ones discussed above, psychologists and other social science researchers have made a number of interesting findings, which are corroborated by long-term observations in the courtroom. In hindsight, some of these findings may seem like mere common sense. However, the point of the research and our discussion is to identify the elements of the process by which pretrial publicity can affect a juror's pretrial perceptions, and how counsel can respond effectively on behalf of a client. Therefore, following are some of the more important conclusions reached by these researchers:

(1) Pretrial publicity influences jury verdicts even after jurors hear all the evidence.

(2) Negative information is cumulative. That is, if pretrial publicity is consistently negative against one party, and if all of the key elements of a negative verdict are included in the publicity, a juror is more likely to begin and end a trial with a negative view of that party.

(3) Pretrial publicity that has emotional content is significantly more powerful than publicity that is purely factual.

(4) Pretrial publicity can influence a juror's memory and impressions of the evidence in spite of contrary actual testimony.

(5) Global judgmental negative information about a party or a party's actions is more damaging than information that is limited to a particular facet of the party's actions or the trial issues.

(6) Positive pretrial information about a party's character traits can undermine negative information and make defending that party easier.

(7) Jurors, judges, and arbitrators do not generally believe that they are biased by pretrial publicity, and they will vehemently disavow any bias or influence by that publicity. Ironically, jurors often state that they believe that *other people* are influenced by the same pretrial publicity.

(8) Inadmissible information that is included in pretrial publicity can influence a juror's perceptions.

(9) Trial courts' assessments of the influences that pretrial publicity has had on particular jurors and the ability of a particular juror to disregard any resulting prejudice are often based upon judicial common sense,

and frequently reveal misappraisal or misunderstanding of the abilities and frailties of human decision making.

(10) The longer the time between pretrial publicity and the beginning of trial, the less likely that pretrial publicity will influence a particular juror's perceptions. Conversely, when little time has elapsed, jurors are more likely to have stronger opinions and make prejudgments about the parties and issues in the case.

(11) Pretrial publicity does not generally lead to formation of opinions and attitudes. However, it can frame the issues and trigger the effect of existing—perhaps subconscious—juror attitudes and opinions.

(12) Jurors and other fact finders tend to believe news reports unless there exists some fundamental reason to mistrust them. In those cases where trial teams have created an appearance of distrust in media accounts, the resulting verdicts of those jurors who mistrusted the media did not differ from verdicts of jurors who had not been exposed to the publicity at all.

(13) Potential jurors are significantly more biased by exposure to both television broadcasts and printed articles on the same subject than exposure to mere print media in and of itself.

(14) Potential jurors will retain the story or message conveyed by pretrial publicity in their long-term memory if that story or message is repeated. However, jurors are more likely to remember the themes and messages of the story than the details.

(15) Because of the anonymous nature and neutral questioning style of professional researchers, community attitudes surveys tend not to influence a jury pool to any measurable degree.

(16) Information about a party's prior bad or good behavior included in pretrial publicity—even if it is inadmissible at trial—can have a profound effect on juror beliefs about that party's culpability.

[3]—Reducing Prejudicial Effects of Pretrial Publicity

Obtaining positive effects and avoiding negative effects of pretrial publicity are both possible, depending upon the situation, but neither should be attempted by the fainthearted. Influencing public opinion is infinitely more difficult than influencing twelve jurors or three arbitrators. The legal profession is rife with inept lawyers who attempted to influence the media or public opinion without the proper tools or understanding.

Creating a positive public perception of a case requires effective public relations. Those who attempt to influence the public know how complex and difficult it can be to create positive images in people's minds (including those of the jury pool). Conversely, dealing with the effects of negative publicity can be just as complex and difficult. We will discuss these matters in greater detail later in this chapter.

However, there are many alternatives for dealing with the negative effects of pretrial publicity in trial. In some instances, where publicity is extensive and localized, it is possible to change the venue of the case. However, in most cases publicity is either not extensive or is not localized and, therefore, a change of venue is either not available legally or may not even be necessary. In such cases, the primary alternatives are continuances, extended voir dire, judicial statements and admonitions, trial evidence and argument, and commonsense moderation imposed by jurors during deliberation. Let's discuss the effectiveness of each of these, plus change of venue, from the viewpoint of researchers who have tested their effects.

[a]—Continuances

A party who seeks a continuance assumes—or at least hopes—that the negative effects of pretrial publicity will dissipate over time. Extensive pretrial publicity only occurs in a few high-profile cases—such as tort cases brought by smokers, their representatives, or third parties who have been exposed to tobacco smoke against tobacco manufacturers—whereas most pretrial publicity is momentary and fleeting. Researchers have concluded that continuances may be very effective when pretrial publicity is factual in nature, such as a news announcement which merely makes a neutral acknowledgment that a lawsuit has been filed. Moreover, continuances are not likely to be effective for publicity which is highly emotional, such as breast implant cases or cases involving catastrophic losses and death that are widely publicized. Such cases often are accompanied by news commentary and documentaries that tend to raise the profile of the case in the public's eye and, in the process, cause great public reaction. The emotional connection of the information contained in the pretrial publicity tends to resonate with some jurors and is not likely to vanish. As a result, refreshing the memory of such jurors about the case or the issues in the case is likely to rekindle the jurors' original feelings about the parties or evidence.

[b]—Extended Voir Dire

One of the most widely used pretrial publicity remediation measures of trial attorneys—supported by trial courts—is extended written and oral voir dire. The premise behind extended voir dire is that inappropriate biases and opinions influenced by pretrial publicity are identifiable so that jurors who are inappropriately biased or influenced can be eliminated from the jury pool. Sometimes this may appear to be the only alternative because pretrial publicity in a particular case may have been so extensive that it may be difficult to find jurors who have not seen or heard something about the case.

One of the fundamental weaknesses in using voir dire as a safeguard is that judgments about a juror often turn upon a juror's own judgment of his or her ability to be fair and impartial. To compound the problem, some courts take a juror's statements about his or her own impartiality at face value. They seem to agree with any juror's assertion that he or she can disregard any pretrial publicity and will do so under all circumstances.

Extensive research experimentation has indicated that only a fraction of the jurors who are actually prejudiced by pretrial publicity can articulate their bias and prejudice. Many studies have indicated that most jurors who denied being influenced by pretrial publicity to which they were exposed voted nevertheless in accordance with their reactions to the pretrial publicity. Most of the time jurors are not aware that their perceptions of the case are being influenced or biased by pretrial publicity.

One might therefore ask whether an attorney's use of peremptory challenges can help to mitigate the problem by eliminating jurors who are inappropriately biased. Most studies indicate that attorney decisions about a juror's biases without the benefit of information about the juror's case-specific attitudes and life experiences are not generally very effective.

Researchers in one interesting study mailed videotapes of mock jurors' responses to voir dire in a criminal case to a national sample of criminal defense attorneys, prosecutors, and trial judges.[3] Summaries of the pretrial publicity in the actual case were enclosed with the videotapes, questionnaires from the jurors, and summaries of the case prepared by the litigants. The attorneys and judges did not receive information about the mock jurors' verdicts. In the study,

---

[3] Kerr, Kramer, Carroll & Alfini, "On the Effectiveness of Voir Dire in Criminal Cases with Prejudicial Pretrial Publicity: An Empirical Study," 40 Amer. U. L. Rev. 665-701 (1991).

the attorneys and judges were requested to indicate which prospective jurors they would strike.

The results of the study indicated that without the benefit of detailed voir dire information about each juror's specific attitudes and life experiences, the hypothetical strikes were used on the wrong jurors. Although prosecutors were somewhat better at identifying sympathetic jurors than defense counsel or judges, there was little or no correlation between how the jurors actually voted and the juror disqualifications made by the attorneys and judges. Excused jurors were just as likely to convict as jurors who were accepted by the judges and defense attorneys. Jurors who had been exposed to pretrial publicity were more likely to find culpability than those who had not been exposed. Therefore, extended voir dire did not help to ameliorate the negative effects of the pretrial publicity.

The results from this study have been duplicated in many other studies in different scenarios. Findings from the subsequent studies indicate that extended voir dire alone generally does not vitiate the effects of negative pretrial publicity. In fact, many times the words and sentence formations used by attorneys who are referring to the pretrial publicity during voir dire can actually cause bias or prejudice to occur. Although a well-written pretrial jury questionnaire and well-executed oral voir dire can identify and eliminate some biased jurors and begin the persuasion process, a more comprehensive strategy of acknowledging and dealing with pretrial publicity as part of the case development is more likely to be effective. In addition, there are public relations measures which can be taken.

[c]—Judicial Statements and Admonitions

Research studies over the past thirty years indicate that judicial instructions and admonitions for jurors to disregard pretrial publicity are not very effective at reducing bias due to the effect of exposure to either factual or emotional pretrial publicity in general. In one of the most comprehensive and well-designed studies on the subject, researchers examined the effectiveness of both (1) instructions from the trial judge prior to and during deliberations and (2) continuances in dealing with the negative effect of different types of pretrial publicity on juror judgment.[4] The instructions

---

[4] Kramer, Kerr & Carroll, "Pretrial Publicity, Judicial Remedies, and Jury Bias," 14 Law & Human Behavior 409-438 (1990).

admonished the jurors to disregard the information. The researchers studied 617 adults from a local jury roster. Half the jurors were given a pattern jury instruction about pretrial publicity and the other half were given jury instructions with no mention of pretrial publicity. In this study, the researchers found that there was no difference in bias due to exposure to pretrial publicity exhibited by those jurors who were given the pattern jury instructions and by those who were not.

This research is consistent with the general body of jury instruction scientific research. It is possible that stronger and more extensive judicial instructions than those in current use could be more effective. However, it is doubtful that instructions, by themselves, can completely resolve problems caused by pretrial publicity.

[d]—Trial Evidence and Argument

Another alternative safeguard relied upon by many courts consists of trial evidence and argument. One of the assumptions of our judicial system is that jurors and judges will decide the case based upon the evidence and argument of counsel. Jurors, judges, and arbitrators all agree that they will try to lay aside any preconceptions and will decide the case based upon the evidence.

With respect to dealing with the effects of pretrial publicity, we assume that fact finders will decide the case based only on the evidence and arguments of counsel, and that they will set aside any preconceptions based upon pretrial publicity. Perhaps one of the most complicated subjects for scientific study is the role of trial evidence vis-à-vis other factors that may influence the decisions of judges and jurors. Thus far, the most rigorous and well-designed research has indicated the likelihood that preconceptions by judges and jurors influence their view of the evidence and, of course, the verdict. However, this research has indicated that roughly 34% of the differences in judgments can be attributed solely to the evidence in the case, with the remainder of the differences explained by other factors such as characteristics or preconceptions of the parties, attorneys, or even the jurors themselves.

Of the alternative safeguards we have discussed, the development of effective evidence and argument appears to obviate pretrial publicity best. However, no single alternative by itself appears to be effective in eliminating effects of negative pretrial publicity.

[e]—Juror Moderation

A fifth safeguard against pretrial publicity is reliance upon jurors themselves to moderate the influences of that publicity during jury deliberations. The underlying premise is that the group deliberation process may facilitate creation of an array of different viewpoints held by various jurors, and since deliberation is a consensual process, inappropriate influences will be filtered out. This alternative is also supported by the concept that some jurors will take the judges' instructions seriously and will intervene when other jurors attempt to discuss information that was not entered into evidence at trial, such as pretrial publicity. There is currently debate between those who subscribe to this theory (known as the *suppression theory*) and those who believe that deliberations which involve discussion of pretrial publicity can actually enhance bias rather than eliminate it.

Thus far, research indicates that deliberation does not significantly reduce bias attributed to pretrial publicity. In fact, several studies have indicated that deliberation may actually magnify the effect of the publicity. Research and experience have indicated that some jurors feel more powerful when they can introduce information into the deliberation process that they gained from their own personal experience.

Most of the safeguards are not effective because they are premised upon removing bias after it has developed. When people are first exposed to pretrial publicity, they have no reason to believe that the information is either unreliable or inadmissible. Because this safeguard is not present when the information is encoded into memory, potential jurors may see no reason to discount or disregard it. According to psychological research, the timing and efficacy of interrupting the encoding process is complicated and not often effective. About the only time information can be edited at the time of encoding is when someone is deciding whether to pay attention to the information or when such information is believed to be incomplete, misleading, or unreliable.

In addition, extended voir dire, judicial instructions, and deliberation require jurors to disregard pretrial publicity immediately after giving it much attention. It is essentially impossible for someone to actively suppress a thought or memory when attention to it is great and emotionally stimulating.

Perhaps the most difficult aspect of controlling the effects of pretrial publicity is that thoughts and feelings generated as a result of pretrial publicity are so integrated into a person's thinking processes that they cannot be neatly excised as the law would prefer. Everyone makes his or her own unique connections between information, perceptions, and judgments. We are hopeful that future research will give us more information about this area of study.

[f]—Change of Venue

Change of venue is perhaps the most extreme solution to problems caused by bad publicity. Most plaintiff attorneys spend a great deal of time studying possible venues before filing suit. They have an obligation to their clients to choose the venue that reflects the attitudes and culture that will be most favorable to their case. Once a civil suit has been filed, judges are generally reluctant to order a change of venue. Trial judges tend to believe that the fairness requirements in a civil case are not as constitutionally mandated as they are in a criminal case and, therefore, that a change of venue is too extreme a solution for bad publicity. They sometimes believe that bad publicity or bad feelings in a community are just part of "doing business."

However, there are a number of possible arguments that might persuade the trial judge to order a change of venue. You might start with the determination of most trial judges to give each side a fair trial. As a result, most trial judges will take notice if there is real evidence that the jury pool is so tainted by bad publicity that one or more of the parties cannot get a fair trial in the venue. Jury researchers who are familiar with community attitude surveys can usually conduct a reliable, useful study that can describe and quantify the effects on the jury population. They can also testify about the effects of such publicity in a jury trial. You should not overlook the possibility that such a survey will tell you that the effects of the pretrial publicity are not as great as you had suspected. You can then determine how best to deal with the problem in your later jury (or judge) research.

However, this information is simply evidence, and must still be woven into themes for an effective argument if you decide to move for a change of venue. Although there are many possible ways to argue for a change of venue, there are two particularly effective arguments to consider. One is a direct argument, and the other is the converse. First, and most likely to be successful, is an argument that sets a standard for fairness that approaches the standard that applies to criminal cases. After all, everyone is entitled to a fair trial. The survey evidence and expert testimony of a jury researcher will be helpful and enlightening to the court if you present such an argument.

Conversely, you will also want to argue that you believe in a fair fight. You might argue that if your opponent wins in a venue where there is no prejudice against your client, then, at least, the fight would have been a fair one.

In response, some trial judges may feel that the real reason for your request for a change of venue is that you are not happy with the court (i.e., the judge) where the case is pending. You might consider reassuring the court that you respect the judge and that if it were not for this issue, you would want to try your case there.

Depending upon the case situation and budget, prior to making a motion for a change of venue you might also consider conducting a mock bench hearing to test the arguments for both sides of the issue. Most attorneys who have used scientific research techniques to study judge decision making have been delighted with what they learned.

[4]—Conclusion

Scientific jury research tends to concentrate on the potential effects of pretrial publicity during the development of the case. Most full-service trial consulting firms regularly study these effects in the course of their work with a trial team and client, and make specific recommendations for the most effective strategy in dealing with these effects. A few such firms also offer special media schools for members of the trial team who will be dealing with media on behalf of clients.

In the final analysis, dealing with the effects of pretrial publicity requires clear thinking about how jurors are affected by it and the different means of dealing with its effects. After considering all of the research in this area, the prudent practitioner will develop a plan for dealing with pretrial publicity that includes proactive elements of a public relations nature prior to trial plus utilization or at least consideration of each of the alternative safeguards discussed above.

§ 9.03 | HANDLING PRETRIAL PUBLICITY FOR YOUR FIRM AND THE CLIENT

This section offers suggestions developed by attorneys, trial consultants, and public relations professionals for dealing with the media regarding pretrial matters. The recommendations included here have proved helpful to attorneys in the past. However, these suggestions and ideas should not be relied upon to the exclusion of specific advice from public relations professionals. Because the field of public influence is so complicated and because one simple misstep could be catastrophic, a trial attorney and client are generally best served by retaining a public relations professional to work with the trial team and trial consultant.

[1]—Communicating with the Media in High-Profile Matters

Working with the media requires giving attention to the messages that you want to publicize for the client and maintaining diligent awareness that media people must transmit information to the public that is not overtly influenced by either side of the case. You must work as hard at preparation of themes and messages as if you were preparing for trial. Here are some tips:

(1) Do your own investigation. As soon as possible, determine the basic who, what, when, where, and how. Do not worry about explaining the "why" early in your communications with the media.

(2) Make sure that you or someone on the client's behalf is trained at dealing with the media. Use a trained spokesperson to give an initial press briefing as soon as possible.

(3) If you refuse to give official information, reporters will use unofficial material, i.e., rumors, speculation, etc., to fill their broadcasts and stories.

(4) Be precise and focused.

(5) Treat national and local media people with respect and help them do their job. Do not become impatient if they ask questions that seem dumb or repetitive.

(6) Media people appreciate being treated equally, without favoritism.

(7) Offer the media access to key information and evidence.

(8) Prepare your most effective themes and messages and state them clearly and precisely.

(9) Demonstrate concern and empathy for the people involved. Show the humanity in your position.

(10) If you are defending a company, tell the media what you are doing to fix the problem and to help those affected. There is no need to admit any guilt, however. Research has shown that contrition is often a strong antidote to angry jurors and punitive damages.

(11) Review all media accounts quickly and correct any errors without delay. You cannot assume that reporters are always accurate.

(12) Declarations of "No comment" are usually counterproductive. The public (including potential jurors) often become angry when high-profile people say, simply, "No comment." If you truly have no comment, the best thing to do is to say, "We are very concerned about the situation. We have nothing to add at this time. We will make further statements later."

(13) Plaintiffs and defendants should avoid fixing blame until their investigations are complete. At that point they should be allowed to make whatever lawful statements will further their cases.

(14) In on-going situations, frequent updates will be helpful.

(15) Always tell the truth.

(16) Always present an image of calm and control.

(17) Try to avoid the use of legal terms, acronyms, and technical jargon.

[2]—Avoiding Missteps with the Media

There are a number of important considerations that trial attorneys and other client representatives must understand before they appear before the media. Following are a few:

(1) *Misunderstanding the Role of the Media.* Many people confuse public relations opportunities with free advertising. This confusion has often led to frustration for the spokesperson and reporters. Reporters and their editors do not want to be an advertising outlet for anyone. The most professional media people feel strongly that their role is to provide interesting and useful information to their audience. As a client spokesperson, you are generally more effective and your image is enhanced if you remain focused on the primary goal of getting out the client's message.

(2) *Confusion About Your Role.* As a trial attorney in front of the media, your ostensible role is to inform, not to sell. You can take some comfort in knowing that when you state your position in court, you will have ample opportunity to state the themes and messages of the case. In this sense you are selling, but in a more sophisticated way. Attorneys who are focused and deliver simple messages without hyperbole are generally more effective, and more sought after by future clients.

(3) *Getting the Message Out.* The key to excellence in content is delivering brief, clear, powerful messages. The themes and messages that you present in public tend to be the same or similar to those you will use in trial. Your client will benefit if you conduct the proper research to accurately describe the messages and clarify your target audience. Many times the target audience includes the general public, the likely juror pool, customers of a company, and shareholders. It is also beneficial to delay making a statement until you get the messages right.

(4) *Why Your Message Is Important.* The ultimate goal in going public is to establish a connection for that public which has meaning. Taking the extra step to tell the media why your messages are important can determine whether those messages actually get out. Tell the reporter and the public why your message is important and what it means to them.

(5) *How Much Is Too Much?* Under the glare of cameras and the heat of the lights, it is easy to let your mind wander while you talk. Answers should be brief and focused. Learning to talk in sound bites is like learning a different dialect of English. However, it's a good idea to practice speaking in short, powerful phrases and then stopping.

(6) *Learn to Listen.* It is a good idea to listen carefully to the interviewer's questions and not to interrupt. The reporter is a colleague just like any person in your firm or your company. Treat the reporter with respect.

(7) *Minimize the Jargon.* Someone who is reading or listening to your interview will likely know nothing about the details of the case or its context. He or she most likely will not have any understanding of the jargon or terms that you use if they are too technical. Jargon is like a foreign language to most people. Using acronyms or technical jargon impedes the message that you are trying to get out and might even cause the information you are giving not to be used at all.

(8) *Do Not Criticize the Opposing Party.* It is so tempting at times to make a nasty remark about the other party in public. But what does that accomplish? It should be enough to be dignified and professional, and state your position in a powerful way. In the course of the interview you will be asked your response to the other side's arguments. It is best to simply refute them without criticizing the character or ability of the opposing party or attorney. You would not do that in trial. Do not do it in public.

The best advice I ever heard about working with the media is to "leave your ego at the door." He who controls the ink, gets the victory.

[3]—Developing Your Most Powerful Appearance and Mindset

In reality, you will have only a few seconds to get your messages out—in roughly forty words. During that time you must be cautious and alert. There is no room for error. You must look and sound impressive. Here are some ideas to help you in maintaining a powerful appearance and having a confident mindset:

(1) Begin with your overall conclusion, state the evidentiary support, and close with what it means to the audience. For example, if you represent the plaintiff in a medical malpractice case, you might say "We believe that most hospitals are safe, but on March 12, 2001 the surgical staff in the hospital did not follow proper procedures. We believe that a jury will find that the hospital staff was negligent, and that as a result, hospitals everywhere will be more diligent about following proper procedures." In defense you might say, "The people at the hospital are hard-working people who did everything they could to save the patient's life. Our hearts go out to the family and we have offered to help in any way we can. We are confident that our hospital is safe and all patients who come here will receive the best of care."

(2) Use themes and highly descriptive words to flavor your comments.

(3) Use analogies and everyday phrases to make points and explanations.

(4) Discuss the subject and point of the interview (as well as what the reporter hopes to gain) before the interview begins.

(5) Look at the interviewer and give him or her your full attention.

(6) Smile genuinely. Smiling builds rapport and credibility.

(7) Stand and move with confidence. Your powerful personality will reveal itself automatically as you talk.

[4]—Giving Effective Interviews

Following are other tips that have proven helpful in giving effective interviews:

(1) Maintain a positive mindset and do not become defensive. Scrutiny is part of the game. Expect to be scrutinized and learn to enjoy it. Confident answers are short and focused.

(2) Welcome discussion about the conflict. Reporters will often test you by asking for assurances that you really believe what you are saying. They might test the strength of your response to the other side's case by asking you hard questions. Welcome them.

(3) Prepare for the interview by knowing the material so well that you can discuss all the key details and messages spontaneously.

(4) Never just say, "No comment." Why waste an opportunity to help your client appear to be right about the controversy? There are so many things which are safe to say that can also leave a good impression.

(5) It is never wise to speculate about facts or situations. If you do not know an answer, say so, and then offer to find the answer and provide it to the interviewer.

(6) Talk in sound bites as discussed above. Interviews are not free-flowing conversations even though they seem that way on television.

(7) Look at the interviewer, not at the camera or the audience unless you have some special reason to do so that is a natural consequence of the interview.

(8) Always be honest.

§ 9.04 | REFERENCES

Caywood, *The Handbook of Strategic Public Relations and Integrated Communications* (New York: McGraw-Hill, 1996).

Center & Broom, *Effective Public Relations*, 8th ed. (Upper Saddle River, NJ: Prentice-Hall, 1999).

Dexter, Cutler & Moran, "A Test of Voir Dire as a Remedy for the Prejudicial Effects of Pretrial Publicity," 22 J. Applied Social Psychology 819-832 (1992).

Fein, McCloskey & Tomlinson, "Can the Jury Disregard That Information? The Use of Suspicion to Reduce the Prejudicial Effects of Pretrial Publicity and Inadmissible Testimony," 23 Personality & Social Psychology Bul. 1215-1226 (1997).

Fein, Morgan, Norton & Sommers, "Hype and Suspicion: The Effects of Pretrial Publicity, Race, and Suspicion on Jurors' Verdicts," 53 J. Social Issues 487-502 (1997).

Greene, "Media Effects on Jurors," 14 Law & Human Behavior 439-450 (1990).

Hans & Dee, "Media Coverage of Law: Its Impact on Juries and the Public," 35 Amer. Behavioral Scientist 136-149 (1991).

Imrich, Mullin & Linz, "Measuring the Extent of Prejudicial Pretrial Publicity in Major American Newspapers: A Content Analysis," 45 J. Communication 94-117 (1995).

Moran & Cutler, "Bogus Publicity Items and the Contingency Between Awareness and Media-Induced Pretrial Prejudice," 21 Law & Human Behavior 339-344 (1997).

Moran & Cutler, "The Prejudicial Impact of Pretrial Publicity," 21 J. Applied Social Psychology 345-367 (1991).

Ogloff & Vidmar, "The Impact of Pretrial Publicity on Jurors: A Study to Compare the Relative Effects of Television and Print Media in a Child Sex Abuse Case," 18 Law & Human Behavior 507-525 (1994).

Otto, Penrod & Dexter, "The Biasing Impact of Pretrial Publicity on Juror Judgments," 18 Law & Human Behavior 453-469 (1994).

Riedel, "Effects of Pretrial Publicity on Male and Female Jurors and Judges in a Mock Rape Trial," 73 Psychological Rep. 819-832 (1993).

Steblay, Besirevic, Fulero & Jimenez-Lorente, "The Effects of Pretrial Publicity on Juror Verdicts: A Meta-Analytic Review," 23 Law & Human Behavior 219-235 (1999).

Studebaker & Penrod, "Pretrial Publicity: The Media, The Law, and Common Sense," 3 Psychology, Public Policy & Law 428-460 (1997).

Studebaker, Robbennolt, Pathak & Penrod, "Assessing Pretrial Publicity Effects: Integrating Content Analytic Results," 24 Law & Human Behavior 317-337 (2000).

Voir Dire and Jury Selection

CHAPTER CONTENTS

> *"Every man is a prisoner of his own experiences. No-one can
> eliminate prejudices—just recognize them."*
>
> — Edward R. Murrow (1908-1965)

§ 10.01 | INTRODUCTION

Does this scene seem familiar? You arrive at the courthouse with other members of your trial team for the last pretrial conference five days before trial. The case is a big one. You are involved in a product liability suit in which there are 130 plaintiffs of all descriptions and eight Fortune 500 corporate defendants. Everything seems to be going well during the conference. The trial judge grants most of your pretrial motions and reserves the rest for later. As the judge closes the conference she says, "By the way, counsel, since this case is more complex than most, I will give each side forty-five minutes to conduct voir dire instead of the usual thirty minutes."

A number of questions arise:

(1) What is your reaction to the judge's comments?

(2) If you could say or do something meaningful, what would it be?

(3) Regardless of whether you represent plaintiffs or defendants, if you sense that the court is not sensitive to your clients' rights to ask enough appropriate questions to determine juror bias, what should you do?

(4) Should you make an informal or formal request for more time to voir dire the panel?

(5) How would you justify such a request so that the court would be persuaded?

(6) When should you ask the court for permission to use a written pretrial juror questionnaire?

(7) If all else fails, how do you use forty-five minutes most effectively to ensure that your clients have a fair trial before an impartial jury?

(8) Should you rely on the scarce demographic information you have about each juror even though you have no information about each juror's attitudes or life experiences?

(9) Should you abandon all hope of a meaningful voir dire and just accept the first group of potential jurors?

All or some of these questions have become routine as we prepare for jury selection. This chapter will focus on jury selection as an essential element of the jury persuasion process, and suggest ways to accomplish the most in the time you are allotted to question the jury panel.

Jury selection is clearly one of the most challenging parts of a trial. In a real sense, a lawyer's performance in voir dire is akin to doing complex surgery. There are many legal and psychological processes taking place at the same time. To be successful, a trial attorney must (1) be well-organized and fully prepared to deal with many spontaneous expressions from jurors about the case, (2) have a clear vision of how the issues in the case should be discussed with the panel, and (3) rate each juror against the ideal juror profile of the case.

Implementing a successful jury selection strategy means knowing in advance how to uncover inappropriate juror biases and how to work with the jury panel to begin the persuasion process for your case. After all, voir dire is the only time during trial that you can dialogue directly with jurors.

Voir dire offers a unique opportunity for you and each juror to begin communicating with each other and building a relationship between you. If you and the jurors get to know each other as intimately as the court will allow, everyone should be satisfied that each juror is free of any biases that would predispose that juror against your client's case. In the final analysis, two of the goals of this chapter are to take much of the uncertainty out of voir dire and to give you more control over the results.

§ 10.02 | Historical Composition of Juries and the Role of Jury Selection in Trial

Most historians believe that the jury system as we know it is a direct descendant of the citizen juries which sat in judgment of civil and criminal disputes in ancient Greece. With the growth of democracy and the enthusiasm with which it was applied in early Western civilization, many of the city-states in early Greece convened large gatherings of citizens (with as many as 400 people) to be the judges of the facts and the law. Whenever citizens would indicate that they were interested or biased in the case, they were expected to recuse themselves. In other instances, the remainder of the group knew in advance of other jurors' biases and would make allowances for them.

As philosophies about the use of juries to decide disputes migrated westward, they went through a multitude of changes until finally reaching the shores of Great Britain after the Norman conquest of 1066 A.D. At first, villagers convened eye witnesses to events, who in turn became the judges over people with disputes or who were accused of breaking the laws. With the growth of towns in Britain, formal courts were developed and disinterested citizens were convened to hear the evidence of witnesses in order to ensure that jury decisions were unbiased and disinterested. Judges were selected by noblemen and the king to administer the courts, and to record and carry out the decisions of the juries.

With the consolidation of Great Britain into one kingdom, jury trials and the rules of law were integrated into one common law. Under common law, other forms of trial such as trial by combat were replaced by civil and criminal decisions made by courts and juries. Finally, in 1215 A.D., King John of Great Britain was forced to sign the Magna Charta, Clause 39 of which guaranteed judgment by one's peers. Thereafter, jury trials became commonplace throughout the British Empire.

The American judicial system replicated jury trials directly from the English common law as a guarantee of freedom and liberty from governmental tyranny. Limitations on jury decision making have been instituted in certain types of federal and state court matters, but for the most part, the right to a trial by a fair and impartial jury is a sacrosanct part of the American philosophy of justice.

Although the right to trial by a fair and impartial jury developed over many centuries of common law, legislatures, court systems, and trial lawyers in the United States have struggled to modernize and standardize jury selection procedures over the past 100 years. Interestingly, modern views of the right to vote and the right to a trial by a fair and impartial jury of one's peers have developed along parallel paths in American culture. Cultural efforts to extend suffrage to all citizens and to extend equal rights to all citizens in the courtroom were a hallmark of the twentieth century. At this point these concepts appear to be linked philosophically in the minds of the American public.

In the past thirty years courts and legislatures have carved out certain types of decisions—many made by administrative agencies—that do not use juries (e.g., hearings regarding the scope of patents, certain labor-related matters, and certain sentencing matters). Otherwise, the trend in the United States has been to faithfully adhere to the fundamental principle that every party is entitled to a trial by a fair and impartial jury.

Over the past 100 years, state and federal court systems have struggled with the question of how to go about ensuring parties a fair trial without subjecting jury panels to inappropriate questions that unnecessarily invade a juror's privacy or try to induce a juror to adhere in advance to one side of the case. The truth is that many of the tactics used by some trial attorneys in voir dire to curry favor with jurors or to investigate jurors' backgrounds are considered by many trial judges and trial advocacy experts to be useless. Many of these tactics evidence a lack of understanding about how jurors make decisions. Unfortunately, in response to these tactics, many trial judges have chosen to severely restrict voir dire to the point that often little meaningful information about inappropriate juror biases can be detected.

Recently, however, as trial attorneys have begun to utilize more artful methods of interviewing jurors in voir dire, trial judges have in response relaxed the rules of procedure to allow appropriate questions that afford careful inquiry into a prospective juror's mind relating to the specific issues in a case. In the process, court systems have instituted guidelines for permitting jurors to be asked case-specific questions about their attitudes, life experiences, values, beliefs, and demographic influences. Recognizing that some of the questions relating to specific jurors and specific issues might seem invasive, courts have allowed jurors to respond to written questions that afford more privacy than is available during oral voir dire.

A review of the most recently recommended guidelines established by committees of the American Bar Association and local and state bar associations indicates that more open voir dire processes where juror attitudes and life experiences can be freely discussed orally or in writing appear to be developing. At the same time, however, courts appear to be more insistent that trial attorneys use the court's and the prospective jurors' time wisely to ask intelligent and thought-provoking questions in appropriate ways.

§ 10.03 | THE IMPORTANCE OF JURY SELECTION IN THE PERSUASION PROCESS

In a realistic sense, when we engage in voir dire we are trying to seat the most receptive audience for our case by identifying (and disqualifying) jurors who are predisposed against us. At the same time, we are also trying to use this precious time to begin the persuasion process for our case. The opposing trial team is doing the same thing. We know from many scientific studies and from experience that jurors start making up their minds about the case very early in the trial process—which begins in voir dire. And as our parents have told us, "You never get a second chance to make a first impression."

Like most trial counsel, this writer has been involved in many cases where it was clear that the seeds for victory or failure were planted during voir dire. One case involved a business dispute between a wealthy investor in a gas well-drilling partnership who alleged that the gas exploration company had not drilled as many wells as it had orally promised.[1] During discovery it was revealed that the investor had secretly tape-recorded the negotiations before the agreement was signed. In the taped conversations, the executives at the exploration company expressed their desire to drill more wells although they alleged in their answer to the suit that they had not "exactly" promised to do so.

The jury panel consisted of forty-six citizens, none of whom had any connections with the oil or gas industry. During voir dire the plaintiff's able attorney raised every issue in the case except for the tape recording. The jury panel as a whole did not seem interested in making a wealthy man even wealthier, but they also did not seem to have any concern for big oil and gas exploration companies. One of the first issues raised by the defense attorney was the issue of secret tape recordings. He was legitimately concerned about the effects of those recorded statements on his defense. However, in helping the defending trial team to develop their most persuasive case, we had already determined through prior jury research that jurors would likely be more incensed about the character of a man who secretly taped conversations than the benign statements that were actually recorded.

As we had forecast, the jury panel contained some people who felt very strongly about the issue and were quite vocal against the plaintiff. Even more interesting, however, was the fact that the two or three most vocal defendants' jurors would otherwise have been great jurors for the plaintiff. Unfortunately, the plaintiff had no choice but to disqualify them, thus depleting badly needed peremptory strikes.

A secret tape recording is an example of an issue that would certainly receive a lot of attention during trial, but it is also an appropriate issue to raise in voir dire. The contents of the recordings and the manner in which they were

---

[1] The plaintiff's complaint had survived an attempt to dismiss based on the defendant's purported defense that any promises violated the statute of frauds.

made are the kinds of issues that are likely to provoke strong reactions that might indicate inappropriate biases in a jury. At the same time, however, issues such as secret tape recordings also help to generate themes about parties and their behavior.

There are several important lessons to be learned from this example of how items of evidence can help to foster themes that become part of the persuasion process for any opposing party. First, every important issue that might affect juror biases should be raised in voir dire in order to gauge juror reactions. Second, when you interview jurors in voir dire, the themes of your case should be revealed to test their power with the actual jury panel. Sometimes we learn that our themes must be revised in order to make our story more persuasive. One of the blessings of voir dire is that it occurs early in the case, before jurors have learned enough about the case to begin to form solid opinions. There is usually enough time to make necessary revisions to a case approach if we respond quickly and decisively to juror feedback during voir dire. Third, advance jury research to test the issues and preliminary themes for trial can help prevent nasty surprises, like the ones experienced by the plaintiff in our example.

§ 10.04 | PURPOSES AND GOALS OF VOIR DIRE

Voir dire is undoubtedly the most fragile part of a trial presentation. At that point, the characteristics of the potential jury and how each juror will be best persuaded are unknown, except for the valuable information obtained during advance scientific juror research. Truly scientific research tries to measure the breadth and depth of reactions of likely jurors in a case and can help a great deal in the preparation process so that there should be very few, if any, surprises in jury selection or later in trial. Testing the case prior to trial can provide warning about likely juror attitudes and relevant life experiences. An ideal juror profile can provide a standard against which to measure actual jurors. An experienced trial lawyer will often even rehearse voir dire with a representative group from the actual juror pool, as you might do in a scientific jury research study. There is no substitute for being open-minded and comfortable when you interview jurors during jury selection, and such a rehearsal can be very enlightening.

A lawyer must attend to two groups of necessary demands when he or she determines the purposes and goals for voir dire: legal demands and human nature demands (i.e., psychological matters). Court procedures and due process provide the logistics and legal rationale for the legal aspects of voir dire. Even though different courts and court systems may have different rules that govern courtroom procedure, the objectives are similar—to seat a fair and impartial jury.

However, the persuasion or psychological process for the case begins as soon as jurors are allowed to see and hear information about that case. Persuasion is a natural process that operates automatically once stimuli such as argument and evidence are provided to the jurors. Despite court admonitions to jurors and attempts to edit and censure lawyers' questions in voir dire, jurors want to know what the case is all about, as much out of curiosity as to determine whether they can be fair and impartial.

If jurors are deprived of the highlights of the case during voir dire, they will use their imagination to fill in the blanks (which may be an inaccurate picture of the case) and then determine on their own whether they can be fair and impartial. Experience tells us, however, that if anyone is asked if they can be fair and impartial, they will usually answer "yes."

Perhaps the most apprehension experienced by trial attorneys arises from (1) determining what questions to ask, (2) assessing jurors' responses to those questions, (3) understanding how each individual juror is likely to process the case with the other jurors, and (4) resolving conflicting messages that jurors send out. There are many solutions to these difficult procedures. We will present some of them here. Others are better addressed in graduate courses in psychology.

Considering these parameters, we can say that there are three goals for voir dire: (1) to uncover bias and prejudice of prospective jurors and eliminate those jurors from the panel, (2) to educate (or preferably self-educate) the jurors about the case in a way that emphasizes and supports your position toward the case, and (3) to establish a relationship of trust and likeability with the jury.

In discussing these purposes and goals, we will discuss procedural tools that can be helpful regardless of the time the court allots to voir dire, methods to accomplish your goals in oral voir dire, and ways to use supplementary information about the jurors to your advantage in voir dire.

Trial attorneys who follow these suggestions and trial judges who cooperate to help parties adequately conduct voir dire will find that the voir dire process can indeed work efficiently to accomplish everyone's goals and protect everyone's rights. We will therefore take a closer look at the concept of bias among prospective jurors, and then examine ways to accomplish the goals of voir dire.

§ 10.05 | HOW BIAS AFFECTS JURORS, JUDGES, AND TRIAL ATTORNEYS IN JURY SELECTION

[1]—What Are Bias and Prejudice?

Because bias and prejudice play such a central role in jury selection and jury persuasion, we will first explore the nature of bias and prejudice and their meaning in the trial process. Experience in the courtroom and decades of scientific research tell us that jurors, judges, and attorneys all have biases and prejudices that affect their perceptions during jury selection and trial. Biases and prejudices seem to operate freely in the courtroom despite the court's admonitions to jurors that bias and prejudice should play no part in their consideration of a case. It is necessary, therefore, for an experienced trial lawyer to have an understanding of how bias and prejudice operate in the courtroom, and how to obtain the best results for the trial team during jury selection.

[a]—Bias

The term "bias" is one of those concepts that can mean different things to different people. For the most part, it is human nature to believe that people who do not agree with us must be biased. However, if you ask most people who come to the courthouse if they are biased, they will most certainly deny it. Nevertheless, people often accuse others who do not agree with them of being biased. It is easy to become confused about the concept of bias. For example, to most people pro-tort reform advertisements imply that jurors are routinely biased against corporations and health care providers, despite the statistical evidence that plaintiffs generally win only 27% to 43% of trials against these defendants, depending on the subject matter.

Like many terms we use every day, there is an everyday definition of bias and a scientific definition. *Black's Law Dictionary* defines bias as:

> "Inclination, bent, prepossession; a preconceived opinion; a predisposition to decide a cause or an issue in a certain way, which does not leave the mind perfectly open to conviction."[2]

Civil and criminal procedural rules rarely attempt to define bias any more clearly than the dictionary definition. In the process of applying this definition, however, trial judges and trial attorneys are forced to make decisions based upon interpretation of the statements of jurors and upon intuition about whether a particular juror is predisposed regarding a particular issue. Some trial judges require that jurors openly admit bias in order to be stricken for cause, whereas others are willing to listen to juror comments and observe juror behavior to make more subjective decisions about juror predispositions.

Most trial judges and trial lawyers operate under the theory that the existence of inappropriate bias or prejudice is an amorphous concept (except by admission of a juror) that can only be determined by individual interpretation. Although most lawyers would be hard-pressed to objectively measure bias in a particular person, they generally believe that the existence of bias is like the existence of pornography as per Supreme Court Justice Potter Stewart's unforgettable definition—you know it when you see it. In addition, most trial judges and trial lawyers think of bias and prejudice as indistinguishable in many respects.

For psychologists and other scientists, the terms "bias" and "prejudice" are distinct and have very specific definitions. Scientists have also found that the existence and the extent of bias or prejudice can be measured objectively in a number of ways. Social psychologists have found that bias exists as a natural part of social information processing and is present in everyone. They have found that assessing bias is usually a question of degree rather than whether it actually exists.

---

[2] *Black's Law Dictionary,* rev. 6th ed. 162 (1990).

EXAMPLES OF NORMAL BIASES IN SOCIAL INFORMATION PROCESSING

Processing Level	Type of Bias	Example
Information selection	Confirmation of bias	If you start with the belief that a juror is conservative, you might ask what is bad about modern jury verdicts rather than trying to test the juror's limits by asking when jury verdicts are justified.
Attention	Salience effect	Instinct causes us to notice something or someone that/who is distinctive. A lone female in a group of males or a lone male in a group of females automatically attracts attention.
Interpretation of information	Belief-consistent encoding	Jurors who believe that corporate officers are usually greedy and self-serving may also believe that a witness or representative for a corporation is greedy and self-serving until those beliefs are proven wrong to the jurors' satisfaction.
	Priming	If you have recently seen a documentary film about the pollution of local rivers by toxic waste, you might believe that every manufacturing plant in your area pollutes rivers (and groundwater.)
Retrieval of information	Belief-consistent memory	If you recently learned that a law school friend was charged with an ethical violation by the state bar association, you might begin recalling memories of questionable behavior by that person. Similarly, if you learned that this friend was selected by the state bar association as the chairperson of the ethics advisory panel, you might recall memories of how this person always acted with honesty and integrity.

Identifying and measuring bias among jurors in a panel requires:

◆ strategy,
◆ skill,
◆ organization,
◆ effective use of language to create a vibrant stimulus to which jurors can respond,
◆ the ability to craft questions that elicit responses which are really useful in assessing a juror, and
◆ a system of tools for quantifying and assessing the responses.[3]

Voir dire and jury selection strategy that is well-planned and focuses on the objectives is generally brief, interesting, and effective in achieving the goals of uncovering bias, educating the panel, and creating a strong rapport with jurors.

[b]—Prejudice

In the scientific community, prejudice also has its own meaning. Bias is generally considered as a "leaning" or belief about the interpretation of events or behavior that influences one's decision making. Prejudice, however, is a set pattern of conditioned thinking brought about by biases, personality traits, and life experiences. Prejudice is, therefore, prejudgment. Prejudice is an unwarranted, inflexible generalization about a group or a particular member of that group.

Social psychologists first became interested in the formation and maintenance of prejudice near the end of World War II when people became aware of the nightmarish behavior of the Germans in their treatment of the Jews and other cultural groups. Although the existence and effects of prejudice had been acknowledged before that time, the Holocaust created a new urgency for the scientific study of prejudice.

Prejudices are usually accompanied by *stereotypes*, or set patterns of labels and values that people ascribe to members of a cultural or other group. Stereotyping is a kind of mental shorthand. It is brought about by the need to classify people and their behaviors quickly in order to make sense and meaning out of events. It is a normal part of human judgment to assume that people around us have simple personalities and characteristic unity in their appearance and behavioral patterns.

---

[3] And you thought voir dire was just a friendly chat!

In addition, people perceive more consistency in the behavior of others than in their own behavior. People perceive others as more predictable than they are. In other words, people (including jurors) perceive that others' personality traits and behaviors are part of an unchanging holistic structure as opposed to independent or isolated characteristics. We have an intrinsic need to develop an organized impression of other people and to imbue this impression with prominent themes.

Whenever we perceive inconsistencies in others, most of us try to resolve these inconsistencies and to search for the most sensible way in which the characteristics can co-exist. For this reason, we, like most jurors, tend to spend more time thinking about inconsistencies than consistencies. We attempt to explain away the inconsistencies which we observe by making attributions about the people, the events, and the behaviors of everyone involved in a transaction. We tend to file away information about the inconsistencies in our memories. However, a memory about another person's inconsistencies is generally the first information to be recalled when one tries to explain the other person's behavior.

Stereotypes also serve as an explanatory framework for interpreting causation. Stereotyping is a powerful tool for constructing one's social reality. It shapes human experience and provides subjective meaning by categorizing people and their behavior. For example, a number of hospital corporations are operated by orders of Catholic sisters. Since the chief executive officers of the corporations are members of their orders, they often appear in court as the corporate representatives. Fortunately for these hospitals, people generally have a favorable stereotype associated with nuns. However, another hospital corporation may be represented in court by a man with a pin-striped suit or a woman wearing the latest Italian fashion. Which stereotype of hospitals will be reinforced in each situation?

Nonetheless, there are pitfalls to assuming that favorable stereotypes will always inure to one's advantage in the courtroom. The strength of positive stereotypes, such as the nun example, often give a party an advantage throughout the trial. However, if jurors discover that someone with such a strong positive stereotype has done something that contradicts the stereotype, they can become especially angry because their expectations were not met.

Conversely, there are examples of people with negative stereotypes who sometimes win trials. For example, many surveys of actual and potential jurors have indicated that they believe that corporate executives and salesmen would lie to protect their jobs. However, an entrepreneurial president of a company who terminated a relationship with a major client because the client asked him to do something he thought was unethical, will likely win jurors' approval.

[2]–Assessing the Effects of Bias and Prejudice in Jurors

All of this discussion about bias, prejudice, and stereotypes is important for trial attorneys in jury selection in two respects. First, in order to uncover real bias or prejudice about the issues in a trial, concerted inquiries must be made about jurors' attitudes, life experiences, stereotypes, and other perceptions of the fact witnesses' behavior in the case. Second, trial lawyers must be wary of their own biases and prejudices about jurors so that objective decisions can be made in the best interest of the client.

Experienced trial attorneys and trial scientists have found that every juror is biased to some degree about many issues. However, for jury selection purposes the central question must be whether the juror is so biased or so prejudiced that he or she cannot be fair to one or both sides of the case. Scientists believe that the answer to this question can be measured objectively for every juror. The most effective way to measure bias or prejudice is to ask precise and focused questions of a potential juror, the answers to which can be objectively reviewed and rated.

For example, some of the important questions for jury selection are:

(1) *Does this juror have attitudes about specific issues in the case?*
    (a) If so, how strongly does the juror hold these attitudes?
    (b) How were these attitudes formed and can they be easily changed or disregarded?
    (c) Would these attitudes cause the juror to filter out much of the evidence for either party in the case?

(2) *Does the juror have life experiences that are relevant to specific issues in the case?*
    (a) Were these life experiences important and fundamental to the juror's views of the world around him or her?
    (b) How does the juror feel about the outcomes of other trials of similar cases?
    (c) Does the juror have any opinion about how a dispute like this one should be resolved?

(3) *What are the juror's stereotypes of the people in the case?*
    (a) How and when were these stereotypes formed?
    (b) Under what circumstances has the juror found that the stereotypes are wrong or inapplicable?

For the most part, the trial team that asks questions about juror attitudes, life experiences, and expectations about people and their behavior should accumulate a fairly reliable picture of how a particular juror thinks, including any unacceptable thought pattern that indicates inappropriate bias or prejudice.

That does not mean that we can or should try to commit a juror to a particular way of thinking about the facts of a particular case. Such a goal would be repugnant to our legal system, and is psychologically premature in any event. Jurors generally resent efforts to pressure them to commit before they know what the case is about. They feel that they are somehow being tricked.

Jurors expect to be asked about their attitudes and experiences. Although they generally do not enjoy being interviewed in public, they tend to accept it as a part of public service. Those few jurors who object to public interviews can easily be accommodated by private bench sessions and written questionnaires.

Although we will discuss the art of listening and asking questions in other parts of this chapter, let's look at a specific example of how scientific questioning techniques can help uncover bias. Following are typical questions that are often asked by the defense during voir dire in a toxic waste trial: "Who does not like oil and gas companies?" (no juror raises a hand), or "Who does not trust oil and gas companies" (Juror No. 21 raises her hand and is subjected to ten minutes of interrogation).

Suppose, however, that we ask about the issue in a different way. What about a question such as, "Is anyone here familiar with a situation where an oil or a gas company was accused of polluting?" (Thirteen jurors raise their hands.) We would then ask those jurors follow-up questions such as:

(1) "How did you hear about the accusation?"
(2) "Did you have any reaction to the information or accusation?"
(3) "How did it make you feel about oil and gas companies?"
(4) "When was the last time you saw something that was part of an accusation against an oil and gas company?"
(5) "As a result of what you saw or heard, how do you feel about whether oil and gas companies pollute?"
(6) "Did it make you less trusting of oil and gas companies?"

(7) "On a scale of 1 to 10—not trustworthy at all to always trustworthy—how would you rate oil and gas companies?"

Written juror questionnaires are great tools for identifying and measuring bias. Jurors generally feel more comfortable being honest about their attitudes, life experiences, and beliefs when they answer private written questionnaires. Questions can be more precise and uniform for everyone on the panel when they are asked and answered in writing. Measuring tools such as scales and open-ended questions can be better utilized. Juror responses can be more accurately compared so that the most biased jurors can be more readily identified.

Common sense tells us that jurors who have had life experiences that involved pollution by chemical or oil and gas companies or who have developed strong attitudes about oil and gas companies and possible links to pollution—either pro-plaintiff or pro-defense—must be identified for further assessment. The dilemma often lies in developing an interview structure that will lead a juror to openly discuss his or her inner thought processes.

There is no good reason for the trial court and trial team not to use simple and efficient tools for uncovering and measuring bias in the courtroom. Perhaps we might adopt our own statement to jurors, i.e., "There are no right answers or wrong answers, only honest ones."

Therefore, if we are really serious about seating jurors who can be fair and impartial, trial advocates must research and understand the biases that will affect likely jurors in a case, and plan how best to work with the court and the jury panel to obtain answers to salient questions about the issues in the case.

§ 10.06 | ASSESSING JURORS DURING VOIR DIRE

Over the years many scholars and scientists have published their opinions about the effectiveness of different means of assessing potential juror characteristics. Research about effectiveness of jury selection methods is usually conducted on the trailing edge of a wave of activity in the courts. For example, in the twenty-year period from 1950 to 1970, the only inquiries that trial courts tended to allow related to a juror's demographics and any direct interest in the case. Scientists who studied the effectiveness of such inquiries in determining juror bias found very few relationships between demographics and verdicts that would predict bias. As a result, scholars rightfully concluded that jury selection based upon an assessment of a juror's demographic characteristics alone was not very effective.

During this same period, however, independent studies were conducted of jurors who had served in many trials to ask about both their perceptions of each case and their general perceptions and biases before trial began. The researchers were startled by the results. Many jurors admitted that they held strong beliefs and biases about the issues in their trials that affected their decisions. Many of these same jurors stated that if they had been asked about their attitudes and biases, they would have admitted them and would probably not have been seated in their juries.

On the heels of all this research activity, trial courts began allowing attorneys more flexibility in asking jurors about their attitudes, life experiences, values, and beliefs. Over the next twenty years (1970 to 1990) a great deal of intense research activity into the effects of juror predispositions began, which has continued until the present time. Most of the research has centered around the possibility of relationships among case-specific attitudes, relevant life experiences, personality traits, moral reasoning patterns, values, beliefs, or demographics, and verdict preferences. Strong relationships might reveal the presence of bias or prejudice.

At the risk of triggering the reader's hindsight bias (i.e., "I knew that all along"), we now believe that there are often significant relationships between a juror's attitudes about specific issues in a case and his or her verdict preference. Hence, asking a juror to define his or her attitudes about specific issues in the case is often effective in revealing whether that juror has a bias or prejudice that is inappropriate. Inquiry about case-specific beliefs or values can result in a similar revelation of bias or prejudice.

There may be significant relationships between a juror's life experiences and that juror's verdict preference. Inquiry about life experiences will often reveal strongly held perceptions that constitute inappropriate bias or prejudice.

Conversely, research has also indicated that inquiry about a juror's demographics alone almost never reveals the existence of inappropriate bias or prejudice.

A review of twenty years of published scientific studies of jurors' pretrial characteristics (involving specific attitudes, life experiences, moral reasoning levels, personality traits, general values, general beliefs, and demographics) provides us with a general checklist of factors that should be considered in assessing jurors during jury selection. Such a list might include:

(1) Attitudes about specific issues in the case

(2) Relevant life experiences

(3) Certain personality traits

(4) General values and beliefs

(5) Demographics

Obviously, the perfect juror scores a "10" in all categories. However, experience tells us that fewer than 10% of jurors in any panel will ever receive perfect scores. Conversely, fewer than 10% of jurors will be deemed absolutely unacceptable and score only "1"s. Most jurors will receive different, often conflicting scores in the various categories. For example, although a juror may receive an "8" in attitudes, he or she may score only a "3" in general values and beliefs. Scientific research and knowledge offer us explanations for these conflicts as well. In such a situation, like so many others, trial advocates and trial scientists often make beautiful music together.

The lesson from this exercise is that science offers attorneys a new world of knowledge and a set of tools to use in doing the job of a trial advocate. In reality, there is no substitute for hard work and preparation. Psychology and the other sciences have been part of our lives for thousands of years. Even though the application of scientific knowledge to trial advocacy may be new in one sense, the role and responsibilities of a trial advocate have not changed. However, applying new methods to traditional practice improves both productivity and results.

§ 10.07 | PROCEDURAL LEGAL TOOLS TO ENSURE ADEQUATE VOIR DIRE

In the natural course of things, we might believe that it would take several hours to accomplish all the purposes and goals of voir dire. However, proper and thorough voir dire can be accomplished in many ways, most of which may take only a short time—and certainly with less anxiety.

The first step, which should occur long before the last pretrial conference with the court, is to take a hard look at both what you must communicate to jurors and what the prospective jurors must communicate back to you. Normally you will have some very definite ideas about the demographics, life experiences, attitudes, and beliefs of people you would like to empanel on the jury (ideal juror profile) and, correspondingly, a list of the life experiences, attitudes, and beliefs that are unacceptable to you. You will know the most powerful themes of your case, the important events that must be discussed during voir dire, and the story you want to tell the jury.

Once you have these things clearly in your mind, you should consider the following options to take in requesting adequate time and content for voir dire:

(1) An informal or formal motion or request to extend time for voir dire,

(2) An informal or formal motion or request to submit a written questionnaire of reasonable length (preferably with agreement from your opposing counsel), or

(3) If the judge prefers to conduct voir dire, an informal or formal motion or request that the court ask additional questions (prepared by you) of the panel.

A word of advice: Take your request for adequate voir dire as seriously as you take voir dire itself. If you shortchange yourself during voir dire, you may wind up with one or more jurors who did not reveal something about themselves that will steal a winning case from you and your client.

The trial judge will usually appreciate any efforts that will save the court some time and also ensure that the parties receive the information they need to do their job. Your opposing counsel is just as interested in an adequate and informative voir dire process as you are.

§ 10.08 | UNDERSTANDING JURORS IN JURY SELECTION

Jury selection is perhaps the most complex and challenging part of trial because of the many active participants (jurors, trial attorneys, and the trial judge) and the variety of spontaneous behaviors that occur. Preparation, organization, and rehearsal are critical, of course. However, effective jury selection strategy also requires that you understand jurors' thinking processes ahead of time and plan how to work with the jurors to produce the most favorable result.

[1]—What Jurors Are Thinking and Feeling During Jury Selection

Interviews of thousands of jurors have revealed some remarkable similarities in the way they think and feel when they arrive for jury service. For example, regardless of the venue, age, gender, or other demographic characteristic, jurors tell us that they are predominantly anxious and angry about being forced to serve as jurors. For this reason, an attorney who acknowledges these feelings and sympathizes with them gains instant rapport.

At the same time, jurors tell us that they are curious about the parties to the case and want to know more. They are curious about the personalities and character traits of the trial attorneys as well, which motivates them to want to learn more about the litigants and the case, and ultimately to make firm judgments about them. When the trial judge and the trial attorneys respond to jurors' natural instincts to know what the case is all about, everyone wins. The trial court can fulfill its role in seating a fair, impartial, and happier jury because everyone in the room has been honest and open about what the case concerns, and jurors can be equally honest about their attitudes, opinions, and biases. The trial attorneys and clients will be more content because they can rightfully feel that they were treated fairly in jury selection.

Toward the end of the jury selection process, jurors begin to accept their fate, and when they are officially selected for service, they shift their attention to making concerted efforts to understand the task ahead of them. Because the jurors are thrust into a public forum, each juror wants to master whatever task is required in order to support his or her self-image. As a general rule, jurors listen closely to the judge to determine what tasks are going to be required. They begin listening and learning early in the process so that when the ultimate task is given to them (reaching a verdict), they will be able to perform with distinction.

Because jurors initially do not know much about the case, they want someone in the legal process to care about their lack of information and to help them understand the case and make their job easier. Attorneys who clearly assist jurors with their learning and decision-making process have a distinct advantage. Conversely, attorneys who are vague and make learning and decision making difficult, are at a distinct disadvantage.

Ultimately, jurors want to feel good about themselves throughout their jury service, just like everyone else in the legal process. They generally work very hard to make decisions about which they can be proud. They want the trial and its outcome to be a meaningful experience for them that will last for the rest of their lives (even though they seem to say that they "just want to go home").

[2]—Getting Jurors to Be Honest

Research has indicated that at least one-third of jurors do not tell the whole truth in oral voir dire. The reason is obvious: jurors are afraid of saying something that will embarrass them in front of people they do not know.

For similar reasons, jurors who are shy or have low self-esteem do not easily reveal their feelings and thoughts. Jurors who are more sensitive about some subjects than other jurors also are less revealing about their thoughts and feelings.

There are many techniques to help jurors feel more comfortable about revealing their innermost thoughts and feelings. Generally, an attorney who feels comfortable revealing his or her own embarrassing thoughts and feelings is better able to help jurors open up with their emotional responses, attitudes, and even biases. During voir dire, an attorney can also create an environment where honesty is rewarded by validating the comments of jurors when they are honest, even when they dissent. Research in social psychology has confirmed that an attorney who encourages dissent not only obtains more honest answers, but also creates more credibility. Written juror questionnaires also allow jurors to answer questions honestly and in private.

[3]—How and When Jurors Make Decisions

Although the intricacies of the jury decision-making process are complex, there are some simple aspects that are particularly applicable to voir dire.

Generally, jurors will form a story of "what happened" early in voir dire and opening statement and will use this story as a basis for early decision-making processes. The story that a particular juror forms after he or she filters through the information presented will be a product of his or her attitudes, life experiences, and personalities.

The decision-making process for any juror also contains a cognitive structure made up of values, beliefs, and attitudes which the juror uses to rationalize information presented in the courtroom and then place that information into a perspective which the juror can understand and accept. Essentially, jurors reason deductively by developing a feeling about who they believe is worthy of winning the case, and then filtering through the information presented to find support for their decision. Conversely, lawyers generally reason inductively by sorting through the available evidence and arriving at a somewhat rational conclusion.

Therefore, the most important parts of the story and the most important themes and messages should be presented clearly during voir dire, helping jurors to accept your version of the case (assuming that the themes and messages are powerful and persuasive).

As the trial progresses, jurors will continually "test" their original impressions of the case, primarily looking for information to support those impressions. Occasionally, however, something dramatic will happen in a trial that will cause a juror to change his or her original opinion. Often it takes a number of dramatic turns of events for jurors to change their minds.

During jury deliberations, jurors will look for acceptance and support from other jurors as the jury socializes itself to reach a verdict. It is no secret that the more powerful and persuasive members of the jury generally sway undecided votes, but jurors tend to "harden" their positions over time as in any group decision-making process.

[4]—Factors in Jury Decision Making That Are Important for Voir Dire

Research has indicated that there are a number of important factors that lead to jury verdicts. They include:

- psychological messages
- emotional impact
- consistencies that lead a juror to attribute causation
- jurors' perceptions of money and damages
- how a particular juror processes emotions
- intellectual capacity
- memory capacity
- personality type
- persuadability
- interpersonal feelings about the parties, attorneys, and other jurors
- demographics

As a general proposition, the psychological messages that a juror perceives in a case constitute the most important factor. However, a juror's emotional and intellectual make-up and relationship to other members of the jury can also be important factors in the decision-making process. Ultimately, jurors will make individual decisions and will make efforts to synthesize their decisions with other members of the jury group.

[5]—The Importance of the Message During Jury Selection

Many years of jury research have confirmed that verdicts are "issue"-driven. That is to say, although the facts, parties, attorneys, and evidence are important factors, the overriding factors in a juror's decision-making process are the themes and psychological messages—and the resulting story that develops in the juror's mind. For this reason, the most important aspect of preparation and delivery of voir dire and opening statement is the development of the most powerful and persuasive psychological messages that are consistent with the facts of the case and the needs of jurors.

§ 10.09 | PREPARATION FOR ORAL VOIR DIRE

Like every other part of trial, successful jury selection strategy requires planning, organization, and rehearsal of the oral phase of voir dire.

Here are some suggestions when preparing for oral voir dire.

[1]—Prepare the Psychological Side of the Case

The single most important persuasive aspect of a case is the theme or story in a case. Therefore, you should have a clear focus of the most powerful theme(s) that you want to pervade every aspect of your case. Whether you use your own experience and research or borrowed ideas, you should get feedback from other people who are not involved in the case. Some of the best feedback comes from experienced trial scientists who can help you present your case in private under simulated courtroom conditions long before the actual trial—including a mock jury that has similar characteristics to the expected jury—and can take the information obtained to make recommendations to the trial team about the most powerful trial themes and strategies.

[2]—Production of Demonstrative Aids

Using demonstrative aids (e.g., anticipated evidence, charts, photographs, etc.) can save you much time and difficulty in telling your story to the jury panel in order to stimulate valuable responses from the prospective jurors. The best demonstrative aids are simple, clear, and interesting.

[3]—Written Juror Questionnaires

The use of written juror questionnaires is rapidly growing in popularity with trial judges and trial attorneys for a number of reasons. If used properly, they:

- ◆ decrease the amount of court time necessary to discuss the same information with each juror,
- ◆ allow each juror to respond in private and, therefore, more openly, honestly, and thoughtfully, and
- ◆ can identify bias and prejudice more quickly than oral voir dire alone.

As we have discussed, at least one-third of prospective jurors do not tell the full truth in voir dire. In fact, you can question jurors all day about certain sensitive issues, and they will not divulge highly relevant information orally in front of the other jury panel members. Juror questionnaires offer an opportunity to the court and to the attorneys to find out more meaningful, truthful information about jurors to ensure that the ultimate jury is fair and impartial.

The lengths of questionnaires vary widely and are usually a matter of choice by the court and the parties. Generally, the court will prefer a shorter questionnaire, probably because it offers less of an opportunity for the parties to take advantage of each other and is less cumbersome. Generally, four to six pages are adequate so long as the information requested is case-specific and relevant to the issues.

The contents of the questionnaire should be well-organized and easy for everyone to follow. They should contain questions about the juror's attitudes toward specific issues in the case, pertinent life experiences, relevant personal and business background, and demographics. The questions should be precise, and should be constructed so that the responses can be evaluated easily in the context of the issues in the case.

A well-constructed juror questionnaire should try to exhaust the possibilities that any particular juror may be biased about the specific issues and give some insight into the juror's mind that will allow for further follow-up during oral voir dire. No evaluating instrument will give a complete picture of a juror's mindset with respect to the issues in the case, just like a doctor or psychologist should never treat a patient based upon written responses alone. Face-to-face discussion in oral voir dire will likely clear up any lack of clarity in a juror's written responses, and in some cases may change the trial team's initial post-questionnaire view of the juror.

We have learned a great deal about the effective use of a pretrial juror questionnaire in the past five years. We have learned that standardized or generic questionnaires used by courts or taken out of form books are not as useful as those which are tailored to the case. However, using a standardized form questionnaire may be better than not using one at all. We have learned that although certain questions about a juror's choice of bumper stickers or favorite books and television shows may be interesting to us, in the absence of other information, they have never been found to reveal bias or a mindset that will help us understand how the juror thinks. For example, some men who prefer to watch World War II movie re-runs all day long may make great plaintiff jurors in a personal injury tort case.

Most jurors are more willing to admit bias in their written responses to a pretrial juror questionnaire than in oral voir dire. They are more willing to discuss their views and personal life experiences that are relevant in most trials and that may form the basis for biased influences on a juror's thinking. Here are some typical kinds of cases and the subjects that are better discussed in written questionnaires:

- Previous on-the-job sexual encounters and views of control issues in sexual relationships: sexual harassment cases
- Current or previous health or medical experiences and personal views of health care issues and providers: medical malpractice and HMO cases
- Current or previous employment problems and difficult issues: employment or trade secret cases
- Current or previous business experiences in the development of new ideas and products: antitrust, patent, and trade secret cases
- Current or previous problems with the use of products or injuries: product liability and personal injury cases

In most cases, courts have found that it makes sense to have the prospective jury panel meet in the courtroom the day before oral voir dire begins and to complete the juror questionnaire at that time. The responses are then gathered by the court clerk, copied for each party the same day, and given to the trial teams overnight to review in preparation for oral voir dire.

In the event your request for a jury questionnaire is opposed, you are well-advised to be assertive and to be prepared to argue the relative benefits of the questionnaire to everyone involved, including opposing counsel. Often opposing counsel is more concerned or opposed because he or she is uncomfortable with the use of the questionnaire or believes it is biased in your favor. It is a good idea to negotiate the questionnaire in ways that benefit both sides of the case. A questionnaire that contains questions benefiting both sides is fair in concept. A court would probably consider it unfair to force the opposing party to be subjected to a questionnaire that does not include even-handed questions that that party needs to make informed decisions.

It is better practice for a trial team to focus on outperforming the other side in jury selection than to try to disadvantage it unfairly in the development of a written questionnaire. And of course it is the responsibility of all attorneys to be diligent so that their clients receive fair consideration in the jury selection process.

In reviewing the information contained in the questionnaire, you must be organized. You do not have much time and you probably now have much interesting information that you cannot obtain any other way. However, most trial attorneys and trial consultants find that the better the questionnaire, the more useful the information collected for review and assessment. It is common for the parties in a case to be inundated with information. Whereas some of the information will be highly relevant, most of it is simply available for consideration.

It is possible in most instances to develop a statistical model and scoring formula that allow you to rate the jurors and compare them to each other. The pretrial jury research you did will likely reveal an ideal juror profile that can be used as a good standard for measuring the actual jurors. Regardless of how you organize the information you receive, it will quickly become important to find a way to resolve conflicting information and place all the information into a usable format at trial. Some trial teams prefer to use a brief profile of each juror based upon his or her responses to the questionnaire. Others prefer to bring the questionnaires themselves to the courtroom with the most relevant responses highlighted for further follow-up with the jurors.

It is a good idea to set up a way to ascertain jurors who may be biased against you based on the information in the questionnaires, and then to identify the one or two questions you may have to develop with them during voir dire. Most important, you must identify statements that each such juror makes that might be grounds for challenge based upon cause.

There are a couple of caveats in the use of juror questionnaires. The first is that they should never be a substitute for strong and effective oral voir dire. Questionnaires are a tool to make oral voir dire more focused and effective, and in most cases shorter. The second is that if you are trying a case in a venue where you know that there is a likelihood that more than 80% of the jurors will be predisposed against your case, the opposing party will be able to identify the few jurors that may be sympathetic to your case and eliminate them from the juror pool. In such a case you might be better off forcing the other side to make less-informed strikes (just as you will do) by writing fewer, less detailed written voir dire questions, since the statistical probability is that you will both mostly strike jurors favorable to your opponent.

This second caveat is a kind of Russian roulette that should be used sparingly. Ninety-eight percent of the time you are much better off obtaining a more-informed view of the jury panel members than restricting your questionnaire unduly. Even in this unusual situation, if you have conducted reliable jury research you will likely have developed a clear profile of those jurors who would be most strongly supportive of your opponent (i.e., highly pro-plaintiff or highly pro-defense). It would likely be better to use a written questionnaire to identify these jurors and force the resulting panel to be more moderate.

[4]—Planning the Presentation

Regardless of the length of time you have to conduct voir dire, you can succeed at accomplishing your goals only if you have determined the issues you will cover and how you will cover them.

Ideally, you should spend only 30% of your time talking and presenting, and 70% of the time listening. During your questioning, you must decide how you will get jurors to open up with you immediately and tell you about themselves. You must decide what questions will motivate jurors to open their minds to the issues in your case, and what questions will motivate them to see things the way you do. In the process, you should ask questions that will identify those jurors who might view things differently. You must know what questions you can ask to force biased jurors to admit bias and to "save" jurors who might agree with your views.

Often the key to getting a useful answer from a juror is to ask a question that is framed so that it both (1) allows the juror full latitude in answering and (2) focuses the response tightly. Crafting questions using the guidelines discussed above in this chapter will be helpful.

Perhaps the most important part of getting ready for voir dire is gaining the right mindset as a trial attorney. It will be helpful to maintain a warm respect and affection for jurors. Having such a mindset will help us to prevent those Freudian slips we see lawyers make whereby jurors feel embarrassed and angry. For example, a city employee who handles the filing of applications for building permits might prefer to be called by his or her title, "Engineering Assistant," rather than "office clerk." Jurors of all ages, but especially those over forty, may resent your using their given names rather than addressing them with their surnames as Dr., Mr., Mrs., Miss, or Ms. Matters we consider to be of little importance may be very important to other people.

[5]—Juror Seating Charts, Notes, and Checklists

The purpose of juror seating charts, notes, and checklists is to further organize yourself so that the administrative part of voir dire does not interfere with your performance. It is important to know ahead of time where each person is going to be seated and to have that person's name or number in the appropriate space on your chart.

This will enable voir dire to proceed more smoothly and more quickly.

[6]—Assistance During Jury Selection

If you are able to present your case, explain demonstrative aids, observe the entire panel, and talk to individual jurors all at the same time, you do not need any assistance. I respectfully submit, however, that doing all of that is a good day's work for at least two people.

You should always have someone who is trained to observe people in the courtroom to assist you by observing and taking notes while you make your presentation and talk to the jurors. Also, having knowledgeable feedback from another person while you make your jury challenge decisions can be critical to the success of the case.

In particular, if you have as little as only thirty minutes to conduct voir dire, the more information you obtain from a second or even a third person can make up for the lack of time you have been allotted to question the panel.

§ 10.10 | CONDUCTING ORAL VOIR DIRE

[1]–Uncovering Bias and Prejudice

Jurors come into court with life experiences that have produced some unalterable attitudes and beliefs. For numerous reasons they are ordinarily too afraid or intimidated to tell counsel about these attitudes and beliefs when they first enter the courtroom, if ever. Research and experience have shown that these feelings, opinions, and experiences will affect their verdicts.

No instruction from a judge, lecturing from a lawyer, or advocacy from a lawyer is going to make these attitudes and beliefs magically disappear. Jurors are human beings, not machines run by computer chips. They generally know how they feel, and they can quickly determine how to get you to stop questioning them and/or not make them risk saying something that might embarrass them.

People who are frightened or intimidated will not communicate openly unless the atmosphere encourages them and assures them of safety if they "open up." The simplest and certainly the quickest way to get jurors to open up with you is for you to reciprocate—to openly communicate *your* ideas and feelings to them.

Some counsel develop "fear lists" that they discuss with jurors. For example, an attorney representing a plaintiff in a bad-faith suit against an insurance company might say, "I am afraid of something that I want to share with you. I am afraid that some of you might think that insurance companies do not make mistakes. How do you feel about that?"

By expressing yourself in an honest way, you make yourself more likable to jurors, and you encourage them to be more open about their views. In addition, when a juror has been honest with you, you should express your sincere approval of that juror for being honest, thereby encouraging others to be honest as well.

It is also important to be able to sense when a juror is harboring attitudes that might be biased against you or your client. In that case, respectfully ask the juror about his or her view or if there is something he or she would like to say. Reassure jurors that they may disagree with you. Encouraging jurors to dissent will help you to gain credibility in addition to motivating more adverse jurors to speak out. It makes them like you and respect you more than if they sense you are afraid to ask.

[2]—Educating and Persuading

Except in rare instances, it is usually a waste of time to spend most of your voir dire trying to "sell" the jury on your case. If you have only a few minutes to communicate with them, this is perhaps the worst thing you can do. Jurors expect you to try to sell your client's side of the case, and in the process, you have learned nothing about the jurors.

Conversely, jurors tend to trust each other's views and opinions, so the wise lawyer creates ways for the jurors to educate themselves about your case, and particularly, the morals or themes in your case. For example, suppose that you are defending a doctor who was sued by some of a patient's family members for making the lone decision to remove feeding tubes from an elderly patient who was in great pain and who then died without nutrition. The family members had been unable to reach agreement, so that the doctor had no legal authority to withhold treatment. Instead of preaching the merits of what the doctor did, you might ask Juror No. 4, "Mr. Abernathy, have you ever heard of situations where an elderly member of a family was being kept alive only by feeding tubes? Do you know if there were disagreements within the family about whether to remove the feeding tubes or not? Under what circumstances do you believe that it would be permissible for a doctor to make the decision to remove the tubes?" You might continue from there. The more thoughtful, accepting, and interesting the voir dire conversation, the more that jurors will want to participate.

It is likely that jurors who are obviously and heavily predisposed to your case will be stricken from the potential jury by opposing counsel. Experienced attorneys will advise you to use that juror to educate the panel on your views, knowing that the juror will not survive the strike process.

It is important to ask many open-ended questions in voir dire that home in on the issues in your case. For example, you might try questions such as:

- "What are your feelings about _____?"
- "What do you look for in _____?"
- "How should people in the _____ industry handle this dilemma?"

These questions can be your key to success if you present the jurors with enough facts to help them form meaningful responses. Attorneys who try to hide some facts of a case extrapolate no meaningful information about the jurors.

[3]—Establishing a Good Relationship with Jurors

You will have a better chance of winning the case if jurors like you. Building a solid rapport with jurors requires that you project sensitivity to their feelings, listen to their answers, show them that you care about them and about your clients, and let them know that you are human and have thoughts and feelings also. A lawyer should be courteous and respectful at all times.

Lawyers who are phony, condescending, or show disrespect will not achieve the rapport needed to establish a strong relationship with the jurors. Note that it is also a sign of disrespect to speak in legalese instead of everyday language.

[4]—Reading Jurors' Behavior and Body Language

Courtroom experts agree that body language is a good communicator of someone's feelings and character in some situations. For the most part, the more observable characteristics of a person are the least reliable in predicting their attitudes and beliefs. Therefore, body language and behavior can be an invitation for further investigation, but should be used cautiously in making any assumptions. The most common problems I see in the courtroom are misunderstanding or overanalyzing what a juror was doing. For example, we all like to think that jurors who smile at us like us, but the truth is they may not agree with us.

The same traits in different people do not always mean the same thing. A man who comes to court with immaculate clothes and shoes shined might always dress that way, or he might usually be a slob who is scheduled for a job interview as soon as he leaves the courtroom.

However, you can tell a lot about a person's rapport with the subject or an attorney by how the person responds physically in the courtroom. You can obtain a great deal of information about how a person views himself or herself by his or her carriage and dress. You can often determine how sincere a person's responses are by how he or she behaves. You can learn a lot about a juror's role in the ultimate jury by how the juror interacts with others socially.

It is important to observe the behaviors of jurors in response to things that people say and do during voir dire. Seemingly unimportant physical motions, uses of phrases or words, or expressions (or lack of them) can be signals to the observer of feelings, attitudes, or beliefs that jurors may have about the case, the parties, or the attorneys.

Special but respectful attention should be given to jurors who are silent. Sometimes silence is simply shyness, but sometimes there is a hidden agenda in the juror's mind. Either case requires your taking the time to assist the juror in speaking up.

Observing people and then intuiting reliable meaning requires organization of one's thinking and observation patterns. Observing a person is like observing a painting. It requires an open mind and a willingness to "step back" and observe a person as a whole. Only then can you readily identify those few points of a person's behavior that are strikingly different from other parts of the person's image and different from people around him or her. Once those interesting traits are identified, it is helpful to separate those that are under the control of the person and those that are not.

Behavior and body language are more helpful as indicators if we can separate the behaviors that are voluntary (which a juror wishes to portray) from those that are involuntary (physical reactions). Some voluntary behaviors such as choice of jewelry, hair style, clothes, and other characteristics are not as helpful in jury selection as those that are involuntary behaviors such as nervous fidgeting, frequent blinking, body turns, leg or arm crossing, and some facial expressions. Voluntary behaviors often mask a juror's underlying characteristics whereas involuntary behaviors tend to reveal more aspects of one's inner character and emotional responses.

Let's look at some examples of involuntary behavior that may help in voir dire. Honest people are more relaxed and comfortable, and dishonest people often are more fidgety and avoidant, and give clipped answers to questions. Angry people may become tense and lock-jawed, develop a change in their skin tone, breathe harder, scowl, and/or become more rigid in their movements.

Vocal tones, speech traits, and related behavior often reveal how jurors really feel versus what they say they feel. I recall an interesting situation during jury selection in a trade secrets trial in which Juror No. 21, who looked like Madame DeFarge in *A Tale of Two Cities*, was knitting in the courtroom during jury selection. She acted almost completely disinterested in the entire proceeding. Finally, one of the trial attorneys asked if she had any thoughts about the case, and she responded by saying, "You want me to think that this small company should have to pay this big Goliath for using a few ideas that were not very secret. Doesn't sound very complicated to me." The attorney would never have known if she had not asked a silent juror to speak.

As trial attorneys we are trained to focus on the words someone uses. However, we must train ourselves to focus on a juror's style of speaking, involuntary qualities of speech, and body language used in speaking. I have witnessed situations where a juror clearly indicated by his or her life experiences that there was a clear bias for one party, but the juror disavowed bias when asked by the judge. I believe the most outrageous such case I have seen concerned a juror who lived six houses down from one of the attorneys, their sons played on the same soccer team, and the two families had dinner together twice a month. The juror even winked at the friendly lawyer before stating to the judge that he could be fair and listen to both sides before making a decision. The trial judge, knowing the situation and having seen the winking, refused to strike the juror for cause.

There are a few voluntary behaviors in jurors that are helpful in jury selection. A juror who dresses conservatively and carries himself or herself with quiet confidence is very likely to be resolute and confident when expressing opinions during jury deliberations. This person could be an opinion-maker or foreperson on the jury. Interestingly, it has been my experience that if such a person appears better dressed and more confident each day of trial, that person is likely quietly positioning himself or herself to be the foreperson.

[5]—Challenges for Cause

Identifying jurors who have deeply ingrained, even enthusiastic feelings against you or your case is extremely important. Indeed, there will be cases where you have so many jurors on the panel who you believe are biased against you that you do not have enough peremptory challenges to eliminate all of them. Therefore, it is important to have a practiced strategy for identifying biased jurors and inducing them to commit themselves publicly.

The only way to identify those jurors is to present your case so clearly and ask questions so directly that you draw out such jurors' expressions of bias and prejudice against you. A trial attorney should never be afraid to draw out jurors who are opinionated against the attorney's case and to commit them strongly to their feelings. Almost without exception, there will be enough people left on the panel who do not feel that way. Moreover, if there are not enough jurors left on the panel to survive peremptory strikes, then it is best to deplete the panel to the point that the court must add more jurors until a fair and impartial jury can be seated. No-one wants a mistrial. But a mistrial is a small price to pay for justice.

Once jurors have admitted that they are "prejudiced in their way of thinking" or "cannot be fair," and that they "feel strongly about it," they should clearly be eliminated by the court for cause once you make a motion to strike them.

§ 10.11 | WORKING WITH TRIAL CONSULTANTS IN JURY SELECTION

Experienced trial consultants can offer advice that will give trial counsel a number of significant advantages in the planning and execution of an effective voir dire strategy. Experience and good intuition are helpful, but psychological skills and objective scientific methodology can enhance results in many ways. Helpful techniques include:

- Development of more effective written juror questionnaires
- Scientific development and use of a detailed ideal juror profile
- Development of a more effective jury selection strategy
- Suggestions for making good decisions about individual jurors who present complex or conflicting characteristics
- Suggestions for more effective voir dire presentation strategy
- Development of analyses for completed written juror questionnaires and rating jurors to make jury selection decisions more effective
- Leading the trial team to more carefully think through the relationship between the case story and the jury selection process
- Development of recommendations that blend the most effective psychological techniques with the most effective trial advocacy strategy

Even the most experienced and intelligent trial attorneys have their hands full during voir dire, and all of us have mental blind spots. We cannot engage in the complex interactions required in voir dire and remain completely detached, objective, and organized in order to make the most rational decisions about empaneling a fair and impartial jury.

How many times have we heard a trial attorney exclaim with pride that, "I do not need any help in jury selection. I have done this for thirty years. I'll just go in there and wing it." Although self-confidence in a trial attorney is admirable, overestimation of one's skills is not. Intuition and experience may play key roles for any professional in jury selection, but taking advantage of new and traditional scientific methods can usually improve results. Collaboration between an experienced trial attorney and an experienced trial consultant can yield powerful and creative ideas for making jury selection for a client highly effective.

Scientific experiments which have compared the thinking processes of trial attorneys, law students, and recent graduates of doctoral psychology programs have yielded interesting findings. Studies show that unless an attorney is trained in scientific observation and methods, an attorney's skills in jury selection are no different from that of a layperson who is not trained in science. Studies of jury selection decisions comparing the factors and stereotypes used by experienced trial attorneys and those used by law students indicate no measurable differences between the two groups. A number of studies have indicated that trial attorneys often make important decisions about individual jurors based solely on one or two characteristics, rather than gathering a broader picture of a juror by recognizing and assessing a wider range of characteristics. Some research has even indicated that when trial attorneys base decision making in jury selection upon standard factors and stereotypes that trial attorneys learn to use in trial advocacy training, often they select jurors who should have been stricken based solely upon characteristics available, but unrecognized, during jury selection.

This is not to say that one can predict with certainty how a juror will vote at the end of a trial. Rather, trial counsel should recognize that there are many valuable tools developed in the fields of psychology, sociology, and other sciences that provide powerful methods of extracting more information about prospective jurors during the jury selection process and evaluating their fitness as jurors in a particular case. In addition, people trained in these sciences and experienced in the courtroom are a valuable resource for navigating the complex interactions that take place in jury selection.

In essence, experienced trial consultants can support a trial team in doing their traditional jobs in more effective ways. The argument that trial consultants somehow subvert the legal process by unfairly targeting jurors who may be sympathetic to the opposition is not supported by any legal or scientific study. Such an argument seems to be based upon a lack of understanding about the role of science in the trial advocacy process. To be sure, the use of scientific techniques to support a trial team can give a client a clear advantage. However, professional trial consultants are trained to be supportive of the roles and objectives of trial advocacy in the courtroom.

One caveat. Trial consultants, like trial attorneys, come in all shapes and sizes. In the trial consulting business, there is no regulating body. There are no training or performance standards other than those dictated by the academic field of the trial consultant. Therefore, in evaluating a particular trial consultant's abilities to help your trial team, it is important to get a clear picture of the consultant's academic and professional experience. These credentials will probably predict how much the consultant can help.

For example, there are hundreds of kinds of doctoral degrees. A consultant trained in drama should have a clear understanding of how to develop and present a story on stage, but will not have a grasp of psychology or social science. A consultant trained in trial advocacy (law) should have a clear understanding of how to comply with courtroom procedure, but will not have a working knowledge of either science or drama. A consultant trained in psychology or another science may be very effective in applying knowledge and research methodologies to solving difficult problems, but may not necessarily be trained in developing or executing courtroom strategy. Trial consultants who are cross-trained in all these fields are hard to find, but they are extraordinary assets to a trial team.

Certainly, no matter how a consultant is trained, he or she must be able to communicate well and help the trial team develop and reach clear goals.

§ 10.12 | POWERFUL PERSUASIVE TOOLS FOR VOIR DIRE

Research in social psychology has revealed a number of important principles of decision making and perceptions that have taught us many things about how to present cases in court so that they are more persuasive. Following are a few pointers from social psychology that are useful to a trial attorney during voir dire.

[1]—Inoculate for Bad Facts or Circumstances

"Take the wind out of their sails" is a familiar expression to attorneys. Inoculating for bad facts or circumstances is a broader form of the same principle. That is, bringing out the negative facts of a case early in the proceedings (not first or last) can help immunize a party from the full force of a jury's negative perceptions.

In addition, creating a "straw man" standard of even worse bad acts as a comparison to show that a client's actions were not so bad is another type of inoculation. Whenever a jury's perceptions are broadened beyond the central focus of inquiry, a client's actions might seem innocent by comparison. For example, suppose a corporation refuses to pay a former chief executive officer a performance bonus based upon the increase in profitability of the company and in accordance with the officer's contract, and the officer then sues. If the company alleges that the officer sold assets of the company that should not have been sold for the sole purpose of increasing the profitability for a financial quarter, the officer's attorney might make that point first and then also present evidence that the company's directors had recommended and approved the action.

[2]–Admit Something Intimate

In the same way that jurors are asked to reveal their innermost thoughts and feelings, an attorney who leads the way by example is viewed to be more credible and likeable than people who are not willing to reveal something private or intimate about themselves.

The most helpful admissions are those which are case-specific. If you are defending in an employment case, you might admit that you once worked in a job where you had problems with your boss, but you were afraid to tell anyone at work. You might state that you later realized that the experience had left a bad taste in your mouth about employers, and that you would not be a fair juror in this case.

For example, you might say something like, "Last night as I was getting ready to talk to you, I realized that I was afraid of something. I was afraid that somebody here might not like my client just because she is a businesswoman from Korea."

[3]–Build Credibility through Genuine Honesty in Style and Content

Credibility is built through a process of observation of someone else and reassurance of trustworthiness of that person. In the same sense that revealing something private gives a lawyer an advantage, a clear and unequivocal demonstration of honesty in style and content can be highly persuasive.

Like everyone else, jurors tend to judge others quickly. Especially in the first parts of the trial process, jurors observe closely and assess character and trustworthiness.

Voir dire is the best time to begin building credibility and trust through honesty and body language that communicate fairness, honesty, and zeal about the case.

[4]—Repeat Important Themes Throughout the Trial

Research has demonstrated that people are best persuaded about the merits or weaknesses of a case when they perceive similar messages about right and wrong from the parties. That is to say, jurors are persuaded by consistent messages that emanate from the trial presentation, even though the particular pieces of evidence which include that message differ in their format. All of us learn through repetition.

For example, suppose one of the themes in a plaintiff's patent case is, "They copied our ideas." Voir dire questions about what that phrase means to jurors can start the persuasive process. Opening statement phrases such as "the evidence will show that the defendant copied our ideas" reinforce the earlier statements. Fact and expert witness testimony to the effect that the defendant had the motivation, opportunity, and results, including advantages of copying, adds to the persuasive power.

Adding cross-examination and rebuttals that echo the same messages increases the persuasive power. Finally, cross-examination that highlights every instance in which the message appeared reinforces the persuasive process to the maximum.

[5]—Anchor Psychological Messages to Principles, Facts, and Evidence

The principle of anchoring originated in research related to clinical psychology and was later adapted by neurolinguistic programming experts. Essentially, whenever something that is new to us is connected to something that we already accept, the new information is more easily acceptable.

For example, jurors feel more comfortable with a position in the case if the psychological messages and evidence are connected to a basic principle or message that they already accept. One defensive anchoring technique in a medical malpractice case might be to connect the doctor accused of wrongdoing to the stereotype of a warm, caring family doctor—which most jurors want to accept. Of course it is also important that there be evidence to support that thematic anchor and that the doctor demonstrate that role or characteristic when he or she takes the witness stand.

[6]—Use Visual, Oral, and Tangible Demonstrative Evidence

Most people learn through visual, oral, and other sensory means. However, only one sense tends to be dominant for any particular person. Someone who relies primarily on his or her visual sense to learn new information is usually disadvantaged as to auditory and other non-visual methods of learning. In other words, hearing and other non-visual sensing of new information requires more effort.

Since we cannot easily know what representational system is dominant for a particular person, we must use all three methods to present information to make sure we are communicating well with all people on a jury. In this way, using all methods of presentation can aid persuasion, and not using them can be an obstacle.

[7]—Simplify the Case Story and Case Themes

There are many reasons to simplify the case story to its most elementary form. Some purists would say that simplicity is beauty. However, research has demonstrated that simplicity itself is persuasive because it comports with the most basic messages we learned early in life and have lived with ever since. Another way of assessing the valuable effects of simplicity is by noting that most jurors have a tendency to accept a simple, powerful message more easily than a complex, powerful message. Certainly a message that is both complex and weak has little chance of persuading against an opposition's message that is both simple and powerful.

[8]—Use Everyday Analogies

In the same sense that anchoring is powerful, the use of everyday analogies helps a juror to learn the gist of a message more quickly. Similarly, an analogy which draws a parallel between the case story of a party and an everyday circumstance for jurors can be very persuasive. For example, a trail of cookie crumbs left on the countertop to indicate that your son had taken cookies is an ingenious way to understand the concept of circumstantial evidence. In medical malpractice cases that involve circulatory problems, we often analogize the circulatory system to a plumbing system. We analogize business breakups to divorces. We analogize some patent disputes and theft of trade secret disputes to a school yard fight where the school bully wants to take something that belongs to someone else. Another close analogy is such cases is the Biblical story of David and Goliath.

When we choose analogies, our experience determines that the most persuasive analogies are those that involve household and family, since almost everyone can identify with these images. Other analogies that are part of the common experience are also helpful. Conversely, analogies that are not part of the common experience are usually not helpful or persuasive. In this regard, counsel should be alert to ethnic differences that may affect individual jurors' responses to particular analogies.

The development of powerful analogies involves a great deal of hard work and testing, even though their use may appear to be spontaneous to the casual observer. In scientific jury research, much attention is often given to the development of persuasive analogies.

[9]—Use Powerful Stereotypes

Stereotypes—whether accurate or not—are a kind of shorthand version of life experience that we use to quickly understand a situation with which we are faced. Stereotypes about groups of people or life circumstances help us to make assumptions that allow our daily lives to be more predictable and less complex.

Jurors, like the rest of us, have developed stereotypes about certain types of people or situations, some of which are derogatory and some of which are complimentary and positive. Counsel can suggest positive stereotypes or solicit them from jurors by drawing parallels with one's clients in trial. The same is also true for unfavorable stereotypes, which an attorney might develop when referring to the opposition.

§ 10.13 | SOME FINAL TIPS FOR VOIR DIRE

Here are some additional tips that seem to help in voir dire:
* Be respectful of everyone in the courtroom at all times.
* Encourage both honesty and dissent from jurors.
* Isolate adverse jurors by painting them into a corner.

- Protect your own jurors by soliciting their acknowledgments and agreements that they will remain fair and impartial until after the trial is concluded.
- Listen 70% of the time and talk only 30% of the time.
- Interview the jury panel like a focus group.
- Test your messages clearly.
- Be open, honest, and fair at all times.
- Ask open-ended questions, but get closure on what a juror means.
- Enjoy voir dire.

A FINAL WORD: VOIR DIRE

The curtain rises at voir dire. Your opening statement begins at voir dire. This is when your "audience" begins its evaluation of you as an attorney and of your client as a party. From the moment the panel walks in the courtroom, they are watching you. Everything you do and say is important and conveys a message. Regardless of what has happened during last-minute pre-trial motions, when voir dire begins you are relaxed, prepared, and confident. Everyone and everything around you mirrors your persona. Your full attention, as well as that of everyone on your team, is on the prospective jury.

Get to know your audience. As soon as you get the list of prospective jurors, begin memorizing their names, where they work and any other information about them that may be unique. Don't ever call a juror by his or her number—they are people with names and they like to hear you say their names. It's a sign of respect.

Give your audience a part in the play. Use the voir dire panel to tell your story. Every good story has a few basic themes. Know your themes, stick to them, and use the jurors to help you develop them. Personalize your themes based on their experiences. If your case involves unfair restrictions on competition, develop your "right to work" theme with a worker on your panel who has changed jobs.

CONTINUED

Remember the cast of characters you chose. Don't forget who your jurors are during the trial. They are the most important people in the courtroom. Remember their names and something about them that sets them apart from the rest of the panel. Use opportunities as you question witnesses to continue to identify and relate to the personal experiences and knowledge of your jurors. You can also do this in closing argument. If you are describing what makes your client's process a trade secret and you have a cook on your jury, talk in terms of ingredients in a recipe—the trade secret may not be what the ingredients are in the sauce, but how they are put together.

– R. Laurence Macon, Partner
Akin Gump Strauss Hauer & Feld LLP

---

§ 10.14 | REFERENCES

Brodsky, Knowles, Cotter & Herring, "Jury Selection in Malpractice Suits: An Investigation of Community Attitudes Toward Malpractice and Physicians," 14 International J. Law & Psychiatry 215-222 (1991).

Cutler, "Introduction: The Status of Scientific Jury Selection in Psychology and Law," 3 Forensic Rep. 227-232 (July/Sept. 1990).

Frederick, *Mastering Voir Dire and Jury Selection: Gaining an Edge in Questioning and Selecting a Jury* (Chicago: American Bar Association, 1995).

Fulero & Penrod, "Attorney Jury Selection Folklore: What Do They Think and How Can Psychologists Help?" 3 Forensic Rep. 233-259 (July/Sept. 1990).

Moran, Cutler & DeLisa, "Attitudes Toward Tort Reform, Scientific Jury Selection, and Juror Bias: Verdict Inclination in Criminal and Civil Trials," 18 L. & Psychology Rev. 309-328 (Spring 1994).

Narby & Cutler, "Effectiveness of Voir Dire as a Safeguard in Eyewitness Cases," 79 J. Applied Psychology 724-729 (Oct. 1994).

Olczak, Kaplan & Penrod, "Attorneys' Lay Psychology and Its Effectiveness in Selecting Jurors: Three Empirical Studies," 6 J. Social Behavior & Personality 431-452 (Sept. 1991).

Penrod, "Predictors of Jury Decision Making in Criminal and Civil Cases: A Field Experiment," 3 Forensic Rep. 261-277 (July/Sept. 1990).

Starr & McCormick, *Jury Selection: An Attorney's Guide to Jury Law and Methods* (New York: Aspen Publishers, 1993).

Werchick, *Civil Jury Selection* (New York: John Wiley & Sons, 1993).

CHAPTER 11

The Opening Statement

CHAPTER CONTENTS

> *"Let us therefore brace ourselves to our duty, and so bear*
> *ourselves that, if the British Commonwealth and the Empire*
> *last for a thousand years, men will still say,*
> *'This was their finest hour.'"*
>
> — Sir Winston Churchill (1874-1965)

§ 11.01 | THE IMPORTANCE OF THE OPENING STATEMENT

According to the opinions of actual and mock trial jurors in thousands of interviews, we now know that the vast majority of jurors reach a clear judgmental predisposition in a case by the end of the opening statements— before there is any evidence in the record. Preliminary decisions recorded immediately after opening statements have shown an astonishing consistency with final verdicts reached at the conclusion of the trial.

Why do jurors begin making up their minds so quickly? In a word: *conditioning*. For centuries human beings have been accustomed to making quick assessments of situations just to survive. In the twenty-first century the sheer volume of information and the number of demands for attention that are constantly assailing each of us make rapid assessment and decision making a necessity. At work most people have to make "snap" decisions just to get through the day. We expect summaries and "head notes" to accompany all lengthy documents or publications we receive. At home we expect to watch news "summaries" on television, and we want everyone in the household to "get to the point."

When we bring jurors into the courtroom and charge them with observing a trial and reaching a verdict, we must anticipate that they will assess the situation and make decisions in such a venue in the same manner they do outside the courtroom. In essence, therefore, jurors need to first hear a general overview (story) and then a retelling with more detail, just like the evening news.

Research and experience tell us that the opening statement offers the jury a preview of the evidence and the story of the case through which they will likely filter testimony and evidence. At this stage of trial, jurors are especially attentive to the judge, the trial attorneys, and the courtroom environment. They are becoming acclimated to their new role and are trying to resolve the tension they feel between their fear of being inadequate for the job and their natural curiosity about the case. At this point they have the capacity and motivation to focus on and recall more information than at any other time in the trial.

Whether one considers an opening statement from a trial advocacy or psychological perspective, the opening statement is one of the most critical phases of trial. It is the most opportune time to make a case to the jury directly and to persuade them that your party should prevail. From a psychological standpoint it is most helpful because it occurs when jurors are most impatient about obtaining an understanding of "what happened" and forming conclusions and judgments.

However, the critical importance of the opening statement does not diminish the significance of the remaining elements of the trial. The effect of the opening statement does not necessarily mean that the initial judgments which jurors make at the beginning of trial cannot change. Nevertheless, if both opposing trial teams have told strong and convincing stories, and if jurors feel their predispositions strongly enough, persuading these jurors to change their minds is a difficult proposition.

It is probably an overstatement to say that a case is won or lost before the evidence is presented. Even so, jurors bring all of their personality and character traits, life experiences, values, beliefs, and attitudes to a trial, and they tend to reach conclusions quickly. For this reason, it is good policy to make a substantial effort to win the case in voir dire and the opening statement.

As we have discussed, "You never get a second chance to make a good first impression."

§ 11.02 | THE PURPOSE OF THE OPENING STATEMENT

Although most of the essential themes and fact issues will have been discussed in voir dire, the opening statement is the first and best opportunity to tell the client's story to the jury. An effective opening statement is both a preview of what the key evidence will show and much more than that: it is a *story*.

For centuries storytelling has been a tool we have used to teach each other about important and unimportant events in our lives. Our ancestors sat around campfires describing the day's events and relating lessons from their ancestors. They talked about gods, wars, monsters, love, discoveries, tragedies, and comedies. They taught their family members about the successes and failures of each day which often would make the difference in future life or death decisions.

Even today we have learned about the world around us through stories we heard as young children. Our parents have relayed their daily observations and taught us right from wrong. Our friends have told us about events in their lives which led to their joys and sorrows. We have been saturated with stories of events happening around us through newspapers, magazines, television, radio, and cyberspace.

If an attorney realizes the importance of storytelling, then the purpose of the opening statement is to tell the most powerful, persuasive story that can be told about the case, using as many persuasive tools as possible.

§ 11.03 | JUROR PSYCHOLOGY AND THE OPENING STATEMENT

[1]–Understanding Individual Juror and Group Psychological Needs

From studying small group behavior, we have learned a great deal about how jurors perceive their roles in jury group activities and how they go about filling their new role. Their chief motivation is to perform their tasks in a way that is consistent with maintaining high self-esteem.

Jurors know instinctively that they have a job to do. They are fearful about their new role and they would prefer to be someplace else. But by the time they are sworn in as jurors in the case they have accepted their fate and want to get on with business. They need someone to help them understand what the case is all about in a manner that they can digest without a struggle. The trial lawyer who helps them understand the case, the central issues, and how to do their job will be their friend.

For reasons that may be speculative and are probably best left to history, courts and lawyers have had a tendency in the past to play "hide the ball" with jurors and to force them to figure out what happened only after days, weeks, or months of detailed and tedious testimony complete with objections and mid-trial arguments and delays. Despite this tortured process, however, jurors have tended to adjust to the oddities of the courtroom, and their decision-making processes in the courtroom have been no different than their decision-making processes outside the courtroom. Jurors continue to form lasting impressions in the early stages of trial, and they continue to have the same questions that need answering.

Even when they are deprived of all the facts they would like to know, jurors persevere by imagining or, in some cases, fantasizing, the answers based on what little information they have been given. And as we now know, once jurors have determined what they believe happened, they will examine the evidence and consciously or subconsciously filter out conflicting portions in order to corroborate their version of the story.

It seems, therefore, that the well-prepared trial attorney would prefer to anticipate juror questions and answer them as early as possible in the trial so that jurors will spend less time trying to figure out what happened and more time paying attention to the details and messages of the case. In this way, the trial advocate gains more control over the story and the "filters" that jurors will use to decide the outcome.

Perhaps the best way to understand how potential jurors might process a case and to gather information to develop a powerful case presentation is through live jury research. Some attorneys prefer to conduct their own live jury research whereas others prefer to retain a psychologist or other behavioral scientist trained in law to assist them.

[2]—Consistency and How Jurors Understand Causation

We have learned through the study of anthropology, psychology, and sociology that each of us has a need to understand events around us by comparing them to other events we are currently perceiving or have perceived in the past. This learning and understanding technique has been an integral part of human mental processing since prehistoric times.

How do we know whether a person walking toward us intends to harm us? How do we know when the gas tank is almost empty? How do we know who left clothes strewn all over our son's bedroom?

The avid desire people have to understand the causes of our own and other people's behavior is so fundamental to human psychology that it is probably part of our genetic code. Our need to attribute causation to someone or something is instinctive. As a result, jurors are driven to want to know why events happened and the motivations that caused the parties and witnesses to behave as they did.

Basically, we attribute causation in accordance with our previous life experiences. For example, we will respond differently if the man walking toward us is a friendly, smiling neighbor from across the street than if he is a grimacing, pipe-wielding stranger. Although we cannot see inside the gas tank, we know from experience that it is time to buy gas when the fuel gauge indicates the tank is empty. Even though we did not actually watch our son toss his clothes around the room, we have seen him do it before, and no-one else has been in the room.

Research tells us that jurors ask three questions when they are trying to understand what caused events to occur as they did:

(1) What is consistent behavior for the people involved?
(2) What is normal behavior in my own experience?
(3) What is consistent or acceptable behavior for people under the same circumstances as those involved?

To the chagrin of many trial advocates, a juror's perception of causation is rarely based on a rational process after the juror marshals all the factual evidence. To the contrary, jurors determine causation and form their perceptions in a case as part of an irrational process. They automatically apply the stereotypes and perceptions of the world they have previously formed in an effort to efficiently determine what must have happened. This process we often refer to as applying "*common sense.*"

In this "rush" to understand events quickly, accuracy is usually sacrificed for efficiency. Critics of jury behavior often criticize jurors for their irrational thinking processes and for making "errors" in judgment. In response, however, one might argue that only computers make truly rational choices, and that the critics would be better off spending less time criticizing jurors and more time understanding them.

In order to better understand how jurors formulate causation, it is also important to understand how jurors create the stereotypes and explanations for events that shape their thinking. In essence, jurors build up a "databank" of knowledge about the world around them based upon their life experiences beginning in early childhood. Based primarily on their previous perceptions of the chronology of events and character traits of the people involved in those events, jurors form "*schemas.*" Schemas are essentially short-hand versions of events that are stored in short-term and long-term memory for future reference.

In the courtroom, judges and jurors try to match the events and messages they perceive taking place with their previously stored schemas to determine if there is a "fit" that can help them understand the new circumstances quickly. If they identify a matching circumstance, they will make an effort to interpret the new events to conform with that schema. They will cease looking for other alternative schemas unless they believe there is no match and, hence, that a fresh look at the situation is necessary.

For example, General George S. Patton, while visiting New York City, once observed some men trying to pull a screaming woman into a wagon. He automatically assumed she was being abducted by the men, and in an effort to come to the woman's aid, he pulled out his ivory-handled revolver and ran to save her. He then discovered that one of the men in the wagon was the woman's husband, who was trying to help her into the moving wagon. The woman's screams resulted from excitement, not terror.

To the chagrin of most trial advocates, judges and jurors do not generally share identical schemas. Because there is such a wide variance in the life experiences and perceptions of each person, no two people will envision identical stories after observing the same evidence even though they may agree on the ultimate decision about who should prevail and who should not. In other words, judges and jurors may agree on the message even though their perceptions of factual detail or story progression may vary.

For all of these reasons, it is important during an opening statement to develop the case story in a way which respects the need for jurors to understand certain "consistencies" that would lead them to make a favorable decision.

[3]—Contrast and Comparison

After working through a case for months or even years, a trial lawyer instinctively knows the context of all the facts and issues in the case. It seems innocent enough, therefore, to believe that to make a point as directly as possible one just says it. However, a point which trial counsel believes to be brilliant may be totally wasted on a jury which has no understanding of the context or "reason" that the point was made. That is, the jury may not understand the "meaning."

One of the strongest methods of creating context and making a powerful point at the same time is the technique of "*contrast and comparison.*" We have learned from studying cognitive and social psychology that setting up an opposing argument or evidentiary point as a "straw man" argument (including, perhaps, its unreasonableness) followed by an argument or point creates context and distinction. In other words, it converts the opposition's point into being untenable in comparison.

Contrast and comparison are so powerful because they derive from our most deeply held belief that every object of our judgment fits on a continuum with opposite values at each end. A simple example is that in order for us to judge something or someone as being "good," we must have an opposite value or perception we call "bad" with which to compare it. As with most mental processes, we are unaware that we are performing a comparison when we make the judgment.

If this technique is used at the beginning of trial, it also sets up a point/counterpoint conversation that instantly appears in each juror's mind whenever the opposition alludes to its case. This conversation is a result of the instinctive need of every person to understand the context of everything that goes on around him or her.

One of the most persuasive ways to set up this contrast and comparison is by creating a visual list of the points and counterpoints that many times can, in themselves, deliver a powerful message.

§ 11.04 | CREATING A POWERFUL STORY IN THE OPENING STATEMENT

[1]—Why Storytelling Is Important Psychologically

The most recent research in developmental and cognitive psychology tells us that people begin learning about the world around them immediately after birth by observation and experimentation. For example, children between the ages of two and three years observe an average of 8.5 new vignettes of life each day through the stories and revelations of their parents. In this process of learning, children begin to record these vignettes or "storiettes" as if they were actual life experiences, and they even adopt the judgments and conclusions relayed to them by their parents.

If we examine this process more closely, we understand that each of these storiettes contains all the elements of any other story. They have a beginning, a middle, and an end. They occur in chronological sequence. They contain characterizations of other people, of the storyteller, and of the circumstances. They contain facts. They contain emotional appeal.

As a result, we can understand how people would feel comfortable with this process as the most acceptable way to learn new information. Imagine, for example, that you are sitting in an audience when a speaker stands up to give a speech. You know nothing about the subject. You may even be somewhat skeptical about the subject. The speaker begins with the usual appreciative comments and then says, "I want to tell you a story." The likelihood is that the room will suddenly become silent as people stop fidgeting and talking in order to hear the story. The likelihood is also that the listener will suspend any skepticism long enough to listen to the story in order to determine whether the resulting feelings are justified or should be modified.

Storytelling is the most powerful vehicle for delivering a compelling message and persuading listeners. We will further discuss how to develop a psychologically powerful story later in this chapter.

[2]—Visual, Auditory, and Kinesthetic Representational Systems

Everything we know comes to us through our senses. All of our mental images, thoughts, beliefs, attitudes, and perceptions are constructed through something that we have seen, heard, felt, touched, smelled, or tasted. When we think about something we ordinarily think in sensory terms, that is, we see things in our minds, we hear voices of ourselves or others talking in our minds, or we feel a sense of our relationship with something outside ourselves.

Most people consult each of their representational systems all day long, every day of their lives. Interestingly, not everyone relies upon the same senses to the same degree. Research in the area of cognitive psychology indicates that approximately 50% of people rely primarily upon their visual sense, 30% tend to rely upon their auditory sense, and 20% of people rely primarily upon feelings, touch, movement, smell, and taste.

The degree to which a person relies upon one representational system more than another is influenced most by his or her previous life experiences. Some of those experiences are more intimate and contained within the family developmental structure, but most of the influences which affect the way we form our perceptions have developed through changes in our culture. For example, our prehistoric ancestors were forced to become adept in their reliance upon all of their senses equally in order to survive. Information came to them in usually predictable ways and at a fairly slow pace.

These days, however, with the advent of modern telecommunications, cable and satellite television, fiber-optic transmission, high-speed computer processing, and the fast pace of community life, we are saturated with a constant flow of information which assaults us without advance warning. As a result, we must rely upon the most efficient means possible to obtain sufficient information, assess circumstances, and make rapid decisions.

It is in this environment that jurors are called upon to make decisions about important matters. They use the same methods in understanding information and making decisions in the courtroom that they use in the rest of their lives. They look, they listen, and they use their senses in response to the presentations being made to them, all in an urgent quest to understand what happened, evaluate the circumstances, and decide the outcome of the trial.

This means that the most effective trial presentation will include visual, auditory, and sensory methods of presenting key evidence and key messages of the case.

[3]—Reinforcement

Generally, jurors feel more comfortable if there are multiple separate indicators that reinforce their perceptions. Since jurors are always looking for the consistencies in what they are seeing, hearing, and sensing, the most effective trial advocates will use themes, visual aids, body language, and other tools to restate the same message. For example, in a medical malpractice case an animation of the surgical history and related body processes provides an effective complement to the actual events of the story. In defending a patent case, side-by-side working models of two machines in dispute can be an effective way to demonstrate their differences.

Any method used to reinforce a case should be focused on reinforcing themes, not on factual detail. Jurors generally welcome repetition of themes and messages, whereas they may resent repetition of evidence.

§ 11.05 | STRATEGY FOR A WINNING OPENING STATEMENT

Most trial advocates agree that the strategy for a winning opening statement is a lot like the strategy for winning an athletic event—a powerful competitor will start strong, remain strong, and finish strong. Mastery of an event, however, requires more than a simple agreement on an objective. A winning opening statement requires awareness of the perceptions and issues that will be important to judges and jurors and presentation of psychological messages that resonate well.

The most powerful strategy to use in a particular case is usually determined by the hierarchy of themes and case story that experience and jury research tell us are important to judges and jurors. Often, however, by the time discovery has been concluded the viewpoint of the trial teams for one or both sides of the case is quite different than that of a likely jury. The following story is a good illustration.

In a toxic waste case tried in an east coast state court, the plaintiffs were local residents who were suing a large corporation that owned a chain of convenience stores which sold gasoline. The corporation purchased the stores in 1992, although previous companies had operated the stores dating back to 1968. In 1994 the new owner discovered gasoline traces in the soil near its underground tanks, notified state and federal authorities, and began cleaning up the ground, thinking that gasoline was leaking from the tanks. The tanks were quickly replaced, after which the corporate owner discovered that its old tanks were not leaking. Tests were subsequently run which indicated that the chemical composition of the gasoline in the ground differed from the gasoline sold by the corporation.

The effect of these findings was that the corporation's position with various regulatory bodies changed from being the polluter or responsible party to being a nonpolluter or innocent party. During most of the next eight years the corporation continued to clean the site amid running battles with regulatory agencies. In the middle of the clean-up, the situation became even more complicated when local residents sued the corporation for contamination of their properties and diminution of land values.

The case took six years for discovery, most of which focused on the dealings between the new owner and the regulatory agencies. By the time the case was destined for trial, the plaintiffs had dismissed the claims against all previous owners of the polluting property as party defendants and were focusing their energy on obtaining liability and punitive damages against the newest (corporate) owner, insisting that the corporation was the "responsible party" as designated by the regulatory agencies. In response, the corporation was building a defense around the difference between a "responsible party" that must clean a waste site and a "responsible party" that is liable for damages to nearby affected landowners.

However, jury research in the case indicated that jurors were more interested in the entire chronology of gasoline distribution from the site, including the behavior of all the previous owners and their employees and agents and whether everyone involved—including the nearby landowners— was acting responsibly. Research also indicated that the local community was both alarmed by the lawsuit's waste of financial and judicial resources and more concerned about the health of the community than any of the parties. Clearly, a party which focused on issues important to a jury would have a better chance of winning. Before trial the corporation, supported by local, state, and federal governmental agencies, did extensive vapor and groundwater testing and found no safety hazard. Luckily, therefore, the corporation was able to bolster its technical defenses with defenses that were of more importance to jurors.

For example, the owner company refocused its defense on a longer time chronology (1965 to the present) to support its allegation that the contamination had seeped into the ground over the thirty years prior to its ownership. Scientific experts were able to demonstrate that there was no existing health hazard. The trial team was also able to prove that after the company discovered the contamination it promptly reported it to public agencies, and undertook a clean-up campaign for most of the time it owned the property, thereby mitigating the plaintiffs' efforts to denigrate the corporation's character and prove the existence of a cover-up. In this case the corporation altered its defense prior to trial and obtained a favorable verdict.

Regardless of the nature of any particular case, there are "real life" human issues in all cases that beg to be addressed by trial lawyers. The most successful trial presentations are those which identify key issues to actual jurors and express psychological messages and themes in accordance with jurors' attitudes and life experiences relative to those issues.

Once the key issues and most powerful themes are identified, developing a compelling opening statement is a simple process of matching up anticipated evidence that supports those themes, ordering them by placing the most important either first or last, and delivering them visually, orally, and kinesthetically in an effective manner. Weaving themes and evidence into an overall case story is generally the most effective form of delivery. However, because cases and lawyers differ, strategies which "stretch" a trial advocate to achieve new challenges often prove to be the most effective.

§ 11.06 | DEVELOPING THEMES FOR THE OPENING STATEMENT

According to the most recent research in the fields of psychology and communication, verdicts are determined by the issues and psychological messages in a case. In trial advocacy we refer to the psychological messages as "themes." It follows, therefore, that the themes which are the most powerful and compelling to a judge or jury will have the most effect on the outcome of a trial.

Although we discussed themes in more depth in Chapter 5, there are three principles which affect strategy for an opening statement. First, there are two types of themes: *descriptive themes* (which characterize particular pieces of evidence) and *evaluative themes* (which characterize the overall principles for which the case stands). Descriptive themes are rarely determinative of case outcome because they are often localized to a particular event or transaction. However, evaluative themes are so important to a case that if the lawyers fail to provide them jurors will articulate their own. For example, a descriptive theme which alleges that a particular signature was forged is not nearly as powerful as an evaluative theme that the forger was "greedy," "dishonest," and "didn't care who he hurt."

Second, compelling themes help jurors to organize case information as the presenter intends and helps the jurors to overcome disputes or conflicts about specific evidence. For example, a medical malpractice theme which asserts that "the doctor didn't care enough to help a mother in distress" assists jurors to identify information in the trial that substantiates that the doctor "did not care" (did not return telephone calls, did not go to the hospital for ten hours after getting an emergency call, etc.). This theme would also help jurors to overcome some inconsistent but isolated evidence which might indicate otherwise.

Finally, compelling themes have to be consistent with jurors' preconceived attitudes and life experiences, and must outrank or "trump" the opposing party's themes in fundamental importance. Themes and messages are as important, if not more so, than the key facts of the case.

Determining the best themes and psychological messages prior to trial should always involve intense research. Places to search for effective themes are ubiquitous because themes are all around us every day. Newspapers, television shows, movies, fiction books, children's story books, collections of fables and fairy tales, mythology books, and similar sources provide excellent basic themes that might apply to a particular case. Ideas can also come from a review of previous jury verdicts, news stories about other cases, and post-trial interviews in similar cases to focus on the issues and rationale of a likely jury. The most effective, reliable method of identifying the most powerful themes and case story for a particular case is to conduct scientific jury research which focuses on the specific circumstances of the case.

The most persuasive themes will generally have the following characteristics:

(1) They contain emotionally powerful messages (generally taking the moral high ground).
(2) They transcend the facts of the case.
(3) They address the greater significance of the case.
(4) They evoke powerful images.
(5) They can be expressed in three ways: visually, in words, and through tangible (kinesthetic) means.
(6) They match juror needs to "do the right thing."
(7) They are consistent throughout the case presentation.
(8) They are consistent with other themes.
(9) They are consistent with the testimony and other evidence.

As with any other presentation, the audience (the judge and jurors) will pay more attention and become more involved when case messages are important enough to transcend the case itself. Therefore, the themes that are presented in court must be significant enough to touch the hearts and minds of the judge and jury. In addition, expanding one's consciousness beyond the case facts exponentially increases the possibilities for powerful themes.

For example, in a hypothetical patent infringement case a wealthy middle-aged man is suing a Fortune 500 company, alleging that the company has begun using an interactive software product that he developed to conduct business on the Internet with the company's clients. Let us assume that the evidence will show that the plaintiff had loaned a demonstration copy of his software to the defendant Fortune 500 company a year before the defendant's new Web product was launched.

Plaintiff's counsel might include themes such as "the inventor deserves the rewards of his work" or "the company should not profit from someone else's work." However, these themes focus only on the parties and not on any greater significance. Evaluative themes such as "in our community we will not tolerate stealing of ideas by big companies" or "we must send a message that big companies who steal ideas from little people will be punished" greatly expand the significance of the messages in the case.

Perhaps one of the biggest obstacles in developing themes is the difficulty in stepping back to view the case through the perspective of a potential juror. By the time discovery is essentially completed in the case, a trial attorney is so immersed in the facts and legal issues in the case that it is difficult to take a fresh look at the images that are presented. For this reason it is often helpful to have another attorney, a trial consultant, or some other disinterested person(s) to help with theme development.

§ 11.07 | STRUCTURING A POWERFUL OPENING STATEMENT

[1]—Putting It All Together

There are three basic principles for developing the structure of a winning opening statement:

(1) Presentation of the information must be organized so that it is sensitive to how jurors can best absorb and accept counsel's ideas.
(2) The presentation must seem to be organized.
(3) There must be a genuine commitment to development, practicing, revising, and rehearsing the presentation.

As for the first principle, jurors tend to learn information best that starts with simple and global truisms, and which adds detail in simple, yet natural ways. Presentations which are too detailed too early in a case tend to cause jurors frustration. In the early stages of a case, jurors are trying desperately to get their bearings and want a trial attorney to (1) "tell them what you're going to tell them," (2) "tell them," and (3) then "tell them what you've told them."

As discussed, jurors also tend to learn new case information best if it is presented chronologically. A narrative presentation such as a story which focuses on the themes, the actors, the facts, and the physical evidence is usually the best way to organize material.

The most effective use of a story in case presentation should try to accomplish three goals. The first is that the story should incorporate likely existing juror attitudes about specific issues, relevant life experiences, values, beliefs, and information. Second, the story must be consistent with the evidence and other themes in the case or jurors will feel some dissonance and be uncomfortable with the presentation. Third, the most effective themes must be woven into the narrative and must then be highlighted.

As a general rule, the contents of the opening statement provide jurors with a mental framework with which to assimilate evidence in the case and, simultaneously, a filtering mechanism with which to enhance evidence that is consistent with their perception of the case and to disregard evidence that is not consistent.

Whether the opening statement is organized solely around the central chronology of the case or around the themes of the case (but referring back to a chronology) is a matter of choice. Jurors are more interested and persuaded by content than by choice of organization. So long as the advocate tells the listener about the chronology of the case in some fashion, jurors can fit the parts together into the overall story presented by the advocate.

Ordinarily there are two types of chronological styles that are effective. The first, most often used is to introduce the "big picture" and then to focus on specific "subchronologies." The second style, which can be very effective in cases where the advocate wants the jury to see things from the point of view of a party who was at a disadvantage (for example, where the truth is alleged to have been concealed), is to focus on subchronologies leading up to a "big picture."

[2]—Using Analogies

It is helpful to make key points by using analogies to which a juror can likely relate day-to-day experiences. Generally, the most persuasive analogies are quite simple and can best be developed in brainstorming with other people. Some reference should also be made to analogies which parallel the life experiences of the particular jurors who are sitting in the jury box. References to such analogies should not obviously point to a particular juror to avoid embarrassing that person and/or appearing to be manipulative. However, using references with which a juror is familiar is respectful and aids in the learning process.

[3]—Primacy and Recency

According to many important studies of short-term and long-term memory, we have learned that people tend to recall the first and the last things that are said or shown to them more often than information presented in between. Some recent studies have also indicated that over the long term, information learned last tends to be recalled the longest.

In applying these study results to trial advocacy, we learn that the first and last things a lawyer presents in opening statement (or any other phase of trial) will be the points most remembered by judges and jurors. Therefore, aside from an initial pleasantry, the first and last things said or presented should include the most powerful themes and messages of the trial.

Some researchers have tried to determine whether primacy (the first item) or recency (the last item) is more often recalled. However, the results of such studies have been inconclusive.

[4]—Length of an Opening Statement

Most opening statements are much too long. The average person's attention span is about twelve minutes. At the beginning of trial, it might be as long as twenty-five minutes if a juror is highly motivated. In practical terms, this means that jurors will likely be "tuning out" and "tuning in" several times during an average forty-five-minute opening statement. Experience tells us, therefore, that the most powerful opening statements should be no more than thirty minutes long. If more detail is required to guide jurors, perhaps a series of additional five-minute "mini-openings" should be presented at strategic points during trial.

§ 11.08 | PRESENTING A WINNING OPENING STATEMENT

Communications specialists tell us that there are three factors involved in presenting powerful opening statements: (1) the self-interest of the listener, (2) the character and credibility of the speaker, and (3) the skill with which the presentation is delivered. Essentially, therefore, trial advocacy focuses on effective delivery of persuasive messages.

[1]—Addressing the Jury's Self-Interest

The self-interest of the judge or juror is best addressed by the substance of the opening statement. The themes, case story, and content of the presentation can, if properly presented, satisfy the jurors' emotional needs in the long term. Jurors instinctively know that they will have to make an important decision about who is right and who is wrong after both sides have presented their cases. They are anxious to obtain the most important facts and messages they will need to perform their task.

Therefore, in addressing the self-interest of the audience the most powerful presentations are those which respect the needs of the judge and jury to "get down to business" quickly and decisively. Because the listeners' senses are heightened during the opening statement, every sentence, every nuance, every characterization, every gesture, every tone of voice, and every other action a lawyer takes is under a microscope. More than at any other time during the trial, first impressions are important. In preparation, therefore, no detail should be spared careful scrutiny.

Jurors do not separate the story from the story-teller. They participate in the trial, much as a theater patron participates in a play on stage. A trial attorney is both a narrator and an actor. Jurors want to believe what they are hearing and seeing in the courtroom. They want a lawyer to be honest, interesting, respectful, committed, caring, and warm, and they become irritated when a lawyer does not display some or all of those traits. Jurors tell us that they actually judge a trial lawyer by asking themselves, "Would I want this person to represent me in court?"

Although it is important in the opening statement to discuss the key witnesses, it is also important to give jurors a glimpse of other people who are significant in the client's life and who therefore make an unspoken statement about the character of the client and the importance of the client's position. In cases where a person (rather than a business entity) is a party, it is often helpful to have family members in court to show support for their relative. In cases where a business is a party, it is important to have employees or key decision makers of the business in the courtroom. Since jurors are just beginning to know the case during the opening statement, it is important to refer to these people during the statement so that their significance is clear and so that jurors will not misunderstand their identities.

During opening statement jurors are beginning to accept their new role as court officials. However, they are feeling unsure of themselves, despite the power they have been given. They take their new role very seriously and are searching for an important meaning to attach to the task they must perform. It is therefore important that the trial lawyer give recognition to the jurors for their power as well as express confidence that the jury will discharge their duty well and honorably. This approach indicates the attorney's respect for the courtroom and informs the jury that you notice and respect them.

In setting out the themes, case story, and evidence, an effective trial lawyer will use every appropriate visual and tangible means to support an oral presentation. Jurors must see, hear, and touch every critical aspect of the case during opening statement. They desperately want to form an understanding of the case and begin making decisions right away. Therefore, the presenter must pose the ultimate trial questions at that time and indicate where to look for the answers.

[2]—Personal Style

The style of presentation that a lawyer uses is generally the result of the personal style with which the lawyer is most comfortable and the image that he or she wishes to create while "on stage." In essence, the most effective trial attorneys reveal something of themselves in their presentations. That is, presentation style is a process of revealing what is inside one's heart and mind, not an adaptation of some trait we have seen in other people.

In this sense, effective presentation is a process of self-revelation. For some people, public self-revelation might seem risky or even terrifying. However, the risk of *not* revealing honest thoughts and feelings about a case is even more dangerous.

As stated by cartoonist Walt Kelly's character Pogo in a famous cartoon, "*We have met the enemy and they is us!*"[1]

---

[1] In the book of the same name: Walt Kelly, *Pogo: We Have Met the Enemy and They Is Us* (New York: Simon & Schuster, 1972).

Developing personal style is a continual process of experimenting, getting feedback, and changing over one's lifetime. However, most people intuitively know when they are feeling comfortable, open, and "in flow" (when everything the speaker is doing seems to work effortlessly). Getting there is usually a process of experience and practice.

Developing an effective style is a dynamic process. As a lawyer progresses through professional life, both personal perspective and environment will change. Consequently, in order to be most effective, a trial lawyer's personal style will change to be consistent with other changes that the lawyer will experience.

Discovering one's most effective style and expressing it is also an empowering process. It feels good to break through previous limitations and to discover unexpected strengths and talents. Self-discovery is a matter of letting things happen, as opposed to making them happen.

[3]—Establishing Credibility with the Jury

Establishing credibility is an intuitive process. It is essentially a process of observing a multitude of small behaviors in another person and provoking a visceral reaction in that person that tells us whether he or she is trustworthy.

Regardless of jurors' backgrounds and experiences, jurors are experts at judging credibility. They hear and see subtle differences between the words one uses and the behaviors that accompany those words. Their senses detect consistencies or inconsistencies instantly.

Ironically, it is often fear of not saying the right thing which causes us to lose contact with our nonverbal behavior. As a result, a disconnection between the verbal and nonverbal aspects of a presentation occurs and credibility suffers. The problem lies in our efforts to "control" expressions with our reasoning ability and thus suppress much of our natural self-expression, which includes our true thoughts and feelings. In order to be most effective we must have the courage to express the whole truth about ourselves and about the case.

If there are any doubts about the case, they should be resolved prior to trial. Jurors immediately sense hesitancy and uncertainty in a trial lawyer. Jurors believe that a trial lawyer who tells the truth is unequivocal in words and behavior.

Therefore, gaining credibility is not merely a matter of technique but involves telling the whole truth about oneself and the case. It is a process of revealing our feelings, especially our fears. All jurors understand fear. They understand the pain of being afraid and the truthfulness of someone who admits being afraid.

Another aspect of establishing credibility is revealing our honest wishes to the jury. We must ask for what we want. And that something should be worthy and valuable. For example, if we seek a substantial sum of money in damages, we ask for justice and a good deal of money as damages. Research tells us that the more money one requests, the more money a fact finder will award.

There are a number of ways to establish credibility in the courtroom. The first is to be consistently respectful and professional at all times. However, within the confines of respectfulness and professionalism, there is considerable flexibility which can include the entire range of appropriate thoughts and feelings about one's case. For example, the use of righteous indignation or passion in the proper factual situation by a lawyer who is generally good-natured or low-key can be a powerful, persuasive tool.

Jurors also judge credibility by the integrity a lawyer displays in the presentation when discussing both small issues and larger issues. There is an old saying that, "He who is faithful in little things, is faithful also in much." In the context of a trial, a lawyer must uphold every large or small promise he or she has made to the judge and jury, whether it is a technical promise such as the time limits of a speech or a substantive promise such as the testimony of key witnesses. To fail to keep any promise could be detrimental or even fatal to the establishment of credibility.

One of the most useful tools to gain credibility is to admit something that is against the interest of one's case. Research in the field of social psychology tells us that to admit a weakness or fear about one's position can increase credibility dramatically. In order to blunt the impact of negative information, however, it is also helpful to demonstrate how the admission or weakness is inconsequential with regard to the case as a whole.

By far the most powerful tool for gaining credibility is to be completely honest.

[4]—Laying Out the Agenda and Headlining

It is helpful to jurors to know one's agenda from the beginning of the opening statement. It can be painful for them not to know what is going to be discussed in advance. It feels comforting to know the lawyer's position and agenda near the beginning of the case.

The delivery of the "silver bullet" (the first two minutes of opening statement where the hard-hitting core of the case is presented) at the outset satisfies the jury's immediate need to know, much like a "top story" or "head note." Telling the jury where the presentation is headed and why it is important can be essential to the opening statement's effectiveness. Laying out the agenda can be as simple as merely listing the topics that will be discussed.

Once the topics are stated, the advocate should discuss each topic in greater depth by using *headlines* (topic sentences) to begin new topics and *transition statements* to move from one topic to another. Jumping around in an apparently disorganized fashion can be painful and hard to follow. Identifying the order and content of topics and bullet points is simply a matter of identifying the key themes and evidence that will be used to make the case, ranking them in order of chronological and psychological importance, and delivering them directly and succinctly.

The use of headlines and transition statements is important because people learn at different speeds, and they must be able to organize the ideas presented in the opening statement in whatever fashion has meaning for them. It is also helpful to recap each topic sentence before making the transition to the next one.

[5]—Speaking and Using Words Carefully

For a number of reasons, mostly cultural in nature, Americans have become somewhat careless in their use of the English language. Such carelessness has become so commonplace that most of the time we think nothing of it. By contrast, we are startled and interested when a speaker chooses words carefully to create pictures or punctuates speech with words so that the meaning is more powerful.

Perhaps it would be helpful for us to remember the purpose of words. Words are sounds or characters that represent pictures or ideas and convey a message. Spoken clearly, they allow us to communicate information. Spoken well, they are an art form.

Words also allow us to encode an experience so that the person we wish to communicate with can decode it and obtain useful information. However, words by themselves mean very little unless they convey images and concepts that are clear, carry emotion, and contain experience gained through one's senses.

Consider the following examples of how different word choices can be used to tell the same story:

Alternative No. 1

> *"The Lincoln Property Company stands here accused of fraud and deceit toward the owners of houses in the Shady Oaks neighborhood. The Company deliberately set out to take control of the neighborhood at the lowest price possible and to redevelop it into a shopping center. In so doing, the Company lied and defrauded the owners into selling their homes under false pretenses. Damages requested are in the amount of the money it will take to restore the owners to the position to which they are entitled."*

Alternative No. 2

> *"The Shady Oaks neighborhood was an oasis of solitude in the middle of a bustling city. The streets were quiet except for the sounds of children laughing and playing among the tall and stately oak trees, which provided the neighborhood with a canopy of shade and protection from the elements. An occasional lawn sprinkler cascaded water over well-manicured lawns. The houses in the neighborhood were large and provided homes for seventy-five families. In the fifty years that the neighborhood had existed, everything had been peaceful and quiet. Until June 14th. On that day, the Lincoln Property Company sent an army of real estate agents into the neighborhood. They had instructions to go house by house and frighten the residents into selling their homes at prices below their market value so that plans for a shopping center to be built by Lincoln could be realized. And they were successful. Panic set in among the families in Shady Oaks. Before six months had passed, the neighborhood was a ghost town. Why? Because the Lincoln Property Company cares more about profits than about people. Its owners are greedy and selfish. They are dishonest. They must be forced to pay for what they did."*

The reason for painting pictures and concepts with words is simple enough. We know from our study of neuropsychology (study of the brain) and cognitive psychology (study of how we learn and think) that people remember concepts more easily than details or facts. Once a concept is simplified enough for storytelling, it is probably already a familiar part of the listener's experience and is embedded in that listener's long-term memory. The concept might even be so deeply engrained in the listener's mind that it is instinctual. However, the specific facts of a case or unfamiliar concepts (such as legal terms) are not part of long-term memory and, consequently, are not part of most jurors' experience. Therefore, until the facts or new concepts are either tied to old concepts or are re-emphasized often enough to become part of long-term memory, they are not easily absorbed into a juror's mental processing.

In addition to the use of words for creating pictures and concepts, words and speech should also be used to emphasize and punctuate key issues in the opening statement and make them easier to recall during deliberations. Some of the more frequently used techniques include:

(1) Creation of a *"catch phrase"* (for example, "convenient memory" or "ostrich syndrome").

(2) Repetition of a word or phrase.

(3) Silence (at the end of an important thought, to give the listener time to reflect).

(4) Voice modulation (changing the tone and style of voice to reflect the importance of the words).

(5) Highlighting importance (telling jurors what is important to remember).

(6) Re-capping (recapitulating).

[6]—Powerful Nonverbal Communication

We communicate constantly by how we sit, how we walk, how we smile, how we speak, how we hold ourselves, and how we interact with other people. Nonverbal communication is two to seven times more significant and influential in the persuasion process than the words we speak. Only about 15% of our communication is related to the actual words we use. Another 35% can be attributed to vocal cues such as rate of speech, tone, pitch, volume, and emphasis. The remaining 50% is generally attributable to physiology, including facial expressions, posture, body movement, and eye contact.

Nonverbal communication is a physical manifestation of what the speaker is really thinking. If the verbal communication and nonverbal communication are congruent, focused, and filled with passion and messages, the result is powerful. However, if the verbal communication and nonverbal communication say different things or either is tentative and fearful, the result is weak.

Much of our social communication is superficial and disingenuous. There is often a disparity between verbal and nonverbal communication. Because such incongruous communication is commonplace, jurors find it to be boring, uninteresting, and perhaps irritating.

Conversely, lawyers who communicate the same message with both their words and their behavior capture jurors' attention. When the complete persona of a lawyer is focused on the message and displays openness and warmth, jurors are drawn in and powerful communication can begin.

Eye contact is an important part of communication. Looking at someone during communication makes a symbolic connection that is perhaps the most powerful form of connection between two people. We look into someone's eyes to discover the meaning behind their behavior. We allow others to look into our eyes to discover the meaning in our behavior.

Our eyes reveal qualities about us that are an important component of the effectiveness of our communication with others. When one looks at someone else, a commitment to the communication is established. Looking at someone tells the other person that he or she is an important part of the communication. An advocate who looks at each juror spontaneously, intentionally, sincerely, and/or momentarily establishes the advocate's respect for the juror and his or her desire to persuade. Looking at each juror is a sign of confidence and of willingness to be vulnerable to the juror's judgment.

Making eye contact with each juror requires that an advocate "speak" with his or her eyes. In return, the intimacy of brief, but focused attention with each juror is an energizing experience. It builds a connection between the advocate and the juror that is unique and powerful.

§ 11.09 | Conclusion

Making the effort to develop a really powerful opening statement is clearly a process of hard work and understanding the audience in an intimate way. Perhaps the most important character trait of a lawyer who wants to deliver a winning opening statement is a burning desire to help the jury understand and to want to know how jurors view the world. At this juncture it is clear that the jurors are the most important people in the room. The client deserves a trial lawyer's best efforts to learn what a likely jury will think about the case by using any jury research tools that the case budget will allow.

A FINAL WORD: OPENING STATEMENTS

The opening statement is the opportunity to win the hearts and minds of jurors. Do this by making a movie in the mind that touches the heart of each juror.

First, forget you're a lawyer. Be a storyteller. Be a teacher. Practice your story everywhere with every person. Develop your theme into a thirty-second sound byte that repeats throughout the trial. Work the complete story into a two-minute summation focused on the who, what, where, how, and, most importantly, why of the story. Reach your listeners' hearts. Be the person whom the jury trusts and, ultimately, the side for which the jury will root throughout the trial.

Second, choose words that create pictures in the minds of the jury. Invite the jury to hear your story as if they were watching a movie. Avoid the nit-picking details. Relate the facts to everyday experience. Be descriptive, but avoid hyperbole and emotion. Talk about the real people with first-hand knowledge. Use the words of the witnesses. Emphasize the words and events with color. Use blow-ups, timelines, charts, and other technology to put snapshots of your movie in the mind's eye of each juror.

Finally, return to the hearts of the jurors. Make fairness the goal of your story. Tell your story so that the jury reaches the moral before you. Choose words that enroll the jury in righting wrongs committed by your opponent. Every person wants to be treated fairly and given a fair opportunity. Focus the jury on the unfair actions/decisions of the other side. Jurors want to reach a fundamentally fair result even where that result may not be the legally correct result.

In a recent trade secret theft/unfair competition case, two corporate giants sued each other on similar theories. To a lay person, critical components of the competing products appeared disturbingly similar. The defense story started in the lab of its scientist, continued with e-mails between the scientist and the corporate plaintiff, and finished with the corporate plaintiff preventing the

> **CONTINUED**
>
> scientist from working in her field of expertise for three years. As a result, the corporate defendant was unable to bring its competing product to market for one and one-half years. Counsel for the defense focused the opening story on two points: (1) the plaintiff's failure to identify the specific trade secrets that the scientist was prohibited from using and (2) the plaintiff's business strategy to use the litigation to keep the competitor's products from coming to market. The jurors may not have understood the technology at issue in the case, but they certainly understood that the corporate plaintiff destroyed the scientist's ability to continue her life's work.
>
> – Nancy J. Geenen, Partner
> Foley & Lardner

§ 11.10 | REFERENCES

Ajzen, "The Directive Influence of Attitudes on Behavior," Gollwitzer & Bargh, eds., *The Psychology of Action: Linking Cognition and Motivation to Behavior* (New York: The Guilford Press, 1996).

Aronson, *The Social Animal,* 7th ed. (New York: W. H. Freeman & Co., 1965).

Benson, "Attributional Measurement Techniques: Classification and Comparison of Approaches for Measuring Causal Dimensions," 129(3) J. Social Psychology 307-323 (1989).

Boyll, "Psychological, Cognitive, Personality and Interpersonal Factors in Jury Verdicts," 15 Law & Psychology Rev. 163-184 (1991).

Eagly, Mladinic & Otto, "Cognitive and Affective Bases of Attitudes Toward Social Groups and Social Policies," 30 J. Experimental Social Psychology 113-137 (1994) .

Gergen, *The Saturated Self* (New York: HarperCollins Publishers, 1991).

Hastie, ed., *Inside the Juror: The Psychology of Juror Decision Making* (New York: Cambridge University Press, 1994).

Hastie & Pennington, "Cognitive and Social Processes in Decision-Making," in Resnick, Levine & Teasley, eds., *Perspectives on Socially Shared Cognition*, pp. 308-327 (Chicago: American Psychological Association, 1996).

Kerr & Bray, *The Psychology of the Courtroom* (San Diego: Academic Press, 1982).

Linz, Penrod & McDonald, "Attorney Communication and Impression Making in the Courtroom: Views from Off the Bench," 10(4) Law & Human Behavior 281-302 (1986).

Packel & Spina, *Trial Advocacy: A Systematic Approach* (Philadelphia: American Law Institute, 1995 Supp.).

Pzyszczynski & Wrightsman, "The Effects of Opening Statements on Mock Jurors' Verdicts in a Simulated Criminal Trial," 11(4) J. Applied Social Psychology 301-313 (1981).

Roberts, *Trial Psychology: Communication and Persuasion in the Courtroom* (Charlottesville: Lexis Law Publishing, 1987).

Tigar, *Persuasion: The Litigator's Art* (New York: Prentice-Hall, Inc., 1998).

CHAPTER 12

Psychology and Demonstrative Aids

CHAPTER CONTENTS

"Visualize winning."

— Gary Player

§ 12.01 | Introduction

A good way to begin our discussion about demonstrative aids is to visualize a trial during which all of the different types of demonstrative aids were considered, and most were used. One such trial comes to mind.

The two-month-long trial that fits these criteria began early on a December morning in a Florida federal courtroom. A health care industry giant was pitted against a smaller competitor in a patent infringement dispute. Both parties were working with trial consultants and companies that specialized in high-tech courtroom presentations. The courtroom was filled with easels, charts, boards, overhead projection equipment, and television screens. Each side had prepared juror notebooks that contained key documents, photographs, and copies of some of the demonstrative exhibits.

The jury consisted of average citizens, none of whom had any experience with the companies' products, but all of whom had had experiences with hospitals and doctors. Pretrial jury research indicated (1) that the smaller competitor, who was the plaintiff, had an uphill fight to prove its claim because the U.S. Patent Office had granted both companies patents on their nearly identical products, but (2) that the party who was more successful in framing the issues would likely prevail.

Despite its jury research, things did not begin well for the defendant. The plaintiff highlighted key evidence that indicated that trade secret information about its product development had been stolen by the defendant through its sales force. The production and technical staff who handled the multimedia presentation that accompanied the plaintiff's opening statement were seamless in tracking their lawyer's presentation. The plaintiff's lawyer was focused and energetic in his castigation of the defendant giant corporation as he stated what the evidence would show. Whenever that lawyer turned to the multimedia operator and whispered an exhibit number, it magically appeared on a large screen and on the jury monitors with relevant passages already highlighted.

The defendant's counsel responded by expressing indignation that anyone would accuse the defendant's salesmen or executives of being dishonest, but he did not expressly deny the plaintiff's allegations. At several points in the defendant's response, the defendant's multimedia production abruptly failed as the lawyer's technical support staff continually fumbled with wires and gadgets. Soon the defendant's attorney became visibly irritated and distracted. In sum, the defendant's opening statement was an unmitigated fiasco.

Five years of widespread discovery, battles over legal issues, and intense jury research had resulted in this day, this scenario. What effect would a dispassionate observer believe the different themes might have had on this jury? What role might the multimedia productions have played? What, if anything, went right or wrong with either attorney's presentation?

The typical debate that takes place over visual aids is primarily internal. Lawyers are trained and conditioned in the use of language and verbal skills but are generally untrained in the development of effective visual aids. As lawyers, we spend a great deal of time and anguish over our word choices. We spend most of our time crafting oral and written statements and questions which focus on specific legal issues.

Most jurors, however, are conditioned quite differently. Today, most jurors spend a good deal of their day in front of a computer or television screen where they learn most of the information that is relevant to their lives. They have become adapted to receiving short, highly focused, and meaningful messages. They have also become adapted to filtering out most of the information with which they are bombarded. They have become impatient and easily irritated with information sources that they believe take excessive time to deliver a simple message. Most people in modern America feel saturated with information and irritated with constant demands for their attention.

A trial attorney who vigorously seeks the judge's and jury's attention (as well as a favorable decision), must therefore appear on this already crowded stage. If there is to be any hope of success, the attorney must know how to both procure and hold attention, as well as motivate the judge and jury to reach a favorable decision. This chapter will discuss some specific ways in which demonstrative aids can help in that process.

§ 12.02 | PERSUASION AND VISUAL AIDS

In the chapter on the psychology of communication[1] we discussed a number of principles that help us understand the persuasive role that visual aids can play. For example, the rate at which judges and jurors can assimilate information is several times faster than the pace of most trial presentations. Moreover, the most persuasive presentations are those that use varied means of presenting central themes and the case story. In this section, we will concentrate on how those principles apply to the use of courtroom demonstrative aids.

[1]—The Psychological Connection Between Visual Aids and Persuasion

Much jury and marketing research has focused on the connection between visual aids and persuasion. In studies that have examined the relationship between the manner in which consumers process the visual content of television commercials and the persuasive effect of those commercials, researchers have made findings that are directly applicable to the courtroom. First, viewers have more frequent "peak responses" to highly persuasive commercials than to less persuasive commercials. Second, highly persuasive commercials encompass stronger connections between visual content and the advertising message.

[a]—Reinforcing Key Messages

In several chapters we have discussed principles and methods of presenting persuasive themes and stories. Visual aids serve two important functions in the learning and persuasive presentation of those themes and stories. The first is that they reinforce key points to make them more ingrained and acceptable than in verbal form alone. The second is that they help to explain and simplify complex ideas.

Visual aids are powerful reinforcers for several reasons. From a physiological and neurological perspective, we are conditioned to expect various sensory impulses to lead to corresponding sensory impressions of someone or something that helps us confirm what we observe. There are examples of this phenomenon in our lives all day, every day.

---

[1] See Chapter 2 *supra.*

For example, suppose you are in your office late on Friday afternoon before a long holiday weekend. You have just asked your secretary to come into work the next morning (Saturday before a Monday holiday). If your secretary then marches into your office and slaps down a stack of papers on your desk, what would you sense is happening? You hear her footsteps and the papers as they hit your desk. You see her approach in a brisk manner and throw the papers on your desk. You may hear her say something that explains why she behaves so unexpectedly. In this scenario your eyes and ears give you information so that you know what is happening. However, different senses (visual and auditory) communicate with different parts of your brain to create some spatial or definitional understanding of what is happening. All of this sensory information is communicated to you and interpreted by you within milliseconds. You do not even realize the process is happening. But you do know that your secretary is resentful at being asked to work part of a holiday weekend.

In addition to our physical comprehension of unusual happenings, we also have internal experiences which are confirmed by external observations. In our example, during the interaction with your secretary you are probably having some internal intuitive and emotional reactions that are confirmed by what your physical senses are telling you. Imagine how strange it would be for your secretary to be taking these actions without you having any internal reaction whatsoever. Imagine how bizarre it would seem for you to see her marching up to your desk, perhaps red-faced, angrily slapping down a stack of papers on your desk, with no internal reaction from you at all.

While you tell your story to a jury or arbitration panel, they visualize the scenario. However, they have nothing but your words to validate their own experiences with that of your story unless you provide them with something that corroborates, confirms, and explains the experience.

Since we now know how most sensory experiences are communicated and confirmed, we should give judges, jurors, and arbitrators the benefit of that knowledge. By presenting information to decision makers in a way that helps them learn and confirm it, we provide them with greater depth of understanding and a more meaningful experience. The messages contained in a communication become more persuasive according to the manner in which they are communicated. If we limit our communication with jurors to speech alone, the jurors may be unable to see and sense corroborative aspects of our story that can breathe life into it.

[b]—Improving Memory Recall

Another advantage of the use of visual aids is reinforcement of memory and recall. Research indicates that information which is communicated orally and reinforced with visual aids is retained in memory much longer and has a better chance of being referred into long-term memory than information which is only communicated orally.

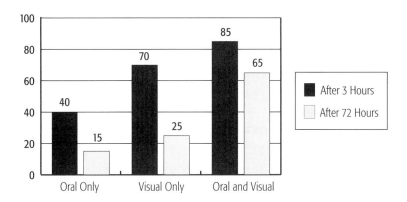

Percentage of Information Recalled After
Oral, Visual, and Combination Styles
of Communication

Most fact finders, therefore, have a limited ability to observe and retain information. Some people have trained themselves to expand their observation and retention levels, but rarely does this apply to judges, jurors, or arbitrators. Even people who undertake special training can improve their observation and retention skills only marginally. Presentation of key points both orally and visually gives a party a statistical advantage, regardless of a message's content.

[c]—Explaining and Simplifying Key Concepts

In many contexts, complex information is best presented with a visual element. One of the challenges of thirty-minute news programs on television is how to tell a story that contains many complexities within thirty seconds or less. Over the years most news networks have mastered the task of relaying to viewers highlights of the factual and emotional content of a news story within that time.

In an increasingly technical world it is inevitable that more and more complex evidence will be presented in the courtroom. Although patent cases are typically complicated in their fact patterns, there are many other kinds of complex cases, such as medical malpractice cases. However, one of the challenges to your trial team is to simplify the complex elements of the case in order to fit them into a simple case story. Different types of visual aids often make wonderful tools for this purpose.

[d]–Improving Accurate Encoding of Information

Visual aids can also present information more accurately than words alone. Suppose you were to close your eyes and envision a rock. Focus on its color, its location, its size, and any other characteristic that makes the rock unique. (This is not a rhetorical suggestion. If you "play" with the exercise you should learn something. You might even ask someone else to join you in this exercise in order to compare the different images that you each generate in your minds.)

Note that the writer did not make any suggestions to you about the color, location, size, or other particulars of the hypothetical rock. If he had, he would have told you that he was visualizing a rock that is gray, mostly round, and about the size of a Volkswagen. It sits at the top of the Logan Pass Trail as it crosses the Going to the Sun Road in Glacier National Park in Montana. It overlooks a scenic glacier lake at about 12,000 feet above sea level.

Most people who try this exercise enjoy comparing rocks. However, it is unlikely that you will ever meet any two people who envision exactly the same rock, unless it is a famous rock such as Mount Rushmore.

When we were young, we played a game called "Rumor" in which ten or more children sat side by side in a long row with enough space between them so that they could not hear something whispered to the person next to them. The person on one end would begin by quickly whispering a short, simple rumor to the next person. The rumor could not be repeated. The listener had only one chance to hear it. That person would then turn to the next person and repeat the rumor, and so on until it was repeated to the person on the opposite end of the row. By the time the rumor reached the opposite end, it bore little resemblance to the original rumor (and generally was highly amusing to the participants). Of course, we could have simply passed a note with the rumor clearly stated on it down the row, but that would have spoiled the fun.

Applying the above ideas to visual aids, the only way to ensure accuracy regarding text, a graphic, an incident layout/map, or a photograph is to prepare the aids with scrupulous care. At the same time, fact finders dislike repetition of facts or evidence. They usually understand both the first time counsel presents either, and may be bored and/or insulted by trial presentations which include repetitive testimony and facts. Visual aids can ensure that the evidence is accurate the first time it is presented.

[e]—Involving the Fact Finder

Visual aids can also involve the audience mentally, unlike oral communication. By presenting the audience with visual content, you heighten its interest in the trial and invite its members to actively participate mentally in presentation of the evidence. Demonstrative aids stimulate thinking and bring closure to ideas and images that the judge, jury, or arbitrator may already have incorporated in his, her, or their thinking.

In a very real way, demonstrative aids make the communication between the trial lawyer and the fact finder a two-way process rather than a dry monologue. Visual aids change the character of the jury's listening from passive to active.

[f]—Creating Powerful Contrast and Comparison

One of the most powerful techniques for persuasion that we have learned from social psychology researchers is that of contrast and comparison. When a trial lawyer stands up and tries to explain why his or her idea is correct and the opposing lawyer's idea is not, the lawyer in effect is explaining two different points of view—and why his or hers is superior and more worthy. Accomplishing this task can be a challenge.

However, if the lawyer can reduce the two arguments to visual aids (e.g., side-by-side lists or pictures), the comparison argument can be much more powerful and starkly visual. This method is by far one of the most effective, efficient persuasive techniques. The images make further argument unnecessary.

For example, let's examine a case involving an explosion at a Missouri chemical plant in which three workers died in the resulting fire. The plaintiff workers' estates and defendant chemical company have opposite arguments to make, both related to the question of whether the plant management and employees observed good safety practices. One of the first arguments for either side of the case is to create a checklist of good safety practices and tell the jury whether the company abided by them. A checklist made by the plaintiffs might look like the following:

The Company's Report Card

Good Safety Practice	Average Company's Grade	Defendant Company's Grade
1. Written Safety Practices	A	C
2. Classroom Training	A	F
3. Field Training	A	F
4. Weekly Safety Meetings	A	F
5. Weekly Safety Inspections by Company Official	A	D
6. Weekly Safety Inspections by Outside Company	A	F
7. Full-Time Safety Official in the Company	A	B

Conversely, a checklist made by the defendant might look like the following:

The Company's Report Card

Good Safety Practice	Average Company's Grade	Defendant Company's Grade
1. Written Safety Practices	C	B
2. Classroom Training	F	B
3. Field Training	D	A
4. Weekly Safety Meetings	F	A
5. Weekly Safety Inspections by Company Official	C	A
6. Weekly Safety Inspections by Outside Company	F	B
7. Full-Time Safety Official in the Company	B	A

Each of these simple tables tells a clear—although very different—story about the safety conditions within the defendant company. The central idea behind contrast and comparison is creating a basic norm and then comparing it to the practices of a person or a group. Both the norm and the particulars about the group or person being compared to that norm must appear visually at the same time for maximum effect. In a matter of seconds one gets a clear picture of the core idea being presented.

The same technique can be used to compare the arguments of two parties. Political parties use this technique constantly. In essence, the person making the argument will set up a "straw man" (i.e., someone or something which serves as the norm or good standard), and then at the same time criticize the position of the opposing party by comparison.

[g]—Adding Credibility

Visual aids also add credibility to important ideas. Take, for example, an idea that may be expressed to you on the street by someone you may or may not know very well. This person may say, "Someone from Washington, D.C. told me that there was a conspiracy to kill President Bush." Depending upon your own beliefs, you will probably have some doubts about the veracity of this statement. However, if you were to pick up a copy of the local newspaper and you saw a statement which read, "Sources in Washington, D.C. have stated that there was a conspiracy to kill President Bush," you might tend to believe it to be true.

Let's try another example that might arise during a trade secret case. The plaintiff might say something during oral opening statement such as, "The evidence will show that the ABC Company's research executives stole information from technical documents belonging to the plaintiff." The oral statement alone has some power because it contains compelling language. However, if at the same time the attorney makes this statement, the key words appear on a large screen followed by a list of the evidence that will show the statement to be true, the total effect can be very powerful.

Visual words and images add extra weight to messages contained in the argument and provide an external anchor that confirms and adds credibility to the messages. Visual words in images also provide a perception of objectivity in the psychological sense, even though in truth the information contained in the visual aid is anything but objective.

[h]—Explaining and Simplifying the Context

Demonstrative aids can also provide a context for counsel to make a point or an explanation as part of the educational and learning process in trial. Visual aids are frequently used to explain to a judge, jury, or arbitrator how the key actors fit into the entire scheme of things. They are a great tool for displaying all the parts of a complicated scenario to get a "big picture" effect, or alternatively, to draw attention to one component of a larger scenario to show the context.

[i]—Making the Process More Enjoyable for Everyone

The final advantage to using visual aids is that they can be enjoyable to use. Certainly they remind us of when we were school children learning to express ourselves through pictures and drawings. After all, developing visual aids that demonstrate to the court the themes and story of the case is as much a creative process as it is a logical one. Because considerable research and thinking are required to develop the most powerful messages for a case and the expression of them through the use of visual aids, developing demonstrative aids is hard work. However, the most powerful and compelling visual aids are those which evolve through a creative, playful process.

Visual aids are also more enjoyable for our audiences. There is nothing more painful for a juror than being forced to listen to lawyers drone on at the courthouse in the middle of a hot summer afternoon. However, at the first sight of interesting visual aids, the agony seems to abate and be replaced with more pleasant feelings.

[2]—The Psychological Connection Between Attitudes and Visual Attention

There has been a great deal of psychological research relating to the relationship between attitudes and visual attention. The marketing research that we discussed above indicated that the most highly persuasive commercials on television are those which incorporate key messages with a visual experience. But what does that mean to us in terms of incorporating our messages in a court case? What is the relationship between jurors' pre-existing attitudes and beliefs and the specific visual aids to be used in the courtroom? We may have the world's greatest visual artist working with our trial team, but what is the message that should be conveyed?

We know from our discussion about the psychology of decision making and research into the likely perceptions of judges, jurors, and arbitrators prior to trial that there are some specific methods that we can use to identify the most significant primary messages. Our mock trial or mock arbitration research has given us important information to develop our best themes and story. But how do we transfer that knowledge to development of the most powerful and compelling demonstrative aids?

Decades of research provide a number of hypotheses. We know, for example, that people use attitudes to express aspects of their social identity. We also know that we consult our existing attitudes and beliefs about situations when we have insufficient time to learn or consider details of a new situation carefully.

Research has also indicated that attitudes are useful in helping us become oriented to new stimuli that we continually encounter. An interesting study that dealt with this hypothesis concerned the reactions of 120 adults to a number of different pictures, images, and visual displays to determine the pre-existing attitudes of the participants, their choices of images, and their judgments about the images.[2]

The researchers found that a person's attitudes do indeed serve an orienting function. People pay more attention to visual stimuli that contain images or messages that correspond with one of their active attitudes or beliefs. That is, people pay more attention to visual stimuli when they have some interest in what the stimuli portray. The research in the study also indicated that this effect is so powerful that people will pay attention to visual contents even when some other matter has the potential to distract them.

Pre-existing attitudes of judges, jurors, and arbitrators influence them at every stage of their processing of visual information. This influence results both from the effects of memory recall and from self-interest. It is therefore important to conduct pretrial research into the mental processing, attitudes, and life experiences of the likely audience. Otherwise, how will we know which attitudes, life experiences, and pretrial characteristics of the fact finder will be stimulated by the case?

---

[2] Roskos-Ewoldsen & Fazio, "On the Orienting Value of Attitudes: Attitude Accessibility as a Determinant of an Object's Attraction of Visual Attention," 63 J. Personality & Soc. Psychology 198-211 (1992).

[3]–Why Multimedia Is So Powerful: The Psychological Connection Between Visual and Verbal Communications

One of the most interesting developments in our culture has been the widespread use of multimedia presentations, such as computer-generated slide shows. As recently as the mid-1990s, public speakers who were using visual aids relied primarily on slide projectors and overhead projectors or charts. Occasionally they would use videotape to support their presentation.

The cost of slides at a local photography shop could easily exceed $300 and took two or three days to generate. Once the slides were created, they could not be altered. If the speaker had a sudden "brainstorm" just prior to a speech and wanted to make changes in the slides, this would be either impossible or very difficult. For these and other reasons, slides were rarely used in trials.

If counsel wanted to show a judge or jury key portions of an important document, one made transparencies for use with an overhead projector and brought along a highlighter pen to mark significant portions of the document. Overhead projectors were usually dim and could only be shown on a screen like the ones we used in grade school.

Now it seems that people everywhere are using multimedia presentations. Every television news program is essentially one long multimedia presentation. People in the sales profession have found that multimedia is a fantastic tool for conveying information in a persuasive way. Business executives have found that multimedia technology makes the presentation of ideas much more interesting and effective.

The advantages to business people in the use of multimedia include:

- Presentations can be customized;
- Multiple presentations of the same information can be consistent;
- Stories are more compelling if they include integration of text, animation, and other visual images;
- A more complete message may be presented (e.g., pop-up screens, etc.);
- Presentations can be changed, updated, and improved constantly with no time delay and at little extra cost (e.g., a presentation slide show can be updated seconds before the presentation);
- The need for carrying around charts, boxes of slides, and other materials is reduced;

 * Information from the Internet can be presented directly on the presentation screen; and
 * The qualities of the medium educate and inspire people.

Advances in technology have made an amazing array of tools available to a trial lawyer for use in integrating visual and verbal messages that are both interesting to view and highly effective in communicating information. One can create a simple multimedia presentation on a laptop computer in a few hours with the right software. Then you can display your presentation on any video screen or blank wall using almost any video projector on the market.

The central issues for experienced trial attorneys are: (1) why this mode of presentation is so effective, (2) when and how to use it, and (3) how to create visual and verbal content that is stimulating and persuasive. Until now, the advances in multimedia technology have been driven by the technology itself and have left trial lawyers and other courtroom professionals in doubt about its effectiveness, when and how to use the technology, and how to integrate what we know about the psychology of persuasion into the technology.

[a]—The Contiguity Principle

There are two psychological principles that are relevant to the development of multimedia presentations. The first is the _contiguity principle_, which states that the effectiveness of a multimedia presentation increases when the words and visual images are presented alongside each other (contiguously) at the same time and in the same space. The second principle is the _modality principle_, which states essentially that words should be presented as auditory narration rather than as visual on-screen text. We will discuss each of these principles briefly. By understanding some of the reasons why multimedia presentations can be so effective, we can make better decisions about when to use them.

The spatial aspects of the contiguity principle indicate that communication is more effective when there is minimal physical space between the printed text and the pictures in a presentation. Recall, for example, the last time you bought something such as a light fixture that required assembly. If the instructions contained only diagrams and pictures and no text, you probably became confused because you could not understand how some of the illustrations related to parts in the box (does that picture show the 1/4" screw or the 1/2" screw?). Or the instructions might have contained illustrations on a different page from the text descriptions. Another possibility is that you were confused because there was no visual relationship between the illustrations and the text.

The best alternative is for the illustration drawings and the text to be adjacent to each other in order to create a mental relationship.

The psychological research studies that have been conducted in this area are quite interesting. Researchers report that people find 50% to 75% more useful and creative solutions to problems when verbal and visual explanations are integrated than when they are separated.

The temporal aspects of contiguity are also interesting and instructive for us. That is, are verbal and visual materials better presented simultaneously or successively? Research indicates that words and pictures presented together outperform words presented before pictures in the learning and creative problem-solving process. Similar research has indicated that voice and pictures presented together outperform voice presented before pictures. However, pictures followed by voice created an effect which was almost as powerful as voice and pictures presented together.

The modes of assimilation for text, voice, and visual images are very different. Each image has a different rate of presentation and assimilation. Each has differing amounts of factual and emotional content. In order to accept the contents of a multimedia presentation, judges, jurors, or arbitrators must split their attention so that the separate senses will be able to comprehend the information coming from different media forms. Moreover, if the content of the information is not well-integrated, the fact finder may become distracted, and the effect of the communications may then become diluted and perhaps lost altogether.

[b]—The Modality Principle

With respect to the modality principle (words should be presented as narration rather than on-screen text), researchers have found that for short-term memory tasks, auditory presentation of words almost always results in greater recall than visual presentation. Of course, the effective capacity of our working memory can be increased by using both visual and auditory methods.

Research related to multimedia learning methods found that students who studied visual presentations with narration outperformed students who studied the same visual presentations, but with text. These studies indicate that dual presentation methods may increase working memory resources by activating both auditory and visual working memory simultaneously, rather than each one separately.

The best trial presentation of multimedia (or any other) material should be developed and presented with these principles in mind. Since people usually encounter new information in everyday life by seeing and hearing it at the same time, the most persuasive presentations of multimedia-based information echo that learning path.

§ 12.03 | JUROR PERCEPTIONS OF DEMONSTRATIVE AIDS: HIGH TECH VS. LOW TECH

We know from our discussion about the psychology of persuading judges, jurors, and arbitrators that they will try to form a story of what happened as quickly as they can. In the process, they will piece together information in a way that makes sense to them. They will form mental pictures. It helps them to absorb new information rapidly and thoroughly enough to satisfy their need to comprehend their version of the case story and decide how the conflict should be resolved. Each fact finder will form his or her unique version of the story including unique pictures in his or her mind.

You will have the best opportunity to win a case if you (1) focus all your energy and resources on helping the jury understand your story in a simple, clear, and interesting manner and (2) tell the story with the jury's perspective in mind. Using visual aids is one of the best strategies for influencing the jury in these ways. Every time you try to make a key point about a fact, relationship, direction, dimension, document, or any other aspect of the transaction(s) that created the conflict between the parties without the use of visual aids, you create a situation where jurors have to substitute their own version instead of yours.

Because today's judges and jurors live in a high-tech world, they do not believe that using the newest technology to display simple, interesting messages is unusual or incomprehensible. We have progressed to the point that jurors often become irritated when trial lawyers use slow, lumbering, painstaking methods for presenting information when jurors themselves know there is a better way to present the same material.

There is hardly a place in the United States where high technology is not in regular use. Digital technology and satellite signals are available in every urban and rural area of the country. The same computer technology and high-technology news broadcasts which are part of regular life in big cities are part of ordinary life on the farm or ranch.

In essence, therefore, the effectiveness of any demonstrative aid depends primarily upon the quality of its content rather than the nature of the high-tech or low-tech tool used.

§ 12.04 | USING FOCUS GROUPS AND MOCK TRIALS TO TEST EFFECTIVENESS

In Chapter 6 we discussed the general use of scientific jury research techniques in the development and presentation of a compelling trial presentation. Research has taught us that we can test the effectiveness of every aspect of a prospective trial presentation with a representative sample from the likely jury pool. The same research techniques can also be used to study both judge and arbitrator reactions.

The effectiveness of demonstrative aids can either be tested separately from other research in the case or combined with a study of the entire case presentation. There are generally two aspects of demonstrative aids that we study scientifically: The first—and most important—is how well the exhibit makes the point or tells the story, and the second is the physical make-up of the exhibit and its design as a factor in making the point or telling the story.

There are many ways to use focus group or mock trial studies in the development of demonstrative aids. Regardless of the method used, you will want to use research wisely and creatively. You will want to get specific reactions to prospective visual aids, and you should obtain original ideas from the research participants you have engaged to participate in the study.

In most cases, it is a good idea for the trial consultant and graphic artist to work together both in the development of the prospective exhibits and in the testing phase. Experienced trial consultants have substantial knowledge (research materials) and good insight about what works in the courtroom and what does not. The best graphic artists have a genius for creativity and visual display of ideas, but very little practical knowledge of the courtroom and little knowledge of psychology. Hence, the two would be most effective if they work closely together on your client's behalf.

§ **12.05** | **GENERAL STRATEGY FOR DEVELOPING AND PRESENTING DEMONSTRATIVE AIDS**

Generally, demonstrative aid strategy will be dictated by the themes and messages to be delivered. However, identifying the best alternative methods of presenting the information and deciding between them requires a great deal of objective decision making and a little intuition.

Most trial attorneys are so accustomed to making split-second decisions about demonstrative aids that substituting a more considered, rational process may initially seem uncomfortable. However, it is shortsighted to create ideas for demonstrative aids without the benefit of objective sources of information. Fortunately, there now exist a substantial body of information and a growing number of highly skilled experts, both of which can help. The more we learn about how different demonstrative aids affect the fact finder, the more effective choices we can make about which strategies to use in developing visual aids to support trial presentations.

It helps to develop a checklist of steps for developing demonstrative aids. This process expands your awareness of ways to develop powerful, creative demonstrative aids for your own trial presentations. Following are some steps to take:

(1) Developing the most powerful themes and case story;
(2) Testing and refining themes and case story;
(3) Identifying key points and themes that can be strengthened with a visual aid;
(4) Developing a list of the most likely visual aids that would help support the point or theme;
(5) Ranking these aids according to their likely strength with the fact finder;
(6) Testing the strengths and weaknesses of your choices with a focus group or mock trial; and
(7) Refining the visual aids.

Although this process of developing and refining demonstrative aids may seem tedious, it is the most effective strategy. Too often members of the trial team become so accustomed to the details of the case that it is difficult for them to distance themselves from the case to foster creative thinking. It is difficult to immerse oneself in the details of complicated litigation and discovery disputes and then step back from the case and generate fresh new ideas about how the case would best be presented to the fact finder.

One of the reasons that trial teams utilize trial consultants and media experts in the development of demonstrative aids is to assist in the generation of powerful and creative ways of expressing the themes and case story. Depending upon their experience and training, these consultants and experts can often generate ideas that help resolve difficult, perplexing problems.

There are a few other fundamental concepts about the use of demonstrative aids in the courtroom that we should now discuss that address some recurring problems during courtroom presentation of demonstrative aids.

[1]—Limiting Information for Each Visual Aid: Focusing vs. Overloading

Whenever counsel first reveals any visual aid or visual evidence to judges, jurors, or arbitrators, they go to work at once trying to understand everything they see. They immediately try to comprehend the details of everything in view. They cannot and will not wait for your explanation of each part of the visual aid. By displaying the entire visual aid at once, you have given the audience permission to scan the entire exhibit and try to understand it. Unfortunately, while you are reviewing the first part of the exhibit, the audience's attention has shifted to the rest of the exhibit.

The best way to use a demonstrative aid is to reveal only the portion that you want the audience to focus on at that time. Later you can add to or build onto that portion as your presentation progresses.

[2]—Use a Building Block Approach

We have a tendency as trial lawyers to want to tell the audience everything at once. We forget that the audience has no familiarity with the subject of our presentation and that information should therefore be provided to them in a natural progression. Sometimes it is helpful to look at the trial presentation as a series of "baby steps." In essence, you take a step and stop to make sure that the audience has comprehended the point you are trying to make; then you take the next step, and so on.

This suggestion may seem to contradict the idea that fact finders tend to absorb information faster than the speed of most trial presentations. However, the progression of the presentation should not be confused with its speed and efficiency.

Note that *control* of the presentation as it unfurls is paramount. Once information is placed before the audience, control over it is lost. Therefore, it is a good idea to pace the presentation and reveal aspects of it in a natural progression.

Setting up an exhibit and revealing its contents in a pre-planned progression of steps also contains an element of showmanship. By moving slowly to set up an exhibit, you create a sense of anticipation in the audience. Then, by slowly revealing the contents of the exhibit step by step, you build upon that sense of anticipation in a controlled, powerful way.

[3]—Visual Aids Should Speak for Themselves

The most powerful visual aids stand on their own. By looking at the title of the exhibit and its contents, the viewer should immediately be able to understand the exhibit's story. One of the primary problems that trial advocates have in the development and use of demonstrative aids is that they assume the fact finder will understand the "thrust" of the exhibit even though the exhibit's context may not be clear from the exhibit's face. In a sense, lawyers tend to wear "blinds" as they develop a case; they understand the details of the case and how the exhibit fits in, but they forget that the judge or jury may not.

It is a good idea to put together a test exhibit and then step back to determine whether it tells a story by itself. Sometimes it is helpful to get the reaction of other people. Focus groups are an excellent tool for testing effectiveness.

[4]—The Scale of Visual Aids Should Match the Courtroom

When counsel prepares the courtroom for the use of visual aids, do not guess where everything should be placed and how everything will work. Painful experience teaches us that some courtrooms are not very friendly to high technology. Moreover, many courtrooms are just too small or irregularly shaped for using your preferred technology. Still others are too large, preventing the judge or jurors from seeing important details across the room.

The only remedy for these kinds of problems is to pretest the demonstrative aids in the actual courtroom where they are to be used. You should sit on the judge's bench and then in the jury box, and go through the exhibits one by one to determine whether each exhibit is effective in that setting.

[5]—Tell, Then Show

As we learned from our discussion about the psychological connection between verbal and visual elements of the presentation, you should tell the judge or jury what you are going to show them, and then show them. You might think of this process as laying a foundation for an exhibit you will be using. By telling the fact finders what you are going to show them, you create interest and give them an opportunity to orient themselves to the exhibit once it is revealed. The first impression of an exhibit is critical to its success.

[6]—Let the Jury Touch Key Documents and Materials

As we have discussed in other contexts, judges, jurors, and arbitrators all learn by engaging their senses of sight, hearing, and touch. Although people primarily rely upon their eyes and ears, they also take great comfort in being able to touch key trial exhibits. For most people, their tactile sense is a kind of anchoring device, whereas for others it is a primary source for learning. In any event, allowing the fact finder to inspect and touch a key exhibit or demonstrative aid can engage him or her in a physical way that can be very powerful.

Almost every case that goes to trial has a few pieces of evidence that should be handed or shown to the jury for physical inspection. Product liability and patent cases are good examples of cases where physical objects can be brought into the courtroom for the jury to inspect.

[7]—Always Consider a Time Line

Time lines are powerful persuasive tools because most people learn about life through chronologies of events and their reactions to these events. Time lines are flexible in their appearance and relative to the events they describe. They can be fashioned to fit virtually every kind of case.

Time lines are also a good tool for a lawyer to use in thinking through a case story. The first time line that we draft for use in a case may be too detailed. It must usually be scaled back to just the essential events that reveal the core issues in the case. Occasionally more than one time line is necessary in a particular case. A general time line will tell the overall story of the case, whereas a more focused time line will tell the story of specific parts of the case.

[8]—Make Sure Everyone Can See the Aid

Unfortunately, one of the most common problems in trial is that an attorney will show a document or demonstrative aid that one or more of the fact finders cannot see. Some jurors become very angry when they are not respected enough to be shown a visual aid that everybody else is able to see.

There are generally two things you can do to avoid this problem. The first is to test out the exhibit prior to trial to make sure that it can be easily seen. The second is to develop the ability to constantly survey the jury to make sure everyone can see and hear what is being presented.

[9]—If the Visual Aid Is Really Important, Refer to It Often

If a visual aid is important to your key themes and story, it should be referred to throughout the trial. An important exhibit should be referred to in voir dire, and then again during opening statement, witness testimony, and closing argument.

Repetition of themes and visual aids that represent themes is important in both the learning and persuasive aspects of trial. In some cases, jurors have even re-created demonstrative aids during jury deliberation when the aids were not admitted into evidence. In these instances, the demonstrative aids were so powerful that they became a central part of the jury's learning and decision process.

For example, in one high-profile trade secrets case, the sequence of events and their meaning were important to the jury. One of the trial attorneys had created a time line as a demonstrative exhibit to indicate that, because of the chronological sequence of events, his client could not possibly have stolen the plaintiff's trade secrets. Even though the trial court would not allow the time line to go to the jury, during deliberations the jury taped key documents to the wall in chronological order to create their own time line.

[10]—Practice Using the Visual Aid with Witnesses

One of the most disheartening experiences in trial occurs when an important witness who is being questioned on direct examination is unfamiliar with one or more important visual aids or fumbles with the aid(s). The story is interrupted and the jury's attention is lost. Even worse, the jury can get the impression that the trial attorney and witness are unprepared.

Clearly, a little practice can go a long way toward telling a story smoothly and effectively. Whether or not the witness has worked with a trial consultant, the trial team should set aside time for the witness to practice testifying with the demonstrative aids that will be used during the witness's testimony. The best place to practice is in the same courtroom where the trial will take place, or at least another similar courtroom environment.

§ 12.06 | DETERMINING THE BEST DEMONSTRATIVE AID TO USE

There are three fundamental principles to guide counsel in determining the best visual aid to use in a particular situation. The first is that the message you wish to convey is more important than the format of visual aid you use. The second is that each medium has its own built-in advantages and disadvantages that will dictate the type of message that can be conveyed by that medium. Finally, there is the comfort factor. Both the trial lawyer and the jurors are probably more comfortable with the use of certain media for particular purposes.

All three principles affect when the following kinds of visual aids are considered for inclusion in a trial.

[1]—Easel Pads and Chalkboards

Large stand-up, multi-page easel pads should be a part of every trial lawyer's arsenal. They are flexible and can be used for many purposes. They are a general visual support tool. One of the most important functions that they serve is give counsel a means to record the key points that each witness makes for the jury. Easel pages can easily be referred to in closing argument for psychological support and as anchoring mechanisms. Jurors will more readily recall the testimony of particular witnesses when easel paper that was used to record the key points during the testimony is exhibited to them during cross-examination of witnesses and/or summation.

Most people are familiar with chalkboards and most courthouses have chalkboards available. Jurors feel comfortable with chalkboards. Most of the boards are large and can be used by counsel to make spontaneous lists and drawings during witness testimony and argument. Of course, chalkboards by their very nature have some irritating qualities. The scraping sounds some people make with chalk can completely disrupt a trial presentation. It is also hard to see some of the markings that are made on chalkboards with ordinary chalk.

[2]—Photographs and Enlargements

Whether a picture "is worth a thousand words" has never been measured with precision. However, following is an example of how it can be worth, say, seventy-one words. The example deals with a cigarette lighter that was recalled by the U.S. Consumer Product Safety Commission. No-one had been hurt by the lighter, but it was deemed to be dangerous nonetheless. *Try covering the photograph with your hand and just reading the text to determine if you can envision what the recalled lighter must look like.* The text description of the lighter reads as follows:

> "The disposable cigarette lighters being recalled are oval tubes shaped with a roll and press type ignition mechanism. The lighters have a blue, orange, red or clear transparent case and a chrome metal windshield surrounding the flame port. Stamped into one side of the windshield is the brand name 'youjie.' A warning label on the back of the lighters reads in part, 'WARNING: KEEP AWAY FROM CHILDREN' and 'MADE IN CHINA.'"

Now here is a photograph of the same lighter.

U.S. Consumer Product Safety Commission
http://www.cpsc.gov/CPSCPUB/PREREL/prhtml01/01120.html

In another example the Commission was working with Fisher-Price Toy Company to recall a table toy that had knobs that some children had tried to chew or swallow. No-one had been hurt by the toy at the time of the recall. Here is the text description provided by the Commission. *Again, cover the photograph with your hand and read the text description. Try to envision what the toy looks like based upon the description.*

> "The Intelli-Table is a round, plastic activity table with a blue, removable top that uses three interchangeable play rings to help children learn numbers, music, and games. The toy is intended for children ages nine to 36 months. The base of the Intelli-Table is red with three legs that are blue, yellow and teal green. The play rings are colored white, yellow and teal green. The red knobs on the yellow ring and white ring can break off. The toy has a Fisher-Price logo on the blue removable top; and has the model number, 77148, and the words, 'Mattel, Inc.' and 'China' molded into the bottom of the red base. Only models manufactured from September 25, 2000 through October 7, 2000 are being recalled. The recalled models have a date code from 269(0) through 281(0) molded into the underside of the blue, removable top."

Now here is the photograph.

U.S. Consumer Product Safety Commission
http://www.cpsc.gov/CPSCPUB/PREREL/prhtml01/01115.html

Photographs are a great tool for use as a tangible exhibit that appeals to all of the jurors' key senses.

[3]—Juror Notebooks

Juror notebooks with identical contents to be distributed by counsel to each juror should be considered for every trial. These notebooks can contain key evidence and demonstrative aids that will help the jury learn about the case. Juror notebooks may only contain documents and materials which would otherwise be shown to the jury anyway. For this reason, it is best for the parties to reach agreement or obtain court rulings about these materials in advance of trial and in time for their inclusion in the juror notebooks

Juror notebooks provide many advantages. The primary advantage for litigants is that all jurors, regardless of their learning habits, have a better chance of learning about the case and absorbing the details of each of the exhibits and demonstrative aids during the trial presentations.

Advantages for jurors are two-fold: First, jurors can get a closer look at key materials in order to better understand their relevance to the case and obtain answers to some of their individual questions about these materials. Second, by having their own individual copies of these key materials, jurors can search back and forth between the materials in order to better study their interrelationships.

Imagine what it would be like if you were taking a class in a complicated subject area and you were not allowed to refer to any study or text materials. The only way you would be able to learn in this class would be from the professor's lecture and demonstrations. How would you feel if on the second or third day of this complicated class, someone suddenly walked up to you and handed you a textbook containing all the reference materials? Would you feel a sudden sense of relief? Would you be grateful that someone cared enough about you to give you these materials?

That's how jurors feel when the court or the attorneys give them juror notebooks.

[4]—Videotaped Deposition Excerpts

The vast majority of videotaped depositions wind up on the cutting room floor. Less than 5% of most videotaped depositions and trial testimony actually is shown to the jury. Most of the tape shown to the jury includes testimony of people who for various reasons do not testify in person at trial. Occasionally some of the tape is used during cross-examination for impeachment and other purposes.

Unfortunately, jurors generally despise videotaped deposition excerpts, unless they are used briefly and judiciously. They much prefer live testimony so that they can witness some interpersonal reaction by counsel with the witness. This preference is supported by research which indicates that live testimony is given more credibility and weight than the same testimony which has been videotaped.

For this reason, we are sometimes concerned when one of our witnesses has created a problem during a videotaped deposition which we believe will be used by the opposing party during the trial. Sometimes a witness's testimony has changed since the time of the deposition. However, jury research indicates that jurors will forgive problems or changes in videotaped testimony as long as the witness provides a reasonable explanation.

[5]—Videotaped Demonstrations and Scene Re-creations

Videotaped demonstrations and scene re-creations are a powerful way of taking the fact finder to the scene (without an actual view) for purposes of teaching and persuading. Most jurors will recall the use of videotapes as learning tools in school. Others will think of them as a source of entertainment.

There are a number of considerations for their use. Videotapes can be expensive to make. Most courtroom experts believe that it is best to have a professional, experienced video team prepare and edit videotaped demonstrations and scene re-creations. Videotapes that are made outdoors are especially expensive.

However, sometimes "homemade" videotaped demonstrations can be made to seem humble and even charming. An expert witness can often use a self-made videotaped demonstration or scene re-creation that is down-to-earth and in keeping with the expert's casual, likeable style.

Editing videotape is generally pretty simple and not very expensive compared to some other types of visual aids such as animations. Even so, editing should be done by a professional. Amateur editing jobs on a ordinary VCR look sloppy at best and are irritating to the fact finder, but professional editing jobs that include titles and transitions can be a pleasure to watch. A thorough editing job will also help cull out those portions of the videotape that are really not essential to the story. Most videotapes should be no longer than ten minutes.

The trial lawyer should always introduce a videotape before it is shown in court. The introduction should explain why the videotape is being used and why it is the best medium to demonstrate certain matters. If jurors are not given an introductory explanation, they tend to believe the videotape is some kind of public relations gimmick and they will not be interested.

As with all demonstrative aids, a videotaped demonstration or scene re-creation should be developed with the team and case story in mind. No videotaped demonstration or scene re-creation should be undertaken until counsel prepares a storyboard which lays out the natural progression of the tape demonstration. If there are changes to be made in the development of the visual scene, they should be done before the taping, not during it. Changes made during the taping often cause the natural flow of the videotape to be disrupted and may arouse jurors' suspicion.

Videotapes are very good tools to take the fact finder to a scene and experience the setting where key events took place. It is a very effective learning and persuasive medium. Often a speaker—trial counsel or witness—will use videotapes to guide the fact finder through a scene while he or she narrates.

Videotapes are not a good medium for demonstrating complex ideas and concepts. Complicated images and ideas are best communicated directly between the trial attorney and the fact finder by the use of other media.

[6]—Live Demonstrations

Jurors and other fact finders generally enjoy live demonstrations. Demonstrations are exciting and interesting by their very nature. However, we are not always sure how demonstrations will turn out. Demonstrations are conducted in the presence of the fact finders, who then may feel as if they are a part of the demonstrations. Demonstrations use the very same products and materials that are at issue in the case and, therefore, fact finders feel more involvement with the subject matter. Because demonstrations are conducted before our very eyes, we trust them.

Like other visual aids, demonstrations should be tested in advance and should be preceded by introductions and explanations.

[7]—Charts and Graphs

Charts or graphs should be chosen as a medium only when they are the best medium for the subject of the visual aids. Often charts and boards are used by lawyers who either have no imagination or fail to think about the effect of those charts and boards. Consequently, most of the charts and boards used in courtrooms are boring and awkward to use. Computerized slide presentations are often much better, but they are frequently overlooked.

Charts, graphs, and boards are useful because they are clear and concise. They are tangible, which adds some finite credibility to them. Charts can be placed side by side for comparisons, whereas other media cannot. Charts are permanent visual aids that can be sent into the jury room for deliberations with the court's approval.

However, in cases where charts and boards are the best media to use, there are a number of considerations for their best use. The first is to reveal only the salient parts of the chart or board at a time. Velcro strips are useful for hiding portions of the chart as you begin your presentation. You can create interest by making a transitional statement or asking a rhetorical question just before you remove a strip and reveal more of the chart or board. (You can also achieve the same effect with computerized slides.)

Following is a set of raw data from information provided by the National Center for Injury Prevention and Control ("NCIPC") at the HHS Centers for Disease Control and Prevention ("CDC"). These data indicate leading causes of death in the State of New York in 1998.

Leading Causes of Death in the State of New York (1998)

1.	Heart Disease	724,859
2.	Malignant Neoplasms (Cancer)	541,532
3.	Cerebrovascular	158,448
4.	Bronchitis, Emphysema, Asthma	112,584
5.	Unintentional Injuries and Adverse Effects	97,835
6.	Pneumonia and Influenza	91,871
7.	Diabetes	64,751
8.	Suicide	30,575
9.	Nephritis	26,182
10.	Liver Disease	25,192

The data are interesting, but to understand the relationships or rank order between the causes of death can require considerable imagination, calculation, and visualization—unless you have a chart to help draw a picture like the following one:

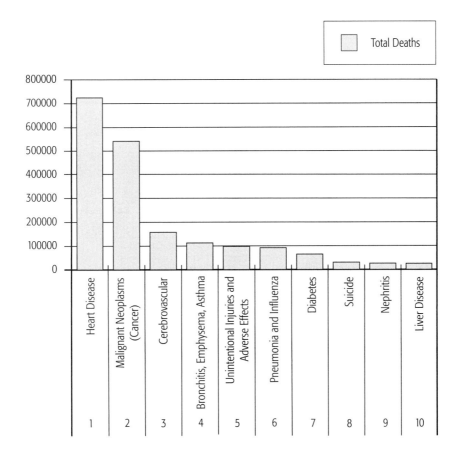

Leading Causes of Death in the State of New York (1998)

[8]—Models

Models are interesting because they re-create real life, generally on a smaller scale. (Some models enlarge a small or even microscopic item to make it available for examination by the fact finder.) Psychologically, models help draw the observer into the mechanism or scene. Models can help simplify and explain complex situations or things that are difficult to visualize.

For the most part, full-scale models are best to use because they are closest to real life, and jurors therefore tend to accept them best. The authenticity that a model conveys to jurors can be very persuasive.

Models can be fairly expensive to use because an artist must study the original, create the design, locate the proper materials, create the model, and then transport the model to the courtroom safely. If models are broken, they are sometimes difficult if not impossible to repair. As a result, often an animation is a better choice than a model because it can be changed easily without much expense, whereas a model can cost a good deal to change. In addition, animation can be changed quickly as the need arises, frequently within minutes, whereas a model often requires several days to change.

[9]—Computer-Generated Animations

One of the most amazing recent technological developments is computer-generated animation. Scientific studies of the effects of animations in the persuasion process have indicated that they can be very powerful influences on a fact finder's perceptions. One study compared the persuasive effect of a computer simulation of an air crash, an audiotape with written transcript of a cockpit voice recorder, and a speaker reading the cockpit voice recorder transcript.[3] The researchers studied the reactions of seventy-two adults by dividing them into small mock juries and then asking them to decide whether there was pilot error based on the evidence to which they had been exposed.

The researchers found that the jurors who were shown the computer animation—which was designed to place the observer of the animation in the pilot's seat—believed the flight crew to be significantly less negligent than the other jurors. In effect, the animations created a rapport between the jurors and the flight crew, and made finding the crew guilty of negligence very difficult.

Animations are also powerful because they can take us to places where human beings cannot go. They can take us inside the human body to see the processes that occur. They permit us to "observe" an incident when no-one was actually present as an eyewitness. They create circumstances based upon the facts of a case and the reasonable inferences that can be drawn from them.

---

[3] Houston, Joiner, Uddo & Harper, "Computer Animation in Mock Juries' Decision Making," 76 Psychological Rep. 987-993 (1995).

Animations are helpful in compiling parts of events and launching them into continuous motion. They help the jury learn the position of the party who offers the animation in some instances better than any other type of medium.

Animations also have the advantage of consistency regardless of the number of times they are repeated. Whether you play animations once or 10,000 times, they will always repeat the same images.

General advantages of the animations that make them powerful include the fact that they are colorful and interesting. Animations bring facts to life in a memorable fashion, particularly when they are repeated in different phases of the trial and with different witnesses. Another advantage is that the most compelling animations incorporate themes and messages that support the case story. Most experienced trial consultants and graphic artists are very knowledgeable about the best elements to use in your case, and help test animation effectiveness.

One objection usually raised by an opposing party to animation is that it constitutes argument. However, a properly prepared animation presents no more argument than any other demonstrative aid. Any argumentativeness can be easily cured by an introduction of the animation that explains that it is only a representation of one side's version of what happened. Another objection that may be encountered is the opposing party's allegation that the animation is misleading and manipulates the uncontested facts unfairly. Generally, the judge must determine whether such an animation is admissible in evidence or would be unduly prejudicial.

[10]—Traditional and Electronic Overhead Projectors

Overhead transparency projectors are not often used in the courtroom these days. Many practitioners believe that they are cumbersome and old-fashioned. However, new electronic overhead projectors that utilize a videocamera pointed down to an original document and then displayed on a screen are very popular.

This popularity is a result of the fact that no preparation of the document or of transparencies is necessary. The projectors can be used to display any kind of photograph, drawing, or text document at a moment's notice. Recent developments have included a built-in "switcher" which allows a trial lawyer to click a button to change the images on the screen from the overhead projector to any other projection equipment.

[11]—Computer-Generated Slides

By far the most popular type of demonstrative medium in use these days is computer-generated slides. The reasons for this popularity are discussed above.[4]

In addition to the advantages stated above,[5] jurors appreciate simple, interesting visual images to support a trial presentation. Most computer-generated slide presentations are smooth and seamless. They can incorporate text, images of documents, photographs, video images, and many other media all in the same slide presentation.

Jurors understand that high-tech equipment is being used to display the slide show, but they do not view the use of high-tech equipment as being extreme or intrusive unless wires and equipment seem to swallow the courtroom. Otherwise, a very effective computer-generated slide show can be produced from an inconspicuous laptop and shown on the same screen as an old-fashioned overhead projector. For this reason, much of the consternation that some lawyers feel about using computers in the courtroom is baseless.

§ 12.07 | PAPERLESS TRIALS AND COMPUTER-GENERATED IMAGING

The term "paperless trial" is more an ideal than a reality. It will be many years before all documents and materials in a court case are saved in digital or microfiche format. However, there is some very useful technology in place that can improve organization and reduce clutter at trial.

[1]—Advantages of Computer-Generated Imaging

With the development of high-powered desktop and laptop computers and more flexible, quick database software programs, we are able to manipulate large data files that contain trial exhibits and images faster and more efficiently than ever before. In addition, with the widespread use of CD-ROMs recording drives on computers, it is very simple to copy trial exhibits, video deposition

---

[4] See § 9.02[3] *supra* relative to the psychological connection between visual and verbal communications.

[5] *Id.*

excerpts, demonstrative aids, and virtually any materials that can be stored digitally onto CDs (that can hold millions of megabytes of data). These CDs can be created by a trial team or an audio/video professional and then used in any computer in the courtroom to display their contents.

A great deal of time and money must be spent in scanning documents and other materials manually onto the software, but as law firms become more adept at the use of imaging and replay equipment, the cost is decreasing. Not surprisingly, the benefits of using computer imaging are substantial.

Computer imaging can greatly increase the effectiveness of a trial presentation by managing a natural flow and mixture of different documents, photographs, video deposition excerpts, and other materials without the traditional avalanche of papers and other materials. Computer files which contain these different materials can be located or called up at will and rearranged in different order by a simple computer keystroke.

Computer imaging also makes the discovery phase of a case much more thorough and effective. Documents can be scanned and imaged as they are produced along with identification numbers that can be logged and recalled in seconds. Traditional discovery methods required rooms and warehouses in which to store discovery materials and copies of them. If there were any questions about discovery, boxes of documents would have to be retrieved and carried to the courtroom for inspection by the trial judge.

With computer imaging, the process of resolving discovery problems is much less expensive and burdensome. If there are problems with discovery, the trial judge can view the problematic or missing documents using CD-ROMs and a laptop computer.

[2]—Juror Perceptions of Computer-Generated Imaging

The advantages of the imaging for jurors are a little more complex. Jurors are aware of the cognitive aspects of seeing and hearing computer-generated images. They appreciate the benefits of being able to learn about a case in a much more interesting and naturally flowing presentation. However, jurors also like to be able to touch and sense key materials. Therefore, the most compelling, effective computer-generated demonstration of exhibits and documents will also provide a hard copy of key materials for jurors to inspect at close hand.

[3]—Choosing and Working with Technical People in the Courtroom

A few law firms have audio/visual technical people on staff, but most trial lawyers prefer to use professional audio/visual technicians from outside companies. There are a number of important considerations for working with technical people in the courtroom.

The first is that the trial presentation will be smoother and more effective if the technician operating the system is experienced and communicates well with the trial lawyer. If the technician is not experienced or does not communicate well with the trial lawyer, the presentation will most likely be a nightmarish experience.

There are many technical people in the world who know a great deal about computers and can make them do amazing things. But the proportion of these people who are good communicators and are easy to work with in the courtroom appears to be very small.

It is wise to search for technical people by their reputations and references from other trial lawyers. However, there is no substitute for experience. If you have any doubts about the audio/visual technicians with whom you will be working in a trial, it is best to conduct a dress rehearsal either in the courtroom to be used for the trial or one that is similar. (In fact, a dress rehearsal is a good idea for every case under almost all circumstances.)

We can offer one more piece of advice: Positioning another trial lawyer on your team next to the technician during key presentations can be invaluable. Despite the skill and communication levels of technicians, they are not lawyers. They will sometimes be called upon to produce an image on the screen and suddenly lack critical understanding about a legal issue that can potentially be solved by a second trial lawyer in close proximity who is able to make necessary judgment calls.

§ 12.08 | THE FUTURE OF COURTROOM PRESENTATION TECHNOLOGY

We are rapidly moving into an era where the new capabilities of presentation technology will transform courtroom presentations from simple old-fashioned storytelling into high-technology theater. The superficial debate about whether to use "high-tech" or "low-tech" will be moot. We will automatically consider a wide variety of visual techniques to support every trial presentation that uses traditional methods (e.g., pads and easels or videotapes), as well as more colorful, organized methods (e.g., computer-based slides, animations, or streaming technology).

The most recent developments in high-tech hardware and software are both more sophisticated and "user-friendly" than those which we have been using. They allow trial teams to easily tell a story such that the technology support is seamless and invisible to the audience. With these new tools, the themes and story of a case may be portrayed in ways that are more interesting and meaningful to judges, juries, and arbitrators in an age in which popular culture is saturated with storytelling through technologically enhanced television shows and movies.

Presentation technology can be divided into topics about *things* (e.g., computer hardware and software) and *techniques* (e.g., special strategic planning and storyboards). Because there are so many recent developments in presentation technology, we will discuss them in relationship to new developments in the courtroom environment, how new developments can be integrated into telling your story, how the perceptions of courtroom decision makers are impacted, and how to develop an effective strategy for using advanced technologies in your case.

[1]–High-Tech Courtrooms

In an age when most courtrooms in America are aging and ill-equipped to accommodate advances in computer and visual technology, it may seem inappropriate to give much credence to discussion of high-tech courtrooms. However, judges, court administrators, and legislators are discovering that advances in courtroom technology are becoming more of a necessity than a luxury. When the rest of the business and academic world operates moment by moment with the latest computerized or high-tech visual systems, at some point it becomes absurd for courts to persist in requiring cases to be tried with thirty- to fifty-year-old presentation systems.

If litigators must provide real-life information about a case to judges or jurors, antiquated courtrooms force their clients to make tough choices about how much of the truth to omit. Most of the older courtroom presentation systems may be compared to two-lane highways through which sixteen lanes of traffic must pass.

Judges and jurors who are now accustomed to learning case information quickly and adequately via the new technology, are often forced in older courtrooms to learn about the details of a controversy in limited ways to which they have not been exposed for decades. In the days of the movie *Twelve Angry Men,* which still provides an exemplar for juror learning and jury deliberations, most jurors were still accustomed to learning about the world through word of mouth, newspapers, or radio. In those days people took more time to think about the news and to listen to other people's views.

Today's judges, jurors, and arbitrators learn about the world primarily through their computer screens or television sets. Fewer and fewer people are reading newspapers, although a substantial audience still listens to hourly radio news and weekday talk shows. Today most people take only seconds to listen to new information and seconds to make day-to-day decisions. On more important matters, they expect to receive all the relevant data quickly, easily, and in a way that helps them make immediate decisions. Over time, judges, jurors, and arbitrators have become conditioned to making "snap" decisions as a matter of course. Trial lawyers must grab decision makers' attention immediately, or risk losing it altogether.

If a controversy involves complicated transactions or facts, courtroom decision makers are often at a serious disadvantage in courtrooms that are technologically inferior because of the lack of presentation systems to help them learn the details and meaning of complex situations. In courtrooms with advanced hardware and software presentation systems that can present any type of human scenario, decision makers can more fully comprehend complicated facts and circumstances. Enhanced presentation systems help judges, jurors, and arbitrators use their time more efficiently and productively. Although there is little scientific research that has studied the effects of high-tech systems in the courtroom *per se,* there is a significant body of scientific data that supports the principle that higher quality presentation systems make high-quality decisions more likely.

In essence, then, the concept of a modern courtroom will inevitably change. Instead of an environment where only selected (and antiquated) means of admitting information is allowed, courtrooms will become places where modern life in all of its technological and complicated facets will be welcomed and re-experienced by all trial participants.

The enhancements in technology that will occur in the new generation of courtrooms will also be designed to serve the needs of everyone who participates in the litigation process, including the judge, courtroom staff, attorneys, witnesses, court reporters, and the jury. All of these participants have specialized needs, many of which overlap.

The new high-tech systems in courtrooms will have a number of important features. They include:

- ♦ Enhanced display of information
- ♦ Enhanced room quality audio systems
- ♦ Mechanisms for instantaneous preparation and maintenance of an accurate trial record in a high-tech environment
- ♦ Videoconferencing
- ♦ Physical control by the judge or court staff
- ♦ Functional, comfortable furniture
- ♦ Technologically enhanced courtroom infrastructure

Perhaps we should discuss some of the components we expect to see in high-tech courtrooms in the future.

[a]—Presentation and Visual Communication Systems

The presentation systems that we will see in courtrooms in the future will include some equipment with which we are familiar, but will also include many new and sophisticated items of hardware and software that will help us to enhance and revolutionize the quality of our presentations. In the old days, we would expect to see a chalkboard, pad and easel, overhead projector, and perhaps a television and VCR.

In the future, we will expect to see document cameras (such as the Elmo, DOAR, or Sony models), large viewing screens and/or flat screen monitors, enhanced sound systems, DVD and CD players, and video projectors flexible enough to accommodate any laptop computer and audio input device currently used in homes and offices. To give the trial team centralized control of all the presentation equipment, central control systems will be available within a lectern-like cabinet that will allow a trial lawyer to present information from a variety of visual sources with just a touch of a few buttons. The prototype for these systems has already been installed in such courtrooms as United States District Courts in Cleveland, Indianapolis, Orlando, Portland (Oregon), and other venues.[6]

---

[6] The DOAR company in Rockville Centre, New York has already installed DEPS™ (Digital Evidence Presentation Systems) in these federal courts.

Even though large-screen monitors will often be used in courtrooms, we will likely find that the use of smaller, high-resolution flat-panel monitors is more conducive to the courtroom environment and enhances the learning experience of judges and jurors better than other types of viewing systems. Because flat-panel monitors are hardwired into a central computer in the courtroom, they allow the trial attorneys and the judge to review information together before displaying it to the jury. In addition, individualized monitors are more familiar to judges and jurors because of their increasing familiarity with computer screens and television sets.

To complement these viewing systems, most courtrooms in the future will have audio systems to enhance the quality and consistency of sound for all the trial participants. These enhanced audio systems will allow judges and jurors to hear recorded statements (such as videotaped depositions or audio tapes) much better than the primitive sound systems that are predominantly in use today. The sound quality in well-designed courtrooms in the future will be similar to the sound quality that you expect in a movie theater.

Because control of trial proceedings is so important to the court, trial judges will be provided with "kill switches" or "delay switches" that will allow the judge to review information prior to its dissemination to the jury. These and other devices will allow a trial judge to exert traditional control over the courtroom environment while at the same time allowing a fuller, more meaningful decision-making experience for the jury.

Another new feature that will be in more courtrooms is videoconferencing equipment that, historically, is an innovative two-way communication tool that can be used to enhance the work of courts in many ways. Videoconferencing permits trial judges to hold meetings and hearings with trial lawyers, judges, and other people who may be located anywhere in the world. Trial attorneys can present witnesses and other evidence to judges, juries, and arbitrators. Moreover, court proceedings can be televised without filling the courtroom with cameras and media people.

[b]—Maintaining a Trial Record in a High-Tech Environment

Court reporters and other court staff members must be considered in any high-tech courtroom environment. Traditional court reporting methods would clearly be inadequate to handle the onslaught of visual and technical data presented in a high-tech courtroom. In addition, trial teams often need access to the details of the trial record at the end of each day in order to prepare for the following day's proceedings.

In response to these needs, real-time court reporting systems have been developed which have special advantages for keeping an adequate record in a high-tech environment. Not only can trial judges, court reporters, and trial attorneys see the text record as it is being created, but they can also reproduce it as necessary to support motion hearings, further trial proceedings, and appellate proceedings. In addition, because real-time court reporting systems are digitally based, they can include audio and video computer files. In essence, therefore, the entire court record, including all visual and oral presentations and evidence, can be kept on a computer without one piece of paper record ever having been created.

Voice recognition software will be widely used to allow the voices of trial judges, court reporters, trial lawyers, and witnesses to be transcribed into a digital court reporting system in order to create a text readout of what was said during the trial proceedings. Those of us who remember the days when court reporters made a trial record with manual stenography will likely require a lengthy adjustment period to this development.

Finally, trial participants who require foreign-language translators or who have a hearing impairment can read and contribute to such high-tech proceedings more easily and accurately, speeding up a communication process that has been traditionally slow and tedious.

[c]–Advanced Courtroom Infrastructure

For decades, trial attorneys have complained about courtrooms not having enough power outlets. If you have ever experienced a situation where you had no place to plug in a simple overhead projector or laptop computer, you know how frustrating older courtrooms can be.

In courtrooms that have been enhanced or designed with the ability to accommodate high-tech equipment, old-timers will feel that their prayers have been answered. In the future, courtrooms will have an infrastructure that will accommodate any of the traditional presentation equipment, as well as newly developed hardware and software systems. You will be able to simply plug in the most advanced presentation equipment and allow the images and sounds to instantly be seen and heard anywhere in the courtroom.

In addition to additional electrical wiring and added power outlets, future courtrooms will be built with universal cabling standards that will support multiple audio, visual, and data technologies. In effect, the courtroom of the future will be "plug and play."[7]

[2]—Advances in Storytelling Technology

As we have discussed in other chapters, judges, juries, and arbitrators learned about the world through narrative storytelling from the time they were children. As they grew older, their learning experiences continued through direct life experiences as well as through their observations of other people in the media or in movies. Television and movie directors and their technological support groups are constantly developing ways to enhance the power and depth of their storytelling capability by using technological advances. It is remarkable how movie directors can now tell stories by integrating themes, characters, and plot using powerful, but almost invisible technology. These directors have studied the basic storytelling model (using beginning, middle, and end formats), and they innately understand the need to develop characters and plots slowly and deliberately. They know how to tell a story that carries a compelling message, but they do it with great technical virtuosity.

One of the most often used techniques of movie directors (now in use by trial lawyers and trial consultants) is the creation of a storyboard to help distill a story down to its key components. There are many benefits to a good storyboard. It helps the trial team to integrate the key physical and visual parts of the case to the themes and persuasive story. The storyboard helps to identify key information in the case that can be told by demonstrative aids, and suggests which demonstrative aids would be most helpful and persuasive to a jury. Finally, a good storyboard also acts as a real-life checklist to make sure that the demonstrative presentation is complete.

One of the benefits of new technology is that it helps persuade people quickly. As we have discussed, judges, jurors, and arbitrators have become conditioned to obtaining the most highly relevant information within seconds and making decisions within minutes. In hour-long television shows, the entire story minus commercial breaks, including the trial, takes about forty-three minutes. At the end of that time, you know what happened, why it happened, how it was resolved, and what it means to you. On television news programs, you learn about an event in fifteen to thirty seconds.

---

[7] Adopting the reference from the Universal Plug and Play Forum, an industry initiative begun by Microsoft Corporation designed to enable simple, robust connectivity among stand-alone devices and PCs from many different vendors.

In addition to art-enhanced videotapes and audiotapes, courtroom animations will continue to be used more and more as we explore how to adapt them to courtroom storytelling. Animators will continue to develop ways of helping trial lawyers tell whole stories or parts of stories. In the psychological sense, a well-done animation can help a trial lawyer to frame an issue or tell a story better than any other device. In the future, animation software and technology will be able to make courtroom animation seem like real life. Plane crashes, explosions, nefarious business practices, and every other aspect of life can safely be re-enacted through animation. A caveat to such presentations might well be the opposing party's efforts to keep such an animation from being presented to a jury on the grounds of relevance, materiality, speculation, and prejudice. A court may well rule against the admissibility of such an animation.

[3]—The Psychology of the Decision Maker in an Age of Advanced Technology

As we have discussed often in this book, the psychology of judges, jurors, and arbitrators is complex. However, there are two basic principles that will help us put the subject of technology into a more useful perspective. First, the underlying needs of decision makers to find the true meaning of the case and to make a decision that supports their self-esteem do not change, no matter what type of technology is used to present information. Second, the learning strategies that decision makers use to understand new facts and circumstances often change as the world around them changes.

If we lose sight of the underlying needs of courtroom decision makers, we are disadvantaged. Therefore, even though we may find the use of advanced technology to be fascinating, we should remember that technology is a tool to serve the goals of a presentation. Technological innovations are not a solution in and of themselves.

There are a number of trends that we have noticed in the psychology of decision makers in this age of advanced technology. The first has to do with cognitive and learning issues. As we have noted, judges, juries, and arbitrators want information in rapid, complete, and meaningful formats. They need to understand the basics of a case quickly. A second trend we have noticed in studying juror attitudes is that jurors believe that there are readily identifiable good guys and bad guys. Increasingly over the past twenty years, movie producers and news media professionals have saturated the public with information about the battles between opposing forces in international relations, business matters, and personal struggles to overcome overwhelming odds. As a result, jurors' fundamental beliefs that the world is full of good guys and bad guys has been reinforced.

In today's culture there is often a void of meaning felt by people of all ages. Young people are struggling to find themselves in an age where they are saturated with conflicting stimuli and multiple distractions. Older people feel left behind in a high-tech, fast-paced world. Single people and married people alike find themselves awash in details all day as they try to cope with demands for their attention. They struggle to sort through the mind-boggling avalanche of information that assails them just to stay focused on a few important, meaningful elements in their lives.

By the time these people get to the courtroom, they are anxious to get on with business and to have a rare and meaningful experience. They are willing to work hard to understand the circumstances of the case and to find its essential meaning.

They are familiar with allegations of alleged whining plaintiffs and greedy corporations. They have already observed hundreds of movies, documentaries, and news programs wherein exposés or investigations examined the wrenching experiences of people during personal or business crises. Most likely, they are just as familiar with the themes of your case as you are.

Judges, jurors, and arbitrators have become accustomed to the matter-of-fact use of high-tech means to make a point. For example, in the recent Rodney King police brutality trial in Los Angeles, defense attorneys representing the police officers used a digitized videotape of the police officers beating King to enhance their argument that King caused the officers to beat him and that he was in control of the situation. By digitizing visual images of an event or a person's behavior, a trial team has the ability to stop the action instantly, play it back, and cause the decision makers to focus on it. In communications terms, this allows a trial team such as the defense team in the King case to frame an argument and use actual visual images from the key evidence in support.

Generally, contemporary judges, jurors, and arbitrators find nothing unusual or high-handed about the use of presentation technologies such as the ones we have discussed. In fact, most of the presentation technologies that trial attorneys use are considerably less sophisticated than those used in movie production and news programs with which courtroom decision makers are quite familiar.

Based upon our study of decision-making processes, there are a number of conclusions we can reach about how to choose presentation systems. First, the messages and story of a case presentation must be decided before we address the question of presentation format. Second, the visual images and stories we present will be impressed in the minds of people you are trying to reach and will greatly influence their decisions. Third, we must focus our visual presentation system strategy on the perceptions of the decision makers, not our own perceptions. Finally, we must boil down a case story quickly, visually, and in a way that conveys the complete meaning of the case to the decision maker.

[4]—Your Decision-Making Process

There often seems to be an inverse relationship between experience and planning. In other words, the more experienced we are in our professional work, the more we tend to take our decision-making process for granted. However, in an age where there are so many important decisions to make about the visual presentation of a case, more care must be taken in the planning and development process. We have to set aside more time to organize our case presentations.

There are several reasons that the planning process is more important today than it was a few years ago. First, there are now many more alternatives from which to choose in developing the visual presentation of a case. Second, there are more people who must be involved in the development of a case presentation because of the specialties that need to be incorporated. Third, some of the choices can be very expensive. Enormous amounts of money can be wasted on aspects of visual presentations that are never completed or used in trial. Enormous cost savings for the client(s) can be effected if you devote enough time planning and refining the visual presentation before spending development money.

Generally speaking, groups make better decisions than individuals, no matter how intelligent an individual may be. Therefore, instituting an organized brainstorming process with others who share goals is usually wise. Brainstorming should begin at least four months prior to trial. Everyone on the trial team, particularly the senior members of the team, must be involved in every session. The team should also include legal assistants and other members of the support group, as well as graphics experts and your trial consultant.

The reason that complete cooperation and involvement from everybody in the team is necessary is simple. There is a direct relationship between the quality of your result (an integrated, persuasive case presentation) and the complete involvement of all of the trial team members. The more all team members are involved and the more complete information the group has about the substance of the case and the technical information necessary to create visual support for the trial, the more consistent and compelling the trial presentation is likely to be.

To enhance the productivity of the brainstorming sessions, it will be helpful for everyone to know his or her task and the rules of the discussion. From an organizational standpoint, someone should then take the lead as moderator and someone should act as secretary to take detailed notes about information that the group needs and decisions that the group makes. This person might also keep a record of the types of visual systems that the group is considering and the relevant descriptive, cost, and production information necessary to produce each visual aid. A simple table or database can be developed that will include the identifying name or number for a particular visual aid, the type of media to be used, the purpose for the visual aid, who will produce it, the cost, and its production status.

The decision-making process to develop demonstrative aids and visual presentations is different from the decision-making process in most legal matters. There are many constraints imposed by the judicial system regarding presentation of legal issues, procedure, and introduction of evidence. However, developing demonstrative aids is artistic in nature and requires a great deal more freestyle thinking and creative ideas. For this reason, members of the trial team should be encouraged not to eliminate ideas that may seem far-fetched at the time, but could with some "polishing" result in a brilliant trial presentation.

[5]—Sources of Information about Courtroom Technology

A complete list of books, Web sites, and other sources of information about courtroom and presentation technology would be huge and is impossible to compile. Not only are there thousands of products on the market and people who produce them, there are also thousands of technicians, artists, and consultants who have developed different ways of using the technologies that are available. Furthermore, some products and techniques are more advantageous than others.

Nevertheless, following are a few sources that might be helpful in developing ideas for your next trial presentation. Many of these sources will also point you to specific hardware, software, and systems that you should review.

[a]—Web Sites

www.courtroom21.com

www.law.com

www.lawtechnews.com/r4/home.cgi

www.law.ufl.edu/lti/

www.indatacorp.com/

www.presentations.com/presentations/index.jsp

[b]—Books

Halverson, *DesignSense for Presentations*™ (Portland, ME: Proximity Learning, 1999).

Joseph, *Modern Visual Evidence* (New York: Law Journal Press, 1984), updated biannually.

Kantor, *Winning Your Case with Graphics* (Boca Raton, FL: CRC Press, 1998).

Mital, *Advanced Litigation Support and Document Imaging* (New York: Kluwer Law International, 1995).

Rothschild, *Easy Tech: Cases and Materials on Courtroom Technology* (Notre Dame, IN: National Institute for Trial Advocacy, 2001).

Siemer, Effective Use of Courtroom Technology: A Lawyer's *Guide to Pretrial and Trial* (Notre Dame, IN: National Institute for Trial Advocacy, 2001).

Siemer, Rothschild, Stein & Solomon, *PowerPoint for Litigators: How to Create Demonstrative Exhibits and Illustrative Aids for Trial, Mediation, and Arbitration* (Notre Dame, IN: National Institute for Trial Advocacy, 1999).

§ 12.09 | REFERENCES

Fishfader, Howells, Katz & Teresi, "Evidential and Extralegal Factors in Juror Decisions: Presentation Mode, Retention, and Level of Emotionality," 20 Law & Human Behavior 565-572 (1996).

Foley & Pigott, "Race, Age, and Jury Decisions in a Civil Rape Trial," 15 Amer. J. Forensic Psych. 37-55 (1997).

Gergen, "*The Saturated Self*" (New York: HarperCollins, 1991).

Houston, Joiner, Uddo & Harper, "Computer Animation in Mock Juries' Decision Making," 76 Psychological Rep. 987-993 (1995).

Mayer & Sims, "For Whom Is a Picture Worth a Thousand Words? Extensions of a Dual-Coding Theory of Multimedia Learning," 86 J. Edu. Psychology 389-401 (1994).

Moreno & Mayer, "Cognitive Principles of Multimedia Learning: The Role of Modality and Contiguity," 91 J. Edu. Psychology 358-368 (1999).

Oestermeier & Hesse, "Verbal and Visual Causal Arguments," 75 Cognition 65-104 (2000).

Roskos-Ewoldsen & Fazio, "On the Orienting Value of Attitudes: Attitude Accessibility as a Determinant of an Object's Attraction of Visual Attention," 63 J. Personality & Social Psychology 198-211 (1992).

Young & Robinson, "Visual Connectedness and Persuasion," 32 J. Advertising Research 51-59 (1992).

Fact Witnesses

CHAPTER CONTENTS

> *"She always says, my lord, that facts are like cows. If you look them in the face hard enough they generally run away."*

> – Dorothy L. Sayers (1893-1957)
> English author

> *"You never know how much a man can't remember until he is called as a witness."*

> – Will Rogers (1879-1935)

§ 13.01 | INTRODUCTION

Every experienced trial lawyer has stories to tell about fact witnesses who appeared to be composed and competent to testify prior to trial, but who fell apart once they took the witness stand. However, every lawyer also has stories to tell about witnesses who seemed ineffective prior to trial, but were amazingly skilled on the witness stand.

One such amazing witness was the owner of a small company in Arizona that manufactured a special machine on wheels for cleaning cooling towers at electrical power plants. That is, he and an inventor who worked for his company had developed a truck that could be rolled up to the tower equipment to clean it more easily than anything else on the market at that time. This invention saved the company's clients millions of dollars in labor and material costs.

Soon after the new truck was placed on the market, another company which marketed this truck for the owner and inventor realized that it could design its own truck that would accomplish the same task, enabling the marketing company to keep all the sales profits. The marketing company's engineers thereafter created a competitive cleaning truck and began marketing it. Soon the company which owned the original truck began to lose sales because of the competition from its marketing company. Not surprisingly, the small company sued the marketing company for theft of trade secrets, patent infringement, and breach of contract.

At trial, both parties were represented by excellent trial attorneys. During the trial, the three key witnesses were the president of the small company, the inventor, and the sales manager of the marketing company. The president, whom we will call "Mr. Valdez," was a successful entrepreneur and was commonly known to have a "Type A" personality. He liked controlling the conversations in which he engaged. He liked being the "star" in any group discussion. During the pretrial preparation phase, he had spent two days with a member of the trial team and an experienced trial consultant to help him to feel more comfortable in the witness box.

Mr. Valdez was articulate and likeable, until he felt constrained by the rules of court procedure and the process of being confined to the witness chair. When he remembered that his role was to help the jury understand the case, he was charming. However, when he felt oppressed, he appeared angry and agitated.

During trial, the first twenty minutes of his testimony were a disaster. From the counsel table perspective, he looked diminished and shy. He seemed frustrated and anxious, even though he was being asked simple questions by his own attorney. The jurors were fidgeting in response, paying more attention to his uncomfortable behavior than the substance of his testimony. The trial team and trial consultant realized immediately that the president's testimony was not going well and that something dramatic needed to be done. The trial team created an excuse for a break and a quick conference was held.

During the break, a decision was made to skip some of the foundation material and refocus the testimony on the development of the idea which led to the invention. The decision was also made that Mr. Valdez would come out of the witness box, stand in front of the jury, and explain the development of the inventions using the toy models which had been created for the trial.

When the trial resumed, Mr. Valdez was therefore asked to step down from the witness stand and answer questions using the toy models which were sitting on a table in front of the jury box. When he stood up, his demeanor completely changed. Instead of looking red-faced and sad, he was energized and happy. When he walked over to the table, he looked dignified, even though there was a little bounce in his step.

The lawyer began by asking him how the idea of the truck originated. Mr. Valdez then turned to the jury and engaged them in the same way he would engage a group of potential investors. He sounded excited about the ideas. This was his chance to tell his story. He talked about how each of the key engineers in his company worked with the inventor twelve to fifteen hours every day for months to design this exciting new machine. He talked about how he traveled all over the world to find investors to help make the machine a reality.

His transformation was amazing. He did not appear to be the same person who had been imprisoned in the witness box. He was so powerful and effective that one of the jurors asked if the witness could elaborate on his testimony.

During Valdez's cross-examination, the opposing attorney had developed questions which would take advantage of the president's feelings of helplessness and loss of control. However, these questions were not very effective. Because Valdez had had an opportunity to release his momentary feelings of confinement and frustration, and because the jury had had an opportunity to see the kind of person he really was, the opposing attorney could not cause him to feel bad about the situation.

The next witness was the inventor. We will call him "Sammy" because he was called by his first name during his testimony. At the time of the trial, he was about sixty-four years old. He was short with white hair. He wore a light-colored suit and a non-descript tie. He was a modest man, an engineer. He was accompanied every day in court by his wife. Their adoration for each other was apparent as they stood quietly together and talked only to each other during trial recesses. As with all witnesses, the trial team assumed that jurors also noticed his characteristics.

During his testimony, Sammy was soft-spoken and direct. He did not appear to be concerned about seeking anyone's approval. He was asked by the trial team to discuss the invention process for the creation of this new machine. In his response he simply turned to the jury and explained the process briefly and clearly. He looked warm and friendly. He seemed to be genuinely interested in helping the jurors understand what had happened during the invention process. During cross-examination, his demeanor did not change. When he was asked to explain something, he simply turned to the jury and gave his answer briefly and clearly. Later, when the trial was over, the jurors approached him as a group to congratulate him on winning the case. In the process, they called him by his first name.

The third witness called by the plaintiffs was the sales manager of the marketing company, to whom we will refer as "Mr. Darden." Mr. Darden was a tall athletic man with very white teeth. He had a great smile and a strong handshake. He had been chosen to be the corporate representative. No other executives from the company appeared in the courtroom until closing argument.

During his testimony, Darden exhibited many good behaviors. He leaned forward even though he was the target of a hostile examination. He did not fidget. He seemed thoughtful. However, he exhibited two characteristics that were not helpful. The first was that he seemed too "smooth." He spoke in a monotone and smiled a lot, even when smiling was not appropriate. The second adverse characteristic Darden exhibited was that his eyes continually darted toward his company's attorney after each answer, as though he were looking for approval to make sure he said the right thing. Later, after trial, the jurors had a number of critical statements to make about the witness's superficial behavior.

These stories illustrate only a few of the many issues that counsel encounter with fact witnesses. Most fact witnesses have never testified in court before. All of them have developed behaviors and mental processes over their lifetimes which often present problems in telling the story of the case.

In this chapter we will provide an in-depth description of the behavior and mental processes of fact witnesses, and how we can use that information to develop more effective, credible testimony to present our cases to judges, juries, and arbitrators.

§ 13.02 | JUDGE AND JUROR PERCEPTIONS OF FACT WITNESSES AND THEIR TESTIMONY

The interaction between fact witnesses, trial attorneys, and fact finders (judges, jurors, or arbitrators) is a much more complicated process than simply asking and answering questions. For example, during the first five minutes of a witness's testimony, the fact finders are trying to get their bearings regarding the witness and are assessing the witness's credibility. At the very outset of the testimony, the eyes and ears of the judge, jury, or arbitration panel are riveted on the witness. The fact finders want to know immediately whether this witness can give them reliable information that they can use to make a decision. They want to know whether the witness's account of the facts will corroborate their initial leanings that they have begun to formulate. They require an immediate assessment of the witness's credibility. They have a need to decide whether they like or dislike the witness.

In this section we will discuss how judges, jurors, and arbitrators go about making these assessments.

[1]–Assessing Credibility

When fact finders are presented with a new witness, they immediately begin to assess the witness's credibility. Truthfulness is only one aspect of credibility. The witness can be truthful in every respect but have no credibility because of other factors. There are a number of factors that affect whether the witness is credible.

[a]–Logical Structure of the Testimony

As in most situations where credibility is being assessed, fact finders observe closely to determine if the testimony essentially makes sense, if it is coherent and logical, and if the different parts fit together. Fact finders want to know if the witness's testimony is corroborated by other testimony, the evidence, and the lawyers' arguments.

[b]–Structured vs. Unstructured Testimony

In the perceptions of fact finders, testimony which is presented slowly, carefully, and unemotionally should be fairly well-structured. It might be presented chronologically, or using some other logical format. Testimony which is genuinely emotional is often characterized by more unstructured aspects, including digression, reiterating back to pick up missed facts, spontaneous emotional breakdowns, etc. If a witness is testifying about an emotional matter, but the testimony is characterized by slow, careful, unemotional demeanor, fact finders will not understand and will likely believe that there is some dishonesty in progress. The fact finders will be experiencing some dissonance that they are at a loss to explain or alleviate.

[c]–Quantity of Details

Generally, when someone is telling a true story, the account is filled with detail such as people's names, places, times, events, etc. The story's chronology will be clear. Some of the facts included in the detail will be strikingly unique to the story rather than generalized to similar situations.

Judges and jurors expect to hear unique detail in truthful testimony. They do not wish to be inundated with detail, but do want enough specifics to convince them that the story is genuine. They need sufficient information to help make a decision about the case.

[d]—Context

One of the most important considerations for a trial lawyer in helping a witness be effective is the framework or context of the testimony. We know from many years of research that whether someone's behavior was appropriate depends upon the circumstances that were taking place around that person.

For example, if a corporate executive takes the witness stand and states that the first priority of the corporation is to be humanitarian, the witness will likely instantly lose credibility. However, if the witness states that the first priority of the corporation is to make a profit, but to do it in a way which is humanitarian, fact finders will more likely believe him.

[e]—Interactions Between People

Witnesses usually concentrate during their testimony on describing the interactions and transactions they observed between various people. If their recollections coincide with the fact finder's life experiences, i.e., relate to the experiences of other people known to the fact finder when they were in similar situations, the witness's account of the story will be more believable. However, if the witness's testimony includes observations of interactions that are at odds with the fact finder's life experiences, the testimony will not be as readily accepted without further explanation.

[f]—Recounting Speech from Past Transactions

In our daily interactions with others, we often ask questions such as, "What exactly did she say?" We do that for two reasons. The first is that we are trying to visualize the situation, and knowing the exact words used helps us to formulate a clearer picture in context. Second, we have a better feeling that the story is true if we know the exact words that the speaker used. The same is true for judges, jurors, and arbitrators.

[g]—Complications and Unusual Details

Let's imagine that two business executives are testifying for opposite sides of a case. The crux of the testimony is a dispute about what was said in a particular meeting. One executive can only recall general aspects of the meeting such as the date, the time, and the place. The other executive, however, recalls the color of the other executive's suit and the name of the first executive's secretary who ushered him into the office. If both witnesses are equally likeable, fact finders will generally tend to believe the witness who recalls more of the unusual and/or unnecessary detail.

This is also true if your witness recalls momentary complications that interrupted the natural flow of events during the transaction which is the subject of the testimony. Simple accounts of unusual aspects of the transaction give the testimony a ring of truth and credibility

[h]—Details That the Witness Does Not Understand

One of the most interesting tools that fiction writers use in creating an air of truth about the story they are telling is a recounting of a fact or circumstance that the character in the story does not understand at the time of the event. In the courtroom, testimony about a factual detail that the witness did not understand at the time gives the same air of truth.

For example, in a medical malpractice case which involves giving the wrong medication to a patient in a hospital, the patient might testify that she took a capsule with a red ring around it given to her by a nurse. The patient might testify that she had previously been given capsules with blue rings around them, but that she did not question the nurse. In this circumstance, unless the judge or jurors concluded for other reasons that the witness is lying, they will likely believe the patient.

[i]—Thoughts and Feelings at the Time of the Events

In everyday interactions between people, their observations and reactions to the thoughts and feelings of others are quite normal. Most of the time we are unconscious of our reactions to others, but often we are quite conscious of them. Testimony which includes observations by the witness of the witness's own thoughts and feelings and those of others who participated in the events often has a ring of truth. Note that such testimony is usually inadmissible unless an appropriate evidentiary exception is cited by counsel.

[j]—Admissions and Corrections

Just as with attorney argument, admissions against a witness's own interests can convince the fact finder that the witness's testimony is honest and credible. In the courtroom, admissions can be painful and embarrassing. Fact finders are usually impressed when a witness takes the initiative to say something that would ordinarily be against his or her interest.

Similarly, whenever a witness spontaneously corrects either his or her own attorney or the witness's own previous testimony, the witness's credibility is enhanced. It is helpful in those circumstances if the attorney who is conducting the direct examination graciously accepts the correction.

[k]–Integration

Fact witnesses are more believable when all of their characteristics are fully integrated. That means that the visual, auditory, and behavioral characteristics of a witness must be coordinated well with the substance of the testimony. For example, a female witness who is dressed as an aristocrat, but who slouches and is not careful with her testimony, would seem strange to most judges and jurors. The witness might be completely truthful in every respect, but the witness does not seem credible even though the fact finder may not fully understand why. In spite of the witness's technical truthfulness, the effectiveness of the witness's testimony is impaired.

The witnesses who are most successful are those who understand their role in the case, are mentally coordinated with the themes and story of the case, and can genuinely relate their testimony without interference from emotional or mental obstacles.

[2]–Testifying from Memory

The process of remembering facts and emotions and later recalling them is fascinating. We know from psychological research that no two people will experience or recall the same facts in the same way. Different people will focus on different aspects of events and, perhaps, experience different emotions in reaction to the same occurrences.

There are two primary theories to describe the process of recalling memories. The first is the *reconstructive theory*, in which the original memory is adjusted by the influence of later events. Under this theory, a witness's account of past events is influenced by conversations or other information which occurred at a later time. The second theory is the *"exact copy" theory*, in which we assume that the original memory is stored accurately. Under this theory, a witness's account of past events may be intact, but cannot be recalled in its original form without the help of hypnosis.

Very rarely do people naturally recall the exact details of past events. In this sense, our brains are not like computers that recall the exact details of data that were input regardless of the length of time that has passed. In order for someone to recall the exact details of a past event, at least one of two factors must be present. The first is that the events were very recent. The second is that the memory must be corroborated or reinforced by external means.

Judges, jurors, and arbitrators will not readily believe that the witness can recall exact details from the distant past without some assistance. Fact finders know that memory is fallible. However, they also know that important or dramatic events and facts often can be recalled in vivid detail. Therefore, if a witness appears to be resolute and confident in his or her recall of past events and the substance of the testimony appears to be credible, fact finders will generally find the witness's testimony to be credible even though it includes recollection of events from the distant past. An eyewitness's level of confidence can account for up to 50% of a fact finder's decision to believe the testimony.

However, if other characteristics of a witness would cause doubt about the witness's credibility, the apparent confidence of the witness in his or her testimony might still be discounted. For example, an older person who has suffered from some cognitive impairment might not be believed even though the person sounds very confident and resolute about the facts described in the testimony.

Another factor which greatly affects the recalling of events for memory is the content and style of the question that is asked of the witness. As we know from years of experience in cross-examination techniques, the recounting of memory can be altered simply by the nature of the question that is asked. Our training in trial advocacy questioning techniques under typical court rules is designed to help us elicit credible testimony during direct examination and to test the credibility of a witness by using leading questions.

For example, let's consider the example of a female plaintiff in an apartment security case. The question in the case is whether she latched the security gate when she entered the apartment complex. During direct examination, if she is asked a question such as, "What did you do next?" and she responds by saying, "I latched the security gate and dropped my groceries in the process," she will more than likely appear to be believable. Alternatively, if she is asked, "Did you latch the security gate?" and she responds by saying, "Yes," the fact finder does not have much opportunity to assess the credibility of the witness's memory.

During cross-examination, if the same witness is asked, "Are you certain that you latched the security gate?" and she responds by saying, "Absolutely," her credibility will likely be enhanced if the rest of her demeanor and credibility is intact. But if she is asked, "Isn't it true that the intruder came through the gate right behind you without a key?" and she responds by saying, "Yes," her credibility about locking the gate is diminished (without directly attacking her truthfulness). This indirect attack by inserting circumstances that fact finders will likely believe rather than the witness's testimony is a more skillful way of casting doubt on someone's credibility.

The preparation of direct or cross-examination of witnesses' accounts of events from memory requires understanding the process of remembering and recalling facts and emotions. Once this process is understood, the number of options and alternatives for developing the testimony is greatly increased.

[3]—General Perceptions of Witnesses by Judges, Jurors, and Arbitrators

Regardless of the amount of experience we have in listening to witnesses and assessing credibility, we make our assessments based upon intuitive, untrained faculties. Often, fact finders will judge the truthfulness and credibility of a witness's testimony based upon peripheral detail about the witness's demeanor or the recollection of facts and events. A more important factor, however, is the fact finder's assessment of the witness's character, integrity, likeability, and general behavior.

[a]—Under the Microscope

Judges, arbitrators, and particularly jurors will place every witness under a microscope. They will not overlook any detail about the witness's demeanor, appearance, character, ability to recall events, or general credibility.

Most fact finders will also sympathize with almost anyone who is called as a fact witness. Jurors might even empathize with witnesses. Although judges and jurors view the act of asking questions of witnesses differently, they all understand that questioning witnesses in a trial proceeding is an aggressive process that can be very manipulative. They realize how helpless they would feel in the same circumstances. They experienced this feeling of helplessness when they were part of the voir dire panel.

Because the witness box is so close to the jury box and the bench, the witness's mental state and behavior are so vivid to the fact finders that they easily sense nervousness, fear, uneasiness, lack of self-confidence, and every other characteristic that reveals how the witness is really feeling and what the witness is really thinking. The more idiosyncratic a witness is, the more a jury will be distracted by the witness's characteristics. In other words, the more unusual a witness appears to be, the more jurors will be unable to concentrate on the witness's testimony. Before any fact finder can really listen to the substance of a witness's testimony, the fact finder must be comfortable with the witness as a person.

Judges, jurors, and arbitrators use the same methods of assessing witnesses that they would use in any social gathering. For example, at a party one listens to an inner voice that is talking about another person during any encounter. As a result, people tend to trust their instincts about another person more than the logical aspects of the encounter.

[b]—Internal Dialogue of Fact Finders That Influences Their Perceptions

Part of the internal dialogue that occurs in the minds of judges, jurors, and arbitrators is influenced by previously held attitudes, beliefs, and stereotypes about people. For this reason, we are sometimes concerned about characteristics of jurors during jury selection and how they will influence the jurors in response to a particular key witness's characteristics.

Preconceived attitudes, stereotypes, schemas, and beliefs are as much a part of our assessment and learning processes as oxygen and hydrogen are elements of air and water. Fact finders' views of ethnic groups, occupations, educational levels, social status, and other human traits color the fact finders' impressions and judgments of witnesses. Most fact finders are perceptive enough to realize that their impressions are being influenced by their own internal dialogue. However, they are generally powerless to do much about it.

The same issues arise when jurors are assessing the attorney as he or she questions the witness. In the sense that the courtroom is a stage, the attorney who is conducting a direct or cross-examination is a character in a play who is having a dialogue with another character. During an examination, the spotlight is on both the attorney and the witness. The judge or jury assesses both characters independently in addition to their relationship to each other. As in any relationship, the quality of the interactions is governed by the quality of the participation of both the attorney and the witness.

Judges, jurors, and arbitrators ask many questions about the attorney who is questioning the witness. Does the attorney like the witness? Does the attorney respect the witness? Is the attorney prepared with regard to this witness's testimony? What kind of personality does the attorney have? Do I like the attorney? Do I trust the attorney? Is the attorney the kind of lawyer I would want to have for my own lawyer?

[c]—Lawyer Blind Spots During Direct and Cross-Examination

Direct and cross-examination of witnesses can be a particularly troublesome area for most attorneys. Often attorneys lose perspective of the entire case while they develop the testimony of a particular witness. They often forget about the themes and case story as they focus on the witness's detailed testimony.

The most important goal of direct and cross-examination is to effectively communicate the story of the case to the judge, jury, or arbitration panel. Sometimes, in an effort to establish a good dialogue with a witness, attorneys will adapt their communication style to the witness with little thought of the overall effect. Although having a free-flowing, revealing dialogue with a witness is important, it is even more important to tell a powerful story.

In the next section we will discuss considerations for preparing fact witnesses for direct examination.

§ 13.03 | CHOOSING FACT WITNESSES AND PREPARING THEM FOR DIRECT EXAMINATION

In this section we will discuss how to choose a fact witness, understand that witness, and help the witness prepare to testify effectively. We will discuss the mental states that witnesses experience and how we can help them overcome problems.

[1]—What Witnesses Are Experiencing at the Beginning of Preparation

Most of the witnesses whom you will encounter have no experience in a live courtroom. They have seen many televisions episodes set in courtrooms that involved interesting interactions between lawyers and witnesses, in some of which witnesses are embarrassed and vilified by the actors who portray the trial attorneys. The television cameras show close-ups of witnesses in distress and jurors glaring at them from across the courtroom. In some cases, like the Perry Mason series, witnesses are often browbeaten into admitting to performing horrible crimes.

Images like these plague most witnesses when they are already suffering from stress related to the underlying events and to their nervousness about telling their story in front of a judge or jury in a live courtroom. These witnesses might be experiencing a great deal of anger about the underlying events or about being forced to come into a courtroom to give testimony.

Perhaps the most critical factor for every trial attorney to remember is that each fact witness is experiencing the case and his or her role in the case in a unique way. Each witness is feeling quiet desperation with which he or she is trying to cope. Each witness wants to excel and perform in a way that makes him or her feel good about himself or herself.

Nevertheless, witnesses feel that they will be on stage in the courtroom and must perform. They have varying assessments of their ability to do well, and they usually perform consistent with their own expectations of themselves. For example, sometimes entrepreneurs and salespeople believe that they can walk into a courtroom and "sell" the judge or jury. These entrepreneurs and salespeople have trained themselves to be able to do that in the business environment, and generally assume that they will perform the same role in the courtroom.

Realistically, witnesses know instinctively that very few people are good performers. They also know that at times even the best performers have a bad day. Witnesses have a constant stream of internal conversation going through their minds as they prepare themselves to testify.

Witnesses appreciate your help in preparing them to testify. They are generally willing to listen and try to cooperate. They usually have two streams of mental activity moving through their minds while they are with you. On the surface, they may appear to be paying attention and actively participating. Below the surface, however, they may be experiencing doubts about their ability to do what you request or doubts about their ability to perform well at all. For this reason, sometimes they appear to be in agreement with you, but are unable to follow your suggestions during subsequent role play.

[2]—Choosing the Right Witnesses

Choosing the right fact witness to testify about a particular aspect of the evidence and to relay particular themes is a lot like hiring people for certain jobs or casting characters in a play.

Sometimes we might believe that we are "stuck" with a certain witness and we have to live with our fate. For example, suppose you are prosecuting a medical malpractice case in which a woman was treated for migraine headaches in a hospital emergency room. She was given a sedative at the hospital and then released. On the way home, while driving (and sedated), she struck a tree and was killed instantly. Her husband was an alcoholic underachiever. Physically, he presented a terrible appearance in the courtroom despite every suggestion made by his attorney. He also failed to follow suggestions for giving testimony that had been made by counsel. However, it seemed that the husband was the best witness to talk about the loss of support that he and the family would experience because of his wife's death even though he did not seem too distraught about his wife's death.

What would you recommend to the attorney? Should he present the witness despite his appearance and hope that the jury would be sympathetic? Should he put on a more credible witness to talk about the relationship between the man and his deceased wife? If the attorney used such a witness, would that witness's testimony completely supplant the testimony of the husband, or simply lay the foundation for the husband's later testimony and perhaps allow the jury to forgive the man for his poor appearance and apparent lack of distress? Should the attorney bring in a trial consultant to assist with helping the husband give more effective testimony?

These questions demonstrate that we often have more options than we first realize. Certainly a man such as the husband in our story will gain sympathy from some jurors and perhaps from a judge or arbitrator. However, fact finders often do not sympathize with people who come into court asking for a remedy, but who do not present a respectable appearance. Jurors are sympathetic toward people who are trying hard to help them understand the evidence, but who are laboring under some obvious distress. However, jurors are not sympathetic toward people who seem to be nonchalant about their testimony. After all, jurors are being forced to make sacrifices to participate in the trial and they expect attorneys and witnesses to make extra efforts to be respectful and helpful to them.

Sometimes it is difficult to choose the best witness to testify about a particular point. For example, one witness may have significant familiarity with the facts, but may make a poor appearance. Another witness may make a great appearance but have no familiarity with the facts. Yet a third witness may make a poor appearance, but may be called as a witness for the opposition.

The more difficult the choice, the more important it is to create a short decision-making outline (e.g., a "decision tree") and to test the alternatives in order to assure a rational decision. Such a decision-making outline could list the witness choices on separate sheets of paper with identical criteria for making the decision on each sheet. The sheets might look something like the accompanying chart.

Husband		Family Friend	
Criteria	*Points*	*Criteria*	*Points*
1. Credibility (1-10)	4	1. Credibility (1-10)	8
2. Knowledge (1-10)	10	2. Knowledge (1-10)	5
3. Appearance (1-10)	3	3. Appearance (1-10)	8
4. Ability to Get Sympathy (1-10)	3	4. Ability to Get Sympathy (1-10)	4
Total Points:	**20**	**Total Points:**	**25**

As we have observed, one of the most important developments in trial science has been the ability to provide consulting and testing mechanisms for making decisions about witnesses. Experienced trial consultants can provide a great deal of information to the trial team that will help make these kinds of important decisions.

In addition, well-organized focus groups and mock trials can often provide important insights into likely judge and jury reactions to proposed fact witnesses. In most focus group and mock trial studies, excerpts from videotapes of key witnesses are usually played for the research jurors. Even though this procedure limits the exposure that research participants have to the witnesses, the information gained about a witness in the context of the whole case can be very valuable.

In other situations when a particular key witness's testimony is pivotal in a case with a substantial budget for trial preparation, it might be helpful to bring in a representative panel of research jurors to observe a live rehearsal with that key witness prior to trial. Such a session will be completely focused on helping the witness be more effective, which in turn can sometimes help with making important decisions about that witness's role in trial.

[3]—Order of Witnesses

The story outline or chronology will normally dictate the order of witnesses. However, there are several other considerations. Fact finders will generally remember the first and last witnesses better than the others. For this reason, it is best to "bury" the less presentable witnesses somewhere in the middle of the case.

All fact finders will appreciate hearing initially from a witness who can give an overview of the facts and story of the case, and express the central themes of the case as he or she testifies.

Moreover, jurors (and sometimes judges and arbitrators) are not aware of the alternative choices we have had about when and how to present witnesses. Therefore, even if the order of witnesses is not perfectly in sync with the best psychology of the case, all is not lost. By the end of opening statement, jurors have likely already have formed a basic understanding of the case, and the role of witnesses is to provide further detailed information so that each fact finder can test his or her understanding of different parts of the case and augment that understanding.

Rarely does one witness provide all of the information that a fact finder needs to make a decision. Testimony usually comes in bits and pieces. Therefore, practically speaking, the choices of first and last witnesses are critical, but choices about the order of testimony of the remaining witnesses are not as pivotal. However, if there is an opportunity to choose the order of witnesses, one should give careful consideration to making the presentation of the case as easy to learn and as compelling as possible.

[4]—Preparing a Witness Mentally and Emotionally

In many respects, preparing a witness is similar to conducting psychotherapy. The first thing you must do is to develop a relationship of trust with the witness. By letting the witness know that you are genuinely sympathetic to his or her concerns, you will eventually earn the witness's trust and faith that will be necessary in presenting the testimony.

There are three phases of preparation that are necessary for most key fact witnesses. The first phase is determining the exact role of each particular witness in telling the story of the case. In this phase, you will want to identify which themes and evidence each witness can relate to the fact finder. This planning phase is absolutely critical to the success of the rest of preparation and the presentation of the witness's testimony.

The second phase is what we generally refer to as "woodshedding." In this phase, the attorney and the witness cull through the evidence to determine which facts and issues the witness will testify about and what the witness will say.

The third phase is devoted exclusively to the mental preparation of the witness. Although most experienced trial attorneys have experience in helping their witnesses to get into their most effective mental state, often it is helpful to have a trial consultant or mental health professional work with the witness to help him or her maximize his or her potential effectiveness.

Most witnesses are processing their role in the case on two levels. On the surface, they are trying to use their best logic and presentation skills to do what counsel has asked them to do. Silently, however, a completely different dialogue is taking place. A witness's "self talk" dialogue is constantly critiquing both his or her performance and your performance. The mindset of the witness may be positive or negative.

Whether or not a mental health professional is involved, it is critical that the trial team have a working knowledge of the underlying mental processes that each of the key witnesses is experiencing. Every witness in every case is a unique individual. Every witness processes the same information differently. Rarely can any one witness follow your demands to the letter. It is therefore more important to establish the direction and goals of the testimony and gain agreement about them.

Next, it is helpful to teach the witness about the role and mental processes of the other people who will be present in the courtroom. And finally, as part of this teaching process, it is important to let the witness practice what he or she has learned in order to demonstrate that the witness understands his or her role and how to present his or her testimony effectively.

Most witnesses are experiencing stage fright on some level. Most presenters (including most trial attorneys) experience some form of stage fright every time they speak in public. We can all understand and sympathize with witnesses who are nervous about their appearance in the courtroom. One of the most effective ways to deal with stage fright is to acknowledge it and visualize mental pictures to help us to relax and to focus. We want to use our stage fright to help motivate us to do our best.

Most of the time the witness cannot articulate these feeling of stage fright, which can take the form of a vague feeling of dread. It is helpful for members of the trial team to be forthright and good-natured about the existence of stage fright and how to work with it.

Other remedies for stage fright include forgiving oneself for not being perfect and feeling prepared. At the core of stage fright is a fear of failure to meet both the witness's own expectations and counsel's expectations, in addition to a fear of disapproval by the fact finder.

By acknowledging that perfection is not required or possible, a witness can reduce some self-induced pressure. However, the most effective remedy for stage fright is a feeling that the witness is prepared for any eventuality. It has been said that that preparation "helps the butterflies to fly in formation."

Much of the witness preparation process is simply helping the witness become accustomed to the courtroom setting. Most witnesses know the substance of their testimony. They simply need someone to help them identify which information they must recall and how to present their testimony most effectively.

Witnesses should expect to be continually at the mercy of a questioning attorney, and should learn how to remain unruffled even when they are being interrupted. They must not visibly react to such aggressive lawyer tactics. They also need to know how loudly to speak and how to teach the judge or jury what they know.

For the most part, all the important testimony that a witness will give should be made while the witness is looking at the jury. Of course, judges and arbitrators generally do not want witnesses to look at them during their entire testimony, so the witness should be trained to use some judgment in this regard. Since there has been some disagreement about whether the witness should look at the lawyer or at the jury, the best directive is that the most effective witnesses can do both.

Think about how odd it is if you are sitting across the table from two people who are talking to each other and who ignore you during the entire conversation. Now let's stretch that conversation to six hours a day for a week or more. During that whole time, neither of these people looks at you. They both ignore you. At what point will you feel left out? At what point will you become offended?

Witnesses who turn to the jury to give answers to important questions are dramatically more effective at persuading the jury than someone who never looks at the jury. In one trial, a woman who had been the controller of a company which went out of business due to the failure of two investors to raise sufficient capital, was called to testify in the trial of the civil case against the two investors. The woman testified in a gray suit and looked very dignified. She was quiet and thoughtful in her testimony. She had worked with an experienced trial consultant and had practiced turning her witness chair slightly toward the jury to prompt her to look at the jury when she gave most of her important testimony.

Her demeanor delighted her company's attorney because the jurors seemed so attentive and accepting during her testimony. Even during the beginning of the cross-examination, she was turning to the jury to give her answers. However, the opposing attorney was not amused. He asked her why she turned to the jury instead of looking at him. She responded, "Because I like them more than I like you."

This witness had the benefit of a supportive trial team and a trial consultant, all of whom were dedicated to her success. She had even been videotaped so that she could watch herself testify and identify areas that could be improved.

The witness was taught that no-one in the courtroom would be able to express any approval as she testified, and that she should be as honest as she could. The way her testimony unfolded, the jury adored her.

There are two final points relative to witness preparation. The first is that counsel should not try too hard to control and direct the witness. During direct examination, the witness is the star and it is critical that the witness's true personality and strengths come through and are not diluted by excessive control. By giving witnesses too many "dos and don'ts," we increase their frustration and diminish their individuality.

Second, counsel should try to be constructive at all times. Sometimes witnesses are difficult and in those instances, a creative solution might be necessary. However, it is important to maintain a positive nature throughout the relationship with each fact witness.

[5]—Overcoming Problems with Difficult Witnesses

Witnesses will listen to your suggestions and try very hard to incorporate them when they give their testimony. However, they sometimes have mental or emotional blocks which prevent them from being able to perform the way you would like. Sometimes the situation is very frustrating.

In these circumstances, it helps to correctly identify the problem. First we must ask if the problem is simply poor communication between the attorney and the witness. If so, any issues need to be gently, but firmly, addressed and resolved. For the most part, increasing the intensity of demands and punitive actions against a witness are counterproductive. These tactics only increase the frustration of everyone involved and perhaps create a permanent obstacle to communication between attorney and witness. An obstacle like this will certainly surface during the actual testimony and might cause permanent damage to the case presentation.

Keep in mind that most problems can be resolved. Usually the best course of action is to begin by obtaining an acknowledgment from the witness that a problem exists and that the witness wants to overcome it. Most witnesses want to be free of the stresses that are causing obstacle(s) and they are frustrated. By approaching this problem in a good-natured way, we help diffuse the situation enough to fashion a solution in a warm and supportive environment.

The third phase of preparation is designed to identify and remedy problems with witnesses. Sometimes, however, problems might best be resolved with the assistance of a trial consultant who is trained to provide the kind of support that a witness needs in order to excel.

[6]—Orienting Fact Witnesses to the Themes and Story of the Case

Traditionally, we have treated witnesses as if they were making a cameo performance. We have at times intentionally hidden the themes and story of the case from witnesses in an effort to not "contaminate" them.

A better approach is to fully inform the witnesses of the themes and story of the case. When counsel articulates the essence of the case and the role that the witness will play, the witness has a better opportunity to conceive of the task ahead and to be able to perform it skillfully. In addition, most of the time fact witnesses can provide valuable suggestions to the trial team when it is determining how best to present the themes and story of the case with the witnesses' testimony.

Inviting a witness to participate in the development of the testimony also helps the witness to deal with the witness's own anxieties. When counsel takes the time to explain the overall organization of the witness's testimony, the witness can then answer questions in context, which is critical to judge and jury persuasion.

It is also helpful to let the witness know in advance how you will transition from one subject to another. Witnesses have a general fear that they will not know what to say next. Telling them in advance that you will guide them through their testimony with particular themes or questions is very reassuring.

In the next section we will talk about designing and implementing direct examination.

§ 13.04 | DIRECT EXAMINATION OF FACT WITNESSES

Developing and presenting a direct examination is a process of planning and execution. Developing direct examination is perhaps the most tedious part of trial preparation. There is often a temptation to cut corners and present the witness spontaneously. This temptation should always be resisted.

Therefore, let's begin by talking about how to design the structure of the direct examination.

[1]—Structure of the Examination

Each direct examination should be viewed as a story within a story. Most trials involve complicated stories, sometimes of epic length. However, within the overall story lie a number of other smaller stories with plots and subplots.

Similarly, every story has a beginning, middle, and end. Every story has themes and messages to relate to whoever is listening. Therefore, it makes sense to develop the direct examination of each fact witness as part of the overall outline of the case, but having its own outline as well.

It might be helpful to list the points and parts of the story that you wish to make with each witness as bullet points. These bullet points should be placed in a logical order that makes learning and understanding simple. Facts and circumstances that relate to each other should be presented together in the direct examination. There should be a flow that resembles everyday life.

Since we were children, we have learned about life through stories filled with chronologically ordered events. We have learned that there are certain sequences in which events occur. For this reason, time lines can be powerful teaching tools to be used during direct examination. Time lines help judges, jurors, and arbitrators understand the sequence of events in order to provide a mental structure for understanding issues of causation, motivation, and other essential factors in a case.

There are two ways to relate a story chronologically. One is to start with the big picture and identify key events and issues that arose during the course of the transactions that took place. This view of the big picture is then followed by more focused questions about the events which resulted in the big picture. The second method of relating chronology is to begin with a description of a scene or event at the beginning of the chronology and then build up to an eventual big picture.

Generally it is best to begin with the big picture in order to help the fact finder become oriented to your themes and case story. Theoretically, once the fact finder understands and agrees with your themes and case story, he or she might be more willing to apply the details to the overall picture that you have created. This approach is often used with the first witness who is called by a party to testify.

However, focusing on events or scenes at the beginning of a chronology and developing them forward in time can be helpful in developing the case story in a different way. This approach can be an effective way to develop rapport between a party and the fact finder by placing the fact finder in the role of a person who has been injured by someone else's behavior in circumstances whereby the injured person claims to have been uninformed. Similarly, this method of development can be helpful in defending someone who has been accused of conduct involving information which the defendant claims not to have known at the time the alleged injury occurred.

Whether the direct examination begins or ends with the big picture, it will be helpful to the fact finder to ask questions which create transitions from one subject to another. Transition questions allow the witness and the fact finder to follow the sequence of events more closely.

In addition, it is helpful to have a mixture of questions which focus on the overall picture, a medium-sized picture, and a close-up picture. You might consider thinking of direct examination as a movie camera which moves in and out of a scene. You might recall a recent television show or movie in which the camera provided wide-angle shots to give the viewer a broad picture and then moved in more closely to examine someone's behavior. The same principle governs whenever we are driving a car. We are constantly looking about to get a clear picture of the cars around us.

In this sense, the direct examination is akin to presenting parts of a play or movie. It is helpful, therefore, to consider that the lawyer's role is similar to that of a director who is guiding the performance of the character who is sitting in the witness box.

Regardless of the method used to develop a story, the objective is to help the fact finder learn about the case and build a persuasive argument which is easy to follow and compelling in a simple yet powerful way.

[2]—Conducting an Effective Direct Examination

[a]—Beginning the Examination

The first question(s) in a direct examination will be the most important question(s). We know from our discussion about primacy and recency that the first statement and the last statement in any part of a discourse will be most vividly remembered by the fact finder. The jury is most attentive and focused at the beginning of the examination. Therefore, the first question should accomplish something memorable that will help the jury learn about your case and persuade them that your view of the case is correct.

That first question might tell the jury the role the witness plays in your case in chief, and might even repeat one of your key themes in the story. You can always double back to lay the foundation for the witness.

As we stated earlier in this chapter, at the beginning of the examination the jury is watching you and the witness closely to determine your relationship to each other. When you handle a witness with respect and courtesy, the jury will have more respect for you and your witness. Your overall behavior with the witness will tell the jury a lot about both you and your witness. For example, instead of asking, "Will you state your name for the record?" you might ask, "Sarah, I know you, but will you introduce yourself to the jury?"

In addition, your behavior also sends signals to the witness about how you will treat him or her during the examination. The more reassuring and supportive you are with the witness, the more the witness will be supportive to you in presenting your case.

In the past, there has been some disagreement about whether to sit or stand during the examination. In some federal courts and state courts, counsel is required to stand behind a lectern during most of an examination. Although it is good practice to stand rather than sit during the examination since standing allows you to maintain a position of power in the room while your questions allow the witness to be the "star," there is often a choice of using a lectern or merely the counsel table if you do stand. If it is possible to work without a lectern, it is best to do so because a lectern will separate you from the jury or other fact finder. Some lawyers will use a pad and easel as a stage prop and to record the key points made during a witness's testimony and will thus avoid the problem of deciding whether to use a lectern, to stand next to the counsel table, or to sit if possible.

When presenting a witness's background, counsel should proceed slowly instead of rushing through the facts. The judge and jury are curious about the witness. They want to know what kind of person he or she is. They want to know whether the witness is interesting enough for them to listen to. They have an important need to decide whether they like the witness and whether the witness is credible.

Years of practice and experience have shown that, despite a trial judge's insistence on moving a case along, it is best to present some revealing aspect of a witness's background for every fact witness even if that aspect is treated briefly. Otherwise, you will be presenting substantive testimony before the jury has even decided whether they like or can believe the witness. In such a case, much of the important information you want to present to the fact finder could be overlooked or lost by the time the fact finder decides whether to believe the witness.

[b]—Questioning Style

No matter how experienced we are in the courtroom, our questioning style is constantly changing, just as many of our personal qualities change throughout our lives. Developing an individual style of questioning is a matter of preference plus lots of practice and experimentation. In addition, as we grow in competence, we learn about new techniques with which we want to experiment. To make matters even more complicated, every questioning situation is unique.

In reality, your questioning technique will usually be an adaptation of your normal speaking style in front of groups of people. The more comfortable you are working and talking while people are watching you, the more comfortable you will be during direct examination.

Since you are in effect on stage, you will have to project yourself. However, your role is that of a supporting actor or actress whose job is to help the witness's testimony come alive in the courtroom. In this role, your job is to help the witness be effective in delivering testimony. If the witness is speaking too softly, ask the witness to speak more loudly. If the witness is speaking too quickly, respectfully remind the witness that the court reporter is trying to take down each word (or the tape recording will be impossible to transcribe) and that it is important to speak more slowly. Whenever you make a request to a friendly witness, speak confidently and respectfully, but never in a condescending fashion.

The tempo of your examination will be set either by you or the witness, depending upon which of you takes the initiative. It is generally better practice if counsel determines the tempo of the examination and maintains it. The witness will usually follow. Sometimes the witness will try to take control and you might need to break his or her stride by interrupting the testimony with some movement about the courtroom. Regardless, the tempo between you and the witness must be smooth in order for the jury to feel that you and the witness are communicating with each other.

Sometimes in the courtroom we are so busy with various distractions that we fail to look at the witness and listen carefully enough to what the witness has said. Even a momentary distraction sometimes signals to the fact finder that we do not think our witness is very important, so we are not listening. This seemingly innocent behavior can be devastating to a witness's credibility and should be avoided. When we have a witness on the stand, we should give that witness our undivided attention.

Throughout our courtroom experience, we have heard people talk about "looping." Looping is asking a question with information from the witness's previous answer. The following questions and answers are an example of looping:

Attorney: "What did you do next?"

Witness: "I immediately notified the president of the company."

Attorney: "How did you notify the president of the company?"

Witness: "I wrote her a letter."

Attorney: "What did you say in the letter?"

Witness: "I told her that we were broke because the vice president had taken all our money and fled to South America."

Attorney: "How did you know that he had taken all the money and fled to South America?"

Witness: "'Cause I was sneaking around his office and found a bank receipt and a copy of his airplane itinerary showing a late night flight to Rio."

Looping is effective for several reasons. First, it shows that the attorney is interested enough in the witness to focus on the witness's answer. Second, it provides a "stepping stone" effect for jurors to follow in piecing together the information coming from the witness. Finally, it has a psychological anchoring effect that makes the testimony more believable.

Counsel will discuss several topics with most witnesses. You know when you will change topics, but usually no-one else will be able to anticipate the change without your help. Judges, jurors, and arbitrators work very hard to listen and determine what they need to remember from the testimony. Making the transition from one topic to another is easier for the fact finder if you ask questions or make statements that signal the listener you are about to change topics.

Therefore, as you are about to change subjects, signal the witness and the jury by a making as statement such as, "I want to change subjects for a moment and talk to you about what happened when you checked into the hospital." Making these kinds of transition statements helps fact finders group information into subject areas. Eventually, it will make their decision-making process less arduous. More important, it will help them categorize the information you are presenting within the themes and story of the case that you wish them to accept.

Two psychologically powerful techniques for speaking or asking questions are to modulate your voice and to punctuate your speaking with silence. When you stop talking, everyone in the room will pay attention to make sure that they do not miss something. When a speaker is silent, people in the audience (such as the judge and jury) who may not be paying attention suddenly perk up, self-consciously thinking that everyone is watching them. In addition, when counsel is silent, the last thing that was said is still resounding in everyone's memory.

Your voice is a kind of musical instrument in addition to being a communication device. To create interest you can raise your voice, lower your voice, or be silent. You can use your voice to highlight an important witness remark by simply repeating it or asking a rhetorical question that embodies the witness's testimony. For example, if the witness says, "'Cause I was sneaking around his office and found a bank receipt and a copy of his airplane itinerary showing a late night flight to Rio," you might follow with a question like, "You found a bank receipt and a copy of an airplane itinerary showing a late night flight to Rio?"

[c]—Handling Sensitive or Unusual Issues

There are several difficult issues that most experienced trial lawyers often face in the courtroom. One of the most challenging is how to handle emotional or sensational issues. Another is how to handle unusual witness situations, such as when witnesses are handicapped.

Most personal injury trials involve evidence that is both sensitive and emotional, and sometimes gory. Presenting this kind of evidence without first warning the jury can, along with the initial shock, create the impression that the trial lawyer is insensitive to both the witness and the jury. Moreover, the shock itself may deflect the fact finders' attention from evidence that follows immediately thereafter. It is good practice to let the fact finder know that something sensitive or gruesome is about to be discussed and to ask the fact finder's indulgence. (This practice is also good when presenting this kind of information during jury selection or opening statement.)

One approach to making the transition into the sensitive or grisly evidence is to state something to the witness that alerts the jury or other fact finder about the information that is about to be presented. You might say something like, "Mr. Donovan, I need to ask you some questions that might be difficult for you to talk about. We must tell the jury about your relationship with your wife before she died in the airplane crash." When gruesome photographs are about to be shown, you might say something to the judge like, "Your Honor, we have some photographs that contain graphic images of Ms. Donovan's injuries that we must show briefly to the jury." These kinds of statements allow the jury to prepare themselves. The jurors will also appreciate the respect indicated by the sensitivity of the statements.

Other kinds of cases contain equally sensitive information. Employment cases may involve embarrassing information about employee behavior that deserves sensitive handling. Business and commercial cases may involve issues relating to interpersonal conflicts. Even patent cases can involve sensitive issues about personal behavior. Regardless of the content of the material, you will increase your credibility with the fact finder if you handle such evidentiary situations with humanity and respect for the individuals involved.

Working with witnesses who have unusual characteristics such as very young or advanced age, language problems, physical, emotional, or developmental disabilities, or an unattractive appearance are not necessarily devastating to your case. It is best to anticipate the kinds of reactions that the fact finder can have to these witnesses and plan ahead to handle them. Sometimes focus group research can help us to find ways to deal with these issues.

If a witness has a disability, you might begin by anticipating the kind of reactions people generally have to the particular disability. It usually is best to insert questions at the beginning of the examination which address the issue and dispose of it. For example, an older witness with mild Parkinson's Disease might shake slightly when beginning the testimony. You might ask questions such as, "Mrs. Rogers, during the time that I've known you, you have told me that you have Parkinson's Disease. Do you feel comfortable coming here to testify today?" and "Does the Parkinson's Disease affect your memory?"

Witnesses in wheelchairs deserve the same sensitivity and respect as other witnesses who are challenged in the courtroom. It is best to begin with an understanding that people who have not been around people who must use wheelchairs have a secret uncertainty about how to treat wheelchair users. On balance, it is generally accepted that it is okay to talk about the wheelchair whether or not it has some relation to the case. Simply acknowledging it and dismissing it, perhaps even with humor expressed by the witness, can take the issue off the jurors' minds.

The same principles apply to children, elderly people, and others with characteristics that might momentarily distract fact finders. Eliciting testimony from them that reveals their humanity or character is helpful.

It also helps the witness and the fact finder if you will rehearse with the witness how he or she will enter the courtroom, where he or she will sit if there will be a delay before that witness testifies, and where the witness will actually testify. Rehearsal is important to make sure that the movement of the witness about the room does not become an issue. People in wheelchairs or with other disabilities are no different than anyone else. Most disabled or otherwise different witnesses are gracious enough to overlook the pandering and undue attention they receive, but they prefer not to be the center of attention merely because of their unusual characteristics. We can all identify with this feeling.

§ 13.05 | CROSS-EXAMINATION OF FACT WITNESSES

Imagine this scene. You are sitting in the courtroom watching a sexual harassment case unfold. The plaintiff is an executive secretary who has just finished testifying that her former boss made suggestive comments to her when she worked late. She testified that he would put his hands on her shoulders and talk about his strained relationship with his wife. Sometimes he would ask her to come sit by him on the sofa in his office just to talk. She also testified that after she complained to him and to his superior, she was transferred to a different department and, in effect, demoted.

What are the dilemmas facing the company's lawyer? Should he cross-examine her? If he decides to cross-examine her, what tack should he take? Should he be aggressive or caring and concerned? What should his cross-examination points be? Should he attack the secretary's credibility? Should he question her motives? What will the judge and jury think? What themes should the lawyer "blend in" with the examination?

These are some of the types of questions that arise every time you begin preparation for a cross-examination. In this section, we will discuss the goals of cross-examination, juror perceptions, considerations for use in preparing for cross-examination, and some ideas for executing a powerful, compelling cross-examination.

[1]—Purposes and Goals

Cross-examination is essentially the use of your opponent's witnesses to help make your case. There are two primary goals for cross-examination: (1) to bolster your client's position and (2) to diminish the persuasiveness of the opposing case. These principles are no doubt familiar from your trial advocacy training.

However, one of the most important aspects of cross-examination is not generally discussed in early trial advocacy training. To be effective, cross-examination must repeat the themes and story of your case and undermine those of the opposing party. It is helpful to discredit or impeach a witness's direct testimony, but it is important to do this so that the entire story of your case is supported and that of the opposing party is diminished.

[2]—Perceptions of Fact Finders During Cross-Examination

For many jurors, cross-examination is one of the highlights of trial. Even for judges and arbitrators, cross-examination is stimulating. It is a process whereby the credibility and substance of the witness's testimony are tested. In our minds, we all have memories of scenes from the Perry Mason or Matlock television series, in which witnesses were reduced to admissions of guilt in committing murder or were forced to acknowledge extremely embarrassing behavior. We continue to wonder whether the next cross-examination is going to completely destroy a witness's direct testimony.

Amidst this excitement, however, judges, jurors, and arbitrators are also continuing to evaluate the witness, even though their perceptions of the witness's credibility are generally determined by the time cross-examination begins. They want to know whether there is anything about the witness's direct testimony that is incorrect or incomplete regarding the information they will need to make their decision. They assume that a cross-examination will reveal important truths about the case. They are even a little excited to know whether the points made in the cross-examination will support or undermine their existing conception about the case. They can become very upset if the cross-examination seems to be pointless. They do not like having their time wasted.

In early trial advocacy classes, we are taught to "control" the witness. We are not usually given much guidance on how to do that other than to ask leading questions and maintain control of the points that emerge during the testimony. Some attorneys take this edict very seriously and literally try to control the witness and his or her behavior from their positions as interrogators. However, sometimes an attorney will be more focused on controlling the witness than making persuasive points, and that can have serious negative consequences.

All fact finders are sensitive about lawyers who browbeat a witness or unfairly interrogate a witness. Judges, jurors, and arbitrators can all appreciate a tough, rigorous cross-examination. They understand that a lawyer's job includes cross-examination. But they will not easily forgive a lawyer for being unfair. Poor or unfair treatment of a witness during cross-examination will diminish the trial lawyer's credibility and likeability.

Judges will generally allow and jurors will generally accept an aggressive cross-examination with a witness that they do not like or trust. However, they may identify with witnesses who are not involved in the dispute as people whom they like. Witnesses who are only involved in the trial because of something that they innocently witnessed should usually be treated gently. As we have noted, jurors will want to protect witnesses whom they like. They try to prevent anyone from hurting them, and will punish a trial lawyer and his client who attempt to hurt a such a witness.

One of the biggest mistakes in conducting a cross-examination is to drag it out. The most powerful cross-examiners make their points and move on quickly to another subject. Once jurors have the information they need, they quickly lose interest in the subject and want the trial lawyers to go to the next issue.

[3]—Organizing and Choosing Points for Cross-Examination

Most successful cross-examinations are efficient and effective. Judges, jurors, and arbitrators are impatient throughout a trial. They prefer that every cross-examination be interesting and brief. They want the trial team to bring out those cross-examination points that they need to remember and that are meaningful as they decide how they will vote in the case. They are usually angry and often offended when trial lawyers take too much time making points that nobody really cares about. In those situations they believe that the trial attorneys in the case do not care enough about them or respect them enough to use their time wisely.

In addition to considerations of jurors, we know from decades of research and experience that the most effective presentations are lean in content and strong in meaning. For this reason, preparation for cross-examination is a process of organizing material for inclusion followed by culling out those points which are not essential to making a strong, persuasive case.

Ideally, there should be no more than three points to be stressed for each cross-examination. Any additional points should be considered very cautiously. Jurors and other fact finders have a difficult time remembering more than three points per witness. In fact, most post-trial interviews have indicated that jurors remember only one or two points per witness regardless of the total number of issues that were presented in a witness's cross-examination. The more points that are raised, the more likely the fact finder will be lost in the detail and unable to determine which points the trial attorney actually believed were the most critical.

During preparation, it is generally a good idea to list all of the possible points to cover with a witness and to list the themes that the witness's cross-examination might support. These lists can provide a first step to the creation of an outline of the cross-examination.

In choosing the themes to present, we should remember that the most powerful themes are those which transcend the facts of a particular case and are meaningful to most people. Themes are either factual or evaluative in nature. Most witnesses who are competent to talk about the facts of the case are also quite confident in talking about the character and behavior of the primary actors in the case, even though the latter topics are more subjective.

We often refer to cross-examination that deals with credibility as an "attack." It is probably more effective to think of impeachment as an "undermining" of a witness's credibility. Jurors and other fact finders are much more intrigued by cross-examination that is artful and intelligent (even if it is direct and brutal) in most cross-examinations of fact witnesses. In other words, it is usually more effective to take the high road in cross-examination despite the temptation to do otherwise.

One of the biggest mistakes in many cross-examinations is not having a clear and decisive point. One of the general rules in trial advocacy is to have a purpose for every action and for every statement made. This is particularly true in cross-examination. Jurors (and other fact finders) are very attentive and interested in cross-examination. If the substance of the cross-examination is either boring or not relevant to their job in making a decision in the case, they can become frustrated and angry at the trial lawyer who is conducting the cross-examination.

A FINAL WORD: WORKING WITH FACT WITNESSES

For a trial lawyer, the keys to effective preparation of a fact witness are rapport and knowledge. The advantages of multiple interviews, beginning early in the case, outweigh impeachment value of your contact with a witness. Your walk-through of a scene with a witness will trigger memories, photos, and side remarks which will prove invaluable. Multiple visits impart the story and theme of a case more effectively than a hurried meeting the week before trial. Assume your visits or calls will be discovered and act accordingly. Remember, though, that you may affect the case since a witness may revisit scenes, ideas, and other witnesses after speaking with you.

Which witness to choose for direct? Go for quality, not quantity. Think about such factors as stability and length of job and marriage, attractiveness, and similarity to the jury, as well as quality of memory and testimony.

Cross-examination of fact witnesses is based on knowledge and intuition. Do your homework. Contact the other side's witnesses. Fight for *ex parte* contact with medical practitioners where the law

> **CONTINUED**
>
> permits such interviews. Medical professionals and witnesses with no apparent interest can carry great weight with fact finders. Portrayal of an opponent's slanting of the playing field, with money, favors, and overwhelming attention to the witness can be effective impeachment techniques.
>
> A good lawyer also conducts background searches and explores all relationships. You might ask, "Which relative of which party married the ex-spouse of what child of which witness?" Investigating hardly noticeable relationships can yield a treasure trove of information. It happens all the time. You can discover hidden, but powerful stories with hard work and a little luck.
>
> – Barbara Radnofsky, Partner
> Vinson & Elkins L.L.P.

§ 13.06 | REFERENCES

Defense Counsel Training Manual (Chicago: Intern'l. Ass'n. of Defense Counsel, 2000).

McGehee, *The Plaintiff's Case: From Voir Dire to Verdict* (Austin: Texas Trial Lawyers Ass'n., 1997).

Memon, Vrij & Bull, *Psychology and Law: Truthfulness, Accuracy, and Credibility* (London: McGraw-Hill Publishing Co., 1998).

Pozner & Dodd, *Cross-Examination: Science and Techniques* (Miamisburg, OH: Lexis Law Publishing, 1993).

Small, *Preparing Witnesses: A Practical Guide for Lawyers and Their Clients* (Chicago: American Bar Ass'n., 1998).

Tigar, *Examining Witnesses* (Chicago: American Bar Ass'n., 1993).

Younger, *Mastering the Art of Cross-Examination* (Notre Dame, IN: National Institute of Trial Advocacy, 1987).

CHAPTER 14

Expert Witnesses

CHAPTER CONTENTS

"The man who can make hard things easy is the educator."

– Ralph Waldo Emerson (1803-1882)

§ 14.01 | INTRODUCTION

From the perspective of both judge and jury, the role of an expert witness is to help the fact finder understand parts of the case that are not normally part of everyday experience. From the trial lawyer's point of view, the role of an expert is to help the fact finder understand the case *and* to persuade the fact finder that his or her expert opinion is more acceptable than that of the opposing expert. Based upon the principles contained in this book, there is one additional goal for an expert—to testify about his or her opinion such that the themes and case story of one of the parties are enhanced.

The use of expert testimony has become increasingly common in all kinds of civil litigation. Expert testimony these days is pervasive in actions involving personal injury, product liability, trade secrets, professional liability, medical malpractice, securities, patents, and most other types of trials and arbitration hearings.

One such trial in Illinois was a bad faith case against an insurance company that involved toxic waste contamination. The plaintiff in the case was a dry cleaning plant that used a gooey substance called "perc" (perchloroethylene) as a chemical solvent to clean garments and textile products. Approximately 85% of dry cleaners use perc as their primary solvent. It is a clear, colorless liquid that has a sharp, sweet odor and evaporates quickly. It removes stains and dirt from common types of fabrics.

However, perc also has some serious side effects when people are exposed to it, the severity of which depends upon the amount of perc used and the length of exposure. People who are exposed to high levels of perc can develop dizziness, fatigue, headaches, confusion, and nausea, as well as skin, lung, and mucous membrane irritation. Repeated exposure to high levels of perc can also irritate the skin, eyes, nose, and mouth, and can cause liver damage and respiratory failure. For some particularly sensitive people, perc might cause these effects at lower levels of exposure as well.

Experiments with laboratory animals have indicated that exposures to levels of perc can produce effects on a developing fetus that include altered growth, birth defects, and death. The studies involving humans are limited and inconclusive. Scientists are still debating whether perc exposure can cause adverse effects in pregnant women, such as increased incidents of miscarriage or reproductive damage.

Extensive laboratory studies have also shown that perc can cause cancer in rats and mice when ingested or inhaled. Several studies of workers in the laundry and dry cleaning business have suggested a causal connection between perc and increased risk of cancer.

Occupational studies have shown that dry cleaning workers and people exposed to perc frequently should take special precautions. In the past, high levels of perc in the air were caused by poorly maintained machines, equipment leaks, open air exposure, and other direct exposure to the chemical. Perc can get into groundwater during the cleaning, purification, and waste disposal facets of dry cleaning.

Once outdoor contamination of perc occurs, perc can remain in the atmosphere surrounding a dry cleaning plant for several weeks. After that, perc breaks down into other chemicals, some of which are toxic. Perc can enter the ground in liquid form through spills, leaky pipes, tanks, or machines, and improperly handled waste. Perc can seep through the ground and contaminate the groundwater and, potentially, the drinking water of a community.

Procedurally, the case involving perc was complicated. The plaintiff was a dry cleaning plant that had suffered a fire. According to the plaintiff's complaint, much of the perc, which had been stored in barrels at the plant, had leaked into the soil and seeped into the groundwater supply of a local community. As a result, members of the community and government agencies brought claims against the dry cleaning plant. The plant owners, in turn, filed claims with their insurance carrier.

However, the insurance company believed that the perc in the groundwater had originated from poor handling of the perc at the plant over a period longer than that covered by the policy and from reckless conduct by the plant in its release of toxic chemicals into the environment, which was not covered under the insurance policy. There was evidence that the plant's sewer and drainage systems were old and broken, and that perc had been leaking from the plant for decades.

After an investigation, the insurance company denied the claim, stating that it would pay for the fire damage to the plant, but not for the toxic chemical cleanup. The carrier realized how expensive it would be to clean up the massive pollution that had occurred. However, the dry cleaning plant owners believed that they had a legitimate claim, and they filed suit against the carrier alleging breach of contract and related bad faith allegations. They wanted to force the insurer to pay for the damage to the plant and for the cleanup of the toxic chemicals in the ground. They realized that the cost of the toxic chemical cleanup might put the company out of business.

At trial, both the dry cleaning plant and the insurance company used expert testimony to present their respective views. The plaintiff's expert was a man who was known as an industry expert on the effects of the use of perc in dry cleaning and the process involved in cleaning perc out of the ground. His job was to convince the jury that the perc in the ground was placed there suddenly by a catastrophic event.

He was youthful, well-dressed, athletic, and very likeable. He exhibited warm professionalism similar to a nightly news anchor being interviewed on an evening talk show. He spoke about how his wife ran their small business while he traveled around the country as a forensic chemical expert.

He testified primarily from the witness box. His testimony was polished and directed squarely at the jury. The jury listened carefully to his testimony, but it was not clear how the jury perceived him or his testimony.

In contrast, the insurance company's perc expert was a chemistry professor at a local university. His job was to convince the jury that perc is too thick and gooey to be absorbed quickly into the ground and down to the groundwater level within only a few days. He wanted to convince the jury that it would take years for perc to migrate down to the groundwater level and, therefore, that the plaintiff's theory that the fire caused the groundwater contamination was not possible.

He looked like a chemistry professor. He wore a tweed jacket and olive green pants. He was obviously excited about teaching the jury what he had discovered in his experiments with perc. He had even made a home video of some of his experiments with perc with the help of some of his students.

During his testimony, he spent most of this time standing in front of the jury teaching them information about how perc is usually released into the environment and about its effects. He was deferential and not polished in his presentation. Yet his enthusiasm for teaching the jury was apparent. On the second day of his testimony, as he began to testify, he said "Good morning" to the jurors, to which they replied, "Good morning" in unison as they smiled at him. He obviously reminded them of their school days or some teacher they had encountered long before.

At the end of the trial, the jurors handed down their verdict for the insurance company within just a few hours. Although a few of the jurors left the courthouse immediately after delivering the verdict, some stayed to discuss the case with the trial attorneys and the judge. When they were asked about the expert testimony, the jurors were candid and unapologetic. They felt that the expert for the dry cleaning plant was intelligent and knowledgeable, but too smooth. They said he sounded like a paid expert who did not necessarily believe the plaintiff's case. They felt that he would have testified for either side of the case for enough money.

In contrast, the jurors felt that the professor for the insurer believed everything he said, and that his commitment and enthusiasm for his opinion were persuasive. They liked his teaching style and felt that he was committed to helping them understand the complexities of the case, rather than trying to merely sell them on the insurance company's case. They said that he did not seem to be the kind of person who would sell his opinion to the highest bidder. Most important, the jurors' comments showed that the professor's testimony echoed the themes and case story for the insurance company.

This story illustrates the complexities that are associated with the presentation of experts in trial. The superficial characteristics of the experts in this story are quite attractive to most trial lawyers. One expert was skilled in the relevant industry and polished in his presentation. The other expert witness came from academia and was skilled at teaching. Both witnesses were well-trained and well-prepared. Choosing whether to retain each of them would be difficult for most of us.

However, superficial characteristics can often be misleading to the most experienced trial attorneys and trial consultants, as we have discussed in other contexts in this book. We sometimes forget to take into account both the external and internal characteristics of an expert before putting him or her on the witness stand. Judges, jurors, and arbitrators are best persuaded by those experts who exhibit coherence between their inner characteristics and the substance of their testimony.

Although a physically attractive expert witness may find it easier than an unattractive witness to persuade others in the courtroom, any expert who lacks a persuasive message and the inner characteristics to engender confidence is no help to a trial team. Many complex details must come together during an expert's testimony.

This chapter will address the perceptions that jurors have of experts and expert testimony, as well as the process of preparing and presenting successful expert testimony in trial.

§ 14.02 | FACT FINDER PERCEPTIONS OF EXPERT WITNESSES AND THEIR TESTIMONY

Fact finders have mixed feelings about expert witnesses. On one hand, they realize that experts can be helpful and they want to hear what they have to say. This perception gives a trial attorney and an expert a head start from the beginning. Judges, jurors, and arbitrators want the expert to be successful in helping them to understand the issues in the case that are not within their normal experience.

On the other hand, they also realize that experts are being paid to testify and that they are therefore testifying by choice. As a result, fact finders are generally less sympathetic toward experts when they are being cross-examined.

At the outset of expert testimony, a juror is likely to feel that the expert is intelligent, but distant, and operating outside his or her normal experience. Judges and arbitrators can more easily identify with courtroom experts in some ways because they all share a certain level of professional camaraderie. However, all fact finders, even judges and arbitrators, have some common perceptions about experts.

They wonder if the expert witness is arrogant and self-absorbed, or pleasant and genuinely interested in helping the fact finder. For certain experts, there are some common perceptions among judges, jurors, and arbitrators. Doctors might be pompous or they might be caring and warm. Accountants might be cold and abrupt or they might be helpful and glad to teach the details. Engineers might be aloof and speak in jargon, or they might be friendly and careful to explain things in simple terms.

All of the preconceptions that jurors, judges, and arbitrators have about certain experts can be reinforced or eliminated according to the personal characteristics of the particular expert and with due regard for the needs of the case. The most important consideration, however, is that an expert witness have the ability and the mental attitude necessary to play the role of a caring, understanding teacher who is committed to helping the fact finder understand the case.

This same principle is important whether the fact finder is a judge, jury, or arbitration panel. Unless the fact finder is also an expert in the same field as the expert witness, the fact finder needs the help of the expert in order to get a good grasp of the case and make an informed, comfortable decision.

Most fact finders inherently believe that whenever there is an expert witness prepared to testify in a case, there must be something about the issues in the case that will be hard for them to understand. They also assume that the subject matter of the testimony will be very technical and will require their careful attention.

Conversely, judges, jurors, and arbitrators believe instinctively that they do not really *need* an expert's testimony in order to make a decision in the case. They believe that they have the capability of making a decision based upon their life experiences, and hence, if the expert's information was important in real life, they would already know what the expert wants to teach them. They believe that at the core of every case, even those cases with highly complicated and technical facts, lies a human story to which they can relate without the help of an expert. They do appreciate an expert's assistance, however, in explaining technical information.

Therefore, most judges, jurors, and arbitrators may appear to be deferential to an expert, but they will not be motivated to listen unless the expert is interesting and the information is easy to absorb and use in their decision-making process. Of course, a few fact finders will be highly motivated to listen under any circumstances.

Under these conditions, it is easy for a jury to become disinterested and bored during an expert's testimony. If the expert witness does not carefully and slowly take fact finders through a journey of understanding the expert's opinions in the case, he or she runs the risk of leaving jurors behind mentally and, worst of all, causing them to feel stupid and resentful.

Most of the expert qualifications that are presented to fact finders prior to actual testimony are given little explanation and are literally shoved at the fact finder *en masse*. As a result, judges, jurors, and arbitrators have a difficult time attaching meaning to a simple list of academic degrees and certifications. They do not know how to evaluate the quality of the expert's information based upon a list of meaningless attributes. However, they can attach meaning to an expert's spontaneous, subjective summaries about what he or she has learned, and why it is important for the fact finder to understand what the expert knows in order to make an important decision in the case.

Judges, jurors, and arbitrators respect most expert witnesses for making the effort to help them understand the issues in the case. They particularly admire scientists and professors who have dedicated themselves to learning and teaching. For this reason, trial attorneys should be careful about their style of cross-examination of expert witnesses whom the fact finder likes.

The most recent research about the perceptions of expert witnesses in trial suggests that in most trials, opposing expert witnesses neutralize each other's efforts. The only exception is that in a trial where one party has retained an expert who is totally ineffective or, worse, angers the fact finders, the trial can be lost for this reason alone. Even jurors are keenly aware that in all probability, both opposing parties have scoured the countryside for an expert who will say what a trial lawyer wants him or her to say on the witness stand. Although jurors appreciate the assistance provided by an expert in most instances, they also realize that an expert is a well-paid mercenary.

§ 14.03 | RETAINING THE RIGHT EXPERT

Retaining the right expert can be as complicated as retaining the right lawyer. There are numerous factors to consider. We will therefore break down the important decisions about experts into categories and try to simplify the process.

[1]—Is an Expert Needed?

In our trial system parties may retain both consulting experts (to help us understand aspects of the case) and testifying experts (to help the fact finder understand the case). Of course, using experts presupposes that experts are needed. If we, as trial lawyers, fully understand the case without resort to an expert, we should not waste our client's money or our time in hiring and conferring with a consulting expert unless we have decided to use him or her as a testifying expert.

Although there are many possible reasons to hire a testifying expert, two categories of reasons are usually paramount. The first is that the fact finder might genuinely need assistance in understanding the case. The second is that some expert witnesses can provide a broad context for the case in a way that fact witnesses alone cannot.

[a]—Understanding Specific Aspects of the Case

In the first category, a number of issues immediately arise. One is a legal issue. Most federal and state trial courts are interested in acting as "gatekeepers" to ensure that the expert testimony offered in the courtroom is based upon competent expert experience and acceptable scientific or technical expertise. Certainly, the most credible experts are those who base their testimony on solid research experience and widely accepted principles. The more traditional the expert appears to be, the more acceptable the expert will be to the judge or arbitration panel. Since the institution of the "gatekeeper" rules, a number of scientific research studies have been conducted to determine their effectiveness. The findings from these studies indicate that trial judges rarely have any advantages over jurors in understanding scientific or technical information. The findings also indicate that separating reliable scientific or technical principles from those that are unreliable can be adequately accomplished through the regular trial advocacy process. Trial judges and jurors are equally skilled at distinguishing truth from fiction.

Another issue is whether the fact finder actually needs the help of an expert. Judges, jurors, and arbitrators may resent being forced to listen to an expert in a subject area with which they already feel very comfortable. Occasionally, the trial team will anticipate that the fact finders must consider an unusual aspect of a familiar subject area, but the foundation for a new look at an old subject should be laid as early as possible to ward off resentment.

The discussion then brings us back to the real purpose of employing expert witness testimony, i.e., to help the fact finder understand certain key issues in the case story. In cases where expert testimony is helpful, the need will be apparent.

[b]—Delineating the Broad Picture

The second category for expert testimony that we should discuss is the use of an expert to describe the broad picture of the case story. This use of an expert is also very helpful to the fact finder, but for a different reason than the first category. Using an expert to give an overview can give an impression that the expert witness is a narrator (similar to a narrator of Greek mythology). He or she draws together parts of the story to help the judge, jury, or arbitration panel make sense out of the various parts of the case. The use of expert testimony for this purpose can be a very powerful, persuasive tool.

[2]—Qualifying the Expert

Rule 702 of the Federal Rules of Evidence provides that opinion testimony may be given by the witness whose "scientific, technical, or other specialized knowledge will assist the trier of fact to understand the evidence or to determine a fact in issue." The United States Supreme Court has held, in *Daubert v. Merrell Dow Pharmaceuticals, Inc.,* that a trial judge can make a preliminary assessment of the validity, reasoning, and methodology of an expert's opinion.[1] In making this assessment, a judge can determine whether the proposed testimony of an expert witness is reliable enough to be helpful to a judge, jury, or, conceivably, an arbitration panel.

Using the *Daubert* analysis, a trial judge can assess the validity, reasoning, and methodology of an expert's opinion to determine whether any novel theory is involved and whether such a theory is sufficiently supported by acceptable scientific principles. It is unclear whether the trial judge's analysis should be based upon subjective or objective reasoning. For this reason, both trial attorney and expert witness should appeal to the sensitivities of the trial judge on both a subjective and objective level.

By knowing in advance how a trial judge will perceive both the scientific reasoning of an expert and the theory upon which the expert's opinion is based, the trial team and the expert can develop the best themes and psychological reasoning that will persuade the trial judge that the expert testimony should be admitted into evidence. In essence, therefore, the expert's opinion must persuade the court that it is composed of solid, traditional scientific or academic reasoning.

However, a two-pronged approach might be helpful in opposing the admissibility of the other side's expert opinion. The first tactic is to simply describe the expert in question as a non-traditional, unacceptable theorist who propounds unusual opinions. Second, opposing counsel may present another expert of its own who has traditional and widely accepted views in order to debunk the testimony of the opposing side's questionable expert.

---

[1] Daubert v. Merrell Dow Pharmaceuticals, Inc., 509 U.S. 579, 113 S.Ct. 2786, 125 L.Ed.2d 469 (1993).

Those jurisdictions which still follow the rule set forth in *Frye v. United States* (i.e., methods and opinions must have "general acceptance" within the relevant scientific community)[2] make the inquiry much simpler. All the trial lawyer and the expert need show is that the method and opinion of the expert have been published in peer-reviewed journals. In most fields of science and expertise, there are mainstream and fringe elements in the community that publish methods and opinions that might be innovative. Therefore, in the *Frye* jurisdictions the need for good advocacy is just as strong as in the *Daubert* jurisdictions.

Therefore, a major concern is whether the expert under consideration will make a good impression on the judge for purposes of admissibility. Sometimes a questionable expert can gain admissibility with a little extra preparation regarding persuasive themes and points that have been known to favorably impress the trial judge who will be ruling on the admissibility of that expert's testimony.

[3]—The Expert as a Persuasive Witness

An expert witness is an advocate just like a trial lawyer. The primary difference is that an expert witness is advocating an opinion on a particular topic whereas a trial lawyer is advocating an entire case theory. Whenever an expert witness tries to become an advocate for the entire case, he or she is stepping out of the proper role for an expert and, as a result, will become less persuasive.

As an advocate, an expert witness must be able to teach and to persuade a judge, jury, or arbitration panel that his or her opinion is correct and applicable to the case. As we have discussed before, fact finders are interested in the expert witness as a whole person. They want to trust and learn from an expert witness, but only if the expert is credible and interesting.

Many of the finest experts in life may be successful and accomplished in their fields of expertise, but they may make terrible expert witnesses at trial. Conversely, many very effective expert witnesses have questionable or unrelated credentials. Therefore, the dilemma of balancing knowledge versus testifying skill often arises in choosing expert witnesses.

Perhaps the best way to resolve the dilemma is to first determine how best to frame the expert opinion that is necessary in the case and then to determine

---

[2] Frye v. United States, 54 App. D.C. 46, 293 Fed. 1013 (D.C. Cir. 1923).

which expert can best persuade the fact finder that the opinion is correct and applicable. Sometimes negotiations with the expert witness are necessary.

However, once the opinion that is applicable to the case is determined, it is best to find an expert who has the persuasive skills necessary to convince the fact finder that the opinion should be adopted. In some cases, this may mean that two experts may be necessary to prepare and present expert testimony necessary in the case—one expert to consult and prepare the opinion and another expert to present it to the fact finder. Developing an expert opinion and persuading others require different sets of skills, and many experts acquire one set but are deficient in the second.

One of the most important traits for an expert witness is the ability to understand his or her role as a supporting actor at trial. This means that the best expert witnesses follow the trial agenda necessary to be persuasive in the case, rather than their own personal agendas. For example, expert witnesses have their own vision of what they should testify about and how they should present themselves. This vision may or may not be synchronous with the themes and story that the trial team wants to tell. Therefore, the best expert witnesses are willing to listen and learn about the case before making conclusions about how they should testify.

Conversely, a trial lawyer must learn from the expert as well. In fact, there must be two-way communication between the expert and the entire trial team. In most instances, this means that there must be good chemistry between the expert and each lawyer on the case.

There are a number of ways to determine whether an expert can meet all the criteria for the case. The first step is to ask for references from other trial attorneys who have used the expert in a case. The second is to interview and audition the expert as if he or she were being cast in a play. The third is to test the expert more scientifically with a panel of jurors from the jurisdiction in which the case is pending. If the budget is limited, it would still be a good idea to rehearse key experts before a panel of local jurors even if the jurors do not live in the specific jurisdiction where the case is pending.

[4]—Choosing Among Possible Experts

Choosing the best expert witness for a case is probably best accomplished by using a combination of logic and intuition. Logically, the trial team will want to obtain references, make a list of characteristics that they want an expert to have, and then prepare a list of the people who have those characteristics. Care should be taken to allow some flexibility regarding preferred characteristics, however, since no-one will be a perfect match.

Most trial teams will want to interview the best candidates. However, it might be helpful for each candidate to provide a short videotape of real or mock testimony for a real or fictitious case in which that expert has participated. A live audition would be even more helpful.

Despite these methodical steps, however, the final choice of an expert is generally the result of strong feelings and intuition. There really is no substitute for good personal chemistry between the expert witness and members of the trial team. A strong personal rapport with experts can help enhance the power and persuasiveness of expert testimony, and can be of assistance in overcoming any problems that might occur after the relationship has been formed.

§ 14.04 | INTEGRATING AN EXPERT WITNESS INTO THE CASE

Imagine that you are about to begin preparation of an expert witness for an upcoming trial. Before the expert arrives, you sit down to map out the themes and case story for the expert to learn and the points for direct examination and cross-examination that you anticipate the expert will encounter. You have worked with this expert before during the consulting phase of your relationship and you believe you have good rapport with each other.

What is the next step to most effectively assist the expert witness to testify effectively? Is it best to list the points that the expert must learn to testify about and expect him or her to figure out how to perform on the witness stand? Is it best to walk the expert through the case themes and case story, although the opposing attorney might ask about the substance of such conversations? Is it best to put the expert through an intensive training mini-course to learn about the case and to practice delivering his or her testimony?

The answer to these questions and others depends upon the witness and the case. However, we must remember that expert witnesses, like everyone else, experience the world on two levels: internal and external. Internally, an expert usually has a dialogue about the case and his or her role in it that may or may not be reflected in the trial team's vision of the case. Internal dialogues are a normal part of human experience, and there is nothing unusual just because an expert first experiences the case differently than anybody else. Externally, an expert sees and hears information about the case and his or her role in it that stimulates the expert to envision a role and to behave in a certain way.

[1]—Establishing a Strong Rapport with Expert Witnesses

The most effective expert witness testimony is a result of hard work and a strong alliance between an expert witness and a trial team. Judges, jurors, and arbitrators can sense when there is a strong rapport between an expert and a trial lawyer. They can sense when a trial lawyer and an expert witness like each other and respect each other. Conversely, they can also sense when a trial lawyer and an expert witness do not like or respect each other.

Before working with an expert, it is generally a good idea to reflect about the personal and professional needs of the expert and the strengths and possible weaknesses that he or she brings to the case. Taking a little time to think about the mental state and needs of the expert can be an important first step to integrating the expert witness into the case.

To begin this first step, it is important to read the expert's résumé, previous deposition testimony, articles and books written by the expert, and any information that may help you to understand the personal and professional background of this expert who may become an important part of your professional life. It might be helpful to call other trial attorneys who have used the expert to get their thoughts about how best to work with him or her. During this process of background review, it might also be helpful to begin forecasting ways to integrate the expert's skills and background into the case development. That is, one of the purposes of using an expert is to find ways to strengthen the case by using the expert's personal and professional skills and experience.

When counsel integrates an expert into the case, it is fundamentally important to demonstrate respect and admiration for the expert. As in any other aspect of life, people will go out of their way to help you if you will demonstrate genuine respect and admiration. Under these circumstances, the witness is being retained solely because of his or her superior knowledge in an area that is critical to your case, and that witness will hence expect even more respect and admiration than the average person.

There are many ways to show respect to an expert that will generate respect in return. First, create an atmosphere whereby the expert is treated as a peer rather than a subordinate. An important characteristic of a peer relationship is the ability of both parties to listen carefully to each other; therefore, be sure to include the expert's observations and thoughts in the development of the case and the trial preparation. Another important characteristic of a peer relationship is to occasionally meet that peer—the expert—on his or her home turf. Visiting the expert's office and seeing the expert in his or her own environment will usually generate a lot of interesting, helpful ideas for the case in addition to developing a better, stronger relationship between the expert and the trial team.

Another important way to gain mutual respect with the expert is to ask for the expert's thoughts before formulating ideas or dictating instructions. Although the trial team is responsible for the case, never forget that the expert can impart knowledge to the trial team that is not within the natural purview of the team and that will make the case stronger and more persuasive to the fact finder. Most experts are skilled at creative thinking, which brings a fresh perspective to the case. Since the creative thinking process works better in an atmosphere of friendliness and support, everyone on the trial team will benefit from a positive working relationship with the expert witnesses.

Most experts realize that they have a responsibility to work at developing a positive relationship with the trial team. Occasionally, an expert presents difficulties in this respect, however. In these instances, it might be helpful to have a third party, such as a trial consultant, visit with the expert to try to identify whether a long-term problem exists or whether the problem is a simple one that can be easily remedied. After all, relationships involve interactive communications.

At the same time the trial team is trying to cultivate a positive relationship with the expert, it is important to relay information to the expert and gather responses that will help the trial team evaluate how helpful the extra witness can be in the consulting and testifying process. Sometimes this may involve role-playing and videotaping exercises while the expert is still in a consulting status. It might also be helpful to ask the expert to make an oral or written evaluation of the issues in the case and to develop an initial opinion about relevant issues that will reveal the expert's thought processes.

If counsel takes the time to integrate the expert into the case slowly, the expert can become a more helpful member of the trial team and a more effective expert witness.

[2]—The Role of the Expert in the Themes and Story of the Case

Most experts will have a specific area of expertise that will enhance the themes and story of the case. They are cast in the dual roles of supportive actor and adviser. Therefore, it would be inappropriate for an expert to also take on the role of directing the case. Direction of the case is the responsibility solely of the trial team.

Most skilled expert witnesses will have experienced situations and formulated ideas that will assist in the development of the themes and story of the case. These ideas should be considered carefully and included in the testing of the case during the decision-making research phase of case development. However, the expertise of most expert witnesses does not include expertise in the decision-making process of the fact finders.

Therefore, the expert witness must understand the needs of the judge, jury, or arbitration panel in order to be able to do his or her job. As a result, it may be helpful to explain the psychological and decision-making processes of the fact finder in a particular case. The expert should understand that it is not enough just to tell the fact finder about the expert's opinion and supportive data. The expert should also understand that it is perhaps even more important to relate information to the fact finder in a way that (1) helps the fact finder understand the information, (2) is interesting, and (3) is persuasive.

The expert should understand that today's judges and juries require that information which is given to them must be both concise and in easily understood terms. It is not helpful for the expert to simply "dump" massive amounts of technical data on fact finders and expect them to understand the data's relationship to the case story.

For example, consider a business breach of contract and tort case in which a movie actor is suing a movie production company. The case involves allegations that a movie production company withheld money from the actor, claiming that some of the expenses of the production should have been the responsibility of all parties before any royalties or profits were distributed. In response, the actor claims that the movie production company has been using accounting tricks to force everyone to share the expenses that should be the sole responsibility of the company.

The actor's causes of action include breach of contract, fraud, breach of fiduciary duty, and conversion. The actor's best themes and case story would reveal that the company was stealing money from the actor and other people out of greed. The actor might try to prove that the company tried to cover up its theft by lying in the financial statements that accompanied the production.

In response, the movie production company states that it has been truthful and honest at all times. It states that it respects the actor, but that he is mistaken. It states that it has commissioned an independent audit of the financial statements and that they are accurate.

In this instance, the financial experts for both sides have choices to make. On the one hand, they can simply repeat their reviews of the details of their audits and opinions. On the other hand, they can state that their audits and reviews show clearly that the case story for their respective parties is correct. The financial expert for the actor will state that his audit and opinion support the finding that the movie production company was stealing money and covering up its theft. The financial expert for the company will state that his audit and opinion support the finding that the actor is mistaken and that his or her client is honest and truthful.

The most effective expert witnesses are good teachers. In the example given above, the prospective experts must have the ability to demonstrate through personal persuasive skills and the use of demonstrative aids that their respective opinions are correct. Part of these persuasive skills will involve making the subject matter interesting and helpful to the fact finder. Otherwise, judges, jurors, and arbitrators have no motivation to listen to the expert.

[3]—Overcoming Problems with Expert Witnesses

Expert witnesses, like everyone else, have strengths and weaknesses. Some experts are more skilled at testifying than others. Some expert witnesses make great experts but poor testifiers. Some expert witnesses are shy whereas others are quite gregarious. Some expert witnesses like to tangle with opposing lawyers while others are more respectful. Some expert witnesses can easily sound interesting but others are inherently boring. Some expert witnesses can easily help support and strengthen the case story even as others appear to be somewhat uncertain.

There are hundreds of reasons why an expert witness may be having difficulty in testifying effectively. Understanding why an expert may be having difficulties is not always an easy task. Most experts have developed their personal and public personas over many decades. They have spent many years understanding their area of expertise and relatively little time testifying. Even those experts who have testified many times may be having problems with their effectiveness because of personal issues that have never been properly addressed.

Even in situations where there do not appear to be any significant problems, the effectiveness of an expert witness can always be enhanced by additional practice. There are significant similarities between the effectiveness of an expert witness and the effectiveness of a trial lawyer. Introspection, insight, and practice are tools that all professional people use to improve their skills and effectiveness.

Helping an expert witness to improve his or her effectiveness requires some intervention that, in turn, involves information gathering, information sharing, and practice. One should not presume to know why an expert is behaving in a certain way. It is a helpful, however, to sit down with the expert and ask him or her to share his or her thought processes. By conducting some investigation into the mind of the expert, the real problems, if any, and perhaps the solutions to those problems will become apparent.

It is usually helpful to share information with the expert that will help to correct any misunderstandings that the expert may be having about the case or about the courtroom. This information-sharing phase should also be followed up with role-playing or practice that can help the expert implement what he or she learned during the information-sharing phase.

Most experts take great pride in their work. They go to great lengths to study and think about the case. They want to perform for you in a way that is professional and reinforces a strong self-image. They want to give testimony that is effective and memorable. They want and need your approval. However, most experts are not trained to understand how lawyers think and they have no real life experiences as trial attorneys. Hence, we must forgive them for these shortcomings.

Perhaps the most serious problems between lawyers and their experts occur because of lack of real communication and lack of effort in trying to accommodate each other. On the one hand, lawyers and experts come from two different worlds. Lawyers are trained in advocacy and have responsibilities imposed upon them by law, practice, and our culture, whereas experts tend to be academicians, teachers, researchers, or the like. On the other hand, lawyers and experts have a great deal in common. Each of them is an expert in his or her field. Each of them has an agenda that overlaps that of the other. Each of them has superior knowledge about the subject matter in which he or she is expert. By reaffirming respect for an expert witness, a trial attorney can achieve a greater level of rapport with the expert that will help to smooth over any specific problems that the expert may have in preparing or delivering testimony.

In addition to showing respect for experts, we must also command and earn respect as trial attorneys when working with experts. Your clients have given you the responsibility of representing them in court. Although experts are encouraged to have independent opinions, their role in the case is limited to giving opinions about important issues. Rarely is the entirety of an expert's opinions about a matter going to agree exactly on all points with your case. Part of what an expert knows is irrelevant. Other parts of an expert's knowledge are relevant, but can be expressed in ways that are either helpful or harmful to the themes and thrust of your case. Still other parts of an expert's knowledge are clearly relevant and squarely on point with your case.

Making choices about what part of an expert's knowledge is relevant and how much information should be delivered to the fact finder is primarily the trial attorney's job. Most experts are not good communicators and will not be star performers in the courtroom without assistance.

The most successful expert witnesses know that they may be experts in a subject matter, but also that they can use some assistance in making choices about the content of their other testimony and in enhancing their testifying skills. Trial attorneys are too often overconfident about the quality and effectiveness of their expert witnesses. Most experts try to give the impression that they are comfortable and effective in giving courtroom testimony. However, experience tells us that putting important expert witnesses through a practice and learning experience before testifying can correct problems with some weak experts and enhance the effectiveness of others. Most experienced trial consultants are trained to assist expert witnesses in overcoming obstacles to giving effective testimony.

Occasionally the trial team will be locked into using an expert witness with whom the trial team feels uncomfortable either because the expert lacks good testifying skills or for some other reason. Rather than summarily dismissing the expert, sometimes it is helpful to bring in a trial consultant or someone who is experienced at diagnosing the cause of behavioral problems with witnesses to make suggestions to both the trial team and the expert on how to resolve these problems.

An example might be a patent case in which an engineering expert with a doctoral degree seems hesitant about giving strong opinions on some issues and combative about other issues. From the trial attorney's point of view, an engineering expert in a patent case should be friendly, helpful, and able to simplify details in a way that is responsive to specific questions about those details. If the expert is not meeting expectations, it is often tempting for the trial team to "beat up" the witness and demand different behavior.

Keep in mind, however, that from an engineer's point of view, the world can only be viewed through a maze of complex detail, so that questions that are too narrow risk containing the wrong assumptions, thus causing the engineer to balk during his testimony. After all, engineers are mathematicians at heart. If you will recall your days in math class, you were taught that if you use the wrong formula, you get the wrong answer.

Therefore, if you ask an engineer or a mathematician for the correct formula before asking him or her for the answer to the formula, your chances of success will skyrocket. However, this alternative way of approaching the expert may not occur to the trial team, and some additional outside assistance can be helpful (and not necessarily expensive).

§ 14.05 | PREPARING AN EXPERT WITNESS FOR DIRECT EXAMINATION AND CROSS-EXAMINATION

It has been said that success is 90% perspiration and 10% inspiration. Certainly this is true for expert testimony. The effectiveness of an expert witness depends upon how well the expert is prepared to understand the content of the testimony *and* to present it in a way that is interesting and persuasive. The more adept an expert is in teaching the fact finder(s) and in maneuvering through cross-examination, the more persuasive and effective he or she will be.

[1]—Contents of the Expert's Testimony

Like the rest of the case development, the expert's testimony must relate to relevant issues and themes in the case. As stated in most rules of court and case law, the testimony must persuade the fact finder that an issue or fact is more likely or less likely. In doing so, it is incumbent upon a trial lawyer and an expert witness to get to the point early and powerfully. Giving expert opinion is not an exercise in avoidance. It is an exercise in creating powerful impressions.

The development of the contents of an expert's testimony should be a mutual effort between the trial team and the expert. Even the most experienced trial attorneys can benefit from the input of a skilled expert witness. Often, expert witnesses can identify issues that the trial team has missed in the development of the case for trial.

Moreover, expert witnesses can be an important addition to the trial team in a group brainstorming effort to determine the most effective ways to develop issues and persuade the fact finder. Expert witnesses bring fresh perspectives to the creative thinking process that can help enhance the persuasive power of the case story.

The preparation of the case presentation, including the development of expert witness testimony, is a process, not an event. Ideas that sound good one day may sound terrible the next. Therefore, one of the benefits of establishing a strong rapport with expert witnesses is to motivate them to be helpful and creative in the development of the case presentation and their own testimony.

As preparation of the expert's testimony proceeds, it is important to continually focus and simplify the opinions and supportive testimony of the expert. Ultimately, the more simple and powerful the opinion testimony, the more persuasive the entire case presentation for the client will be.

Once the expert witness has become attuned to the case and has substantially completed the process of focusing and simplifying his or her opinions and supportive testimony, the expert will rely upon members of the trial team to furnish him or her with the case materials and the demonstrative tools necessary to teach the fact finder. In most instances, the expert witnesses will have read the complete pleadings and depositions carefully and will have reviewed the other documents and case materials. It is generally important for expert witnesses to know as much about the case as possible in order to give context and relevance to the issues about which the expert witnesses will be testifying. Nothing is more disquieting to an expert (or to a trial lawyer) than to be blindsided by an issue that the expert did not anticipate.

Therefore, for practical and legal reasons, it is best for a trial team to share all of the case materials with the expert witnesses, unless there is a special legal reason for not doing so. In those cases where some of the case materials are not available, a time schedule should be developed for the trial team to obtain the materials and furnish them to the expert witness.

Preparation for expert witness testimony usually includes dealing with the deposition testimony given by the expert or other people in the case. Although it is true that deposition testimony is given under oath and is recorded, depositions generally result in more flexibility during trial once the deposition witness's live testimony is given in the courtroom. Most experienced expert witnesses realize that a question asked in a deposition generally does not cover all the bases, and that an honest and truthful expert opinion must address all the issues raised in the question.

In general, juries are quite forgiving of both trial lawyers and witnesses in deposition, although judges and arbitrators are sometimes less forgiving. Regardless, all fact finders seek the truth and want to know what the expert has to say about the subjects addressed in the trial. Therefore, if an expert witness gives an answer in the courtroom that is different from his statement in a deposition, most judges, jurors, and arbitrators are generally satisfied as long as there is a simple explanation for the variance.

Certainly, an expert who states one opinion in deposition and a very different opinion in the courtroom will be subjected to a vigorous cross-examination; moreover, rarely does a trial judge intervene with some sort of sanction. The most common explanation for a variance in testimony is a difference in the question asked or in the circumstances under which the question is answered. For example, an expert may give an opinion during deposition that a car was speeding and yet at trial state that, after reviewing more data or reviewing the data more closely, it was not speeding. Most fact finders would be satisfied with these types of simple explanations.

Judges, jurors and arbitrators often comment about the quality of expert testimony after proceedings are completed. Although they will sometimes comment about the personal characteristics of the expert, they most often comment about the helpfulness of the content of the expert's testimony. Even though research has indicated that many jurors believe that the experts for each side of a case "neutralize" each other, it is also true that the quality and effectiveness of expert testimony reflects on a party's entire case.

If both parties have strong cases and strong expert testimony, the slightest increase in the level of excellence can mean the difference between winning and losing. In developing the content of an expert's testimony, therefore, great care should be given to blend important themes, facts, and expert opinions in such a way that makes the testimony both informational and persuasive.

[2]—Preparing an Expert for Direct Examination

The process of preparing an expert for direct examination can be smooth and productive or rough and painful. To be smooth and productive, the process is best served by a combination of mutual respect and cooperation as well as good organizational skills.

[a]—General Considerations

As we have discussed, trial lawyers and expert witnesses often have different agendas and needs, most of which can be accommodated easily. To make sure that everyone is on the same page, it would be best to start out in a neutral way. It is usually a mistake to begin in a commanding or demanding stance with an expert witness. That is, we all function on two different levels. The first and more superficial level is our surface behavior. Although an expert may be doing and saying the right things initially, there may be a fundamental misunderstanding that is lurking below the surface. The second level beneath the surface contains our feelings and unconscious thoughts. To make sure that everything is on the table, it is best to ask many open-ended questions and attempt to understand how the expert feels about the issues in the case and his or her testimony. It is also important for the trial attorney to constructively express his or her feelings and thoughts about the issues and about the expert's testimony as well.

There are some specific things that you can do to get the preparation process off to a good start. In order to give the expert the feeling that he or she is a trusted comrade, it is often wise to locate the first meeting somewhere other than the trial team's office. Meeting in a neutral environment where the expert feels comfortable is often a good way to show respect and give the expert a feeling that you are confident enough in him or her to allow independence outside the control of the law office. Restaurants are great places to meet because they are conducive to building rapport, relaxing, and listening to each other without interruptions.

[b]—Including the Expert in Decision Making

Regardless of where you meet with expert witnesses, it is critical to include the expert in decision making about the witness's opinions, field of expertise, and testimony. One of the most common complaints we hear from successful expert witnesses is that trial attorneys do not listen to or are not willing to consider the witnesses' recommendations. Sometimes experts have helpful ideas that may at first seem to be far-fetched, but after some consideration and discussion, turn out to be quite useful.

A related issue that arises many times in the preparation process is that the trial team is "too busy" to discuss certain issues with the expert witness because they may seem trivial or misguided. One of the problems in this scenario is that often trial preparation begins too late for some of the discussion that should occur with the expert before trial.

To avoid problems where issues should have been more extensively discussed with experts before trial, it might be useful to develop a schedule that would allow for thorough discussions before trial and to appoint someone on the trial team to be in charge of communicating with experts to make sure there are no undiscussed issues. In those rare instances where unanticipated issues arise in trial, it would be helpful for the expert to have a way of communicating with the trial team by notes or through an intermediary on the trial team.

Most trial consultants who train expert witnesses have prepared special programs for assisting the trial team with developing the testimony of expert witnesses. Most of the special programs follow three steps:

(1) Interviewing the witness to find out the witness's mental state and the witness's concerns;

(2) Teaching the witness about the psychology of the courtroom and how to testify effectively; and

(3) Letting the witness practice what he or she has learned by demonstrating testimony on the two or three key points about which he or she will testify.

[c]—The Expert's Mental Focus

Getting the expert witness in the right mental state to testify is also important. If the witness is experiencing inappropriate anxiety or is so concentrated on his or her own feelings and thoughts that the overall perspective of the case is lost, the testimony can be disastrous. In order to be successful, the expert witness must be mentally focused on helping the audience (judge, jury, or arbitration panel) understand the expert's opinions in such a way that they are persuasive and more compelling than those of the opposing expert.

There are myriad ways in which the effectiveness of an expert witness can be compromised by his or her thoughts and feelings about the courtroom in general or the case in specific. Whether it be unnecessary combativeness, shyness, or some other mental state, each of these problems can and should be addressed constructively early in the preparation process.

The next step in preparing a witness mentally for trial is to teach the witness through lectures and demonstrations about the psychology of the courtroom and how to testify effectively. Of course, the best place to teach someone about the courtroom is in a courtroom-like environment. By taking some of the mystery out of the courtroom, expert witnesses (indeed, all witnesses) can spend more time focusing upon their effectiveness than upon their musings and anxieties.

The teaching process should include observations about judges, jurors, or arbitrators and how they make decisions. The most important part of this process is teaching the expert witness how to be most effective in helping the fact finder understand the expert's opinions and their important meaning to the case.

Perhaps one of the most often heard expressions among members of the trial team is, "Aw, don't worry, this expert doesn't need any help. He has testified hundreds of times and knows what he is doing." Comments like this should signal someone on the trial team that some attention should be given to determining whether this opinion is correct. After all, if an expert is important to a case, it is equally important to make sure the expert is practiced, rehearsed, and ready to testify.

Jurors have expressed many complaints about experienced expert witnesses who were too glib or too arrogant, or who failed to talk to the jury on its own level. Sometimes a feeling of self-importance gets in the way of effective expert witness testimony. Sometimes expert witnesses have managed to testify for many years without realizing that there are personal expressions or behaviors that the fact finders have considered offensive.

[d]–Presentation Style and Technique

Aside from behavioral issues, most expert witnesses need some help with presentation style and technique. After all, most expert witnesses are experts in fields other than communication and persuasion. Counsel will no doubt have many suggestions based upon actual trial experiences that will help an expert to testify more effectively. Some trial consultants also will have suggestions for an expert witness based upon their own experiences in the courtroom and their discussions with jurors.

In the lecture and demonstration process, we have found it helpful to have the expert witness sit in the seats of the fact finders to get a feel for the experience of being a judge, juror, or arbitrator. The empathy that is created in this process often makes it easier for an expert witness to accept the trial team's suggestions.

[e]—Practice and Role Play

The next phase of preparation for an expert might be practice and role play. If enough "woodshedding" (i.e., elimination of unnecessary detail) has been conducted for the expert to be familiar with the issues and questions that will be asked of him or her on key points, rehearsal and feedback are very important.

In trial advocacy training, we have learned that practice in a courtroom environment, immediate critique, and videotape replay are very useful tools in persuading judges, jurors, and arbitrators. The same tools are useful in helping expert witnesses to prepare to testify. Although a life-like mock courtroom is also helpful, it is not essential. Mock courtrooms can also be set up in conference or meeting facilities such as hotel meeting rooms. Most expert witnesses have had enough experience with courtroom environments either in person or through television that they will automatically feel the effects of rooms which have been altered to include rows of chairs for the jury, two tables for opposing counsel, and a mock judge's bench with state and federal flags on each side.

The role play process can be as formal or informal as counsel prefers. We have learned a great deal from drama professors and actors about the rehearsal process, just as we have learned a great deal from psychologists. In the preparation process for direct examination, there are no better preparation tools than practice and rehearsal. The closer we get to trial, the more formal the process should be. However, in its early stages, the preparation process might be less formal in order for the trial team and the expert witness to become comfortable with their roles and the subject matter of the testimony.

[f]—Woodshedding

The woodshedding process will usually take place on a different time track than the preparation for actually testifying. It is possible to overload experts with so much information so that they end up not absorbing any of it. However, the most important reason for having a two-track preparation process is that the focus and intent for each of the two tracks is different. The woodshedding process is designed simply to hammer out the details of the witness's testimony. This process may take hours or days and will focus on simplifying and expressing the meaning of the expert's opinions and the basis for them.

However, the courtroom presentation part of the preparation process deals more with behavior and psychology. In order to be effective, an expert witness must be able to integrate information from the woodshedding process into a style of testifying that is compelling and persuasive.

There are a few suggestions that might be made to an expert throughout the preparation process. These suggestions are characteristically important in any kind of expert testimony.

[i]—Keep the Presentation Simple and Interesting

Whether the fact finder is a judge, juror, or arbitrator, each will begin thinking about the case based upon his or her own experience with the subject matter. In addition, if the fact finder is a group of people such as a jury or arbitration panel, an expert would be well-advised to appeal to each of the members of the group in a way that takes into account their individual experiences and needs. Some judges, jurors, or arbitrators may be very sophisticated or knowledgeable in the subject matter, but most of them will not have a great deal of knowledge or experience with the subject of the expert's testimony. (Otherwise, an expert would not be needed to tell a judge, jury, or arbitration panel things that they already know.)

For the most part, an expert should assume that the fact finders stopped learning about the subject matter of the case while they were in school. In addition, the more technical the subject matter, the more the fact finders probably avoided taking the time to learn and understand it while they were in school.

Nevertheless, there are ways to help jurors overcome their anxieties about a subject and make the learning process interesting and motivating. The first is to use analogies whenever possible to help make the transition between (1) experiences, objects, and concepts with which the jury is familiar and (2) experiences, objects, and concepts about which the expert will testify. For example, in a patent case, a telecommunications engineer might explain to a jury the process and relationship between a base station controller, a telephone central office, and a communications path leading to a cellular telephone call.

In all probability, a technical discussion about circuits, transceivers, software, and hardware would leave the judge or jury in a fog. They would be perplexed, anxious, and perhaps angry that they cannot understand the subject matter.

However, using an analogy—say, to basic military command structure—could help most fact finders understand the foregoing telecommunications information. That is, if the central office is referred to as an Army general, the base station controller as an Army captain, and the circuit going to the cellular telephone as an Army private, fact finders will better understand the command and control relationships in wireless telephone systems.

The best ideas for simplifying testimony result from a process of brainstorming alternatives.

[ii]—Use Simple Language

Although it is sometimes necessary to use technical jargon, the most successful expert witnesses and trial attorneys realize that judges, jurors, and arbitrators appreciate explanations for technical terms and the use of simple language. Even though the fact finder may have an idea about clarifying the definition of the jargon, judges, jurors, and arbitrators always feel more comfortable with testimony that can be expressed in the simplest terms.

Occasionally, cases are so complex that familiarity with technical terms is essential to understanding the case and reaching a verdict. However, even in those cases fact finders feel more persuaded and more comfortable if the essence of the case can be reduced to simple, non-technical terms.

It may take a little more work for the trial team and the expert to simplify the terms used, but the result will be well worth the effort. For example, a healthcare product liability case may involve the "initiation of hypoglycemic episodes due to catalytic fluctuations during the migration of fluorochloride compounds in the blood system." In such a case, judges and jurors would greatly appreciate an understanding of the basic issues before heading off into technical Never-Never Land. To accomplish this, an expert might say simply, "This case is really simple. It is about allegations that a drug made by the XYZ Company had dangerous side effects even though the Company intended for the drug to be helpful to people who need to control blood sugar problems."

[iii]—Use Visual and Demonstrative Aids

One of the most important ways for an expert to teach and explain key concepts is to use visual and demonstrative aids. As we learned earlier in this book, the majority of people learn faster and more thoroughly with the use of visual aids. In addition, experience and scientific jury research with the subject matter of any given case will help to identify issues that can be made more understandable with the use of visual aids.

A simple visual aid can often clarify a complex point instantaneously. Just as important, it can help the individual fact finder or a group of fact finders to focus on key points together with others in the courtroom. Otherwise, not only will a trial team be faced with as many as twelve different points of view, but it may be faced with up to twelve *widely different* points of view.

Visual aids also help make an expert witness's testimony more memorable. Even though we realize that judges and jurors sometimes view experts as neutralizing each other, it is always possible for one expert to be more persuasive in the final analysis with the use of helpful, interesting, and memorable visual aids that are more persuasive than those of the opposing expert.

As we have discussed in other parts of this book, using visual aids as building blocks for teaching the fact finder is a good idea. There are many ways to begin using a series of visual aids with simple concepts and then add to or overlay them with information or concepts that coincide with the expert's testimony.

One of the most important reasons for using frequent visual aids is that they provide important anchors for the decision maker. The use of demonstrative aids in the courtroom provides the jury with physical reproduction of the spoken information (the testimony). If these two sources coincide well, judges, jurors, and arbitrators get a more comfortable feeling that the information they are receiving is solid and reliable.

The use of visual aids also provides the expert witness with support material that enhances the witness's authority and persuasiveness. Visual aids often provide the witness and the trial lawyer with added focus and structure for parts of the testimony. This gives the decision maker a feeling that the lawyer and the witness are organized, credible, and reliable. Visual aids help to reinforce the testimony and thus, the feeling that the points that the expert is making are important and constitute a good use of the court's time.

As we have also discussed, visual aids help to motivate interest in the information about which the expert is testifying. It provides a respite from the tendency of some courtroom presentations to be merely overwhelming, endless streams of meaningless rhetoric.

It is preferable for the expert witness to leave the witness stand at times when drawings or demonstrations must be made. The trial team's case gains more credibility if the expert witness maintains center stage. Even in situations where it is preferable for the trial attorney to create a structure for the discussion by using visual aids, it is very important to invite the expert witness to be the real focus of attention. After all, the expert witness is the source of the information and is a more reliable teacher on the subject of the testimony.

There are other practical reasons to keep the expert witness on stage, out of the witness box, and in the center of the courtroom as the focus of attention, rather than the trial lawyer. During an expert's testimony, the trial attorney is more of a director and producer than an actor. As the director, the trial attorney should be watching the judge, jury, or arbitration panel for feedback that may indicate areas that might be unclear or need further explanation. By maintaining his role as an observer, the trial attorney can also spot questions that should be addressed or areas in which the subject of the expert's testimony might be unclear. In addition, by maintaining his role as director, rather than participant, the trial attorney can have a better opportunity to control the direction, speed, and flow of the testimony.

The choice of visual aids during the expert's testimony will depend upon the identification of choices available for particular subjects and the selection of those that are the most persuasive. As we have discussed in other parts of this book, there are many possible types of visual aids that are persuasive in different ways.

Although there are continual debates about whether to use high-tech or low-tech methods of presenting visual aids, the better argument seems to be that a combination of methods is preferable. Simple easel pads are versatile and familiar to people in the courtroom. However, computer-based presentations are simple to create and often more powerful and persuasive. Men and women who serve as decision makers in the courtroom will be comfortable with any type of visual aid. Most judges, jurors, and arbitrators are accustomed to high-tech presentations.

[g]–Meaning vs. Volume of Information

You might recall our previous discussion about the relative importance of details versus the meaning of details. That is, the meaning of information is more important than the details of the information itself.

Nowhere is this more true than with expert witness testimony. Sometimes experts are more interested in showing how much they know rather than in persuading people about the meaning of the information they have to share.

It is a bad idea for an expert witness to throw everything he or she knows at the judge or jury, hoping that something will be remembered. It is much more effective for an expert to state simple and clear conclusions, provide supportive data, and explain those conclusions about the key issues in the case.

[3]–Preparing an Expert for Cross-Examination

The same preparation process that we discussed in preparing an expert for direct examination is useful in preparing an expert for cross-examination. It is easy to incorporate information about the psychology of cross-examination and how to handle cross-examination into the lecture and demonstration phase of the preparation process. Similarly, practicing cross-examination on key issues is an important part of the practice and role-play phase of preparation.

During this preparation phase, there are some key suggestions that you will want to review with the expert.

[a]–Efforts to Control the Witness by Opposing Counsel

It is usually a good idea to explain to expert witnesses that attorneys are taught in law school to "control the witness." It is also a good idea to explain to the witness at the same time how to avoid being controlled by the opposing attorney.

Before discussing specific behavioral techniques to use, counsel will often find it more helpful to help the expert witness gain a mindset which is conducive to self-confidence and independence. Often, expert witnesses view the other party's attorney as a powerful, bullying personality. Once this mindset has taken hold, the expert has probably visualized and fantasized ways of meeting challenges from people who bully other people.

There are a number of problems with the visualization and fantasy "games" that most fact and expert witnesses play in their minds. The first is that these mind games are generally motivated by fears and feelings of helplessness that, unresolved, could lead to disastrous results in the courtroom. The way a witness deals with threats from street bullies might be inappropriate in the courtroom and would certainly not be persuasive there.

Experience has taught us that it is more useful to help the witness visualize the opposing attorney as a somewhat less threatening figure, such as a wayward student who just does not understand the subject matter. By reducing the image of the opposing attorney to someone with less power, the trial team can help the expert to devise more "compassionate" ways of responding to the tactics of the opposing attorney.

Expert witnesses will also benefit from realizing that the challenges posed by the opposing attorney are simply invitations, which do not have to be accepted. Realizing that they have the option to decline temptations to do battle or temptations to accept the words of the cross-examiner, experts often feel more confident and relaxed. Once experts realize that they have complete control over their own answers, they often become more effective.

The struggle for power and control between cross-examiners and expert witnesses generally delights cross-examiners and frightens expert witnesses, some of whom who will not admit it. Even the most experienced expert witnesses are afraid that they could be humiliated or their reputations annihilated in the heat of battle.

However, when expert witnesses have the luxury of understanding the course of the cross-examination as it is unfolding they are better prepared to avoid traps. Once experts feel comfortable not controlling the entire discussion (but merely controlling their answers), they generally relax and become more effective. After all, it is not important to control the discussion to be effective, but it is important to not *feel* controlled.

The most successful expert witnesses are those who are comfortable with the course of the cross-examination as it develops, but who maintain control of their answers. A high level of performance in cross-examination can often be attributed to thorough preparation and practicing rigorous cross-examination.

Two frequent scenarios should be anticipated. The first is opposing counsel's demand for a "yes" or "no" answer. Even trial attorneys who are new to the courtroom are familiar with questioning techniques in which they demand that the witness answer simply "yes" or "no." Although counsel may generally ask the witness to answer the question first and then explain, *the answer does not necessarily have to be "yes" or "no."* It is generally important to consider the possibility of longer answers, such as "Sometimes that is true," or "Yes, but not in this situation," or "I cannot answer that with a yes or a no."

A few experienced experts occasionally like to have fun with the cross-examiner. Consider the following exchange from a medical malpractice case:

Attorney: "Dr. Smith, according to your deposition, X is true, isn't it?"

Expert: "Yes, that's true."

Attorney: "And you also believe that Y is true, don't you?"

Expert: "Yes, I believe Y is true."

Attorney: "Well, Dr. Smith, if X is true and Y is true, then Z must be true?"

Expert: "Wait a second. I want to make sure I am following you. You are saying that if X is true and Y is true, then Z must be true?"

Attorney: "Yes, Doctor. That's right. If X is true and Y is true, then Z must be true. Isn't that right?"

Expert: "No. That's not right."

(Whereupon the cross-examiner must either leave the jury hanging by not asking why the expert does not agree, or ask the expert why he does not agree and risk forfeiting an important point.)

[b]–Compensation Questions

At trial the issue of paying an expert money is one that plagues many experts and trial attorneys. Some trial attorneys feel obligated to ask the opposing expert how much money he is being paid in exchange for his testimony. The reason that this issue keeps coming up in trial is that sometimes jurors do not understand why experts are paid large amounts of money for their services and believe that such payments cause the experts to be biased.

In truth, jurors believe that each side has hired the best expert testimony they can get and that the amount of money each expert earns should be considered. For this reason, a trial attorney will want to hold down the "righteous indignation" about the amount of money that an opposing expert is paid lest the backlash become untenable. A loss of credibility for a trial attorney is more costly than the value of pointing out the cost of an opposing expert.

Jurors also believe (sometimes rightly so) that the amount of money experts are paid is commensurate with the quality of their testimony. From their own point of view, they have a job to do, part of which is to figure out the technical aspects of a case and what they mean. Experts who are better at helping them, even if they cost more, are preferred and appreciated by the jury.

Certainly, you will remind expert witnesses that they should respond to a question about their compensation by emphasizing that they are being reimbursed for their time and expense in providing information to the attorneys and the jury. They should emphasize that they are not being paid for their opinions—which are not for sale.

Of course, the best way to handle the issue is to casually raise it with your own expert during the direct examination. However, if the subject comes up for the first time during cross-examination, the issue should be clarified in redirect examination if there are any lingering issues.

[c]—Trial Consultants and Communications Experts

These days, trial teams frequently use trial consultants and communications experts to assist with the preparation of witnesses. The trial team has many things to do in preparation for trial, and trial consultants and communications experts are equipped and trained to take a leading role in helping witnesses present their most effective testimony.

However, the revelation that a witness has received advice and help from a communications expert sometimes disturbs trial attorneys. The reason for this anxiety is not always clear. Certainly, if the substance of a witness's testimony has been biased or become tainted by someone, there is fertile ground for examination. However, most professional trial consultants have sufficient integrity to realize that their services are designed to help the witness be more comfortable and effective from a behavioral standpoint, rather than offering substantive information about which they have no knowledge.

Therefore, it is helpful for a witness who is asked about who assisted with his preparation to simply respond by saying, "The attorneys and other people working with them." If asked to name names, the witness should simply testify from general memory. If asked what was discussed, the witness can simply say that they discussed ways to help the jury better understand the case. The more matter-of-fact and casually a witness handles the subject, the more unimportant the subject will be to the fact finder.

The subject of communications experts seems to be more important to lawyers than to fact finders. For judges, jurors, and arbitrators, the use of someone to assist with the task of helping a witness prepare for trial is not an important issue. To jurors, it makes sense to get someone's help before making a court appearance. They would want the help if they were going to testify in court.

In addition, some trial consultants are attorneys as well as psychologists. Their roles in a case are no more interesting to judges, jurors, or arbitrators than that of any other attorney in the case.

The uncomfortable feelings that trial attorneys sometimes have are more related to defensiveness that an outside expert was used rather than simply relying on old-fashioned "do-or-die" trial methods. Experience has shown that lawyers who try to take advantage of an expert during cross-examination have been disappointed with the results.

From a judge or juror's point of view, the use of communications experts is not an issue in the case. At best, it is a sideshow and a distraction. It does not help the fact finder make a decision about who is right and who is wrong. Moreover, attempting to humiliate a witness about who helped him or her get ready to testify risks the loss of an attorney's credibility.

As time goes by, the use of trial consultants and communications experts is becoming more common and usual. The uncomfortable feelings are being replaced with feelings of respect for trial teams that demonstrate thorough preparation, including the use of trial consultants and other experts who help the trial team achieve its goals for clients.

[d]—Behavior on Direct Examination vs. Cross-Examination

During direct examination, most expert witnesses are supportive, friendly, careful, and smooth. Even jurors know that for a witness, direct examination is a "snap" compared to cross-examination. Jurors anticipate cross-examination. It excites them. They move to the edge of their seats when they hear the direct examiner say, "Pass the witness" or "I have no more questions for this witness."

They scrutinize the witness carefully at the beginning of cross-examination. They ask themselves, "Is he nervous?" "Is he confident?" "Is he going to change his behavior now that he is being cross-examined?" and "How much of what he said during direct examination can I believe?"

The best advice for an expert witness is to use the same behavior and body language on cross-examination that he or she used during direct examination. To fact finders, if a witness is just as supportive, friendly, careful, and smooth during cross-examination as he was during direct examination, the substance of the testimony is more reliable and credible. Using the same behavior dispels any notion that the witness is hiding something or unsure of himself. In addition, judges, jurors, and arbitrators tend to genuinely like a witness who is confident and cool under pressure.

[e]—Tips for Handling Hard Questions

Here are some tips for expert witnesses that deal with common issues:

(1) When asked about a learned treatise, always ask to see it to make sure that the quotation is accurate and that the context of the opposing party's use of the quotation is appropriate.

(2) Do not accept a learned treatise as the last word unless you are the author.

(3) Listen carefully to the exact words used by the opposing attorney. The seed for your answer is contained in the details of the question.

(4) Look at the jury when giving substantive answers. Jurors need to feel connected with you in order to be persuaded.

(5) Do not be apologetic for not knowing all primary sources on a subject.

(6) When the opposing attorney is trying to make you feel guilty or shamed, ignore those efforts. Rather, respond by being confident and good-natured.

(7) Readily agree with points that are not contestable.

(8) Use silence to relax and observe everything and everyone in the room.

(9) Show respect at all times, including acknowledging the judge, the attorneys, the parties, and the witnesses by name.

(10) If you make a mistake, correct it voluntarily and as soon as possible.

§ 14.06 | CONDUCTING DIRECT EXAMINATION OF EXPERT WITNESSES

We will now provide a few insights and recommend some ideas for direct examination of expert witnesses. As an experienced trial advocate, you will have already studied and practiced basic and advanced techniques for conducting an examination. Therefore, to make good use of your time, you should focus on the dynamics of the examination that involve the fact finder and some germane questioning techniques.

[1]—Structuring the Examination

There are a number of questions that will be uppermost in judges' and jurors' minds when the expert witness begins to testify. Until these questions are answered, fact finders will spend a great deal of time trying to determine why they should listen to the expert and what the expert can say that could possibly make their job easier.

For this reason, it is helpful to begin the examination by telling the jury why the expert has been called to testify. Contrary to the technique favored by some litigators, it might be best to defer asking for the expert's core opinions until some credibility has been established. Once an expert has given an opinion, interest in the expert's testimony diminishes somewhat. As a result, the opinion has been stated without the aura of authority and reliability that accompany an opinion from a recognized expert. In some courts, it is required that counsel establish credibility and authority of the expert before the expert may give an opinion.

Once the fact finder understands why the witness has been called, he or she will want to know why one should like the witness and find the witness credible. At this juncture, giving concise information that will help the judge, jury, or arbitration panel feel some rapport with the witness is important. In the rush to get the court testimony on the record, trial attorneys may overlook the importance of brief, powerful information that will personalize the witness.

Humanizing a witness can be critical to establishing credibility. Allowing a witness to tell a story about how he became interested in the field, why he was motivated to study the subject, and why he feels it is important to understand the information is much more compelling than simply listing the witness's credentials.

Establishing witness credibility with the court and with the jury can be measured on a continuum of too little information up to too much information. On the one hand, you will want to the witness to testify about his or her education, training, experience, skill, and knowledge on the specific subjects that are being discussed in the case. Pointing out one or two key accomplishments of the expert should be enough to illustrate practical experience. On the other hand, permitting the witness to testify regarding all of his continuing education classes, occasional teaching assignments, general licenses and certifications, and every professional membership may include such an overload of information that this process will shift the fact finder's reactions from being impressed with a witness to being overcome with the boring details of the witness's background.

We have learned through research that experience is generally more significant to fact finders than one's academic background. For example, an expert who worked in the engineering department of Boeing for twenty-five years commands more respect than someone who has a mechanical engineering degree from a major university.

Once a witness's expertise has been established, the trial team has a great deal of flexibility about how to present the witness's opinions and support for those opinions. For the most part it is more important as a next step for the witness to state his or her opinions clearly and concisely (and visually) without interruption than to present the opinions separately interspersed with explanations and supportive data.

Visual aids can be useful to provide a list of the opinions as a logical structure for the witness's testimony. Once the opinions have been listed, the direct examination can then turn to each one in order. At the conclusion of the discussion of each opinion, a brief restatement of the opinion would be helpful to bring closure and give the fact finder a point to disengage and regroup mentally for the next opinion.

All fact finders are interested in how an expert arrived at his or her opinions in order to gauge the witness's reliability and to understand the meaning that the opinions have in the case. One effective style of testifying about the process of arriving at opinions is to adopt the method used by fictional detectives such as Columbo, Miss Marple, or Poirot. Each of these detectives conducts an investigation by explaining the problem, the alternatives, and how he or she solved the mystery. Each explanation is peppered with references that indicate how the detective approached the problem from a neutral point of view.

Once the expert's opinions are proffered, it is important for the expert to discuss the opposing expert's opinions and why they are incorrect or inappropriate. Differentiating the opinions and explaining why the opposing expert's opinions are wrong requires clarity and an air of professionalism. Your expert must be able to state precisely the differences between the two opinions and explain why adopting the opposing expert's opinions would yield an unreliable result for the fact finder. At the same time, however, your expert will not want to attack the opposing expert personally or unfairly. It would harm the case for your expert to forfeit his likeability and credibility with the fact finder gained during a strong direct examination by inappropriately attacking the opposing expert.

There are a number of techniques that can be useful in helping an expert witness give effective testimony. For example:

(1) Help the witness intersperse his opinion testimony intermittently with technical jargon explanations.

(2) Help the witness use powerful, direct language rather than equivocal language that some experts prefer in a professional setting. Hammering out the most powerful words should begin long before trial.

(3) Provide graphic artistic support for the expert from the trial team rather than asking the expert to produce his or her own visual aids. As we have discussed, experts are not necessarily proficient in persuasion or in graphic design, whereas the trial team will generally have such resources at its disposal.

(4) Use transitional phrases and questions to provide headlines for letting the jury know the subjects that are about to be discussed and understand the importance of the information that will follow.

(5) Be sure the expert progresses from information that is familiar to the fact finder to information that is more complex and/or less familiar.

(6) Rather than constantly focusing the expert on the jury with questions such as, "Please tell the jury," vary the questions with phrases such as, "Please tell us" and "Please explain." Focusing too much on the jury appears to be patronizing.

(7) Interrupt or redirect a witness when he or she has strayed from the question or has launched into an explanation that is too narrative. If you have noticed that the witness has lost direction, you can be certain that the jury has also noticed.

(8) Avoid using the term "briefly explain." Subtle word choices affect the fact finder's evaluation of testimony. Using the words "briefly explain" signals the listener that the information is going to be boring and unimportant. If the objective is to provide a brief explanation, then have the witness simply do it. Sometimes visual aids are helpful in making important points quickly.

[2]—Developing Credibility of the Expert Witness

Establishing the credibility of an expert witness is as important as the testimony itself. After all, the purpose of utilizing expert testimony is to present reliable, credible information and conclusions to the fact finder. If the information from the expert is not reliable and/or if the expert is not credible or believable from the viewpoint of the fact finder, everyone's time has been wasted.

What makes an expert witness credible in the eyes of a judge or jury? The best answer is that credibility is a positive feeling about someone rather than a body of information about that person.

A feeling that an expert is credible often results from information offered by the expert that shows that the expert has genuine expertise *and* can relate opinions and conclusions in a friendly, careful way. Often jurors comment after trial about how smart and educated an expert was, but that they were uncomfortable with personal aspects of the expert. This can indicate that the expert had some difficulty in relating to the jury panel. Conversely, jurors have commented that experts seemed to be nice, likeable people, but that the opposing expert seemed to have a better grasp of the subject and appeared to have done more homework.

Credibility is enhanced when an expert puts forth a coherent theory or set of opinions that are believable and that coincide with the primary themes of the case presentation. Jurors will not believe an expert witness who presents a theory that does not coincide with their beliefs of how the world works.

Credibility is also enhanced when an expert can express his or her views in a way that helps the judge, jury, or arbitration panel to make sense out of the case. Even the ancient Greeks in their classic dramas and comedies realized the importance of narrative accounts in helping the audience discover the meaning of complex events. If the expert helps the fact finder understand the context of facts and opinions, the substance of the expert's testimony itself can enhance credibility.

One of the most important things that a witness can do before trial that will aid in developing credibility is simply to study the subject matter of his or her testimony in detail and then to practice being challenged by trial counsel. The more comfortable a witness is being challenged, the more comfortable the fact finder will be with the witness's testimony.

There is an important body language component to the establishment of credibility. Witnesses who seem relaxed and confident generally convey more credibility. Witnesses who have good posture and eye contact, who appear to be well-organized, and who are respectful to everyone are generally well-received in the courtroom. Witnesses who appear to welcome challenges and are careful and thoughtful in their responses generally have more credibility.

However, witnesses who fidget or stroll around the courtroom, have poor eye contact, seem disorganized, act disrespectfully, or dress inappropriately rarely gain credibility.

In the final analysis, the development of credibility is the result of a strong, supportive internal dialogue as much as coherent, responsive opinions and testimony. The more focused and effective an expert feels, the more effective he is likely to seem to others who observe him on the witness stand.

§ 14.07 | CONDUCTING CROSS-EXAMINATION OF EXPERT WITNESSES

Regardless of the experience level of a trial lawyer, he or she may often have an inclination to annihilate the opposing expert witnesses. The only question seems to be how to go about it. Some people prefer baseball bats and shotguns, whereas others choose laser-guided bombs or more covert methods. It's war! After all, anything is fair in war.

Generally, however, public execution is frowned upon and would interrupt the flow of the trial (too much blood). So that we can have a chance to persuade the decision maker without making him or her cringe from incoming missiles, we have chosen more civilized methods of dealing with expert witnesses in cross-examination.

In our culture we show respect and honor to people who have accomplished important things. Judges, jurors, and arbitrators expect deference to experts who have demonstrated such accomplishments. If they perceive that a trial lawyer is being rude, arrogant, offensive, impatient, unfair, or manipulative, they will question the tactics of the lawyer more than they will question the information obtained from the witness. It is much more effective to challenge the opinions and ideas of a witness than to try to humiliate him.

However, if an expert witness has presented himself in a way that makes him unlikeable, it can be more effective to step back and let the witness further expose his unlikeable persona than to try to steal the jury's disapproval by attacking him. Jurors generally appreciate a clever, subtle attack on a witness more than one that is crude and abrasive.

From a structural standpoint, cross-examination is more effective when it is simple and focused on a few clearly defined points. The initial points should be clear and brief. The final point on cross-examination should be the most persuasive point, even if it requires development that is more complex. The most recent research with regard to primacy and recency indicates that people remember the last point longer than the first point. The cross-examination should make succinct use of this fact.

A FINAL WORD: ① EXPERT WITNESSES DONE RIGHT

One of Robert F. Kennedy's favorite lines went something like, "The three most overrated things in the world are the FBI, the State of Texas, and . . . ." He then added whatever he was aggravated with at the time. The first two targets of scorn for Kennedy were the result of his frustrations with Hoover and LBJ. I would add expert witnesses to the list because they have often been a source of frustration for me.

Expert witnesses can be overrated. At best, they can tie your case together in a pleasing way that helps the jury to understand what it all means. At worst, they are punching bags for cross-examination. They can be great or terrible. The keys to presenting the great ones are simple:

1. **Like your experts.**

   I will not use an expert whom I do not like as a person. This doesn't mean that I have to socialize with experts or even have anything in common with them, but I have to like them. If I find them to be arrogant, slow, ill-prepared, or prickly, the jury will see those qualities too. Further, if you like your expert, you will communicate with him or her better—in preparing for trial and on the witness stand. Chemistry matters.

CONTINUED

Checklist for expert witness selection:

a. "Affidavit" face
b. Plainspoken
c. Admits minor mistakes
d. Brilliant
e. Well-prepared

2. Challenge your experts.

I cringe every time I hear someone say, "I don't know if my case is any good. I need to find out what my experts have to say." Experts are not lawyers; they don't always know what is important to the case. You must work with them every step of the way. Read their references. Do they say what they are claimed to have said? Do they also include damaging information? Check their calculations. Are there faulty assumptions? How would your opponent pick them apart?

Only you know how the expert's testimony will fit into the rest of the case. It is your job to make sure that your experts do not stray beyond the area they are supposed to address. It is your job to let them know what other experts are going to say and to ensure that there are no inconsistencies between them.

Checklist for expert witness preparation:

a. Tell them what you hope to find.
b. Check their work as closely as you would that of an opposing expert.
c. Tell them when they are wrong.
d. Coordinate their work with that of other witnesses.
e. Eliminate them if they will hurt you.

3. Make expert testimony live.

The days when juries believed experts because they had a degree or title are long gone. We are a cynical society. The expert who testifies that his or her opinion is true "because I told you so" is worthless. Prove it.

Whenever possible, I run a test or create a demonstration for the jury. You say the pipe fractured due to stress? Then stress one and fracture it for me. You say the clearance is very small? Show me how small.

Expert witness examinations are the only time you truly have the freedom to make the courtroom live. The liver is a stiff and brittle organ? Let the jury feel a cow's liver. Your expert is a pole-climbing expert? Have him put on the spikes and climb a pole. Talk is cheap. Reality is credibility.

Before the jury gets educated, they need to know the teacher. Humanize your expert. Have him talk about himself. Does he have a family? Did he fight in Vietnam? Is he a competitive hang glider?

You must also deal with the negatives. Some lawyers shy away from weak spots in their presentation because it makes them uncomfortable. This is exactly what your opponent wants you to do. Address up front the amount of money an expert is paid, that his qualifications are the result of experience rather than fancy degrees, or that he has previously taken a different position. Embrace these facts and turn them to your advantage.

Checklist for presenting expert witnesses:

a. Humanize your expert.
b. Deal with any negatives up front.
c. Test, test, test.
d. Make it interesting.
e. Keep it moving.

The key to having an expert who is not "overrated" is to create an environment in which he can perform well. The harder you work at it, the easier it will look to others.

– Scott D. Lassetter, Partner
Weil, Gotshal & Manges LLP

A FINAL WORD: ② DEALING WITH AN EXPERT'S MINDSET

During my over thirty years of trial practice, I have had an opportunity to present, as well as cross-examine, numerous expert witnesses. These witnesses have testified on many subjects including economics, technology, the environment and damages. I have found that experts (like many trial lawyers) can be easily disrupted because their own egos get in their way. My practice has been to read everything ever published or publicly uttered by the expert witness. This is true whether I am presenting a witness on behalf of my client or cross-examining a witness adverse to my client. Most experts have taken both sides of almost any question during their careers. This is particularly true with economics. It is useful and also devastating to be able to throw back at an expert prior inconsistent positions that he has taken.

Obviously, a good expert might be able to put the prior inconsistent testimony into context; or if he is handled by a good trial lawyer, he can be led back to the right spot. If you are trying a jury case in trial, the inconsistent positions can often totally discredit the expert's testimony and negate any positive direct testimony. We must keep in mind that if we plan to attack an opposing expert, we must ensure that our experts are prepared to be dealt with in a like manner, particularly when our adversaries are up to the task.

In closing, it has been my experience that any good trial lawyer can learn the subject matter of his or her expert or adversary's expert sufficiently to be able to do a very credible direct or cross-examination. This information may not be retained for any period of time after the expert leaves the courtroom; however, it can often carry the day.

– Job Taylor, III, Partner
Latham & Watkins

§ 14.08 | References

Cooper & Neuhaus, "The 'Hired Gun' Effect: Assessing the Effect of Pay, Frequency of Testifying, and Credentials on the Perception of Expert Testimony," 24(2) Law & Human Behavior 149-171 (April 2000).

Lubet, *Expert Testimony: A Guide for Expert Witnesses and the Lawyers Who Examine Them* (Notre Dame, IN: National Institute for Trial Advocacy, 1997).

Malone, *Persuasive Expert Testimony* (Notre Dame, IN: National Institute of Trial Advocacy, 1990).

Memon, Vrij & Bull, *Psychology and Law: Truthfulness, Accuracy, and Credibility* (London: McGraw-Hill Publishing Co., 1998).

Pozner & Dodd, *Cross Examination: Science and Techniques* (Miamisburg, OH: Lexis Law Publishing, 1993).

Tigar, *Examining Witnesses* (Chicago: American Bar Association, 1993).

Final Argument

CHAPTER CONTENTS

"How invincible is justice if it be well spoken."

– Marcus Tullius Cicero (106-43 B.C.)

§ 15.01 | INTRODUCTION

Final argument is an opportunity for you to tap into your unique power as an advocate. During final argument you acknowledge the supremacy of the fact finder(s) and empower him, her, or them with the evidence, themes, and meaning of the case that will lead to a favorable verdict.

In the annals of judicial history, final argument has become known as the moment at which truth and justice are revealed. It is a time when advocates fearlessly stand up for the client who needs your spirit, your intellect, and your magic.

Many great men and women have come before you and stood in the same spot where you will deliver your next final argument. Each of them had a different style and way of organizing his or her presentation to the judge, jury, or arbitration panel. A few of them may have dressed alike, but in general, each of them had individual behavior and characteristics that set them apart from anyone else in the legal profession. They explored their individuality and took pleasure in it.

However, there is one characteristic that all successful trial lawyers have in final argument—a passionate commitment to persuading their audiences by using the most compelling themes and demonstrative aids they can develop. They create a kaleidoscope of logical and emotional expressions that help judges, jurors, or arbitrators to move from a mundane and disinterested mindset to one which is spiritual and meaningful.

Consider the following excerpts from the two-hour conclusion of Clarence Darrow's twelve-hour-long plea to the court in the sentencing hearing at the 1924 murder trial of Nathan Leopold and Richard Loeb:[1]

---

[1] The case captured national attention during the summer of 1924 as nineteen-year-old Nathan Leopold, Jr. and eighteen-year-old Richard Loeb, both brilliant young psychopaths from wealthy families, were tried for the murder of a teenage boy named Bobby Franks. The evidence indicated that Leopold and Loeb conspired to commit "the perfect crime" by kidnapping a child of wealthy parents, collecting a ransom, and then murdering the victim so that they would not be identified. The prosecution proved that Leopold and Loeb rented a car, kidnapped Franks as he walked home from school, killed him with a chisel as they

"Nature is strong and she is pitiless. She works in mysterious ways, and we are her victims. We have not much to do with it ourselves. Nature takes this job in hand, and we only play our parts. In the words of old Omar Khayyám, we are only

> "'Impotent Pieces of the Game He plays
> "'Upon this Chequer-board of Nights and Days;
> "'Hither and thither moves, and checks, and slays,
> "'And one by one back in the Closet lays.'

"What had this boy had to do with it? He was not his own father; he was not his own mother. . . . All of this was handed to him. He did not surround himself with governesses and wealth. He did not make himself. And yet he is to be compelled to pay.

* * *

"Your Honor knows that in this very court crimes of violence have increased growing out of the war. Not necessarily by those who fought but by those that learned that blood was cheap, and human life was cheap, and if the State could take it lightly why not the boy? There are causes for this terrible crime. There are causes, as I have said, for everything that happens in the world. War is a part of it; education is a part of it; birth is a part of it; money is a part of it—all these conspired to compass the destruction of these two poor boys. Has the court any right to consider anything but these two boys? The State says that your Honor has a right to consider the welfare of the community, as you have. If the welfare of the community would be benefited by taking these lives, well and good. I think it would work evil that no one could measure. Has your Honor a right to consider the families of these two defendants? I have been sorry, and I am sorry for the bereavement of Mr. and Mrs. Frank, for those broken ties that cannot be healed. All I can hope and wish is that some good may come from it all. But as

---

drove off, poured hydrochloric acid over his body to make identification more difficult, and then stuffed his body into a concrete drainage culvert. The murderers were identified from a pair of horn-rimmed glasses which had fallen from Leopold's pocket as Leopold struggled to hide the body. It was widely believed that Leopold and Loeb had had a protracted sexual and romantic relationship. There was a public outcry for the conviction and execution of the two young criminals. To avoid the possible wrath of a jury, Darrow had his clients waive their rights to a jury trial and plead guilty, and he then tried the sentencing hearing before Judge John R. Caverly in Chicago. The question before the court at the hearing was whether the defendants should receive the death penalty.

compared with the families of Leopold and Loeb, the Franks are to be envied—and everyone knows it.

* * *

"I care not, your Honor, whether the march begins at the gallows or when the gates of Joliet close upon them, there is nothing but the night, and that is little for any human being to expect.

"But there are others to consider. Here are these two families, who have led honest lives, who will bear the name that they bear, and future generations must carry it on.

* * *

". . . I know the easy way. I know your Honor stands between the future and the past. I know the future is with me, and what I stand for here; not merely for the lives of these two unfortunate lads, but for all boys and all girls; for all of the young, and as far as possible, for all of the old. I am pleading for life, understanding, charity, kindness, and the infinite mercy that considers all. I am pleading that we overcome cruelty with kindness and hatred with love. I know the future is on my side. Your Honor stands between the past and the future. You may hang these boys; you may hang them by the neck until they are dead. But in doing it you will turn your face toward the past. In doing it you are making it harder for every other boy who in ignorance and darkness must grope his way through the mazes which only childhood knows. In doing it you will make it harder for unborn children. You may save them and make it easier for every child that sometime may stand where these boys stand. You will make it easier for every human being with an aspiration and a vision and a hope and a fate. I am pleading for the future; I am pleading for a time when hatred and cruelty will not control the hearts of men. When we can learn by reason and judgment and understanding and faith that all life is worth saving, and that mercy is the highest attribute of man."

As you read Darrow's arguments, you can almost hear Darrow's passionate pleas for mercy in a hot and crowded courtroom filled with hundreds of spectators who listened intently to every word. The drone of the rotating fans blended into the background as Darrow commanded attention.

For most of us, it is difficult or impossible to separate the messenger from the message. In his speech, Darrow was brutally honest and totally committed to his ideas. He held nothing back. Although he may have rehearsed his speech, he appeared to be spontaneous.

Even though the excerpts of Darrow's argument deal with issues that arise most often in criminal cases, what can we learn from arguments like his that would be useful in final arguments in all types of courtroom presentations? After all, even Clarence Darrow had to learn to develop and present persuasive arguments. What had he learned that would be helpful for all of us?

In reviewing the excerpts from his speech, you can see that there are a number of interesting tools that Darrow used that coincide with some of the ideas we discussed in Chapter 5. For example, his themes transcended the facts of the case. Darrow wanted the judge to realize that the meaning of the case was not confined to the behavior and plight of the two defendants, but rather dealt with important issues that affected all of humanity.

He went to great lengths to tell the judge how unimportant the lives of the two defendants were in the scheme of things. He told the judge that no matter what decision he made, the defendants would experience "nothing but the night." He framed the argument so that the judge might have the perception that his role was to relieve the suffering of the families involved and to make a decision that would help the American people heal from the cruelties of war.

The timelessness of the subject matter of Darrow's speech also tells us something about memorable speeches. The most effective speakers realize that they are not speaking about themselves; they are speaking about their audiences and the meaning of the speech to them. No-one else matters. Most interesting of all, they tell the audience something that the audience *already* believes. In Darrow's case, the notions of helping bereaved families and eliminating violence from society are integral to democratic cultures.

What is it about compelling final arguments that makes them so powerful and motivating? Is the speaker, himself, the most influential part of the speech, or is the message (ideas and themes) more influential? What relationships exist between the speaker and the message that makes them well-matched? What aspect of powerful final arguments are remembered most by judges, juries, and arbitrators?

In this chapter we will discuss what your audience needs from you, how to prepare yourself to give the best closing argument you have ever given, and how to develop the structure of a powerful final argument.

§ 15.02 | Psychology and Purpose of Final Argument

Final argument is your contribution to help the judge, jury, or arbitrators understand the case as a whole and to determine what it means to them. It is your opportunity to empower and motivate the fact finders to make a decision for your client. The most successful final arguments have a number of psychological components, which we will discuss below.

[1]–Summing Up the Case

You might remember your last speech class where you learned that it is important to tell the audience what you are going to tell them, actually tell them, and then tell them what you told them. Reminding the audience what you told them is more powerful than may first appear.

Final argument helps the jury recollect the key elements of the case and place them in a perspective that helps them understand the case as a whole. By the end of trial, judges, jurors, and arbitrators are trying to recollect all the key points of the trial and what they mean. Even if the fact finders may have been permitted to take notes during trial, assembling the evidence in a coherent manner so as best to emphasize your client's theory of the case takes considerable skill. This process is of consummate importance.

As final argument begins, jurors and arbitrators come to a sudden realization that they will shortly be confronted with the views of the other decision makers. They want to feel confident that they have the information and arguments necessary to support their points of view.

Each fact finder encodes the information received in trial in his or her own individual way. Each fact finder's memories of the evidence and other components of the trial contain all the logic and emotion that the fact finder attached to the information at the time it was perceived. However, memories are often incomplete and fallible. People are not computers. Yet, fact finders seek a level of comfort that they have not forgotten something important.

Closing argument, then, is your opportunity to help the jury recollect the important evidence and themes of your case to help them attach the important meaning they need to experience so as to interpret that evidence favorably to your client's case. Your organization of the material in a way that is simple and compelling will help them, and will ultimately help you.

[2]—Clarifying and Simplifying the Case

The most powerful closing arguments are those that clarify and simplify the case to its most meaningful points. Within every case, there is a simple truth waiting to be revealed.

There should come a time in every case when you ask yourself, "What do they really need to decide?" At the heart of every dispute is at least one core question that is pivotal to the case. In all likelihood, the judge, jurors, or arbitrators realize that there is such a core question, even though they may not be able to articulate it.

These central questions must be answered before the jury can answer the jury charge. For example, in a tobacco case a core question might be, "Whose fault is it that Mr. Smith has lung cancer?" We know from previous research that jurors are asking this question in most tobacco cases and in order for them to resolve each case, they must answer it for themselves.

By condensing the entire case down to one or two questions during closing argument and answering them by reference to appropriate evidence and a few powerful themes, you develop a strong "epicenter" for your argument that should reverberate (with "aftershocks") during jury deliberations. In addition, you have continued to establish yourself as an honest, straight-shooting advocate.

Conversely, by not asking or addressing the core question(s), you lose the opportunity to frame the arguments during deliberation. You relinquish the opportunity to create necessary strength for your case.

[3]—Explaining the Evidence

As you talk about the meaning of the case, you will be explaining the reasons why you presented the case as you did. You will be laying out your strategy for telling the fact finders what you believe they want to know.

It would be helpful to explain what issues you proved, how these issues were proven, and why you proved them as you did. By giving the jurors a logical path to follow, you provide the jury with the rationale for your position.

[4]—Proving Your Case Theory

Your entire case presentation will come down to your theory of the case. Your theory should reflect the key evidence, the important themes (which help provide meaning to the case), and the fair and just decision that you want the fact finders to make.

Closing argument is a time for you to remind the judge, jury, or arbitration panel what you have said about the case throughout the trial. It is a time for you to demonstrate that time-honored principles of life are applicable to the case (in addition to legal principles), and that they point to the correctness of your position.

In proving your case, you have an opportunity to frame the issues in the case. To do so, you can emphasize which points are most important, which evidence is key to deciding the case, and the most effective way to weigh all of the information that the fact finders have received in the case.

In proving your case, you might consider using one of the most powerful persuasive techniques we have discussed—contrasting and comparing your position and that of the other party with the "truth" of the case. If you decide to use this technique, you might explain the true context of the case in real life and how your position conforms to acceptable behavior under the circumstances, and then contrast the inappropriate position of the opposing party. We have already discussed other powerful techniques in Chapters 2 and 3.

[5]—Disproving the Other Side's Case

Even though you are advocating one side of the case, fact finders must consider both sides. Therefore you should always address the central elements of the other side's case. Until you have done so, your job is only half-finished.

By addressing your opponent's case, you have an additional opportunity to frame the argument for both sides in a way that puts the opponent on the defensive. By addressing the opposing allegations and theories of the case, you underscore your own confidence, and you provide the jury with ammunition to "shoot down" the opposing arguments. If you are first to present final argument, you imply by discussing the other side's case that your client does not fear nor ignore evidence that appears to weaken his own case. You therefore seem to use largesse, but then demolish any substantive opposing arguments in the most effective way possible. Your opponent must then resuscitate his own case.

[6]—Guiding and Motivating Fact Finders

Of all the roles that you will play as an advocate, your role as a leader is more apparent in closing argument than at any other time in trial. Rather than continuing the combative role you have played during trial vis-à-vis the opposing attorney, you have the opportunity during final argument to be human, i.e., to guide and empower the decision makers.

What quality about you will make other people want to believe you? Is it your honesty, your ability to see the truth, your commitment to justice, or some other passion that you feel and have communicated to the fact finders?

By telling fact finders that you believe in their ability to do the right thing, you empower them, reassure them, and show them respect. By telling them that you have confidence that they will judge the case fairly, you motivate them to show that they are committed to fairness.

You might also consider ways to overcome obstacles that jurors will feel in making their decision. Most jurors will be struggling with the conflict between their hearts and their heads. Plaintiff attorneys will use this opportunity to ask jurors to trust their feelings in making judgments about the case in accordance with how they feel. Defense attorneys will often use the opportunity to ask jurors to overcome their sympathy and think logically instead.

The most powerful arguments address both logical and emotional elements of the case. Most juries will include people who rely upon both logic and emotion to varying degrees depending upon the situation. Of course, many jurors are guided more heavily by either logic or emotion, and you must hope that your closing argument will convince them that both may be important in different ways. Judges and arbitrators also rely to varying degrees on logic and emotion to make important decisions.

Even though you may have some idea how the fact finders in your case will approach the issues, you should consider ways to integrate both logic and emotion in your argument. Jurors feel much better about their decisions if their logic and their emotions intersect in agreement.

§ 15.03 | WHAT DECISION MAKERS ARE THINKING AND WHAT THEY NEED

In order to motivate and inspire judges, juries, and arbitrators to render a decision in your favor, you must first understand what they are thinking and what they need so that you can motivate them to do what you ask.

[1]–Jurors

By the time closing arguments ensue, most of the jurors have already made important decisions about who they like and who they do not like, as well as who they believe and who they do not believe. Each of them has developed a version of the case story that he or she believes is likely to have happened. Most important, the jurors have already determined which issues are most significant to them and what they believe the case means.

However, most of them are not quite ready to "sign on the dotted line." They want to be persuaded that what they want to do is the right thing to do. They want someone to help erase their doubts and give them the motivation to do what they believe in their hearts is appropriate.

Sometimes there is a tendency to believe that juries can be manipulated, and that they are under the spell and control of a trial lawyer. Indeed, by the time closing arguments begin, most of the jurors may have decided that they like one lawyer rather than the other lawyer, that they like both lawyers, or that they think one lawyer is a better lawyer than the other lawyer. Sometimes they have decided that that one lawyer is more credible and believable than another lawyer.

In almost every jury there are people who tend to believe the plaintiff on one or more issues and people who tend to believe the defendant. The remaining jurors are still undecided about something. A few jurors do not have strong feelings about the case and perhaps never will.

In simplified terms, your primary job in closing argument is to provide your friends on the jury with the tools they need to prevail in the deliberations. This means that you must make the strongest arguments that favor your positions and at the same time undermine the opposition. Conversely, you want jury members who are supportive of your client to neutralize or even demoralize your "enemies" on the jury.

You should address many juror needs in your closing argument. The most important need—which we have discussed before—is that jurors want to feel good about themselves when they make their final decision. Jurors take their job seriously. They work hard to understand the case and to discover its most important meaning. They want to go to sleep the night after the verdict feeling good about themselves and about the world around them.

Studies of post-trial interviews of jurors have indicated that even when the evidence in the case would appear to lead to a close verdict, jurors generally feel compelled to differentiate clearly between the parties and their positions so that they will feel better about making a decision for one party and against the other. Jurors do not want to feel that they might be wrong and that the decision should have been made differently.

In most situations where juries "split" verdicts, they genuinely believe that both parties are right or both parties are wrong. In these rare situations, jurors do not feel totally committed to either of the two opposing positions.

Your job as the advocate is to make every closing argument your best closing argument. You must be totally committed to your positions so that the jury can feel good about choosing between two opposing views.

Jurors also need some logistical help from you. They need your help in organizing the information. Even though each one of them has a method of sorting out information in important circumstances like this, their methods are highly individualized. They will have twelve different ways of separating important and unimportant details and determining the hierarchy of importance.

They need your leadership in resolving all of the many different perspectives that have arisen in the case. They need a simple, clear way to understand the facts and the meaning of the case. They need to know the reasons and arguments that support your version of the case theory. They need your help in easing any doubts about your position and any doubts about the verdict that they want to render.

[2]—Judges

As we discussed in Chapter 8, judges are people too. They lived through the formative years of life just like millions of people who are not judges. They are shaped by the same types of environmental and natural influences as everyone else.

Judges have responsibilities that weigh heavily on them. They feel the importance of making decisions that are fair and that will set an important precedent. They feel powerful and are sometimes afraid of their power. They are aware of their humanity and concerned about the possibility that they might do the wrong thing.

Judges work hard to understand the circumstances of each case. They want to discover the meaning in the case. They want to make decisions in the case that make them feel good about themselves and about the world around them.

Nevertheless, judges have some additional needs. Judges need to understand your view of how the facts and circumstances in the case should lead them to make both legal and factual determinations that coincide. When you wish to persuade a judge, it is generally a mistake to use histrionics. Judges want to hear and understand the human story of the case, but they usually feel uncomfortable being drenched by an overly emotional argument.

Judges also require that the attorneys be informed and prepared regarding the circumstances of the case and the law pertaining to the case, and that they keep the judge informed about where the argument is heading. One of the strongest criticisms by trial judges has been that lawyers forget that judges do not read minds, and that they therefore need "roadmaps" to help them understand the case.

Judges need just as much help understanding the circumstances of the case as juries do. They need important information given to them in visual, oral, and tangible formats. They must know simple things such as the chronology of events, just like juries.

Perhaps it is helpful for us to forget that the judge is a lawyer. We should treat the judge as a powerful decision maker, but one who is unfamiliar with the circumstances of our case. At the same time, however, judges like to be treated like human beings, not like emperors.

Judges generally insist that you use court time wisely and efficiently. In other words, judges want you to get to the point quickly and make your best argument.

If you listen to judges' questions carefully, you will often detect that the trial judge is searching for a specific meaning in whatever you may be discussing. Final argument is an opportune moment for you to weave together the most potent aspects of the facts and the law in the case. You should make an argument to a trial court as passionately and logically as you would an argument to the United States Supreme Court.

[3]—Arbitrators

One of the most interesting characteristics of arbitrations is that the advocates and the members of the arbitration panel are peers (or at least it feels that way to many advocates). Yet arbitrators view the world somewhat differently. They view themselves as powerful and competent, but they feel some humility since they are not trial judges.

Arbitrators approach their work in the same way that they approach their regular jobs. A few people are full-time arbitrators. But most of them are lawyers, accountants, engineers, stockbrokers, and other professionals. In order to understand what will be important to an arbitrator, you must understand the background of that particular arbitrator and, perhaps, how he or she views the subject matter of your case.

Nevertheless, as arbitrators become socialized into a case, they begin to feel the mantle of authority and the weight of the burden to make a fair and impartial decision. At this juncture, they begin to take on some of the same characteristics as trial judges and jurors. They work hard to understand the circumstances of the case, and they want to find the personal meaning for themselves in the case. They also want to feel good about themselves in the process of making a decision.

Therefore, it is helpful to overcome the initial feeling that arbitrators are peers. In this setting, they are not peers. You must treat them the same way that you would treat a judge or a jury. They want you to treat them as human beings. They do not want you to pander to them.

You may be fooled by your feelings about arbitrators. You may believe that because an arbitrator is a lawyer, an accountant, or an engineer that he or she will not be swayed by a story that relies on some human or emotional appeal. Although most arbitrators are educated and intelligent, it is a mistake to rely only on factual and logical arguments. Arbitrators must feel the human story that is embedded in the circumstances of a case.

Arbitrators take cases seriously in the same way that judges and jurors do. They want to be proud of their decision in the case and feel that they have done the right thing. They also want to go to sleep the night after the decision feeling strongly that they made the right decision.

§ 15.04 | How Jurors Make the Decision

In Chapter 3 we discussed the general process by which jurors make decisions in the case. For purposes of enhancing the power of your next closing argument, it will be helpful for us to highlight some of the important aspects of jury decision making as you develop your argument.

[1]–Morality

Like everyone, jurors make judgments about the world around them based upon the morals and values that they learned during their childhood and adapted over the years. Individual views of the differences between right and wrong, good and bad ethics, as well as acceptable and unacceptable behavior, are deeply ingrained in most people.

Some of the most interesting psychological studies deal with how people resolve moral dilemmas. For example, one of the typical fact scenarios in these studies involves a destitute father who breaks into a warehouse to steal medical supplies for his son, who is suffering from a severe injury received during some innocent activity. The moral dilemma: Should the father be prosecuted for burglary?

Although there may be no perfect answer for resolving a dilemma like this, we ask juries to answer these kinds of questions every day. In your next case, there is likely to be such a dilemma for jurors.

We know from studying judge and juror reactions to various themes that the most powerful themes are those that transcend the facts of a particular case and address moral questions (dilemmas). If it is true that one of your goals in closing argument is to challenge the decision makers and empower them, then it would be beneficial to you to direct them to the moral issue and to help them feel good about taking the moral high ground by deciding for your client.

[2]–Life Experiences

Our view of the world is colored by our life experiences. In your next jury trial, the jurors will likely react most powerfully to circumstances and themes in the case that remind them of similar circumstances that previously touched them deeply.

In the past, jurors have been affected by their successes and failures, their joys and their sorrows, and by the lessons that they learned from their experiences. Their individual experiences will play a large role in how they filter the evidence and how they make their decision.

[3]–Perceptions of Themselves and Others

Self-esteem is important to everyone. It is true for jurors in every courtroom. They need to believe that they are fair and competent in making a decision in the case. By the time they have entered the jury box, they believe that they are powerful. As counsel, we want them to feel powerful.

Jurors feel more comfortable with judges, lawyers, and witnesses who share their perceptions, standards, life experiences, and attitudes. If they feel that you reflect their moral values and beliefs, they will feel more rapport with you. Conversely, if they feel that your values and beliefs conflict with theirs, your chances of persuading them are diminished.

Jurors are judgmental, like everyone else. They tend to be critical of parties, witnesses, and attorneys. In the case of personal injury plaintiffs, jurors often feel somewhat more capable than a plaintiff, and that the plaintiff needs protection.

The great equalizers between jurors and attorneys are ideas, attitudes, and themes. If your arguments and themes are powerful and are shared by the jurors, you become their hero or heroine.

[4]—Attitudes and Stereotypes

As we have discussed in earlier chapters, jurors come into trial with preconceived attitudes and stereotypes about the world. These shorthand ways of summarizing how the world works influence how jurors will perceive your case. If your summary of the case coincides with their view of the world, then they believe you must be right. If your summary is at odds with their ideas of how the world works, you have a real challenge ahead.

[5]—Intuition

Closely akin to a juror's preconceived attitudes is a juror's intuition. Like everyone, jurors have gut reactions to people and circumstances that help them understand a situation and what, if anything, should be done about it.

Intuition is like radar. It can sense things that cannot be learned otherwise. Even though a theme or case theory may seem acceptable on paper, it may not pass the "smell test" with jurors.

Even in situations where a case would be resolved by logic in one fashion, the inner voices of jurors may point in another direction.

[6]—Sympathy and Empathy

Sympathy and empathy are two feelings that we can sense in others, but we cannot sense very well in ourselves. *Sympathy* is an appreciation of the circumstances that someone else is experiencing. *Empathy* goes farther, and is an actual identification with someone else's circumstances. Both allow us to share someone else's experience and perhaps to understand on a personal level how we would act if we were in the other person's circumstances.

When jurors are sympathetic to parties, witnesses, or lawyers, they are generally motivated to make a decision that coincides with their feelings of sympathy. Because it is a natural phenomenon to have these feelings, in most circumstances they cannot be avoided.

However, as with other natural feelings, you want to roll with the punches. A plaintiff's attorney might argue that the plaintiff does not want anyone's sympathy (allowing sympathetic jurors to use their logic to support their emotional side, and thus to act on their sympathy). A defense attorney might acknowledge the sympathy that jurors might feel in a case and then give the jurors permission to act logically, in spite of their sympathy. In either instance, however, jurors will do whatever they are inclined to do anyway.

[7]—Perceptions of the Law

As a group, jurors are usually respectful of the law and they try to follow it. The problem is that they only have a layman's understanding of the law. Therefore, they pick up bits and pieces of discussion during the trial about the law, and they imagine what the law really says. Afterwards, they do their best to apply their understanding of the law to their understanding of the case. Consequently, the trial decision-making process often goes awry.

It is better for everyone if the court or the attorneys inform the jurors very specifically about the applicable key provisions of the law. Jurors understand the importance of the law and know that their decision must be placed in the context of legal principles. However, it puts the jury at a disadvantage in making a completely fair decision if everyone involved in the trial knows the principles of law except the jury.

Occasionally, jurors disagree with a legal principle as they perceive it. Because they take their jobs so seriously and they want to make a decision that helps them to feel good about themselves, they will usually try to fit their decision into an existing jury charge. However, it is possible that more juries would "nullify" the law if they believed they had the power to do so.

[8]—Relations Among the Jurors

Although jurors form individual perceptions about a case, their relationship with the other jurors can significantly affect their decisions during deliberation. Most jurors are shocked to find out that other jurors look at the case differently. They are not sure how to react, so they rely upon their previous patterns of dealing with other people in their work groups.

Most jurors want to go along with the majority of other jurors. They feel uncomfortable being the "lone wolf" or taking a stand which is not popular within the group. Since most jurors are not accustomed to fighting for a cause, if they are strongly committed to their view of the facts, they will try to find ways to be accommodating to others and to subtly manipulate others to be accommodating to them so as to sway opinion to accord with their own.

Jurors begin bonding with each other as soon as they first enter the courtroom. Once the jury is seated in the jury box, the individual jurors begin looking for ways to make friends with the other jurors. This socialization process is a powerful element in the decision-making process.

By the time deliberations begin, the jurors have already established a pecking order that identifies the people with various resources who will be helpful to the group. Some people will be leaders, some will be information-gatherers, and some will be conscientious objectors.

As deliberations progress, the jury group tends to become more cohesive and the opinions of the jurors become clearer and more defined. Jurors tend to become polarized and to become more firm in their opinions as the discussion continues. They need strength and clarity from the attorneys' closing arguments.

[9]—Need to Feel Good about the Decision

Above all else, jurors (as well as judges and arbitrators) need to feel good about their decisions. Their self-esteem is at stake. This basic principle is one of the most powerful that helps make our judicial system work so well. Although the authors of the Magna Charta and the United States Constitution assumed that the right to a trial by jury was best for protecting the common man against tyranny, it turns out that jurors are generally very conscientious about their work and are highly motivated psychologically to make the best decision in a case.

§ 15.05 | Getting Ready for Closing Argument

Getting ready for closing argument is a time for meaningful reflection and powerful visualization. This portion of your preparation process is critical and can often spell the difference between success and defeat.

As you already know, most trial judges will not give you much time to prepare for closing argument once the last witness has testified. However, preparation for final argument can begin long before it is to be presented at trial. After all, the most persuasive case presentations tend to be cohesive and consistent from voir dire through final argument.

[1]—Empowering Yourself

When you are preparing for closing argument, you might start from the inside and work outward. That is, it is a time to look within your soul and feel the powerful emotions that are driving you to win the case. Whenever you take the time to reflect, you allow yourself to let down personal barriers and feel the flood of passion about the case as well as the dreadful fear of embarrassing yourself or maybe losing the case. You cannot selectively experience some feelings about the case and not others. It's an all-or-nothing situation.

All the emotions that you feel about the case are normal and natural. To gain your power, you must be willing to experience the discomfort of being vulnerable and accept the possibility of failure. It is out of this confrontation with potential failure that we inspire ourselves to rise to the occasion. Your experience will tell you that no matter what happens, you will instinctively do your best.

As Gerry Spence, the great trial lawyer, has said, "You have a power of your own that no one else can ever match."[2] One of the reasons that you have been successful is because your mind is programmed for success. If you could step

---

[2] Spence, *How to Argue and Win Every Time* (New York: St. Martin's Press, 1995).

back to watch yourself, you would be amazed at what you would discover about your ability to handle stressful situations brilliantly. Whenever you inhibit yourself from acting on your basic instincts, you interfere with your natural processes for striving no matter what the challenge and your innate abilities.

In our early years as lawyers we picked up a few bad habits. One of these is the habit of comparing ourselves to other well-known trial attorneys such as Johnnie Cochran. We may even compare ourselves to our opposing counsel in a particular case and momentarily believe that we are outgunned.

Although great trial lawyers like Spence and Cochran may be very effective at trial and highly celebrated in the media, they must work hard at enhancing their skills just like you. Although both are talented, each will also tell you how intensely he works to be able to produce those moments of brilliance that we see in public. They realize that they cannot afford to be too arrogant in believing that they can be so inspiring without putting in long hours and hard work. Many lawyers have learned the hard way that too much arrogance can be costly.

In the context of closing argument, it is a mistake to try to hold on to all of the power. After all, in closing argument you are trying to empower the jury to do something meaningful and important. In order to do this, you must give them power rather than steal their power from them.

In our enthusiasm to win a case, sometimes we are afraid to be vulnerable and to show humility. We feel that it is important for us to be powerful, argumentative, dogmatic, and sometimes very emotional.

Nevertheless, there is a problem with holding onto all the power. It may deprive the jury of the spontaneous combustion that is needed to motivate them to make the decision you seek. By focusing the closing argument on yourself and what you think should be done in the case, you may actually drive away the very jurors you need. If you present a closing argument that is in effect a stage production about you, some of your best jurors may become unresponsive and might even feel angry that their "thunder" has been "stolen."

There is a better way. From your experience with actors and stage drama, you may recall that the real goal of an actor is to make the audience feel the joy and the pain of the story. The real goal of a lawyer must be the same. Lawyers must help the audience to become cognitively and emotionally active in the drama. We do not want jurors to sit in the audience observing other people do things. We want them to be mentally involved in the activity.

In final argument, therefore, you must inspire the audience. You must make them care about what you are saying. You must help them feel the deep emotions necessary to motivate them to take action. You must convince them that the action you suggest will give them the satisfaction and closure they need.

Persuading a jury is hard work and requires extremely heightened sensitivity. It would be easier to dictate to jurors how they should decide the case and force them to feel the emotions that you believe are appropriate. However, telling the jury what to do and demanding a favorable verdict are likely to be counterproductive.

[2]–Inspiring Your Audience

There is an important difference between convincing and inspiring someone. Convincing fact finders that you are correct is only half the battle. The other half is inspiring them to take action. Unless you have motivated the audience to take the action that you need, you cannot achieve your goals.

In closing argument your objective is to convince and empower the judge, jury, or arbitrators to make a decision that is favorable to your clients. To do this, you must draw on your natural power, charisma, or whatever you call the spirit within you that motivates others to take action. Contrary to popular beliefs, inspiring your audience is not simply a matter of magic and chemistry. It is a matter of organizing yourself and your presentation in a way that is oriented toward the audience.

[a]–Clarifying Objectives

Before you can inspire an audience, you must understand what your audience thinks, what they need from you, and what they expect. We have discussed this concept in general terms, but there are some clearly defined steps you can take to clarify the objectives for your presentation.

You might consider a channeling or narrowing process as follows:

(1) *Identify the specific action that you want the fact finders to take.* Be sure that you identify not only the responses you want in the jury charge, but also the answers to core questions that you believe will precede the responses in the charge.

(2) *Define the characteristics of the fact finders.* You might study the attitudes, life experiences, and other characteristics that you believe will

influence the fact finders in their decision. It will also be helpful to identify the opinion-makers among the jury or arbitration panel.

(3) *Determine your needs and those of the fact finders.* Take the time to clarify your own thoughts and feelings and determine how to help the fact finders satisfy their needs.

(4) *Link the needs of the fact finders with your case theory and themes.* Develop arguments that summarize the case, which at the same time respond directly to the needs of the fact finders. This part of your process allows you significant opportunities to incorporate meaningful principles that you have learned over your lifetime to help the fact finders relate to your case theory in a powerful, meaningful way.

[b]–Creating and Rehearsing

By the time of final argument, you will have already determined the key issues that will affect the decision in the case. You will know your most persuasive themes and the most compelling way to marshal the evidence in your favor. However, creating and delivering your most powerful argument will be a process of creation of the entire argument followed by whittling down the details to the most important part. Much of the process of developing the most powerful closing arguments will draw upon your most creative talent and skills.

Rehearsal is so important. It gives you an opportunity to polish the rough spots in your argument and help it flow and gain strength. It also gives you an opportunity to practice with the equipment and visual aids that you will be using during the argument. In those cases where you will be working with a computer technician or other staff person during the actual presentation, extensive rehearsal will make a great difference in keeping your presentation flowing without technical interruptions. There is an inverse relationship between the intensity of your practice and the problems that you experience in the actual argument. The more you practice, the fewer problems you will have.

Taking a mental walk through the presentation is important. However, it is just as important to have someone else watch and listen while you practice.

[c]–Managing Stress

Everyone feels butterflies before standing up and making a closing argument. You have experienced them hundreds of times. The only difference between an amateur and a professional is that the professional's butterflies fly in formation. By now, you have developed ways of managing stress. In addition, you should spend time doing things that replenish your energy and enthusiasm. You work long hours and withstand a lot of pressure. You deserve to repay yourself with activities that are mentally and physically pleasurable.

Here are some tips for managing stress before and during final argument:

+ Prepare thoroughly and rehearse until you have reached a level of confidence whereby you feel comfortable;
+ Give yourself permission to speak from your heart and your best intellect;
+ Visualize yourself making the most powerful closing argument you have ever made;
+ Maintain a comfortable schedule for exercising regularly, even during trial;
+ Breathe deeply and often;
+ Continue to use rituals that worked for you in the past;
+ When you are making the argument, consciously look at each member of the jury or arbitration panel deliberately, but briefly, to create powerful bonds.

One of the most stressful moments in closing argument may come when you forget what you want to say next. Since your mind and your body are linked together, you might consider taking some spontaneous action that has no real purpose other than to force your mind back into gear. For example, walk over to the exhibit table, pick up an exhibit in silence, ponder it briefly, and lay it back down. This sequence is perfect for jogging your mind while giving the jury the impression that you are thoughtfully preparing your next comment.

[d]—Focusing on the First Four Minutes

Perhaps the most wasted four minutes in trial for many trial lawyers are the first four minutes of closing argument. Even some of the most experienced trial lawyers use this time to ingratiate themselves with a jury, when the time would be better spent making powerful statements at the very beginning, when you have their greatest attention.

Even though the judge, jury, or arbitrators have come to know you during the course of the trial, they have high expectations and needs at the outset of final argument. Their attention is at its highest level and will last about four minutes. You have only one chance to use those first four minutes wisely. Are you going to spend them commiserating with the jury about how long the trial has taken and how much you appreciate their attention? Or are you going to say something to them that is powerful and moving?

There are several sure ways to ruin final argument. The first is to begin with an apology. The second is to say something that is either unrelated to the case or inappropriate. The third is to ramble. The fourth is for your visual equipment to fail.

Within the first four minutes you want to show respect for the jury by saying something important to them that rewards them for their attention. They are ready for action and they are ready for the trial to conclude. They need your help to move into deliberations with your thoughts and words uppermost.

[e]—Establishing Credibility

Credibility is something that is bestowed upon you by your audience. It is not something that you can give yourself. You have to earn it.

By addressing the hard issues directly, acknowledging opposing allegations, and speaking honestly, you establish and maintain credibility. Judges, juries, and arbitrators who listen to you will know whether you have integrity. If you have consistently told the truth throughout the trial and have demonstrated conviction and knowledge about your positions, your credibility should increase.

Because judges, juries, and arbitrators take their jobs so seriously, they deserve all the truth. They will reward you for giving it to them.

[f]—Creating the Right Atmosphere

Your mental state about your case is infectious. If you feel powerful and confident, it will show in your behavior and in fact finders' responses to you. You are an actor and you are on stage.

You have the power to set the mood and the atmosphere. At this point, a lot of little things are really big things. For example, body language, eye contact, enthusiasm, word choice, openness, and commitment will each affect the tone of your argument and the extent to which it is accepted.

The key to setting a powerful atmosphere is to relax and let yourself deliver the closing argument without restraint; that is, just let it happen. You already know what the judge or jury must hear because you developed the argument carefully, you have thought through the details, and you have rehearsed. In order to be really powerful at the time it counts the most, you have to trust yourself enough to transcend your inhibitions.

Fact finders take pleasure in closing arguments where the atmosphere is relaxed, serious, exciting, entertaining, energetic, and thought-provoking. They do not feel comfortable when the atmosphere is too serious, formal, wordy, showy, or artificial.

The perceptions that fact finders will have of you is as important as setting the right tone for your argument. They respond well to attorneys who are open, conversational, accessible, confident, humble, knowledgeable, forthright, and entertaining. They do not respond well to lawyers who want to lecture them or who are aloof, or those who are arrogant and feel the need to swagger.

[g]—Surpassing Expectations

Most fact finders will expect you to try to sell your case during final argument. They expect you to be argumentative and to tell them why they should find for your client. They do not expect you to really understand what they need.

You might consider giving them more than they expect. If you understand that they need to feel good about their decision, to be respected, and to feel motivated to do the right thing, why not provide them with the means to have their needs fulfilled?

By acknowledging to fact finders that you understand the problems and questions they face, you begin to surpass their expectations. They will probably be amazed that you are tuned into their needs without shameless, ingratiating comments.

Another important technique is to acknowledge something important that a juror (who was seated on the jury) said during jury selection. It shows that you were listening and that you respect that person's idea. To speak to individual jurors directly is not a good idea. They feel singled out and embarrassed. But by acknowledging an idea—not the person who expressed the idea—you anchor your argument to a comment that was important to a juror and, thus, honor the entire jury. The same is true for comments that were made by judges and arbitrators at some point in the proceedings. It is important, however, to be careful not to pander.

[h]—Holding Their Attention

The average adult has an attention span of between seven and ten minutes. In addition, fact finders can comprehend information five to six times faster than you can relate it. This means that they will tend to race ahead of you and perhaps miss part of your presentation.

There are a number of important things you can do to hold their attention. The first is to use headlines and transition statements to tell jurors where you are heading and keep them on the same track. Use silence occasionally to let important points sink in, but also to let the jury mentally relax momentarily. The second method of commanding jury attention is to continually vary your body language and speech so that you maintain the jury's interest. By continually using the same gestures and the same tone of voice, you risk losing the fact finders quickly.

The third way to keep the jury's attention is to state your key points both visually and orally. Judges and jurors will be more interested if you vary the stimuli. In addition, visual text-based statements and images (boards, charts, computer slides, video excerpts, demonstrations, etc.) provide a nice psychological anchor for the key point you wish to make as you are discussing it orally.

The fourth method you can adopt is to repeat your themes at appropriate times so that you have a better chance of catching the judge and all of the jurors when they are "tuned in," lessening the chance that you stated your theme when their attention was diverted.

§ 15.06 | TELLING A POWERFUL STORY

As we discussed in Chapters 3 and 5, all fact finders (judges, jurors, and arbitrators) will develop a story to help them make sense out of the case and remember key elements in the evidence. During final argument, the jury must hear your version of the case story. Although they feel compelled to follow their instincts about the case, jurors are still somewhat uncertain about how all of the details flow together and how they fit in with your persuasive arguments. In addition, they are concerned that the trial is almost finished and that they will shortly be required to make a final decision about the case.

All of their needs can be addressed by the telling of a powerful story. A well-constructed story will not only summarize what happened, but will also weave together the themes and meaning of the case so as to point to the obvious decision.

Throughout most of a trial, the evidence is presented to fact finders in a disjointed and disorganized way much like a jigsaw puzzle. Witnesses may have testified in a jumbled chronological order, and the "he said, she said" format of testifying does not lend itself to any one simple story. The story that you will tell will help the jury organize the information and make sense out of any conflicting evidence. It will help them to organize the evidence into structures that are meaningful to them.

The most powerful stories are those which blend logical and emotional elements of the case together so that the fact finder's intellect and interest are both engaged. Such stories are based primarily on a chronology of events and explanations of the meaning of those events.

So how do themes fit into the story? The themes are the underlying messages that tie together the characters, the plot, and conclusions about them. They are the meaning that fact finders will attach to the case long after the trial is over.

Unfortunately, there is no repository of good themes sitting in a library waiting for our use. We have discussed in Chapter 5 many good sources for ideas about themes. However, the best, most reliable method for constructing powerful themes is to utilize scientific pretrial focus group or mock trial research.

In pulling together a powerful story, you may want to address the three stages of a good story:

(1) Establishing the setting,
(2) Developing the plot and struggle, and
(3) Resolving the conflict.

Setting up the story may be as simple as asking a rhetorical question or describing the opening scene in a novel. Jurors need you to take them back to the beginning of the chronology.

Most of the adventure in your story will take place as you develop the plot and discuss the conflict and struggle that arose. There are essentially four elements that are used in developing the plot. They include:

(1) Describing what happened,
(2) Characterizing the actors (who did the acts that caused events to happen as they did),
(3) Describing how and why the actors behaved as they did, and
(4) Describing the circumstances.

Of course, your story will not yet have an ending or resolution of the conflict. That is the province of the fact finder. You should ask the judge, jury, or arbitrators to resolve the conflict and end the story. In this way, you involve your audience in the story and give them the opportunity to satisfy their need to reach a decision about which they can feel good.

A FINAL WORD: CLOSING ARGUMENTS

Most literature about closing arguments is directed toward persuading jurors to vote for your client. While it is important to present an effective and persuasive closing argument, studies of juror behavior demonstrate that most jurors have decided whom they will support by the time the lawyers give their closing arguments. This is particularly true the longer a trial lasts. Jurors hear the lawyer's position and theories during voir dire and opening statements. The jurors evaluate those theories against the evidence presented at trial. By the end of the trial, the jurors have definite opinions regarding which side to support. Therefore, the lawyer's opportunity to persuade jurors at the end of the trial is severely limited.

The real purpose of closing argument is to teach your supporters on the jury how to successfully argue with your opponents on the jury panel. Herbert J. Stern[*] is correct that the final argument does not take place in the courtroom, but in the jury room. The task of arming your friends on the jury (even if you do not know who they are) can be done with references to testimony, exhibits, the burden of proof, and the judge's instructions. As a result, I present my closing arguments to my supporters on the jury so that they are prepared to argue my case in the jury room.

                    – Kerry E. Notestine, Partner
                    Littler Mendelson, P.C.

---

[*] Stern, "The Purpose of Summation," 18 Trial Diplomacy J. 131 (May/June 1995).

§ 15.07 | REFERENCES

Bell, *Developing Arguments* (Belmont, CA: Wadsworth Publishing Co., 1990).

Easton, *How to Win Jury Trials: Building Credibility with Judges and Jurors* (Philadelphia: American Law Institute/American Bar Association, 1998).

Lubet, *Modern Trial Advocacy: Analysis and Practice* (Notre Dame, IN: National Institute of Trial Advocacy, 1997).

Spence, *How to Argue and Win Every Time* (New York: St. Martin's Press, 1995).

CHAPTER 16

Advocacy in Mediation and Settlement Negotiations

Chapter Contents

"Peace is not only better than war, but infinitely more arduous."

— George Bernard Shaw (1856-1950)

§ 16.01 | INTRODUCTION

In this section we will discuss how we can use the information we have about trial advocacy, communication, and persuasion to achieve certain goals in the mediation process. It is not the purpose of this section to describe logistics and structure of mediations, although we will refer to them. (There are many authoritative texts that adequately address these topics.)

However, there seems to be little information that provides meaningful suggestions for using trial advocacy skills and psychology in achieving a lawyer's goals in mediation. What information is available is chiefly provided by conventional wisdom, books and courses on negotiation, and personal experience. There is relatively little data about how to use scientific knowledge and research to strengthen persuasive skills in mediation.

There is a widely held belief that an opposing party settles a case because it is convinced by the moving party that the former has a weak case. But in most mediations, *both* parties usually negotiate a settlement and each makes concessions and/or gives up something of value in order to reach a compromise.

In reality, people settle because they believe it is in their own best interest to settle, not because the opposing party frightened them. Something happened in the mediation process that triggered their belief that they should settle the case and in a certain way.

§ 16.02 | INTERACTION BETWEEN MEDIATION AND ADVOCACY

Once we have progressed beyond the issue of whether trial or mediation is philosophically better, our primary job is to help the client to obtain the most advantageous outcome in both the short term and the long term. Mediation and trial (or arbitration) have relative advantages and disadvantages that we must consider in determining our strategy.

Mediation is particularly challenging for trial advocates because there is no set structure for most settlement discussions. The opportunities for effective advocacy are limitless in the negotiation process. However, it is important that we begin with a clear understanding of our goals and of our strategies for achieving those goals.

For example, if you are representing a plaintiff in a products liability suit and your goal is to settle the case, making threats to "bury" the manufacturer and to send it into bankruptcy may not be the most effective strategy. If you were defending the company and your goals are to minimize risk and settle the case, expressing the company's compassion for the plaintiff while at the same time offering to pay nothing is also not likely to be very effective.

[1]—Obstacles to Settlement

[a]—Fuzzy Thinking

Perhaps the biggest obstacle to settlement of a case is what psychologists call "fuzzy thinking." Fuzzy thinking occurs when we have a goal to reach but our perceptions of the goal are not clear or our perceptions about how to reach the goal become influenced by irrational thoughts about the process. In the examples above, a plaintiff's attorney who makes threats may have clear goals and may have studied the opposing party's mental processes enough to believe that threats will work. Clearly, when the lawyer assumes that threats will work without realizing that the opposing attorney and client will simply dig in their heels—whether justifiably or not—the lawyer's behavior defeats his or her own goals.

[b]—Incongruence

The second obstacle to resolution of the case by mediation is incongruence between the feelings of the parties and attorneys and their behavior. Often in mediation we find parties who would much rather be engaged in battle. They have no commitment to the mediation process. We have also found that some people really wanted to settle their case during mediation, but declined to do so and went to trial because they were afraid that they would appear weak.

Perhaps the best place to begin this part of our discussion is to determine when it is best to talk peace and when it is best to fight.

[2]—Elements of Conflict: When to Talk Peace and When to Fight

We can learn a lot about when to talk peace and when to fight from the study of international conflict. Experts who have studied conflict and conflict resolution have discovered that the elements of conflict and the formulas for peace are the same in international disputes and civil law case disputes. Regardless of the subject of the conflict, similar incompatibilities exist in almost every human conflict. We can therefore learn a lot about the resolution of civil law conflicts from studying how parties handle international disputes.

For example, we might look at the Cold War scenario between the United States and the former Soviet Union. Although the Cold War conflict manifested itself in many more arenas than most civil disputes, the United States and the Soviet Union perceived that each had wronged the other, that one would take advantage of the other, and that, indeed, one would "kill" the other given the right opportunity. This scenario closely resembles the dynamics of many civil lawsuits.

The difference between the Cold War and most civil disputes is that in the Cold War, both sides tacitly agreed that the consequences of all-out nuclear warfare were unthinkable, even though they would bare their teeth and growl at each other, whereas there are enough civil constraints in place that parties to a civil lawsuit are not fearful of all-out legal warfare.

However, we learned during the existence of the Cold War standoff that there was a time for peacemaking and a time for making war. As long as both parties maintained the perception of parity in power, neither side would take advantage of the other. When one party appeared weak, the other party would take advantage of the situation and make a limited incursion into the other's territory.

An example is the Cuban Missile Crisis in 1962. The Soviet Union perceived that the political leadership in the United States was distracted by domestic affairs and was not resolute about world affairs. The Russians thought it was an historic opportunity to gain an intimidating advantage against the Americans. Fortunately, they were mistaken. A discussion of choices between peacemaking and fighting assumes that a party has both the option of making peace or making war and some influence or control over events. In most civil cases, it is common for one party to believe that it has superior power, but secretly doubt this. This same perception system is common in most human conflicts.

[3]—Testing the Relative Strength of the Case

One of the central premises of Sun Tzu, author of the ancient Chinese treatise *The Art of War*, is that in order to win a war, one must know the strength of the opposing party's forces. Sun Tzu believed that wars are won or lost before they are even fought.

The author recommends watching and listening to every move of the "enemy" (i.e., the opposing party) so that ultimate decisions about strategy can be based upon good intelligence. Probing the enemy's defenses to determine its character and strength is an important part of the strategic planning process.

Among combatants on the battlefield or in the courtroom, it is common for one side to test the other side's strength by making limited incursions to probe the other side's defenses. In civil cases, the mechanisms we have for testing the other side's strength are actually more sophisticated than those used on the battlefield.

In civil cases, we have developed a number of ways to challenge the opponent's case and to test the relative strength of our own case before the real contest begins. From experience we know that we can test the strength of our opponent's case before trial or mediation in courtroom pretrial battles. However, we can also test the strengths and weaknesses of our own case and that of our opponent with scientific research using mock jury trials, mock bench hearings, and mock arbitrations.

One of the important points upon which Sun Tzu and recent scientific developments agree is that the challenging and testing process must be thorough and reliable. The author of *The Art of War* and scientists agree that haphazard testing and challenging is a waste of time and can lead to dangerous consequences.

In Chapter 6 on scientific jury and decision-maker research, we discussed the parameters for reliable scientific testing. We explored how to apply the information and scientific research study methods from the social sciences to gain a better understanding of the effectiveness of our case presentation and to discover ways to enhance the persuasive power of the case presentation.

The assumptions to be used in testing the relative strength of a case are based upon four factors:

(1) That the case presentation include the key evidence and themes for each of the opposing parties;

(2) That the research jurors, judges, or arbitrators be similar in their attitudes, life experiences, personality traits, values, beliefs, and demographics to the likely jurors, judges, or arbitrators in the case;

(3) That the question(s) to be answered and the data gained by the research be useful and clear; and

(4) That the questions asked, data received, and findings of the research not be skewed or distorted by bias or inappropriate assumptions.

Sometimes even an innocent question in research might result in misleading findings. For example, attorneys often ask whether a jury will "like" their arguments on a certain point. The answer might be "yes," they will "like" the argument, but "no," they will not vote for your client because the other side's argument is more compelling.

You must therefore conduct scientific research the same way you might conduct intelligence operations on the battlefield. If opposing commanders meet to discuss the possibility of peace, they will certainly have already conducted complete, thorough assessments of their chances of winning on the battlefield.

[4]—Advantages and Disadvantages of Trial, Mediation, and Arbitration

Decisions about when and how to use different dispute resolution methods can be confusing. Many trial attorneys (and their clients) believe that the majority of cases should be tried in open court or in arbitration so that the parties can obtain "justice." Many proponents of alternative dispute resolution believe that few, if any, cases should be tried and that every case can be settled if the parties simply have the proper frame of mind for "giving peace a chance."

The truth is that there are advantages and disadvantages to each type of dispute resolution process. Most cases would benefit from exploring all the options. In the end, trial attorneys, corporate counsel, risk managers, and parties will most likely be more satisfied with the process that allows them to feel the most vindicated (or relieved) when the process is complete.

[a]—Jury Trials

The advantages and disadvantages of jury trials are well known. The jury trial is the most common method of formal dispute resolution in Western culture. Jury trials take place in public. Trial judges supervise them. Juries of citizens who have no interest or stake in the case decide them. The procedures for ensuring that jurors are fair and impartial are quite elaborate.

In a jury trial, the procedures are tightly structured and the rules of evidence are well-defined to help ensure the reliability of evidence and information for the judge and the jury. There is little possibility that one party will have control or power over the other party in a jury trial.

The actual cost of a trial itself is minimal. Jury trials are publicly funded. Most of the costs in taking a case to trial are attorney's fees and expenses associated with developing a case for trial. However, these costs can be substantial.

The outcome of a trial is dependent upon the persuasiveness of the case presentation that each party makes to the judge or jury. The chances of winning a verdict are directly related to the attitudes and beliefs of the judge or jury and a party's ability to tell a compelling story which coincides with those attitudes and beliefs. (One of the basic tenets of courtroom dispute resolution is the belief in our culture that a judge and jury are essential to enforce cultural mores.)

Scientific research has helped to better identify the attitudes and beliefs of judges and jurors and, thus, lower the risk of telling a story at trial that has no appeal to the judge or to likely jurors. Nevertheless, there are inherent risks in taking a case to trial since there are so many factors that a jury will consider in rendering a decision.

[b]—Bench Trials

Contrary to conventional wisdom, bench trials have many characteristics in common with jury trials. Even though the audience is one person rather than six or twelve, judges make decisions the same way jurors do. Judges will listen carefully to try to understand what happened so that they can form a story in their minds. Once they begin to understand what happened, they will begin to filter through the evidence to cull out information that supports their version of the story, while remaining receptive to evidence that will require adjusting the story. Judges want to feel good about their decisions just as jurors do.

The only differences between judges and jurors is that judges have certain conditioning as lawyers, and judges therefore view their story through a "prism" of law. Most of the time, judges will be able to reconcile any differences between the outcome they prefer and the outcome that the law prescribes. Judges are also conditioned to try to ignore or set aside their natural conscious biases, to the extent possible.

However, bench trials are generally somewhat more risky unless a judge's record reveals a clear pattern of making decisions on certain issues that are documented in written opinions. A great deal of research has indicated that jury decisions are more predictable than judge decisions on identical issues, although judge and jury decisions will generally agree. In civil cases the differences between the decisions of judges and juries are not significant. Most of the differences between judge and jury decisions appear to be in the area of criminal law, where judges tend to be stricter on punishment than jurors.

Decision making by judges is just as complex as that of jurors. Judges are influenced by their attitudes about specific issues, their relevant life experiences, and other factors. But because a judge is the single decision maker in the case, there are no moderating influences on a judge similar to those exerted by members of a jury panel. There is no-one to discuss the case with other than fellow judges (who did not hear the evidence) or perhaps the judge's clerk, and no-one with whom the judge must reach a consensus.

For this reason, judge decisions are often more surprising than those of juries. Judges often defy expectations either intentionally or unwittingly. Sometimes, for example, a conservative judge will render a large judgment for a plaintiff on both liability and damages issues if he or she believes the facts of the case warrant such a judgment.

Recent innovations in scientific research have allowed us to study the decision-making process of a particular judge in an upcoming decision. By employing the services of retired judges who have characteristics similar to those of the sitting judge, we can begin to understand the thinking and feeling process that a particular judge will likely experience. This type of study is possible for two reasons. First, we have learned through the study of social psychology that people with similar attitudes, beliefs, and life experiences will tend to share the same or similar perspectives. Second, the longer a trial judge sits on the bench, the more acclimated the judge becomes to approaching cases in the same manner as other judges who sit in the same venue or on the same panel. This is simply a socialization process.

Despite the information counsel may receive about a judge, however, there are still risks that are inherent in a bench trial. Frequently trial judges will resist the urge to make decisions that favor attorneys with whom they are friendly. In this respect, their decisions are often difficult to predict. Because a trial judge is independent, the trial team for each party is subject to the control of the fact finder himself or herself. In this respect, the fact finder is highly sophisticated about behind-the-scenes lawyering taking place and may be influenced by it. In a jury trial, that would not likely be true.

[c]—Mediation

Mediation seems to be the only dispute resolution process in which the parties and the attorneys are theoretically in complete control. If there is parity (equal power, control, and knowledge) in the process, the possibilities for reaching creative solutions are limited only by the parties' resources and imagination. In a few instances, mediation can even restore the parties to a previous working relationship.

Most of the time mediation itself is inexpensive. Most of the cost in the case occurs during the discovery phase of the case development and in preparing for trial. Most parties feel more comfortable trying to mediate a case after they have completed discovery and learned whatever information is available to decide the case. Often parties will attempt mediation to explore the possibility of settlement without incurring any further cost related to trying the case or experiencing the risk of losing a trial.

Considering that the parties have theoretical control over the mediation process, they also have the advantage of setting their own goals in mediation and perhaps determining how best to persuade the other side to settle the case. Later in this chapter we will discuss ways to develop persuasive arguments and persuasive strategies for mediation.

However, there are a few disadvantages to mediation. Some people have experienced a lack of quality control in the mediation process and have felt that the cost and time associated with a particular mediation was wasted effort. There are no public standards with which a mediator or the mediation process must comply.

Many times parties settle their differences in the mediation process because they are fearful of encountering the risks associated with trial. Sometimes settlement does not truly satisfy the parties. They continue to wonder what would have happened if the case had proceeded to trial. They do not feel vindicated. There is no feeling of closure.

Attorneys and companies acquire reputations for how they handle negotiations and view the possibility of going to trial. Companies that are involved in many different lawsuits continue to wonder whether their strategy for negotiating or not negotiating will lead to more lawsuits or different strategies of prospective opposing litigants.

[d]–Arbitration

Arbitration also offers a number of advantages. The arbitration process is private and generally designed by the parties unless they have specified in their contract to utilize or voluntarily defer to an outside organization such as the American Arbitration Association. Although the parties have significant control over the organization of the arbitration, they often have little or no control over the resolution process. Most arbitrations have three judges rather than one. The difference is that, unlike the situation in most courts where a judge is assigned by some established court process to preside over a case, the parties can choose who the arbitrators will be.

From an advocacy standpoint, arbitration may be more advantageous than mediation if one party has considerable power when compared to the other party. Arbitrators generally wield enough power during the arbitration to help level the playing field. Arbitration is also a good venue for large companies that face a volume of small claims that should be resolved fairly but inexpensively and efficiently for everyone's benefit.

Although arbitration is generally conducted in a more relaxed environment than in trial, the arbitrators generally have the power to supervise the proceedings and maintain adherence to evidentiary and procedural rules. Arbitration awards are generally enforced through the judicial process if non-voluntary enforcement is necessary.

There are a few disadvantages with the arbitration process for some people. Although the arbitration fee itself may be small, the overall cost of arbitration can be fairly steep considering daily or hourly payments for arbitrators, the expenses of discovery, and the cost of trial lawyers to develop and present the case at arbitration.

[e]–Summary Jury Trials

A summary jury trial is simply a "private" jury trial. The trial judge, the facilities, the jurors, and any other staff necessary to design and carry out the summary jury trial are paid for by the parties rather than the government. The parties can decide in advance whether the results of the private jury trial will be binding or not.

One advantage of a summary jury trial is that truly disinterested parties (i.e., jurors) will decide the case. (Usually a third party who is agreed upon by the attorneys and clients will designate the jurors, subject to approval by the parties.) In addition, the cost of a summary jury trial can be substantially influenced by the parties and the trial can be held at a time in the development of the case when discovery may not be complete, so that some of the expense of developing a case as if it were to be presented in a courtroom for trial can be spared.

There is generally more closure for the parties if they are bound to accept the verdict of the summary jury trial jurors. However, you can also choose a nonbinding summary jury trial and use the results as a live jury experiment if the parties decide to avoid the summary trial verdict. Since summary jury trials simply adopt the procedures used normally in a trial court in the local venue, the attorneys and parties are generally familiar with the courtroom procedures.

Note that there are also a few disadvantages to summary jury trials. Summary jury trials are expensive. The out-of-pocket expenses for the trial alone (in addition to attorneys' fees and related expenses) can cost as much as $10,000 per day. Most cases that are candidates for summary jury trials are cases in which the risks are great. Therefore, the parties will generally spend as much money to prepare for a summary jury trial as they would for a courtroom trial.

[5]—When to Use Mediation

From an advocate's standpoint, there are a number of reasons for utilizing mediation. Mediation is supposed to resolve all or part of the dispute. But there are many other reasons why parties come to the negotiating table:

(1) Mediation is most often used by attorneys and parties to try to reach an agreement on all or part of the liability and damages issues in the case. If they can agree on the liability issues, then mediation is helpful to evaluate the case for purposes of determining the range of damages. If they can agree on damages but not on liability, then sometimes mediation is helpful to facilitate agreement on liability. In cases with multiple liability and damages issues, mediation is often helpful to resolve whatever part of the case can be resolved during that process so that the trial advocates can focus on the more disputed parts of the case.

(2) Many mediators, particularly those who are experienced trial attorneys or former trial judges, often help the parties gain a better perspective of how a trial judge will view the issues in the case and whether the claims or defenses have a chance of success.

(3) One of the more disputed reasons to use mediation is to obtain information about the opposing party's case outside the normal discovery process. Since most of the information that will be obtained

is also discoverable, using the mediation process to obtain information in an informal atmosphere often allows the parties to resolve discovery issues without wasting resources and effort on issues that need not be the subject of a battle. This method of obtaining information from the opposing party is often more successful if the tone of the dialogue between the parties is more peaceful and assertive rather than combative.

(4) The mediation process is also helpful in working out interim agreements in cases that involve procedural complexities. These cases may have multiple parties, many claims and counterclaims, more than one venue, or complex problems associated with discovery. It is often less expensive and more productive for the parties to bring these issues to a mediator rather than to fight about them in a courtroom.

[6]—The Role of Advocacy in Mediation

To some extent, the mediation process is a bit unsettling for many lawyers. We have never had any mediation advocacy training either in law school or in practice. There are almost no rules and procedures to follow. There is a natural tension between protecting the client's interest (and trial strategy) while at the same time revealing enough about the case to persuade the other side to settle on terms that are favorable to the client.

However, it is in precisely these circumstances that the highest form of advocacy can take place. How much more challenging can it be than to persuade your enemy to settle?

Your skill and experience in the courtroom has many applications for mediation. The only real difference between advocacy in the courtroom and advocacy in mediation is that the audience in mediation is distinctly different and the goals to be reached are slightly different.

In order to be successful in persuading the opposing attorney and client in mediation, you will have to use all of the knowledge and skills that you have learned as a trial advocate; in addition, you will have to be willing to understand and engage your opponent. Using advocacy skills to present your client's case will be familiar to you. However, developing a genuine understanding of the mental processes of your opponent and engaging him or her in a way that is persuasive may not be so familiar, and you may lack enough information to be successful.

Later in this chapter we will discuss ways to obtain information about the mental processes of your opponent and about strategies for persuading him or her to work with you in settling the case.

§ 16.03 │ NEGOTIATING TACTICS

There are a number of basic principles that apply to all successful negotiations:

(1) A successful negotiator always asks for more than he expects to get. Most original offers are equally distant from a reasonable resolution. That is, most offerors first take a somewhat extreme position either greater or less than what is probably a fair compromise. From a psychological standpoint, the reason this tactic is so successful is that, upon resolution, your opponent gains a more euphoric feeling of satisfaction when he receives something that he perceives to be a loss to you.

(2) Successful negotiators rarely say "yes" to the first offer. You want to give the impression that something you are giving up is of great value to you. By saying "yes" to the first offer, you send a psychological message that what you are giving up is of little value, thus prolonging the negotiations until the opponent perceives that something you are willing to give up is of great value to you. There is also an interesting symbiosis that takes place between negotiating parties such that when one party begrudges giving up something, the opponent often begins to place a higher value on that item. When the opponent begins to place a higher value on the item, he is likely to become more satisfied if and when it is given to him.

(3) It is helpful to "flinch" in response to proposals from your opponent. If you do not act surprised, then you have tacitly given a signal that the proposal is a possibility. Also, by flinching or appearing to be skeptical or surprised, you tend to raise the value of an item that you might be willing to give up at a later time and which might satisfy the opponent.

(4) It is counterproductive to argue with your opponent at the outset of negotiations. Arguing can stiffen the opposition, and then you risk making the opponent less interested in becoming involved in your negotiation tactics. In other words, by causing resistance to your

communications, you might be defeating your own efforts. It takes at least two parties to settle a matter.

(5) It is helpful to demonstrate reluctance in making offers. By appearing reluctant, you tend to raise the perceived value of the offers.

(6) Responding to offers by stating, "You will have to do better than that," generally results in a better offer.

(7) Always imply that you have no authority to finalize a decision. This tactic tends to create value for any offer or response you might make.

(8) If an impasse occurs regarding an issue, suggest laying that issue aside for the moment. Most impasses occur as a result of an emotional block. Emotions tend to subside with time.

(9) If a true deadlock exists, defer to the mediator, but be prepared to walk away. Sometimes there is no way to resolve an impasse either during the mediation or later.

(10) Always ask for something in return for any concession. By conditioning the opponent to give something in return for receiving something, the negotiations tend to proceed more energetically and successfully.

(11) Using a "good guy/bad guy" technique can be an effective way of negotiating an issue without confrontation. Becoming entrenched in a standoff can be counterproductive. By alternatively being implacable and then more compliant, you gain flexibility in how to make and respond to offers.

(12) Always ask for a little more.

§ 16.04 | EFFECTIVE ADVOCACY SKILLS IN MEDIATION

[1]—Effective Speaking and Body Language

Most of the effective presentation tools that you have used in the courtroom will also be helpful in mediation. The only difference is that in the mediation context it is usually more effective to present your positions in a tone of voice and style which make the other side feel more comfortable. Speaking across a negotiating table is significantly different from presenting a court case before a judge and jury, with witnesses, all while making a record and abiding by the rules of evidence. Some attorneys prefer to be intimidating during mediation when presenting a case to the opposing party. However, unless there are other reasons to settle, intimidation is not generally considered to be a successful tactic.

Using simple, focused language also helps settle the case. Using abstract words and phrases usually raises unnecessary questions and leaves the listener with the impression that you may not be entirely clear about what you are saying.

The most important characteristic of a successful presentation in mediation is that it be knowledgeable. It is important to the persuasion process that you give the impression that you have been thorough in your preparation for both the case and mediation. It is also persuasive to focus your presentation in a way that shows your understanding or gauge of your opponent's needs and interests. In this regard, attacking the opposing attorney will only cause more barriers to arise and will not likely help you reach your goals.

Conveying commitment, confidence, and enthusiasm for your client's case is also important to the persuasion process. Your adversary and his or her client will certainly evaluate the case with reference to your own beliefs about the case as revealed in your behavior.

Direct eye contact is important in persuading the opposing party and client to settle the case. Good eye contact helps you to establish a respectful communication and gives you immediate feedback about how well your message is being received. In addition, strong eye contact gives the impression that you are confident about your case and not afraid of walking away from the settlement discussions.

[2]—Applying Communication Skills to Mediation Advocacy

The effectiveness with which you transmit and receive verbal and nonverbal information is important in persuading your opponent. To be successful in the mediation process one must be able to (1) express oneself effectively, (2) use purposeful body language, (3) listen well, and (4) understand the other people in the process through their body language.

Some of the things that we learned when we studied the psychology of mediation can also be applied to communicating and persuading during mediation. First, we must be able to directly engage our opponents and motivate them to listen to us. Second, we must express ourselves clearly and fully by using visual aids. Settlement brochures, excerpts of videotapes, charts, and other visual aids are helpful examples. Third, we must appear credible and trustworthy. Fourth, we must present our positions in a way which conforms to the values, attitudes, and beliefs of the opposing attorney and party. Finally, we must motivate the opposing attorney and party to do something constructive.

In the mediation process, themes are just as important as they are in trial. The themes will express our thoughts about the case to reveal our character, arouse a positive emotional response from our opponents, and present logical arguments that appear to be true and accurate.

§ 16.05 | USING SCIENCE TO ENHANCE EFFECTIVENESS IN MEDIATION ADVOCACY

For some people, the use of scientific methods to improve the effectiveness of a persuasive argument is an organized way of obtaining information to help build the most compelling presentation. To these people, scientifically based information is reliable and contains ideas that might not be available from any other source. For others, using scientifically based information seems "unromantic" and perhaps even distasteful.

Regardless of your thoughts on the matter, there is an enormous amount of information available about how to persuade opponents that has been developed using scientific methods. Counsel disregards this body of information at his or her peril.

[1]–The Role of Science in Developing Effective Mediation Advocacy

As we have discussed earlier, science is simply a tool we use to gather knowledge. In the mediation process we are trying to persuade the opposing attorney, the opposing party, and perhaps the mediator. Each of these people has needs and interests that he or she is trying to fulfill. At the same time, our opponents and the mediator possess information that we want and that is related to the subject of the lawsuit.

In this context, it is important to know how to gather information about the other people in the mediation and how they might be persuaded to give you and your client what you want. Of course, the opposing attorney and party have the same objective. They want to persuade you and your client to give them what they want.

Within this framework, there are a lot of blanks to be filled in. Just as with judges and jurors, we need to know a few things about our opponents. We need to know their attitudes about specific issues related to the mediation, their life experiences related to the subject of the lawsuit and the mediation process, their personality traits, and any other factors that may influence their thinking during the mediation process. We need to know what they want to achieve, both materially and psychologically. We need to know the strategy that is most likely to succeed in persuading them to settle the case on terms that make them feel successful.

There are many negotiation consultants and books about negotiation techniques that have useful suggestions for presenting a persuasive strategy in mediation. However, most of these suggestions are generic and may or may not work in a given situation. Scientific research methods have helped provide reliable information that can be applied to your case.

[2]—Using Scientific Knowledge and Research Methods

There are two specific applications of scientific research to the mediation process. The first is the study of the strengths, weaknesses, and value of the case using a mock trial format to obtain information about how the decision makers at trial will perceive the evidence. This information is helpful in evaluating the case objectively and preparing the client for the mediation process. Often clients are more successful in mediation once they understand how a likely judge or jury will perceive the case. The second application of science deals with the study of the mental processes of the opposing attorney, opposing party, and perhaps the mediator.

[a]—Available Scientific Research Information

Over the past twenty years, relatively little scientific research has been conducted into the mental processes that people use in the resolution of conflicts or in negotiations. We do know, however, that people are more motivated to resolve matters peaceably when they are considering what they will lose rather than what they will gain as a result of a negotiated settlement.

Some of the scientific research that has been published is available in a few scientific journals, psychology textbooks, and other publications. Most of this material will be available in major public or university libraries as well as on some Internet sites.

[b]—Consultations with Psychologists and Other Experts

There are a few people who are recognized as experts in the development and presentation of persuasive negotiation strategies. Some of these experts are available as consultants who can help the trial team to devise a strategy which should be successful in the mediation context.

Before you hire an expert, however, you should think about what you want to accomplish in the mediation process and how an expert will help. For example, if you want to understand how the opposing parties will approach mediation and how you might be successful in persuading them, either a trial or mediation psychologist or negotiation specialist may be helpful. If you want to develop some useful negotiating tactics, a specialist will probably provide the best suggestions.

In addition, if you want to understand how to incorporate previous jury research you have done into the mediation process, you will want to talk to the trial scientist who conducted the research or someone similar. If you need assistance in developing visual aids for the mediation presentation, there are many graphic artists who can work with you alongside a psychologist or other consultant.

[c]—Mock Jury Trials, Mock Bench Trials, and Mock Arbitrations

Research tools such as mock trials, mock arbitrations, mock bench trials, and focus groups are familiar to most trial attorneys and corporate counsel, and we have discussed these research techniques in Chapter 6.

There is little doubt that the information gathered from these research tools is helpful in preparing for trial. However, much of the information gathered in decision-maker research is also helpful in facilitated settlement discussions.

It is common these days for all parties to a major lawsuit to have conducted jury research prior to mediation. If the parties have engaged in scientifically designed research, they should know how juries will perceive the case and they should know the range of a likely verdict. If the parties are aware that each side has conducted such research, both the attorneys and the clients will try to gauge how well the opposing party(ies) will use that information. However, if one party has conducted jury research and the other has not, the attorneys who have not conducted research will likely expose their lack of knowledge during their case presentation during mediation. An attorney who appears weak through lack of awareness about jurors' perceptions in the case will likely be at a disadvantage in the mediation process.

Conversely, attorneys and clients who have conducted mock jury trials, mock bench trials, or mock arbitrations will generally use the information they have gained in developing a presentation to the opposing side that has an air of confidence and the ring of truth. A presentation which is based upon a sophisticated understanding of one's case is also helpful in persuading the mediator that that presentation most accurately defines the issues and appropriate resolution of the case.

[d]—Should Jury Research Be Revealed to the Opposing Party?

The decision whether or not to reveal the contents and data collected in a jury research project depends on several factors. First, if the party who possesses this research information realizes that the opposing party will be skeptical of the research, the former should only commission research that is conducted by trial scientists who have a good reputation and whose work product and research design appear to be reliable. Second, the research should directly address the positions and issues taken by the opposing party. Otherwise the research will simply be dismissed as being "off point." Finally, you or the trial scientists should be prepared to discuss questions about the research with either the mediator or the opposing party.

The results of jury research are most often shown to the mediator in private before the subject is mentioned to the opposing party. There are two reasons for first presenting the research material only to the mediator. First, the mediator may be persuaded by information that is helpful in persuading the opposing party. Second, if he knows that the information exists, the mediator will be able to gauge if and when to present that information to the opposing party in a way that will facilitate settlement.

[e]—Mock Mediations

Research tools such as mock jury trials, mock arbitrations, mock bench trials, and focus groups are familiar to most trial attorneys and corporate counsel. Mock mediations are a new technique that has been developed to study the likely decision-making process of the opposing attorney and client and to develop methods of persuading them to settle the case. It also gives a trial team the opportunity to rehearse the case presentation before the actual mediation.

The design of a mock mediation research study is based upon the same principles as any other kind of scientific research:

(1) Determine the goals of the research and the ultimate questions to be answered. For example, you may simply want to know how the other side views the case and how to persuade them to settle the case within the range of damages that are acceptable to your client.

(2) Locate people who have personal characteristics and backgrounds similar to those of the opposing attorney, opposing party, and mediator. These people must be pledged to confidentiality and advised about the purpose of their role in the process. Their primary tasks will be to learn about the case and the positions of the parties and to engage in a negotiation process which resembles that of the actual mediation.

(3) Arrange a mock mediation environment at a facility which resembles that of the actual mediation that is expected to take place.

(4) Arrange for professional mediation or trial consultants to observe and perhaps moderate the process, and who will facilitate a discussion at the end of the process that is designed to understand how the opposing party, client, and mediator perceived the participants and the case.

(5) Obtain recommendations from the consultants to augment your own observations and ideas based upon the mock mediation process.

Attorneys and companies that have used mock mediations to help prepare for an upcoming mediation have found the process to be meaningful and helpful in developing a persuasive mediation strategy.

A FINAL WORD: ① MEDIATION ADVOCACY

Mediation provides the best opportunity for counsel to convince the opposing party that counsel (and the client's position) is reasonable, and that a negotiated settlement is preferable to continued litigation. If counsel uses this opportunity simply to impress his or her own client and to argue with the opposing party, the effort may be counterproductive. My experience is that honest concessions and agreement with the opposing party, where appropriate as to specific issues, increases the likelihood that the opposing party will give serious consideration to our side of the contested issues. While mediation may be used to give both sides

Continued

the chance to vent their grievances, this approach may be more divisive than constructive.

I have found that, even when the relationship between the parties is extremely contentious, I can best represent my client if I can establish my credibility with the opposing party. I would rather have the opposing party believe me and give credence to what I say than be convinced of my skills as a trial advocate. To accomplish this objective, understatement rather than exaggeration of my case may be more effective; and use of a single letter or other piece of documentary evidence or precise language from a court decision may produce better results than eloquent or passionate argument.

Credibility is also enhanced by not drawing lines in the sand. If you have told the mediator that the absolute bottom line your client will accept, or the absolute maximum your client will pay, is $1 million and if this is conveyed to the other side, either you have to stick to this position or you will undermine your credibility. Better to discuss ranges or approximate amounts with your own client and with the mediator so that your credibility and that of your client is not at stake at each stage of the mediation.

Finally, I recommend that an attorney be creative. If he or she gets to the point that the parties are very close to settlement but the client will not take a penny less and the other side will not pay a penny more, consider other alternatives. We settled one case by having the other side pay all the costs of the mediation. The other side preferred to pay their share and our share of those costs rather than pay another cent to our client.

— Edward M. Waller, Jr., Partner
Fowler White Boggs Banker

A Final Word: ② Thoughts About Working with Opposing Counsel

I learned from personal experience as a young lawyer the value of accommodating your opponent in a situation in which you do not compromise your client's interests. I had a huge docket at the time, over 100 active cases. Late on a Friday night, I realized that an important deadline for making a filing with the Court ran that day, and there was no way I could meet it.

Following a sleepless weekend, I conferred with two of the firm's senior partners about the best way to deal with the situation. We concluded that I should meet with the other lawyer, explain the mistake I had made, and see if we could work something out. The meeting took place, the other lawyer, after apprising me of the weakness of my position, graciously agreed that: I could file my response; he would not raise the issue of the missed deadline; and we could allow the judge to decide the matter in controversy on the merits.

As it turned out, the other lawyer's assessment of my client's position was correct, and the judge ruled against us. The missed deadline never became an issue, and I was saved from embarrassment, or perhaps worse, in dealing with my client. Obviously, there were several lessons learned from this experience, but the most important one is how to conduct yourself in dealing with other lawyers. I had always respected the lawyer on the other side, but, after this incident, he became one of my heroes.

When difficult situations arise and someone needs a favor, as long as it doesn't adversely affect my client, I try to be accommodating. Who knows, I may need another favor myself someday.

– Frank G. Jones, Partner
Fulbright & Jaworski L.L.P.

§ 16.06 | REFERENCES

Cooley, *Mediation Advocacy* (Notre Dame, IN: National Institute for Trial Advocacy, 1996).

Dawson, *Secrets of Power Negotiating*, 2d ed. (Franklin Lakes, NJ: Career Press, 2000).

Levinson, Smith, Wilson & Wilson, *Guerrilla Negotiating: Unconventional Weapons and Tactics to Get What You Want* (New York: John Wiley & Sons, 1999).

Purdy & Nye, "The Impact of Communication Media on Negotiation Outcomes," 11 Intern'l. J. Conflict Management 162-187 (2000).

Salacuse, "So, What Is the Deal Anyway? Contracts and Relationships as Negotiating Goals," 14 Negotiation J. 5-12 (1998).

Stark, *The Power of Negotiating: Strategies for Success* (Littleton, CO: TriMark Publishing, 1996).

Weiss, "Analysis of Complex Negotiations in International Business: The RBC Perspective," 4 Organization Science 269-300 (1993).

CHAPTER 17

Improving Jury Trials:
Perceptions and Reality

CHAPTER CONTENTS

> *"There is one thing stronger than all the armies in the world: and that is an idea whose time has come."*
>
> — Victor Hugo (1802-1885)

§ 17.01 | INTRODUCTION

Although jury trial innovation and jury reform issues may seem like new topics, the jury trial system in the United States has been the recipient, and sometimes the victim, of reform-minded people almost since its inception. For example, a search of appellate records indicates that state and federal courts have been examining and making decisions about juror note-taking and juror questions of witnesses since 1825.

Concerns about the organization and efficacy of modern jury trial operations have been expressed by a variety of sources relative to many non-related issues. For example, civil rights proponents have been concerned that disadvantaged people and minorities are not fairly represented on jury panels. Defendants who have incurred high jury verdicts against them want to control the issues that go to a jury and put a cap on verdicts. Court officials and others who seek efficient operation of trials have sought to eliminate attorney participation in all voir dire or at least prevent lawyers from "wasting time" in oral voir dire. Conversely, advocates, litigants, and others who defend a party's right to conduct adequate voir dire wish to preserve the right to inquire about jurors' attitudes and life experiences regarding specific issues in a case while at the same time educating attorneys to improve voir dire skills.

Legal scholars, courts, and bar associations that have studied and experimented with various types of jury innovations and jury reforms over time have not arrived at a consensus regarding the advantages and disadvantages of different proposals. A review of the various proposals and completed studies indicates that many of the proposals have been made and supported by people who have narrow, perhaps vested interests. Other proposals appear to have broad support but are opposed by influential people who also have narrow, vested interests. As a result, regardless of the nature of the proposals and the identities of the interested parties, improvements in the jury trial system developed very slowly.

The lack of agreement on various proposals does not appear to be based on disagreement about proper procedures to effect innovations or reform. Most recent studies indicate that similar if not identical procedures for considering changes are used in almost every venue where reforms are introduced or examined.

Similarly, the lack of agreement does not appear to be based on inadequate information or experience with new proposed procedures. Many proponents and opponents of various jury trial innovations appear quite satisfied with the information and experiences they have accumulated.

A close review of the arguments of most proponents and opponents of jury reforms indicates that the basis for disagreement is that until recently, there has been no reliable empirical research into the purported advantages and disadvantages of jury trial innovations. Therefore, attorneys, judges, and legal scholars have relied upon limited experimentation and opinions based upon preconceived notions.

For the most part, judges who have instituted jury trial innovations are the same judges who take bold steps in other areas of court practice and who consistently search for ways to improve the satisfactory operation of their courts and court systems. Recently, however, judges and attorneys all over the United States have taken progressive steps toward instituting changes in the trial of cases, which have enhanced jury performance and resulted in increased satisfaction about the operation of trials.

Some people say that one of the problems in addressing these issues is that there has been too much "opinion" and too little objective research. In this chapter we will review the current status of discourse and research into the some of the most widely recognized types of jury trial innovations and jury reforms which have been examined. The reader is encouraged to consider the proposals, form his or her own opinions, and join the debate.

§ 17.02 | THE CONTROVERSIES AND THE DEBATES

Issues regarding potential changes in jury trials can be divided into two categories. The first category concerns critics of the jury trial system itself. The second category includes various proposals to improve satisfaction with jury trials.

[1]—Voices of Dissatisfaction with the Jury System

Some observers have stated their beliefs that the jury trial system in the United States is fundamentally flawed. For example, some official observers of the American Medical Association's task force that studied the effect of malpractice trials have concluded that juries are not competent to judge medical malpractice, and that all such cases should therefore be reviewed by a panel of lawyers or only medical experts. In response, proponents of jury trials point to research that has indicated that the decisions of trial judges and medical experts in most medical malpractice disputes would be similar to jury decisions in which medical expert testimony is admitted.

The primary criticism of the jury trial system focuses on the allegation that jurors are not competent to evaluate the evidence and make appropriate decisions in the face of aggressive trial lawyers and complex evidence. Much of the dissatisfaction with the jury trial system seems to center around intolerance of jurors' human nature. When jurors try to understand litigants and their transactions, the jurors' abilities are enhanced or limited by those jurors' individual characteristics. These characteristics include attitudes about specific issues, life experiences, personalities, general values and beliefs, and demographic backgrounds. These characteristics are generally an indelible part of a juror's make-up, but are somewhat malleable depending upon the psychological messages and the nature of the information to which the jurors are exposed in trial.

Criticisms of jurors and jury decision making have come from politicians, media commentators, corporate leaders, and countless other sources. Juries have been criticized for knocking down "legal guardrails,"[1] for consuming too much court time, and for being unreliable. Other critics simply maintain that the average lay jury is not capable of understanding the details of highly technical evidence such as DNA or most patent applications.

Ironically, the same human characteristics that our forefathers admired have caused the most criticism of jury decision making. Critics of juries and jury decision making find these human characteristics to be failings, and believe that the jury's ability to hear all the evidence and to make ultimate and binding decisions should be limited. Conversely, these same critics are silent about proposals to make jury trials more comprehensible and "friendly" to jurors.

---

[1] Tackett, "Dole Fires a Salvo at Clinton Judges," Chicago Tribune, p. 1 (April 20, 1996).

[2]—Responses to Criticisms

In response to these criticisms, juror proponents argue that the critics do not understand or trust jurors to do the right thing. As one report of this controversy has stated:

> "Innovations in jury trial procedures are both necessary and long overdue. The institution of trial by jury is not fatally flawed, as some critics have suggested. Rather, the problem lies with rigid trial procedures and evidentiary rules that reflect false assumptions about jury comprehension and decision making."[2]

The report goes on to add:

> "Debates over the competence of jurors to decide cases have prompted some commentators to argue that judges should assume more decision-making responsibility. Others advocate reforming the trial process to make the jury's task more manageable. Empirical research on jury decision making has revealed that in many cases juries perform their duties quite competently. When problems arise, it is often the quality of the presentation that is implicated, rather than inherent deficiencies in jurors' abilities to process the information provided."[3]

It is difficult to determine whether the reasons for these criticisms and responses are political, philosophical, or ideological, or reflect some perceived personal interest. However, there is considerable disagreement about both the nature of the proposals and their underlying bases.

Defenders of broadened jury discretion and involvement in trial point to a number of aspects of courtroom procedures which might cause misplaced criticisms of jurors. For example, many observers blame inadequate presentation of information by trial attorneys as a contributing cause of juror inability to completely comprehend a party's position in a case.

Other commentators note that, unlike in other settings, jurors are brought into a trial with no orientation to the events under scrutiny, are given no

---

[2] Munsterman, Hannaford & Whitehead, eds., *Jury Trial Innovations,* p. 3 (Williamsburg, VA: National Center for State Courts, 1998) (a joint report of the National Center for State Courts and the Jury Initiatives Task Force of the American Bar Association Section on Litigation).

[3] *Id.* at 7.

resources to record information or to refer to for information, are given no opportunity to ask questions to complete their understanding of a case, are not told in advance what the ultimate issues will be, and finally are thrust into a decision-making mode with little or no guidance.

Finally, jury supporters point out that although some jurors may not understand the technical aspects of some evidence, the central legal issues are not technical, and juries have a tendency to correctly spot and deal with the core dynamics of a case even though there may be some technical information that they do not fully understand.

[3]—Debate over Improvements in Jury Trial Procedure

The controversies and debates about ways to improve certain aspects of the jury trial system seem to mirror the same ideological differences that are reflected in the debate over the efficacy of a jury trial as a whole. For example, some of the same critics who would eliminate jury trials would also restrict attorney participation in voir dire and restrict jury trial innovations such as jury note-taking and jury questions to witnesses.

Until recently, the arguments for all sides of the argument relied only upon untested observations and opinions. Over the past few years, however, a number of important scientific studies have taken place which add valuable, reliable information to the debate. We will discuss both the arguments and the recent scientific findings in this chapter.

Let's first review the purpose of a jury trial and how jurors make decisions. This information is helpful in framing the debate.

§ 17.03 | BASIC CONSIDERATIONS FOR CHANGES IN THE JURY TRIAL SYSTEM

The jury trial is a fundamental concept of many cultures in Western civilization. For both early Greeks and modern Americans, the Western system of justice, including a strong jury trial system, has been instrumental in preserving individual rights and serving the interests of the public in maintaining common standards of justice.

Throughout our history, American men and women of ordinary capacities have sat in judgment of others in an attempt to decide disputes based upon common sense principles. The original authors of the United States Declaration of Independence, Articles of Confederation, and Constitution believed strongly that ordinary citizens had the right and the resources to determine how disputes should be resolved. Through the centuries we have called upon juries to use their best efforts to understand the basis for each dispute and to fashion a decision which is in keeping with their sense of values and beliefs.

Our system of justice and its protection of citizen rights with the use of a jury says as much about our values as it does about the logistics of courtroom decision making. Historically, our forefathers were concerned about the protection of freedom from tyranny by providing that justice be applied by ordinary citizens. The authors of our system of justice were not as concerned about the "correctness" of a jury's decision as they were about a litigant's right to have a fair trial.

Over time, with the extraordinary revolutions in technology and communications, the focus has changed from guaranteeing freedom to making "correct" decisions. The great advances in mass communications have facilitated wider distribution of information about courtroom cases and have generated avenues for millions of people to express their opinions and attitudes about pending legal cases.[4] As a consequence, although only twelve members of a jury will hear the details of the evidence and case presentation, millions of Americans may be expressing strong opinions about the outcome during the course of a trial and afterwards.

As a result, there seems to be a growing tension among those who wish to maintain tight control over jury verdicts, those who wish to increase the effectiveness of juries, and those who would make jury verdicts a matter of democratic decision making.

Supporters of broadened jury discretion and enhanced involvement of jurors in trial tend to accept the human element in jurors and seek to augment human characteristics with the same learning and decision-making tools that are available to the rest of the public when they make important decisions. These proponents of jury trials also want to influence courts to make innovations to help jurors in understanding cases. They argue that the innovations they support would decrease the criticisms of jury decisions and increase juror satisfaction.

---

[4] Aronson, *The Social Animal,* 7th ed., p. l (New York: W. H. Freeman & Co., 1995); Gergen, *The Saturated Self: Dilemmas of Identity in Contemporary Life* (New York: Basic Books, 1991).

In an effort to respond to criticisms from the bar, the public, and jurors, trial judges have attempted to fashion simple procedures intended to enhance jury learning and competence. Two of the innovations involve note-taking and questioning of witnesses by jurors.

§ 17.04 | SCIENTIFIC RESEARCH AND JURY TRIAL REFORMS

Because of the mounting rhetoric about the efficacy of jury trials in general or the value of some of the proposals to improve jury trials, a number of court systems have instituted various improvements and then measured the results. Some of the results were measured scientifically and others were not. Regardless, valuable information has been obtained by those court systems that have instituted improvements.

Most of the comments and statements made about jury trials amount to hypotheses. As such, they are subject to testing to determine whether or not they are true. Although some nonscientific experiments have been conducted by individual courts and court systems, a great deal of empirical research has been conducted by social science and psychology researchers that is designed to understand whether criticisms of the competency of a jury are well-founded.

Academic researchers have also studied the effectiveness of some of the various improvements that have been instituted. For example, they have studied whether jurors are capable of comprehending and making informed decisions about complex fact and legal matters, as well as the effectiveness of specific proposals for enhancing the quality of attorney participation in the voir dire process and for enhancing jury comprehension.

Substantial research has been conducted to determine whether implementing specific proposals to improve interactions with the jury would really be helpful and/or meaningful. For example, a number of empirical studies have focused on juror note-taking and questions about the jury decision-making process. Much of this research took place in the 1970s and 1980s, but it has been largely omitted from the discussion until now.

Typically, scientific research follows real life experiences. In other words, scientific researchers tend to study the hypotheses that have been created by other people in our culture to determine whether they are true. The purpose of most of the scientific research that has been conducted about the efficacy of jury trials has been to determine whether the proposed improvements would accomplish their goals, and if not, how they might be enhanced in order to better accomplish those goals.

It would be helpful for us to discuss some of the specific hypotheses and proposals that have been made and to review them in light of the available research.

§ 17.05 | JURY COMPETENCY IN COMPLEX MATTERS

One of the more fundamental challenges in the debate is whether a jury is competent to make decisions in disputes with complex fact patterns. This section will explore the position of the challengers and the available scientific research which addresses the issue.

[1]—Jury Competency: Positing the Argument

The argument that citizen juries are not competent to understand disputes involving complex factual matters is not a new phenomenon. Until the twentieth century, juries were highly regarded as arbiters of truth and justice. However, with the arrival of modern technology and high-speed communications, doubts about the competency of juries began to surface. Along with the development of new technologies, there has arisen a mind set that, in order to understand the nature of a dispute, one must have a working knowledge of the complexities of the underlying fact patterns. Previously, when fact patterns were simpler, there were no reasons to challenge the intellect or experience of jurors. With the development of modern technology, however, jurors are often accused of being generally incompetent as fact finders.[5]

Along with challenges to jurors' intellectual capabilities, some legal scholars have also challenged jurors' ability to place trial attorney comments into perspective and to resist being too impressionable. The argument is made that jurors are too gullible to be competent as fact finders.[6]

---

[5] Skidmore vs. Baltimore & Ohio Railroad, 167 F.2d 54 (2d Cir. 1948).

[6] *Id.*

A number of important and often cited appellate opinions over the past few years reflect doubts about the competency of jurors to make decisions in complex cases. The most frequently cited case is that of *Markman v. Westview Instruments, Inc.*[7] In *Markman* the underlying dispute centered around the alleged infringement of a patent involving dry-cleaning equipment tracking processes. At trial the jury decided that Westview's tracking process was so similar to that of Markman that Westview infringed Markman's patent. Despite the jury's verdict, the trial judge granted the defendant's motion for judgment as a matter of law and found that Westview's process did not infringe the patent.

Markman appealed the judge's ruling all the way to the United States Supreme Court. Writing for the majority, Justice David Souter said:

> "[J]udges, not jurors, are better suited to find the acquired meaning of patent terms.
>
> "The construction of written instruments is one of those things that judges often do and are likely to do better than jurors unburdened by training in exegesis. Patent construction in particular 'is a special occupation, requiring, like all others, special training and practice. The judge, from his training and discipline, is more likely to give a proper interpretation to such instruments than a jury; and he is, therefore, more likely to be right, in performing such a duty, than a jury can be expected to be.'"[8]

The statements about jurors made by Justice Souter are typical of some of the more recent court opinions which have indicated support for limiting the involvement of jurors in making decisions. Many appellate court opinions have reflected similar views of jury competency in different contexts.[9] Justice Souter's comment about the superior skills of a judge in interpreting patents is merely a hypothesis, as are all statements about human nature. Since the *Markman* opinion there have been many research studies that have tested Justice Souter's hypothesis, but there are no research findings which would support a conclusion that jurors are not competent to understand and make decisions

---

[7] Markman v. Westview Instruments, Inc., 517 U.S. 370, 116 S.Ct. 1384, 134 L.Ed.2d 577 (1996)

[8] *Id.*, 517 U.S. at 388-389, citing Parker v. Hulme, 18 F. Cas. 1138, 1140 (No. 10,740) (Cir. Ct. E.D. Pa. 1849).

[9] Cecil, Hans & Wiggins, "Citizen Comprehension of Difficult Issues: Lessons from Civil Jury Trials," 40 Amer. U. L. Rev. 727 (1991).

about complex matters such as patent infringement. We will discuss the research that has been conducted in more detail later in this section. Although the Justice could be correct in his statements, there is no empirical research which would support his statement that judges, because of their training and practice, are more competent to interpret patents than are jurors. We might assume that the Justice considered that expert testimony was presented at trial to help the jury understand the patent, and that some of the jurors might have been engineers and/or scientists who had training and experience that the trial judge did not have.

Nonetheless, the position of jury challengers is provocative. One might ask, is it true that jurors do not have the intellectual capacity to comprehend the nature of the dispute and to make informed decisions in complex cases? Second, if the jury cannot comprehend adequate information to make a decision, which is the better cure for the problem: replacing the jury with a judge as a fact finder or improving the courtroom educational process through better trial advocacy and implementation of more modern learning tools?

The response to criticisms of jurors' intellectual ability has two parts. First, jury supporters state that all of the research studies and observations of individual jurors indicate that juries are quite capable of making informed decisions in the most complicated matters. These supporters show that there is no research finding that would support an allegation that juries are not competent to understand the necessary facts in a complicated case and, therefore, to make informed decisions. Second, jury supporters state that a jury's ability to comprehend complicated factual patterns would be enhanced if juries were given the same learning tools that other groups in our culture are given. Third, jury supporters point out that jury critics are unable to point to any specific deficiency in juror capabilities, such as lack of memory recall capabilities or lack of intellectual capacity to grasp complicated facts or why the jury deliberation process is not sufficient to assist less intellectually sophisticated jurors in understanding the case.

Jury supporters state that it would be unfair to handicap a jury by not providing them with information by using the same simple learning tools that are available in schools and other forums, and then criticizing them for not understanding the case. They also state that trial attorneys should take responsibility for making their case presentations easier to understand by using the same presentation techniques that professionals in the fields of education, marketing, and politics use every day.

[2]–Jury Competency Research

The research relating to jury competency is comprehensive. Because questions about jury competency have been raised periodically over the past seventy years, published and private research has been conducted for several decades to test the hypothesis that jurors are not competent to decide cases involving complex facts. In addition to the research studies themselves, other scientific researchers and academic scholars have reviewed the research to determine whether the methods used and the findings obtained were valid and/or reliable.

A review of the forty years of research into jury competency reveals that juries are quite competent at comprehending cases with complicated fact patterns and concepts, even though some individual jurors may have difficulties in the absence of jury deliberation. In addition, the research indicates that simple learning tools can easily be implemented during trial to assist a jury in comprehending complicated cases.

[a]–Juror Intellectual Capacities Research

There are two methods that have traditionally been used in research to test whether juries are competent to understand complicated cases and make informed decisions. The first method is to compare the decisions of judges to those of jurors in the same case to determine whether judges make different decisions than jurors, and if so, why. The second is to measure how well jurors understand the issues and the necessary facts, and how well they remember them during jury deliberations. The second method utilizes both subjective determinations by jurors and others as well as objective measures developed by the various research teams.

[i]—Judge Decisions vs. Jury Decisions in the Same Case

One of the ways to determine if a judge is more competent than a jury to decide fact issues is to compare the decisions of judges and jurors in the same case to measure any differences and, if there are any, to understand the reasons for the differences.[10] One of the earliest studies of this nature was conducted in the 1950s by the University of Chicago Law School's Jury Project. In this study the researchers compared jury verdicts in a great number of criminal and civil

---

[10] Kalven & Zeisel, *The American Jury,* 63-65 (Boston: Little, Brown, 1966); Kalven, "The Dignity of the Civil Jury," 50 Va. L. Rev. 1055-1075 (1964).

cases to the decisions that the actual trial judges would have made in the same cases. The civil cases contained cases of all types, including cases with both simple and complex fact patterns.

Taking all cases together, the researchers found that the trial judges' decisions agreed with the jury verdicts 78% of the time. Looking at the differences, in criminal cases, juries were more likely to acquit the defendant than were judges, and in civil cases, the differences were evenly divided between plaintiffs and defendants. There was no trend that would indicate that jurors or judges favored any party's position differently.

The researchers also looked closely at the civil cases where there were differences between the judge and jury decisions in order to determine if the differences could be characterized or explained by differences in the complexity of the cases. However, the findings indicated that the rate of differences in the decisions were the same in both simple and complex cases. Therefore, any differences in the intellectual or competency levels of judges and jurors did not account for the differences in the verdicts.

The only factor that the researchers found to explain the differences in verdicts were differences in how juries applied community values and norms and how judges applied them. Other studies that have reviewed the differences in judge and jury verdicts have also noted that the great majority of jury verdicts are strongly tied to legally relevant evidence that would be supported by legal rulings.[11] Researchers have noted that juries' departures from the law can usually be explained by differences between the law and community norms or values.

Further research indicates that although certain aspects of complicated cases do challenge jurors' ability to comprehend and understand technical evidence, there has been no finding that the judgments of jurors tend to be wrong. Regardless of the complexity of the evidence, jurors continue to actively process evidence and apply their common sense and common experience in making informed decisions.

[ii]—Subjective and Objective Determinants

Researchers have also studied jurors' perceptions of the jurors' own ability to comprehend complicated cases, as well as objective measures of the accuracy

---

[11] Myers, "Rule Departures and Making Law: Juries and Their Verdicts," 13 Law & Society Rev. 781 (1979); Poulson, Brondino, Brown & Braithwaite, "Relations Among Mock Jurors' Attitudes, Trial Evidence, and Their Selections of an Insanity Defense Verdict: A Path Analytic Approach," 82 Psychological Rep. 3-16 (1998); Visher, "Jury Decision Making: The Importance of Evidence," 11 Law & Human Behavior 1 (1987).

of juror recall of complicated facts. The research findings indicate that most civil jurors believe that despite long trials, complicated fact patterns, and court procedures which are an impediment to easy learning, they comprehend the evidence and make informed decisions.[12]

Other studies have found that, realistically, some jurors are able to follow and understand complex facts and ideas more readily than others. As a result, jury deliberation is a helpful equalizing tool whereby jurors who more easily comprehend the evidence tend to help other jurors understand the information and, together, they make a reasoned decision.

Researchers in these studies have concluded that juries which include people with at least moderate levels of education generally have little difficulty in comprehending complex evidence and issues. However, juries which contain only people with low levels of education are often at a disadvantage and must work harder to comprehend complex matters. In some instances, juries selected for longer trials are often composed of people with lower levels of education for a variety of reasons, including their availability for longer periods of time.

In situations where juror education level is low, the central question might be, whose responsibility is it to help the jury comprehend the complexities of the case? Is it the responsibility of the trial court to improve the learning environment so that jurors' learning tasks are less challenging? Is it the responsibility of the trial team to go to greater lengths to simplify the evidence and the issues?

Many observers have noted that the education level of a typical jury in the United States is rapidly increasing. Is it possible that juries with only people who have little education is a thing of the past? Or does the statutory elimination in recent years of many exemptions for various professionals (including lawyers) result in a more varied jury pool than previously?

Perhaps the most difficult kind of evidence for a jury is scientific, technical, and statistical data. From the time they are school children, many people have

---

[12] Cecil, Lind & Bermant, "Jury Service in Lengthy Civil Trials" (Washington, D.C.: Federal Judicial Center, 1987); Lempert, "Civil Juries and Complex Cases: Let's Not Rush to Judgment," 80 Mich. L. Rev. 68 (1981), reprinted in part in Monahan & Walker, eds., *Social Science in Law: Cases and Materials* (New York: Foundation Press, 1985), and Levine, Doernberg & Nelken, *Civil Procedure Anthology* (Cincinnati: Anderson Publishing Co., 1998); Lempert, "Civil Juries and Complex Cases: Taking Stock After Twelve Years," in Litan, ed., *Verdict: Assessing the Civil Jury System,* p. 181 (Washington, D.C.: The Brookings Institution, 1993).

trouble understanding scientific and mathematical information. For example, theories of probability and statistical measurement are difficult subjects for many jurors.

In addition to the inherent complexities in evidence, our system of trial advocacy promotes competing expert testimony, which further complicates matters. Ordinarily, juries anticipate that the opposing parties will present expert testimony which is consistent with their core themes. However, jurors and trial attorneys report that courtroom presentations which make the learning process simpler and more comprehensible for average jurors have a better chance of persuading jurors.

In order to better sort out the complexities in the testimony of competing experts, jurors tend to look closely at an expert's credentials and other characteristics that help determine the credibility and usefulness of the expert's testimony. Such evaluation of an expert's testimony based in part on evaluations of the expert's credibility is part and parcel of decision making for judges, jurors, or arbitrators.

In the final analysis, jurors take their role in the courtroom seriously. They use every faculty at their disposal as individuals and as a group to understand the information that is presented to them and to make a decision of which they can be proud. Compared to judges and other observers of the evidence in specific cases, jurors rarely make wrong decisions. When they do, a review of the adequacy of courtroom procedures and trial team presentations would likely reveal some deficiencies in either or both relative to helping the jurors better understand the case.

In the next part of our discussion we will focus on specific proposals that have been made to improve the learning environment in the courtroom.

[b]—Improvements in Court Procedure to Aid the Jury

Over the past forty years, legal scholars and academic researchers have studied various methods of improving the quality of the courtroom learning environment that would benefit jurors in their comprehension of cases of all types. As many observers have noticed, jurors are traditionally treated rather poorly relative to the learning tools that are available to them to help understand the evidence and issues in a case. Jurors are traditionally given little guidance about the task they are to perform, the ultimate questions they will have to answer, and a framework for the body of evidence that will be presented to them. Essentially, they are placed in the jury box and told to listen and observe everything. Jurors generally anticipate that they will be asked to render a verdict of some sort, but they rarely are given any guidance to the specific subject matter of the case or the questions that will be asked.

If the jurors were students in school, they would be provided with a course outline and textbooks or other materials to assist them in learning about the subject matter. In addition, they would have daily lectures to help in understanding the material and an opportunity to ask questions about any aspect of the subject matter that they did not understand. That these tools have traditionally been withheld from jurors is, at times, incomprehensible.

The tools that have been the subject of discussion and research include:[13]

+ Jury tutorials in complex cases
+ Juror notebooks
+ Juror note-taking
+ Juror submission of questions to witnesses
+ Pre-instructing the jury
+ Mini-openings or interim commentary
+ Jury instructions before closing argument, rather than afterwards only
+ Plain English jury instructions

Outside the legal context, most of these tools seem benign. However, applying each tool requires additional effort and time invested by the trial judge and the parties. Moreover, the litigants might have to pay additional expenses. Other objections concern perceived loss of control by the litigants.

However, the general research findings have concluded that jurors welcome these learning tools. They make the work of being a juror less burdensome and arduous. Trial judges who have experimented with these tools have indicated consistently that, with moderate controls, the use of these tools can assure the litigants a fair and impartial trial, while at the same time improving the courtroom learning environment. For example, trial judges who have allowed jurors to submit written questions to witnesses have found that the active involvement of jurors in the trial increases everyone's satisfaction without any known harmful consequences.[14]

---

[13] Munsterman, Hannaford & Whitehead, eds., *Jury Trial Innovations,* pp. 89-193 (Williamsburg, VA: National Center for State Courts, 1998). A joint report of the National Center for State Courts and the Jury Initiatives Task Force of the American Bar Association Section on Litigation.

[14] Saltzburg, "Improving the Quality of Jury Decision-making," in Litan, ed., N. 12 *supra* at p. 341.

In the remaining sections of this chapter we will explore juror reactions to certain learning tools that have been studied extensively.

§ 17.06 | Juror Note-Taking

Permitting jurors to take notes both during trial and deliberations was, until recently, a novel idea. Juror note-taking is a matter of discretion for the trial court. Some of the questions that have been raised with reference to juror note-taking are helpful to our assessment of the procedure. Should note-taking be encouraged by the trial court? Should note-taking be limited to longer or more complicated trials? Should jurors be allowed to use their notes during deliberations? Should jurors' notes be destroyed after trial? Are the notes part of the court record? Will juror note-taking distract jurors from paying attention to the evidence? Will note-taking improve juror learning about the case?

[1]—Procedures Used or Tested

Some of the earlier research conducted in the 1970s and 1980s was successful in comparing the effects of note-taking vs. non-note-taking or questioning vs. no questioning. However, much of the research suffered from methodological limitations (e.g., conducted in a laboratory vs. courtroom) or focused exclusively on juror reactions while excluding those of judges and attorneys.

More recent experiments have included large-scale field experiments in actual courtrooms, and have incorporated the experiences and observations of trial judges and attorneys. One such study used data collected from sixty-seven trials in the state of Wisconsin, involving twenty-nine different judges, ninety-five attorneys, and 550 actual jurors.[15]

Another experiment used a national sample of trials that included seventy-five civil trials and eighty-five criminal trials located in thirty-three states and involving 103 judges, 220 trial attorneys, and 1,229 actual jurors.

---

[15] Heuer & Penrod, "Increasing Jurors' Participation in Trials: A Field Experiment with Jury Notetaking and Question Asking," 12 Law & Human Behavior 231-262 (1988); Penrod & Heuer, "Tweaking Common Sense: Assessing Aids to Jury Decision Making," 3 Psychology, Public Policy & Law 259-284 (1997).

Other recent studies that have been conducted in this area and utilized laboratory settings and simulated juries produced findings identical or similar to those obtained in the Wisconsin and national studies.

In all of the scientific experiments, jurors were permitted to take notes during all phases of trial, including deliberations, and were given that permission as soon as the jury was empaneled. In some instances, judges did not allow note-taking during closing arguments, but jurors were allowed to take notes up to that point in the trial.

In those trials conducted under "non-note-taking" circumstances, judges instructed jurors not to take notes and stated their reasoning on the record.

Juror note-taking was permitted in a total of 135 trials, including the Wisconsin and national studies. When jurors were given the opportunity to take notes, most jurors took advantage of the opportunity (66% in the Wisconsin study and 87% in the national study), but did not as a rule take extensive notes.

In the Wisconsin study, jurors took an average of 5.4 pages of notes over the average trial length of 2.3 days. In the national study, jurors took an average of 14.4 pages of notes in civil trials and 7.1 pages of notes in criminal trials. The average trial was ten days for civil trials and six days for criminal trials.

[2]—Evaluation of Perceived Advantages

[a]—Notes Are an Aid to Memory

Although jurors who took notes believed that their memories had been aided, a comparison of information recalled by jurors in the Wisconsin and national studies who took notes with those who did not indicated that there was no memory advantage to note-taking per se.

However, subsequent laboratory-based experiments have indicated that, with regard to the quality of recall, note-takers outperform non-note-takers by a significant margin.

[b]—Increase in Satisfaction

Jurors were asked in both the Wisconsin and national studies if they perceived that the ability to take notes increased the satisfaction of their jury experience. Juror respondents in the Wisconsin study noted only a marginal increase in their satisfaction and the national study did not produce any real increase in satisfaction. However, the researchers noted that in those trials where notes were allowed, juror satisfaction with the trial procedure overall was quite high compared to trial procedures where note-taking was not allowed. In essence, the jurors expected that note-taking would be allowed as in most other learning experiences in life, and did not believe that granting one the freedom to take notes deserved special attention.

[3]—Evaluation of Perceived Disadvantages

[a]—Does Note-Taking Distract Jurors?

In the Wisconsin study, judges and trial attorneys who participated in trials where jurors were allowed to take notes stated almost unanimously that they did not find the note-taking to be distracting. Conversely, in other studies judges and trial attorneys reported that they believed that note-taking actually motivated jurors to pay more attention to the case.

[b]—Do Note-Takers Have Influence Over Non-Note-Takers?

Some people have theorized that jurors who take notes wield more influence or dominance during deliberations. However, in the Wisconsin study no evidence was found that note-takers participated to a greater degree in jury deliberations when they were aided by notes. Similarly, earlier studies also found that, of the factors that determined which jurors gained more influence during deliberations, juror note-taking was not predominant.

One laboratory study indicated that jurors in note-taking trials were less reliant on other jurors for information. A few jurors reported that they were persuaded by jurors who had taken notes, but it was unclear from the results as to whether the ability of note-taking jurors to win over the other jurors was attributed to the note-takers' compelling communication skills or simply because they took notes.

[c]—Must Notes Be Accurate Trial Records?

The Wisconsin and national studies both found that juror notes tended to be fair, accurate records of trial proceedings. One of the trial judges even wrote to the researchers stating that he was surprised that individual juror notes tended to agree with the transcript of the trial as well as with other jurors' notes.

One pervasive note-taking criticism is that note-taking constitutes a distraction for jurors. The argument is that jurors cannot listen and watch while they are taking notes.

However, 85% of jurors in the Wisconsin and national studies reported that the trial did not proceed too quickly for them to keep pace with the proceedings while taking notes.

[d]—Does Note-Taking Favor One Side?

Laboratory studies have shown that note-taking has no effect on the verdict or on the jurors' rating of attorney competence. Similarly, the Wisconsin and national studies did not reveal any relationship between extensive note-taking in the early phases of trial and ultimate jury decisions.

However, attorneys in criminal trials were more likely than their civil counterparts to believe that the prosecution benefited from juror note-taking. Ironically, judges presiding over those same trials believed that the defense benefited more from note-taking.

Other research has determined that verdicts are issue- or message-driven, and that the mechanics of trial are rarely a significant factor.

[e]—Does Note-Taking Consume Too Much Time?

Laboratory research, as well as the Wisconsin and national studies, have all indicated that note-taking did not affect jury deliberation time. There had been some speculation that jurors would take more time during jury deliberations to resolve discrepancies in notes. However, jurors stated clearly that little deliberation time had been devoted to discussing notes.

Similarly, judges and attorneys did not characterize any delays as attributable to note-taking.

[4]—Conclusions and Recommendations

As a learning tool, note-taking is a benign activity which allows jurors to process information and record it for later recall. In both the Wisconsin and national studies, judges and attorneys were asked their general impressions of note-taking. In both studies, judges and attorneys stated that they had not expected note-taking to be problematic and did not find it to be so.

§ 17.07 | Juror Questions to Witnesses

The Federal Rules of Evidence do not explicitly permit or prohibit a procedure whereby jurors ask questions of witnesses.[16] Conversely, Rule 61(A) states that

> "[a] court must exercise reasonable control over the mode and order of interrogating witnesses and of presenting evidence so as to (1) make the interrogation and presentation effective for the ascertainment of truth, (2) avoid needless consumption of time, and (3) protect witnesses from harassment and embarrassment."

Historically, the trial judge has had the discretion to permit or deny juror questioning, and most judges have demonstrated a preference or bias toward reserving to the court and the attorneys the exclusive right to ask all questions of the witnesses. Some courts have been reluctant to either encourage or discourage questions from jurors.[17] However, published opinions in both federal and state courts indicate that the implementation of simple courtroom procedures can provide for written juror questions about the facts of a case while safeguarding the rights of all parties.[18] Excerpts from the court's opinion in *United States v. Hernandez* are included in Appendix C of this book.

Some observers have stated that biases against allowing jurors to ask questions are based on objections to form as much as to substance. Judges and attorneys are sometimes irritated by the lack of artfulness or proper trial advocacy form that characterizes many juror questions. Other irritations arise when jurors raise questions about matters which are inadmissible or which appear on the surface to favor one side or the other.

Trial judges and attorneys who favor allowing jurors to ask questions either orally or in writing weigh the potential benefits to jurors against the potential harm to the parties. In complicated or complex cases such as conspiracy, patent, or antitrust cases, trial judges have found that the facts are so

---

[16] DeBenedetto v. Goodyear Tire and Rubber Co., 754 F.2d 512, 80 A.L.R.Fed. 879 (4th Cir. 1985).

[17] Penrod & Heuer, "Improving Group Performance: The Case of the Jury," in Tindale et al., eds., *Theory and Research on Small Groups* (New York: Plenum Press, 1998).

[18] See United States v. Hernandez, 176 F.3d 719 (3d Cir. 1999), and Cohee v. State, 942 P.2d 211 (Okla. Crim. App. 1997).

complicated that jurors should be allowed to ask questions in order to perform their duties as fact finders.

Certainly, in bench trials when trial judges act as fact finders, the court frequently asks the witnesses questions. Supporters of jury questions would allow jurors to also ask questions in order to clarify the subject matter of the trial.

[1]—Procedures Used or Tested

The standard procedure used and tested when jurors are allowed to ask questions permits jurors to prepare written questions that are delivered to the trial judge. The court then determines the relevancy and admissibility of the information requested and either asks, reformulates, or disallows the question.

In the Wisconsin and national studies, recommended instructions for participating trial judges are generally stated as follows:

> "In this trial, we request that you allow the jurors to direct written questions to any witness. After direct and cross-examination of each witness is complete, please ask jurors to submit any additional questions they may have, in writing, to you. If you find any such question patently objectionable, decline to ask it and explain to the jury that no adverse inference should be drawn from your ruling. If the question is facially acceptable, confer with counsel and rule on any objection (outside the hearing of the jury) raised before posing the question to the witness. If an objection is sustained, explain to the jury that no adverse inference should be drawn from your ruling."

In the Wisconsin study, juror questioning was permitted in thirty-three trials, and in the national study questioning was permitted in seventy-one trials. In the Wisconsin study eighty-eight questions (2.3 questions per trial) were asked, of which two-thirds were directed to the prosecution or plaintiff witnesses and one-third to defense witnesses.

In the national study, jurors chose to ask questions in only fifty-one of the seventy-one trials, with an average of 5.1 questions per civil trial and 4.4 questions per criminal trial. Of these questions, 79% of questions were directed to plaintiff witnesses in civil trials, and 77% to prosecution witnesses in criminal trials.

[2]—Evaluation of Perceived Advantages

[a]—Do Questions Promote Juror Understanding or Alleviate Juror Doubts?

Common sense dictates that the ability to ask questions and receive answers is a method that would enhance the understanding of trial evidence and the transactions which are the basis of a dispute. In most instances courts look favorably upon questions that are formulated to elaborate or explain evidence that has been presented by counsel.

One concern is that juror questions will go beyond matters that have been previously raised. Therefore, one of the focuses of research has been to determine the kind of questions jurors raise.

Laboratory and field research has consistently found that juror questions serve an explanatory or clarifying function. For example, in the national study, juror questions generally sought to clarify evidence, clarify the law, or in some other way get to the truth.

In the Wisconsin study, jurors who asked questions expressed a higher degree of satisfaction that the questioning of witnesses had been thorough, and that the jury had enough information to reach a just verdict. In both the national and Wisconsin studies, trial attorneys expressed fears before trial indicating that juror questions might cause havoc with an attorney's trial strategy. However, attorneys who had participated in trials where questions were asked reported that juror questions did not adversely affect their strategy.

Conversely, attorneys discovered that the questions jurors asked had been anticipated in the normal course of case development. In those instances where juror questions had not been anticipated, attorneys were suddenly alerted to present information on aspects of the case which they had overlooked.

[b]—Do Juror Questions Improve Satisfaction?

In both the Wisconsin and national studies, jurors universally stated that they were quite satisfied with their experiences and that the ability to ask questions enhanced their ability to serve as jurors. In addition, jurors stated that satisfaction with their verdict was not affected by their ability to ask questions.

Interestingly, judges indicated more satisfaction with juror questions than did trial attorneys. Some attorneys were still ambivalent about the uncertainties inherent in allowing disinterested parties to ask questions in a public forum.

[3]—Evaluation of Perceived Disadvantages

[a]—Are Juror Questions Inappropriate?

In both the Wisconsin and national studies, researchers found that jurors asked appropriate questions even though they were unfamiliar with the rules of evidence and procedure.

In the Wisconsin study, trial judges and attorneys stated that they had not expected juror questions to be inappropriate, and that their expectations were met. In the national study, attorneys were more skeptical than judges if they had had no prior experience with juror questions. However, after trial both judges and attorneys believed that the questions jurors had asked were appropriate.

[b]—Is Attorney Reluctance to Object a Problem?

Most jurisdictions require that attorneys raise objections to evidence when counsel first attempts to introduce it and to questions when they are first asked, or any objections to the evidence or questions are waived. However, some attorneys felt that they might be reluctant to object for fear of offending a juror.

Research has indicated that those fears are unfounded, particularly when a curing instruction is made from the bench.

In the Wisconsin study, attorneys objected to 17% of the questions submitted by jurors. In the national study, attorneys objected to 20% of questions submitted by jurors. In these instances, the trial judge was asked to explain the basis of his or her ruling so that jurors would not draw an adverse inference.

In the national study, sixty-five of the 145 jurors who asked questions indicated that one or more of their questions had drawn an objection. Of these sixty-five jurors, fifty-two of them indicated on a nine-point scale that they were neither embarrassed nor angry about the objections. In addition, most of the jurors in the Wisconsin study indicated that they understood the basis for the attorney's objection.

[c]—Do Jurors Make Inappropriate Inferences When Objections Are Sustained?

Another fear of counsel has been that if an objection is sustained, the jurors might draw an inappropriate inference about the disadvantaged counsel from the unanswered question. However, trial judges and attorneys who participated in the Wisconsin and national studies typically indicated that they did not expect and did not observe such a consequence.

[d]—Do Jurors Become Advocates?

Several cases have contained opinions of appellate judges that indicate a concern that allowing juror questions would cause a "gross distortion of the adversary system and a misconception of the role of the jury as a neutral fact finder in the adversary process."[19]

Other courts have expressed concerns about the "risks" of allowing jurors to ask questions or to interrogate witnesses.

However, laboratory and field research has found that jury questions had no recognizable effect on verdicts. In the national study, for example, researchers examined the agreement between judge and jury verdicts. In 69% of cases, the verdicts were identical.

Agreement between judges and jurors was actually higher in those cases in which questions were permitted. In those cases, 74% of verdicts were identical. Also, jurors in both studies felt that neither attorney in the case was perceived less favorably as a result of juror questions.

[e]—Do Jurors Place Undue Emphasis on Their Own Questions?

In *United States v. Johnson*[20] the court indicated a concern that jurors would place more importance on the reactions and questions of each other than on questions presented in the normal adversarial process.

However, findings from the national study refute that position. For example, jurors indicated that the ultimate value of the questions that jurors had asked was modest. In addition, jurors indicated that less than 10% of their deliberation time (an average of fifteen minutes) was spent discussing questions jurors had raised.

[f]—Do Juror Questions Have a Prejudicial Effect?

Another concern expressed in *United States v. Johnson* was that juror questions might cause a legally prejudicial effect against one party or the other.

---

[19] United States v. Johnson, 892 F.2d 707, 713 (8th Cir. 1989).
[20] *Id.*

One of the advantages of scientifically based research is that trends and relationships become apparent with a large sample size. In this instance, researchers could measure the existence of questions against trends in jury verdicts or reactions from judges or jurors.

However, no such trend was observed in either the Wisconsin or national studies. The results of the studies clearly found that jury questions did not affect either the pattern of jury verdicts or the agreement levels between judge and jury verdicts.

Judges, attorneys, and jurors typically agreed that there appeared to be no prejudicial effects even though some attorneys had expected them to occur.

[4]–Conclusions and Recommendations

Written juror questions have proven to be benign. They do not appear to cause an adverse effect in trial and, at the same time, they greatly enhance jurors' understanding of evidence and information at trial.

Clearly, as in all instances where an adverse effect is feared, court-established limiting instructions and procedures help remove doubts and establish confidence in the system.

§ 17.08 | REFERENCES

American Bar Association, Judicial Administration Division, Committee on Jury Standards, *Standards Relating to Juror Use and Management* (Washington, D.C.: American Bar Association, 1993).

Dann, "Learning Lessons and Speaking Rights: Creating Educated and Democratic Juries," 68 Indiana L. J. 1229-1277 (1993).

Diamond & Casper, "Blindfolding the Jury to Verdict Consequences: Damages, Experts, and the Civil Jury," 26 Law & Society Rev. 513-563 (1992).

Hans, "The Contested Role of the Civil Jury in Business Litigation," 79 Judicature 242-248 (1996).

Hans & Vidmar, *Judging the Jury* (New York: Plenum Press, 1986).

Hastie, Penrod & Pennington, *Inside the Jury* (Cambridge: Harvard University Press, 1983).

Hayes, "Bronx Cheer: Inner-City Jurors Tend to Rebuff Prosecutors and to Back Plaintiffs," The Wall Street Journal, pp. A1-A6 (March 24, 1992).

Heuer & Penrod, "Juror Notetaking and Question Asking During Trials: A National Field Experiment," 18 Law & Human Behavior 121-150 (1994).

King & Munsterman, "Stratified Juror Selection: Cross-section by Design," 79 Judicature 273-279 (1996).

Munsterman, Hannaford & Whitehead, eds., *Jury Trial Innovations* (Williamsburg, VA: National Center for State Courts, 1998). A joint report of the National Center for State Courts and the Jury Initiatives Task Force of the American Bar Association Section on Litigation.

Penrod & Heuer, "Improving Group Performance: The Case of the Jury," in Tindale et al., eds., *Theory and Research on Small Groups* (New York: Plenum Press, 1998).

Saks, "The Smaller the Jury, the Greater the Unpredictability," 79 Judicature 263-265 (1996).

Saks, "Reducing Variability in Civil Jury Awards," 21 Law & Human Behavior 243-256 (1997).

CHAPTER 18

Working with
Trial Consultants

Chapter Contents

"The General who wins the battle makes many calculations in his temple before the battle is fought. The General who loses makes but few calculations beforehand."

— Sun Tzu (ca. 480-221 B.C.)
The Art of Strategy

§ 18.01 | Introduction

The poet Samuel Taylor Coleridge (1772-1834) once said,

> "To most men, experience is like the stern lights of a ship which illumine only the track that it has passed."

There is no better teacher than experience for developing and presenting cases for trial. However, if one relies only on experience, two problems arise. First, experience lives in the past. It can give us some ideas about what might lie ahead, but we have no way of knowing whether experience will accurately predict an unseen future. It usually does not.

Second, the world is full of new information that was not available to us in the past. We have statistical information about persuading judges, juries, and arbitrators that did not exist even ten years ago.

If we spend our time practicing in one area of substantive law, we might be able to accurately predict the *legal* issues that will arise in an upcoming case. We may know with some precision how judges, jurors, and arbitrators have viewed specific issues in the past. But without fail, past cases involved specific evidence, opposing attorneys, fact witnesses, experts, judges, jurors, and perhaps arbitrators that are not likely to constitute part of your next case.

As a result, there is some danger in generalizing from lessons learned from past cases to future cases. Similarly, it can be perilous to adopt themes, argument styles, case theories, and other aspects of previous cases in the belief that a pleasant experience with those elements in the past will bring about a favorable result in the future.

Trial consultants help us better understand what we are likely to encounter in an upcoming trial and prepare us to do battle. They shine some light into the misty future.

Trial consultants are more than just an intelligence unit for a trial team. As you know from your experience, the development and presentation of a powerful, persuasive case is the result of thousands of human interactions that have taken place over many months that must produce a compelling case to decision makers. Every word spoken, every idea, and every gesture used by anyone in the courtroom can influence the outcome.

Trial consultants often have important information and a number of important skills that can help a trial team. The most talented trial consultants have developed the ability to sense the cause of problems in time for remedies to be utilized.

Trial consultants are not silver bullets. They are just people who have special skills and training for persuading important decision makers. Except in extraordinary circumstances, they cannot help a trial team win a case that is fundamentally weaker than the opposing case.

In this chapter, we will discuss the background and history of trial consultants, factors to consider in using a trial consultant, types of services offered by trial consultants, some criticisms of trial consultants, and a few suggestions on how to use the services of trial consultants to maximize their benefit to your case.

§ 18.02 | HISTORY OF TRIAL CONSULTANTS

Written historical records from ancient Greece indicate that lay citizens consulted with advocacy experts about the persuasiveness of their presentations as far back as about 450 B.C.[1] At that time, the city states of Greece practiced various forms of judicature from large lay jury trials (with fifty or more jurors) to judicial tribunals that had many similarities to the jury trials, arbitrations, and bench trials that we use today.

However, at the time, citizens commonly represented themselves in criminal, civil, or family matters or called upon well-spoken professional

---

[1] Covino & Jolliffe, *Rhetoric: Concepts, Definitions, Boundaries* (Boston: Allyn & Bacon, 1995); Guthrie, *The Sophists* (Cambridge: Cambridge University Press, 1971); Waterfield, *The First Philosophers: The Presocratics and Sophists* (Oxford: Oxford University Press, 2000).

advocates to represent them. In some cases, they paid people who were knowledgeable about oratory and persuasion to argue for them or to teach them how to best present their case. These oratory experts were called "Sophists." They were respected scholars and advocacy professionals trained in the art of persuasion who were consulted to assist citizens and professional advocates to develop and present their cases to decision makers.

Protagoras of Abdera, who appeared in the historical record about 445 B.C., is believed to be the first Sophist. The next most important Sophists were Gorgias of Leontini, Prodicus of Ceos, and Hippias of Elis. These men were celebrities in their own right. Wherever they appeared, people flocked to hear them. Even such public figures as Pericles, Euripides, and Socrates sought them out.

In those early days, the art of advocacy developed along different paths from the sciences (e.g., mathematics, psychology, and astronomy). Scholars who studied mental processing and behavior were making the same types of inquiries as scholars who studied the stars and physics. They wanted to know how the human mind worked and what relationships and meaning existed between the mind and the external world.

For ancient Greeks and Romans, advocacy was a necessary practical tool for persuading others to agree with one's philosophical and political positions. Effectiveness in the art of advocacy was related to oratorical and persuasive skills in the same sense that they are related today.

Most of the advocacy experts during the time of the ancient Greeks were scholars and philosophers who had developed their own advocacy skills and knowledge because of their chosen professions. A few of these people were scientists in the true sense, but most of them were trained in many disciplines, since specialties were rare in those days. Most scholars prided themselves on the breadth of knowledge that they had accumulated. They believed that in order to have sufficient knowledge of the world to be able to understand and persuade others, one must have studied the workings of the world as well as human nature.

As civilization has developed since that time, the body of general knowledge about the universe and the tools to deal with scientific inquiry and the application of knowledge have grown so large that scientists tend to master certain limited areas of knowledge and inquiry. In the process, trial attorneys have been delegated the role of being the advocacy experts on persuasion in the courtroom, since it was their job historically to perform the advocacy function.

The demands on trial attorneys over the past 100 years have led to a growth in trial advocacy schools, instructors, and publications aimed at enhancing advocacy skills. In addition, trial attorneys have looked for ways to better understand their audiences (judges, jurors, and arbitrators). Because trial attorneys have the responsibility of developing and presenting their clients' most persuasive case, they have spent a great deal of time learning new ways to be more effective in their work.

Over the past forty years, trial attorneys and their clients have begun to take advantage of the recent growth in the specialized knowledge and methods that have originated in many academic fields to further enhance the effectiveness of their trial advocacy skills. From about 1970 until about 1986, most of the growth in the use of trial consultants came from a few attorneys who wanted to experiment with new sources of information and with assistance regarding jury selection and witness training. During that time, most trial consultants in the United States were scientists who did not have training in law or trial advocacy. Their assistance was limited to conducting surveys and jury research by using mock trials and focus groups. A few people trained in theater were helpful in witness training and in helping trial attorneys better utilize the skills they were learning in trial advocacy classes.

There were three obstacles to the more widespread use of trial consultants. First, the research methods used in the 1970s and 1980s were expensive and not cost-effective from a business perspective. As a result, trial consultants often gained a reputation for being too high-priced and not worth the money. Second, most trial scientists were not trained in business matters and therefore were ignorant of the service and budgetary needs of trial lawyers and their clients. They were also not very effective at communicating the value of their services to trial attorneys. Third, trial lawyers who were not trained in behavioral science were unaware of the value of the scientific information offered to them.

Over the past ten years, there has been a noticeable shift toward the use of professional trial consultants to assist trial teams. This change likely occurred because of the increased ability of trial consultants to deliver valuable services to meet business needs of trial lawyers and their clients.

The trend toward increasing the use of behavioral science in developing and presenting cases at trial is likely to continue. The effectiveness of the trial advocacy system is improved when trial attorneys learn more about how courtroom decision makers think. Trial attorneys and their clients are becoming more sophisticated in understanding how to use scientific knowledge in the development of their trial presentations. Conversely, trial consultants are becoming more experienced in knowing how to meet the needs of trial attorneys and their clients.

§ 18.03 | TYPES OF TRIAL CONSULTANTS

Trial consultants come from many backgrounds. There is no special career track, academic discipline, or certification for people who wish to be trial consultants. The depth and breadth of skills offered by particular trial consultants therefore can vary widely and is generally dictated by their academic backgrounds and experiences.

As a result of this eclectic mix of those who are deemed to be qualified trial consultants, there are a number of issues we should consider in order to understand the capabilities and different types of consultants.

[1]—Single vs. Multiple Disciplines

A close look at the trial-consulting profession reveals that the 400 or so people who practice trial consulting on a regular basis tend to come from various academic disciplines such as trial advocacy, psychology, theater, sociology, and marketing, and from a variety of experiential backgrounds.

The needs of a trial team and the requirements of the case will often dictate whether a trial consultant with a background in a single discipline will be competent to provide the specific services needed with the level of skill required. For example, if a trial team needs assistance in helping a witness give effective testimony, a trial consultant who is trained in theater or trial advocacy will be able to help the witness with stage performance issues. A psychologist will be able to help the witness with developing a successful mental attitude and with visualizing and practicing effective performance.

If a trial team needs assistance in understanding how a jury will perceive the circumstances of a case and recommendations for enhancing the persuasive power of a case, the training and skill of trial consultants becomes more specialized. The more knowledgeable the trial consultant is in the areas of scientific behavioral research and trial advocacy, the more valuable he or she is likely to be in meeting these needs.

[2]—Education vs. Experience

Until recently, there was no particular educational training program designed for trial consultants. Most of the people who are currently working as trial consultants have some graduate training in standard psychology, sociology, or some other behavioral science. They may also have training in law, theater, and trial advocacy. Several major universities now offer graduate programs with training in law and psychology.

Occasionally a debate arises that pits education against experience. Sometimes people argue that successful prior experience as a trial consultant is more important than educational background. Others argue that education is more important than experience.

In reality, however, they are both essential. Just as in the legal profession, the requisite educational background for a trial consultant is an important foundation for developing skill and successful experience.

If a trial consultant claims that he or she can conduct scientific research to understand how jurors will mentally process the circumstances of a case, then that consultant should have an educational background and experience in behavioral science. If a trial consultant proposes to help witnesses and lawyers perform better in the courtroom, he or she should have an educational background and experience in theater or trial advocacy. Otherwise, the trial consultant may be offering services for which he or she is not highly qualified.

[3]—Psychologists

People trained in psychology at the master's or doctoral level will likely have a working knowledge of how people think and behave. They are also trained in scientific research and statistical analysis. The academic requirements for people trained in psychology include the study of social psychology, group psychology, organizational psychology, abnormal psychology, cognitive psychology, individual differences and personality, neuropsychology (brain functioning), and other areas that examine how people process information and conduct themselves. The study of psychology includes the study of how people learn new information and attach meaning to that information.

[4]—Sociologists

People who are trained in sociology at the graduate level should have a working knowledge of how people interact with each other in cultural settings. This field is highly relevant to how jurors perceive the world around them and interrelate with each other. People trained in sociology also have a working knowledge of statistical research methods.

[5]—Marketing Research Professionals

People trained in the field of marketing research focus their research on the perceptions and motivations that prospective consumers of information will have when presented with ideas or products. These professionals offer helpful information about how to "package" ideas in the courtroom so that it is persuasive and convincing.

[6]—Lawyers and Trial Advocacy Instructors

Lawyers and trial advocacy instructors have special insights about how the world inside a courtroom operates. They understand courtroom procedure and the performance requirements of barristers and trial lawyers. Most successful trial advocacy instructors have a great deal of knowledge about sophisticated presentation techniques that have been proven successful.

[7]—Drama and Theater Professionals

People who are trained at the graduate level in the field of theater and drama have special information to share with trial lawyers. They have developed the ability to tap into the mindset of audiences and know how to develop an effective stage presence. Their greatest value to trial lawyers is their ability to help members of the trial team and witnesses to convey their story convincingly and draw the audience into the performance.

[8]—Other Professionals

No-one has a monopoly on knowledge. There are many bright trial consultants who have learned something that might be of value to a trial team regardless of their unorthodox credentials or lack of the more usual academic or experiential background. Like everybody else, they will help or hinder your case based upon their talents, skills, and knowledge.

§ 18.04 | CHOOSING A TRIAL CONSULTANT FOR A CASE

[1]—Factors to Consider

There are many factors to consider regarding whether to use a trial consultant and, if so, which trial consultant is right for a particular case. Following are a few of these factors:

- Needs of the case;
- Academic background of the consultant;
- Experience level of the consultant;
- Attitude of the consultant;
- Personal chemistry; and
- Cost.

[2]—Clarifying the Services Needed

Most attorneys will have good instincts about the needs of a case. You might not be able to articulate the source of any psychological problems with the case, but you know when they exist. Something does not feel right. When this happens, you should trust your instincts.

Diagnosing problems with the development or presentation of a case at trial can be compared to diagnosing health problems. You know when something is wrong and you may have an idea about the cause.

For example, it is common for trial lawyers to know when there are mental or behavioral problems with a key fact witness. They may not understand the cause of the problems and may feel incapable of effectively dealing with them. Sometimes witnesses have perceptions and emotions that cause them to behave strangely. In these circumstances, it would be beneficial to both client and the witness to consult with a trial consultant who is trained in helping witnesses to be more effective.

Brainstorming ideas with a trial consultant can help sort out the problems and develop a method for dealing with them. Seeking out someone who is trained to help the trial team is not an admission of weakness. It is a sign that a trial attorney wants to intelligently utilize sources of information that are important to the successful resolution of a case.

[3]—Individuals vs. Firms

Of the approximately 400 trial consultants in the United States, about 70% are solo practitioners. The others are members of small firms ranging in size from two to twenty trial consultants.

Almost all trial lawyers and corporate counsel have a philosophy that has worked for them in choosing between individual trial consultants and firms. Many attorneys believe that regardless of the size of the firm they hire, they are essentially designating one or two individuals to work with them. Other attorneys believe that it is important to hire firms that have several experienced trial consultants who can offer more total resources and personnel.

[4]—Budgeting the Cost

Law practice and trial consulting practice have many similarities. Because lawyers and trial consultants are businesspeople, discussions about cost and budgets should be second nature. In today's economic climate, productivity, value, and cost are important factors in determining how professional work is planned and performed. Perhaps the most important consideration is that all three parties to the trial consultant's work (i.e., trial team, client, and trial consultant) should have clear understandings and expectations about the nature of the consultant's work and its cost. Whether or not the understandings and expectations are reduced to writing is simply a matter of preference. Many people believe that written confirmations are helpful.

[5]—Finding a Trial Consultant

The most productive way to find a trial consultant who will do the best job for your case is to conduct an investigation on your own of available and recommended consultants for the needs of a particular case. You can obtain the names of experienced trial consultants through referrals of people whom you trust and from the American Society of Trial Consultants (ASTC).[2]

---

[2] The American Society of Trial Consultants is the only national trade organization of trial consultants. Their Web site is located at www.astcweb.org.

Personal chemistry and personal working style are important to most people, so plan to visit with consultants you are considering hiring. If your visit is constructive, you should feel comfortable that the consultant will be committed to your case, that his or her knowledge is substantial in the area of the case that you need to address, and that the consultant will listen to you.

§ 18.05 | TRIAL CONSULTANTS' SERVICES

[1]—Prior to Filing

Decisions about where a suit should be commenced and the psychological effects of various allegations on different jury populations in different venues are important considerations at the outset of a case. Some trial consultants have the ability to conduct scientific community surveys or analyses of previous verdicts in a particular venue.

[2]—Early Pretrial

Many trial attorneys believe that effective control of a lawsuit starts early in the life of a case. They believe that by framing the issues early they can force opposing parties to adopt a defensive posture. To assist attorneys, some trial consultants can provide recommendations through the use of consultation services, community attitude surveys, analyses of previous verdicts, and focus groups. In addition, because pretrial motions can often be dispositive in a case, some trial consultants provide recommendations for prosecuting or defending against such motions by using mock court hearing research.

[3]—Discovery Assistance

Because effective development and presentation of litigation strategy often depends upon the success of effective discovery tools, some trial consultants offer services that can help a trial team and party to effectively utilize discovery tools to control and frame the issues in a case. These services include consultations, the use of focus groups, and witness effectiveness training to prepare witnesses for depositions and court hearings.

[4]—Settlement and Alternative Dispute Resolution

One of the most recent developments in the field of trial consulting has been the use of scientific information and research to assist in developing effective settlement and alternative dispute resolution strategies. To accomplish this, trial consultants sometimes provide recommendations and research services such as mock trial jury studies, mock arbitration studies, and mock mediation studies.

[5]—Trial Preparation

The largest array of trial consulting services offered to trial teams involves techniques for assisting in the development of persuasive trial presentation strategies in the courtroom or in arbitration. These services include case consultations, focus groups, mock jury trial studies, mock bench trial studies, mock arbitration studies, mock court hearing studies, witness effectiveness training, development of a written jury panel questionnaire, attorney style coaching, media coaching, development of demonstrative aids and exhibits, and neurolinguistic analysis of pleadings and briefs in order to enhance their persuasive power.

[6]—At Trial

Many attorneys have used the services of trial consultants during trial. Their services include consultations during trial recesses, scientific jury selection, trial observation, and the use of shadow or mirror juries.

[7]—Post-Trial

Regardless of the outcome of a trial, trial attorneys have sometimes found it helpful to bring in a trial consultant for specific purposes. One purpose might be to conduct post-trial interviews of jurors to better understand how they made their decisions. Another purpose might be to help the trial team develop a persuasive strategy for winning a case on appeal by using a mock appellate panel study.

[8]—Media Coaching and Other Special Services

Some types of litigation have special requirements. For example, federal courts often hear pretrial motions in patent cases to determine the scope of a patent.

Consultants sometimes offer special consultations or scientific studies that are helpful in developing an effective strategy in these special circumstances.

Moreover, because pretrial publicity can be so powerful in framing jurors' opinions before a trial even begins, some attorneys and litigants have sought help from trial consultants or media consultants to help them develop effective pretrial presentations to the public.

A FINAL WORD:
① WORKING WITH TRIAL CONSULTANTS

After all the pleadings, discovery and motion practice ends and the preliminary case dust settles, the obviously critical issue is what the jury thinks of your themes, your client's documents and witnesses, and the evidence that your opponent can muster. Working with trial consultants provides a relatively inexpensive but frequently invaluable tool to evaluate how the jury will perceive your case.

Trial consultants offer a wide variety of services, such as focus groups, mock jury presentations of an entire case (or portions of it), and surveys. It is important to work closely with the consultant to decide what your case budget can accommodate and what you *need* to know about how a jury might evaluate your case.

The kinds of insights that jury consultants help with include:

○ Do you want to try the case to a jury at all? If you learn that a jury would consider major factual challenges in your case to be fatal flaws, can you convince your opponent to agree to waive a jury?

○ How will a "real" jury perceive your client? Are the themes you're considering too aggressive? Are a handful of themes "winners" that should become the centerpiece of your case, and be touched upon in some manner by all of your witnesses and in cross-examination of the opposing witnesses?

CONTINUED

❍ Is the applicable legal standard likely to be followed, or will the jury be more apt to apply a "fundamental fairness" standard? Is there a way to frame the case in a more basic way to address such a phenomenon?

❍ Do you want any, or extensive, jury interrogatories? How closely do you want the jury to parse the facts?

In short, the type and usefulness of information generated by an experienced jury consultant is limited only by your imagination.

– Robert S. Walker, Partner
Jones, Day, Reavis & Pogue

A FINAL WORD: ② USING FOCUS GROUPS, MOCK TRIALS, AND JURY CONSULTANTS

1. Why and When to Use Jury Consultants

From initial investigations to depositions, discovery, and trying a case before a jury, a lawyer must remain focused on the ultimate goal—presenting a persuasive and convincing case to a jury. The more complex or serious the case, the easier it becomes for lawyers to become too involved and lose sight of their goals. Jury consultants are a more objective source for helping lawyers develop and evaluate cases.

Often the jury consultants are brought in at the last minute before a pending trial setting and after all witnesses have been deposed. Although bringing in jury consultants at the end of discovery may be helpful to test case theories, if the case is not persuasive, it is often too late to change theories, and the only

CONTINUED

option at that point may be to settle. In my experience, the earlier a lawyer begins to talk through case themes, the more likely the lawyer will stay with those themes and develop them throughout discovery.

If the case is complex or severe, a lawyer may decide to use a jury consultant early in developing the case. A jury consultant can help a lawyer to structure arguments, choose which arguments will persuade a jury, and remain focused on those arguments throughout discovery.

2. Services Provided by Jury Consultants

a. Focus Groups

In my experience, focus groups are a valuable feedback tool a jury consultant can provide to review the whole case or some aspect of it. Although focus groups can be structured many ways, especially early in a case, a simple presentation of objective data with a moderator and discussion about the issues is helpful to the client and the trial team. The best evidence to present to a focus group might be records, photos, videos, videotaped deposition excerpts, or other tangible information. This way the focus group can see the evidence a jury will ultimately see during trial.

When using a jury consultant to set up a focus group, you should outline all points and issues that you would like to have tested and provide all relevant materials to the jury consultant.

b. Mock Trials

In my experience, a mock trial is a useful tool that more closely duplicates an actual trial or summary jury trial, and it typically lasts one or two days. A mock trial involves presenting an abbreviated form of relevant case materials to a jury as lawyers act as both plaintiff and defense counsel.

CONTINUED

A mock trial allows a lawyer to present his theory of the case to a jury and try to identify the best arguments for the other side. A mock trial can produce feedback about how a jury may receive your theories and presentations. Working with a jury consultant after a mock trial helps identify weak arguments to be discarded, strong arguments to emphasize or develop, as well as a witness's effectiveness. Any emotional videotapes, pictures, and other demonstrative aids should be shown to mock jurors to test their effectiveness. A mock jury trial can give you a useful test of both the key evidence and themes you are considering.

There are two other aspects about the use of jury consultants and mock jury trial research that I like. First, they can give attorneys the ability to practice advocacy skills and get feedback on how to improve their presentation. Second, mock trials allow an attorney to view videotaped jury deliberations. Watching a representative group of jurors talk about your case is always an eye-opening experience.

c. *Jury Selection*

In many cases today, one or both sides take advantage of a jury consultant to help with jury selection. A jury consultant can help draft a jury questionnaire, assist in reviewing demographic information, and even analyze who may be a good juror. Having said that, many experienced lawyers follow their own instincts in terms of their interaction with jurors during voir dire. In my experience, an experienced trial lawyer's instincts are often as good as a jury consultant's advice about how a particular juror will perform. But it is helpful to have instincts confirmed by another reliable source.

Continued

d.   *Shadow Juries*

In some cases a jury consultant can arrange for shadow juries to mimic the demographic data of actual jurors and give feedback to a trial team on a daily or twice daily basis. Many times shadow jurors can objectively identify the effectiveness of a party's presentation and themes. Also, with shadow jurors, a jury consultant can help a lawyer understand how one shadow juror's opinions may or may not affect how a twelve-person group reaches a decision and translate those opinions into useful recommendations. I would be careful about relying on shadow juror comments without input from someone trained to interview shadow jurors and interpret their comments.

3.   **Using Other Services**

a.   *Simplifying Themes and Case Story*

Many lawyers believe, as I do, that every case must be explained in one or two persuasive sentences. When a lawyer takes fifteen or twenty minutes to explain his case, he often winds up confusing and overwhelming a jury. A consultant can help identify basic themes that will resound with jurors and condense these themes to one or two sentences.

b.   *Staying Focused*

Often by the time a case comes to trial, bad blood exists between the parties, and the attorneys are tempted to make personal attacks on each other. These situations are dangerous because even if an attorney wins debating points, he may lose the jury since the jury may come to the defense of the other party. In these cases, a jury consultant can help an attorney remain focused on the issues and stay away from self-destructive behavior.

CONTINUED

c. *Difficult Issues*

In addition to cooling tempers, a jury consultant can help identify effective ways to communicate difficult issues to a jury at the earliest opportunity.

d. *Focusing on Particular Jurors*

Jury consultants who have tested and studied a case can provide specific assistance in picking individual jurors. Although most defense attorneys would not want jurors who had been plaintiffs on their jury, a jury consultant once persuaded me to keep a former plaintiff on my panel. In that case, the juror had been a plaintiff in a lawsuit, but we decided not to strike her after questioning her during voir dire. She ended up being one of our best defense jurors, and we never would have allowed her on the jury if the jury consultant we used had not encouraged us to question her further during voir dire. During voir dire, we asked her if she could distinguish between the case she had filed and the plaintiffs in our suit. When she assured us that she could and that she thought that the two cases were dramatically different, she remained on the panel.

e. *Countering the Opposition*

Finally, a good jury consultant can come up with effective counterarguments to the opposing party's themes that no-one on the trial team had proposed.

f. *Preparing Witnesses*

Although I have not often used jury consultants to prepare witnesses, I have found them helpful in complex and serious cases. They are most helpful preparing witnesses who have language barriers, attitude problems, or personality problems. Although most lawyers have a standard checklist they run through when they prepare witnesses, I have found that a jury consultant can help by

CONTINUED

identifying why a person makes a poor witness. In these cases, the consultant acts more as a psychologist to help the witness make the most effective presentation possible.

g. *Settlement Negotiations and Mediation*

During mediations, attorneys will often confidentially tell the mediator about focus group or mock trial results. Sharing this information helps illustrate a case's strengths and helps the mediator evaluate the case. The more data a mediator has, the more likely a case can be resolved through mediation. I have found that showing mediators portions of a mock jury's deliberations or the actual data from a focus group or mock trial, helps resolve cases in mediation.

4. Clients and Jury Consultants

Jury consultants can be expensive, so it is important to communicate clearly with both the client and jury consultant about the fees involved. I have occasionally seen lawyers get in the middle of a fee dispute between a client and a consultant. This is a no-win situation.

Tell your client about any concerns you may have with a focus group outcome and identify points that may be emphasized differently at trial that would make a difference in the case's outcome. It can be helpful for a client to observe a mock jury discussing a case to help communicate issues that come up regarding liability or damages.

5. The Chances of Losing

Even when focus group or mock trial results are favorable, an attorney must ask a jury consultant to calculate a party's chances of winning at trial and to calculate potential verdict ranges. I have won a defense verdict in a mock trial but had the jury return a dramatically different verdict in the actual trial. Jury consultants can explain the possibility of this happening in your case and tell you how frequently it has happened in their test groups.

6. Conclusion

A good trial lawyer must be an excellent advocate. Advocacy involves marshalling facts in the most persuasive way possible to a jury. Although you may feel that you have compelling legal positions in a case, if these positions do not resound with your jury, you may not win your case. Reducing your message points in a case down to a handful and ensuring that those message points are proved in a variety of ways to the jury during the course of a trial is critical. Having a jury consultant help you reduce your message points to a handful of easily understood and persuasive themes can be invaluable and help you become a better advocate for your client.

— John S. Serpe, Partner
Sheehy, Serpe & Ware, P.C.

§ 18.06 | REFERENCES

Abbott & Batt, eds., *A Handbook of Jury Research* (Philadelphia: American Law Institute/American Bar Association, 1999).

American Society of Trial Consultants, www.astcweb.org.

Roberts, *Trial Psychology* (Austin: Butterworth Legal Publishers, 1987).

Scientific Journal Articles
on Courtroom Decision Making

Following is a list of scientific research articles that have appeared in peer-reviewed professional journals on the subject of courtroom decision making. The articles listed contain only a sample of such articles that have been published and are available to the public.

1. *Attorney Presentation Style*

   Hahn, "The Effects of Attorney Presentation Style, Attorney Gender, and Juror Gender on Juror Decisions," 20 Law & Human Behavior, 533-554 (1996).

2. *Bifurcation*

   Greene, Woody & Winter, "Compensating Plaintiffs and Punishing Defendants: Is Bifurcation Necessary?" 24 Law & Human Behavior, 187-205 (2000).

3. *Causation: Juror Perceptions*

   Wright, MacEachern, Stoffer & MacDonald, "Factors Affecting the Use of Naked Statistical Evidence of Liability," 136 J. Social Psychology, 677-688 (1996).

4. *Class Action Cases: Effects of Plaintiff Sample on Jury Decisions*

   Bordens & Horowitz, "The Limits of Sampling and Consolidation in Mass Tort Trials: Justice Improved or Justice Altered?" 22 Law & Psychology Review, 43-66 (1998).

5. *Comparative Negligence: Juror Perceptions*

    Zickafoose & Bornstein, "Double Discounting: The Effects of Comparative Negligence on Mock Juror Decision Making," 23 Law & Human Behavior, 577-596 (1999).

6. *Computer Animations: Effects of Decision Making*

    Houston, Joiner, Uddo & Harper, "Computer Animation in Mock Juries' Decision Making," 76 Psychological Rep., 987-993 (1995).

7. *Confessions and Admissions: Juror Perceptions*

    Kassin, "The Psychology of Confession Evidence," 52 Amer. Psychologist, 221-233 (1997).

8. *Courtroom Decision Making: Effects of Preexisting Attitudes*

    Eagly, Mladinic & Otto, "Cognitive and Affective Bases of Attitudes Toward Social Groups and Social Policies," 30 J. Experimental Social Psychology, 113-137 (1994).

    Fisher, Derison, Cadman & Johnston, "Religiousness, Religious Orientation, and Attitudes Towards Gays and Lesbians," 24 J. Applied Social Psychology, 614-630 (1994).

    Larsen, "Environmental Waste: Recycling Attitudes and Correlates," 135 J. Social Psychology, 83-88 (1995).

    Maurer, Park & Judd, "Stereotypes, Prejudice, and Judgments of Group Members: The Mediating Role of Public Policy Decisions," 32 J. Experimental Social Psychology, 411-436 (1996).

    Rogers, "Assessing Right to Die Attitudes: A Conceptually Guided Measurement Model," 52 J. Social Issues, 63-84 (1996).

9. *Criticisms of Juries*

    McClintock, "Is the Jury Trial a Lottery?" 8 J. Forensic Psychiatry, 118-126 (1997).

10. *Damages Arguments*

    Marti & Wissler, "Be Careful What You Ask For: The Effect of Anchors on Personal-Injury Awards," 6 J. Experimental Psychology, 91-103 (2000).

11. *Death Penalty Attitudes of Jurors*

    Dillehay & Sandys, "Life Under *Wainwright v. Witt*: Juror Dispositions and Death Qualification," 20 Law and Human Behavior, 20, 147-164 (1996).

Haney, Hurtado & Vega, "'Modern' Death Qualification: New Data and Its Biasing Effects," 18 Law & Human Behavior, 619-633 (1994).

12. *Defendant's Conduct in Civil Cases: Juror Perceptions*

Bornstein, "David, Goliath, and Reverend Bayes: Prior Beliefs About Defendants' Status in Personal Injury Cases," 8 Applied Cognitive Psychology, 233-258 (1994).

Greene, Johns & Smith, "The Effects of Defendant Conduct on Jury Damage Awards," 86 J. Applied Psychology, 228-237 (2001).

13. *Disregarding Evidence: Judge Instructions*

Fein, McCloskey & Tomlinson, "Can the Jury Disregard That Information? The Use of Suspicion to Reduce the Prejudicial Effects of Pretrial Publicity and Inadmissible Testimony," 23 Social Psychology Bulletin, 1215-1226 (1997).

Schul & Goren, "When Strong Evidence Has Less Impact Than Weak Evidence: Bias, Adjustment, and Instructions to Ignore," 15 Social Cognition, 133-155 (1997).

14. *Evidence: Its Role in Courtroom Decision Making*

Poulson, Braithwaite, Brondino & Wuensch, "Mock Jurors' Insanity Defense Verdict Selections: the Role of Evidence, Attitudes, and Verdict Options." 12 J. Social Behavior & Personality, 743-758 (1997).

15. *Expert Witnesses: Effects of Expert Testimony*

Greene, Downey & Goodman-Delahunty, "Juror Decisions About Damages," in Griffith, Liblcuman, Dodd, Shafir & Dickinson, eds., "The Effects of Expert Testimony on Mock Jurors' Decision Making and Memory," 20 Amer. J. Forensic Psychology, 69-80 (2002).

16. *Expert Witnesses: Eyewitness Memory*

Leippe, "The Case for Expert Testimony About Eyewitness Memory," 1 Psychology, Public Policy & Law, 909-959 (1995).

17. *Expert Witnesses: Mental Health Professionals*

Williger, "A Trial Lawyer's Perspective on Mental Health Professionals as Expert Witnesses," 47 Consulting Psychology J.: Practice & Research, 141-149 (1995).

18. *Fact Witnesses and Eyewitnesses: Juror Perceptions*

Berman, Narby & Cutler, "Effects of Inconsistent Eyewitness Statements on Mock-Jurors' Evaluations of the Eyewitness, Perceptions of Defendant Culpability and Verdicts," 19 Law & Human Behavior, 79-88 (1995).

Davenport, Penrod & Cutler, "Eyewitness Identification Evidence: Evaluating Commonsense Evaluations," 3 Psychology, Public Policy, & Law, 338-361 (1997).

Penrod & Cutler, "Witness Confidence and Witness Accuracy: Assessing Their Forensic Relation," 1 Psychology, Public Policy, & Law, 817-845 (1995).

Pickel, "Evaluation and Integration of Eyewitness Reports," 17 Applied Cognitive Psychology, 569-595 (1993).

19. *High-Tech Courtroom Presentations*

Houston, Joiner, Uddo & Harper, "Computer Animation in Mock Juries' Decision Making," 76 Psychological Rep., 987-993 (1995).

Kassin & Dunn. "Computer-Animated Displays and the Jury: Facilitative and Prejudicial Effects," 21 Law & Human Behavior, 269-281 (1997).

20. *Judge's Behavior at Trial: Influences on a Jury*

Halverson, Hallahan, Hart & Rosenthal, "Reducing the Biasing Effects of Judges' Nonverbal Behavior with Simplified Jury Instruction," 82 J. Applied Psychology, 590-598 (1997).

Hart, "Naturally Occurring Expectation Effects," 68 J. Personality & Social Psychology, 109-115 (1995).

21. *Juror Comprehension: Generally*

Cooper, Bennett & Sukel, "Complex Scientific Testimony: How Do Jurors Make Decisions?" 20 Law & Human Behavior, 379-394 (1996).

ForsterLee & Horowitz, "Enhancing Juror Competence in a Complex Trial," 11 Applied Cognitive Psychology, 305-319 (1997).

Horowitz, ForsterLee & Brolly, "Effects of Trial Complexity on Decision Making," 81 J. Applied Psychology, 757-768 (1996).

22. *Juror Comprehension: Note-Taking*

ForsterLee, Horowitz & Bourgeois, "Effects of Notetaking on Verdicts and Evidence Processing in a Civil Trial," 18 Law & Human Behavior, 567-578 (1994).

Hartley, "Notetaking in Nonacademic Settings: A Review," 16 Applied Cognitive Psychology, 559-574 (2002).

Penrod & Heuer, "Tweaking Commonsense: Assessing Aids to Jury Decision Making," 3 Psychology, Public Policy & Law, 259-284 (1997).

23. *Juror Morals and Values: Developmental*

Kochanska, Padavich & Koenig, "Children's Narratives About Hypothetical Moral Dilemmas and Objective Measures of Their Conscience: Mutual Relations and Socialization Antecedents," 67 Child Development, 533-554 (1996).

24. *Jury Decision Making: Factors of*

Boyll, "Psychological, Cognitive, Personality and Interpersonal Factors in Jury Verdicts," Law & Psychology Review, 15, 163-184 (1991).

Fishfader, Howells, Katz & Teresi, "Evidential and Extralegal Factors in Juror Decisions: Presentation Mode, Retention, and Level of Emotionality," 20 Law & Human Behavior, 565-572 (1996).

25. *Jury Decision Making: Resistance to Persuasion*

Zuwerink & Devine, "Attitude Importance and Resistance to Persuasion: It's Not Just the Thought That Counts," 70 J. Personality & Social Psychology, 931-944 (1996).

26. *Jury Decision Making: Small Group Behavior*

Hill, "Rating of Interpersonal Conduct in Small Groups by Aggregated Peers and Self: Replicated Factor Analyses," 136 J. Social Psychology, 597-611 (1996).

27. *Jury Decision Making: Story and Narrative Formation*

Covington, "No Story, No Analysis? The Role of Narrative in Interpretation," 40 J. Analytical Psychology, 405-416 (1995).

Downing, "Learning the Plot: Emotional Momentum in Search of Dramatic Logic," 28 Management Learning, #1, 27-44 (1997).

Jackson, "Anchored Narratives and the Interface of Law, Psychology, and Semiotics," 1 Legal & Criminological Psychology, 17-45 (1996).

Parry, "Why We Tell Stories: The Narrative Construction of Reality," 27 Transactional Analysis J., 118-127 (1997).

Sarbin, "The Poetics of Identity," 7 Theory & Psychology, 67-82 (1997).

Singer, "Putting Emotion in Context: Its Place Within Individual and Social Narratives," 5 J. Narrative & Life History, 255-267 (1995).

Voss & Van Dyke, "Narrative Structure, Information, Certainty, Emotional Content, and Gender as Factors in a Pseudo Jury Decision-making Task," 32 Discourse Processes, 215-243 (2001).

Weiner, Richmond, Seib, Rauch & Hackney, "The Psychology of Telling Murder Stories: Do We Think in Scripts, Exemplars, or Prototypes," 20 Behavioral Sciences & the Law, 119-139 (2002).

Welch-Ross, "An Integrative Model of the Development of Autobiographical Memory, 15 Developmental Rev., 338-365 (1995).

28. *Jury Deliberations: Dynamics*

Aldred, "Citizens' Juries: Discussion, Deliberation and Rationality," 6 Risk Decision & Policy, 71-90 (2001).

Bourgeois, Horowitz, ForsterLee & Grahe, "Nominal and Interactive Groups: Effects of Preinstruction and Deliberations on Decision and Evidence Recall in Complex Trials," 80 J. Applied Psychology, 58-67 (1995).

Devine, Clayton, Dunford, Seying & Pryce, "Jury Decision Making: 45 Years of Empirical Research on Deliberating Groups," 7 Psychology, Public Policy & Law, 622-727 (2001).

Manzo, "Taking Turns and Taking Sides: Opening Scenes from Two Jury Deliberations," 59 Social Psychology Q., 107-125 (1996).

Neck & Moorhead, "Jury Deliberations in the Trial of *U.S. vs. John DeLorean:* A Case Analysis of Groupthink Avoidance and an Enhanced Framework," 45 Human Relations, 1077-1091 (1992).

Sandys & Dillehay, "First-Ballot Votes, Predeliberation Dispositions, and Final Verdicts in Jury Trials," 19 Law & Human Behavior, 175-195 (1995).

Scudder, Herschel & Crossland, "Test of a Model Linking Cognitive Motivation, Assessment of Alternatives, Decision Quality, and Group Process Satisfaction," 25 Small Group Research, 57-82 (1994).

Tindale, Davis, Vollrath, Nagao & Hinsz, "Asymmetrical Social Influence in Freely Interacting Groups: A Test of Three Models," 58 J. Personality & Social Psychology, 438-449 (1990).

Winship, "Jury Deliberations: An Observation Study," 33 Group Analysis, 547-557 (2000).

29. *Jury Deliberations: Leaders and Opinion Makers, Emergence of*

Burpitt & Bigoness, "Leadership and Innovation Among Teams: The Impact of Empowerment," 28 Small Group Research, 414-423 (1997).

De Souza & Klein, "Emergent Leadership in the Group Goal-Setting Process," 26 Small Group Research, 475-496 (1995).

Estlund, "Opinion Leaders, Independence, and Condorcet's Theorem," 36 Theory & Decision, 131-162 (1994).

Fielding & Hogg, "Social Identity, Self-Categorization, and Leadership: A Field Study of Small Interactive Groups," 1 Group Dynamics, 39-51 (1997).

Foley & Pigott, "The Influence of Forepersons and Nonforepersons on Mock Jury Decisions," 15 Amer. J. Forensic Psychology, 5-17 (1997).

Hawkins, "Effects of Gender and Communication Content on Leadership Emergence in Small Task-Oriented Groups," 26 Small Group Research, 234-249 (1995).

Hebl, "Gender Bias in Leader Selection," 22 Teaching of Psychology, 186-188 (1995).

Kassin, Smith & Tulloch, "The Dynamite Charge: Effects on the Perceptions and Deliberation Behavior of Mock Jurors," 14 Law & Human Behavior, 537-550 (1990).

Kolb, "Are We Still Stereotyping Leadership? A Look at Gender and Other Predictors of Leader Emergence," 28 Small Group Research, 370-393 (1997).

Patterson, "Interaction Behavior and Person Perception: An Integrative Approach," 25 Small Group Research, 172-188 (1994).

Schultz, Ketrow & Urban, "Improving Decision Quality in the Small Group: The Role of the Reminder," 26 Small Group Research, 521-541 (1995).

Wheelan & Johnston, "The Role of Informal Member Leaders in a System Containing Formal Leaders," 27 Small Group Research, 33-55 (1996).

30. *Jury Instructions: Effects on Jurors*

Bourgeois, Horowitz, ForsterLee & Grahe, "Nominal and Interactive Groups: Effects of Preinstruction and Deliberations on Decision and Evidence Recall in Complex Trials," 80 J. Applied Psychology, 58-67 (1995).

Greene & Bornstein, "Precious Little Guidance: Jury Instruction on Damage Awards," 6 Psychology, Public Policy & Law, 743-758 (2000).

Lieberman & Sales, "What Social Science Teaches Us About the Jury Instruction Process," 3 Psychology, Public Policy & Law, 589-644 (1997).

Wiggins & Breckler, "Special Verdicts as Guides to Jury Decision-Making," 14 Law & Psychology Review, 1-41 (1990).

31. Jury Nullification

Niedermeier, Horowitz & Kerr, "Informing Jurors of Their Nullification Power: A Route to a Just Verdict or Judicial Chaos?" 23 Law & Human Behavior, 331-351 (1999).

Sommer, Horowitz & Bourgdois, "When Juries Fail to Comply With the Law: Biased Evidence Processing in Individual and Group Decision Making," 27 Personality & Social Psychology Bul., 309-320 (2001).

32. Jury Selection: Felony Cases

Johnson & Haney, "Felony Voir Dire: An Exploratory Study of Its Content and Effect," 18 Law & Human Behavior, 487-505 (1994).

Moran & Cutler, "Jury Selection in Major Controlled Substance Trials: The Need for Extended Voir Dire," 3 Forensic Rep., 331-348 (1990).

33. Jury Selection: Race and Gender Issues

Golash, "Race, Fairness, and Jury," 10 Behavioral Sciences & the Law, 155-177 (1992).

Rose, "The Peremptory Challenge: Accused of Race or Gender Discrimination? Some Data from One County," 23 Law & Human Behavior, 695-702 (1999).

Schutte & Hosch, "Gender Differences in Sexual Assault Verdicts: A Meta-Analysis," 12 J. Social Behavior & Personality, 759-772 (1997).

34. Jury Selection: Scientific Information and Methods, Use of

Cutler, "Introduction: The Status of Scientific Jury Selection in Psychology and Law," 3 Forensic Rep., 227-232 (1990).

Fulero & Penrod, "Attorney Jury Selection Folklore: What Do They Think and How Can Psychologists Help?" 3 Forensic Rep., 233-259 (1990).

Lennox, "Applications of Structural Equation Methodologies to Jury Selection Research," 3 Forensic Rep., 349-360 (1990).

Patterson, "Scientific Jury Selection: The Need for a Case Specific Approach," 11 Social Action & the Law, 105-109 (1986).

Strier, "Whither Trial Consulting? Issues and Projections," 23 Law & Human Behavior, 93-115 (1999).

35. *Jury Size; Effects of*

Davis, Hulbert, Au, Chen & Zarnoth, "Effects of Group Size and Procedural Influence on Consensual Judgments of Quantity: The Examples of Damage Awards and Mock Trial Juries," 73 J. Personality & Social Psychology, 703-718 (1997).

Saks & Marti, "A Meta-Analysis of the Effects of Jury Size," 21 Law & Human Behavior, 451-467 (1997).

36. *Medical Malpractice: Juror Perceptions*

Feigenson, Park & Salovey, "Effect of Blameworthiness and Outcome Severity on Attributions of Responsibility and Damage Awards in Comparative Negligence Cases," 21 Law & Human Behavior, 597-617 (1997).

Vidmar, Lee, Cohen & Stewart, "Damage Awards and Jurors' Responsibility: Ascriptions in Medical Versus Automobile Negligence Cases," 12 Behavioral Sciences & the Law, 149-160 (1994).

Worthington, "Making Attributions to the Physician Following Closing Arguments of a Simulated Medical Malpractice Suit: Jurors' Sex, Health, Locus of Control, and Locus of Authority," 80 Psychological Rep., 943-946 (1997).

37. *Predicting Juror Decisions*

Penrod, "Predictors of Jury Decision Making in Criminal and Civil Cases: A Field Experiment," 3 Forensic Rep., 261-277 (1990).

38. *Pretrial Publicity: Effects of*

Fein, McCloskey & Tomlinson, "Can the Jury Disregard That Information? The Use of Suspicion to Reduce the Prejudicial Effects of Pretrial Publicity and Inadmissible Testimony," 23 Social Psychology Bul., 1215-1226 (1997).

Imrich, Mullin & Linz, "Measuring the Extent of Prejudicial Pretrial Publicity in Major American Newspapers: A Content Analysis," 45 J. Communication, 94-117 (1995).

Moran & Cutler, "Bogus Publicity Items and the Contingency Between Awareness and Media-Induced Pretrial Prejudice," 21 Law & Human Behavior, 339-344 (1997).

Mullin, Imrich & Linz, "The Impact of Acquaintance Rape Stories and Case Specific Pretrial Publicity on Juror Decision Making," 23 Communication Research, 100-135 (1996).

Studebaker & Penrod, "Pretrial Publicity: The Media, the Law, and Common Sense," 3 Psychology, Public Policy & Law, 428-460 (1997).

39. *Responsibility Determination and Damage Awards: Juror Perceptions*

Bothwell & Duhon, "Counterfactual Thinking and Plaintiff Compensation," 134 J. Social Psychology, 705-706 (1994).

Foley & Pigott, "Belief in a Just World and Jury Decisions in a Civil Rape Trial," 30 J. Applied Social Psychology, 935-951 (2000).

Hastie, Schkade & Payne, "Juror Judgments in Civil Cases: Effects of Plaintiff's Requests and Plaintiff's Identity on Punitive Damage Awards," 23 Law & Human Behavior 445-470 (1999).

Kovera & Cass, "Compelled Mental Health Examinations, Liability Decisions, and Damage Awards in Sexual Harassment Cases: Issues for Jury Research," 8 Psychology, Public Policy & Law, 96-114 (2002).

Laughery, Laughery, Lovvoll, McQuilkin & Wogalther, "Effects of Warnings on Responsibility Allocation," 15 Psychology & Marketing, 687-706 (1998).

Olsen-Fulero & Fulero, "Commonsense Rape Judgments: An Empathy-Complexity Theory of Rape Juror Story Making," 3 Psychology, Public Policy & Law, 402-427 (1997).

Robbenolt, "Punitive Damage Decision Making: The Decisions of Citizens and Trial Judges," 26 Law & Human Behavior, 315-342 (2002).

40. *Scientific Decision-Maker Research: Blending Qualitative and Quantitative Approaches*

Maio, Roese, Seligman & Katz, "Rankings, Ratings, and the Measurement of Values: Evidence for the Superior Validity of Ratings," 18 Basic & Applied Social Psychology, 171-181 (1996).

Cioffi, "Who's Opinion Is This Anyway? Self-Inferential Effects of Representing One's Social Group," 13 Social Cognition, 341-363 (1995).

41. *Scientific Decision-Maker Research: Trial Simulations, Use of*

Diamond, "Illuminations and Shadows from Jury Simulations," 21 Law & Human Behavior, 561-571 (1997).

Kramer & Kerr, "Laboratory Simulation and Bias in the Study of Juror Behavior: A Methodological Note," 13 Law & Human Behavior, 89-99 (1989).

42. *Sexual Harassment and Rape: Juror Perceptions*

Gowan & Zimmerman, "Impact of Ethnicity, Gender, and Previous Experience on Juror Judgments in Sexual Harassment Cases, 26 J. Applied Social Psychology, 596-617 (1996).

43. *Stereotypes: Juror Perceptions*

Dane, "Applying Social Psychology in the Courtroom: Understanding Stereotypes in Jury Decision Making," 22 J. Applied Communication Research, 309-321 (1992).

Elkins & Philips, "Evaluating Sex Discrimination Claims: The Mediating Role of Attributions," 84 J. Applied Psychology, 186-199 (1999).

Fisher, Derison, Polley & Cadman, "Religiousness, Religious Orientation, and Attitudes Towards Gays and Lesbians," 24 J. Applied Social Psychology, 614-630 (1994).

Memon & Shuman, "Juror Perception of Experts in Civil Disputes: The Role of Race and Gender," 22 Law & Psychology Rev., 179-197 (1998).

Nunez, McCoy, Clark & Shaw, "The Testimony of Elderly Victim/Witnesses and Their Impact on Juror Decisions: The Importance of Examining Multiple Stereotypes," 23 Law & Human Behavior, 413-423 (1999).

Ross, Duning, Toglia & Ceci, "The Child in the Eyes of the Jury: Assessing Mock Jurors' Perceptions of the Child Witness," 14 Law & Human Behavior, 5-23 (1990).

Schutte & Hosch, "Gender Differences in Sexual Assault Verdicts: A Meta-Analysis," 12 Violence & Victims, 115-126 (1997).

Wittenbrink, Gist & Hilton, "Structural Properties of Stereotypic Knowledge and Their Influences on the Construal of Social Situations," 72 J. Personality & Social Psychology, 526-543 (1997).

44. Tort Reform: Juror Perceptions

Moran, Cutler & De Lisa, "Attitudes Toward Tort Reform, Scientific Jury Selection and Juror Bias Verdict Inclination in Criminal and Civil Trials," 18 Law & Psychology Rev., 309-328 (1994).

Robbennolt & Studebaker, "Anchoring in the Courtroom: The Effects of Caps on Punitive Damages," 23 Law & Human Behavior, 353-373 (1999).

Trial Science in the Life of a Lawsuit

The most powerful cases for either plaintiff or defendant are those which apply trial science techniques throughout the life of the lawsuit. If these techniques are applied early, a trial team can focus discovery efforts and development of the lawsuit so that (1) the party's position is more solid and persuasive, and (2) fewer resources are wasted on aspects of the case that will not be important to a judge, jury, or arbitration panel. The following chart demonstrates some specific trial science techniques that are applicable to each stage of a lawsuit.

Stage of the Suit	Technique	Benefit
Pre-suit/pre-answer	• Case consultation/ strategic planning	⇨ Decision whether to file or defend; frame the suit or defense
	• Venue and verdicts analysis	⇨ Determine where suit is more advantageous
Early pretrial	• Case consultation/ strategic planning	⇨ Generating ideas for direction of the case using scientific jury research from the past
	• Focus group (live or online)	⇨ Determine most powerful favorable issues

Stage of the Suit	Technique	Benefit
	• Venue and verdicts analysis	⇨ Analysis of community attitudes and previous verdicts
	• Community attitude survey	⇨ Study of community attitudes and ideal jurors
	• Study of the persuasive power of pleadings	⇨ Develop the most persuasive arguments in written pleadings and motions
	• Mock court hearing study	⇨ Develop the most compelling courtroom argument
Discovery assistance	• Case consultation/ strategic planning	⇨ Determine strengths and weaknesses of witness testimony; generate ideas for enhancing effectiveness of witnesses
	• Mock trial study	⇨ Test the strength of the case early enough for changes
	• Focus group (live or online)	⇨ Discover strongest initial on themes/ theories
	• Witness effectiveness training	⇨ Development of persuasive witnesses
Settlement or mediation	• Case consultation/ strategic planning	⇨ Generate creative ideas for achieving a favorable settlement of the case
	• Mock trial study • Mock arbitration study	⇨ Measure the strength of the case; determine range of likely verdict
	• Mock mediation study	⇨ Develop a powerful strategy for persuading the opposing parties and attorneys to settle the case on favorable terms

Stage of the Suit	Technique	Benefit
Trial preparation	• Case consultation/ strategic planning	⇨ Strategic planning for trial preparation and trial compared to strongest themes
	• Focus group (live or online)	⇨ Identify juror perceptions regarding specific issues, witnesses, visual aids and case presentation
	• Mock jury study • Mock bench trial study • Mock arbitration study	⇨ Test themes, theories, witnesses, attorney style, overall presentation to enhance the persuasive power of the case
	• Mock court hearing study	⇨ Develop the most compelling courtroom argument
	• Witness effectiveness training	⇨ Develop effective and persuasive witnesses
	• Juror questionnaire	⇨ Allows for advance in-depth venire review
	• Attorney style coaching	⇨ Assistance from a trial advocacy/psychological point of view
	• Media training	⇨ Enhance client/attorney effectiveness with the media
	• Demonstrative aids/ exhibits	⇨ Develop strongest themes/ theories into visual format
	• Study of the persuasive power of pleadings	⇨ Develop the most persuasive arguments in written pleadings and motions
Trial	• Case consultation/ strategic planning	⇨ Strategic planning during trial
	• Jury selection	⇨ Assistance in selection of fair jury panel

Stage of the Suit	Technique	Benefit
	• Trial scientist observation	⇨ Experienced trial consultant observation to assist attorneys with instant feedback to enhance courtroom persuasiveness
	• Shadow/mirror jury	⇨ Lay person feedback each day of trial
	• Attorney style coaching	⇨ Assistance to attorneys from a trial advocacy/ psychological point of view
Post-trial	• Case consultation/ strategic planning	⇨ Strategic planning for appeal
	• Post-trial jury interviews	⇨ Determines strengths and weaknesses of case presentation; uncovers any misconduct
	• Mock appellate study	⇨ Determine strongest themes for argument
Special services	• Intellectual property mock hearing study	⇨ Develop compelling cases; courtroom presentations relating to intellectual property
	• Media coaching	⇨ Enhance client/attorney effectiveness with the media

Should Jurors Be Allowed to Ask Questions of Witnesses?[1]

. . . The District Court allowed jurors to pose questions by handing the court written questions for the court's review. It appears from this record (and appellant does not argue to the contrary) that the court would then allow the attorneys to see the question so that counsel could make whatever objections they deemed appropriate, and the court could thus determine the admissibility and propriety of a question outside the hearing of the jury before asking the question.

One juror did submit a question in this manner. The juror asked: "[w]hat kind of rear doors are on the rear of the trailer?" . . .

* * *

[The question of] the propriety of allowing juror questioning is an issue of first impression in this circuit. Although we have not previously addressed this issue, several other courts of appeal have. Although those courts have consistently expressed concern over the dangers of the practice, they have refused to adopt a rule prohibiting juror questioning of witnesses during the course of a criminal trial. See *United States v. Bush*, 47 F.3d 511 (2d Cir. 1995); *United States v. Ajmal*, 67 F.3d 12, 14 (2d Cir. 1995); *United States v. Cassiere*, 4 F.3d 1006, 1017-18 (1st Cir. 1993); *United States v. George*, 986 F.2d 1176, 1178 (8th Cir. 1993); *DeBenedetto v. Goodyear Tire & Rubber Co.*, 754 F.2d 512,

---

[1] Excerpts from United States v. Hernandez, 176 F.3d 719 (3d Cir. 1999), involving the hijacking of a truck. Footnotes and some italics omitted.

516 (4th Cir. 1985); *United States v. Callahan*, 588 F.2d 1078, 1086 (5th Cir. 1979); *United States v. Gonzales*, 424 F.2d 1055, 1055 (9th Cir. 1970). We take this opportunity to approve of the practice so long as it is done in a manner that insures the fairness of the proceedings, the primacy of the court's stewardship, and the rights of the [parties].

In *United States v. Polowichak*, 783 F.2d 410 (4th Cir. 1986), the court disapproved the practice of posing juror questions in front of other jurors. The court stated that the trial judge should require questions to be submitted in writing, without disclosure to other jurors, "whereupon the court may pose the question in its original or restated form upon ruling the question or the substance of the question proper." *Id.* at 413.

In *United States v. Stierwalt*, 16 F.3d 282 (8th Cir. 1994), the court held that the District Court did not err where questions were submitted in writing and all evidentiary issues were resolved before the judge read the questions to the witness. See *id.* at 286. See also *George*, 986 F.2d at 1178-79 (holding that despite the fact that the jury submitted 65 written questions to the court, the court employed proper formal procedures in that the questions were discussed with the attorneys and ruled upon by the judge).

In *United States v. Bush, supra*, jurors directly questioned witnesses, including the defendant. Defense counsel failed to object, and even engaged in a dialogue with the jurors. The practice of allowing such questioning was therefore reviewed for plain error. The court first noted that "we have already held . . . that direct questioning by jurors is a 'matter within the judge's discretion, like witness-questioning by the judge himself.'" 47 F.3d at 514. The court noted that "every circuit court that has addressed this issue agrees. State courts, moreover, have overwhelmingly placed juror questioning of witnesses within the trial judge's discretion, and indeed its common law roots are deeply entrenched." *Id.* at 515 (citations omitted). Nevertheless, the court expressed concern over this practice. "Although we reaffirm our earlier holding . . . that juror questioning of witnesses lies within the trial judge's discretion, we strongly discourage its use." *Id.* The court listed several dangers endemic to the practice including "turning jurors into advocates, compromising their neutrality," the "risk that jurors will ask prejudicial or otherwise improper questions," and counsel's inability to respond for fear of antagonizing, alienating, or embarrassing a juror. *Id.* The court noted that

> [b]alancing the risk that a juror's question may be prejudicial against the benefit of issue-clarification will almost always lead trial courts to

disallow juror questioning, in the absence of extraordinary or compelling circumstances.

Id. at 516. However, the court affirmed the conviction because the challenged questioning had been "limited and controlled" and because the defendant could not demonstrate prejudice. *Id.*

In *United States v. Sutton*, 970 F.2d 1001 (1st Cir. 1992), the court voiced similar concerns about allowing jurors to question witnesses even though the procedure used involved the court asking questions that the jurors had submitted in writing. *Id.* at 1005. Once again, the court allowed the practice though it was clearly troubled by it. "Although we think this practice may frequently court unnecessary trouble, we find no error in the circumstances of this case." *Id.* at 1003. There, at the beginning of the trial, the trial court had informed the jurors that they could ask questions by handing written questions to the jury foreman who would then give them to the judge. "If your question even possibly could make any legal difference . . . if it's relevant as the lawyers say, I'll ask it for you." *Id.* On appeal, the court stated:

> Allowing jurors to pose questions during a criminal trial is a procedure fraught with perils. In most cases, the game will not be worth the candle. Nevertheless, we are fully committed to the principle that trial judges should be given wide latitude to manage trials. We are, moreover, supportive of reasoned efforts by the trial bench to improve the truth seeking attributes of the jury system. Consistent with this overall approach, and mindful that the practice . . . may occasionally be advantageous, especially in complex cases and under carefully controlled conditions, we hold that allowing juror-inspired questions in a criminal case is not prejudicial per se, but is a matter committed to the sound discretion of the trial court.

Id. at 1005. Although the court allowed the practice, it was quick to discourage it." We hasten to add that the practice, while not forbidden, should be employed sparingly and with great circumspection." *Id.* The court also added to the list of concerns enunciated in *Bush*, though it acknowledged that the practice could further the search for truth by allowing jurors to clear up confusion. The court also recognized that allowing jurors to participate in questioning could enhance the attentiveness of jurors. Nevertheless, the court concluded "in most situations, the risks inherent in the practice will outweigh its utility." *Id.*

In *United States v. Ajmal, supra,* the court did reverse a conviction based upon juror questioning of witnesses, even though the judge had "incorporated prophylactic procedures to lessen the potential prejudice. . . ." 67 F.3d at 15. The Second Circuit noted that the trial judge's decision to invite such questioning

> was not necessitated by the factual intricacies of this banal drug conspiracy, nor . . . prompted by the urging of jurors themselves. Rather, the District Court, as a matter of course, established at the outset of the trial that jurors would be allowed to question witnesses. Indeed, the District Court encouraged juror questioning throughout the trial by asking the jurors at the end of each witness's testimony if they had any queries to pose. Not surprisingly, the jurors took extensive advantage of this opportunity to question witnesses, including Ajmal himself.

Id. at 14 (emphasis added). The trial judge there had taken precautions. He had required questions to be in writing, and the court, rather than the attorneys, asked the questions. In addition, the court only asked those questions that it believed were proper under the Federal Rules of Evidence. Nevertheless, the Court of Appeals held that the trial judge had abused his discretion.

> Although the District Court substantially complied with the procedures this Court advocated in *Bush,* . . . such measures alone cannot purge the harm caused by the extensive juror questioning in the case at hand. Regardless of the procedures adopted by the District Court to vet questions, there must be ample justification for adopting the disfavored practice in the first instance. To hold otherwise would sanction juror questioning of witnesses in any circumstance, so long as appropriate prophylactic measures are adopted. We cannot accept such a proposition.
>
> In light of our discussion above, the District Court's encouragement of juror questioning of witnesses . . . was an abuse of discretion.

67 F.3d at 15 (emphasis added). Thus, although the court was once again concerned with the practice of allowing juror questioning absent circumstances sufficient to justify the risk inherent in the procedure, the court clearly based

its reversal upon the trial court's encouragement of such questioning, and the frequency with which jurors had accepted the judge's invitation.

Here, the court received only one question from the jury. It was a fact question that was not even asked. We do not think that one fact question which is submitted to a judge in writing . . . can be labeled an abuse of discretion. See *United States v. Lewin*, 900 F.2d 145 (8th Cir. 1990). In *Lewin*, jury questioning was deemed proper where the jury tendered six questions to the court and the court only asked four of them. The questions that the court allowed were "specific and factual in nature," and no questions were asked of the defendant. *Id*. at 147-48. The court of appeals noted that "this [was] not a case in which juror questioning was allowed to become disruptive or abusive." *Id*. Moreover, the court suggested appropriate safeguards. "If [the District Court] decides to permit jurors to ask questions in future trials, it should consider requiring jurors to submit their questions in writing, or orally out of the presence of the other jurors, without prior discussion with the other jurors." *Id*. at 148.

We agree that a trial judge who allows such questioning in a given case should adopt a procedure to first screen the questions. However, we conclude that the dangers of allowing jurors to ask questions orally far outweighs any perceived benefit of allowing juror questioning of witnesses. Thus, the judge should ask any juror-generated questions, and he or she should do so only after allowing attorneys to raise any objection out of the hearing of the jury.

The procedure utilized here is consistent with our admonitions and consistent with the sound exercise of judicial discretion. The court did not surrender its discretion as to whether to allow a given question to be asked, and the judge, not the attorneys (and certainly not the jurors), was to have asked any questions posed by a juror. This procedure is consistent with the holding of every court of appeals that has addressed this issue. We hold that the trial judge did not abuse her discretion.

Index

A

B

C

F

I

J

T

U

V

W

About the Author

Dr. Richard Waites is one of the nation's leading authorities in the field of jury decision making and trial advocacy. He has been quoted in nationwide and local media including *The National Law Journal*, *The Wall Street Journal*, *USA Today*, and ABC News. Waites has authored or contributed to eleven books and more than forty articles dealing with persuading judges, jurors, and arbitrators and with the use of scientific information to enhance performance in the courtroom.

Dr. Waites is a board-certified civil trial lawyer licensed in Texas. He is the founder and chief trial psychologist of Advocacy Sciences, Inc. and The Advocates,[1] one of the nation's most respected trial consulting firms. He obtained his law degree from the University of Houston Law Center and his doctorate in psychology from Walden University. He is a member of the American Bar Association, the American Psychological Association, the American Psychology-Law Society, the American Society of Trial Consultants, Defense Research Institute, and the American Corporate Counsel Association.

Over the past twenty years Dr. Waites has worked with hundreds of trial lawyers and corporate clients. Prior to becoming a national trial consultant, he appeared in more than seventy trials as lead attorney.

---

[1] Offices in Atlanta, Chicago, Dallas, Houston, Los Angeles, Miami, and Phoenix. On the Internet at www.theadvocates.com.

ALSO FROM **ALM PUBLISHING:**

Game, Set, Match: Winning the Negotiations Game
by Henry S. Kramer

The Essential Guide to the Best (and Worst) Legal Sites on the Web
by Robert J. Ambrogi, Esq.

Full Disclosure: The New Lawyer's Must-Read Career Guide
by Christen Civiletto Carey, Esq.

On Trial: Lessons from a Lifetime in the Courtroom
by Henry G. Miller, Esq.

Going Public in Good Times and Bad: A Legal and Business Guide
by Robert G. Heim

Inside/Outside: How Businesses Buy Legal Services
by Larry Smith

Arbitration: Essential Concepts
by Steven C. Bennett, Esq.

Other publications available from AMERICAN LAWYER MEDIA:

LAW JOURNAL PRESS professional legal treatises—over 100 titles available

Legal newspapers and magazines—over 20 national and regional titles available, including:

The American Lawyer
The National Law Journal
New York Law Journal

Legal newsletters—over 25 titles available

Visit us at our websites:
www.lawcatalog.com
and
www.americanlawyermedia.com